The Law and Slavery

The Law and Slavery

Prohibiting Human Exploitation

By

Jean Allain

BRILL
NIJHOFF

LEIDEN | BOSTON

Also published by Brill Nijhoff:

Jean Allian, Slavery in International Law, 2013
Jean Allian, The Slavery Conventions, 2008

Cover illustration: Image on the front cover produced for Anti-Slavery International by Saachi & Saachi;
© Anti-Slavery International. Image used with permission.

Library of Congress Cataloging-in-Publication Data

Allain, Jean, 1965- author.
[Essays. Selections]
The law and slavery prohibiting human exploitation / by Jean Allain.
pages cm
Includes bibliographical references and index.
ISBN 978-90-04-27988-9 (hardback : alk. paper)
1. Slavery—Law and legislation. 2. Forced labor (International law) I. Title.

K3267.A945 2015
342.08'7—dc23

2015010269

This publication has been typeset in the multilingual "Brill" typeface. With over 5,100 characters covering Latin, IPA, Greek, and Cyrillic, this typeface is especially suitable for use in the humanities.
For more information, please see www.brill.com/brill-typeface.

ISBN 978-90-04-27988-9 (hardback)
ISBN 978-90-04-27989-6 (e-book)

This book is printed on acid-free paper.

FSC www.fsc.org MIX Paper from responsible sources FSC® C109576

Printed by Printforce, the Netherlands

For Gina Bekker

Contents

APPENDICES

Preface

When I first considered the law of anti-slavery there was very little of substance written. That is both a bold and unnerving statement, as few would argue that the prohibition against slavery is a fundamental human rights. And yet, the historical record bears this out: I would invite anybody to find an academic piece written prior to 2006 which makes a substantive point of international law regarding human exploitation whether it be forced labour, servitude, or slavery.

If nothing else, in setting out to consider human exploitation, I had a vision of what I sought to achieve. In October 2005, at a conference in Liverpool on the Transatlantic Slavery held at its Maritime Museum, I had the following to say:

> The Paper I will be presenting today is the first volley of what I expect to be a treatise entitled *Slavery in International Law*.[1] Over the last three years I have immersed myself in historical studies of the various tenets of the rise and fall of the slave trade both occidental and oriental. The task I set myself was rather ambitious – to get a grip on the histories of the European maritime Powers of the sixteenth through the nineteenth centuries, the birth and development the States of the New World, and the interaction between representatives of these countries and the local elite in Africa. In so doing, I had hoped to grasp the fundamentals of the rise and fall of slavery so as to ground my future research of the legal parameters of slavery as it exists today in general international law, the law of the sea, international human rights law, humanitarian law, labour law, refugee law, and international criminal law.
>
> Before proceeding to speak about the content of my Paper I wish to pay my respects and to publicly honour those historians who have, over the last thirty years or more, spent their time in archives here in the United Kingdom and throughout the world so as to bring to life the issue of the international slave trade and save it from what George Orwell called the 'memory hole'. I have been throughout my life a keen student of history, having taken many a course during my first degree in Canadian. Though I have moved away from the discipline, what continues to intrigue me is the many varied discussions about historiography and what it means to write 'history'. I have found, and, in many ways, what has led me to focus on slavery in international law, has been the revolution

1 See Jean Allain, *Slavery in International Law: Of Human Exploitation and Slavery*, 2013.

which has transpired within the discipline of History where issues of slavery and the trade are concerned. The rich vein of scholarship which has transpired, the dedication which has manifested itself in, for instance, the compilation of *The Trans-Atlantic Slave Trade: A Database* [now http://www.slavevoyages.org], is testimony to what can only be described as the most creative, insightful, and far-reaching, research that has transpired in the discipline of History over the last thirty years.

As an outsider, I wish to express my debt of gratitude to those of you who have dedicate your life's work to synthesizing primary research into historical works. You have paved the way for those of us, like me, who wish to take on research in our own disciplines and who must, by necessity, turn to your studies. In my discipline, scholarship is based on a melding together of law and fact. The law and its interpretation, however, are only as strong as the underlying facts which we seek to apply to them. If our understanding of the facts does not mirror the situation which has transpired, then our application of the relevant legal norms lacks a proper foundation and ultimately raises questions of scholarship not only in regard to the factual elements of our work, but our overall reputation both with regard to the facts and the law.

Being rather suspicious of claims of righteousness attached to dominance, I would never have embarked on a study of slavery had the discourse not left the colonial comforts of, say, W.E.H. Lecky who painted British abolition "as among the three or four perfectly virtuous pages comprised in this history of nations."[2] It is clear that in the last thirty years; the discourse is much more nuanced, having originally been challenged by Eric Williams' 1944 work *Capitalism and Slavery*, which for a period of time became the orthodoxy, and its having been displaced, though not completely discredited, where motivations of the United Kingdom are concerned in its move to suppress the international slave trade.[3]

Having read much around the abolition of the slave trade, I continued to consider the evolution of the anti-slavery regime as it developed in international law through the Nineteenth and into the Twentieth Century. That evolution is chronicled in these pages through the publication of a piece on the British

2 See Roger Anstey, *The Atlantic Slave Trade and British Abolition 1760–1810*, 1975, p. xx; where he quotes W.E.H. Lecky, *A History of European Morals*, 1884.

3 Jean Allain, "Rough Seas: The Establishment of a Legal Regime to Abolish the International Slave Trade," Liverpool and Transatlantic Slavery, October 2005.

abolition of the slave trade at sea and the relationship of Ethiopia and the League of Nations seen through the lenses of slavery. The evolution of abolition is further given context through papers presented in Dakar, Senegal, setting out the historical outlines of the Transatlantic Slavery Trade; and at the Tartu University, Estonia which considered the diplomacy of Fyodor Martens (one of the most important international jurist and diplomat of his generation) at the 1890 Brussels Conference, where he mediated agreement of the first multilateral treaty meant to be universal in scope in prohibiting the slave trade at sea.

In carrying out my research, I felt compelled to challenge accepted orthodoxies which had emerged over the intervening 125 years (from 1890 to today, re: 2015). During this period States, at the international level, adopted the 1926 Slavery Convention, the 1956 Supplementary Convention, human rights treaties, international labour law conventions; and agreement related to the laws of war, law of the sea, and international criminal law. Over time, a legal narrative emerged which had no basis in the historical record. Instead, that narrative depended on descriptive elements of the various provisions found in these international agreements being passed down over time from one commentator to the next with no true scholarship being introduced at any point. I have sought to challenge the status quo over the years, by calling out NGOs for failing to utilise the law as an anti-slavery tool; international courts for their dubious case-law on normative elements of the various manifestation of human exploitation; and academic for their reading of the law related to human exploitation and reparations.

Hand in glove with this exercise of tearing down the perceived wisdom on human exploitation was a systematic consideration of the material found in the archives of the League of Nations, and in the libraries and documentation centres of the United Nations, the International Labour Organisation and the International Committee of the Red Cross, all located in Geneva, Switzerland. This material is the brick and mortar of the law of anti-slavery set out over the years in my work. It is with some pride that I find a number of these documents now being quoted with authority, where previously they laid on dusty shelves. Likewise, my development and use of certain terms in framing the law of anti-slavery have become common currency. Having minted such terms as 'human exploitation', 'conventional servitudes', and 'servile marriage', etc., each, in its own way, has become part of the discourse. This is no idle boast: again, I invited the curious to consult the historical record. The sum of the articles, book reviews, case notes re-published in this collection, along with the original papers presented at the International Criminal Court, the Special Court for Sierra Leone, at Harvard Law School and at the Wilberforce Institute for the

Study of Slavery and Emancipation (WISE); set out in further detail my consideration of the law prohibiting human exploitation.

What then are those fundamental tenets of the law of human exploitation which are given more of an in-depth consideration in these pages than could be afforded in *Slavery in International Law*? For instance, that unlike piracy, universal jurisdiction was never established over the slave trade at sea; that forced labour was never a norm of *jus cogens*; that those 'practices similar to slavery' set out in the 1956 Supplementary Convention should in fact be considered conventional servitudes; that the notion of 'slavery-like practice' is a term of art rather than law; and finally, that the 1926 definition of slavery, long thought to be applicable only to *de jure* situations of legal ownership, is in fact and in law, also applicable to contemporary situations where a person is held in a *de facto* condition of slavery.

Acknowledgments

The one constant throughout my years of research has been the hand of Gina Bekker. What a great partner, wife, mother to our children, friend, and confidant. My research has been a big part of our relationship, but she has been the keel, both intellectually and in practical terms, which has keep it steady and on course. The 'big family' rages on and I believe for each of us, we would have it no other way.

In carrying out the research related to human exploitation I have had the support of a number of funding grants. The first of these was provided in 2004 by the School of Law, Queen's University, Belfast, which allowed me to travel to Geneva and carry out a preliminary survey of the material in the Archives of the League of Nations and the United Nations Library. This was followed by a grant by the British Academy entitled 'Suppression of Slavery at the United Nations', which allowed me to return in 2007 for several months to consider the material in Geneva, the product of that stay being my 2008 *The Slavery Conventions*.

On the strength of that work I was granted money by the UK Arts & Humanities Research Council, under their Research Network and Workshops scheme for a project entitled 'Slavery as the Powers Attaching to the Right of Ownership', which allowed me to bring together scholars to form the Research Network on the Legal Parameters of Slavery. Through support provided by the Rockefeller Foundation, the members of the Research Network were invited in 2010 to meet at Bellagio Conference Centre in Italy. A year late, that group met in Cambridge, Massachusetts to completed the drafting of what would become the 2012 *Bellagio-Harvard Guidelines on the Legal Parameters of Slavery* as well as the 2012 (Allain ed.) *The Legal Understanding of Slavery*. The Research Network consists of: : Kevin Bales, Annie Bunting, John Cairns, William M. Carter Jr., Catherine Clinton, Holly Cullen, Seymour Drescher, Stanley Engerman, Paul Finkelman, Bernard Freamon, Allison Gorsuch, Robin Hickey, Richard Helmholz, Antony Honoré, Christopher McCrudden, Aidan McQuade, Orlando Patterson, James Penner, Joel Quirk, Jody Sarich, and Rebecca Scott.

I received a Leverhulme Research Fellowship in 2010 which allowed me to consider the various types of human exploitation found at the domestic level. With the assistance of Dr Marie Lynch, we developed the *Slavery in Domestic Jurisdictions* database which is available at: http://www.qub.ac.uk/slavery. The end product of the totality of that research is both by 2013 *Slavery in International Law* and this collection.

Finally, as of September 2014, I am part of a team (Kevin Bales, John Oldfield, and Zoe Trodd), which has received a five-year grant from the Arts & Humanities Research Council under their *Care for the Future* scheme, entitled 'The Antislavery Usable Past', which allows me, amongst other important and interesting things, to again visit the Archives of the League of Nations and the United Nations Library in Geneva, this time to consider the evolution of the 'white slave' trade and trafficking in law. Stay tuned for that.

In acknowledging these funders, I wish to thank them for their support, as their assistance has been a catalyst in moving my research agenda forward.

The following are acknowledgment of publishing houses which granted permission to reproduce my writings which have previously been published elsewhere. But before noting those, I wish to acknowledge the High Court of Australia for allowing me to reproduce the 2008 *The Queen v Tang* judgment at the end of this collection.

The number of my pieces are reproduced with permission from Oxford University Press, including: "Nineteenth Century Law of the Sea and the British Abolition of the Slave Trade" which first appeared in the *British Yearbook of International Law*; the review of Kevin Bales' *Understanding Global Slavery: A Reader*, in *International Journal of Refugee Law*; and the case note of *Rantsev* v. *Cyprus and Russia* in *Human Rights Law Review*; while the book review of *Trafficking in Human Beings: Modern Slavery*, by Silvia Scarpa, appeared in *European Journal of International Law*. I also wish to acknowledge OUP for permitting the reproduction at p. 95, of the map of the Maritime Zone agreed to at the 1890 Brussels Conference.

Brill/ Martinus Nijhoff grant permission to reproduce the following piece which appeared in the *Journal of the History of International Law*: "Slavery and the League of Nations: Ethiopia as a Civilised Nation"; and "On the Curious Disappearance of Human Servitude from General International Law." As well as acknowledge Hart Publishing for permission to reprint the review of Fernne Brennan and John Packer's collection on reparations which appeared in the *Irish Yearbook of International Law*.

"Property and the Definition of Slavery" co-authored with Robin Hickey, appeared in *International and Comparative Law Quarterly* and is reproduced in this collection with permission from British Institute of International and Comparative Law; the case note of *Hadijatou Mani Koraou v. Republic of Niger* and the review of *The Slave Trade and the Origins of International Human Rights Law* by Jenny Martinez appeared in the *American Journal of International Law* and are reproduced with permission from the American Society of International Law.

Beyond these, the following have been reproduced with the permission of the journals they appeared in: "No Effective Trafficking Definition Exists: Domestic Implementation of the Palermo Protocol," in the *Albany Government Law Review*; "The International Legal Regime of Slavery and Human Exploitation and its Obfuscation by the Term of Art: 'Slavery-Like Practice'," in the *Cahiers de la recherche en droits fondamentaux*; a piece entitled "Slavery and its Definition," which was co-authored with Kevin Bales appeared in *Global Dialogue*; and the case note of *The Queen v. Tang* which is found in the *Melbourne Journal of International Law*.

Introduction

The year 2015 marks the 125th anniversary of the first universal, legally binding, instrument meant to address slavery. Yet, for the first hundred of those years, the emerging law related to slavery and lesser servitudes suffered diminishing returns, becoming effectively inoperative. It has only been during the last fifteen years or so that a project to reclaim the legal from the political has been successful in demonstrating the parameters of what, in law, constitutes forced labour, servitude, slavery, and the slave trade.

Considerations of the law applicable to the slave trade provide context which gets us from international law justifying the trade to the point of dispelling the myth that universal jurisdiction ever was applicable to the slave trade. Where forced labour is concerned, while its limited normative content is set out, the rather interesting issue regarding its *jus cogens* nature is tackled head on. With reference to servitude and to slavery, what follows highlights how each of these concepts fell into disuse but more importantly how, through legal analysis, they have been given a new lease on life, their full potential only now being realised as tools in seeking to combat slavery, various types of servitudes and specific forms of human trafficking. That legal analysis was built on archival research which brought to life the deliberations of the League of Nations era and of the United Nations. Where slavery is concerned, the establishment of the *Research Network on the Legal Parameters of Slavery* assisted in taking the reading of slavery as originally conceived and developing it in a manner which was both internally consistent and captured the lived experience of modern slavery.

The results have been well worth the effort as rich veins have been mined bringing much conceptual clarity to what was previously an area of the law best side-stepped, but more often than not, simply ignored. What follows then is an overall consideration of the legal regime meant to curtail human exploitation – the law of anti-slavery, writ large.

The Legal Instruments

The General Act of the Brussels Conference of 1890 marks a watershed in international relations as previous to this, international law not only allowed slavery and the slave trade, it justified it. While enlightened thinkers, notably Bodin and Montesquieu, demonstrated the bankruptcy of thought which allowed for the enslavement of human beings, the Law of Nations persisted in allowing it, though as we approach 1890, with a growing discomfort for the international

 | DOI 10.1163/9789004279896_002

jurists who considered the issue. While the Powers at the 1814–1815 Congress of Vienna would declare "their wish of putting an end to the scourge, which has so long desolated Africa, degraded Europe, and afflicted humanity," it would take another seventy-five years before such pious wishes would be translated into a first universally binding instrument.

The legal means of seeking to repress the slave trade at sea focused on the eastern Indian Ocean in 1890; this was followed by the 1926 Slavery Convention, which required parties to "prevent and suppress the slave trade" more generally. For the States that consented to that 1926 Convention, it also required somewhat hesitantly that they "bring about, progressively and as soon as possible, the complete abolition of slavery in all its forms." The next milestone of anti-slavery legislation would be 1930 Forced Labour Convention of the International Labour Organisation (ILO) which regulated the use of such labour in the colonies, while banning it for private use and required States Parties "to suppress the use of forced or compulsory labour in all its forms within the shortest possible period."

From a legal perspective, the first international binding instrument of the United Nations era was the 1956 Supplementary Convention, which established forthwith that the "act of enslaving another person [...] shall be a criminal offence," while it returned to the formula of 1926 where the conventional servitudes of debt bondage, serfdom, servile marriage and sham adoption were concerned, as these should be dealt with "progressively and as soon as possible" so as to seek their "complete abolition or abandonment." This was followed the next year by the ILO's 1957 Abolition of Forced Labour Convention which requires States to undertake "to suppress and not to make use of any form of forced or compulsory labour" as a means of discrimination, education, labour discipline, or political coercion; as punishment for participation in a labour strike; or as "a method of mobilising and using labour for purposes of economic development."

It was not until the aspirations of the 1948 Universal Declaration of Human Rights were translated into legal obligations, via the 1966 United Nations International Covenant on Civil and Political Rights, that we can speak of the legal abolition of forced labour (though with a number of exceptions), servitude, slavery and the slave trade. Thus, it is only in my life-time that these types of human exploitation have been universally outlawed. Article 8 of the Covenant reads:

1. No one shall be held in slavery; slavery and the slave-trade in all their forms shall be prohibited.
2. No one shall be held in servitude.

3. (a) No one shall be required to perform forced or compulsory labour;
   (b) Paragraph 3(a) shall not be held to preclude, in countries where imprisonment with hard labour may be imposed as a punishment for a crime, the performance of hard labour in pursuance of a sentence to such punishment by a competent court.
   (c) For the purpose of this paragraph the term 'forced or compulsory labour' shall not include:
      (i) Any work or service, not referred to in sub-paragraph (b), normally required of a person who is under detention in consequence of a lawful order of a court, or of a person during conditional release from such detention;
      (ii) Any service of a military character and, in countries where conscientious objection is recognized, any national service required by law of conscientious objectors;
      (iii) Any service exacted in cases of emergency or calamity threatening the life or well-being of the community;
      (iv) Any work or service which forms part of normal civil obligations.

Since 1966, three instruments which are meant to be universally applicable have been created that fall within the purview of the law meant to curtail human exploitation and expand the remit of the regime's applicability. These are, the 1999 Worst Forms of Child Labour Convention which requires ILO Members to "take immediate and effective measures to secure the prohibition and elimination of the worst forms of child labour as a matter of urgency." The first of these worst forms of child labour being:

> all forms of slavery or practices similar to slavery, such as the sale and trafficking of children, debt bondage and serfdom and forced or compulsory labour, including forced or compulsory recruitment of children for use in armed conflict.

The second such instrument is the 1998 Statute of the International Criminal Court which develops the international crime of enslavement while creating the crime of sexual slavery, wherein it is recognised through its secondary legislation – the Elements of Crimes – that enslavement and sexual slavery may manifest themselves through a deprivation of liberty which in some circumstances might include forced labour, servitude as set out in the 1956 Supplementary Convention, or trafficking in persons. The final instrument of a universal character which has expanded the legal parameters of what is understood as human exploitation is the 2000 UN Palermo Protocol related to Trafficking which requires States Parties to prevent, investigate and prosecute those who would, in essence, move persons against their will for the purposes of exploitation; that is for the purposes of: "the exploitation of the prostitution of others or other forms of sexual exploitation, forced labour or services, slavery or practices similar to slavery, servitude or the removal of organ." Here then are the legal instruments which constitute the foundation of what Joel Quirk has termed the *Anti-Slavery Project*; that is: the law which seeks to address human exploitation in its various guises.[1] These legal instruments, along with the organisations which established them, and the mechanisms both international and domestic, meant to address these harms should thus be understood as the legal regime curtailing human exploitation.

Substantive Elements of the Legal Regime Curtailing Human Exploitation

When, in 1815, the European Powers made their Declaration on the Abolition of the Slave Trade, they recognised that the trade "has been considered, by just and enlightened men of all ages, as repugnant to the principles of humanity and universal morality."[2] And yet, such enlightened men were far and few between, and, in the main, their arguments carry little weight, as the Atlantic Slave Trade grew in importance. Prior to the legal regime curtailing human exploitation developing in the late Nineteenth Century, international law not only allowed for slavery and the slave trade, it justified it. As William Warwick Buckland wrote in his classic 1908 treatise *The Roman Law of Slavery*:

> Slavery is the only case in which, in the extant sources of Roman law, a conflict is declared to exist between the *Ius Gentium* and the *Ius Naturale*. It is of course inconsistent with the universal equality of man which Roman speculations on the law of Nature assume, and we are repeatedly told that it is a part of the *Ius Gentium*, since it originates in war. Captives, it is said, may be slain: to make them slaves is to save their lives; hence they are called *servi, ut servati*, and thus both names, *servus* and *mancipium*, are derived from the capture of war.[3]

---

1 Joel Quirk, *The Anti-Slavery Project: From the Slave Trade to Human Trafficking*, 2011.

2 *Declaration des 8 Cours, relative à l'Abolition Universelle de la Traite des Nègres*, 8 Feburary 1815, *British and Foreign State Papers*, Vol. 3 (1815–1816), 1838, p. 972. The eight Powers at Vienna were: Austria, Britain, France, Prussia, Russia, Portugal, Spain, and Sweden.

3 William Warwick Buckland, *The Roman Law of Slavery*, 1908, p. 1.

Thus, as the argument in international law – *jus gentium*: Roman precursor to international law, being the law applicable to all, including those foreign to the Roman Empire – goes: having spared the life of a prisoner of war, the victor could enslave the vanquished. As Jean Bodin wrote in 1576: "who would deny that it is laudable and charitable to spare the life of a prisoner taken in legitimate warfare who cannot find a ransom, instead of killing him in cold blood, for this was generally the origin of enslavement." And yet Bodin did not accept this argument, unwilling as he was to set down "in words the base humiliation that slaves have been made to suffer," instead noting "where is the man who would spare the lives of the vanquished if he saw more profit in killing than in sparing them?"[4] For Montesquieu, writing in the Eighteenth Century, "these reasons of the jurists are not sensible. It is false that killing in war is permissible except in the case of necessity; but, when a man has made another man his slave, it cannot be said that he had of necessity to kill him, since he did not do so. The only right that war can give over captives is that they may be imprisoned so that they can no longer do harm."[5]

In having considered the issue of slavery within the cannon of international law as set out, in the main, in the *Classic in International Law* series commissioned more than a century ago by the Carnegie Foundation, it becomes clear that a dichotomy existed between the law applicable in Europe and the law beyond its borders. For those wars in Europe, an evolution transpires over time with regard to captives in war: from death, through slavery, to ransom, to being held until the end of war and released through an exchange of prisoners. Beyond those Christian wars, the Law of Nations was remarkably consistent in allowing for enslavement of captives, yet its scope would increase as the Atlantic Slave Trade grew in importance. From Francisco de Vitoria, who provided the legal justification and rationale for the enslavement of the New World population, through the likes of Bynkershoek, Gentili, Pufendorf, and Vattel, enslavement beyond Europe forms part of the Law of Nations. Of note also is Grotius, for whom I have reserved special mention as Hugo de Groot – who is often revered as the 'grandfather of international law' – probably did more than any other person in giving justification for the industrial nature of the Atlantic Slave Trade. This is so, as Grotius went against the trend of narrowing the application of the *jus gentium*. Instead, Grotius, whose work would be used by many in his wake as an "apologist for slavery," would deem slavery

4 Jean Bodin, *Six Books of the Commonwealth*, 1576; as reproduced in Stanley Engerman, Seymour Drescher and Robert Paquette, *Slavery* (2001), pp. 17 and 18.

5 Baron de Montesquieu, *The Spirits of the Laws* (1748); see *id.*, p. 20.

applicable not only to prisoners of war, but would widen its scope to everybody on enemy territory and their progeny.[6]

The Slave Trade

During much of the Nineteenth Century, when States sought to abolish the slave trade, their focus, in legal terms, was on the Atlantic Slave Trade. This in the context where there also existed a trade in European sailors captured on the Mediterranean Sea and held for ransom by the Barbary States of North Africa; as well as an older trade carried out not by caravels, but by camel caravans heading east across the Africa continent with its human chattel destined for the Ottoman Empire, the Arabian Peninsula, and further afield. Yet, the industrial nature of the Atlantic Slave Trade was such that one of the foremost experts on slavery, Robin Blackburn, termed it a different 'species of slavery'.[7] This large scale enslavement of African populations transpired from 1514 to 1866 and was carried out by flagged ships of what is today: Brazil, Denmark, France, Germany, The Netherlands, Norway, Portugal, Spain, Sweden, the United Kingdom, the United States of America, and Uruguay. The most accurate assessment of the scale of the Atlantic Slave Trade is that over 12.5 million human beings were taken from Africa, with 10.7 million surviving to be disembarked in the Western Hemisphere. Of those people taken, over 3.1 million were embarked on the West Central African coast, the epicentre being the port of Luanda, capital of modern-day Angola; while both the regions of the Bights of Benin (re: the Slave Coast) and Biafra shipped more than a million enslaved persons, their busiest ports being Whydah (Benin) and Calabar (Nigeria) respectively. Of those individuals who survived the Middle Passage, 4.8 million came ashore on various Caribbean islands; 3.4 million arrived in Brazil, with less than 365,000 landed in North America.[8]

Throughout the Nineteenth Century no issue of international law occupied more time, energy, and involved more countries than the Atlantic Slave Trade. At play was the fundamental issue of the freedom of the sea, which saw the United Kingdom seek to extend the wartime right to visit ships on the high seas to check for contraband goods, to a peacetime 'right to visit' to suppress the slave trade. The failure to get general agreement on a right to visit to suppress

6 The quote of Grotius as an apologist for slavery is from John Cairns, "Stoicism, Slavery and Law: Grotian Jurisprudence and Its Reception," *Grotiana*, Volume 22/23, 2001/2002, p. 242. For more on the consideration of slavery within the classics of international law, see Jean Allain, *Slavery in International Law: Of Human Exploitation and Trafficking* (2013), pp. 9–55.

7 Robin Blackburn, *The Overthrow of Colonial Slavery*, 1776–1848, 1988, p. 7.

8 See The Trans-Atlantic Slave Trade Database at http://www.slavevoyages.org/.

the slave trade at sea during the Congress of Vienna led the British to create a web of bilateral agreements which, in reality, allowed it to unilaterally police vessels of an ever-growing number of States in its search to stop the slave trade. While the recalcitrant States did not object in principle to ending the slave trade, they sought to emphasise the Grotian notion of the freedom of the seas as being fundamental to maritime commerce. As John Quincy Adams, the United States Secretary of State, would relate when asked if he could conceive of a greater evil than the slave trade, he responded: "yes, admitting the right of search by foreign officers of our vessels upon the sea in time of peace; for that would be making slaves of ourselves."[9] This disagreement over the nature of the seas resulted in the seventy-five year lag- time between the 1815 Declaration and the first legally binding instrument signed in 1890.

While the 1890 General Act of the Brussels Conference was meant to be universal in application, it was not universal in scope, as it was limited to a zone off of Eastern Africa, which extended into the Rea Sea, the Persian Gulf, while taking in the southern coast of the Arabian Peninsula. The Act applied to small, artisan, ships rather than the much larger slavers which had been built in the not so distant past to carry out their nefarious commerce on the Atlantic. The fact that the Atlantic Slave Trade had, for all intents and purposes, ended more than a dozen years previously very much made the United Kingdom's attempts to gain an international treaty more palatable to States but for one: France. France, made a reservation to the 1890 General Act which, in essence, allowed only it exclusive right to visit ships flying the *Tricolore* so as to suppress the trade. The failure of France to effectively police those vessels plying the maritime zone established by the General Act lead the United Kingdom to bring the 1905 *Muscat Dhows* case against it before the Permanent Court of Arbitration.[10] That case would sound the death-knell of the slave trade at sea, as it determined that from 1863 onwards, sailors from Muscat (modern day Oman) could not transmit the use of the French flag from generation to generation or from one dhow to another, thus effectively closing the last avenue for carrying out the slave trade at sea.

With regard to the slave trade, maybe the most interesting substantive question of international law relates to the persistence of a myth, often repeated, that there exists universal jurisdiction to suppress the slave trade on the high

9 See Hugh Soulsby, "The Right of Search and the Slave Trade in Anglo-American Relations 1814–1862," *John Hopkins University Studies in Historical and Political Science Collection*, Series 51(2), 1933, p. 8.

10 *The Muscat Dhows*, Award of 8 August 1905, James Brown Scott (ed.), *The Hague Court Reports* (1916).

seas.[11] As with other elements of the regime meant to curtail human exploitation, there has been a lack of research and analysis into the normative content of the slave trade which has allowed inaccuracies to persist over time, gaining momentum and a life of their own, but ultimately having no basis in law. Universal jurisdiction, it should be noted, is a legal concept which gives the power to act, to any State *vis-a-vis* a criminal act. From 1820 until 1956 it was British policy in developing international law around the issue, to equate the slave trade with piracy. Had the United Kingdom been successful in assimilating the slave trade to piracy, it would have achieved its goal of gaining universal jurisdiction over the slave trade and thus a right to visit any ship on the high seas during peacetime so as to suppress the slave trade. It might be added that such a right would have existed for all States in law, but the reality of the 19th Century was that the Royal Navy was *the* dominant maritime power.

Piracy is the quintessential crime for which universal jurisdiction has been established, in large part because the ordinary means of establishing jurisdiction over vessels at sea is not applicable to pirate ships. Ordinarily, a ship is bound by the obligations and requirements of the State to which that vessels is registered, thus giving it the right to fly that State's flag. An act of piracy, in effect, removes flag-State jurisdiction, creating a status of outlaw; as a result, all States have – hence 'universal' – jurisdiction to act so as to suppress piracy on the high seas. One can see the close quarters the slave trade has to piracy, in the sense that each transpires at sea. However, as opposed to piracy, when the slave trade remained legal, flag-State jurisdiction was applicable and, as between the United States of America and the United Kingdom, this distinction was deemed important enough to go to war. Although not the overriding justification for the War of 1812, the fact that Royal Navy was – illegally – visiting American merchant ships under the pretext of suppressing the slave trade, but impressing its sailor, fed into the American determination to declare war on the United Kingdom.

In the context where States, foremost among them France and the United States of America, balked at the creation of a customary norm of universal jurisdiction allowing for the visiting of any ship on the high seas suspected of being involved in the slave trade, the only means by which a State could visit a foreign ship at sea in peacetime was by agreement set out in a treaty. As part of

11 See James Crawford, *Brownlie's Principles of Public International* Law, 2012, p. 468 where he writes: "The original crime to which universal jurisdiction attached was that of piracy *ius gentium*, which was in turn followed by slavery"; as well as Jenny Martinez, *The Slave Trade and the Origins of International Human Rights Law*, 2012, pp. 114–139. A review of the Martinez book is reproduced in this volume at Chapter 11.

its early consideration, the newly established United Nations International Law Commission mandated, in large part, to assist in codifying existing customary international law, turned to consider the issue of jurisdiction to supress the slave trade at sea. The Commission made plain that "States were not prepared to go nearly so far in the case of the slave trade as in the case of piracy."[12] Indeed it might be noted that the United Kingdom put a proposal to the 1885 Berlin Conference that the slave trade be declared "a crime against the Law of Nations." The draft Declaration read in part that: "The Slave Trade is henceforth a crime prohibited by the Law of Nations, and cognizable by the tribunals of all civilized nations whatever the nationality of the accused."[13] This proposal, however, did not find favour with the fifteen States gathering in Berlin. Instead, the current law of the sea mirrors what was agreed to one-hundred and twenty-five years ago in Brussels: that a warship of one State may board a vessel if it has reasonable grounds to suspect it being involved in the slave trade, for the sole purpose of verifying whether that ship has the right to fly its flag. If that ship is not one of its own flag-ships, no further action is prescribed.[14] As opposed to piracy, which by way of the Law of the Sea Convention, provides for any State to arrest those on board and to seize a pirate ship and its content – thus prescribing universal jurisdiction; the Convention makes plain that no such jurisdiction exist with regard to the slave trade. Article 99 of the Law of the Sea Convention, confirms jurisdiction is in the hands of the flag-State: "Every State shall take effective measures to prevent and punish the transport of slaves in ships authorized to fly its flag and to prevent the unlawful use of its flag for that purpose."

Forced Labour

The issue of forced labour was first considered at the international level by the League of Nations as its Covenant, under Article 23(a), mandated that the organisation "endeavour to secure and maintain fair and humane conditions of labour for men, women, and children." However, the League effectively handed over the issue of forced labour to the International Labour Organisation upon completion of the negotiations of the 1926 Slavery Convention, considering that the ILO's mission "naturally include[s] the problem of forced labour."

---

12 United Nations, General Assembly, International Law Commission, *Yearbook of the International Law Commission,* Vol. I, (Summary Record of the Third Session: 16 May–27 July 1951), UN Doc. A/CN.4/SER.A/1951, 21 October 1957, p. 350.

13 Suzanne Miers, *Britain and the Ending of the Slave Trade,* (Longman, London, 1975), 171–172.

14 See Article 110, United Nations Convention on the Law of the Sea, 1982.

For its part, the 1926 Slavery Convention mentions forced labour in both its preamble and devotes a specific article to the issue. The drafting process of the preambular paragraph is instructive as the provision which states "that it is necessary to prevent forced labour from developing into conditions analogous to slavery," was originally proposed by the United Kingdom to address the issue as "it is desirable to regulate the employment of forced labour."[15] Instructive, as we shall see, the 1930 Forced Labour Convention was precisely that: an instrument meant to regulate rather than outlaw forced labour.

While the article devoted to forced labour in the 1926 Slavery Convention was the most discussed and contentious provision of the whole negotiating process, it ultimately set out the framework for what would become the 1930 Forced Labour Convention. Its contentious nature resulted from the fact that the provisions related to forced labour could have impact both within the borders of the Members of the League of Nations and within their colonies, whereas slavery and the slave trade were deemed to apply beyond the pale of its membership. So as to ensure that forced labour did not develop into conditions analogous to slavery, Article 5 of the 1926 Slavery Convention prescribed that forced labour was only to be "exacted for public purposes," but where it was used for private gain, that this be put to an end "progressively and as soon as possible." Where it did exist, the provisions of Article 5 sought to regulate forced labour: that it be exceptional in character, that adequate remuneration be received, and that labourers not be displaced from their habitual residence.

When a draft of the Forced Labour Convention was first considered by an ILO Committee, the workers representative (rather than the employers' or governments' representatives) objected to its content, making plain that the provisions did not aim to end forced labour, rather, they tended "towards a kind of codification of forced labour."[16] The bulk of the provisions of the 1930 Forced Labour Convention, are taken up with transitional provisions, wherein States Parties were meant "to suppress the use of forced or compulsory labour in all its forms within the shortest possible period." These transitional provisions – included the exacting of forced or compulsory labour only for able-bodied males, between the ages of eighteen and forty-five years; that such labour be

15 See League of Nations, Draft Convention on Slavery, Replies of Governments, Reply from the British Government, A.10.1926.VI, 21 July 1926, p. 2; as found in League of Nations, Publications of the League of Nations, VI.B.Slavery.1926, VI. B. 2; and Jean Allain, *The Slavery Conventions: The Travaux Préparatoires of the 1926 League of Nations Convention and the 1956 United Nations Convention*, 2008, p. 47.

16 International Labour Conference, 14th Session, Item I, Minority Report of the Workers Members of the Committee on Forced Labour, *Forced Labour* (1930), p. 46.

required for no more than sixty days a year; and that work be limited for the same hours and pay as prevailing for *voluntary* work – are no longer applicable. Deemed as being desuetude in law and recognised as such by the ILO in 2007; this was confirmed in 2014 with the signing of the Protocol to the Forced Labour Convention wherein the preamble notes "that the transitional period provided for in the Convention has expired, and the provisions [...] are no longer applicable."[17]

As for the normative content of forced or compulsory labour, it may be said that very little of substance has emerged since the drafting of the 1930 Forced Labour Convention, in part because the United Nations human rights system has failed to engage with the issue, maintaining the clear division between it and the ILO, as first established in 1926 by its predecessor, the League of Nations. This, it might be added, has been to the detriment of victims of forced labour, as it has effectively limited the application of both international human rights and criminal law being mobilised to deal with cases of forced or compulsory labour.

What then is forced labour? Forced or compulsory labour is made up of two elements, the first is the definition which reads: Forced or compulsory labour is "all work or service which is exacted from any person under the menace of any penalty and for which the said person has not offered himself voluntarily." Where the drafting process of this provision is instructive is to be found in the consideration of the term 'penalty' not be read in the strict sense as imposed by a judicial body, rather that it be deemed "any penalty or punishment, inflicted by persons or body whatever." Further, it was confirmed that the phrase 'under the menace of any penalty' should be read to include "the loss of any rights or privileges."[18] Beyond that, the oversight body of the ILO conventions, the Committee of Experts on the Application of the Conventions and Recommendations has stated that the phrase 'the loss of rights or privileges' would include situations "where persons who refuse to perform voluntary labour may lose certain rights, advantages or privileges" such as "promotion, transfer, access to new employment, the acquisition of certain consumer goods, housing or participation in university programmes."[19] In going no further, the

17 International Labour Conference, Text of the Protocol to the Forced Labour Convention, 1930, 9A – Provisional Record, 103rd Session, 2014, p. 2.

18 International Labour Conference, 14th Session, Item I, Report of the Committee on Forced Labour to the Twelfth Session of the Conference, *Forced Labour*, 1930, pp. 11 and 691.

19 International Labour Conference, 96th Session, Item III, Report of the Committee of Experts on the Application of Conventions and Recommendations, *Eradication of Forced Labour*, General Survey concerning Forced Labour Convention, 1930 (No. 29), and the Abolition of Forced Labour Convention, 1957 (No. 105), Report III (Part 1B), 2007, p. 20.

ILO has failed to provide any legal clarity or content to this element of definition of forced labour.

The second element of forced or compulsory labour is the exceptions which, while being recognised as instances of forced labour in and of themselves, they are nevertheless excluded from the requirements set out in the 1930 Convention and the 2014 Protocol. These exceptions are:

(a) Any work or service exacted in virtue of compulsory military service laws for work of a purely military character;
(b) Any work or service which forms part of the normal civic obligations of the citizens of a fully self-governing country;
(c) Any work or service exacted from any person as a consequence of a conviction in a court of law, provided that the said work or service is carried out under the supervision and control of a public authority and that the said person is not hired to or placed at the disposal of private individuals, companies or associations;
(d) Any work or service exacted in cases of emergency, that is to say, in the event of war or of a calamity or threatened calamity, such as fire, flood, famine, earthquake, violent epidemic or epizootic diseases, invasion by animal, insect or vegetable pests, and in general any circumstance that would endanger the existence or the well-being of the whole or part of the population;
(e) Minor communal services of a kind which, being performed by the members of the community in the direct interest of the said community, can therefore be considered as normal civic obligations incumbent upon the members of the community, provided that the members of the community or their direct representatives shall have the right to be consulted in regard to the need for such services.

While I have elsewhere considered in depth the way both international and regional bodies have provided more guidance to both the definition and the exception to forced or compulsory labour,[20] I wish to turn to consider the 1957 Abolition of Forced Labour Convention, before revisiting the definition in light of claims made by the ILO that forced or compulsory labour constitutes a norm of *jus cogens*.

The 1957 Abolition of Forced Labour Convention, which supplements rather than revises the 1930 Convention, was the end product of a mud-slinging exercises

20 See Jean Allain, *Slavery in International Law: Of Human Exploitation and Trafficking*, 2013, pp. 217–235.

resulting from the rivalry of the Cold War. Redundant, as the 1957 Convention simply draws attention to practices which are already covered 1930 definition of forced labour, and could have been addressed simply by reference to that instrument. Instead, the boisterous exchange of Cold War driven accusations resulted in a 1953 joint United Nations and International Labour Organisation Report which noted that a number of Western States were using systems of forced labour for economic purposes against their indigenous populations, while the Union of Soviet Socialist Republics were using systems of forced labour as a means of political coercion against those within their own countries who expressed their "ideological opposition to the established political order."[21]

There is no denying that at the time, in a number of States on both sides of the divide of the Iron Curtain, there existed systems of forced labour utilised as a means of political coercion or economic development. And thus, if nothing else the 1957 Abolition of Forced Labour Convention, drew attention to these systems, which as a result of the decolonisation process and the imploding of the Soviet Union, have now lost their industrialised scale. Article 1 of the 1957 Convention sets out the obligation "to suppress and not to make use of any form of forced or compulsory labour" for the following reasons:

(a) As a means of political coercion or education or as a punishment for holding or expressing political views or views ideologically opposed to the established political, social or economic system;
(b) As a method of mobilising and using labour for purposes of economic development;
(c) As a means of labour discipline;
(d) As a punishment for having participated in strikes;
(e) As a means of racial, social, national or religious discrimination.

Turning now to *jus cogens*, as early as 2009, I developed an argument that challenged the International Labour Organisation's assertion that forced labour constituted a peremptory norm of international law.[22] I am happy to report that during the adoption of the 2014 Protocol to the Forced Labour Convention, 1930, that argument held sway despite the efforts the ILO's Legal Adviser to the

---

21 United Nations and International Labour Office, Report of the *Ad Hoc* Committee on Forced Labour, UN Doc. E/2431, 1953, pp. 124–125.

22 See Jean Allain, *Slavery in International Law: Of Human Exploitation and Trafficking*, 2013, pp. 246–254; and Jean Allain, "The Implications of the Preparatory Works for Debates on Slavery, Servitude and Forced Labour," in Adelle Blackett and Anne Trebilcock (eds.), *Handbook on Transnational Labour Law*, Edward Elgar Publishing, 2015.

negotiation conference. For its part, a *jus cogens* norm is peremptory in character in that what flows from its characterisation is what is often termed 'strict liability' in domestic legal systems. As the 2001 Articles on State Responsibility make plain, no circumstance can be invoked which would seek to preclude the wrongfulness of a violation of a *jus cogens* norm.[23] The claim that forced labour is a *jus cogens* norm was first stated in the 2007 Report of the ILO Commission of Inquiry into forced labour in Myanmar, in which it concluded "that there exists now in international law a peremptory norm prohibiting any recourse to forced labour and that the right not to be compelled to perform forced or compulsory labour is one of the basic human rights."[24] That claim is based on an ill-conceived argument which assimilates forced labour and the conventional servitudes found in the 1956 Supplementary Convention, to slavery; and then rides the prohibition against slavery's – or at least the slave trades' – status as a *jus cogens* norm into a determination that all of these constitute *jus cogens* norms.[25] While I have demonstrated elsewhere the manner in which the original argument used to propagate the notion that forced labour constitutes a *jus cogens* norm was faulty, the States negotiating the 2014 Protocol to the Forced Labour Convention turned to an argument developed in my 2013 *Slavery in International Law*, to estop the notion that forced labour constitutes a *jus cogens* norm.[26]

---

23 See Article 26, United Nations, International Law Commission, State Responsibility, UN Doc. A/CN.4/L.602/Rev.1, 26 July 2001. Note that there are further implications attached *jus cogens* norms which are found at Articles 40, 41 and 50 of the Articles of States Responsibly; and via Articles 53, 64, and 71 of the 1969 Vienna Convention on the Law of Treaties.

24 International Labour Organisation, Governing Body, Forced Labour in Myanmar (Burma), Report of the Commission of Inquiry appointed under article 26 of the Constitution of the International Labour Organization to examine the observance by Myanmar of the Forced Labour Convention, 1930 (No. 29), 2 July 1998, para. 203.

Note that the claim of forced labour as a peremptory norm also appears in International Labour Conference, 96th Session, Item III, Report of the Committee of Experts on the Application of Conventions and Recommendations, *Eradication of Forced Labour*, General Survey Concerning Forced Labour Convention, 1930 (No. 29), and The Abolition of Forced Labour Convention, 1957 (No. 105), Report III (Part 1b), 6 (2007); and International Labour Organisation, Report for Discussion at the Tripartite Meeting of Experts Concerning the Possible Adoption of an ILO Instrument to Supplement the Forced Labour Convention, 1930 (No. 29), TMELE/2013 4 (2013).

25 See Chapter 10.

26 See *id.*, for the discussion regarding the faulty argument used to first designate forced labour as a *jus cogens* norm. As for the argument as it played out at the 2014 ILO Conference, see Jean Allain, *Slavery in International Law: Of Human Exploitation and*

That argument is rather straight forward: that one cannot have a *jus cogens* norm if, built into that very norm, there are exceptions.[27] For its part, the ILO Committee of Experts itself recognises that the exceptions regarding military service, penal labour, emergency assistance, and as part of community or civil obligations, do constitute forced labour.[28] In fact, the need to include exceptions to the norm of forced labour looks to have been the reason why a prohibition against forced labour was not included in the Universal Declaration of Human Rights alongside servitude and slavery.

At the 2014 negotiations of the Protocol to the Forced Labour Convention, the Workers' Group of the Committee on Forced Labour, proposed that the preamble include a provision which reads: "that the prohibition of forced or compulsory labour should be considered a peremptory norm of international law [...]"; its Representative having noted that "it was now part of '*jus cogens*' which included genocide and slavery. Slavery and forced labour were at the core of what was discussed here so there should not be a problem." For his part, when the Legal Advisor representing the ILO at the Conference, Georges Politakis, was requested to clarify whether in law the prohibition of forced labour could be considered *jus cogens*, he noted the Report on Mayanmar and stated that these considerations "had been largely commented and reproduced in academic writings over the past 16 years."

That said, Mr Politakis noted that forced labour was not amongst those norms most frequently cited, but that the "prohibition of forced labour could be considered a peremptory norm of international law – indeed this had been the position taken by ILO supervisory bodies – and it would be now for the Committee to decide whether it wished to echo that view." It fell to the Government member of Canada to note that "she had been advised that this [the concept of *jus cogens*] could only apply to provisions or rights that had no

Trafficking, 2013, pp. 249–252 and more recently, Jean Allain, "The Implications of the Preparatory Works for Debates on Slavery, Servitude and Forced Labour," Adelle Blackett and Anne Trebilcock (eds.), *Handbook on Transnational Labour Law*, 2015.

27 The argument set out here should be distinguish from the one I have made with regard to *non-refoulement*, as in the latter case, states through practice and *opinio juris* have deemed the norm of *non-refoulement* to be peremptory in nature, and thus are estopped from applying the exception as to a person who is regarded as a danger to security, as set out in Article 33(2) of the 1951 Refugee Convention. See Jean Allain, "The Jus cogens Nature of Non-Refoulement," *International Journal of Refugee Law*, Vol. 13, 2001, pp. 533–558.

28 See International Labour Conference, 65th Session, Item III, Report of the Committee of Experts on the Application of Conventions and Recommendations, General Survey on the Reports Relating to Forced Labour Convention, 1930 (No. 29), and the Abolition of Forced Labour Convention, 1957 (No. 105), Report III (Part 4B), 1979, pp. 9–10.

lawful derogations, which was not the case for forced labour." With a number of States questioning the peremptory nature of forced labour, it fell to the representative of EU Members to propose that the provision equating forced labour to a *jus cogens* norm be replaced by the following provision which, in fact, is now to be found in the 2014 Protocol to the Forced Labour Convention, 1930: "Recognizing that the prohibition of forced or compulsory labour forms part of the body of fundamental rights."[29]

Servitude

Much of the lack of clarity previously hovering over the legal regime curtailing human exploitation has been with regard to what constitutes 'servitude' in law and the distinction to be made between cases of servitude and those of slavery. The lack of understanding as to what, in law, constitutes servitude continues to stymie international courts, which have failed to provide any substantive guidance on the issue. The most elaborate reading of servitude to date has been provided by the European Court of Human Rights which has held that what is to be prohibited is a "particularly serious form of denial of freedom"; and that "the concept of 'servitude' entails an obligation, under coercion, to provide one's services, and is linked with the concept of 'slavery'."[30] These elements provide little insight into what constitutes servitude in law and appear to speak more to a link to forced labour than to slavery.

Instead of seeking to provide a reading of what constitutes servitude in law – an exercise which to date has failed – I have demonstrated that in fact the substantive content of 'servitude' should be understood as constituting those 'institutions and practices similar to slavery' set out in the 1956 Supplementary Convention.[31]

The 1956 Supplementary Convention on the Abolition of Slavery, the Slave Trade, and *Institutions and Practices Similar to Slavery* was originally, conceived as the draft 'Supplementary Convention on Slavery and *Servitude*'. The change in the title was not brought about as a result of a re-focus in the substance of this instrument, rather the four servitudes set out in the Supplementary

29 International Labour Conference, 103th Session, Provisional Record, Report of the Committee on Forced Labour, Fourth Item on the Agenda: Supplementing The Force Labour Convention 1930 (No. 29), to Address Implementation Gaps to Advance Prevention, Protection and Compensating Measures, to Effectively Achieve the Elimination of Forced Labour, Number 9, 8 June 2014, pp. 14–15. paras 66, 72, 75, 76, 68, and 77.

30 *Case of M. and Others v. Italy and Bulgaria*, 17 December 2012, paras 149–150.

31 See Jean Allain, "On the Curious Disappearance of Human Servitude from General International Law," as reproduced in Chapter 14 of this volume.

Convention, despite having been recognised as such throughout the League of Nations era, were only re-branded as 'institutions…' or as they have come to be termed simply as '…practices similar to slavery' in 1956, as a result of the obligations tied to that Convention rather than the substance of the enumerated servitudes. Before going on to explain how these four conventional servitudes were rebranded as practices similar to slavery, it might be worthwhile to set out these four conventional servitudes; they are: debt bondages, serfdom, servile marriage, and sham adoption.

From the work of the League of Nations' Temporary Slavery Commission before the adoption of the 1926 Slavery Convention until the penultimate draft of the 1956 Supplementary Convention, it was understood that 'servitude' was not a concept, but instead was a categorisation of types of exploitation which experts had identified as such. The reason for the change in designations from servitudes to practices similar to slavery was the long shadow which the 1948 Universal Declaration of Human Rights cast over the negotiation of the 1956 Supplementary Convention. This is so despite the Universal Declaration stating that "no one shall be held in slavery or servitude," some States at the 1956 negotiations had other ideas. Led by the Representatives of the Soviet Socialist Republic, the Conference negotiating the 1956 Supplementary Convention would revert to obligations set out in both the 1926 Slavery Convention and the 1930 Forced Labour Convention, that the abolition of servitudes take place 'progressively and as soon as possible'. Considering what I have said thus far in this paragraph, readers may be able to guess how the negotiators squared the circle as between what the Universal Declaration said, to how far some States were willing to go during the 1956 negotiations.

The introduction of the penultimate draft of the 1956 Convention was the catalysis prompting not only the change of name to this instrument, but also the term 'servitude' – the very item this treaty was meant to suppress – being expunged from the substance of the 1956 Supplementary Convention. This came to pass as an objection was made to the proposal that the title of the 'Draft Convention on Slavery and Servitude' be modified to read the 'Draft Convention on the *Abolition* of Slavery and Servitude'. Despite the fact that the proposal sought only to add the term abolition to the title, the Soviet Representative feigned linguistic difficulties regarding the term 'servitude'.[32] Yet, Mr Nikolaev was adamant, "the word 'servitude' had no equivalent in

32 Note that the Russian speaking representative of Yugoslavia, Mr. Bozovic, let the cat out of the bag when he challenged Mr Nikolaev that the "Russian text of article 4 of the Universal Declaration of Human Rights successfully drew a distinction between slavery and servitude." See United Nations, Economic and Social Council, Committee on the Drafting of a

Russian and thus it would have to be translated by a paraphrase which would either unduly enlarge its meaning or else would be identical with a definition of slavery and would therefore be redundant."[33] As a result, a diplomatic compromise was reached on the back of an attempt by Mr Nikolaev to have the term 'servitude' removed from the title of the Convention or that the title read as follows: '*Supplementary Convention on the Abolition of Slavery, the Slave Trade and Institutions and Practices Similar to Slavery*'.[34]

As a result, the 1956 Supplementary Convention on the Abolition of Slavery, the Slave Trade, and Institutions and Practices Similar to Slavery requires that States Parties "take all practicable and necessary legislative and other measures to bring about progressively and as soon as possible the complete abolition or abandonment of the following institutions and practices": debt bondage, serfdom, servile marriage, and what might best be termed 'sham adoption'.[35] It might be emphasised here that the Convention also recognised that some of these 'practices similar to slavery' might, in law, also be "covered by the definition of slavery contained in article 1 of the Slavery Convention." Without going into detail, it should be understood that in law both serfdom and the three categories of servile marriage set out in the 1956 Supplementary Convention are indeed already covered by the definition of slavery. While this will become more evident after having read the section on Slavery to follow, it suffices to say that where a person is forced to live and labour on land and they are not free to change their status, such a practice is slavery; likewise, the purchase of a bride, transfer of a wife, or the inheriting of a widow each meet the threshold required to deem such a practice of serfdom is, in law slavery.[36] Thus, what is left of these conventional servitudes is debt bondage and sham adoption, where such practices, as defined in the 1956 Supplementary Convention, do not amount to slavery. It is within these rather narrow confines that we can speak of servitude. Narrow yes, but rather more expansive, in black-letter law,

---

Supplementary Convention on Slavery and Servitude, Summary Record of the Eight Meeting, 20 January 1956 UN Doc. E/AC.43/SR.8, 17 February 1956, p. 3.

33 United Nations, Economic and Social Council, Committee on the Drafting of a Supplementary Convention on Slavery and Servitude, Summary Record of the Ninth Meeting, 23 January 1956 UN Doc. E/AC.43/SR.9, 17 February 1956, p. 3.

34 United Nations, Economic and Social Council, Committee on the Drafting of a Supplementary Convention on Slavery and Servitude, Summary Record of the Ninth Meeting, 23 January 1956 UN Doc. E/AC.43/SR.9, 17 February 1956, p. 3.

35 See Chapter 15.

36 See Jean Allain, *Slavery in International Law: Of Human Exploitation and Trafficking* (2013), p. 202.

than any forward guidance given to the term 'servitude' by international courts or other authoritative bodies.

Having muddied the waters by substituting the term 'practices similar to slavery' for servitude, the waters went from being at least translucent to being opaque as a result of discussion around colonialism and apartheid which transpired within the United Nations in 1966. By this time, newly independent States made up the majority of the United Nations as a result of the decolonisation process and thus could dictate the agenda of the democratic bodies of that Organisation (re: all bodies but for the Security Council). Further, as the work of the United Nations was hobbled by the Cold War, UN Secretary General Dag Hammarskjöld sought to promote the work of those States – the Non-Aligned Movement – which sought to work within the UN to further their goals. This is how colonialism, but more so apartheid, came to dominate most facets of the United Nations during the 1960s and 1970s.

It was in 1966, when Members were asked to provide an update as to the extent to slavery, the slave trade and practices similar to slavery still in existence that the Soviet Union let loose the cat amongst the pigeons in responding that the "main factors upholding and encouraging slavery at the present time are colonialism, apartheid and racism."[37] While the discussions around the UN Economic and Social Council focused on apartheid, they waivered as between equating colonialism, apartheid and racism with slavery or practices similar to slavery. The main proponent of this link was the Representative of the United Republic of Tanzania, Mr. Waldo Waldron-Ramsey, who stated that:

> the policy of apartheid followed by South Africa in its own territory and in South West Africa, by the racist, traitorous and illegal regime in the Colony of Rhodesia and the colonialist methods applied by the Portuguese Government in the so-called Portuguese territories of Mozambique, Angola, and Portuguese Guinea, were flagrant examples of slavery. It was manifest that the methods traditionally used by the colonialist must be regarded as practices similar to slavery.[38]

When such consideration were then to be translated into a resolution, not surprisingly little consensus existed between those newly independent States and the colonial powers and their Western supporters. During the deliberations,

37 See United Nations, Mohamed Awad, *Report on Slavery*, UN Doc. E/4168/Rev.1, 1966, p. 285.

38 United Nations, Economic and Social Council, Social Committee, Summary Record of the Five Hundred and Thirty-Sixth Meeting, 7 July 1966, UN Doc E/AC.7/SR.536, 14 December 1966, p. 5.

the Representative of Greece made the point, that if States sought to expand the concepts of slavery or practices similar to slavery, which were legal terms, by including apartheid and colonialism, then States would need to convene a diplomatic conference to negotiate these concepts into the corpus of international law. With this, the penny dropped as despite holding the majority with the United Nations, at a negotiation conference meant to create an instrument which is legally binding, a two-thirds majority is required; something with the newly independent States could not command. As a result of the Greek intervention, a new tack was taken.

Mr. Waldo Waldron-Ramsey was not impressed:

> The Committee was not asked to go back to the 1926 or 1956 Conventions, to which the Greek representative had referred, but to deal with slavery in 1966. Some delegations interpreted the notion of slavery in a limited technical [re: legal] sense and were endeavouring to restrict its definition to suit their own ends; he was not fooled by their humbug.

Having burnt off steam, the Committee suspended considerations and reconvened the next day with a political compromise which would see a new term enter the lexicon of the United Nations. However, that term would prove to sow so much confusion that it would, for all intents and purpose contribute, to rendering the overall legal regime meant to curtail human exploitation effectively inoperative for nearly two generations.[39] This new term of art – as opposed to a term of law – is to be found in Resolution 1126 passed by the Economic and Social Council referring "the question of slavery and the slave trade in all their practices and manifestations including the *slavery-like practices* of apartheid and colonialism, to the Commission on Human Rights."[40] Thus, beside the legal term 'practice similar to slavery' emerging, the term of

39 For more detail, see: Jean Allain, "The International Legal Regime of Slavery and Human Exploitation and its Obfuscation by the Term of Art: 'Slavery-Like Practice'," as reproduce at Chapter 5 in this volume.

40 United Nations, Economic and Social Council, Resolution 1126 (XLI), 26 July 1966. Where law did emerge on the issue, in the guise of the 1973 International Convention on the Suppression and Punishment of the Crime of *Apartheid*, the link to slavery or practices similar to slavery was never seriously entertained during the negotiation process. Instead amongst the instances of the crime of apartheid is the "exploitation of the labour of the members of a racial group or groups, in particular by submitting them to forced labour." See Article 2(e), International Convention on the Suppression and Punishment of the Crime of *Apartheid*, United Nations, General Assembly, Resolution 3068, 30 November 1973.

art 'slavery-like practice', which while having no legal currency, would catch out many, including the experts within the United Nations system. Thus, as late as the year 2000, David Weissbrodt in a Working Paper for the UN Sub-Commission on Human Rights would write: "ownership is the common theme existing in all of the conventions concerning the abolition of slavery and slavery-like practices."[41]

Slavery

By the start of the Twenty-First Century slavery, as a legal concept, was devoid of any meaningful content. The prohibition of slavery, although often given lip-service, was effectively dead-letter law. Prior to a thorough examination of the material found at the Archives of the League of Nations and at the United Nations Library in Geneva, the most concerted effort in seeking to understand the overall regime curtailing human exploitation was set out by Yasmine Rassam.[42]

Yet Rassam's work lacks the insights garnered from a thorough analysis of the evolution of the regime. As a result, her considerations suffered from a number of the pitfalls that had hobbled the overall regime meant to address human exploitation. Primary amongst these drawbacks was the conflation of the legal with the political, which results in seeking to understand slavery not through its definition but rather as constituting a variety of categories or exploitative practices. As she notes: "instead of limiting the conception of slavery to its definition as it emerged under the Atlantic slave trade, situating slavery and the slave trade in its modern, global context allows for broader interpretations of categories under international law."[43] In her 1999 article, Rassam turns to New Haven School and its policy-oriented approach to interpreting international law to argue that the following categories should also be understood as constituting slavery: "the practices of sex trafficking, forced

---

41 United Nations, Economic and Social Council, Commission on Human Rights, Sub-Commission on the Promotion and Protection of Human Right, *Contemporary Forms of Slavery: Updated review of the implementation of and follow-up to the conventions on slavery*, Working Paper prepared by David Weissbrodt and Anti-Slavery International, UN Doc. E/CN.4/Sub.2/2000/3, 26 May 2000, p. 7. See also paragraph 62 at p. 15 for the same type of conflation.

42 See Yasmine Rassam, "Contemporary Forms of Slavery and the Evolution of the Prohibition of Slavery and the Slave Trade Under Customary International Law," *Virginia Journal of International Law*, Vol. 39, 1999, pp. 304–352; and Yasmine Rassam, "International Law and Contemporary Forms of Slavery: An Economic and Social Rights-Based Approach," *Penn State International Law Review*, Vol. 23, 2005, pp. 809–885.

43 *Id.*, *Virginia Journal of International Law*, p. 320.

prostitution, debt bondage, forced labour and the exploitation of immigrant domestic workers."[44] By 2005, Rassam was ready to jettison the established regime seeking to curtail human exploitation as being "outdated and unresponsive to the basic needs of the enslaved," and to propose a "paradigm shift from abolition to an economic and social rights-based approach" to addressing slavery. In advocating this position Rassam notes that "given the abundance of practices named slavery, a shared agreement among states could find that certain actions are so reprehensible that they constitute the crime of slavery."[45] This, despite the fact that States negotiating Statute of the International Criminal Court in 1998 had, for the second time in almost seventy-five years, confirmed the legal definition of slavery first established in 1926.[46]

The willingness of Rassam to want to give up on the legal regime related to slavery and lesser servitudes is understandable, as I have said: it was for all intents and purposes, dead-letter law. The legal regime had been overtaken by a political agenda which sought to expand the term slavery so as to include any social ill that furthered the aims of the parties making the claim. For instance, at the level of the United Nations, the body mandated to review developments in the field, the Working Group on Contemporary Forms of Slavery, undertook reports on: trafficking in persons, exploitation of prostitutes (in 1989); child pornography, children in armed conflict (1990); child soldiers (1991); removal of organs (1992); incest (1993); migrant workers, sex tourism (1994); illegal adoption (1996); and early marriages and detained juveniles (1997).

The ability to reclaim the legal from the political necessitated a return to the negotiation process and thus to the archives. In the previous section I considered how 'servitude' became inoperative as a result of both the obfuscation created by the introduction of the term of art 'slavery-like practice'; and the diplomatic developments of 1956 which saw the term 'servitude' replaced by 'practices similar to slavery'. Likewise, the norm of 'slavery' would become inoperative, its content effectively nullified as a result of a reading given to it from the 1930s onwards. That reading, which lacked legal rigour, was allowed to persist in a rather thoughtless manner until the archives revealed a different

44 *Id.*, p. 352; for the use of the New Haven School, see fn. 183.

45 Yasmine Rassam, "International Law and Contemporary Forms of Slavery: An Economic and Social Rights-Based Approach," *Penn State International Law Review*, Vol. 23, 2005, pp. 855 and 853.

46 See Article 7(a), 1956 Supplementary Convention on the Abolition of Slavery, the Slave Trade, and Institutions and Practices Similar to Slavery; and Article 7(2)(c), 1998 Rome Statute of the International Criminal Court.

story: a narrative which provides a firm legal grounding in being able to apply slavery to modern situations where a person is not legally enslaved, but where he or she is in a *de facto* condition of slavery.

Let me first spell out the definition of slavery as set out in Article 1 of the 1926 Slavery Convention:

> slavery is the status or condition over which any or all of the powers attaching to the right of ownership are exercised.

The reading of this provision which took hold was first set out in the 1930 Report of the International Commission of Inquiry meant to consider "whether slavery as defined in the anti-slavery convention in fact exists" in Liberia. That Commission was established in the wake of a populist leader having won the 1927 election in Liberia and accusations that the government was allowing slavery to be used within its borders and forcedly shipping labourers to Fernando Po. The International Commission of Inquiry was "convinced that the 'definition' of slavery is not so important to the welfare of Liberia and all its people as the study of the conditions themselves [...] and is therefore content to let the facts both speak and classify themselves."[47] In providing a rationale for increasing the scope of its considerations, the Commission stated that the "definition of slavery as formulated by the anti-slavery convention admittedly avoids detailed description for a comprehensive formula. In its present form it leaves little room for distinguishing between degrees of restrictive freedom." The International Commission of Inquiry then truncated a passage of the Report which accompanied the draft of the 1926 Convention to the Assembly of the League of Nations so as to make it appear that the definition of slavery not only included slavery, but also lesser servitudes and forced labour. In so doing, the Commission, while determining that "classic slavery carrying the idea of slave markets and slave dealers no longer exists as such in the Republic of Liberia," it could still find that servitude (what is called domestic slavery) and forced labour was being used. As a result, "high Government officials"[48] were implicated, which ultimately led to the forced resignation of both the President and Vice-President of the Republic of Liberia.

---

47 *Report of the International Commission of Inquiry into the Existence of Slavery and Forced Labour in the Republic of Liberia.* 8 September 1930; Publication of the Department of State, United States Government Printing Office, 1931, p. 15.

48 *Report of the International Commission of Inquiry into the Existence of Slavery and Forced Labour in the Republic of Liberia.* 8 September 1930 (Department of State, United States Government Printing Office, 1931) 142.

Seventy-years later, David Weissbrodt, a Member of the United Nations Sub-Commission on the Promotion and Protection of Human Right, would – as other had before him – follow the lead of the 1930 International Commission of Inquiry and utilise the same truncated passage to consider slavery not as defined by the 1926 Slavery Convention, but as a concept: "In order for the United Nations or any other international body to carry out a mandate concerned with slavery effectively, it is necessary to develop an international consensus on what practices are included within the concept of slavery."[49] Under this concept, Weissbrodt included "the various forms of slavery and slavery-like practices [sic]," including: serfdom, forced labour, debt bondage, migrant workers, trafficking, prostitution, forced marriage and sale of wives, and child labour and chid servitude.

This reading, which came to dominate the landscape occupying issues of human exploitation – or as it was termed within the United Nations: contemporary forms of slavery – effectively overshadowed another reading set out during the negotiation process of the 1926 Slavery Convention which provides slavery with a clear reading, based on its definition, and allows it to be seen as distinct from lesser forms of servitude. It might be noted that these two readings came to a head in 2008 in the Australian context, where first the Court of Appeal of the Supreme Court of Victoria noted that:

> The understanding of the scope of the definition of slavery stated by Jean Allain is at odds with that of David Weissbrodt in his paper commissioned by the Office of the United Nations High Commissioner for Human Rights. Weissbrodt concluded that the definition was intended to include the broader range of practices that had been addressed by the Temporary Slavery Commission of 1924, including debt bondage, serfdom, practices involving restrictions of liberty and personal control analogous to slavery, practices such as acquisition of women and girls in the guise of payment of dowry, and so forth. It was not limited to chattel slavery, but required examination of the degree of restriction and control exercised over the person, rather than concentration on the criterion of ownership.[50]

---

49 United Nations, Sub-Commission on the Promotion and Protection of Human Right, *Contemporary Forms of Slavery: Updated review of the implementation of and follow-up to the conventions on slavery*, Working Paper prepared by David Weissbrodt and Anti-Slavery International, UN Doc. E/CN.4/Sub.2/2000/3, 26 May 2000, p. 5.

50 Supreme Court of Victoria (Court of Appeal), *Queen v Wei Tang*, [2007] VSCA 134, 2 July 2007, para. 36.

While the Supreme Court of Victoria concluded that "in final analysis, it is unnecessary to resolve the dispute between Allain and Weissbrodt"; on appeal, the supreme court of Australia – the High Courts of Australia – did just that, in its 2008 *Tang* case. This was made most evident in oral proceedings when it was noted before the High Court that there "is perhaps an element of advocacy in Mr Weissbrodt's article about the need to expand the definition of 'slavery', or as Mr Allain was undertaking, a more academic task of investigating the actual *travaux preparatoires* of the 1926 Convention and the 1956 Convention as well."[51]

While considerations of the pertinent negotiation history has been set out elsewhere, what is important to retain here is that in the penultimate draft, the obligations of the 1926 Convention were to apply, in part, to "slavery in every form, notably in the case of domestic slavery and similar conditions."[52] When the draft was considered by States, the Union of South Africa objected to the phrase 'domestic slavery and similar conditions', saying, in essence that one was either held in slavery or not, and that this was to be determined on the basis of the definition of slavery as set out in Article 1 of the Convention. As a result, this phrase was omitted; and the four types of 'domestic slavery and similar conditions' under deliberation would come to form the basis – and precipitate the adoption of – the 1956 Supplementary Convention, as these conventional servitudes were in their embryotic form in 1926, but would mature by 1956, into debt bondage, serfdom, servile marriage, and sham adoption.

For its part, the 1930 International Commission, like Weissbrodt seventy-years later, would abridge the words of the British Delegate introducing the Convention so as to make it appear that those cases of 'domestic slavery and similar conditions' were included in the definition of slavery *ipso facto*. This, despite the Delegate stating that it was possible that these practices did not meet the threshold of Article 1 and that instead the Convention was meant to address "everything which admits the maintenance by a private individual of rights over another person of the same nature as the rights which an individual can have over things."[53]

---

51 High Court of Australia, *The Queen* v Wei *Tang*, [2008] HCATrans 180, 14 May 2008, para. 5595, p. 124.

52 See "A Legal Consideration 'Slavery' in Light of the *Travaux Préparatoires* of the 1926 Convention"; "The Definition of 'Slavery' in General International Law and the Crime of Enslavement within the Rome Statute" as reproduced in Chapters 17 and 18 of this volume; and more generally, Jean Allain, *The Slavery Conventions: The Travaux Préparatoires of the 1926 League of Nations Convention and the 1956 United Nations Convention, 2008.*

53 League of Nations, Slavery Convention: Report presented to the Assembly by the Sixth Committee, LofN Doc. A.104.1926.VI, as found in League of Nations, Publications of the League of Nations, VI.B.Slavery.1926, VI. B. 5, 24 September 1926, p. 2.

This reading of the intension of the drafters was confirmed by the expert group of the League of Nations ten years after the conclusion of the 1926 Slavery Convention. In its 1936 Report, the League of Nations Committee of Experts on Slavery considered the issue of serfdom and stated that it was important "to keep the fundamental distinction clearly in mind, and to realise that the status of 'serfdom' is a condition 'analogous to slavery' rather than a condition of actual slavery, and that the question whether it amounts to 'slavery' within the definition of the Slavery Convention must depend upon the facts connected with each of the various systems of 'serfdom'."[54] Here then we see that the distinction made between slavery and lesser servitudes: that it is only slavery if it falls within that definition as set out in the 1926 Slavery Convention. But also, it points to something more fundamental: that in understanding what constitutes slavery in law we must look to the substance of the relationship rather than its form. In other words, we must consider what is happening (re: an exercise of the powers attaching to the right of ownership) rather than what it is called (re: be it debt bondage, forced labour, serfdom, etc.). To emphasise the point, here is the Committee of Experts on Slavery speaking to the issue of debt bondage, wherein it speaks of *debt slavery*, and seeks to emphasise the distinction it had already made with regard to serfdom, that: it "is not 'slavery' within the definition set forth in Article 1 of the 1926 Convention, unless any or all the powers attaching to the right of ownership are exercised by the master."[55]

What then of this definition, that "slavery is the status or condition of a person over whom any or all of the powers attaching to the right of ownership are exercised?" In 1953 the United Nations Secretary-General turned to consider what constitutes the definition noting that one "does not find in the *travaux préparatoires* of the International Slavery Convention of 1926 any precise indication of the meaning of the 'power attaching to the right of ownership' to which the drafters of that Convention intended to refer, or of the legal system by which they were guided." The Secretary-General then noted that "it may reasonably be assumed that the basic concept which they had in mind was that of the authority of the master over the slave in Roman law, the '*dominica potestas*'. This authority was of an absolute nature, comparable to the rights of ownership, which included the right to acquire, to use, or to dispose of a thing

54 League of Nations, Slavery: Report of the Advisory Committee of Experts, Third (Extraordinary) Meeting of the Advisory Committee, LofN Doc. C.189(I). M.145.1936, VI, 13–14 April 1936, p. 27.

55 *Id.*, 24–25. Emphasis added.

or of an animal or of its fruits or offspring."[56] The Secretary-General then goes on to enumerate what he considers those powers attaching to the right of ownership:

1. the individual of servile status may be made the object of a purchase;
2. the master may use the individual of servile status, and in particular his capacity to work, in an absolute manner, without any restriction other than that which might be expressly provided by law;
3. the products of labour of the individual of servile status become the property of the master without any compensation commensurate to the value of the labour;
4. the ownership of the individual of servile status can be transferred to another person;
5. the servile status is permanent, that is to say, it cannot be terminated by the will of the individual subject to it;
6. the servile status is transmitted *ipso facto* to descendants of the individual having such status.[57]

This was the only authoritative engagement with what constituted those powers attaching to the right of ownership until the 2008 *Tang* judgement delivered by the High Court of Australia. While both the European Court of Human Rights and the International Criminal Tribunal for the former Yugoslavia had considered the 1926 definition, it is clear that to this point international courts had struggled to understand what constitutes slavery, having no jurisprudence or doctrinal studies to assist them in their understanding.[58] However, in light of what was to be found in the archives, the High Court of Australia developed a contemporary reading of the 1926 definition and started to unpack the wording of the definition of slavery.

The High Court first considered the phrase 'status or condition'. Citing a 2007 paper that I had presented at the Guest Lecture Series of the International Criminal Court, the High Court of Australia stated that its criminal law refers only to "'condition', not 'status or condition' [as] legal ownership of a person is

56 United Nations Economic and Social Council, Slavery, the Slave Trade, and other forms of Servitude (Report of the Secretary-General), UN Doc. E/2357, 27 January 1953, p. 40. p. 27.

57 United Nations Economic and Social Council, Slavery, the Slave Trade, and other forms of Servitude (Report of the Secretary-General), UN Doc. E/2357, 27 January 1953, p. 28.

58 See European Court of Human Rights, *Siliadin v France* (Application 73316/01), 26 July 2005; and International Criminal Tribunal for the former Yugoslavia, *Kunarac et als.* (IT-96-23-T &-IT-96-23/1-T) Judgment, 22 February 2001.

impossible." Thus, the Court adjudged that 'status' relates to *de jure* ownership, while condition "is concerned with *de facto* slavery." The Court then went on to explain the essence of such *de facto* slavery: "the reference to powers attaching to the right of ownership, which are exercised over a person in a condition described as slavery, is a reference to powers of such a nature and extent that they are attributes of effective (although not legal, for that is impossible) ownership."[59]

The Court then considered the second element of the definition, that is: "any or all of the powers attaching to the right of ownership," and cited the 1953 Memorandum of the Secretary-General of the United Nations – which had been rescued from the archives – that listed six such powers noted above. The High Court satisfied itself – by reference to some, but not all, of the powers noted by UN Secretary General – that five Thai women working in a brothel in Melbourne, had been held in a condition of slavery. Not surprisingly, the Court did not go beyond what was required in making its finding in the *Tang* case, and thus it was left to a group of property law scholars and experts of slavery both past and present, to give voice to what should be understood as the fullest expression of the exercise of those powers attaching to the right of ownership, where human beings are concerned.

Having met at both the Rockefeller Foundation's Bellagio Conference Centre and at Harvard University in 2010 and 2011 respectively, this Network of scholars and practitioners produced both the 2012 edited collection titled *The Legal Understanding of Slavery*, and the 2012 *Bellagio-Harvard Guidelines on the Legal Parameters of Slavery*. The *Guidelines* bring to bear the foundations of property law so as to provide a coherent reading of the definition of slavery.[60] In so doing, the definition is not only internally consistent – giving it the type of legal certainty needed in a court of law but it also captures the lived experience of modern slavery. Not surprising for those versed in property law, the starting point for engaging with the topic is Antony Honoré's work in developing the standard incidents of ownership.[61] As Robin Hickey has shown, those powers

59 *The Queen v Tang* [2008] HCA 39, 28 August 2008, para. 23.

60 See more generally, Jean Allain and Robin Hickey, "Property Law and the Definition of Slavery," *International and Comparative Law Quarterly*, Vol. 61, 2012, p. 915; as reproduced in Chapter 21 of this volume.

61 A.M. Honoré, "Ownership," A.G. Guest (ed.), *Oxford Essays in Jurisprudence* (1961), p. 105. See also: L.C. Becker, *Property Rights: Philosophic Foundations* (1983), pp. 7 and 18; J. Waldron, *The Right to Private Property* (1988), pp. 27, 28, and 49; S.R. Munzer, *A Theory of Property* (1990), pp. 22–27; J.E. Penner, "The Bundle of Rights Picture of Property," *University of California Law Review*, Vol. 43, 1995–6, p. 711; L. Katz, "Exclusion and

attaching to the right of ownership should be understood as being synonymous with Honoré's standard incidents of ownership.[62]

Before delving into those powers attaching to the right of ownership, it might be worthwhile to start from the most fundamental of questions: what is ownership? What may come as a surprise to many is that ownership – a fundamental tenet of liberal legalism and the basis of the capitalist economic order – has no set definition. Ownership has no fixed meaning, rather it is an elusive concept. A social construct, it is typically understood as a priorital right over something. As Honoré puts it: "those legal rights, duties and other incidents which apply, in the ordinary case, to the person who has the greatest interest in a thing admitted by a mature legal system." That 'greatest interest' thus does not mean that an individual has a sovereign or absolute right over a thing but, rather, the ability to enjoy and dispose of the thing "provided that one abstains from any use forbidden by statute or subordinate legislation."[63] Honoré lists what he calls the eleven 'standard incidents' of ownership, of which the majority are rights, but some are also obligations. These incidents include the right to possess, to use, to manage, to the income of the thing, to its capital, to its transmissibility, and the right of security; along with prohibition of harmful use and liability in instances of insolvency.

Where contemporary slavery is concerned, those incidents of ownership, those 'powers attaching to the right of ownership', start and end with possession – with control tantamount to possession. This is so, as possession allows for the exercise of the other powers attaching to the right of ownership. Yet, without possession – that control which removes agency from a person – slavery cannot exist in law. Thus, as Guideline 2 of the *Bellagio-Harvard Guidelines* makes plain:

> In cases of slavery, the exercise of 'the powers attaching to the right of ownership' should be understood as constituting control over a person in such a way as to significantly deprive that person of his or her individual liberty, with the intent of exploitation through the use, management, profit, transfer or disposal of that person. Usually this exercise will be

---

Exclusivity in Property Law," *University of Toronto Law Journal*, Vol. 58, 2008, p. 275 and J.W. Harris, *Property and Justice*, 1996, pp. 125–130.

62 Robin Hickey, "Seeking to Understand the Definition of Slavery," but also in the same collection J.E. Penner, "The Concept of Property and the Concept of Slavery," in Jean Allain (ed.), *The Legal Understanding of Slavery: From the Historical to the Contemporary*, 2012, pp. 242–252.

63 A.M. Honoré, "Ownership," A.G. Guest (ed.), *Oxford Essays in Jurisprudence* (1961), p. 105.

> supported by and obtained through means such as violent force, deception and/or coercion.

Beyond possession, the powers attaching to the right of ownership applicable in cases of slavery as set out in the *Bellagio-Harvard Guidelines* are: (a) the Buying, Selling or Transferring a Person; (b) Using a Person; (c) Managing the Use of a Person; (d) Profiting from the Use of a Person; (e) Transferring a Person to an Heir or Successor; and (f) Disposal, Mistreatment or Neglect of a Person. Let us unpack the first of these so as to understand the manner in which the *Guidelines* capture the essence of modern-day slavery. In speaking of the buying, selling or transferring a person, *Guideline 4(a)* makes plain that such buying, selling or transferring might well provide evidence of slavery. But this is not enough. Consider the case where a professional athlete is traded from one club to another – she is transferred, it may even be said that she has been 'sold' to another club or 'bought' by it. One would be hard placed to call this slavery. Why? What is missing is the underlying element of possession. Without the exercise of control tantamount to possession, such buying, selling or transferring will not meet the threshold of slavery. Our professional athlete need not accept the transfer, she can take on other employment, but ultimately she will not be forced to take the field against her will – her personal liberty has not be reduced to such an extent. More is needed – only when control tantamount to possession is brought into the equation can we speak of slavery. Thus, while buying, selling or transferring of a person *may* provide evidence of slavery, only in cases where control tantamount to possession are at play can we then speak of slavery. Guideline 4(a) speaks in such terms:

> Buying, selling or otherwise transferring a person may provide evidence of slavery. Having established control tantamount to possession; the act of buying, selling or transferring that person will be an act of slavery.

Beyond buying, selling or transferring of a person, the *Guidelines* speak to the *use of a person*, which is straight forward. The actual use of a person is not enough to constitute slavery, only when, having first established control over a person tantamount to possession, can we speak of slavery in law. The managing of the use of a person provides a good example of the underlying need to establish control tantamount to possession. In any labour relationship, the employee will be managed. In base terms, an employee will be told where to work and the hours they will have to labour. But it would be too much to say such management constitutes enslavement. Here then we recognise that the background relationship of control tantamount to possession is need to constitute slavery.

It is not enough in law to say that the power of managing the use of a person amounts to slavery. Such managing of the use of a person will, in the first instance, help to identify a possible case of slavery, however, in and of itself, it is not enough to constitute enslavement. The background relationship known in property law as possession will slide a banal act of managing the use of a person from being not only permissible and fundamental to any working relationship, to being a case of enslavement if control is such that if it were exercised against a thing, we would recognise it as possession.

Without going into detail as to the other powers attaching to the right of ownership set out in the 2012 *Bellagio-Harvard Guidelines on the Legal Parameters of Slavery*, it should be emphasised that what is required in establishing a case of slavery is the *substance* rather than the *form* of a relationship. Thus, it is of no benefit in law to consider whether a person is in a situation which we might call 'child soldiering', 'debt bondage', 'forced marriage', 'forced labour', or 'trafficking'; rather, one must look to the *substance* of the relationship which has been created by the parties involved. In considering the particular set of circumstances, one must ask whether a power attaching to the right of ownership is being exercised and if so, can it be demonstrated that during such exercise that control tantamount to possession was at play. By such means of determination, one can establish legal parameters around what is slavery in a contemporary situation, where the condition of slavery is *de facto* rather than *de jure*. In so doing, a clear distinction emerges as to those instances which in law constitute slavery and those which amount to lesser servitudes; or, for that matter, between slavery in law and slavery as rhetoric.

Conclusion

Having set out the law applicable to the overall regime meant to curtail human exploitation and considered the normative content of forced labour, servitude, the slave trade, and slavery, a number of substantive issues have been brought to the fore. For more than a century, this legal regime hovered in a shadowland of disuse: accepted by States at the normative level but functionally inoperative as a tool to curtail human exploitation.

Archival research was the key which has unlocked it potential. Without reference to the deliberations of the League of Nations and the United Nations, the legal regime meant to curtail human exploitation was best avoided. Yet, as I have shown, the records demonstrate how 'servitude' was transformed into 'practices similar to slavery' and how the term of art 'slavery-like practice' managed to grind to a halt the conventional servitudes of debt bondage, serfdom, servile marriage and sham adoption. Thus, effectively ensuring that the law was not available in seeking to address these servitudes. As for forced labour, the main stumbling block remains the lack of coordination as between the ILO and the United Nations human rights system in giving normative content to the parameters of forced labour. This despite the possibility that forced labour in theory could capture much of what we understand as human exploitation and be utilised as a tool to better the lives of many people.

Where slavery is concerned, here is where the biggest break-through has transpired. Going back to the negotiation history and showing how the taking out of context of the Report introducing the 1926 Convention had led to a conceptualisation of slavery which lacked legal rigour and effectively rendered it devoid of legal content was but the first step. The archives reveal another path, one based on reading of the definition of slavery as set out in Article 1 of the 1926 Slavery Convention. Despite the definition being opaque in its formulation – *slavery is the status or condition over which any or all of the powers attaching to the right of ownership are exercised* – in substance, it would show itself to be rich enough to capture the lived experience of modern slavery. Analysis developed on the basis of the archives provided the type of legal certainty required for the equivalent of supreme court of Australia to determine that 'status' was applicable to chattel slavery – where one person owns another in law – whereas 'condition' was applicable to *de facto* cases of slavery. Again, based on material pulled from the archives, the High Court of Australia was able to rely on the 1953 considerations of the UN Secretary-General, to give voice to those powers attaching to the right of ownership. From there it was left to a Research Network comprised of the foremost thinkers of – the law of property, including Antony Honoré, Robin Hickey, and James Penner; the law of slavery, including Paul Finkelman, Bernard Freeman, and Rebecca Scott; historical slavery, including Seymour Drescher, Stanley Engerman, and Orlando Patterson; and contemporary slavery, including both Kevin Bales, Aidan McQuade, and Joel Quirk – to think through what constitutes the parameters of those powers attaching to the right of ownership through our 2012 *Bellagio-Harvard Guidelines on the Legal Parameters of Slavery*.

The project to first consider the legal regime of human exploitation has turned out to one of saving it from itself. Historical research and legal analysis have taken the concepts of forced labour, servitude, the slave trade and slavery out of the shadowlands where claims that there was universal jurisdiction to suppress the slave trade or that forced labour was a norm of *jus cogens* could go unchallenged; where the prohibition against servitude could be negotiated away; and where slavery – recognised as a fundamental human rights – could evolve so as to rid it of its normative content.

Let us hope that the 2015 marks not only the 125th anniversary of the first legal instrument meant to curtail human exploitation, but that it also marks a turning point in the operationalization of the law of anti-slavery writ large.

The material set out in this collection should be understood as 'works in progresses'. I am quite conscious that in formulating arguments lawyers will always look to make the strongest case possible. Let me be plain: My thinking on a number of issues has evolved over time. This collection is meant to give the background to arguments which appear in more abbreviated form in *Slavery in International Law*, and thus the academic provisos should apply: (1) that considerations that were given in papers delivered at conference but which are not reproduced in my monograph of 2013 should be considered lines of inquiries which were speculative rather than authoritative; (2) that chronology is important: my argumentation has evolved over time and thus, the most recent should be understood to override earlier pronouncements; and (3) that this Introduction should be understood as my most up to date thinking on the subject...which continues to evolve.

PART 1

The Evolution of Abolition

CHAPTER 1

What We Know Today: A Contemporary Understanding of the Atlantic Slave Trade*

Sir Moses Finley, the Cambridge University Professor of Classic History, reminds us in his work *Ancient Slavery and Modern Ideology* that even the study of something as distant as slavery of the Greco-Roman eras is politically inspired, contextualised, and propagated.[1] That the centrality of the *Classic* eras to the meta-ideology of the West as manifest in the Enlightenment and Modernity, has meant that, until recently, slavery within classic Greece and Rome was downplayed or ignored as challenging those elements of the past which sought to be put forward as part of the Enlightenment Project. Thus, it is rather easy to see that little space would be given to human bondage and exploitation when the fundamental underpinnings of Western ideology are predicated on the classic ideas of *freedom* and *liberty*. In essence then, the study of the Classics was ideologically truncated to give voice to the virtues of the dominant class while disregarding the plight of those people who actually built and allowed the City States of Sparta and Athens and the Roman Empire to prosper.

Professor Finley's consideration of ancient slavery took place in the era when the classical elements of Western ideological hegemony was being challenged not by Marxist-Leninism of the Cold War, but by the North–South rift which, in the era of decolonisation, had its place in overturning the orthodoxies of the West. Granted, the civil rights movement in the United States and the student revolts of Europe also played their part in undermining from below the ideological *status quo* of the 1960s. So too did advances in science which made plain that the Enlightenment Project, which displaced religion by scientific inquiry, could *not*, in fact, explain all, and that ultimately humanity is left no closer to understanding the fundamental questions about our existence, our destiny, then before Galileo or Newton. As a result, the latter half of the twentieth century was marked by the emergence of *Post-Modernity*. An era when the Enlightenment Project, anchored as it was in the deliverance of science, was displaced by a meta-ideology which accepts that there can be no established

* Paper presented at the International Conference on Human Rights in Africa, Dakar, Senegal, August 2007.

1 See Brent Shaw (ed.), Moses Finley, *Ancient Slavery and Modern Ideology*, 1998.

 | DOI 10.1163/9789004279896_003

'right' answer, that ultimately what we know and don't know is politically driven and socially constructed.

Within this evolving social revolution within the Western world, it is clear that the Classics could not withstand the rigours of a post-modern evaluation which not only reconsidered the fundamental tenets of the discipline, but asked probing questions as to why slavery had played such a minor role in the study of Greco-Roman civilisations thus far. With the disintegration of the Western ideological construct from below, it should come as little surprise that the question of slavery generally – and the Atlantic slave trade in particular – moved from the peripheries to become central to the discipline of History. Thus within the last forty years, the study of slavery has gone from being near to naught, to being all encompassing and engrossing. The current doyen of British slavery historians, James Walvin, writes: "When I first began to work on slavery in the British West Indies in 1967, the corpus of relevant secondary literature was relatively thin. Now – in the mid-1990s – it is virtually impossible to keep abreast of current scholarship."[2] Thus, as a result of the last forty years of enquiry, historians have provided the raw material essential to considering the slave trade in a new and well-informed manner, moving away, for instance, from a one-dimensional understanding of the issues which painted, for instance, British abolition of the slave trade "as among the three or four perfectly virtuous pages comprised in this history of nations."[3] The state of this contemporary scholarship will now be considered.

To do so, what now follows is a tour through the Atlantic World of the nineteenth century, following the notorious triangular trade, both at its height and through its legal abolition. As regards this Atlantic Slave Trade, Professor Herbert Klein has noted, in his seminal survey, that: "despite a quarter century of sophisticated multinational studies, the gap between popular understanding and scholarly knowledge remains as profound as when the trade was first under discussion in literate European circles in the eighteenth century." Klein goes on to say that not "only is there been a failure in the dialogue between the academic and general literate world, but there is surprising ignorance even within the scholarly world at large about the nature of the trade."[4] This may be said to be doubly so with regard to legal scholars where, as recently as 2004, a young historian could write: "While the last three decades have seen a reinvigorated

2 James Walvin, *Questioning Slavery*, 1997, p. vii.

3 See Roger Anstey, *The Atlantic Slave Trade and British Abolition 1760–1810*, p. xx; where he quotes W.E.H. Lecky, *A History of European Morals*, 1884.

4 Herbert Klein, *The Atlantic Slave Trade*, 1999, pp. xvii and xx.

interest in almost all aspects of the transatlantic slave trade, legal historians have completely neglected it."[5]

Before departing on our tour of the Atlantic World, it is import to place slavery in context, by noting that with regard to the universal history of the world, it is free labour and not slavery which is the rather 'peculiar' institution the norm having been slave labour; likewise slavery itself has only existed where a distinction was established allowing for private property to exist; and finally, slavery only persisted where economic development allowed for advanced means of production and consumption.[6] It should be emphasised also that slavery has existed since time immemorial, with recorded traces being found in Egyptian hieroglyphics and the Code of Hammurabi.

On the African continent, the nineteenth century was marked by three types of slavery. The start of the nineteenth century, with the end of the Napoleonic Wars, saw so-called 'white slavery' on the Barbary coast, before the United States of America sent its first-ever naval squadron to liberate its merchant seamen from Algiers. That 1815 naval expedition was meant to put to an end the practice by Barbary States (Algiers, Tunis and Tripoli) whereby pirates under their protection captured foreign sailors at sea, enslaved them, and held them for ransom. Before the use of this gunboat diplomacy by the United States, the 'White Slave Trade' had been managed through international agreements which required maritime powers plying in the Mediterranean to pay annual tributes to the Beys of the Barbary States. The end of this type of slavery was ultimately delivered in 1816 by the British who, with the assistance of the Dutch, bombarded Algiers, destroyed its navy, and extracted promises from the Beys of Tunis and Tripoli that the practice would be put to an end.[7]

The second type of slavery which existed in nineteenth century Africa was the so-called 'Oriental Slave Trade' (also referred to in the literature as the 'Arab Trade', the 'Islamic Trade' or 'Sahara Trade'). This slave trade, which was older and more ingrained in the fabric of Africa then the Atlantic Slave Trade, had existed for more than a millennium before it was outlawed in the late nineteenth and early twentieth century. The Oriental Slave Trade, as opposed to the western oriented, capitalist driven, trade generally enslaved two women for every man, with the final destination being domestic service in the homes or concubines of North Africa or what is today termed the Middle East. This trade,

5 Holger Lutz Kern, "Strategies of Legal Change: Great Britain, International Law, and the Abolition of the Transatlantic Slave Trade," *Journal of History of International Law*, Vol. 6, 2004, p. 223.

6 See Brent Shaw (ed.), Moses Finley, *Ancient Slavery and Modern Ideology*, 1998, pp. 299 and 14.

7 Robert Phillimore, *Commentaries upon International Law*, 1879, pp. 320 and 319.

like that of the Atlantic, focused on the enslavement of inhabitants of sub-Saharan Africa, with the main means of transportation eastward being not ocean going caravels, but camel caravans crossing the North African dessert and small dhows sailing the Indian Ocean, the Persian Gulf, and the Red Sea. It is estimated that this trade involved seven million slaves, of which three million were transported during the nineteenth century.[8] By the 1870s, the Oriental Slave Trade had been funnelled into Omani ruled Zanzibar as the primary outlet for the slave trade on the east coast of Africa (which, rather embarrassingly, was under British protection). It was only when the Atlantic Slave Trade ended and European States undertook to conquer the whole of the African continent that the suppression of the Oriental Slave Trade was undertaken. This transpired by means of a British naval presence on the east coast of Africa, the 1890 Final Act of the Brussels Conference establishing the international abolition of the slave trade within a prescribed zone encompassing those areas of the Indian Ocean, Persian Gulf, and Red Sea where the trade was known to persist, and monitoring of State action via the International Maritime Bureau located at Zanzibar – the first ever intergovernmental institutions established on the African continent.

Despite the existence of these two types of slavery, the Atlantic Slave Trade, which emerged in the late fifteenth century should be understood as a new "species of slavery," whereby a type of 'artisan' slavery was replaced by 'industrial' slavery. Or as Robin Blackburn notes, as part of his seminal trilogy, the "slaves of the New World were economic property and the main motive for slaveholding was economic exploitation; to this end at least nine tenths of American slaves were put to commodity production."[9] The Atlantic Slave Trade emerges as a result of the receding of the Islamic threat from Europe at the end of the fifteenth century; rather secure on the home front, advances in maritime technology allowed Iberian States to first, under Prince 'Henry the Navigator' of Portugal (1394–1460), to incrementally make their way further south down the African Coast on an annual basis; ultimately opening the sea lanes to the New World (Christopher Columbus, 1492), around the Cape of Good Hope to India (Vasco de Gama, 1498), and finally to the circumnavigation of the globe (Ferdinand Magellan, 1522).

In the wake of this global adventurism, came the establishment of colonial outposts. This nascent European colonial expansionism of the sixteenth century

8 See James Walvin, *Black Ivory: Slavery in the British Empire*, 2001, p. 267; and also Ralph Austen, "The Mediterranean Islamic Slave Trade out of Africa: A Tentative Census," in Patrick Manning (ed.), *Slave Trades, 1500–1800; Globalization of Forced Labour*, 1996, pp. 1–36.

9 Robin Blackburn, *The Overthrow of Colonial Slavery (1776–1848)*, 1988, p. 7.

manifested itself in New World economies which were plantation based, growing labour-intensive products such as sugar, coffee, rum, and tobacco, that were now made available for larger public consumption in Europe.[10] These plantations were not a new phenomena, *per se*, as slave-based sugar plantation under Spanish and Portuguese control had existed previously in the Levant, on the islands of Mediterranean as well as the West Coast of Africa (the Azores, Canaries, Cape Vertes, Madeiras islands, as well as San Tomé and Principe). Within the New World setting, it was sugar which, by far, was the most relevant as "some 70 per cent of *all* Africans imported into the Americas were destined, in the short term at least, to work in sugar."[11] Professor Walvin has recently put into perspective the importance of the Atlantic Slave Trade in general terms. He writes that the Atlantic Slave Trade had profound consequences not only for Africa, but "it was a major ingredient in the transformation of the West." He continues:

> Slavery was the means by which the West emerged to a position of unrivalled economic and political dominance. Stated simply, African slave labour, transplanted into the Americas, was critical to the creation of Western wealth and the consequent relegation of other regions and peoples to the overarching power of the West.[12]

The legal basis upon which European expansion into the New World during this era took place was a result of religious sanction which divided the globe – beyond Europe – between Portugal and Spain. The *Inter caetera* of 1493 issued by Pope Alexander VI was a Papal Bull granting Ferdinand and Isabella of Spain a monopoly over all lands three hundred miles west of the Azores and Cape Verde Islands; there being a line of demarcation drawn vertically from the Arctic to the Antarctic poles.[13] The Bull precipitated the signing of the Treaty of Tordesillas of 1494 between Spain and Portugal which ended a certain controversy "as to what lands, of all those discovered in the ocean sea up to the present day" belonged to which Iberian State.[14] The Treaty effectively divided

10 See, for instance, Robert William Fogel, *Without Consent or Contract: The Rise and Fall of American Slavery*, 1994, pp. 17–29; or John Thornton, *Africa and Africans in the Making of the Atlantic World, 1400–1800*, 1999, pp. 152–182.

11 James Walvin, *Questioning Slavery*, 1997, p. 32. Emphasis in the original.

12 James Walvin, *A Short History of Slavery*, 2007, p. 2.

13 See *European Treaties Bearing on the History of the United States and Its Dependencies to 1648*, Frances Davenport (ed.), 1917, p. 77.

14 *Ibid.*, p. 95.

the yet to be 'discovered' world between these States; it also moved the demarcation line approximately seven hundred miles westward, thus granting Portugal its Brazilian foothold in South America.

During the sixteenth century, Iberian States busied themselves conquering the New World, introducing sugar estates, and manning them with indentured Europeans and enslaved native-Americans.[15] However, for a number of reasons, including rapid economic growth in Europe and alien diseases brought to the New World, African slaves "became the most desired labour force for Europeans to develop their American export industries."[16] During this period, Portugal opened up West Africa on its side of the line; while Spain, unable to recruit workers from Europe and having more than decimated the native American population, turned to granting *Assientos* – trade monopoly licences – to furnish, in this case, slaves to its colonies.[17] The slave-trade *Assientos* would become amalgamated as one *Assiento* and, by 1701, be fought over and granted to foreign States by way of treaty. However, by 1750, the *Assiento* lost its value as so-called 'interlopers' broke the Iberian monopolies on both side of the line, with colonies and forts being established in the New World and in Africa by the British, Brandenburgs, Danes, Dutch, French, Norwegians, and Swedes.

It should be noted that the involvement of various European States in the Atlantic Slave Trade (which spanned from 1519 until 1867) was part of a well established international market connecting Africa, the Americas, Asia, and Europe.[18] Professor Herbert Klein writes that:

> the Atlantic Slave Trade was one of the more complex of international trades that existed in the modern period. It intimately tied cowry and textile exports from Asia to Africa imports and involved massive movements of people across large land masses and great oceans. It tied up European capital, ships, and crews for long periods of time and involved very complex credit arrangements for the sale of American crops in European markets. [... The] economic ties between Asia, Europe, Africa and America clearly involved a web of relationships that spanned the

15 See Patrick Manning, *Slavery and African Life: Occidental, Oriental, and African Slave Trades*, 1990, p. 30.

16 *Ibid.*, p. 21.

17 See Georges Scelle, "The Slave-Trade in the Spanish Colonies of America: The *Assiento*," *American Journal of International Law*, Vol. 4, 1910, p. 617.

18 For the dates quoted see David Eltis, "The Volume and Structures of the Transatlantic Slave Trade: A Reassessment," *William and Mary Quarterly*, Vol. 58, 2001, p. 17.

> globe. At the heart of this system was a Europe committed to consuming American plantations crops at an every expanding rate, crops that ranged from luxuries to basic necessities within the European population.[19]

In contrast to common perceptions that Europeans raided the African coast to gain slaves, traders in short order tapped into a market which already existed.[20] However, these European traders facilitated the expansion of what would become an industrial scale slave trade not only by creating an ever-growing demand, but also by supporting the commercial and political ambitions of selected local African elite. These ambitions – which, for instance, would lead to the creation of the Ashanti and Dahomey Kingdoms in West Africa – transpired through warfare which, while producing territorial gains, also created as a by-product, the main source of slaves for the Atlantic trade. The human bounty of war were often forced to walk from the interior to the west coast of Africa, where those that survived were offered for sale in places such as St. Louis and Gorée (in modern day Senegal), Elmina and Cape Coast (Ghana), on the so-called 'Slave Coast', must notoriously in Ouidah (Benin), and further south in Luanda (Angola).[21]

While we know little (and never will) of the numbers of individuals captured, or the number of those who died on the African continent awaiting transport, the last forty years has, through historical research, revealed much of what transpired once Africans fell into European hands. A decade long project which started in the late 1980s, under the auspices of the W.E.B. Du Bois Institute of Harvard University, has brought together data on "perhaps 70 percent of all slaving voyages" and provides much well-grounded insight into the various elements of the trade.[22] From this data, it can be said that during the period in which the Atlantic Slave Trade persisted, more than eleven million men, women, and children, are known to have been forcefully enslaved and

19 Klein, *op. cit.*, n. 4, pp. 101–102.

20 See John Thornton, *Africa and Africans in the Making of the Atlantic World, 1400–1800*, 1999, p. 125; where he writes: "In conclusion, then, we must accept that African participation in the slave trade was voluntary and under the control of African decision makers. [...] Europeans possessed no means, either economic or military, to compel African leaders to sell slaves."

21 Eltis notes that on "the African coast, West Central Africa [re: Angola] was an even more important source of slaves that the recent literature credits." See Eltis, *op. cit.*, n. 18, p. 41. West Central Africa accounts for 44.2% of departures of all known slaves from Africa heading to the New World (4,887,500 individuals). See Table II, *ibid.*, 44.

22 David Brion Davis and Robert Forbes, "Foreword," *William and Mary Quarterly*, Vol. 58, 2001, p. 7.

taken from Africa. Of these, approximately one and a half million did not reach the Americas, having died at sea during the so-called 'middle passage'.[23] Over time, as the trade became more sophisticated, it became evident that the most cost effective slave for the New World was a young man, one who could withstand the heavy burden of plantation life. During the 1600s, 60% of slaves transported were male, with 12% being children; by the 1700s, 65% were male, and 23% children, finally, during the 1800s males constituted 72% of all those transported and 46% of the human cargo was comprised of children.[24] Great Britain and Portugal accounted for more than seventy percent of all the slaves transported during the Atlantic Slave Trade. "Broadly," Professor David Eltis notes, "the Portuguese dominated before 1640 and after 1807, with the British displacing them in the intervening period."[25] In the New World, with the exception of "the meteoric rise and fall of St. Domingue – modern day Haïti which gained its independence in 1804 as a result of a slave revolt[26] – the primary receiving regions were Brazil, the British Caribbean and, briefly, in the nineteenth century, Cuba."[27]

As we are aware today, the Atlantic Slave Trade literally changed the face of the Americas, the descendants of enslaved Africans making up the majority of the populations of Brazil and the Caribbean and substantial minorities in various countries most notably the United States of America.

Today, in 2007, there are two markedly different dynamics at play in considered the legacy of the Atlantic Slave Trade, both ideologically driven. The first, is the acknowledged participation in the Atlantic Slave Trade by the United Kingdom wherein former Prime Minister, Tony Blair, expressed his 'deep remorse' for his country's involvement in the trade. Yet, the leading role of the United Kingdom in the Atlantic Slave Trade was acknowledged within the context of the celebration of the 1807 Westminster Bill abolishing the slave trade for British subjects. This year then, the United Kingdom has played host to literally hundreds of events, from primary school projects to the major motion

23 See Eltis, *op. cit.*, n. 18. The dataset is found in David Eltis *et al.* (eds.) *The Trans-Atlantic Slave Trade: A Database on cd-rom*, 1999.

24 See Klein, *op. cit.*, n. 4, pp. 161–162.

25 See Eltis, *op. cit.*, n. 18, p. 20. From the nationality of the ships, the data reveals that Great Britain was responsible for 28.1% of the trade which amounts to 3,112,300 Africans transported (Portugal being responsible for 45.9% of the trade). See Table I, *ibid.*, 43.

26 For a consideration of the revolt in St. Domingue and the emergence of an independent Haïti, see the eloquently written classic, first published in 1938: C.L.R. James, *The Black Jacobins*, 2001. For a consideration of the leader of the Haïtian Revolution written by the foremost French abolitionist of his day, in 1889, see Victor Schoelcher, *La Vie de Toussaint Louverture*, 1982.

27 See Eltis, *op. cit.*, n. 18. p. 41.

pictures focused not on the slave trade, but on its abolition. This then resulted in the secular canonisation of the so-called 'saints', the likes of William Wilberforce, Thomas Clarkson, and Grandville Sharp having re-entered the public consciousness and provided the British State the possibility to utilise its abolitionist past to motivate present interests – most obviously – with regard to global warming. Like the ultimate abolition of the slave trade and slavery, which the United Kingdom spearheaded, the menace of global warming is being sold to the Nation in messianic terms wherein it is part and parcel of being British to lead the fight against global warming, and to impose its will on others in both paternalistic terms, but also on economically terms wherein Britain is best placed to prosper.

The second dynamic at play is that of reparations led, at the international level, by Caribbean States which are seeking compensation as a means of correcting this historical injustice. While Dean Gowok from Jimma University, Ethiopia will consider the issue in greater detail in his presentation, it suffices for me to note, that ultimately, the issue is a political one, not a legal one; as from a legal perspective the issue comes up against the rather sobering doctrine of inter-temporal law, which dictates that State responsibility will only be incurred with regard to violation of laws which have been consented to by States and from that period onwards, with no possibility of retroactivity *unless agreed to*. Whether reparations will ever be forthcoming, or payment in kind, as debt relief, remains to be seen.

What remains true of these two modern dynamics is that they are part of competing historical narratives about the place of the Atlantic Slave Trade in contemporary society. In this, the post-modern era, the glorification of abolition of the Atlantic Slave Trade stands side-by-side with an acknowledgement that Europe was responsible for destroying the Americas, both north and south, and depopulating large tracks of Africa so as to provide slave labour to build the New World in its image. Further, we must recognise that Western motivation for ending slavery in Africa was a pretext for Empire, and for the European colonial project. Historians, for their part have, over the last forty years, unlocked the secrets which laid dormant in archives all over the world, untouched for ideological reasons. What we know today about slavery provides us with a sound foundation from which to address the issue of the Atlantic Slave Trade and its legacy in our contemporary world. Yet, we must also accept that ideology, as Sir Moses Finley reminds us, drives knowledge; and as such the most effective means of acknowledging the Atlantic Slave Trade and its legacy, is to ensure that it becomes and remains part of a discourse which is not bogged down in economic arguments but acknowledges the inhumanity and racism which allowed for the taking of millions of Africans from their homes and families and introducing them to the hell on earth which was the Atlantic Slave Trade.

CHAPTER 2

The Nineteenth Century Law of the Sea and the British Abolition of the Slave Trade*

It would be difficult to underestimate the relevance of the issue of the slave trade in nineteenth-century international relations. The move by Great Britain to suppress the slave trade was *the* issue with global implications during most of that century, as little else required the collective coordination of European States, newly-independent American States and other emerging "civilized nations." However, the process of establishing an international regime which sought to outlaw the slave trade reflected an international system lacking the tools of modern statecraft. In effect Great Britain was left to its own devices in seeking to achieve the suppression of the slave trade at sea. The limited contact between States meant that the establishment of law regarding the slave trade was a slow and awkward process which, though agreed to in principle at the Congress of Vienna in 1815, only emerged as a binding universal instrument at the Brussels Conference of 1890, and ultimately led to the suppression of both the slave trade and slavery with the League of Nations Convention to Suppress the Slave Trade and Slavery of 1926.[1]

The lack of a developed multilateral system during the nineteenth century, however, was not the determining factor in the slow pace by which the slave trade on the seas was outlawed. At the heart of the matter was States' understanding of the nature of the high seas. The challenge was not the slave trade *per se* but rather the conflict between the Grotian notion of freedom of the seas and the right to visit ships suspected of involvement in the slave trade. Over a period of eighty years, Great Britain proposed various understandings of the "right to visit"; first seeking to assimilate slavery to piracy, then arguing for the extension of the French notion of *droit de visite*, an indirect right to visit but not to *search* a ship as a way to suppress the slave trade. Other maritime Powers were originally unwilling to concede *any* right of visit in peace time and baulked at these innovative notions put forward by Great Britain. Yet, a diplomatic compromise was reached in 1890 that accepted the concept of a "right to visit," while limiting its

* This chapter was originally published as Jean Allain, "Nineteenth Century Law of the Sea and the British Abolition of the Slave Trade," *British Yearbook of International Law*, Vol. 78, 2008, p. 342, Copyright © Oxford University Press, 2008.

1 Slavery Convention, Geneva, 25 September 1926, 60 *LNTS* 255.

 | DOI 10.1163/9789004279896_004

application to a specific maritime zone and to the type of ship used in the late nineteenth-century slave trade. For most of the century, then, the battle lines were drawn between Great Britain, which put forward an abolitionist agenda primed on the use of its superior naval forces and on the other hand, lesser maritime Powers including Brazil, France, Portugal and the United States of America, that sought to maintain freedom of commerce for their merchant fleets.

The Slave Trade during the Nineteenth Century

The legal history of the suppression of the slave trade in the nineteenth century revolves around the "Atlantic Slave Trade," where the most significant legal issues regarding the right to visit and the freedom of the seas manifested themselves. But the century started – and ended – with a focus on other slave trades. In 1815 the United States equipped and sent its first-ever naval squadron to liberate American merchant seamen held for ransom by Algiers on the Barbary Coast. Previously, international agreements had existed requiring annual tributes from foreign States to ensure their nationals were not taken at sea, enslaved, and held for payment by pirates under the protection of North African States.[2] The expedition ended the practice by the Barbary States (Algiers, Tunis and Tripoli) of "white slavery" against United States sailors. The decisive blow was delivered in 1816 by Great Britain which bombarded Algiers and destroyed its navy. The Royal Navy, assisted by a Dutch squadron, demanded and received a treaty which mandated "the abolition for ever of Christian Slavery."[3] Likewise, the British Commander-in-chief in the Mediterranean "extracted a promise from the Beys of Tunis and Tripoli that they would not, for the future, make slaves of prisoners of war, but would conform to the practice of European Nations."[4] Thus ended this type of enslavement in North Africa.

During the nineteenth century, Great Britain focused primarily on the "Atlantic Slave Trade."[5] Although slavery had persisted for more than a

2 For American actions see F Leiner, *The End of Barbary Terror: America's 1815 War against the Pirates of North Africa* (OUP, 2006).

3 R. Phillimore, *Commentaries upon International Law* (Butterworths, London, 1879), 320.

4 Ibid, 319.

5 Over the past thirty years, the Atlantic Slave Trade has been the subject of extensive study by historians. Since the 1960s the "academic study of slavery has, in effect, shifted from the margins of scholarly interest (even of respectability) to become the focus of innovative and imaginative work at the very core of modern historical scholarship" (J. Walvin, *Questioning*

thousand years as a continuous oriental trade; the Atlantic Slave Trade emerged as a new "species of slavery."[6] During the sixteenth century, Portugal and Spain introduced plantations on vast tracts of land in the Americas and manned them with indentured Europeans and enslaved Native Americans.[7] However, for numerous reasons, including rapid economic growth in Europe and the introduction of alien diseases to the New World, African slaves "became the most desired labour force for Europeans to develop their American export industries,"[8] which were based on labour-intensive plantations producing commodities such as sugar, coffee, rum, and tobacco.[9]

The Papal Bulls of Donation (specifically, the *Inter caetera* of 1493) and the Treaty of Tordesillas of 1494 established that Portugal and Spain had exclusive right to the undiscovered world, with a line drawn vertically through the Atlantic Ocean from the Arctic to the Antarctic, one thousand miles west of the Azores and Cape Verde Islands. While the Treaty gave Portugal its Brazilian foothold in South America, it excluded Spain from the African coast and direct access to slaves. As a result, Spain turned to granting *Assientos* – trade monopoly licences – to furnish slaves to its colonies.[10] The slave-trade *Assientos* were ultimately amalgamated into one *Assiento* and, by 1701 began to be granted to foreign States by way of treaty. The *Assiento* first went to France. As a result of the Treaty of Utrecht (1713), it was passed to Great Britain, and then, by way of the treaties of Aix-la-Chapelle (1748) and Madrid (1750) reverted back to Spain.

Slavery (Routledge, London, 1997), vii). Further, "[w]hile the last three decades have seen a reinvigorated interest in almost all aspects of the transatlantic slave trade, legal historians have completely neglected it" (H. Kern, "Strategies of Legal Change: Great Britain, International Law, and the Abolition of the Transatlantic Slave Trade," *Journal of History of International Law*, Vol. 6, 2004, p. 223).

6 R. Blackburn, *The Overthrow of Colonial Slavery 1776–1848* (Verso, London, 1988), 7.

7 See P. Manning, *Slavery and African Life: Occidental, Oriental, and African Slave Trades* (CUP, 1990), 30. Such plantations – primarily sugar estates – had previously proven successful in Spanish possessions off the African West Coast.

8 Ibid, 21.

9 See R. Fogel, *Without Consent or Contract: The Rise and Fall of American Slavery* (Norton, New York, 1994), 17–29; J. Thornton, *Africa and Africans in the Making of the Atlantic World, 1400–1800* (CUP, 1999), 152–182. Of these commodities, sugar was by far the most relevant to issues of enslavement: "It is worth recalling, for instance, that some 70 per cent of *all* Africans imported into the Americas were destined, in the short term at least, to work in sugar." Walvin, above n. 5, 32. Emphasis in the original.

10 See G. Scelle, "The Slave-Trade in the Spanish Colonies of America: The *Assiento*," *ajil*, Vol. 4, 1910, p. 617; G. Scelle, *La traite négrière aux Indes de Castilles, contrats et traités d'assiento, étude de droit public et d'histoire diplomatique puisée aux sources originales et accompagnée de plusieurs documents inédits*, (Larose et Tenin, Paris, 1906).

However, by this time the *Assiento* was of limited relevance, as Spain and Portugal's maritime rivals had broken the monopolies on both sides of the line; colonies and forts had been established by "interlopers" (including the British, Brandenburgs, Danes, Dutch, French, Norwegians and Swedes) in the New World and in Africa. The ideology of "empire" had shifted and was now commerce-based.[11] It was within this new imperial paradigm that the Atlantic Slave Trade developed and flourished.

The Atlantic Slave Trade, which spanned from 1519 until 1867, formed part of a well established international market connecting Africa, the Americas, Asia, and Europe.[12] In contrast to common perceptions that Europeans raided the African coast to gain slaves, early European traders actually tapped into a market which already existed. However, they facilitated the expansion of the slave trade by creating an ever-growing demand and by supporting the commercial and political ambitions of African elites. These ambitions were manifested through warfare which, while producing territorial gains,[13] created the main source of slaves for the Atlantic trade. Captured enemies were often forced to walk to the west coast of Africa. Survivors of the journey were offered for sale in places such as St. Louis (modern day Senegal), Elmina and Cape Coast (Ghana), most notoriously on the so-called "Slave Coast," in Ouidah (Benin), and, in greater numbers still, further south in Luanda (Angola).[14]

A decade-long project started in the late 1980s, conducted under the auspices of the W E B Du Bois Institute of Harvard University, has gathered data on "perhaps 70 percent of all slaving voyages," providing much insight into the various elements of the trade.[15] During the period in which the Atlantic Slave Trade persisted, more than eleven million men, women, and children were forcefully enslaved and taken from Africa. Of these, approximately one and a half million did not reach the Americas, having died at sea during the so-called "Middle Passage."[16] Eltis notes that Great Britain and Portugal accounted for

11 A. Pagden, *Peoples and Empires* (Weidenfeld & Nicolson, London, 2001), 94.

12 For the dates quoted see D. Eltis, "The Volume and Structures of the Transatlantic Slave Trade: A Reassessment," *William and Mary Quarterly*, Vol. 58, 2001, p. 17. With regard to the global market, see H. Klein, *The Atlantic Slave Trade* (CUP, 1999), 101–102.

13 E.g. the creation of the Ashanti and Dahomey Kingdoms in West Africa.

14 See Thornton, above n. 9, 125. Eltis notes that on "the African coast, West Central Africa [Angola] was an even more important source of slaves that the recent literature credits": Eltis, above n. 12, 41. West Central Africa accounts for 44.2% of departures of all known slaves from Africa heading to the New World (4,887,500 individuals). See Eltis, Table II, 44.

15 D. Davis & R. Forbes, "Foreword," *William and Mary Quarterly*, Vol. 58, 2001, p. 7.

16 See Eltis, above n. 12. The dataset is found in D. Eltis et al. (eds.), *The Trans-Atlantic Slave Trade: A Database on cd-rom* (CUP, 1999).

more than seventy percent of the Atlantic trade: "the Portuguese dominated before 1640 and after 1807, with the British displacing them in the intervening period."[17] In the New World, with the exception of "the meteoric rise and fall of St. Domingue,[18] the primary receiving regions were Brazil, the British Caribbean and, briefly, in the nineteenth century, Cuba."[19] Finally, Eltis notes that between "1660 and 1807, when the slave trade was at its height, the British and their dependencies carried every second slave that arrived in the Americas, a dominance that would no doubt have continued but for the politically inspired decision to abolish the trade."[20]

The move by Great Britain to abolish the slave trade was inspired by economic, philanthropic, and populist considerations. Heuman notes that until "the 1940s there was a general consensus among historians about the abolition of slavery in the Empire" where it was "maintained that the British abolished slavery largely because of the strength of religious feelings and humanitarianism."[21] This view, however, is challenged by Eric Williams' 1944 *Capitalism and Slavery*, in which he asserts that slavery was abolished because it had become unprofitable, not because it had become morally wrong and unpalatable to the British. While this perspective has been largely rejected, it has not been completely displaced.[22] More recently, greater emphasis has been placed on the public pressure which moved Great Britain towards abolition of the slave trade, with the anti-slavery movement described by Walvin as "*the* most popular political issue in these years [1789–1838]."[23] Finally, the resistance of slaves themselves increased the costs of participating in the trade and placed New

17 Eltis, above n. 12, 20. Great Britain was responsible for 28.1% of the trade which amounts to 3,112,300 Africans transported (Portugal being responsible for 45.9%). See Eltis, above n. 12, Table I, 43.

18 *Viz*, modern-day Haïti, which gained its independence in 1804 as a result of a slave revolt. Davis writes: "The Haitian Revolution impinged in one way or another on the entire emancipation debate from the British parliamentary move in 1792 to outlaw the African slave trade to Brazil's final abolition of slavery ninety-six years later." D. Davis, *Inhuman Bondage: The Rise and Fall of Slavery in the New World* (OUP, 2006), 158. For a consideration of the revolt in St. Domingue and the emergence of an independent Haïti, see C.L.R. James, *The Black Jacobins* (Secker and Warburg, London, 1938).

19 See Eltis, above n. 12, 41.

20 Ibid.

21 G. Heuman, "Slavery, the Slave Trade, and Abolition," in R. Winks (ed.), *Oxford History of the British Empire*, Vol. 5 (Historiography) (OUP, 1999), 322.

22 Ibid. Eric Williams would later become the Prime Minister of Trinidad and Tobago.

23 Heuman, above n. 21, 324. Emphasis in the original. See also C. Brown, *Moral Capital: Foundations of British Abolitionism* (University of North Carolina Press, Chapel Hill, 2006).

World European settlers in a heightened state of anxiety over their safety, especially after the slave revolt and revolution in St. Domingue.[24]

Although individuals had called for the end of slavery and the slave trade during the eighteenth century, these calls came primarily from individual intellectuals and minority religious sects (principally the Society of Friends) and were easily dismissed.[25] However, as the abolitionist movement grew in popularity, spurred on by the ideas of the American and French revolutions and the increases in literacy and leisure time brought about by the Industrial Revolution, it became a major factor in domestic politics. This was not due to the virtue of the cause *per se*, but because it "reflected the needs and values of the emerging capitalist order,"[26] and impelled successive British governments to make abolition a key part of their foreign policy. This policy permitted British administrations to maintain the moral high ground as against those States which continued to allow their ships to be involved in the slave trade. Great Britain, having lost its greatest colonial asset in 1783 as a result of the American Revolution, no longer needed to support the New World's slave-based economy. Likewise the mercantile economy, which had been in existence since the late fifteenth century, was being replaced by a capitalist order, wherein Great Britain was best placed to prosper (and dominate) through the advocacy of free trade and supremacy of its Royal Navy.[27] Thus, Great Britain went from being the main slaving nation from 1640 to outlawing the trade in 1807 and becoming the leading proponent of its international abolition.

As Great Britain's campaign for the universal suppression of the slave trade at sea moved towards successful completion at the end of the nineteenth

---

24 See D. Richardson, "Shipboard Revolts, African Authority, and the Atlantic Slave Trade," *William and Mary Quarterly*, Vol. 58, 2001, p. 69–92; in the British context, see M. Craton, *Testing the Chains: Resistance to Slavery in the British West Indies* (Cornell University Press, London, 1982) and R. Hart, *Slaves Who Abolished Slavery* (University of the West Indies, Mona, 2002).

25 See, e.g., Ch 10 "Religious Sources of Antislavery Thought: Quakers and the Sectarian Tradition," in D. Davis, *The Problem of Slavery in Western Culture* (Cornell University Press, New York, 1966), 291–332.

26 See Heuman, putting forward David Brion Davis' view (above n. 18), 324. For a similar co-opting by States of popular sentiment, consider the evolution of dispute settlement and the peace movements which transpired at the turn of the twentieth century: see J. Allain, *A Century of International Adjudication: The Rule of Law and its Limits* (T M C Asser Press, The Hague, 2000), 6–35.

27 See D. Davis, *The Problem of Slavery in the Age of Revolution 1770–1823* (Cornell University Press, New York, 1975), 351. See also C. Lloyd, *The Navy and the Slave Trade: Suppression of African Slave Trade in the Nineteenth Century* (Cass, London, 1968), xi: "Throughout the nineteenth century the Navy was the chief instrument of preserving the *Pax Britannica*."

century, it brought in its wake the end of the Atlantic Slave Trade. The last recorded slave ship made its way across the Atlantic to Cuba in 1867; however, another slave trade, the "Oriental Slave Trade," persisted "virtually unnoticed" in east Africa.[28] This oriental trade was an older, more ingrained slave trade which existed for more than a millennium before it was suppressed in the late nineteenth and early twentieth century. The Oriental Slave Trade (as opposed to the western-oriented, capitalist-driven trade) generally enslaved two women for every man, for the purpose of work as domestic servants or concubines in north Africa and western Asia. This trade, like that of the Atlantic, focused on the enslavement of inhabitants of sub-Saharan Africa. The main means of transportation was not ocean-going caravels, but camel caravans crossing the North African dessert and small dhows sailing the Indian Ocean, the Persian Gulf, and the Red Sea. It is estimated that this trade involved seven million slaves, of which three million were transported during the nineteenth century.[29]

The suppression of this trade was a rather low priority for Great Britain during the first half of the nineteenth century as, for instance, only two ships could be spared for east coast patrols during Napoleon's stay on St. Helena (1815–1821), and as late as 1854, the Royal Navy "had only three vessels to deploy between Delagoa Bay to Zanzibar, over 1300 miles of coastline."[30] It was only when the Atlantic Slave Trade ended and European States undertook to conquer the whole of the African continent that Great Britain showed any great zeal in promoting the suppression of the Oriental Slave Trade. However, by this time, the legal issues relating to the British wish to establish a right to visit to suppress the slave trade at sea had been settled. The end of the Oriental Slave Trade then was a matter for the British squadrons, the 1890 Final Act of the Brussels Conference, and the International Maritime Bureau. The British naval presence on the east coast of Africa was limited by the means at its disposal until the 1870s. Further, with the abolition of the trade on the Barbary Coast and in Egypt, over the nineteenth century the Oriental Slave Trade had been funnelled into one primary outlet on the east coast of Africa, the island of

28 J. Walvin, *Black Ivory: Slavery in the British Empire* (Blackwell Publishers, Oxford, 2001), 267. Note that the Oriental Slave Trade is also referred to in the literature as the "Arab Trade" the "Islamic Trade" or "Sahara Trade."

29 Ibid. See also R Austen, "The Mediterranean Islamic Slave Trade out of Africa: A Tentative Census," in P. Manning (ed.), *Slave Trades, 1500–1800; Globalization of Forced Labour* (Variorum, Aldershot, 1996), 1–36.

30 See R. Beachy, *The Slave Trade of Eastern Africa* (Collings, London, 1976), 20 where he continues: "and this number was reduced to none, when the *Dee* was laid up for refit, and the *Crecian* and *Dart* were recalled to the Cape."

Zanzibar (which, embarrassingly, was under British protection). The Sultan of Zanzibar had, in 1843, negotiated a treaty with Great Britain that allowed for the free passage of Arab dhows along the African and Arabian coast to Oman, thus excluding this traffic from visits to suppress the slave trade. It was only when dhows ventured outside the prescribed zone that they were susceptible to capture.[31]

In 1873, the "provisions of the existing Treaties having proved ineffectual for preventing the export of slaves from the territories of the Sultan of Zanzibar, Her Majesty the Queen and His Highness the Sultan above-named, agreed that from this date the export of slaves from the coast of the mainland of Africa, whether destined for transport from one part of the Sultan's dominions to another [re: Oman] or for conveyance to foreign parts, shall entirely cease." The 1873 Treaty further stipulated that "any vessel engaged in the transport or conveyance of slaves after this date shall be liable to seizure and condemnation" by the British Navy.[32] In all likelihood, the Treaty itself would not have been concluded but for the fact that the East African Squadron had blockaded Kilwa, the transit port to Zanzibar on mainland Africa, in early 1873. While Lloyd states that by 1883 that wholesale trade had ended, the issue of slave trading in the Indian Ocean, the Red Sea, and the Persian Gulf did persist, although on a much more limited scale and often under French flag.

Common Law Attempts to Outlaw the Slave Trade

Great Britain emerged from the Napoleonic Wars as an unrivalled maritime power. As a means of suppressing the slave trade, it sought to establish a right during peacetime from which all maritime States benefited in war: the right to visit foreign ships. While a belligerent right to visit ships was well established by the end of the Napoleonic Wars, it was limited to visiting neutral ships to ascertain whether they were in fact neutrals or simply flying flags of convenience; and searching to ensure that no contraband material was on board.[33]

---

31 See Lloyd, above n. 27, 234. An Arab dhow has been described by Captain, later Commander, Phillip Colomb as follows: "If a pear be sharpened at the thin end, and then cut in half longitudinally, two models will have been made resembling in all essential respects the ordinarily slave dhow." See Beachy, above n. 30, 68.

32 Article 1, Treaty between Great Britain and Zanzibar for the Suppression of the Slave Trade, 5 June 1873, 63 *BFSP* 174.

33 See L.-B. Hautefeuille, *Des droits et devoirs des Nations neutres en temps de guerre maritime* (3 volumes) (Guillaume et Compagnie, Librairies, Paris, 1858).

During the early nineteenth century a number of cases in Great Britain and the United States considered whether there existed a right to visit foreign ships on the high seas in times of peace so as to suppress the slave trade. While late-Napoleonic municipal judgments on both sides of the Atlantic were willing to admit a right to visit based largely on domestic law elevated to the international level by way of natural law,[34] by 1825 such pronouncements had been reversed by decisions which conformed to a growing trend of positivism as a means of interpreting international law.[35] The decisions of the British High Court of Admiralty and the United States Supreme Court highlighted the need to gain the consent of a sovereign State for foreign warships to visit its vessels in times of peace on the high seas, no matter the jurisdiction. Great Britain then turned to international relations to seek to develop a right to visit in peacetime.

International Jurisprudence Admits No Common Law Right to Visit

During the Napoleonic Wars, the British Admiralty courts were willing, on the basis of a "natural law" right to visit, to condemn ships involved in the slave trade. Such judgments not only violated the rights of neutrals, they were at variance with general international law in seeking to detain foreign ships not in violation of international obligations but merely in breach of the flag ship's own municipal law. In *The Amedie* case of 1810, an American ship carrying one hundred and five slaves from Bonny (on the coast of modern-day Nigeria) to Matanzas in Cuba was condemned by the Vice-Admiralty Court of Tortola (British Virgin Islands) for having engaged in illegal trade. The Claimants failed on appeal. The Lords of Appeals in Prize Causes noted that, ordinarily, they could not be called upon to consider or apply a foreign State's municipal law.

> But by the alteration which has since taken places in our law, the question stands now upon very different grounds. We do now, and did at the time of this capture, take an interest in preventing that traffic in which this ship was engaged. The slave trade has since been totally abolished in this country, and our Legislature has declared the African slave trade is contrary to the principles of justice and humanity. ...
>
> [We] are now entitled to act according to our law and to hold that *prima facie* the trade is altogether illegal, and thus to throw on a claimant the whole burden of proof in order to shew that by the particular law of

34 See A. Rubin, *Ethics and Authority in International Law* (CUP, 1997).

35 See A. Nussbaum, *A Concise History of the Law of Nations* (Macmillan, New York, 1961), 232–234.

> his own country he is entitled to carry on this traffic. As the case now stands, we think that no claimant can be heard in an application to a court of prize for the restoration of the human beings he carried unjustly to another country for the purpose of disposing of them as slaves.[36]

Similarly, in *The Fortuna* in 1811, the High Court of Admiralty considered the case of an American ship which had been re-flagged as Portuguese and, having set out from the Spanish Atlantic island of Madeira, was shortly thereafter captured as prize by the Royal Navy. Lord Stowell noted the principle which had emerged from *The Amedie*:

> that any trade contrary to the general law of nations, although not tending to or accompanied with any infraction of the belligerent rights of that country, whose tribunals are called upon to consider it, may subject the vessel employed in that [the slave] trade to confiscation.[37]

Lord Stowell then turned to consider the nature of the ship to see whether it was, in fact, involved in the slave trade:

> The construction and furniture of the ship had all the accommodations necessary for the conduct of that trade, and of that trade only. She had platforms ready constructed; she had timbers fit for the construction of more; she had iron shackles and bolts, and running chains and collars – all adapted for the purposes of conveying slaves – and the quantity and species of provision and medicine which such purposes require.[38]

He condemned the foreign ship and its cargo as prize, not on the basis of an established treaty between Great Britain and Portugal but as being, in part, "repugnant to the law of nations, to justice and humanity."[39]

---

36 *The Amedie* (1810) 1 *Acton's Admiralty Reports* 240, 250–252. Note that Kern writes: "Yet the reasoning that British rights under international law could depend on the domestic legislation of other countries was hardly consistent with traditional interpretations of international law": see above n. 5, 236.

37 *The Fortuna* (1811) 1 *Dodson's Admiralty Reports* 81, 84. For a general discussion of these case and their relevance in international law to the issue of the slave trade, see W. Lawrence, *Wheaton's Elements of International Law* (Stevens & Sons, Limited, London, 1857) and Phillimore, above n. 3.

38 *The Fortuna*, ibid, 90.

39 Ibid, 85.

By 1813 however, Lord Stowell acknowledged that the Vice-Admiralty Court at Sierra Leone had gone too far in condemning the *Diana*, a Swedish ship carrying one hundred and twenty slaves from Cape Mount, Liberia, to St. Bartholomew (part of the Lesser Antilles) which had been seized by His Majesty's ship the *Crocodile* and taken to Sierra Leone. While the High Court of Admiralty was willing to award prize for ships involved in the slave trade where the flag-State had outlawed such activity in its municipal law, Lord Stowell was unwilling to do so where it was clear that the State had yet to outlaw the trade:

> The…sentence affirms, "that the slave trade, from motives of humanity, hath been abolished by most civilised nations, and is not at the present time legally authorised by any." This appears to me to be an assertion by no means sustainable. This Court is disposed to go as far in discountenancing this odious traffic as the law of nations and the principles recognised by English tribunals will warrant it in doing, but beyond these principles it does not feel itself at liberty to travel: it cannot proceed on a sweeping anathema of this kind against property belonging to the subjects of foreign independent states. The position laid down in the sentence of the [Vice-Admiralty Court of Sierra Leone] that the slave trade is not authorised by any civilised state, is unfortunately by no means correct, the contrary being notoriously the fact, that it is tolerated by some of them.
>
> This trade was at one time, we know, universally allowed by the different nations of Europe, and carried on by them to a greater or less extent, according to their respective necessities. Sweden, having but small colonial possessions, did not engage very deeply in the traffic, but she entered into it so far as her convenience required for the supply of her own colonies. The trade, which was generally allowed, has been since abolished by some particular countries; but I am yet to learn that Sweden has prohibited its subjects from engaging in the traffic, or that she has abstained from it either in act or declaration. Our own country, it is true, has taken a more correct view of the subject, and has decreed the abolition of the slave trade, as far as British subjects are concerned; but it claims no right of enforcing its prohibition against the subjects of those states which have not adopted the same opinion with respect to the injustice and immorality of the trade.[40]

The Diana, however, failed to address the fundamental issue raised in *The Amedie* and *The Fortuna*: the right to visit and capture foreign vessels suspected

40 *The Diana* (1813) 1 *Dodson's Admiralty Reports* 95, 97–98.

of involvement in the slave trade where no international treaty existed. These decisions were superseded by *The Le Louis* in 1817. In that case, a French ship was returning from Africa to Martinique when the Royal Navy attempted to board it on suspicion of involvement in the slave trade. The crew resisted and twelve British and three French sailors were killed. The ship was taken and brought to Sierra Leone where it was adjudged as prize for being outfitted for the slave trade. On appeal before the High Court of Admiralty, Lord Stowell considered whether there existed a right to visit foreign ships in times of peace – if not, the resistance by the crew would be lawful:

> Upon the…question, whether the right of search exists in time of peace, I have to observe, that two principles of public law are generally recognised as fundamental. One is the perfect equality and entire independence of all distinct states. Relative magnitude creates no distinction of right; relative imbecility, whether permanent or casual, gives no additional right to the more powerful neighbour; and any advantage seized upon, that ground is mere usurpation. This is the great foundation of public law, which it mainly concerns the peace of mankind, both in their politic and private capacities, to preserve inviolate. The second is, that nations being equal, all have an equal right to the uninterrupted use of the un-appropriated parts of the ocean for their navigation. In places where no local authority exists, where the subjects of all states meet upon a footing of…equality and independence, no one state, or any of its subjects has a right to assume or exercise authority over the subjects of another. I can find no authority that gives the right of interruption to the navigation of states in amity upon the high seas, excepting that which the rights of war give to both belligerents against neutrals.
>
> …
>
> But at present, under the law, as now generally understood and practised, no nation can exercise a right of visitation and search upon the common and un-appropriated parts of the sea, save only on the belligerent claim.[41]

Lord Stowell held that although the aims of the British Navy were commendable, they were unlawful. If Great Britain wanted to continue with the suppression of the slave trade it would have to do so within the confines of international law:

41 *The Le Louis* (1817) 2 *Dodson's Admiralty Reports* 210, 244–245.

> To press forward to a great principle by breaking through every other great principle that stands in the way of its establishment; to force the way to the liberation of Africa by trampling on the independence of other states in Europe; in short, to procure an eminent good by means that are unlawful; is as little consonant to private morality as to public justice. Obtain the concurrence of other nations, if you can, by application, by remonstrance, by example, by every peaceable instrument which man can employ to attract the consent of man. But a nation is not justified in assuming rights that do not belong to her merely because she means to apply them to a laudable purpose; nor in setting out upon a moral crusade of converting other nations by acts of unlawful force. Nor is it to be argued, that because other nations approve the ultimate purpose, they must therefore submit to every measure which any one state or its subjects may inconsiderately adopt for its attainment.[42]

In 1817 the British admiralty courts settled that the suppression of the slave trade did not allow for a right to visit foreign ships on the high seas during time of peace, but it took a further eight years for this principle to emerge in the United States. Although the Federal Circuit Court of Massachusetts, in *The Jeune Eugenie* in 1822, relied heavily on domestic law to find the slave trade was "prohibited by universal law,"[43] this decision was followed by the United States

42 Ibid, 258–259. Despite having found that the British had illegally seized the *Le Louis*, Lord Stowell was unwilling to award damages, see 264.

43 *The United States v. La Jeune Eugenie* (1822) 26 *Federal Case Reports* 832, 851. Although the Court held that it could indeed confiscate, it handed over the cargo to the French Consul so that it might be "dealt with according to his own sense of duty and right." The following passage emphasises the natural law approach of Justice Story and also vividly portrays the reality of the slave trade:

> It would be unbecoming in me here to assert, that the state of slavery cannot have a legitimate existence, or that it stands condemned by the unequivocal testimony of the law of nations. But this concession carries us but a very short distance towards the decision of this cause. It is not, as the learned counsel for the government have justly stated, on account of the simple fact, that the traffic necessarily involves the enslavement of human beings, that it stands reprehended by the present sense of nations; but that it necessarily carries with it a breach of all the moral duties, of all the maxims of justice, mercy and humanity, and of the admitted rights, which independent Christian nations now hold sacred in their intercourse with each other. What is the fact as to the ordinary, nay, necessary course, of this trade? It begins in corruption, and plunder, and kidnapping. It creates and stimulates unholy wars for the purpose of making captives. It desolates whole villages and provinces for the purpose of seizing the young, the feeble, the defenceless, and the innocent. It breaks down all the ties of parent,

Supreme Court in 1825. *The Antelope* case involved the capture of a vessel on suspicion of involvement in piracy as it had been hovering off the coast of Florida for some time. When seized, it was discovered that the *Antelope* had been captured by Spanish privateers off the coast of Africa and was carrying more than two hundred and eighty slaves to be sold in Surinam. The case was brought by the Vice-Consuls of Portugal and Spain who sought restitution for the property they considered had been improperly seized by the American Government. Chief Justice Marshall took a decidedly positivist approach to interpreting the law regarding the slave trade and the notion of visitation:

> Whatever might be the answer of a moralist to this question, a jurist must search for its legal solution, in those principles of action which are sanctioned by the usages, the national acts, and the general assent, of that portion of the world of which he considers himself as a part, and to whose

---

> and children, and family, and country. It shuts up all sympathy for human suffering and sorrows. It manacles the inoffensive females and the starving infants. It forces the brave to untimely death in defence of their humble homes and firesides, or drives them to despair and self-immolation. It stirs up the worst passions of the human soul, darkening the spirit of revenge, sharpening the greediness of avarice, brutalizing the selfish, envenoming the cruel, famishing the weak, and crushing to death the broken-hearted. This is but the beginning of the evils. Before the unhappy captives arrive at the destined market, where the traffic ends, one quarter part at least in the ordinary course of events perish in cold blood under the inhuman, or thoughtless treatment of their oppressors. Strong as these expressions may seem, and dark as is the colouring of this statement, it is short of the real calamities inflicted by this traffic. All the wars, that have desolated Africa for the last three centuries, have had their origin in the slave trade. The blood of thousands of her miserable children has stained her shores, or quenched the dying embers of her desolated towns, to glut the appetite of slave dealers. The ocean has received in its deep and silent bosom thousands more, who have perished from disease and want during their passage from their native homes to the foreign colonies. I speak not from vague rumours, or idle tales, but from authentic documents, and the known historical details of the traffic, – a traffic, that carries away at least 50,000 persons annually from their homes and their families, and breaks the hearts, and buries the hopes, and extinguishes the happiness of more than double that number. [...] "There is," as one of the greatest of modern statesmen has declared, "something of horror in it that surpasses all the bounds of imagination." Mr. Pitt's speech on the slave trade, in 1792. It is of this traffic, thus carried on, and necessarily carried on, beginning in lawless wars, and rapine, and kidnapping, and ending in disease, and death, and slavery – it is of this traffic in the aggregate of its accumulated wrongs, that I would ask, if it be consistent with the law of nations?

Ibid, 845–846.

> law the appeal is made. If we resort to this standard as the test of international law, the question, as has already been observed, is decided in favour of the legality of the trade. Both Europe and America embarked in it; and for nearly two centuries, it was carried on without opposition, and without censure. A jurist could not say, that a practice thus supported was illegal, and that those engaged in it might be punished, either personally, or by deprivation of property.
>
> In this commerce, thus sanctioned by universal assent, every nation has an equal right to engage. How is this right to be lost? Each may renounce it for its own people; but can this renunciation affect others?
>
> No principle of general law is more universally acknowledged, than the perfect equality of nations. Russia and Geneva have equal rights. It results from this equality, that no one can rightfully impose a rule on another. Each legislates for itself, but its legislation can operate on itself alone. A right, then, which is vested in all by the consent of all, can be divested only by consent; and this trade, in which all have participated, must remain lawful to those who cannot be induced to relinquish it. As no nation can prescribe a rule for others, none can make a law of nations; and this traffic remains lawful to those whose governments have not forbidden it.
>
> ...
>
> If it be...repugnant to the law of nations...it is almost superfluous to say in this Court, that the right of bringing in for adjudication in time of peace, even where the vessel belongs to a nation which has prohibited the trade, cannot exist. The Courts of no country execute the penal laws of another; and the course of the American government on the subject of visitation and search, would decide any case in which that right had been exercised by an American cruiser, on the vessel of a foreign nation, not violating our municipal laws, against the captors.
>
> It follows, that a foreign vessel engaged in the African slave trade, captured on the high seas in time of peace, by an American cruiser, and brought in for adjudication, would be restored.[44]

By 1825, therefore, international jurisprudence – at least of an Anglo-American variety – was settled. The principles which emerged were rooted in positive international law, where State consent was required to establish jurisdiction over its flagged ships. Early common law decisions sought to assert a natural law emphasis on the repugnance of the slave trade which, outlawed for the

44 *The Antelope* (1825), 23 *United States Supreme Court Reports* 66, 121–123.

most part at the municipal level, granted States the *right* to suppress the trade in accordance with a flagged State's domestic laws.[45] From *The Le Louis* onwards, Great Britain could no longer use its own common law to justify suppressing the slave trade; this case made plain that visiting ships on the high seas for that purpose was against international law. Instead the British largely followed Lord Stowell's advice and sought: "the concurrence of other nations... by application, by remonstrance, by example, by every peaceable instrument which man can employ to attract the consent of man." When this failed, Great Britain, as we shall see, was not above using force and coercive means to achieve its ultimate objective of suppressing the slave trade through the establishment of a right to visit.

Early Attempts at Outlawing the Slave Trade

Following *The Le Louis*, it was clear that Great Britain was unable to rely on a common law prerogative to develop the means of suppressing the slave trade. Yet it had also been active at the international level prior to this judgment and had sought, as early as the settlement of the Napoleonic Wars, to establish a universal instrument which would allow for the suppression of the slave trade and provide for a reciprocal right of visit to ensure the end of the trade at sea. While Great Britain maintained this strategic foreign policy objective for seventy-five years, for tactical reasons it spent most of the intervening period establishing a web of bilateral arrangements which were ultimately subsumed into the General Act of the 1890 Brussels Conference. Gradually Britain locked a growing number of States into its web of bilateral treaties and isolated those outside the system, moving closer towards its original goal: the universal outlawing of the slave trade.

In the lead up to the Congress of Vienna of 1814 the British Foreign Minister, Lord Castlereagh, gained the formal support of a defeated France for the end of the slave trade and for his endeavours to internationalise the issue at Vienna.[46] At the Congress itself, Great Britain proposed that the trade should be outlawed within a three-year period; that a permanent institution be established to supervise adherence to the treaty obligations; and that a reciprocal right of visit be established.[47] Yet French support was not forthcoming at Vienna where

45 Rubin, above n. 34, 110.

46 M.T. Barclay, "Le droit de visite, le traffic des esclaves et la Conférence antiesclavagiste de Bruxelles," *Revue de droit international et de legislation comparé*, Vol. 22, 1890, pp. 319–320.

47 S. Miers, *Britain and the Ending of the Slave Trade* (Longman, London, 1975), 10–11.

capitulation was no longer the order of the day. France and the Iberian States opposed the proposal, and Castlereagh was ultimately unable to gain a binding commitment regarding the abolition of the slave trade beyond a Declaration by the Powers which expressed the wish to "bring to an end a scourge which has for a long time desolated Africa, degraded Europe, and afflicted humanity." The Powers declared that they:

> consider the universal abolition of the trade in Negroes to be particularly worthy of their attention, being in conformity with the spirit of the times, and the general principles of our August Sovereigns, who our animated in their sincere desire to work towards the quickest and most effective of measures, by all means at their disposal, and to act, in the use of those means with all zealousness and perseverance which is required of such a grand and beautiful cause.[48]

This pious statement was qualified by a recognition that the Declaration would not prejudice the time it might take any State to conclude its involvement in the trade and that a "determination as to time when this commerce is to universally come to an end would be the object of negotiation as between the Powers."[49]

In the wake of the Congress of Vienna, Great Britain instituted a "formal and permanent conference" in London comprising ambassadors of the Great Powers. With a permanent secretariat, it was intended to represent "both a centre of information and a centre of action." However, although it held sixteen formal meetings between 1816 and 1819, it achieved very little beyond information gathering, as the other Powers remained suspicious of British attempts to promote its abolitionist agenda at the expense of their right to freedom of the seas.[50] The recognition in the Vienna Declaration that the end of the slave trade would have to result from negotiations was picked up by Castlereagh at Aix-la-Chapelle in 1818 at the first meeting of the Concert of Europe.[51] The British Foreign Minister sought the creation of a right to visit and

48 *Declaration des 8 Cours, relative à l'Abolition Universelle de la Traite des Nègres*, Vienna, 8 February 1815, 3 *BFSP* 972. The eight Powers were Austria, Britain, France, Prussia, Russia, Portugal, Spain and Sweden.

49 Ibid.

50 C.K. Webster, *The Foreign Policy of Castlereagh 1815–1822: Britain and the European Alliance* (G. Bell, London, 1925), 457–459. For the Protocols of the London conferences see 6 *BFSP* 23, 25, 50–52.

51 The Concert system was intended to allow European Powers to consider international issues, at intervals, during peacetime, as opposed to their former practice of solely meeting

detain slave ships solely in the Atlantic Ocean north of the equator and the establishment of mixed commissions with the power to adjudicate claims; yet his appeals fell on deaf ears, as the other Powers were unwilling to curtail their freedom of the seas.[52]

At the Congress of Verona of 1822, Great Britain once again sought to achieve an international agreement. By the 1820s, all maritime Powers had abolished the trade domestically and a distinct possibility for success existed. However, the British grand design for a universal treaty outlawing the trade was again thwarted, not because of the principle, but because of a lack of consensus on the modalities to be used. At Verona, the new Foreign Minister, the Duke of Wellington, put forward a proposal to the Powers that included the renewal of the Declaration of Vienna of 1815 and the assimilation of slave trading with piracy.[53] The continental Powers were unwilling to agree to the regime proposed, and what emerged from Verona was not a mechanism to enforce the suppression of the slave trade, but a diplomatic willingness to move beyond the Declaration of 1815 by making the following "Resolution":

> That they invariably persisted in their principles and sentiments which these Sovereigns manifested in their Declaration of 8 February 1815 – That they have never ceased, and will never cease to consider the commerce in Negroes – "a scourge which has for a long time desolated Africa, degraded Europe, and afflicted humanity," and that they are ready to contribute to everything which could assure and accelerate the complete and definite abolition of this commerce.[54]

This Resolution was the end product of earlier attempts by Great Britain to establish a universal instrument prohibiting the slave trade at the expense of the freedom of the seas. Yet the failure at Vienna in 1815, more than any other, resulted in a change of tactics by Great Britain in pursuing the creation of a universal instrument which allowed for a right to visit on the high seas. It is to this tactical adjustment which this study now turns.

---

to settle the peace after war (e.g. Congress of Vienna). Four meetings took place in this manner: Aix-la-Chapelle (1818), Troppau (1820), Laibach (1821), and Verona (1822).

52 Memorandum of the British Government, 27 October 1818, Castlereagh, 6 *BFSP* 59.

53 Memorandum of the Duke of Wellington, 10 November 1822, 10 *BFSP* 95. The Five Powers in attendance at Verona were: Austria, Britain, France, Prussia, Russia.

54 *Résolution relatives à l'Abolition de la Traite des Nègres*, Vienna, 28 November 1822, 10 *BFSP* 109–110.

The Bilateral Outlawing of the Slave Trade

Thwarted in its multilateral attempts to outlaw the slave trade and in the face of the determination by its domestic courts that visitation of foreign ships on the high seas in peacetime had to be a consensual right, Great Britain turned to the establishment of bilateral treaties to outlaw the slave trade. The building of such a bilateral network, however, would prove ineffective if any maritime power remained outside the system. As noted abolitionist, the parliamentarian Thomas Fowell Buxton stated in 1837: "it will avail us little that ninety-nine doors are closed, if one remains open. To that outlet the whole slave trade of Africa will rush."[55] Great Britain persisted in building its network, and through an increasing number of bilateral treaties was able to isolate the few States outside the system, increasing the momentum towards a universally accepted *right* to visit. That it took until 1890 for a universal treaty to be established speaks to the opposition of a number of States, not to the slave trade *per se*, but to granting to Britain the right to visit their merchant ships.

France and the United States were most obstinate in their call to respect the absolute right (in peacetime) to free commerce upon the high seas. While Brazil, France, Portugal, and the United States each had distinct reasons for opposing the British initiative, they all saw in the British wish to suppress the slave trade an attempt to appropriate the policing of the seas and control maritime commerce. While Brazil and Portugal were persuaded by coercive means to join the system, France and the United States remained adamant in supporting freedom of the seas. Ultimately, France and the United States acceded to the British wish to suppress the slave trade, and Great Britain accepted a *limited* right to visit merchant ships of these two States.

Unable to forge a consensus to establish a universal treaty outlawing the slave trade during the Concert of Europe era, Great Britain ultimately entered into treaties with thirty-one States to suppress the slave trade at sea.[56] There was only one instance in which two States, neither of which was Great Britain,

55 W. Mathieson, *Great Britain and the Slave Trade (1839–1865)* (Longman, Greens & Co, London, 1929), 38–39.

56 These thirty-one States included, in chronological order of signature: Portugal, Denmark, France, Spain, Netherlands, Sweden, Buenos Aires, Colombia, Brazil, Mexico, Confederation of Peru, Bolivia, Hanseatic Cities, Tuscany, the two Sicilies, Chili, Venezuela, Uruguay, Haiti, Texas, Austria, Prussia, Russia, The United States of America, The Kings and Chiefs of Cape Mount (Africa), Equator, Muscat, Arabs of the Gulf, New Granada, Zanzibar, Egypt. See Phillimore, above n. 3, 420–421. This does not include agreements with African leaders who were not considered "civilized nations."

entered into an agreement to suppress the slave trade.[57] These bilateral agreements, as we shall see, evolved over time and were generally of two types: those that provided for a right to visit and those which contained "mutual obligation to maintain squadrons on the coast of Africa."[58]

At the beginning of the eighteenth century Great Britain began to solicit agreements whereby other States renounced the slave trade. As early as 1810, Portugal bound itself to such a treaty of principle. Likewise in 1813, in exchange for the island of Guadeloupe, Sweden renounced the introduction of slaves into its colonies and prohibited Swedes from participating in the trade.[59] However, Great Britain realised that it was vital not only to seek agreement with all maritime powers, but that such agreements needed to include enforcement provisions to have any effect on the suppression of the trade. In other words, the right to visit was vital.

In 1817 and 1818, Great Britain concluded treaties with the Netherlands, Portugal, and Spain which went beyond declaratory statements outlawing the slave trade, introducing mechanisms which became the essence of these bilateral agreements over the next half-century. The 1818 Dutch treaty, in which Great Britain and the Netherlands confirmed a "mutual desire to adopt the most effectual measure for putting a stop to the carrying on of the Slave-trade by their respective Subjects, and for preventing their respective Flags from being made use of as a protection to this nefarious traffic,"[60] is exemplary. These early agreements permitted the navies of the contracting parties, under special instruction, to visit merchant ships of the other contracting party suspected of slave trading. If slaves were found on board, the ship was to be brought before mixed commissions to determine whether the ship and cargo were forfeited.[61]

Within a five year period, it was discovered these reciprocal visitation treaties were lacking: ships which did not have slaves on board could not be detained, yet there was a recognition that vessels "employed in the illegal Traffic, have unshipped their Slaves immediately prior to their being visited… [having] thus found means to evade forfeiture, and have been enabled to

57 *Convention entre la France et la Suède*, Stockholm, 21 May 1836, 24 *BFSP* 556.

58 Phillimore, above n. 3, 422.

59 3 *BFSP* 886.

60 Treaty between His Britannic Majesty and His Majesty the King of The Netherlands, for preventing their Subjects from engaging in any Traffic in Slavery, The Hague, 4 May 1818, 5 *BFSP* 125.

61 These treaties, as others that would follow, excluded the right to visit from European waters as well as the Mediterranean. The 1817 Portuguese treaty also excluded the right to visit south of the equator. See Article 2, Additional Convention between Great Britain and Portugal, for the prevention of the Slave Trade, London, 28 July 1817, 10 *BFSP* 88.

pursue their unlawful course with impunity, contrary to the true object and spirit of the Treaty."[62] As a result, a so-called "equipment clause" was introduced into subsequent treaties, which provided that a ship outfitted with certain materiel would be "considered as *primâ facie* evidence of her actual employment in the Slave Trade." Such equipment included open gratings on hatches, spare planks for the creation of a slave-deck, possession of "shackles, bolts or handcuffs," or an overabundance of water and food for needs of the crew on the planned voyage.[63]

Part of the bilateral regime established by Great Britain to suppress the slave trade was the establishment, between 1817 and 1871, of mixed commissions to adjudicate claims arising from the capture of ships suspected of involvement in the slave trade. These adjudicative organs consisted of judges appointed by the two parties: with no third-party involvement. Instead these mixed courts or more properly "mixed or joint commissions" consisted – at least in theory – of a judge and a commissioner of arbitration from each State party. The judges considered the legality of the capture and, failing agreement, lots were drawn to decide which commissioner would settle the case. As Bethell writes in his historical study of the mixed commissions: "[judges] usually – although by no means always – agreed with their senior partners on the commission, with the result that many ships captured without slaves on board were condemned or acquitted literally on the toss of a coin." He continued:

> In December 1841, for instance, two Brazilian vessels, the *Ermelinda* and the *Galianna*, almost identical cases in terms of their fittings, came before the Anglo-Brazilian commission in Sierra Leone, where the judges were unable to agree upon a verdict. In the first case the English arbitrator won the toss and the *Galianna* was condemned; in the second the Brazilian was successful and the *Ermelinda* was released.[64]

The early bilateral treaties allowed for the establishment of two mixed commissions, ordinarily one in West Africa, in the British Crown colony of Sierra

62 See Article 1, Explanatory and Additional Articles to the 4th May, 1818, Treaty between Great Britain and The Netherlands, for the Prevention of the Traffic in Slaves, 31 December 1822, Brussels, 10 *BFSP* 132.

63 Further Additional Article to the 4th May, 1818, Treaty between Great Britain and The Netherlands, for the Prevention of the Traffic in Slaves, 25 January 1823, Brussels, 10 *BFSP* 559.

64 L. Bethell, "The Mixed Commissions for the Suppression of the Transatlantic Slave Trade in the Nineteenth Century," *Journal of African History*, Vol. 7, 1966, pp. 79, 87 [footnote omitted].

Leone, the other in the New World. Thus, for instance, an Anglo-Portuguese mixed commission sat in Rio de Janeiro (later in Spanish Town, Jamaica); an Anglo-Spanish commission in Havana; an Anglo-Dutch commission in Surinam; an Anglo-American commission in New York; and an Anglo-Brazilian mixed commission in the newly independent capital of Brazil, Rio de Janeiro.[65]

The British were at an advantage with respect to these mixed commissions, as their naval squadrons effectively had a monopoly on captures and worked primarily off the coast of Africa.[66] As a result, most captures were adjudicated in Freetown, Sierra Leone, where Great Britain already had a Vice-Admiralty Court whose officials also sat on the various Commissions. While the Brazilian, Dutch, Portuguese and Spanish Commissioners sat in waiting for one of their own nations' ships to be brought in by the British Royal Navy, the British representatives could handle cases involving slavers from the flagship of any State which had agreed to jurisdiction under a bilateral treaty. Sierra Leone was "a notorious white man's grave," and non-British parties which had agreed to mixed commissions in Freetown had difficulty staffing them. The Anglo-Dutch Mixed Commission is a case in point. In line with the Treaty of 1818, the Netherlands appointed a judge and commissioner in 1819. When the judge left in 1820, he was never replaced; the commissioner remained until 1828, acting sometimes as judge sometimes as commissioner. From 1828 onwards "the Anglo-Dutch mixed courts functioned without a Dutch representative until the court was dissolved in 1871."[67]

---

65 Note that although Chile (1839), the Argentine Confederation (1839), Uruguay (1839), Bolivia (1840) and Ecuador (1841) ratified bilateral treaties with Great Britain allowing for mixed commissions, they "waived the right to establish mixed commissions in their own territory," instead allowing the mixed court in Sierra Leone– to which they did not appoint Commissioners – to adjudge captures: ibid, 83.

66 Bethell notes that 95 percent of all vessels captured under the anti-slave treaties Britain had secured from Portugal, Spain, the Netherlands and Brazil were taken by ships of the Royal British Navy: ibid, 83. Bethell also gives a breakdown of the cases that were heard between 1819 and 1845: at Sierra Leone, 528; Havana, 50; Rio de Janeiro, 44; and Surinam, 1. As for cases dealt with in Freetown, the Anglo-Spanish Commission heard 241, the Anglo-Portuguese Commission: 155, Anglo-Brazilian Commission: 111, and the Anglo-Netherlands Commission: 21: ibid, 84.

67 P. Emmer, *The Dutch in the Atlantic Economy, 1580–1880: Trade, Slavery and Emancipation* (Ashgate, Aldershot, 1998), 181. According to Bethell: "British officials in the so-called 'mixed' commissions frequently found themselves sitting alone. Each of the three [Dutch, Portuguese, Spanish] commissions at Sierra Leone started out in 1819 with a full complement of officials, but during the next few years all foreign commissioners left, not to return." Bethell, ibid, 87.

It is estimated that the various mixed commissions involved in suppressing the slave trade were "responsible for the condemnation of over 620 slave vessels and the liberation of nearly 80000 slaves." 528 vessels appeared before the Freetown commissions, of which 501 "were condemned and nearly 65000 slaves liberated."[68] However as a result of a change in British policy in 1845, only a further seven cases were heard in Sierra Leone before the mixed commissions finally closed in 1871. The Palmerston Act, enacted in 1839, mandated, *inter alia*, that ships "not entitled to claim the protection of the flag of any state" be brought before Vice-Admiralty courts. Cases were henceforth increasingly brought, not before what were, in effect, the exclusively British manned "mixed" commissions, but instead to the British Vice-Admiralty Courts of Sierra Leone, St Helena, or Cape Town. Likewise in South Africa, after 1845, only eight cases were brought before the Cape Town mixed commissions, and only three resulted in condemnation.[69] As a result, where slave traders were in actuality in command of a flag ship of a State which sought to take action, not only against the ship, but also against the captain and crew, it was wise for the sailors to quickly "lose" their papers and flag, and thus take command of a "stateless" ship; when captured, they fell under the jurisdiction of the Vice-Admiralty courts where only the vessels faced judicial sanction.[70]

While eighty thousand slaves were liberated as a result of the pronouncements of the mixed commissions, these numbers paled in the face of the continuing trade which, during the first half of the nineteenth century, resulted in the transportation of more than three million slaves to the New World. Yet, the British bilateral regime did have a deterrent effect on the Atlantic Slave Trade as the number of known slaves transported to the Western Hemisphere

---

68 J.P. van Niekerk, "British, Portuguese, and American judges in Adderley Street; the international legal background to, and some judicial aspects of, the Cape Town Mixed Commissions for the Suppression of the Transatlantic Slave Trade in the Nineteenth Century (Part 2)" *The Comparative and International Journal of Southern Africa*, Vol. 37(2), 2004, p. 200.

69 J.P. van Niekerk, "British, Portuguese, and American judges in Adderley Street; the international legal background to, and some judicial aspects of, the Cape Town Mixed Commissions for the Suppression of the Transatlantic Slave Trade in the Nineteenth Century (Part 3)," *The Comparative and International Journal of Southern Africa*, Vol. 37(3), 2004, p. 405.

70 J.P. van Niekerk, "British, Portuguese, and American judges in Adderley Street; the international legal background to, and some judicial aspects of, the Cape Town Mixed Commissions for the Suppression of the Transatlantic Slave Trade in the Nineteenth Century (Part 1)," *The Comparative and International Journal of Southern Africa*, Vol. 37(1), 2004, p. 35.

dropped by one-fifth in comparison to the latter half of the eighteenth century.[71] Eltis, having considered supply and demand, estimates that as a result of the actions of the British Navy, two hundred and thirteen thousand Africans were spared enslavement after 1830.[72] Despite this reduction in the number of slaves transported, the weaknesses in the bilateral system persisted. The total abolishment of the slave trade required that all maritime States join the British system, as slave traders used false flags and forged papers to avoid visit and capture. Slave ships were not above "acquiring" a new nationality at sea:

> During the chase the captain of the *La Fortunée* had been standing on the bow of his ship with two tin boxes in his hand. As soon as the man-of-war had shown the Union Jack, the captain had dropped one of these boxes into the sea. The ship was captured and the remaining box contained only French papers.[73]

In an attempt to complete its bilateral system, during the late 1830s early 1840s, Britain signed a number of such agreements with newly independent Latin American States.[74] However, this did not complete the system, as four States held out, limiting the effectiveness of the British bilateral system for the suppression of the slave trade.

The Recalcitrant States: Completing the Bilateral Regime

For diverse reasons Brazil, France, Portugal, and the United States of America were unwilling to involve themselves in the bilateral treaty regime constructed by Great Britain to suppress the slave trade.[75] While Brazil and Portugal simply needed some "nudging" by the British Navy to join the existing system, France and the United States were not so easily moved. With international law on their side and as "Powers" in their own right, they remained adamant that the freedom of the seas should be respected and that, in the absence of a conventional agreement, a legal right of visitation only existed in times of war. It was only when the domestic situation in both States began to favour abolition that they were willing to seriously discuss the suppression of the slave trade. While France conceded a right to visit for a period of time, it reverted to its former

71 Eltis, above n. 12, Table 1, 43.

72 Davis, *Inhuman Bondage*, above n. 18, 244.

73 Emmer, above n. 67, 182.

74 Buenos Ayres (1839), Chile (1839), Venezuela (1839), Uruguay (1840), Bolivia (1840), Texas (1840), Equator (1841), Mexico (1841), and later, New Grenada (re: Colombia; 1851).

75 Lloyd, above n. 27, x.

position and ultimately accepted a bilateral arrangement whereby joint naval squadrons patrolled the African Coast. For the United States, a war-time measure by the Northern Union during the American Civil War ultimately allowed it to become party to a bilateral treaty similar to the Anglo-French treaty. Thus, one by one, these four States became part of the web of bilateral treaties which Great Britain had been establishing since 1817. Only then, when all maritime powers had agreed to effective means to suppress the slave trade at sea was it possible to look to developing a universal instrument.

1 France

British abolitionist tendencies were viewed in France with great suspicion. As Daget noted, it was thought the "envied rival was using ostensibly humanitarian means to further its ambitions for political, commercial and indeed military hegemony."[76] France was hesitant to join the British bilateral system, instead dispatching warships to the West African coast where, from 1817 to 1831, they seized 65 suspected slavers and condemned 51 of a known total of 482 French slavers.[77] Great Britain simply bided its time, witnessing the rise and fall of the Bourbon Dynasty, and in the aftermath of the 1830 July Revolution found a French government with abolitionist leanings willing to sign a visitation treaty. Yet the treaties of 1831 and 1833 were very restrictive and detailed in laying down procedures for visit. They were to apply in specific maritime zones off West Africa and surrounding the islands of Cuba, Madagascar and Puerto Rico and mandated that jurisdiction over seized ships fell to the flag State's judiciary; thus no mixed commissions were attached to these agreements.[78] Further, these treaties were opened to accession, an option which was later taken up by Denmark, Haïti, the Hanseatic League (i.e.: Bremen, Gdansk, Hamburg, and Rostock), Sardinia, the Kingdom of the Two Sicilies and Tuscany. While the acceding States would remain bound by their agreements with Great Britain, France would not.

The mutual right of visitation agreed to by France in the 1831 and 1833 Treaties proved to be contentious, and its application became embroiled in the

76 S. Daget, "France, Suppression of the Illegal Trade, and England, 1817–1850," in D. Eltis and J. Walvin (eds.), *The Abolition of the Atlantic Slave Trade: Origins and Effects in Europe, Africa, and the Americas* (University of Wisconsin Press, London, 1981), 194.

77 Ibid, 200.

78 For the Treaty of 1831, see *Convention between Great Britain and France, for the more effective suppression of the Traffic in Slaves*, Paris, 30 November 1831, 18 BFSP 641; for the Treaty of 1833, see *Supplementary Convention between His Majesty and the King of the French, for the more effectual Suppression of the Traffic in Slaves*, Paris, 22 March 1833, 20 BFSP 286.

traditional British-French rivalry which was so much a part of that era. The seizing of two French ships by the Royal Navy in particular – the *Sénégambie* and the *Marabout* – was a rallying point for anti-British sentiment in France.[79] Thus, when Great Britain gained the European Powers' agreement on a multilateral convention, succeeding where it had failed in Vienna in 1815, France acted as the spoiler. In 1841, Austria, France, Great Britain, Prussia, and Russia signed a treaty which assimilated the slave trade at sea with piracy. The United States was the first to make this connection, equating slaving to piracy in its domestic legislation in 1820. Great Britain had also managed to include such a provision as early as 1826 in an agreement with Brazil. The appearance of this provision in the multilateral convention among the European Powers indicated that Great Britain was very close to achieving its foreign policy objective of an established right to visit in international law. The assimilation of slaving to piracy meant that ships involved in the trade would have no right to avail themselves of the protection of any State's flag and as such, could be visited by ships of all States; to use modern terminology, universal jurisdiction was established.[80] The 1841 Convention required domestic courts to assume jurisdiction over seizures; it also provided a right to visit in an expanded rectangular maritime zone which included the east coast of the New World from modern day Florida westward to India, extending southward to a parallel line established just south of Buenos Aires and extending east into the India Ocean.[81] Yet the signing of the 1841 Quintuple Treaty "stirred up a veritable hornets nest in France,"[82] in part, for practical reasons – Austria, Prussia, and Russia being land Powers, the provisions only truly applied to France, for geopolitical reasons as Great Britain had recently imposed its will in Egypt and Syria at the expense of France, and also as a result of the actions of the American Ambassador in Paris. The Ambassador, General Lewis Cass, fearing that the

79 S. Daget, *La répression de lat traite des Noirs au XIXe sicècle: L'action des croisières français sur les côtes occidentales de l'Afrique (1817–1850)* (Éditions Karthala, Paris, 1997), 472–475 and 481–486. Daget also considers the historic rivalry as a means of explaining the lack of cooperation proffered by France: "On ne collabore pas avec des Anglais. Parce que cela offre le plaisir de leur compliquer la vie," 599.

80 See "'Quasi-Piracy': The Fight against the Slave Trade," in W. Grewe, *The Epochs of International Law* (Walter de Gruyter & Co, New York, 2000), 554–569; Rubin, above n. 34, 82–137.

81 Article 2, *Treaty between Great Britain, Austria, France, Prussia, and Russia, for the suppression of the African Slave Trade*, London, 20 December 1841, 30 BFSP 273. For a pictorial representation of the zone, see Grewe, ibid, 559.

82 Miers, above n. 47, 17. See also H. de Montardy, *La Traite et le Droit International* (V. Giard & E. Brière Paris, 1899), 87–88.

United States would be isolated and forced to give up its freedom of the seas, produced an anonymous pamphlet, which "excited violent agitation against" the Treaty.[83] In the end, the 1841 Treaty was not ratified by France, though it did came into force for the other four parties, and was later acceded to by Belgium (1848) and Germany (1879).[84]

In 1845, France and Great Britain concluded a ten-year treaty which suspended the treaties of 1831 and 1833 (as between the two parties only), and ended the mutual right to visit to suppress the slave trade. Instead the parties agreed that, in order that their flags "may not, contrary to the law of nations and the laws in force in the 2 countries, be usurped, to cover the Slave Trade, and in order to provide for a more effectual suppression of that traffic," each would station a twenty-six ship naval squadron off the west coast of Africa.[85] These squadrons were to work in concert, within a specific maritime zone, to suppress the trade "jointly or separately, as may be deemed most expedient" but could only visit ships to ascertain if they had a right to fly the *Tricolore* or the Red Ensign on the basis of Instructions which each had communicated to the other party.[86] While these Instructions were modified over time, the original Instructions for the Senior Officers of Her Majesty's Ships and Vessels of 1845 made plain that "[y]ou are not to capture, visit, or in any way interfere with vessels of France," but at the same time "Great Britain, will not allow vessels of other nations to escape visit and examination by merely hoisting a French flag."[87] Thus, the British Instructions continued:

> Accordingly, when from intelligence, which the officer commanding Her Majesty's cruiser may have received, or from the manoeuvres of the vessels, or other sufficient cause, he may have reason to believe that the vessel does not belong to the nation indicated by her colours, he is, if the state of the weather will admit of it, to go a-head of the suspected vessel, after communicating his intention by hailing, and to drop a boat on board of her to ascertain her nationality, without causing her detention.

In seeking to determine the nationality of a ship,

83 Mathieson, above n. 55, 67. See also Lawrence, above n. 37, 188.

84 Miers, above n. 47, 17.

85 Article 1, Convention between Great Britain and France, for the Suppression of the Traffic in Slaves, London, 29 May 1845, 33 *BFSP* 4.

86 Ibid, Article 7.

87 Ibid, "Annex referred to in Article VII," 14.

> the officer who boards the stranger is to be instructed merely in the first instance to satisfy himself by the vessel's papers, or other proof, of her nationality; and if she proved really to be a vessel of the nation designated by her colours, and one which he is not authorized to search, he is to lose no time in quitting her, offering to note on the papers of the vessel the cause of his having suspected her nationality, as well as the number of minutes the vessel was detained.

If the ship proved to be flying fraudulent colours the commander of the man-of-war was to "deal with her as he would have been authorized and required to do had she not hoisted a false flag."[88] That is, either as a stateless ship, or on the basis of one of the bilateral treaties which Great Britain had negotiated.

The Instructions of 1845 were replaced in 1859. These new Instructions, of which the French and British were mirror versions (like all such Instructions), were much more thorough. The Instructions first set down the principle that by "virtue of the immunity of national flags, no merchant-vessel navigating the high seas is subject to any foreign jurisdiction. A vessel of war cannot therefore visit, detain, arrest, or seize (except under Treaty) any merchant-vessel not recognized as belonging to her own nation." The Instructions went on to state that if a ship failed to hoist its flag, that a "first warning may be given her by firing a blank gun, and should this have no result, a second gun warning may be given her by means of a shotted gun, to be levelled in such a manner as not to [strike] her."[89] If a ship did hoist its flag, it was to be understood that the "man-of-war has no right to exercise the least control over her," unless the nationality could be "seriously called into question." On this basis, after hailing the ship and declaring its intentions, a cruiser could send an officer aboard with the understanding that only an examination of papers would be undertaken: "All inquiry into the nature of the cargo; or the commercial operations of the said ships; in a word, on any other subject save that of their nationality; all search, all visit, are absolutely forbidden."[90] In other words, the right to visit had been narrowed, and separated from the right to *search*.

The final set of modified Instructions, issued in 1867, mirrored the above provisions of the 1859 Instructions, but were more focused, allowing an officer to request only specified papers on board a ship suspected of flying a

88 Ibid, 14.

89 Instructions issued to Commanders of French Ships of War in the "Correspondence respecting the Visit of American Vessels by British Cruisers," *British Sessional Papers*, Vol. 34, 1857–1858, p. 427.

90 Ibid, 428.

fraudulent flag. If a ship was deemed to be flying such a flag, the warship then escorted it to the nearest port where a representative of the flag State could determine whether it had a right to fly the flag in question.[91] The 1859 Instructions were crucial to the relationship between France and Great Britain where the suppression of slave trade at sea was concerned, as these Instructions as we shall see remained in force beyond the nineteenth century.

2 Portugal and Brazil

As previously noted, Portugal entered into agreements with Great Britain to end the slave trade in principle in 1810 and also to establish the means of doing so (ie creation of a right to visit and the mixed commissions) in 1817. The Convention of 1817 included a Separate Article which later caused much friction between the parties. As an afterthought to the 1817 Convention, a time limit of fifteen years was imposed; establishing that, short of a further agreement, in 1832 Portugal would effectively opt-out of the bilateral system Great Britain was building.[92] Under the terms of the 1817 Convention, in conjunction with an earlier 1815 Treaty, Portugal was allowed to carry on with its slave trade south of the equator provided the traffic was destined for the "actual Dominions of the Crown of Portugal."[93] With the independence of Brazil in 1825, Great Britain considered that the Portuguese trade would come to an end but, because of internal strife in Lisbon, it was not until 1834 that a stable government emerged which could negotiate a new agreement. However, even a government with abolitionist leanings in Lisbon could not concede the end of the trade for fear of losing Angola and Mozambique which benefited from the trade. As Miers writes: "With a weak navy and an empty treasury Portugal was in no position to force the issue. [Palmerston, the Foreign Secretary] tried in vain to negotiate a new treaty and finally took the radical step of having Britain simply assume by Act of Parliament the right to arrest and try Portuguese slavers. ... Portugal deeply resented this gross infringement of her sovereignty."[94]

---

91 "Instructions as to Vessels under the French Flag," *Documents relatives à la Répression de la Traite des Esclaves publiés en execution des Articles LXXXI et suivants de l'Act Général de Bruxelles*, 1892, 272–274.

92 *Article Separe*, Additional Convention between Great Britain and Portugal, for the prevention of Slave Trade, London, 11 September 1817, 4 *BFSP* 115–116.

93 Article 2, Treaty between Great Britain and Portugal, for the restriction of the Portuguese Slave-Trade; and for the annulment of the Convention of Loan of 1809; and Treaty of Alliance of 1810, Vienna, 22 January 1815, 2 *BFSP* 352.

94 Miers, above n. 47, 24.

The 1839 Palmerston Act created the legal fiction that Portuguese ships involved in the slave trade should be treated as though they were British, and thus susceptible to capture and trial by British courts.[95] Disregarding the advice proffered by Lord Stowell in *The Le Louis* regarding use of force and acting against international law in seeking an end to the slave trade, Great Britain declared it open season on Portuguese maritime commerce in an attempt to end the Portuguese slave trade. In the leading British international law text of the latter half of the nineteenth century, Phillimore did not truly engage with the issue, stating: "This Act has been vehemently attacked as a violation of International Law; it must of course be considered with reference to the previous Treaties, upon which its authority is found."[96] Indeed, Lord Palmerston sought to justify his actions in Parliament on the grounds that Portugal had not faithfully carried out its previous treaty obligations and was unwilling to come to an agreement on a new treaty. "The conclusion," Palmerston said "which Great Britain draws from hence, is, that she is entitled and compelled to have recourse to her own means, in order to accomplish results which she has a right to obtain."[97] Wilson, acknowledging that Great Britain "contended that her action was distinctly authorized by the terms of existing engagements," declared, having considered the evidence presented by the Foreign Secretary, that "[h]is case at least manifested a care for legality."[98]

Despite the challenge the Palmerston Act posed to established international law, in its quest to abolish the slave trade, in 1845 Great Britain introduced the so-called "Aberdeen Act" aimed at the Brazilian trade. Great Britain's willingness to recognise the independence of Brazil was predicated on a number of conditions, including signature of a treaty which mirrored the Anglo-Portuguese agreement of 1817. In 1845, Brazil invoked the termination of that Treaty of 1826 "without making any alternative suggestions," and Lord Aberdeen then successfully advocated an "Act authorizing the Government to take action against suspected vessels sailing under Brazilian flag on the basis of the 1826 treaty."[99] Aberdeen contended that, as the Treaty of 1826 had assimilated the slave trade with piracy and had established the complete abolition of the

---

95 Act for the Suppression of the Slave Trade, 24 August 1839 (2 & 3 Vict. C. 73), 27 *BFSP* 849.

96 Phillimore, above n. 3, 413.

97 Enclosure to a Letter from Viscount Palmerston to Lord Howard de Walden, 20 April 1839, 27 *BFSP* 565.

98 H. Wilson, "Some Principal Aspects of British Efforts to Crush The African Slave Trade, 1807–1929," *ajil*, Vol. 44, 1950, pp. 505, 513–514.

99 J.H.W. Verzijl, *International Law in Historical Perspective: Nationality and Other Matters Relating to Individuals*, Part V (A. Sijthoff, Leyden, 1972), 257.

Brazilian trade within three years; it granted jurisdiction to British admiralty courts over any vessels engaged in the Brazilian slave-trade.[100] In 1850 Palmerston, who had regained his position as Foreign Secretary, on the basis of the Aberdeen Act, ordered the Royal Navy into the territorial waters and ports of Brazil, where it captured, burned, and sank a number of slave traders.[101]

The Palmerston and Aberdeen Acts, it must be said, had their intended effects. For its part, Portugal agreed to a new treaty with Great Britain in 1842.[102] Brazil by contrast was forced to accept the British interpretation of the 1826 Treaty, which ultimately moved Brazil to put an end to its slave trade through domestic legislation and patrolling its waters. Lord Palmerston was delighted with the Brazilian outcome, noting that "naval operations on the Brazilian coast…had apparently accomplished in a few weeks what diplomatic notes and treaty negotiations had failed to achieve over a period of many years."[103]

Great Britain through gunboat diplomacy was able to achieve the near completion of its bilateral web of treaties aimed at universal suppression of the slave trade. However, there remained one maritime Power outside the bilateral regime. As William Law Mathieson explained in considering the effects of the 1839 and 1845 Acts on slave traders: when they were challenged, they "either hosted American colours or threw overboard both flag and papers."[104]

3 United States of America

Just as the three recalcitrant States before it, the United States of America saw ulterior motives in British attempts to abolish the slave trade. In 1895, US Ambassador Eugene Schuyler, a career diplomat, wrote that "the real reason" for attempting to end the slave trade "was fairly well concealed under the mask of philanthropy." The Americans further objected to British attempts to gain the right to visit which they consider had been abused during the Napoleonic Wars. Schuyler points to calls by the colonial agent of Trinidad in the British House of Commons in 1810 for the "effectual" as opposed to "nominal" abolition of the slave trade to counter the advantage of the continued flow of slaves

---

100 L. Bethell, *The Abolition of the Brazilian Slave Trade: Britain, Brazil and the Slave Trade Question 1807–1869*, (CUP, 1970), 263–265. See also An Act of the British Parliament to amend an Act, intituled as an Act to carry into execution a Convention between His Majesty and the Emperor of Brazil, for the Regulation and final Abolition of the African Slave Trade, 8 August 1845 (8 & 9 Vict. C. 122), 34 *BFSP* 1216.

101 Bethell, ibid, 329–330, 355.

102 Treaty Between Great Britain and Portugal, for the Suppression of the Traffic in Slaves, Lisbon, 3 July 1842, 30 *BFSP* 527.

103 Bethell, above n. 100, 344.

104 Mathieson, above n. 55, 74.

to Spanish possessions which "in its effects [was] ruinous to the British colonies. ... He appealed to the British Parliament on the part of our own planters, and trusted that effectual steps would yet be taken for remedying so serious an evil" (i.e. unfair trade not the slave trade).[105] The second reason which Schuyler gives, while also relating to commerce, deals with British attempts at hegemony over the oceans:

> British statesmen soon began to see that, through the right of visitation and search which had been accorded by the treaties with several powers, it might be easy, under the pretext of putting down the slave-trade, to obtain the police of the sea, which once having been granted and made the rule of international law, it would be difficult to take away from them; and this would secure the preponderance of the British navy.[106]

The United States had a further reason for not wanting to cooperate with British attempts to suppress the trade at sea, impressment. As Soulsby wrote in his study focusing on the right to visit and the slave trade in Anglo-American relations:

> Great Britain was the traditional upholder of belligerent rights at sea; she had emerged from the wars the greatest naval power in the world, and in any concerted measures against the slave trade her navy would inevitably take a leading part. Hence it was not remarkable that her European neighbors were not enthusiastic over proposals which promised to strengthen her existing maritime supremacy. Still more serious was the opposition of the United States, which had protested in the war of 1812 against an abuse, as it was considered, of the belligerent right of search – the impressment of seamen...[107].

---

105 E. Schuyler, *American Diplomacy and the Furtherance of Commerce* (Charles Scribner's Sons, New York, 1895), 236–237; H. Soulsby, "The Right of Search and the Slave Trade in Anglo-American Relations 1814–1862," *John Hopkins University Studies in Historical and Political Science Collection*, Series 51(2), 1933, 121 at 134.

106 Schuyler, ibid, 239. See also W. Beach Lawrence, *Visitation and Search; or, An Historical Sketch of the British Claim to Exercise a Maritime Police over the Vessels of All Nations, in Peace as well as War, with an Inquiry into the Expediency of Terminating the Eight Article of the Ashburton Treaty* (Little, Brown & Co, Boston, 1858), 16. Lawrence was the editor of *Wheaton's Elements of International Law*, the leading American international law text of the era.

107 Soulsby, above n. 105, 8.

For the United States, after the War of 1812, the issue of visitation became visceral. It had gone to war against Britain in part because the Royal Navy, during the Napoleonic Wars, had impressed sailors who were American citizens under the pretext of a belligerent right to visit neutral ships to check for contraband.[108] Although, the United States President, James Madison, cited Great Britain's support of a new Indian War and the use of "a secret agent to subvert the Union," his main reason for war was the conduct of the British Navy. The United States took issue with the violation of its territorial waters by the Royal Navy, the establishment of "illegal blockades," and importantly, in the eyes of the general public, the impressing of American seamen which, during the period of 1803–1812, was estimated to be in the range of six thousand American citizens.[109] To what extent this issue touched a raw nerve with the United States is made plain by the conversation in the early 1820s between Stratford Canning, the British Ambassador in Washington and John Quincy Adams, the US Secretary of State: "Canning had inquired if he could conceive of a more atrocious evil than the slave trade, to which Adams replied; 'Yes; admitting the right of search by foreign officers of our vessels upon the sea in time of peace; for that would be making slaves of ourselves'."[110] Although Article 10 of the Treaty of Ghent, which settled the War of 1812, made the following declaration, it made no mention regarding either the issues of visitation or impressment:

> Whereas the Traffic in Slaves is irreconcilable with the principles of humanity and Justice, and whereas both His Majesty and the United States are desirous of continuing their efforts to promote its entire abolition, it is hereby agreed that both the contracting parties shall use their best endeavours to accomplish so desirable an object.[111]

In 1818 John Quincy Adams laid out the United States' objections to allowing British ships the right to visit American merchant vessels in time of peace as

---

108 In 1821, US Secretary of State John Quincy Adams noted that "the United States had very recently issued from a war with Great Britain, principally waged in resistance to a practice of searching neutral merchant vessels for men in time of war, exercised by Great Britain, as the United States deem, in violation of the law of nations." See J. Bassett Moore, *A Digest of International Law*, Vol. 2 (Govt Print Office, Washington, 1906), 919.

109 D. Hickey, *The War of 1812: A Forgotten Conflict* (University of Illinois, Urbana, 1989), 18–24. More specifically, see J. Fulton Zimmerman, *Impressment of American Seamen* (Columbia University Press, New York, 1925).

110 Soulsby, above n. 105, 18.

111 Article 10, Treaty of Peace and Amity between His Britannic Majesty and the United States of America, 4 December 1814, 24 December 1814, Ghent, 2 *BFSP* 364.

being directly related to its wartime abuse of its status as a neutral during the Napoleonic Wars:

> The United States have never disputed the belligerent right of search as required and universally practised conformably to the laws of nations. They have disputed the right of belligerents under *color* of the right of search for contraband, to seize and carry away *men*, at the discretion of the boarding officers, without trial and without appeal; men, not as contraband of war, or belonging to the enemy, but as the subjects, real or pretended, of the belligerent himself, and to be used by him against the enemy. It is the fundamental abuse of the right of search, for the purpose never recognised or admitted by the laws of nations, purposes in their practical operation of the greatest oppression and most crying injustice, that them against assenting to the extension in time of peace of a right of search which experience has shown to be liable to such gross perversion in time of war.[112]

Adams made it plain, in instructions to his Ambassador in London, that the possibility of entering into a treaty regarding the suppression of the slave trade with Great Britain was, for the foreseeable future, impossible:

> That the admission of a right in the officers of foreign ships-of-war to enter and search the vessels of the United States in time of peace, under any circumstances whatever, would meet with universal repugnance in the public opinion of this country; that there would be no prospect of a ratification, by advice and consent of the Senate, to any stipulations of that nature; that the search by foreign officers, even in time of war is so obnoxious to the feelings and recollections of this country, that nothing could reconcile them to the extension of it, however qualified or restricted, to a time of peace.[113]

However, by 1821, Adams proposed a course to Stratford Canning which ultimately broke the impasse between the two States and lead to the signing of a treaty in 1824:

> The expedient proposal on the part of the United States of keeping cruisers of their own constantly upon the coast where the traffic is carried on,

112 Soulsby, above n. 105. Emphasis in the original.

113 Ibid.

> with instructions to cooperate by good offices and by the mutual communications of information with the cruisers of other powers stationed and instructed to the attainment of the same end, appears in its own nature as well as to experience so far as it has abided that test, better adapted to the suppression of the traffic than that of the British Government, which makes the officers of one nation the executors of the laws of another.[114]

In 1820, the United States House of Representatives declared that trading in African slaves by American citizens should be assimilated to the concept of piracy and made punishable by death. Although the slave trade was never accepted as piracy in international law, this link found its way into the proposed 1824 Anglo-American Treaty.[115] The draft Convention allowed the cruisers of each States to visit and search each other's vessels "on the coasts of Africa, of America, and of West Indies."[116] It stipulated that the captain and crew were to proceed against seized vessels and crews "as Pirates involved in the African Slave Trade" and try them in the courts of either State.[117] The Convention, however, did not come into force as the United States Congress, while accepting the Convention in general terms, sought to amend it by inserting a provision allowing for denunciation of the treaty on six months notice, and by deleting the word "America" from the above noted phrase. The latter provision was "deemed insuperable" to Great Britain which then declared that it was unable to ratify the Convention as modified by the United States.[118] In 1834, the same stumbling block appeared as Great Britain sought to convince the United States to accede to the French treaties of 1831 and 1833. The United States President declined to bring the question before the legislature; the British Ambassador in Washington had made plain "that the right of search would be extended to the coasts of the United States."[119]

Although the American Ambassador to Paris was successful in preventing France from consenting to the 1841 Quintuple Treaty, the United States, by this

114 Moore, above n. 108, 921.

115 Moore writes that the declaration was meant "to enable the United States to join in the movement then on foot to assimilate the slave trade to piracy, both in the measure of its punishment and the method of its repression. This movement, however, did not succeed, owing to the opposition to opening the way to the establishment of the practice of visitation and search in time of peace." ibid, 922.

116 Article 1, Convention with Great Britain, 12 *BFSP* 839.

117 Article 7, ibid, 842.

118 Moore, above n. 108, 926.

119 Ibid, 927.

time, found itself isolated by the growing number of British bilateral treaties. As a means of deflecting this mounting pressure, the United States agreed, in the 1842 Webster-Ashburton Treaty, to maintain a naval presence of the coast of Africa to suppress the trade, it being understood that "the said squadrons [are] to be independent of each other."[120] United States President John Tyler noted that the provisions removed "all pretext on the part of others for violating the immunities of the American flag upon the seas, as they exist and are defined by the law of nations."[121] Great Britain having abandoned its attempt to assimilate the slave trade with piracy, changed tack and sought to emphasise the innovation developed in the Quintuple Treaty: the separation of the right to visit from the right to search foreign ships on the high seas, in peacetime, to suppress the slave trade. Great Britain sought to advocate that while there did not exist a right to search ships on the high seas, there did exist a right to approach and visit a ship to inquire, through an inspection of its papers, whether a ship's nationality corresponded to the flag it flew. As the United States and France remained the only two States not party to the British bilateral treaty regime, it was logical that slave ships would gravitate towards flying their flags to avoid capture. By advocating this new understanding of the concept of the "right to visit," Great Britain hoped to close the loophole and include all States in its bilateral treaty regime. Thus, the British Foreign Secretary took issue with the United States President's address and noted that the right to visit had not been part of the discussion leading to the Webster-Ashburton Treaty, nor had any concession on the issue been made by Great Britain. Aberdeen went on to say:

> The President may be assured, that Great Britain will always respect the just claims of The United States. We make no pretension to interfere in any manner whatever, either by detention, visit, or search, with vessels of The United States, known or believed to be such. But we still maintain, and will exercise, when necessary, our right to ascertain the genuineness of any flag which a suspected vessel may bear.[122]

---

120 Article 8, Treaty between Great Britain and The United States, to settle and define the Boundaries between the Territories of the United States and the Possessions of Her Britannic Majesty in North America, for the final Suppression of the African Slave Trade; and for the giving up of Criminals, fugitive from Justice, in certain Cases, Washington, 9 August 1842, 30 *BFSP* 365.

121 Moore, above n. 108, 931.

122 The Earl of Aberdeen to Mr. Fox [United States Ambassador to the Court of St. James], 18 January 1843, 32 *BFSP* 444.

Sir Robert Phillimore, "one of the most ardent champions" of this new right of visit advocated by Great Britain[123] noted that:

> The question of the *Right to Visit* has been a matter of sore contention between Great Britain and the North American United States; the latter refuse to distinguish it from the *Right to Search*, which, they justly say, is an exclusively *belligerent* Right. The British Government, on the other hand, denies the identity of the two Rights, and claims merely to ascertain the nationality of ships hosting, under suspicious circumstances, the flag of the United States, alleging that when once that nationality is ascertained to be that of the United States, they immediately release whatever be her cargo or destination, the vessel; and that it is manifest, that if the mere hosting a particular ensign is to supersede all inquiry, the Slave Trade may be carried out with impunity.[124]

The Secretary of State Daniel Webster addressed the issue in a letter to the British Ambassador in Washington, stating that the Government of the United States:

> maintains that there is no such well-known and acknowledged, or indeed, any broad and genuine difference between what has been usually called visit, and what has been usually called search; that the right to visit, to be effectual, must come in the end to include search; and thus to exercise, in peace an authority which the law of nations only allows in time of war. If such a well-known distinction exists, where are the proofs of it? What writers of authority on the public law, what adjudications in Courts of Admiralty, what public Treaties recognize it? No such recognition has presented itself to the Government of The United States; but, on the contrary, it understands that public writers, courts of law, and solemn treaties have for 2 centuries, use the word, 'visit' and 'search' in the same manner.[125]

The Secretary of State questioned the approach of the British, noting that the Foreign Secretary had indicated that in exercising its right, if errors were committed, prompt reparations would be forthcoming. Webster indicates the

123 L. Gessner, *Le Droit des Neutres sur mer* (Stilke et van Muyden, Berlin, 1865), 287.

124 R. Phillimore, *Commentaries upon International Law* (W. Benning, London, 1854), 326. Emphasis in the original.

125 Mr Webster to Mr Evertt, 28 March 1843, 32 *BFSP* 466.

apparent flaw in such an argument as the "general rule of law certainly is, that in the proper and prudent exercise of our own rights, no one is answerable for undersigned injuries." As such, the British approach to the right to visit "implies, at least in its general interpretation, the commission of some wrongful act."[126] Webster concluded by noting:

> On the whole, the Government of The United States, while it has not conceded a mutual right to visit or search, as has been done by the parties to the Quintuple Treaty of December 1841, does not admit that by the law and practice of nations, there is any such thing as a right to visit, distinguished, by well known rules and definition, for the right of search.[127]

Although the United States dispatched a squadron to the African coast in 1843, the British Instructions to its Naval Officers issued in 1844 were almost verbatim those cited earlier with reference to France, that is: "it is no part of their duty to capture or visit, or in any way interfere with vessels of the United States, whether those vessels shall have Slaves on board or not." But, that, "most, assuredly, Great Britain, never will allow vessels of other nations to escape visit and examination by merely hoisting an United States' Flag."[128] In essence a stalemate ensued and the United States was left to challenge by diplomatic means the continuing visits by British warships to inquire whether ships flying the Stars and Stripes were authorised to do so. This diplomatic impasse became acute in 1858, the year following the appointment of General Lewis Cass – who it will be recalled caused France to decline to ratify the 1841 Quintuple Treaty – as United States Secretary of State; and as a result of the Royal Navy's actions off the coast of Cuba, where the slave trade persisted. As Schuyler wrote, noting that Cass had brought to the attention of the United States legislature incidents of British boarding of American ships in the Caribbean which, in turn, had prompted the United States Congress to approve the dispatch of a naval force to protect its maritime commerce in the region: "This looked very much

126 Ibid, 467.

127 Ibid, 470.

128 British Instructions for the Senior Officers of Her Majesty's Ships and Vessels on the West Coast of Africa, with respect to the Treaty with the United States of America, signed at Washington, 9 August, 1842, *Instructions for the Guidance of Her Majesty's Naval Officers employed in the Suppression of the Slave Trade*, 1844, 16–17. In 1858, the British Commodore of the African Squadron pointed to the fact that the American flag was being used to harbour slave ships, as he "complained to the Admiralty of 'the shameful prostitution of the American flag, for under that ensign alone is the Slave Trade now conducted'." See Lloyd, above n. 27, 56.

like war."[129] Secretary of State Cass, despite his apparent belligerence, opened a diplomatic window to allow for a compromise: if Great Britain renounced the notion of a *right* to visit to ascertain the propriety of hoisted American flags, the United States would admit that Great Britain could, in suspicious circumstances, visit ships flying American colours to ascertain their right to do so:

> The immunity of their merchant-vessels depends upon the rights of The United States, as one of the independent Powers of the world, and not upon the purposes or motives of the foreign officers by whom it is violated. A merchant-vessel upon the high seas is protected by her national character. He who forcibly enters her, does so upon his own responsibility. Undoubtedly, if a vessel assumes a national character to which she is not entitled, and is sailing under false colours, she cannot be protected by the assumption of a nationality to which she has not claimed. As the identity of a person must be determined by the officer bearing a process of his arrest, and determined at the risk of such officer, so must the national identify of a vessel be determined, at a like hazard to him who, doubting the flag she displays, search her to ascertain her true character. There, no doubt, may be circumstances which would go far to modify the complaints a nation would have a right to make for such a violation of its sovereignty.

Cass then provided his diplomatic concession:

> If the boarding office had just grounds for suspicion, and deported himself with propriety in the performance of his task, doing no injury and peaceably retiring when satisfied of his error, no nation would make such an act the subject of serious reclamation. It is one thing to do a deed avowedly illegal, and excuse it by the attending circumstances; and it is another and quite different thing to claim a right of action and the right also of determining when, and how, and to what extent, it shall be exercised. And this is no barren distinction, so far as the interest of this country is involved, but it is closely connected with an object dear to the American people – the freedom of their citizens upon the great highway of the world.[130]

129 Schuyler, above n. 105, 261.

130 General Cass to Lord Napier, 10 April 1858, 50 *BFSP* 715. Also see General Cass to Mr Dallas, 23 February 1859, 49 *BFSP* 1121.

In response the British Foreign Secretary, the Earl of Malmesbury, made known through his Ambassador in Washington that Great Britain was willing to concede the point: "Her Majesty's Government recognize as sound those principles of international law which have been laid down by General Cass in his note." The Foreign Secretary stated that "Her Majesty's Government agree entirely in this view of the case, and the question therefore becomes one solely of discretion on the part of acting officers." As a result, it was proposed that as the burden of the question fell to each officer's discretion which "is one extremely dangerous to entrust, and onerous to bear…,"[131] the parties should negotiate suitable instruction to be give to their naval commanders. In the meantime, however, Great Britain,

> anxious to remove all possible repetition of the acts which appear to have causes so much excitement in the United States, and which might, if repeated at this moment be detriment to the good relations of the two countries, have set further orders to the officers commanding the Cuban squadron to discontinue the search of any vessels of the United States until some agreement, in the sense I have pointed out shall be made.[132]

The American Ambassador in London was informed that the "President desires you would express to Lord Malmesbury his gratification at this satisfactory termination of the controversy which has given so much trouble to our respective Governments, concerning the claim of a right in behalf of a British cruiser in time of peace to search or visit American merchant vessels upon the ocean."[133] Having settled its differences with the United States, Great Britain sought to close the loophole which allowed slave ships to avoid British capture by hoisting either the American or French flag. The negotiation of Instructions with France, which might then be adopted by the United States, would ensure that no ship, in suspicious situations, could avoid being visited to ascertain the propriety of the flag flown. These negotiations, started in February 1859, were concluded successfully in May of that same year.[134]

The United States, in the throes of a civil war that centred on slavery, shifted policy. In 1863, the United States of America (i.e: the Northern Union of States) concluded a bilateral treaty with Great Britain to suppress the slave trade to

131 Earl of Malmesbury to Lord Napier, 11 June 1858, 50 *BFSP* 738 and 739.

132 Ibid, 740.

133 General Cass to Mr Dallas, 30 June 1858, 50 *BFSP* 747 and 748.

134 General Cass to Count de Sartiges, 12 May 1859, 50 *BFSP* 796.

gain British support for its conflict with the Southern Confederacy.[135] The attempted equation of the slave trade with piracy, at the core of the 1824 draft Convention, was dropped from the 1863 agreement. Much like the 1845 Anglo-French Convention, the 1863 Anglo-American Treaty required each State to dispatch a naval squadron to the West African coast. However, unlike France, the United States agreed to patrol a differently demarcated maritime zone, one which ran contiguous to the African coast to a distance of two hundred miles. The United States further agreed to the establishment of mixed commissions, though these never heard a case and were superseded by a 1870 agreement that transferred jurisdiction to each State's respective domestic courts.[136]

By negotiation and coercion Great Britain had, by the mid-1860s, created bilaterally what it had failed to achieve multilaterally during the early eighteen hundreds. The four recalcitrant States had, one by one, been integrated into the British regime of slave trade suppression. By the time the United States had agreed to a bilateral treaty however, the tide had clearly shifted in favour of abolition. According to Klein, the 1860s was a turning point as "the pressure that led to the abolition of the trade now shifted to attacking the institution of slavery itself."[137] The forced migration of enslaved African labours was supplanted throughout the Western Hemisphere in the late nineteenth century by European free labour in what was to be the "great age of immigration,"[138] and more importantly, by large numbers of indentured labourers from Asia – primarily from China and India – who took up employment side by side with newly freed slaves.

In essence, therefore, Great Britain had achieved the primary element of its objective by the 1870s: it had managed to totally abolish the Atlantic Slave Trade. For all the fears expressed by the four recalcitrant States, Great Britain had persisted in moving forward its abolitionist agenda when British hegemony over maritime commerce was no longer at issue, when the policing of the seas had become a concern of the past and when New World slave products no longer challenged British goods. While, throughout the nineteenth century, the suppression of the slave trade remained aligned with Britain's

135 Soulsby, above n. 105, 174.

136 Treaty between Great Britain and the United States, for the Suppression of the African Slave Trade, 7 April 1862, Washington, 52 *BFSP* 50.

137 Klein, above n. 12, 202.

138 Ibid. David Brion Davis goes further, pointing out that "there can be no doubt that black slave labour was essential in creating and developing the 'original' New World that began by the 1840s to attract so many millions of European immigrants." See *Inhuman Bondage* (above n. 18), 80.

strategic imperial interests, it remained true that within Britain, there persisted popular and philanthropic support for the ending of slavery and the slave trade. This required, for much of the nineteenth century, the British Foreign Office to continuously push for completion of its bilateral network of treaties to suppress the slave trade.

While Great Britain had managed to end the Atlantic Slave Trade, its attention now shifted to the east coast of Africa where the Oriental Slave Trade came into play. As a result of the persistence in fighting the slave trade and slavery, Great Britain finally gained in 1890 what it had failed to achieved nearly eighty years previously: a universal right, established by treaty and accepted as international law, to visit ships on the high seas to suppress the slave trade.

The Universal Outlawing of the Slave Trade

In their quest for what historians termed the "Second European Empires," the ideology used to justify usurpation of land shifted once more.[139] Having colonised the New World, European Powers embarked on a civilizing mission. That mission would descend into an all-out "scramble" for Africa by the 1880s. While much of the colonization of the New World had taken place under the banner of "Gold, Glory and God," the British missionary, David Livingstone, made it known throughout Europe that in Africa "slave raiding and trading were devastating large areas, and his appeal to bring Christianity, commerce, and civilization to the heart of the continent" did not fall on deaf ears.[140] A recurring theme throughout much of this period was the European demand to end the slave trade, not only at sea, but on land on the African Continent. Thus, in the latter part of the nineteenth century, as Africa was opened to the pursuit of Empire, European States concluded treaties with local African elite mandating the suppression of the slave trade. Great Britain became party to more than a hundred such agreements "which eventually covered the whole coast from which slaves were exported."[141] During this period, it was clear that the

139 For 'Second European Empires' see A. Pagden, *Lords of all the World; Ideologies of Empire in Spain, Britain and France c.1500–c.1800* (Yale University Press, New Haven, 1995), 2.

140 S. Miers, *Slavery in the Twentieth Century: The Evolution of a Global Problem* (Altiamira Press, Walnut Creek, 2003), 20.

141 Miers, above n. 47, 46. Treaties were concluded by Great Britain with the following regions of Africa up to the 1889–1890 Brussels Conference: *Central Africa*: Gando, Sokoto; *East Africa*: Brava (Somalia), Comoro, Eesa Somal, Habr-Awal, Habr-Gerhajis, Habr-Toljaala, Mohilla, Soomalees (*sic*), Tajowra, Warsangali, Zaila; but primarily from *West Africa*:

suppression of slavery and the slave trade had become part of the discourse of international relations and, though it had been championed by Great Britain, other States with holdings in Africa – France, Germany, Italy, and Portugal (and the private Congolese State awarded to King Leopold of Belgium in 1885) – were agreeable to its inclusion on the agenda of international conferences and in international instruments.

When a dispute arose over an Anglo-Portuguese treaty regarding control of the mouth of the Congo River in 1884, the German Chancellor, Otto von Bismarck, proposed an international conference to settle the question. The Berlin Conference, which ultimately provided for the free navigation of the Congo and, more generally, a framework for the effective occupation of the African coast, also found on its agenda a British proposal which called for universal jurisdiction to be established over the slave trade.[142] The proposal was in the form of a declaration that the slave trade was "a crime against the Law of Nations." The draft Declaration read in part that: "The Slave Trade is henceforth a crime prohibited by the Law of Nations, and cognizable by the tribunals of all civilized nations whatever the nationality of the accused."[143] This proposal, however, did not find favour with the fifteen States gathering in Berlin as they were unwilling to commit to a pronouncement which they considered to raise unforeseeable consequences. Instead they accepted a general declaration that the slave trade was indeed prohibited by international law. The Declaration Relative to the Slave Trade, which emerged from the 1885 General Act of the Conference of Berlin, reads:

> Seeing the trading in slaves is forbidden in conformity with the principles of international law as recognized by the Signatory Powers, and seeing

---

Abbeokuta, Abo-den-Arfo, Aboh, Acassa, Adaffie, Adinnar Cooma, Afflowhoo, Aghwey, Angiana, Badagry, Baddiboo, Bagroo River, Batanga, Bereira, Biafra, Bimbia, Biombo, Blockouse, Bonney, Boom River, Bulola, Bussama, Cabenda, Cagnabac, Calabar, Cameroons, Camma, Cantalicunda, Cape Lopez, Cape Mount, Cartabar, Chacoonda, Congo, Cumbo, Dahomey, Dalu Mahdoo, Dobacconda, Drewin, Egarra, Epe, Fouricaria, Gallinas, Garraway River, Goom Corkway, Grand Bereby, Grand Lahou, Grand Popoe, Grand Sesters, Ivroy Bay, Joboo, Jack Jaques, Joug River, Kambia, Kinsembo, Kittam, Lagos, Little Booton, Little Popoe, Lucalla, Macbatee, Malghea, Malimba, Manna, Monney, Maricaryah, Naloes, New Calabar, New Cestos, Nyanibantang, Okeodan, Old Town (Old Calabar), Omitska, Otanda, Pocrah, Porto Novo, Qua Plantations, Nio Nunez, Pongas, Ro-Woolah, St. Andrew, St. Antonio, Samo, Samoah, Sherbro, Small Scarcies River, Sugury, Soombia, Zanga Tanga. See *British and Foreign State Papers*, General Index, Volumes 64 and 80.

142 See H. Wesseling, *Divide and Rule: The Partition of Africa 1880–1914* (Praeger, Westport, 1996), 113–119.

143 Miers, above n. 47, 171–172.

> also that the operations, which, by sea or land, furnish slaves to trade, ought likewise to be regarded as forbidden, the Powers which do or shall exercise sovereign rights or influence in the territories forming the Conventional basin of the Congo declare that these territories may not serve as a market or means of transit for the trade in slaves, or whatever race they may be. Each of the Powers binds itself to employ all the means at its disposal for putting an end to this trade and for punishing those who engage in it.[144]

Great Britain was satisfied with the outcome of the Berlin Conference and saw little reason to push States further with regard to the suppression of the slave trade, though the trade on the east coast of Africa, in places such as Zanzibar and Pemba, was starting to raise difficulties with other European Powers. It was at this point, shortly after the end of Berlin Conference, that an ally to the anti-slavery cause emerged from the most unlikely of sources, in the Roman Catholic Archbishop of Algiers, Cardinal Lavigerie. In what can only be termed a "one-man" crusade, Lavigerie gained the support of the Pope, and moved to establish a number of anti-slavery societies throughout Europe and aroused public sentiment by describing the horrors of the slave trade on the Africa continent. The long established British and Foreign Anti-Slavery Society noted that in the "Summer of 1888 the eloquent orations of Cardinal Lavigerie created an extraordinary impression on the Continent." Likewise his visit to London "aroused some of the dormant enthusiasm of the people of England, and a Resolution, unanimously passed at the meeting was forwarded to the Foreign Minister which suggested that a Conference of the Powers might be convened."[145] Such a conference, Miers notes, was "infinitely more practical and less hazardous" than Lavigerie's other proposal, which was to establish a religio-military order modelled on the Templers or the Knights of Malta to take the battle to Africa in a crusade to suppress the trade.[146]

144 Article 9, *General Act of the Conference of Berlin, relative to the Development of Trade and Civilization in Africa; the free navigation of the River Congo, Niger, etc.; the Suppression of the Slave Trade by Sea and Land; the occupation of Territory on the African Coast, etc.* 26 February 1885. Sir E. Hertslet, *The Map of Africa by Treaty*, Vol. 2 (Routledge, London, 1967), 474.

145 British and Foreign Anti-Slavery Society, *The Slave-Trade Conference at Brussels and the British and Foreign Anti-Slavery Society* (1890), 6.

146 "Sur les anciens orders religieux-militaires et la possibilité d'une association du même gendre pour l'abolition de l'esclavage, dans les contrées Barbares de l'Afrique," in Cardinal Lavigerie, *Documents sur la Foundation de l'oeuvre Antiescalvagiste* (Belin et fils, St Cloud, 1889), 712–715.

Lord Salisbury, the then British Foreign Minister, saw the suggested conference as a means of addressing the awkward situation which had developed as a result of slave trading emanating from Zanzibar, a sultanate under the protection of Great Britain. At the request of Germany, Great Britain, along with Italy, had agreed to blockade Zanzibar to "restore the Sultan's authority and prevent the export of slaves and the import of arms [used by slave raiders]."[147] While the blockade was effective, it "highlighted the need for an international treaty against the slave trade."[148] Thus, using the momentum created by Lavigerie, Salisbury requested his ambassador in Brussels, Lord Vivian, to sound out the possibility that King Leopold host an international conference to deal with the slave trade. On 18 November 1889, the seventeen invited States met in Belgium to inaugurate the Brussels Conference to discuss the end of the slave trade by land and sea.[149]

The 1889–1890 Brussels Conference

While the General Act of the Brussels Conference dealt with the suppression of the African slave trade on land in countries of destination, it also established an arms agreement and restricted the traffic in spirits. However, the suppression of the slave trade at sea, it was said, was the "most awaited and most delicate point"[150] to be considered; it was, in fact, the point upon which the Conference hinged.[151] Vivian, having been named plenipotentiary, spelled out the British position on the second day of the Conference:

> The Congresses of Vienna and Verona had established the general principles; the Berlin Conference recognized and applied these principles to the territory forming the conventional basin of the Congo. The Powers, therefore, had formally accepted these principles, and the object of this Conference, such as Her Majesty's Governments understands it, is to establish efficient measures to put into practice these principles and to substitute individual action for collective action.

---

147 Miers, above n. 47, 211.

148 Ibid, 219.

149 The following States attended the 1889–1890 Brussels Conference: Austria, Belgium, Congo Free State, Denmark, France, Germany, Great Britain, Italy, The Netherlands, Persia, Portugal, Russia, Spain, Sweden and Norway, Turkey, the United States of America, and Zanzibar.

150 de Montardy, above n. 82, 141.

151 H. Queneuil, *La Conférence de Bruxelles et ses Résultats* (Larose et Tenin, Paris, 1907), 132.

Vivian then turned to the suppression of the slave trade at sea, calling for a universal instrument to encompass the established bilateral regime for the suppression of the slave trade:

> It is the opinion of Her Majesty's Government that the suppression of the maritime trade is the object upon which the efforts of this Conference should be primarily focused.... It may be possible, perhaps, to come to a unanimous international understanding, which, while respecting the right and interests of the Powers not yet linked by the Treaties, to incorporate and even amplify the provisions of the existing Treaties, which it might well be substituted for.[152]

The British delegation took the initiative and presented a proposal which called for the creation of a *cordon sanitaire* around "the most dreadful pest which has ever gnawed on humanity."[153] Within this zone, which would extend south from Port Suez on both coasts of the Red Sea and into the Persian Gulf and follow the African coast southwards, extending to the far extremities of Mozambique, the British proposal called for the right to detain "vessels directly or indirectly suspected of trafficking in Slaves" both in internal and international waters with a view toward bringing them to be judged before mixed tribunals.[154] Yet as the British and Foreign Anti-Slavery Society related to its readers, where the right to visitation was at issue, the "French have more or less taken the place of the Americans in this curious controversy."[155] The age-old Anglo-French rivalry was once again rearing its head, this time directly linked to the African colonial ambitions of the Powers; anti-British sentiment in France remained high – and *vice versa* – throughout this period (from 1881 and the 'Easter Question' to Fashoda in 1891).[156] The Anti-Slavery Society of France foreshadowed French resistance to the right to visit at Brussels, (and later in Paris) in 1888, stating that "we believe it is utterly impossible to obtain the

---

152 Protocol 2, Protocoles de Séances Plénieres de la Conférence de Bruxelles, 19 November 1889, *Actes de la Conférence de Bruxelles (1889–1890)* (Hayez, Brussels, 1890), 21 and 22. All direct quotations which have been taken from French language sources have been translated by the Author.

153 Annex 2, Protocol 10, "Project présenté par les Plénipotentiaries de la Grande-Bretagne," 28 November 1889, *Actes de la Conférence de Bruxelles (1889–1890)* (Hayez, Brussels, 1890), 149.

154 Ibid, p. 150.

155 British and Foreign Anti-Slavery Society, *The Slave-Trade Conference at Brussels and the British and Foreign Anti-Slavery Society*, 1890, 27.

156 See, generally, Wesseling, above n. 142.

consent of Parliamentary and public opinion in France, to the right for English cruisers to search French boats sailing under the national flag."[157] In a Declaration made on 20 December 1889, the French representatives in Brussels stated categorically that if the right to visit was placed on the agenda, they were not authorized to participate in such discussions. Acknowledging that the British proposal had not mentioned a right to visit *per se*, the French plenipotentiaries indicated they were willing to discuss the issue of the suppression of the slave trade at sea and put forward a general sketch of a forthcoming proposal, with the understanding that they would produce a more substantial version in the new year. This French diplomatic declaration pointed to the 1867 Anglo-French Instructions and noted that it would submit a proposal which would provide, *inter alia*, for the verification of the nationality of a boat sailing in the zone "contaminated by the exercising of the trade."[158]

The French counter-proposal was made on 20 January 1890. It provided for a zone enlarged to include the west coast of Africa, and laid down the principle that ships in the zone could only be searched by their own navies, with an exception where the right to fly a flag was in question. The counter-proposal, having laid down the manner in which a ship could be visited, then explained that fraudulent ships would be brought to a port where an international tribunal would be located. The supposed flag state's Consul would then undertake an investigation. If there was a difference of opinion between the Captain of the cruiser and the Consul, the international tribunal would consider the case. While the status of the seized ship would be considered by this mixed tribunal, its captain and crew were to be tried by their respective municipal systems. Finally, the French counter-proposal called for the creation of an international bureau which would act as a registry for ships in the zone.[159]

On 6 February 1890, the British Delegation responded to the French Counter-proposal in a positive manner, saying that it "merited serious attention" and "could probably serve as the basis for effective preventative measures which would receive general applicability in the zone where the trade is taking place."[160] However, it noted with regret that the French Government would not

---

157 British and Foreign Anti-Slavery Society, above n. 155, 20.

158 Annex 3, Protocol 10, "Déclaration des Plénipotentiaires de France," 20 December 1889, *Actes de la Conférence de Bruxelles (1889–1890)* (Hayez, Brussels, 1890), 153.

159 Annex 4, Protocol 10, "Project de Traité et projet de Règlement présentés par les Pléinpotentiaires de France" *Actes de la Conférence de Bruxelles (1889–1890)* (Hayez, Brussels, 1890), 154.

160 Annex 5, Protocol 10, "Déclaration des Plénipotentiaires de la Grande-Bretagne," 6 February 1890, *Actes de la Conférence de Bruxelles (1889–1890)* (Hayez, Brussels, 1890), 159.

accept "under any circumstances, the reciprocal right to monitor sailing ships in the trade zone." For its part the British Delegation refused to discuss "proposals which derogated, in any way, from the treaties to which the Queen is party, or the rights which flow from them." The Declaration said that Her Majesty's Government wanted to go as far as possible to reach an understanding with all Powers, and thus was willing to concede that the "right to visit established in the existing treaties be limited to the zone determined [during the Conference], and to limit the exercise of this right to ships of less than 500 tons [i.e. tantamount to 'native' African vessels], as long as this final condition, related to the dimensions of vessels, be submitted to revision if experience shows that a change was necessary." The Declaration went on to say that Great Britain "could not make these great concessions if the Conference, for its part, did not consent to adopt the strict regulations suggested in the French Counter-proposal, with a look to preventing, within the limits of the zone, the usurpation or abuse of flags of all the signatory States."[161] The British Declaration conceded that it probably made sense to drop the idea of an international tribunal as its bilateral network already had an established network of mixed commissions attached to it. Finally, the Declaration expressed itself in favour of an international bureau as proposed by France.

The Parties having made plain their positions, it was left to eminent international lawyer, Fyodor de Martens – best known today for penning the so-called "Martens Clause"– to step into the breach, though hesitantly, to mediate a solution. Martens benefited from the fact that, as a Russian plenipotentiary, he was seen as a disinterested party where issues of slavery in Africa and the slave trade at sea were concerned.[162] Martens prepared a report and draft articles which later were "entered into the General Act without major modification."[163] In his Report, Martens stated that the more he studied the British and French proposals, the "more I became convinced that there did not exist between them any fundamental contradictions."[164] He acknowledged Great Britain's century worth of experience in suppressing the slave trade at sea; but believed that the conditions in which the trade persisted had changed. The trade was

161 Ibid, 160.

162 For consideration of the 'Martens Clause' see Antonio Cassese, "Martens Clause Half a Loaf or Simply Pie in the Sky?" *European Journal of International Law*, Vol. 11, 2001, p. 187–216.

163 Queneuil, above n. 151, 136.

164 Annex 7, Protocol 10, "Rapport de M. de Martens, second Plénipotentiaire de Russie, sur les projets précédents," 17 February 1890, *Actes de la Conférence de Bruxelles (1889–1890)* (Hayez, Brussels, 1890), 169.

now exclusively taking place in East Africa, by means of indigenous boats, in a region where nearly the entirety of the coast was either under the sovereignty or the protection of European Powers. There was a real possibility for the Powers to work collectively on land and at sea to end the slave trade. With this in mind, Martens laid out draft articles that would become part of the General Act, which took into consideration the various components of the British and French proposals.[165] A contemporary French jurist, Henry Queneuil, wrote of Martens' mediation work: "thus the different principles found themselves reconciled without having compromised the efficacy of the repression of the slave trade by sea. At the same time, a latent and disquieting conflict between France and Great Britain which had existed for fifty years was put to rest."[166]

The provisions regarding the Repression of the Slave Trade at Sea are contained in Chapter III of the General Act of the Brussels Conference relative to the African Slave Trade, signed on 2 July 1890.

The General Act defined a maritime zone which centred on the high seas contiguous to the East Coast of Africa and included both the Red Sea and the Persian Gulf. It acknowledged a right to visit, search, and detain, in established treaties and that these treaties remained in force "in so far as they are not modified by the present General Act."[167] The two major British concessions were also included, namely that the States agreed that all such rights to visit could only transpire in the newly established maritime zone, and only with respect to "vessels of less than 500 tons burthen."[168]

Article 42 introduced the modified regime for visits under the General Act, allowing for visits to suppress the slave trade and to verify the propriety of the use of the flag:

> When an officers in command of a vessels of war of any of the Signatory Powers have reason to believe that a vessel of less than 500 tons burthen, found in the above-mentioned zone, is engaged in the Slave Trade, or is guilty of the fraudulent use of a flag, they may proceed to the verification of the ship's papers.

---

165 See Annex 6, Protocol 10, "Projet de Traité et project de Règlement codifiant les projets précédents et présentés par les Plénipotentiaires de Russie," 17 February 1890, *Actes de la Conférence de Bruxelles (1889–1890)* (Hayez, Brussels, 1890), 169.

166 Queneuil, above n. 151, 148.

167 Article 24, General Act of the Brussels Conference relative to the African Slave Trade, 2 July 1890; Hertslet, above n. 144, 499.

168 Ibid, Articles 21–23.

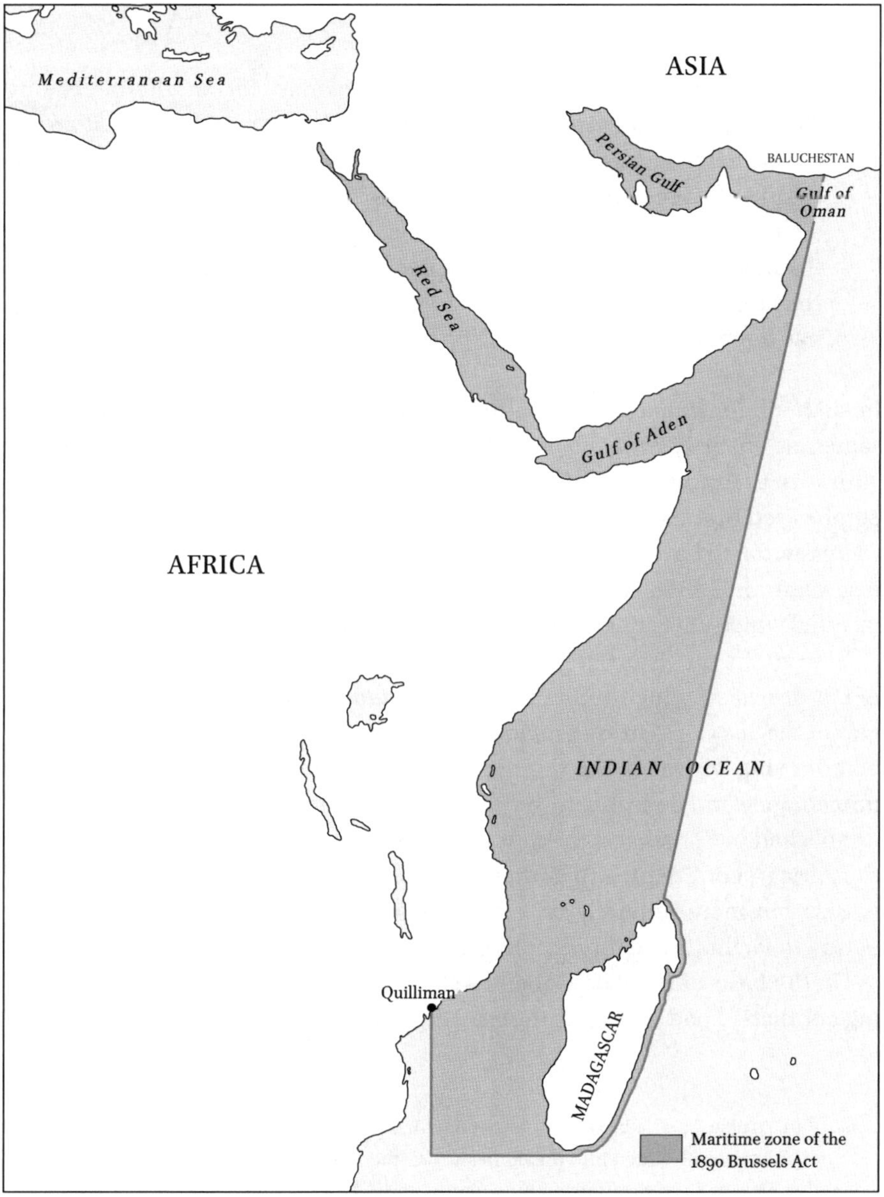

MAP 1 *The Maritime Zone established at the 1890 Brussels Conference.*

Article 46 stipulated:

> If, in carrying out the supervision provided for in the preceding Articles, the officer in command of the cruiser is convinced that an Act of Slave Trade has been committed on board during the passage, or that irrefutable proofs exist against the captain, or fitter-out, to justify a charge of fraudulent use of the flag, or fraud, or the participation in the Slave Trade, he shall take the detained vessel to the nearest port of the zone where there is a competent authority to the Power whose flag has been used.

In such circumstances, a Consul or the commander of a man-of-war of the same nationality as the suspected ship could be considered the competent authority to examine and determine the status of the seized vessel. Martens emphasised that having dropped the proposal for an international tribunal, it was essential to have a means to settle disputes which might arise between the flag state and these involved in the capture: a compromissory clause was inserted which envisioned the possible appointment of an arbitration panel.[169]

Beyond the provisions regarding right to visit, Article 27 of the 1890 General Act, a provision which remains, *mutatis mutandis*, operative under the 1982 Law of the Sea Convention provides: "Any slave who may have taken refugee on board a ship of war flying the flag of one of the Signatory Powers, shall be immediately and definitively freed." Finally, an International Bureau was to be established in Zanzibar – the first inter-governmental entity to be situated on the African continent – to gather information, including the registration of vessels, but more generally, to "centralize all documents and information of a nature to facilitate the repression of the Slave Trade in the maritime zone."[170]

On the basis of the 1890 General Act, it looked like the "latent and disquieting conflict"[171] had been put to rest. Yet, as Miers writes, an "unforeseen and

---

169 Ibid, Article 54. The mixed commission which had, by the 1870s, become a solely British affairs were subsumed into the domestic jurisdiction. For Great Britain this meant either the relevant Supreme Court of the Colony or an Admiralty Court. See *Documents relatives à la Répression de la Traite des Esclaves publiés en execution des Articles LXXXI et suivants de l'Act Général de Bruxelles*; 1892, 260.

170 Ibid, Article 77. For the work of the International Bureau in Zanzibar see: *Documents relatives à la Répression de la Traite des Esclaves publiés en execution des Articles LXXXI et suivants de l'Act Général de Bruxelles*; from 1892 to 1913 under the heading "*Bureau international maritime de Zanzibar.*"

171 See Queneuil, above n. 151, 148.

serious difficulty"[172] arose as the French Ambassador in Brussels wrote to the Belgian Foreign Minister:

> I have the honour to confirm to your Excellency the information which I gave *viva voce* yesterday to Baron Lambermont [the President of the Conference]; after a prolonged discussion occupying the sitting of the 24th and 25th of last month, the French Chamber of Deputies decided to suspend the authorization to ratify the General Act [...]. His Majesty's Government must be aware of the part which the Cabinet had taken in this grave debate, and it was certainly been from no want of effort on their part that the conclusion was not entirely different. Your Excellency is further aware that the consideration which weighed with the Chamber were derived from the nature of the measures to be taken for the repression of the traffic at sea.[173]

The Institute of International Law came on side in 1891 declaring that the General Act did not reinstitute an expansive right to visit and that the Act addressed the concerns of France; expressing its hope that all States which had been present in Brussels would ratify the Act.[174] The issue of French ratification remained unresolved until 2 January 1892 when France deposited its instrument of ratification, with the following reservation:

> His Excellency [the French ambassador to Belgian] declared that the President of the Republic, in his ratification of the General Act of Brussels, has provisionally reserved, for an ulterior understanding, Articles XXI, XXII, and XXIII, and Articles XLII to LXI.[175]

In essence, France agreed to the General Act but excluded the application of the provisions relating to visitation. The content of Articles 21, 22, and 23 was discussed above. Articles 42 to 61 set out the modalities of the regime of

---

172 Miers, above n. 47, 293.

173 See "France," Protocol of a Meeting held at the Foreign Office at Brussels, respecting the Ratification of the General Act of the Brussels Conference, 2 July 1891, Hertslet, above n. 144, 521–522.

174 Institut de Droit International, "Voeu motive de l'Institut tendant à la ratification intégrale de l'Act general de Bruxelles," *Annuaire de l'Institut de Droit International*, Vol. 11, 1889–1892, p. 269.

175 See "France," Protocol of a Meeting held at Brussels, in the Foreign Office, respecting the Exchange of Ratification of the General Act of the Brussels Conference, 2 January 1892, Hertslet, above n. 144, 524–525.

visitation within the General Act. The phrase "provisionally reserved, for an ulterior understanding" was interesting, as the French legislature had determined France would be "governed by the stipulations and arrangements now in force," that is to say, the 1867 Naval Instructions. France further modified its reservation when Belgium, as depositor of the General Act, noted that obligations stemming from Articles 30 to 41, regarding the authorisation of native vessels to fly a State's flag, were only applicable in the zone established by Articles 21 to which France had entered a reservation. France declared that its east coast possessions would form part of that regime, noting that it "will be spontaneously applied by the Government of the Republic in the territory of Obock [Djibouti], and, according to necessity in the Island of Madagascar and the Comoros."[176] The French reservation was accepted by the other Parties and the General Act came into force on 2 April 1892.[177]

Miers, writing about the French reservation, stated that the "solution was unusual in diplomatic history and left France in a privileged position."[178] In reality, as De Montardy noted, it left France disadvantaged: "Only France refused to cooperate with the rest of Europe in its *oeuvre* of civilisation and humanity; and only it was to undertake the policing of ships flying its own colours, while the other State Parties provided mutual assistance: a regrettable situation, as the slavers would tend to cover their operations with the French flag which was less energetically policed."[179] Miers concluded that little had been lost because the French "government agreed to abide by the regulations of 1867 and to put into operation the new rules for the issue of French colours."[180] Queneuil also echoed these sentiments, stating that the differences between the General Act and the 1867 Instructions were not great.[181] However, the limited French acceptance of the 1890 General Act provided at least one means by which slave traders could avoid visits by hosting the French flag; although that practice was effectively ceased by the Permanent Court of Arbitration (PCA) in the *Muscat Dhows* case (1905).

In that case, the panel considered whether the status of subjects of the Sultan of Muscat who had been granted the status of *protégé* by France in 1844, and

176 Ibid.

177 Beyond the parties which negotiated in Brussels (see n. 147 and accompanying text), all of which ratified the General Act, the following States acceded to the instrument: Ethiopia, Liberia, Persia and the Orange Free State. See Hertslet, above n. 144, 488.

178 Miers, above n. 47, 293.

179 Montardy, above n. 82, 159–160.

180 Miers, above n. 47, 293. For the 1867 Instructions see *Documents relatives à la Répression de la Traite* (n. 91 above).

181 Queneuil, above n. 151, 189.

thus benefited from the protection of France and, on the seas, the French flag, was limited by the obligations undertaken by France as a result of the 1890 Brussels Act. The issuance of papers authorising dhows to fly French flags had meant that those "native vessels" had been "commonly employed in the slave trade."[182] In the Award, the arbitrators pointed to Article 32 of the 1890 General Act which set out the conditions under which native vessels were granted authority to fly a flag. This included owners or outfitters "furnishing proof that they enjoy a good reputation, and especially that they have never been condemned for acts of slave trade."[183] The Court determined that after France had ratified the Brussels Act (1892), it was not permitted to "authorize vessels belonging to subjects of His Highness the Sultan of Muscat to fly the French flag, except on conditions that their owners or fitters-out had established that they had been considered and treated by France as her *protégés* before the year 1863." It further determined, with regard to another question, that the "authorization to fly the French flag can not be transmitted or transferred to any other person or other dhow, even if belonging to the same owner."[184] Subjects of Muscat might well benefit from the protection of the French flag, but only during their lifetime or that of their precious dhow. Considering the life expectancy in early twentieth century Muscat and that of "native vessels," the PCA had, at the behest of Great Britain, sounded the death-knell of the slave trade at sea.

Conclusion

While debate concerning the motives of Great Britain in its attempt to suppress the slave trade remains lively today, it cannot be disputed that Great Britain did, in fact, lead and shoulder most of the responsibility in ending the slave trade and slavery itself. Over the past thirty years, historians have busied themselves uncovering the means and modalities of the Atlantic trade which persisted for nearly three and a half centuries. We know much more today about the slave trade and the manner in which it was undertaken and historians can in no way dispute the centrality of Great Britain to its abolition. Abolition was a lengthy process which required Britain to persist with its

182 Syllabus, "The Muscat Dhows Case between France and Great Britain," James Brown Scott (ed.), *The Hague Court Reports* (1916), 93.

183 Article 32, General Act of the Brussels Conference relative to the African Slave Trade, 2 July 1890, Hertslet, above n. 144, 500.

184 *The Muscat Dhows*, Award of 8 August 1905, James Brown Scott (ed.), *The Hague Court Reports* (1916), 99–100.

foreign policy objective for seventy-five years. When it became evident suppression of the trade could not be achieved through common law pronouncements or agreement on a universal instrument during the era of the Concert of Europe, British foreign policy took a tactical shift towards building a bilateral regime of instruments outlawing the slave trade. Brazil and Portugal were unable to resist muscular interventions by the Royal Navy and joined the burgeoning web of bilateral treaties; France and the United States could not be cajoled so easily.

Despite French reservations regarding visitation under the 1890 General Act, the slave trade was, by this time, clearly in its last throes. Through its bilateral network, Great Britain had managed to abolish the Atlantic Slave Trade by 1867. The limited possessions of France in the zone where the slave trade persisted and its lack of willingness to ascribe to the right to visit established by the Brussels Act slowed the momentum towards complete suppression of the slave trade at sea. As the *Muscat Dhows* case indicates, loopholes persisted in which slavers could find protection of a flag to carry on the trade. However, such instances were very limited in nature and scope. In essence, the bilateral web of treaties created by Great Britain in the first half of the nineteenth century had not only ended the Atlantic Slave Trade, but also made it near impossible, legally and politically, for any State to allow its citizens – or for that matter, those under its protection – to continue with the slave trade. It was only in 1890 that Britain finally achieved a right to visit to suppress the slave trade. British ambition to establish a right to visit, despite its overwhelming dominance of the seas during much of the nineteenth century, was ultimately limited for nearly seven decades, not by the moral lassitude of other States, but by the international law imperative to respect the Grotian notion of the freedom of the seas.

CHAPTER 3

Fydor Martens and the Question of Slavery at the 1890 Brussels Conference*

Fydor Martens played a crucial role in the move to establish an international regime to suppress the slave trade. This may come as a surprise as there is nothing in Martens' past which would have pointed to his involvement in issues of slavery or the slave trade during the late nineteenth century, nor was Tsarist Russian implicated, in any serious manner, in the international slave trade. It was, instead, the perception of Russia as a disinterested party on the issue of the slave trade and Martens acknowledge status as a jurist which thrust him into the spotlight during the 1889–1890 Brussels Conference where he mediation the differing interests of France and Great Britain to draft – in effect – the 1890 General Act of the Brussels Conference.

Martens play a fundamental role in the issue of the suppression of the slave trade which, though it is seldom recognised today, was *the* issue which had global implications during most of the nineteenth century. The fact that very little else before required coordination of European States, newly independent American States, and emerging 'civilized nations', meant that the suppression of the slave trade was one of the few items that – as a result of the limited inter-State intercourse during the age of sail – demanded truly international attention. The limited contact between States meant that the establishment of law regarding slavery was a slow and clumsy process which, though agreed to in principle at the 1815 Congress of Vienna, would only manifest itself in a binding universal instrument in 1890 at the Brussels Conference; and ultimately by the suppression of both the slave trade and slavery with the coming in to force of the 1926 League of Nations Convention to Suppress the Slave Trade and Slavery. It was these factors then – the interaction of European Powers with the New World, Africa and on the high seas of the Atlantic, Pacific and Indian oceans, coupled with its time span, which marked every decade of the nineteenth century; that made the suppression of the slave trade *the* international issue of resonance throughout the eighteen hundreds.

At the outset of this paper, it should be made plain that the lack of a developed multilateral international system during the eighteen hundreds was not

* Paper presented at The History of International Law Scholarship in Russia Conference at Tartu University, Estonia, September 2006. Note that quotations from French sources are translated by the author.

 | DOI 10.1163/9789004279896_005

decisive in explaining the slow pace by which the slave trade on the seas was outlawed. What was at the heart of the matter was the very essence of States' understanding of the nature of the seas. The challenge to the abolition of the slave trade on the high seas was not the slave trade *per se*; but, rather, the conflict between the Grotian notion of the freedom of the seas and attempts to establish a right to visit ships suspected of being involved in the slave trade. The introducing of a 'right to visit' into the corpus of international law is fundamental to understanding the move to suppress the slave trade during the nineteenth century. Over a period of eighty years, Great Britain – which was the primary actor in the suppression of the slave trade at sea – sought to advocate various understandings of the concept of a 'right to visit'; first seeking to assimilate it to piracy, then arguing that the term was in keeping with the French notion of *droit de visite*: that is an indirect right to visit to ascertain the right to fly the flag hoisted but not to *search* a ship, as a way to suppress the slave trade. Ultimately, it was a diplomatic compromise marshalled by Martens in 1890 that allowed for the acceptance of the concept of a 'right to visit' – while limiting its application to a specific maritime zone and to the type of ship used in the late nineteenth century slave trade.

This Paper is part of a larger study, which will appear in the 2008 edition of the *British Yearbook of International* Law and focuses on British attempts, during the nineteenth century, to end the Atlantic Slave Trade and outlaw the slave trade internationally by way of a universal instrument; which it only succeeded in achieving after seventy-five years of effort. For most of the nineteenth century though, the battle lines were drawn between Great Britain on the one hand, which put forward an abolitionist agenda primed on the use of its superior naval forces; and on the other hand, lesser maritime Powers that sought to maintain freedom of commerce for their merchant fleet. The larger study brings into focus the manner in which a dominant Power, limited by normative constrains in the guise of established international law regarding the freedom of the seas, was able, over a long period of time, to reach a *modus vivendi* with those States that, by and large, were in opposition to a right to visit. Consideration is given in that study to the failed attempts, in the early eighteen hundreds, by Great Britain to establish a universal treaty outlawing the slave trade, and the change of tactics that would ultimately prove more successful – the establishment of a web of bilateral agreements that would come to include all maritime powers. The larger study also highlights the relationship between Great Britain and Brazil, France, Portugal along with the United States of America, to demonstrate the various dynamics that were at play in getting these recalcitrant States to join the bilateral regime. It concludes with an examination of the 1890 General Act of Brussels, which achieved the decades-long British foreign policy objective of a universal instrument meant to suppress the slave trade at sea. As for this Paper, in considers Russia's role during the nineteenth century as a bit player with regard to the slave trade and then focus on Marten fundamental role played at Brussels in 1889–1890.

British Attempts to Gain a Right to Visit to Suppress the Slave Trade

The slave trade was at its peak during the nineteenth century, as the Barbary States (Algiers, Tunis and Tripoli) were involved in the of so-called 'white slave trade' in the Mediterranean; the Atlantic Slave Trade (1519–1867) having emerged in the late fifteenth century as a new "species of slavery"[1] which ultimately include the known transport of more than eleven million Africans[2]; and the Oriental Slave Trade, an older, more ingrained, slave trade which had existed for more than a millennia and only was suppressed in the early twentieth century. It was during the eighteen hundreds that Great Britain emerged as an unrivalled maritime power. As a result of that privileged position, Great Britain sought to translate a belligerent right to visit ships into a peacetime right so as to suppress the slave trade. During the early nineteenth century a number of court cases both in Great Britain and the United States of America considered whether there existed a right to visit foreign ships on the high seas in time of peace so as to suppress the slave trade. While late-Napoleonic municipal judgments on both sides of the Atlantic were willing to admit a right to visit based, to a large extent, on domestic law lifted to the international level by way of natural law;[3] by 1825, such pronouncements had been reversed in favour of high court decisions which conformed to a growing thread of positivism as a means of interpreting of international law.[4] For instance, in the 1925 *Antelope* case, United States Chief Justice of the Supreme Court, John Marshall,

1 Robin Blackburn, *The Overthrow of Colonial Slavery (1776–1848)*, 1988, p. 7.

2 See David Eltis, "The Volume and Structures of the Transatlantic Slave Trade: A Reassessment," *William and Mary Quarterly*, Vol. 58, 2001, n. 21. The dataset is found in David Eltis *et al.* (eds.) *The Trans-Atlantic Slave Trade: A Database on CD-ROM*, 1999.

3 For discussion of *jus gentium* as general principles of municipal law applicable internationally and *jus inter gentes* as the law of nations, see Alfred Rubin, *Ethics and Authority in International Law*, 1997.

4 This should come as little surprise as the trend in international relations during this era was to leave behind the notion of natural law justified by reference to domestic law in favour of

took a decidedly positivist approach to interpreting the law regarding both the slave trade and the notion of visitation:

> Whatever might be the answer of a moralist to this question, a jurist must search for its legal solution, in those principles of action which are sanctioned by the usages, the national acts, and the general assent, of that portion of the world of which he considers himself as a part, and to whose law the appeal is made. If we resort to this standard as the test of international law, the question, as has already been observed, is decided in favour of the legality of the trade. Both Europe and America embarked in it; and for nearly two centuries, it was carried on without opposition, and without censure. A jurist could not say, that a practice thus supported was illegal, and that those engaged in it might be punished, either personally, or by deprivation of property.
>
> In this commerce, thus sanctioned by universal assent, every nation has an equal right to engage. How is this right to be lost? Each may renounce it for its own people; but can this renunciation affect others?
>
> No principle of general law is more universally acknowledged, than the perfect equality of nations. Russia and Geneva have equal rights. It results from this equality, that no one can rightfully impose a rule on another. Each legislates for itself, but its legislation can operate on itself alone. A right, then, which is vested in all by the consent of all, can be divested only be consent; and this trade, in which all have participated, must remain lawful to those who cannot be induced to relinquish it. As no nation can prescribe a rule for others, none can make a law of nations; and this traffic remains lawful to those whose governments have not forbidden it[...].

---

positive international law. See Arthur Nussbaum, *A Concise History of the Law of Nations*, 1961, pp. 232–234, where he considers this shift:

> In the science of international law, the nineteenth century was the great era of positivism. [...] broad movements of legal and political thought were influential in the advance of positivism. The battle pro and contra the law of nature was fought along all fronts of legal and political science. On the European Continent, where the doctrine of the law of nature had won such notable triumphs, it not only was defeated but fell into utter disrepute. Political bias was a factor in this phenomenon: the law of nature, having furnished the conceptual weapons of the French Revolution, became an easy target for the theorist of the counterrevolution. Moreover, the speculative methods of the natural law school harmonized but little with the intellectual atmosphere of a century in which physical science had so conspicuously demonstrated the value of observation and painstaking research. In international law, too, theories had to be based upon the solid foundation of fact.

> If it be [...] repugnant to the law of nations [...] it is almost superfluous to say in this Court, that the right of bringing in for adjudication in time of peace, even where the vessel belongs to a nation which has prohibited the trade, cannot exist. The Courts of no country execute the penal laws of another; and the course of the American government on the subject of visitation and search, would decide any case in which that right had been exercised by an American cruiser, on the vessel of a foreign nation, not violating our municipal laws, against the captors.
>
> It follows, that a foreign vessel engaged in the African slave trade, captured on the high seas in time of peace, by an American cruiser, and brought in for adjudication, would be restored.[5]

As there was an acknowledgement that domestic law did not allow for a right to visit, Great Britain sought to establish such a right by way of an international instrument. While early attempts failed, Great Britain maintained this strategic foreign policy objective for seventy-five years and, for tactical reasons, spent most of the intervening period establishing a web of bilateral arrangements which would then, ultimately converge and be subsumed into the General Act of the 1890 Brussels Conference. With regard to these early universal attempts, they transpired during the Concert of Europe wherein Russia had a seat at the table.[6] While the British Foreign Minister, Lord Castlereagh, proposed at the Congress of Vienna in 1814–1815 that the slave trade be outlawed within a three-year period; that a permanent institution be established to supervise the adherence to the treaty obligations; and that a reciprocal right of visit be established;[7] this was not to be, as he was unable to gain a binding commitment regarding the abolition of the slave trade beyond a Declaration by the Powers which expressed the wish to "bring to an end a scourge which has for a long time desolated Africa, degraded Europe, and afflicted humanity." The Powers declared that they:

> consider the universal abolition of the trade in Negroes to be particularly worthy of their attention, being in conformity with the spirit of the times, and the general principles of our August Sovereigns, who our animated in their sincere desire to work towards the quickest and most effective of

5 The *Antelope* [1825], 23 *United States Supreme Court Reports* 66, pp. 121–123.

6 The Concert system was meant to allow European Powers to consider international issues, at intervals, during peacetime, as opposed to their former practice of solely meeting to settle the peace after war (ex: Congress of Vienna). Four meeting took place in this manner: Aix-la-Chapelle (1818), Troppau (1820), Laibach (1821), and Verona (1822).

7 See Suzanne Miers, *Britain and the Ending of the Slave Trade*, 1975, pp. 10–11.

> measures, by all means at their disposal, and to act, in the use of those means with all zealousness and perseverance which is required of such a grand and beautiful cause.[8]

While Castlereagh failed to get any cooperation to suppress the slave trade at Aix-la-Chapelle in 1818, his successor the Duke of Wellington, did somewhat better at the 1822 Congress of Verona, though once again, this was in the guise of a the following declaration with no binding commitments from the participants:

> That they invariably persisted in their principles and sentiments which these Sovereigns manifested in their Declaration of 8 February 1815 – That they have never ceased, and will never cease to consider the commerce in Negroes – "a scourge which has for a long time desolated Africa, degraded Europe, and afflicted humanity," and that they are ready to contribute to everything which could assure and accelerate the complete and definite abolition of this commerce.[9]

This Resolution was the end product of earlier, unsuccessful attempts, by Great Britain to establish a universal instrument prohibiting the slave trade. Yet, the failure at Vienna in 1815 more than any other, determined a change in the tactics of Great Britain in pursuing its ultimate foreign policy objective of a universal instrument allowing for a right to visit on the high seas in pursuit of an end to the slave trade. That is, Great Britain turned to building a bilateral system and through it, was able to isolated the few States outside the system and increased the momentum towards a universally accepted *right* to visit. That it took until 1890 for a universal treaty to be adopted speaks to the willingness of a number of States to demonstrate their opposition to, not the slave trade *per se*, but to the granting to Great Britain the right to visit their merchant ships.

It fell to France and the United States of America to be most obstinate in their call to respect the absolute right (in peacetime) to free commerce upon the high seas as against British attempts to limit that right with an aim of suppressing the slave trade. While Brazil, France, Portugal, and the United

---

8 *Declaration des 8 Cours, relative à l'Abolition Universelle de lat Traite des Nègres*, 8 February 1815, *British and Foreign State Papers*, Vol. 3 (1815–1816), 1838, p. 972. The eight Powers at Vienna were: Austria, Britain, France, Prussia, Russia, Portugal, Spain, and Sweden.

9 *Résolution relatives à l'Abolition de la Traite des Nègres*, 28 November 1822, *British and Foreign State Papers*, Vol. 10 (1822–1823), 1828, pp. 109–110.

States of America had individual and distinct reasons for not wanting to participate in this British initiative, they all saw in the British wish to suppress the slave trade as an attempt to appropriate for itself the policing of the seas and control over maritime commerce. While Brazil and Portugal were persuaded by coercive means to join the system, France and the United States remained adamant in their belief regarding the freedom of the seas. In the end, France and the United States would accommodate themselves to the British wish to suppress the slave trade much as Great Britain would come to terms with an agreed to limited right to visit merchant ships of these two States.

Having been unable to forge a consensus to establish a universal treaty outlawing the slave trade during the Concert of Europe era, Great Britain would ultimately enter into treaties with thirty-one nineteenth century States so as to suppress the slave trade at sea.[10] One such treaty, to which Russia was party, was the 1841 Quintuple Treaty which "stirred up a veritable hornets' nest in France,"[11] in part, because Austria, Prussia, and Russia being land Powers were not truly effected by its provisions for the suppression of slavery at sea. The end result was that the 1841 Treaty was not ratified by France, though it did came into force for the other four parties, and was later acceded to by Belgium (1848) and Germany (1879).[12]

While the United States of America would accommodate itself to the British right to visit by sending out its own squadrons to sail the seas in tandem with the British Royal Navy, France sough further restriction on any British pretension to a right to visit. When a ten year treaty lapsed in 1845, the French and British came to a *modus vivendi* on a provisional basis, but which would, in fact, last until the end of the First World War. The 1859 Instructions, of which the French and British versions mirrored each other (like all such Instruction), were very elaborate and included a conceptual understanding of a right to visit. The Instructions first set down the principle that by "virtue

10 These thirty-one States included, by chronological order of the signing of the first agreement with Great Britain: Portugal, Denmark, France, Spain, Netherlands, Sweden, Buenos Aires, Colombia, Brazil, Mexico, Confederation of Peru, Bolivia, Hanseatic Cities, Tuscany, the two Sicilies, Chili, Venezuela, Uruguay, Haiti, Texas, Austria, Prussia, Russia, The United States of America, The Kings and Chiefs of Cape Mount (Africa), Equator, Muscat, Arabs of the Gulf, New Granada, Zanzibar, Egypt. See R Phillimore, *Commentaries upon International Law* (Butterworths, London, 1879), pp. 420–421.

11 Miers, *op. cit.*, n. 7, p. 17. See also Henry de Montardy, *La Traite et le Droit International*, 1899, pp. 87–88.

12 Montardy, *id.*

of the immunity of national flags, no merchant-vessel navigating the high seas is subject to any foreign jurisdiction. A vessel of war cannot therefore visit, detain, arrest, or seize (expect under Treaty) any merchant-vessel not recognized as belonging to her own nation." The Instructions went on to state that if a ship failed to hoist its flag, that a "first warning may be given her by firing a blank gun, and should this have no result, a second gun warning may be given her by means of a shotted gun, to be levelled in such a manner as not to [strike] her."[13] If a ship did hoist its flag, it was to be understood that the "man-of-war has no right to exercise the least control over her," unless the nationality could be "seriously called into question." On this basis, after having hailed and informed the ship of its intensions, a cruiser could send an officer aboard with the understanding that only an examination of papers was to transpire: "All inquiry into the nature of the cargo; or the commercial operations of the said ships; in a word, on any other subject save that of their nationality; all search, all visit, are absolutely forbidden."[14] In other words, the right to visit had been narrowed *stricto senso*, having been decoupled from the right to *search*. The final set of Instructions of note, those issued in 1867, mirrored the above provisions of the 1859 Instructions, but were more focused, allowing an officer to request only specified papers on board a ship suspected of flying a fraudulent flag. If a ship was deemed to have been flying such a flag, the warship was to escort its capture to the nearest port where a representative of the flag State could determine whether it had a right to fly the flag in question.[15]

The 1859 Instructions would become crucial to the relationship between France and Great Britain where the suppression of slave trade at sea was concerned, as these Instructions would persist in their application beyond the nineteenth century. This understanding between France and Great Britain would remain the last word as between the two Powers, despite attempts to gain universal agreement on the modalities by which the suppression of the slave trade should transpire and despite Martens having hammered out an agreement amongst the parties' diplomats in Brussels in 1890.

---

13 Instructions issued to Commanders of French Ships of War, as found in the "Correspondence respecting the Visit of American Vessels by British Cruisers," *British Sessional Papers*, Vol. 34, 1857–1858, p. 427.

14 *Id.*, p. 428.

15 See "Instructions as to Vessels under the French Flag," *Documents relatives à la Répression de la Traite des Esclaves publiés en execution des Articles LXXXI et suivants de l'Act Général de Bruxelles*, 1892, pp. 272–274.

The Brussels Conference

In their quest for what historians termed the 'Second European Empires' the ideology which justify usurpation of land shifted beyond the New World.[16] Having colonised the Western Hemisphere, European Powers embarked on its civilizing mission. That mission would descend into an all out 'scramble for Africa' by the 1880s. While much of the colonization of the New World had taken place under the banner of "Gold, Glory and God"; the British missionary, David Livingstone, made it known throughout Europe that in Africa "slave raiding and trading were devastating large areas, and his appeal to bring 'Christianity, commerce, and civilization' to the heart of the continent" did not fall on deaf ears.[17] A recurring theme throughout much of this period was a demand by Europeans to end the slave trade, not only at sea, but on land: on the African Continent. Thus, in the latter part of the nineteenth century, as Africa was opened to the pursuit of Empire, European States concluded treaties with local African elite mandating the suppression of the slave trade. For its part Great Britain became party to more than a hundred such agreements "which eventually covered the whole coast from which slaves were exported."[18] During this period, it was clear that the suppression of slavery and the slave trade had become very much part of the discourse of international relations and, though it had been championed by Great Britain, other States with holdings in Africa – France, Germany, Italy, and Portugal (and the private Congolese State which was to be awarded to King Leopold of Belgium in 1885) – were willing to see its inclusion on the agenda of international conferences and for it to find voice in international instruments.

Thus when a dispute arose over an Anglo-Portuguese treaty regarding control of the mouth of the Congo River in 1884, the German Chancellor, Otto von Bismarck, proposed an international conference to settle the question. The Berlin Conference, which ultimately provided for the free navigation of the Congo and, more generally, a framework for the effective occupation of the African coast, also found on its agenda a British proposal which called for – in the language of the twenty-first century – universal jurisdiction to be established over the slave trade.[19] The proposal put forward was in the form of a

16 For 'Second European Empires' see Antony Pagden, *Lords of all the World; Ideologies of Empire in Spain, Britain and France c.1500–c.1800*, 1995, p. 2.

17 Suzanne Miers, *Slavery in the Twentieth Century: The Evolution of a Global Problem*, 2003, p. 20.

18 Miers, *Britain and the Ending of the Slave Trade*, p. 46.

19 See H.L. Wesseling, *Divide and Rule: The Partition of Africa 1880–1914*, 1996, pp. 113–119.

declaration making the slave trade "a crime against the Law of Nations." The draft Declaration read in part that: "The Slave Trade is henceforth a crime prohibited by the Law of Nations, and cognizable by the tribunals of all civilized nations whatever the nationality of the accused."[20] This proposal, however, did not find favour with the fifteen States gathering in Berlin as they were unwilling to commit to such a far-reaching pronouncement, instead they accepted a general declaration that the slave trade was indeed prohibited by international law. The Declaration Relative to the Slave Trade, which emerged from the 1885 General Act of the Conference of Berlin, reads:

> Seeing the trading in slaves is forbidden in conformity with the principles of international law as recognized by the Signatory Powers, and seeing also that the operations, which, by sea or land, furnish slaves to trade, ought likewise to be regarded as forbidden, the Powers which do or shall exercise sovereign rights or influence in the territories forming the Conventional basin of the Congo declare that these territories may not serve as a market or means of transit for the trade in slaves, or whatever race they may be. Each of the Powers binds itself to employ all the means at its disposal for putting an end to this trade and for punishing those who engage in it.[21]

Shortly after the end of Berlin Conference, an ally to the anti-slavery cause emerged from the most unlikely of sources, in the person of the Roman Catholic Archbishop of Algiers, Cardinal Lavigerie. In what can only be called a 'one-man' crusade, Cardinal Lavigerie gained the support of the Pope, and moved to establish a number of anti-slavery societies throughout Europe and aroused public sentiment through the detailing of the horrors of the slave trade on the Africa continent. During his visit to London, Cardinal Lavigerie it was suggested that a "Conference of the Powers might be convened" to deal with the issue of slavery and the slave trade in Africa.[22] Such a conference,

20 Miers, *Britain and the Ending of the Slave Trade*, pp. 171–172.

21 Article 9, *General Act of the Conference of Berlin, relative to the Development of Trade and Civilization in Africa; the free navigation of the River Congo, Niger, etc.; the Suppression of the Slave Trade by Sea and Land; the occupation of Territory on the African Coast, etc.* 26 February 1885. Sir E. Hertslet, *The Map of Africa by Treaty*, Vol. 2, 1967, p. 474. The following are the States which participated in the 1884–1885 Berlin Conference: Austria, Belgium, Denmark, France, Germany, Great Britain, Italy, The Netherlands, Norway, Portugal, Russia, Spain, Sweden, Turkey, and the United States of America.

22 British and Foreign Anti-Slavery Society, *The Slave-Trade Conference at Brussels and the British and Foreign Anti-Slavery Society*, 1890, p. 6.

Professor Susan Miers notes, was "infinitely more practical and less hazardous" than Cardinal Lavigerie's other proposal which was to establish a religio-military order modelled on the Templers or the Knights of Malta to take the battle to Africa in a crusade to suppress the trade.[23] The suggestion of a conference was taken up by the British Foreign Ministry and on 18 November 1889, the seventeen States invited met in Belgium to inaugurate the Brussels Conference meant to discuss the end of the slave trade by land and sea.[24]

While the General Act of the Brussels Conference dealt with issues of the suppression of the African slave trade on land, in countries of destination, it also established an arms agreement and restricted the traffic in spirits. However, the suppression of the slave trade at sea, it was said, was the "most awaited and most delicate point"[25] to be considered; it was, in fact, the point upon which the Conference hinged.[26] The delegated British plenipotentiary, Lord Vivian, spelled out his State's position on the second day of the Conference in the following terms:

> The Congresses of Vienna and Verona had established the general principles; the Berlin Conference recognized and applied these principles to the territory forming the conventional basin of the Congo. The Powers, therefore, had formally accepted these principles, and the object of this Conference, such as Her Majesty's Governments understands it, is to establish efficient measures to put into practice these principles and to substitute individual action for collective action.

Lord Vivian then turned to the suppression of the slave trade at sea, calling for a folding of the established bilateral regime for the suppression of the slave trade into a universal instrument:

> It is the opinion of Her Majesty's Government that the suppression of the maritime trade is the object upon which the efforts of this Conference

23 See "Sur les anciens orders religieux-militaires et la possibilité d'une association du même gendre pour l'abolition de l'esclavage, dans les contrées Barbares de l'Afrique" in Cardinal Lavigerie, *Documents sur la Foundation de l'oeuvre Antiescalvagiste*, 1889, pp. 712–715.

24 The following are the States which attended the 1889–1890 Brussels Conference: Austria, Belgium, Congo Free State, Denmark, France, Germany, Great Britain, Italy, The Netherlands, Persia, Portugal, Russia, Spain, Sweden and Norway, Turkey, the United States of America, and Zanzibar.

25 Henry de Montardy, *La Traite et le Droit International*, 1899, p. 141.

26 Henry Queneuil, *La Conférence de Bruxelles et ses Résultats*, 1907, p. 132.

> should be primarily focused [...]. It may be possible, perhaps, to come to a unanimous international understanding, which, while respecting the right and interests of the Powers not yet linked by the Treaties, to incorporate and even amplify the provisions of the existing Treaties, which it might well be substituted for.[27]

Following on the heels of this statement, the British delegation took the initiative and presented a proposal which called for the creation of a *cordon sanitaire* around "the most dreadful pest which has ever gnawed on humanity."[28] Within this zone – which would extend from Port Suez south on both coasts of the Red Sea and into the Persian Gulf before following the African coast southwards, extending to the far extremities of Mozambique – the British proposal called for the right to detain "vessels directly or indirectly suspected of trafficking in Slaves" both in internal and international waters with a look toward bringing them to be adjudged before mixed tribunals.[29] During the Conference the ago-old Anglo-French rivalry was once again rearing its head, this time directly linked to the African colonial ambitions of the Powers; anti-British sentiment in France would remained high – and vice versa – throughout this period (from 1881 and the 'Easter Question' to Fashoda in 1891).[30] The Anti-Slavery Society of France foreshadowed French resistance to the right to visit at Brussels (and later in Paris) in 1888, when it stated that "we believe it is utterly impossible to obtain the consent of Parliamentary and public opinion in France, to the right for English cruisers to search French boats sailing under the national flag."[31] In a Declaration made on 20 December 1889, the French representatives in Brussels stated categorically that if the right to visit was placed on the agenda, that they were not authorized to participate in such discussions. Having acknowledged that the British proposal had not mentioned a right to visit *per se*, the French plenipotentiaries indicated that they were willing to discuss the issue of the suppression of the slave trade at sea, and thus put forward a general sketch of a forthcoming proposal, with the understanding that they would produce a more substantial version in the new year. This French diplomatic declaration pointed to the 1867 Anglo-French Instructions

27 Protocol 2, Protocoles de Séances Plénieres de la Conférence de Bruxelles, 19 November 1889, *Actes de la Conférence de Bruxelles (1889–1890)*, pp. 21 and 22.

28 Annex 2, Protocol 10, "Project présenté par les Plénipotentiaries de la Grande-Bretagne," 28 November 1889, *Actes de la Conférence de Bruxelles (1889–1890)*, p. 149.

29 *Id.*, p. 150.

30 See, generally, Wesseling, *op. cit.* n. 19.

31 British and Foreign Anti-Slavery Society, *op. cit.*, n. 22, p. 20.

and noted that it would submit a proposal which would include, inter alia, for the verification of the nationality of a boat sailing in the zone "contaminated by the exercising of the trade."[32]

The French Counter-proposal was made on 20 January 1890; it provided for a zone which was enlarged to include the west coast of Africa, it laid down the principle that ships in the zone could only be searched by their own navies, but that there could be an exception existed where the right to fly a flag was in question. The Counter-proposal, having laid down the manner in which a ship could be visited, then explained that fraudulent ships would be brought to a port where an international tribunal would be located. The supposed flag-State's Consul would then undertake an investigation. If there was a difference of opinion between the Captain of the cruiser and the Consul, then the international tribunal would consider the case. While the status of the seized ship would be considered by this mixed tribunal, its captain and crew were to be tried by their respective municipal systems. Finally, the French Counter-proposal called for the creation of an international bureaux which would act as a registry for ships in the zone.[33] On 6 February 1890, the British Delegation responded to the French Counter-proposal in a positive manner, saying that it "merited serious attention" and that it "could probably serve as the basis for effective preventative measures which would receive general applicability in the zone where the trade is taking place."[34] However, it noted with regret that the French Government could not accept "under any circumstances, the reciprocal right to monitor sailing ships in the trade zone"; for its part the British Delegation noted that it could not discuss "proposals which derogated, in any way, from the treaties to which the Queen is party, or the rights which flow from them." Having made the point, the Declaration said that Her Majesty's Government wanted to go as far as possible to reach an understanding with all Powers, and thus was willing to concede that the "right to visit established in the existing treaties be limited to the zone determined [during the Conference], and to limit the exercise of this right to ships of less than 500 tons [i.e.,: tantamount to 'native', African, vessels], as long as this final condition, related to the dimensions of vessels, be submitted to revision if experience shows that a change was necessary." The Declaration went on to say that Great Britain "could

32 Annex 3, Protocol 10, "Déclaration des Plénipotentiaires de France," 20 December 1889, *Actes de la Conférence de Bruxelles (1889–1890)*, p. 153.

33 Annex 4, Protocol 10, "Project de Traité et projet de Règlement présentés par les Pléinpotentiaires de France" *Actes de la Conférence de Bruxelles (1889–1890)*, p. 154.

34 Annex 5, Protocol 10, "Déclaration des Plénipotentiaires de la Grande-Bretagne," 6 February 1890, *Actes de la Conférence de Bruxelles (1889–1890)*, p. 159.

not make these great concessions if the Conference, for its part, did not consent to adopt the strict regulations suggested in the French Counter-proposal, with a look to preventing, within the limits of the zone, the usurpation or abuse of flags of all the signatory States."[35] In light of these proposals, the British Declaration stated that it probably made sense to drop the ideal of an international tribunal as its bilateral network had attached to it an already established network of mixed commissions. Finally, the Declaration expressed itself in favour of an international bureau as proposed by France.

The Parties having made plain their positions, it was left to the only international jurists attending the Brussels Conference to step into the breach, though hesitantly, to mediate a solution. The eminent international lawyer, Fyodor Martens benefited from the fact that, as a Russian plenipotentiaries, he was seen as a disinterested party where issues of slavery in Africa and the slave trade at sea were concerned. Martens prepared a report and draft articles which later were "entered into the General Act without major modification."[36] In his Report, Martens stated that the more he studied the British and French proposals, the "more I became convinced that there did not exist between them any fundamental contradictions."[37] At the same time he acknowledged Great Britain's century worth of experience in suppressing the slave trade at sea; but noted his belief that the conditions in which the trade persisted had changed. The trade was now exclusively taking place in East Africa, by means of indigenous boats, in a region where the near entirety of the coast was either under the sovereignty or the protection of European Powers. As such, there was a real possibility for the Powers to work collectively on land and at sea to end the slave trade. With this in mind, Martens laid out draft articles that would become part of the General Act; that took into consideration the various components of the British and French proposals, and expressed them both as over-arching principles and practical rules.[38] A contemporary French jurist, Henry Queneuil, wrote of Martens' mediation work, in glowing terms: "thus the different principles found themselves reconciled without having compromised the efficacy of the repression of the slave trade by sea. At the same time, a

35 *Id.*, p. 60.

36 Queneuil, *op. cit.*, n. 26, p. 136.

37 Annex 7, Protocol 10, "Rapport de M. de Martens, second Plénipotentiaire de Russie, sur les projets précédents," 17 February 1890, *Actes de la Conférence de Bruxelles (1889–1890)*, p. 169.

38 See Annex 6, Protocol 10, "Projet de Traité et project de Règlement codifiant les projets précédents et préséntés par les Plénipotentiaires de Russie," 17 February 1890, *Actes de la Conférence de Bruxelles (1889–1890)*, p. 169.

latent and disquieting conflict between France and Great Britain which had existed for fifty years was put to rest."[39]

The provisions regarding the Repression of the Slave Trade at Sea make up Chapter III of the General Act of the Brussels Conference relative to the African Slave Trade, which was signed on 2 July 1890. The General Act defines a maritime zone which centred on the high seas contiguous to the East Coast of Africa and included both the Red Sea and the Persian Gulf. It acknowledge a right to visit, search, and detain, in established treaties and that these treaties remained in force "in so far as they are not modified by the present General Act."[40] The two major British concessions were also included, namely that the States agreed that all such rights to visit could only transpire in the newly established maritime zone, and this only with respect to "vessels of less than 500 tons burthen."[41] Article 42 introduced the modified regime for visits under the General Act, allowing for such visit to suppress the slave trade and to verify the propriety of the use of the flag:

> When an officers in command of a vessels of war of any of the Signatory Powers have reason to believe that a vessel of less than 500 tons burthen, found in the above-mentioned zone, is engaged in the Slave Trade, or is guilty of the fraudulent use of a flag, they may proceed to the verification of the ship's papers.

Having done so, Article 46 notes:

> If, in carrying out the supervision provided for in the preceding Articles, the officer in command of the cruiser is convinced that an Act of Slave Trade has been committed on board during the passage, or that irrefutable proofs exist against the captain, or fitter-out, to justify a charge of fraudulent use of the flag, or fraud, or the participation in the Slave Trade, he shall take the detained vessel to the nearest port of the zone where there is a competent authority to the Power whose flag has been used.

In such circumstances, a Consul or the commander of a man-of-war of the same nationality as the suspected ship could be considered the competent

39 Queneuil, *op. cit.*, n. 26, p. 148.

40 Article 24, General Act of the Brussels Conference relative to the African Slave Trade, 2 July 1890, Sir E. Hertslet, *The Map of Africa by Treaty*, Vol. 2, 1967, p. 499.

41 'Burthen' refers to the carrying capacity or load of a ship.

authority to examine and determine the status of the seized vessel. In Martens' Report, he highlighted the fact that having dropped the proposal for an international tribunal, it was essential to have a means to settling disputes which might arise as between the flag State and these involved in the capture, and thus inserted a compromissory clause which envisioned the possible appointment of an arbitration panel.[42]

Beyond the provisions regarding right to visit, the 1890 General Act provides, at Article 27, a provision which remains, mutatis mutandis, operative under the 1982 Law of the Sea Convention: "Any slave who may have taken refuge on board a ship of war flying the flag of one of the Signatory Powers, shall be immediately and definitively freed." Finally, an International Bureau was to be established in Zanzibar – the first inter-governmental entity to be situated on the African continent – to gather information, including the registering of vessels, but more generally, to "centralize all documents and information of a nature to facilitate the repression of the Slave Trade in the maritime zone."[43]

On the basis of the 1890 General Act, as Queneuil noted, it looked like the 'latent and disquieting conflict' had been put to rest. But had it? Professor Miers writes that an "unforeseen and serious difficulty"[44] arose as the French ambassador in Brussels wrote to the Belgian Foreign Minister, stating:

> I have the honour to confirm to your Excellency the information which I gave *viva voce* yesterday to Baron Lambermont [the President of the Conference]; after a prolonged discussion occupying the sitting of the 24th and 25th of last month, the French Chamber of Deputies decided to suspend the authorization to ratify the General Act [...]. His Majesty's Government must be aware of the part which the Cabinet had taken in this grave debate, and it was certainly been from no want of effort on their part that the conclusion was not entirely different. Your Excellency is further aware that the consideration which weighed with the Chamber

---

42 See Article 54, *op. cit* n. 40. Note that the mixed commission which had, by the 1870s, become a solely British affairs were subsumed into the domestic jurisdiction. For Great Britain this meant either the relevant Supreme Court of the Colony or an Admiralty Court. See *Documents relatives à la Répression de la Traite des Esclaves publiés en execution des Articles LXXXI et suivants de l'Act Général de Bruxelles*; 1892, p. 260.

43 See Article 77, *id.* For the work of the International Bureau in Zanzibar see: *Documents relatives à la Répression de la Traite des Esclaves publiés en execution des Articles LXXXI et suivants de l'Act Général de Bruxelles*; from 1892 to 1913 under the heading "*Bureau international maritime de Zanzibar*".

44 Miers, *op. cit.*, n. 7, p. 293.

> were derived from the nature of the measures to be taken for the repression of the traffic at sea.[45]

Despite the fact that the prestigious Institute of International Law came on side in 1891, and said that the General Act did not reinstitute an expansive right to visit and that the Act addressed the concerns of France, it thus expressed its hope that all States which had been present in Brussels would come to ratify the Act;[46] the issue of French ratification remained a question mark. That question mark was lifted on 2 January 1892 – at least partially – when France deposited its instrument of ratification, with the following proviso:

> His Excellency [the French ambassador to Belgian] declared that the President of the Republic, in his ratification of the General Act of Brussels, has provisionally reserved, for an ulterior understanding, Articles XXI, XXII, and XXIII, and Articles XLII to LXI.[47]

In essence, France agreed to the General Act but modified its undertaking by excluding itself from the provisions related to visitation. Articles 21, 22, and 23, as noted earlier, related to the *ratione loci* of the treaty; to the rights established in previous treaties now to be applicable solely in the conventional zone; and to the limitation, *ratione personae*, of the treaty to ships of less than 500 tons. Articles 42 to 61 set out the modalities of the regime of visitation within the General Act. The clause "provisionally reserved, for an ulterior understanding" was interesting, as the French legislature had determined that France would be

---

45 See "France," Protocol of a Meeting held at the Foreign Office at Brussels, respecting the Ratification of the General Act of the Brussels Conference, 2 July 1891, Hertslet, *op. cit.*, n. 40, pp. 521–522.

46 Institut de Droit International, "Voeu motive de l'Institut tendant à la ratification intégrale de l'Act general de Bruxelles," *Annuaire de l'Institut de Droit International*, Vol. 11, 1889–1892, p. 269.

47 See "France," Protocol of a Meeting held at Brussels, in the Foreign Office, respecting the Exchange of Ratification of the General Act of the Brussels Conference, 2 July 1892, Hertslet, *op. cit.*, n. 40, pp. 521–522. France further modified its reservation in light of the fact that Belgian – as depositor of the General Act – point out that obligations stemming from Articles 30 to 41, regarding the authorisation of native vessels to fly a State's flag where only applicable in the zone established by Articles 21 to which it had reserved. France responded by declaring that its east coast possessions would indeed be part of that regime, noting that it "will be spontaneously applied by the Government of the Republic in the territory of Obock [Djibouti], and, according to necessity in the Island of Madagascar and the Comoros." *Id.*

"governed by the stipulations and arrangements now in force," that is to say, the 1867 Naval Instructions.[48] The French reservation having been accepted by the other Parties; the General Act came into force on 2 April 1892.

Despite Professor Miers concluding that little had been lost because the French "government agreed to abide by the regulations of 1867 and to put into operation the new rules for the issue of French colours";[49] and despite the French jurist Henry Queneuil echoed these sentiments in saying that the differences between the General Act and the 1867 Instructions were not great,[50] the French limited acceptance of the 1890 General Act did provide at least one means by which slave traders could avoid visits by hosting the French flag; though this would ultimately be put to a stop by the Permanent Court of Arbitration in its 1905 *Muscat Dhows* case.

In that case, the Panel considered whether the status of subjects of the Sultan of Muscat who had been granted the status of *protégé* by France in 1844 (that status having been modified in 1863) – and thus benefited from the protection of France and, on the seas, by the French flag – was limited by the obligations undertaken by France as a result of the 1890 Brussels Act. The issuance of papers authorising dhows to fly French flags had been, it had been noted, had meant that those 'native vessels' had been "commonly employed in the slave trade."[51] It is Award, the arbitrators pointed to Article 32 of the 1890 General Act which set out the conditions under which native vessels was to be granted authority to fly a flag. This included owners or outfitters "furnishing proof that they enjoy a good reputation, and especially that they have never been condemned for acts of slave trade."[52] The Court determined that after France had ratified the Brussels Act (1892), it was not allowed to "authorize vessels belonging to subjects of His Highness the Sultan of Muscat" to fly the French flag, except on conditions that their owners or fitters-out had established that they had been considered and treated by France as her *protégés* before the year 1863. It further determined, with regard to another question, that the "authorization to fly the French flag can not be transmitted or

48 *Id.*

49 Miers, *op. cit.*, n. 7, p. 293. For the 1867 Instructions see *Documents relatives à la Répression de la Traite des Esclaves publiés en execution des Articles LXXXI et suivants de l'Act Général de Bruxelles*, 1892, pp. 272–274.

50 Queneuil, *op. cit.*, n. 26, p. 189.

51 See Syllabus, "The Muscat Dhows Case between France and Great Britain," James Brown Scott (ed.), *The Hague Court Reports*, 1916, p. 93.

52 See Article 32, General Act of the Brussels Conference relative to the African Slave Trade, 2 July 1890, Hertslet, *op. cit.*, n. 40, p. 500.

transferred to any other person or than other dhow, even if belonging to the same owner."[53] In essence, the Permanent Court of Arbitration determined that in this case the slave trade would die a natural death. That subjects of Muscat might well be able to benefit from the protection of the French flag, but only in their lifetime (or that of their precious dhow) had they received such protection some forty-years previous. Taking into consideration the life expectance in early twentieth century Muscat and that of 'native vessels', the Permanent Court of Justice had, at the behest of Great Britain, sounded the death-knell of the slave trade a sea.

Conclusion

While the debate about the motives of Great Britain, regarding its attempts to suppress the slave trade remain lively today; what can not be disputed is that Great Britain did, in fact, lead and shoulder most of the responsibility in ending the slave trade and slavery itself. For Great Britain, the main stumbling block was not the abolition of slavery *per se*, as there persisted throughout the known world a growing ideological aversion to both slavery and the slave trade. Instead, the Grotian notion of the freedom of the seas ran counter to the main means by which Great Britain sough to suppress the slave trade: the wish to create a mutual right to visit ships on the high seas suspected of being involved in the slave trade.

Today, we know that while the freedom of the high seas remains as a guiding principle of the 1982 United Nations Convention on the Law of the Sea, that freedom in not absolute and does, in fact, allow for a right to visit ships suspected of being engaged in the slave trade.[54] The provisions of the Law of the Sea dealing with slavery are very much a reflection of the solution mediated by Fyodor de Martens in Brussels in 1890. Despite France failing to join the regime regarding visitation as envisioned by the 1890, Martens had ushered in the

53 Award of the arbitration tribunal appointed to decide on the question of the grant of the French flag to Muscat dhows, 8 August 1905, James Brown Scott (ed.), *The Hague Court Reports*, 1916, pp. 99 and 100.

54 See Part VII (High Seas) of the 1982 United Nations Convention on the Law of the Sea. That the freedom of the seas has always been qualified, see Hugo Grotius, *De Jure Belli ac Pacis* Libri Tres, (Carnegie' Classics of International Law series, Vol. 2), 1925, pp. 190–191; Hugo Grotius, *De Jur Praedae Commentarius* (Carnegie' Classics of International Law series, Vol 22), 1950, pp. 226–255; and W E Bulter, "Grotius and the Law of the Sea" in Hedley Bull *et al.* (eds) *Hugo Grotius and International Relations*, 1995; pp. 209–220.

framework for the international suppression of the slave trade which would then find voice through the 1926 League of Nations convention and the 1956 United Nations conventions suppressing slavery and the slave trade. As a jurist from a disinterested party, Martens was requested to undertake the specific task of mediated a dispute which had been in existence for more than fifty years. It is to his credit that he was able to convince the diplomats in Brussels to agree to the Final Act. Thought France's *Assemblé Nationale* would opt-out of the system devised by Martens, the provisions of the 1982 Law of the Sea Convention are testimony that Martens solution is the one that survives and is thus one more tenant of the legacy of one of the greatest international jurist of all time.

CHAPTER 4

Slavery and the League of Nations: Ethiopia as a Civilised Nation*

In 1949, the United Nations International Law Commission quietly decided to "refrain from using the expression 'civilized countries'"[1] in its deliberations. An era had apparently died away, only to be resurrected as part of the discourse of the post-September 11, 2001 United States' 'War on Terror'. Despite the resurgence of rhetorical use of 'civilisation', the notion of 'civilised nation' never truly left the stage of international relations, as it remains on the books today, a part of international law. Article 38(1) of the Statute of the International Court of Justice mandates that the International Court apply international law from three sources, not only treaty and customary law, but also: (c) "the general principles of law recognized by civilised nations." This provision is a much needed window onto a bygone era, as some have said an embarrassing reminder that international law acted as an instrument of imperial design. Much needed, as at the time such a designation as 'civilised nations' would have appeared neutral and benign. This begs the questions: Is and does international law remain, structurally, biased in favour of the West and its informal empire, while couched in more benevolent, universal language of say, human rights?

This article considers an instance of the transition from the 'law of Christian nations' and the 'public law of Europe' of the nineteenth century to 'international law' of the twentieth century wherein non-European States were allowed to join the international *qua* European system of international relations on the basis of a fluctuating rule of 'civilisation' dictated to by European colonial powers. The standard of civilisation which was applied in the Ethiopian context,

---

* This chapter originally appeared as Jean Allain, "Slavery and the League of Nations: Ethiopia as a Civilised Nation," *Journal of the History of International Law*, Vol. 8, 2006, p. 213. Copyright © Brill |Nijhoff, 2006.

The author wishes to acknowledge the receipt of a Overseas Conference Grant from the British Academy which allowed for the presentation of this article as a paper at the Conference of the European Society of International Law, at Université Paris 1, in May 2006.

1 For the International Law Commission, see Gerrit Gong, *The Standard of 'Civilization' in International Society*, 1984, p. 90. For the embarrassing nature of Article 38(1) see Gong, at p. 69, where he writes: "It is an embarrassing anachronism to some that Article 38(1) of the statute of the International Court of Justice still directs the Court to apply the general principles of law recognized by civilized nations in such disputes as are submitted to it."

 | DOI 10.1163/9789004279896_006

upon which its admission to the League of Nations was predicated and later used to justify Italian aggression, was the abolition of slavery and the slave trade on its territory. The Ethiopian experience is considered here as a vehicle to study the emergence of slavery as the 'first' human right given voice internationally; the manner in which the League of Nations, having established the abolition of slavery and the slave trade as a criteria of 'civilisation' moved to codify it; and finally, the manner in which Ethiopia, though brought into the fold of the League of Nations, was denied true recognition as a part of the 'community of civilised nations' as European concerns trumped the Covenant as Italy was allowed to once more take on the 'savages' who previously – at Adwa in 1896 – had defeated it.

Of Civilised Nations

The notion of 'civilisation' in international relations was used as a bridge by which a public law developed in Europe among Christian princes was promulgated throughout the world in universal terms. It was this standard which in the late nineteenth century and early twentieth century allowed European States to accommodate those States it could not conquer, in their quest for Empire.[2] Yet, for those States of non-European stock which were accepted into the club of 'civilised nations', sovereign equality did not truly exist. As Martti Koskenniemi writes, there laid at the heart of the notion of 'civilisation' a paradox: "if there was no external standard for civilisation, then everything depended on what Europe approved," and thus: "In order to attain equality, the non-Europeans community must accept Europe as master – but to accept a master was proof that one was not equal."[3] This quote develops a central tenet of the notion of civilisation which Koskenniemi points to: "No stable standard of civilisation emerged to govern entry into the 'community of international law'."[4] For Gerry Simpson, "Civilisation was a usefully elusive term. […] the standard of civilisation was a way of imposing a particular set of values on the international legal order. Failure to meet these values meant

2 See generally, Anthony Pagden, *Lords of all the World: Ideology of Empire in Spain, Britain, and France c.1500–c.1800*, 1995; as well as Niall Ferguson, *Empire: How Britain Made the Modern World* (2004); Henry Kamen, *How Spain Became a World Power 1492–1763* (2003); and C.R. Boxer, *The Portuguese Seaborne Empire, 1415–1825* (1969).

3 Martti Koskenniemi, *The Gentle Civilizer of Nations; The Rise and Fall of International Law 1870–1960* (2002), pp. 135–136.

4 *Id.*, p. 135.

exclusion or unequal sovereignty"[5] Gerrit Gong, in his seminal 1984 study *The Standard of 'Civilization' in International Society*, defines 'civilisation' in general terms, as "an expression of the assumptions, tacit and explicit, used to distinguish those that belong to a particular society from those that do not. [... By] definition, those who fulfil the requirements of a particular society's standard of civilization are brought inside its circle of 'civilized' members, while those who do not so conform are left outside as 'not civilized' or possibly 'uncivilised'."[6]

'Civilisation' as a concept, it should be made plain, become fundamental to a changing international order, one that was European in origin but sought to be universal in application. The distinction between so-called 'civilised'; 'semi-civilised' or 'barbaric'; and 'uncivilised' or 'savage' States was at once a manifestation of a State's ability to counter, in limited terms, European encroachment and a recognition of a State's legal standing internationally. For those States where outright conquest did not transpire; European extraterritoriality in the guise of unequal treaties, capitulations, and protectorate regimes were put into place. For Brett Bowden, the "importance of the classical standard of civilization can not be underestimated" specifically with regard to "the violent European civilizing mission that it helped give rise to."[7] Antony Anghie, for his part, points to the use of the apparently benign term 'civilisation' as being used to justify the continued expansion of the European colonial project: "vocabulary of international law, far from being neutral, or abstract, is mired in this history of subordination and extinguishing alien cultures." This is so, as Anghie notes, in reference to the work of Francisco de Vitoria:

> European practices are posited as universally applicable norms with which the colonial peoples must conform if they are to avoid sanctions and achieve full membership. Vitoria's jurisprudence demonstrates, furthermore that the construction of the barbarian as both within the reach of the law and yet outside its protection creates an object against which sovereignty may express its fullest powers by engaging in an unmediated and unqualified violence, justified as leading to conversion, salvation, civilization. Non-European peoples have been continuously characterised as

5 Gerry Simpson, *Great Powers and Outlaw States: Unequal Sovereigns in the International Legal Order* (2004), pp. 243–244.

6 See Gerrit Gong, *op. cit.* n. 1, p. 3. Note also Mark Salter, *Barbarians & Civilizations in International Relations* (2002).

7 Brett Bowden, "The Colonial Origins of International Law. European Expansion and the Classic Standard of Civilization," *Journal of History of International Law*, Vol. 7, 2005, p. 1.

> the barbarians compelling the further extension of international law's ambit.[8]

Where international law is concerned, the notion of 'civilisation' was quite simply, a criteria of State recognition. Gong, makes clear, having considered international instruments and conducted a genealogical study of the evolution of the concept of civilisation in the writings of leading contemporary international law publicists of the late nineteenth and early twentieth century, that the notion of civilisation, although rather fluid, was very much a principle of public international law. For his part, Georg Schwarzenberger, writing in 1955, laid out the characteristics of the principle:

> The test whether a State was civilised and, thus entitled to full recognition as an international personality was, as a rule, merely whether its government was sufficiently stable to undertake binding commitments under international law and whether it was able and willing to protect adequately the life, liberty and property of foreigners. In a multitude of treaties these minimum standards were codified into rules of international customary law.[9]

For his part, Gong outlines the five tenets of what was required to be considered 'civilised'. A State would have to:

(1) ensures basic rights: life, property, freedom to travel, commerce, religion;
(2) had an organized political structure and the ability to act in self-defence;
(3) accepted the norms of international law;
(4) had the ability to carry diplomatic relations with other States; and

More subjectively, but of specific importance to this study:

(5) a 'civilized' state by and large conforms to the accepted norms and practices of the 'civilized' international society, e.g., suttee, polygamy, and slavery were considered 'uncivilized', and therefore unacceptable.

---

8 Antony Anghie, "Francisco de Vitoria and the Colonial Origins of International Law," in Eve Darian-Smith and Peter Fitzpatrick (eds.), *Laws of the Postcolonial*, 1999, pp. 103–104. Anghie elaborates his views on sovereignty and the exclusion of the uncivilised in Chapter 2 of Antony Anghie, *Imperialism, Sovereignty and the Making of International Law* (2005).

9 Georg Schwarzenberger, "The Standard of Civilisation in International Law," *Current Legal Problems*, Vol. 17, 1955, p. 220.

Having elaborated these tenets, Gong, however, remained cautious, seeing in the incorporation of 'civilisation' in international law a fundamental problem:

> the standard was never much more than a fairly blunt legal instrument. Even after it emerged as an explicit legal concept, the standard was still subject to the admixture of contrasting elements – political and legal, subjective and objective, explicit and implicit – associated with any doctrine of recognition.[10]

It should be said that this elasticity of the concept of civilisation was most evident in regard to legacy of the League of Nations' actions involving Ethiopia. The standard of civilisation that was used in this instance was the rather slippery "norms and practices of the 'civilised' international society," manifest in the outlawing of slavery and the slave trade. This was so as Ethiopia had, by the 1920s, met the first four tenets noted by Gong; but, its consolidation of effective control over territory from the mid-eighteenth century onwards had come as a result of warfare, which had, as a by-product, the production of slaves as prisoners *qua* spoils of war.

Slavery and the Consolidation of the Ethiopian Empire

The consolidation of the Ethiopian Empire was a long process which transpired during the second half of the nineteenth and first half of the twentieth century. Like German and Italian unification during the 1850s and 1860s, Ethiopian State-building was predicated on belligerent co-opting of the peripheries: the requirement of peaceful submission or armed conquest. In the Ethiopian context, the iconic photo of the last King of Kafa, Tato Gaki Sherocho, bound in chains after his defeat in 1897, speaks to the consolidation of modern Ethiopia.[11] The modern move to unify Ethiopia was brought about by Kasa Haylu, who pacified much of the country north of the Rift Valley. Having learnt his military skills through the repulsing of Egyptian troops from his fiefdom on the Ethio-Sudanese frontier in the 1830s,

---

10 *Id.* Schwarzenberger, however, continues with the following caveat:

> At the same time, the distinction between civilised and non-civilised communities served less disinterested purposes of Western imperialism and colonialism whenever it was opportune to treat communities on the fringes of the expanding Western world on a footing other than that of sovereign States.

11 See Bahru Zewde, *A History of Modern Ethiopia 1955–1991* (2001), p. 67.

Kasa – upon becoming Emperor Tewodros II (1855–1868), King of Kings of Ethiopia, in 1855 – turned his attention to the southern half of Ethiopia, in essence moving the country's centre of gravity southwards and away from its Nilitic sources. It was during this southern campaign that Tewodros "made the first attempt to put an end to the slave-trade which had become endemic in Ethiopian society."[12]

The ever-present Egyptian threat to Ethiopia emerged again in the early 1870s, when the importance of the Horn of Africa grew as a result of the opening of the Suez Canal and Egypt's ambitions over the Nile Valley spread. Egypt's Khedive Ismail, having subjugated Sudan, justified his expansion into Ethiopia "in terms of eradication of the slave-trade."[13] Yet, this adventure was ultimately unsuccessful, as the Ethiopian 'victories' at Gundat and Gura in 1875 and 1876 "hastened Ismail's downfall and the subsequent British occupation of Egypt."[14] These victories in battle, however were not consolidated in peace, as the Emperor Yohannes (1872–1889) was faced with a further threat from the north, this time from the Sudanese Mahdist movement. The cooperation undertaken with the British to suppress the Mahdist was to have a long-term price for Ethiopia as, by way of the 1885 Adwa Peace Treaty settling the war with Egypt, Britain gained what is now the Eritrean capital of Massawa which it shortly thereafter handed it over to Italy. As for Yohannes' attempts at nation-building, these were of limited success, as he sought to consolidate his power base through a "loosely united Ethiopia, with autonomous regional rulers under an emperor exercising benevolent political suzerainty."[15]

It was left to Empire Menelik II (1889–1913), therefore, to consolidate the Ethiopian Empire as a sovereign State. "It was to be," historian Bahru Zewde writes, Menelik's "main claim to historical distinction that he presided over the realization of an idea that had first been kindled in the fiery mind of Tewodros. Yet the final result bore little resemblance to the initial dream."[16] This was so, as Tewodros had sought a rather modest Nilitic empire, one in line with a previous medieval incarnation; whereas Menelik created the Ethiopia of today, one which straddles equally both sides of the Rift Valley. Where Menelik's

---

12 *Id.*, p. 34.

13 *Id.*, p. 50. Note, however, that R.W. Beachey writes: "Ismail was soon caught up in grand plans for territorial expansion, however, and he had little time for an anti-slave trade campaign." R.W. Beachey, *The Slave Trade in East Africa* (1976), p. 130.

14 Zewde, *op. cit.* n. 11, p. 53.

15 *Id.*, p. 60.

16 *Id.*

imperial design fell short, however, was with regard to access to the sea, as this was the era of the 'Scramble for Africa' wherein European States first made claims to the African coastal regions before moving inland. Ethiopia was thus made contiguous to Italian (Eritrea and Italian Somaliland); French (Djibouti); and British (British Somaliland) territories on the Horn of Africa. It was left to the Italians, late-comers to Empire, to lay claim to Ethiopia as a colony. As a result of a dispute over the interpretation of the 1889 Wuchale Treaty of Amity (as regards its Italian and Amharic versions), Italy claimed protectorate status over Ethiopia, which was duly recognised by European powers. However, Menelik, who had refused to accept this interpretation, denounced the Treaty in 1893, having prepared Ethiopia for war. The outcome of the 1896 Battle at Adwa "was a remarkable victory for Menelik, and a complete defeat for his enemies"; the Italians were thus forced to agree "on 26 October, to the Peace Treaty of Addis Ababa, which annulled the Treaty of Wuchale and recognized the absolute independence of Ethiopia."[17]

The Ethiopian success at Adwa, the first defeat of a European Power during the colonial period and the only complete defeat of such a Power in the African context had many a repercussion. Most important for Ethiopia, in regard to its international relations, was the consolidation of its territory vis-à-vis its European neighbours, brought on by European "apprehension of the expansive potentialities of post-Adwa Ethiopia."[18] Thus, in just over a decade, between 1897 and 1908, not only were boundaries delimitated on the Horn of Africa, but also with the British in regard to Sudan and British East Africa (Kenya).[19] With respect to internal affairs, Menelik sought to modernise the Empire, he "advanced ideas of social reform, and decreed the abolition of slavery."[20] But as Jones and Monroe note in their 1935 study: Menelik's reforms "would have been more effective had he personally supervised their execution; as it was, he was usually too busy consolidation his frontiers."[21] In his autobiography, Emperor Haile Sellasie (1930–1974) considered his predecessors' measures in regard to slavery and noted that slavery itself had "remained firmly established by custom." "Consequently," the Emperor – writing in exile in 1937 – stated that:

---

17 A. Abu Boahen (ed.), *Africa under Colonial Domination 1880–1935*, UNESCO General History of Africa, Vol. 7, 1990, p. 125.

18 Zewde, *op. cit.* n. 11, p. 113.

19 For a discussion of these treaties see W.B. Stern, "The Treaty Background of the Italo-Ethiopian Dispute," *The American Journal of International Law*, Vol. 30, pp. 196–198.

20 A.H.M. Jones and Elizabeth Monroe, *A History of Ethiopia* (1935), p. 156.

21 *Id.*

> Emperors Theodore (Tewodros), Yohannes, and Menelik, who reigned in Ethiopia from [1855–1913], had promulgated decrees against the sale and purchase of slaves in Ethiopia. But because at the time it was not customary to set up special offices for work of this kind, their intentions remained unaccomplished, as it was impossible to observe and enforce the decree on account of the vastness of the country.[22]

A more detached view which has been expressed regarding Ethiopia, during the reign of these three Emperors, was that Ethiopians were not *per se* against slavery, that "the country was surrounded on all sides by slave raiders and traders," and that no concerted effort was ever made to seek to end the trade or slavery. The failure to act resulted from the following:

> The fact that Ethiopia managed to maintain its independence throughout the nineteenth century and that Europeans were not involved in its internal affairs, left the rulers to a large degree free from outside pressure to suppress the slave trade, even if they opposed it personally. They realized that they lacked both the power and the popular support to accomplish the task. For the same reason, they had no wish to abolish the institution of slavery.[23]

Ultimately, by the time of Haile Sellasie's ascendance to power as the Regent, Ras Tafari Makonnen, in 1916, Ethiopia had consolidated its external borders but had yet to effectuate control over its territory and actively seek the suppression of slavery and the slave trade. The extent to which slavery was not truly an issue in the Ethiopian context might best be exemplified by the short-lived reign of Lej Iyyasu (1913–1916) who had personally gone on a slave-raiding expedition in 1912, "a most nefarious campaign of his career. Against the Dizi in south-western Ethiopia, which ended up with the enslavement of tens of thousands of the inhabitants"![24]

---

22 Emperor Haile Sellasie I, *The Autobiography of Emperor Haile Sellasie I: My Life and Ethiopia's Progress, 1892–1937* (1976), p. 80.

23 Alice Moore-Harell, "Economic and Political Aspects of the Slave Trade in Ethiopia and Sudan in the Second Half of the Nineteenth Century," *The International Journal of African Historical Studies*, Vol. 32, 1999, pp. 416 and 421.

24 Zewde, *op. cit.* n. 11, p. 122. Pankhurst puts the number at 40,000; writing that "half of whom died en route [to Addis] of smallpox, dysentery, hunger and fatigue." See Richard Pankhurst, *Economic History of Ethiopia: 1800–1935*, p. 107.

1923 'Abyssinian' Admission to the League of Nations[25]

Ethiopia's admission to the League of Nations came as an attempt to shield itself from possible outside encroachment from the British, French or Italians, who had agreed in 1906 by way of a tripartite instrument to 'spheres of influence' over it.[26] The acute nature of that threat was revealed in a 1922 Memorandum to the Council of the League of Nations by Sir Frederick Lugard, a member of the Permanent Mandates Commission which pointed to either the three Powers taking control of Ethiopia or, better yet, the League of Nations. Lugard was considered one of the leading experts on issues of slavery of the day and had been very much "in the public eye, taking an active part in the controversy over Ethiopian slavery."[27] In that well-circulated Memorandum, Lugard argued that, as a result of the inability of Ethiopia to suppress the slave trade, it should be placed under a scheme which "would be little different in principle from the B class Mandates. Abyssinia would be recognised as having reached a stage where 'its existence as a independent nation can provisionally be recognised, subject to the rendering of Administrative advice and assistance' – not by a Mandatory, but by the League itself."[28] Where Lugard's calculations in regard to Ethiopia went wrong, however, was in regard to that State's willingness to apply for admission to the League of Nations.[29] Lugard wrote less than a year before Ethiopian entry into the League of Nations that "Abyssinia has not applied, and since her chief desire is to avoid any foreign interference in her

25 Abyssinia is considered a pejorative term by Ethiopians, but was utilized internationally up to, and including, much of the period of Ethiopia's membership in the League of Nations.

26 See Gong, *op. cit.* n. 1, p. 123. This concern for outside encroachment was also manifest in 1918, when "rumours were rife that the victorious allies might attempt to establish a mandate over Ethiopia." See Suzanne Miers, "Britain and the Suppression of Slavery in Ethiopia," Taddese Beyene (ed.), *Proceedings of the Eight International Conference of Ethiopian Studies*, Vol. 2, 1989, p. 253. The 1906 instrument is the *Agreement between the United Kingdom, France and Italy, Respecting the Importation of Arms and Ammunitions into Abyssinia*, 13 December 1906; reproduced in *The American Journal of International Law*, Vol. 1, 1907, pp. 230–231.

27 Miers, *Slavery in the Twentieth Century: The Evolution of a Global Problem* (2003), p. 103.

28 Frederick Lugard, *Slavery in Abyssinia*, 6 November 1922. p. 10. See League of Nations, Mandates, *The Question of Slavery*, 1922, LofN Doc. (R.61) 24628/23252.

29 Note that Pankhurst states that Ethiopia had been interested in joining the League of Nations from its inception, stating: "Ethiopia was prevented from joining the League of Nations at its inception in 1919 because of the existence of slavery." Pankhurst, *op. cit.*, n. 24, p. 112.

affairs – least of all the exposure to scandal – she is not likely to do so."[30] Despite this threat from the League of Nations itself, Ethiopia couched its wish to join the League in terms of an isolated Christian State surrounded by Muslim "heathens," thus seeking a collective security umbrella and wishing to maintain the peaceful co-existence it currently enjoyed with its neighbours.[31]

It might also be noted that Ethiopia's attempted entry into the League coincided with the wishes of the British Anti-Slavery Society, which sought to internationalise issues of the repression of slavery but could not focus on an independent Ethiopia – which it considered the main culprit of the slave trade – as long as it was not a member of the League of Nations.[32] This was to have important ramifications, as France considered that the agitations of the Anti-Slavery Society was a prelude to British intervention in Ethiopia and thus precipitated its support – or as the Professor of African History, Suzanne Miers, writes "instigation" – of Ethiopia's admission into the League of Nations.[33] The wish to join the League was, of course, something which was not forced upon Ethiopia, but was something it sought, as:

> [p]rominent Ethiopians, conscious of the British press campaign and the quixotic crusade of the anti-slavery societies, were alarmed that the league assembly due to convene in September 1923 would adopt measures restricting Ethiopian independence. Equally suspicious of Britain and Italy, the government in Addis Ababa had no option but France.[34]

The fact that the Anti-Slavery Society supported Ethiopia's admission should not be confused with British support of Ethiopia's bid, as the British Government "strongly opposed Ethiopian admission to the League, believing that her application was a French plot to flood the country with arms on the pretext that they were needed to fight slavery."[35] Further, Miers' relates that the "British were outraged. They thought Ethiopia was 'unfit' for membership and that its admission would mean that in the future there would be 'no ground for

---

30 Lugard, *op. cit.*, n. 28, p. 4.

31 League of Nations, *Request for Admission to the League of Nations from Abyssinia*, LofN Doc. A.55.923.VI, 6 September 1923. The Ethiopian Note is dated 12 August 1923.

32 Miers, *Slavery in the Twentieth Century*, *op. cit.*, n. 27, p. 73.

33 Miers, "Britain and the Suppression of Slavery," *op. cit.* n. 26, p. 256. This assertion is also repeated in: Miers, "Slavery and the Slave Trade as International Issues 1890–1939," *Slavery and Abolition*, Vol. 19, 1998, p. 25.

34 See Antoinette Iadarola, "Ethiopia's Admission into the League of Nations: An Assessment of Motives," *The International Journal of African Historical Studies*, Vol. 8, 1975, p. 614.

35 Miers, "Britain and the Suppression of Slavery…," *op. cit.* n. 26, p. 256.

excluding anybody."[36] This lack of British support for Ethiopia's application was made evident by the British Delegate to the League of Nations, Mr. Wood, when he ventured that there were two conflicting motives to be taken into consideration when contemplating the admission of Ethiopia to the League:

> on the one hand, the desire to help Abyssinia to raise herself in the scale of civilisation, which it was possible she might do more effectively if she became a Member of the League, and on the other hand, the feeling that the well-being of the League depended on the level of public opinion in each of the Member States. It was most important that [we] should consider very carefully from this point of view whether Abyssinia was in a position to make a worthy contribution to the League.[37]

Ethiopia's request for admission to the League of Nations was considered by the Sixth Committee (Political) of the Assembly of the League of Nations, which delegated that power to a sub-committee to investigate the issue. The Sub-Committee used a questionnaire that had been employed previously when considering other applications to the League. Gerrit Gong writes that the questions were a "codified expression of the standard of 'civilization' and a predecessor in some ways to the [1933] Montevideo Convention" on the Rights and Duties of States.[38] In its Report back to the Sixth Committee, the Sub-Committee dealt summarily with the first three questions:

1. Is Abyssinia's request for admission into the League of Nations in order?
2. Is Abyssinia recognised *de jure* or *de facto*, and by what States?
3. Does the country possess a stable government and well-defined frontiers?

The Sub-Committee noted that questions one and three returned affirmative answers, while question two elicited the following response: "the Sub-Committee notes that Abyssinia is recognised by and has concluded treaties with several Powers."[39] As for the fourth question: "Is it full self-governing?" the

---

36 Miers, *Slavery in the Twentieth Century*, *op. cit.*, n. 27, p. 79.

37 League of Nations, *Record of the Fourth Assembly, Meetings of the Committee, Minutes of the Sixth Committee (Political Questions)*, 19 September 1923, p. 15.

38 See Gong, *op. cit.* n. 1, p. 125.

39 League of Nations, *Record of the Fourth Assembly, Meetings of the Committee, Minutes of the Sixth Committee (Political Questions)*, Report of the Second Sub-Committee of the Sixth Committee, Abyssinia's Application for Admission to the League, Annex 5, 14 September 1923, p. 34.

Sub-Committee noted that it "was unable to determine exactly the extent of the effective control of the central authority over the provinces remote to the capital" but, nevertheless, "is of the opinion that Abyssinia is fully self-governed."[40]

Finally, the fifth question, although couched in general terms, allowed the Assembly to condition Ethiopia's admission to the League of Nations on the suppression of slavery and its willingness to provide any information which the Council of the League might request on the matter. The fifth question reads as follows:

> 5. What have been the acts and declarations of Abyssinia (a) as regards her international obligations, (b) as regards the stipulation of the League with reference to armaments?

Clearly, the question as posed did not point to issues of slavery nor to any international obligation which Ethiopia might have undertaken on the matter, as it was party to neither the 1890 Final Act of the Brussels Conference[41] or the 1919 Treaty of Saint-Germain-en-Laye;[42] those instruments not having been open to its possible accession. Nevertheless, the Sub-Committee noting Ethiopia's good will, proposed that it be required to sign the following Declaration before being considered for admission:

1 1 Abyssinia adheres to the obligations formulated in Article 11, paragraph 1, of the Convention of Saint Germain-en-Laye on September 10th, 1919, amending the General Act of Berlin dated February 26th, 1885, and the General Act and Declaration of Brussels dated July 2nd, 1890.

2 Abyssinia, recognizing as binding the system at present established with regard to the importation of arms and ammunition, undertakes to conform

40 *Id.*

41 The 1889–90 Brussels Conference dealt with arms agreement and the traffic in spirits but focused, above all else, on the suppression of the African slave trade on land and at sea. Its General Act established a maritime zone of the high seas skirting much of sub-Saharan Africa wherein States had a right to visit, search, and detain ships of a certain tonnage suspected of involvement in the slave trade. See the General Act of the Brussels Conference relative to the African Slave Trade, 2 July 1890, Sir E. Hertslet, *The Map of Africa by Treaty*, Vol. 2, 1967, p. 499.

42 1919 Convention of Saint Germain-en-Laye abrogates the general acts of both the 1885 Berlin and 1889–90 Brussels Conferences but mandated that colonial powers in Africa seek to suppress slavery in all its forms. See Article 11, *Convention revising the General Act of Berlin of 26 February 1885 and the General Act and Declaration of Brussels of 2 July 1890*, 10 September 1919.

> to the principles set forth in the Convention and Protocol signed at Saint Germain-en-Laye on September 10th, 1919, and in particular to the stipulations contained in Article 6 of the said Convention.
>
> 3 Abyssinia declares herself ready now and hereafter to furnish the Council with any information which it may require, and to take into consideration any recommendations which the Council may make with regard to the fulfillment of these obligations, which she recognizes that the League of Nations is concerned.[43]

With regard to the first paragraph of this Declaration, Ethiopia had to agree by way of Article 11 of the Convention of Saint Germain-en-Laye "to watch over the preservation of the native populations and to supervise the improvement of the conditions of their moral and material well-being"; but more specifically, it had to: "endeavour to secure the complete suppression of slavery in all its forms and of the slave trade by land and sea." It was on this basis that Ethiopia's application for admission to the League of Nations rested. For its part, the link between the issue of slavery and 'civilisation' was articulated by the Italian member of the Sixth Committee, Count Bonin-Longare, as he noted that the Sub-Committee:

> had thought it right to ask, and had asked, for one guarantee, namely, that she should accept the principles adopted by the other States with regard to slavery in their most recent contractual form, namely, that found in the Convention of St. Germain. That request contained nothing to wound Abyssinia's susceptibilities, since other States, which had arrived at a higher degree of civilisation, had already consented to undertake special engagements not included in the Covenant.[44]

---

43 This second paragraph was moot; as the Permanent Advisory Commission of the League dealing with issues of disarmament declared that it was "of the opinion that, from a military, naval and air point of view, the present military, naval and air forces of Abyssinia do not constitute an objection to her admission to the League of Nations." League of Nations, Abyssinia's Military, Naval and Air Forces. Opinion of the Permanent Advisory Commission, *Record of the Fourth Assembly, Meetings of the Committee, Minutes of the Sixth Committee (Political Questions)*, Appendix to the Report of the Second Sub-Committee of the Sixth Committee, Abyssinia's Application for Admission to the League, Annex 5, 14 September 1923, p. 35. Article 6 of the 1919 Treaty related to the importation of arms reads in part; "The High Contracting Parties reserve the right to grant, in respect of arms whose use is not prohibited by international law, export licenses to meet the requirements of the Government [...]."

44 League of Nations, *Record of the Fourth Assembly*, *op. cit.* n. 37, p. 18.

Ethiopia's response to this conditional acceptance of membership was sent by telegraph to the Secretary-General of the League of Nations on 20 September 1923, informing him that the "Imperial Government accepts the undertakings proposed by the Sixth Committee and has the honour to inform you that it fully empowers its Delegation to sign such undertakings in its name."[45] This being so, the way was clear for Ethiopia's unanimous admission to the League of Nations on 28 September 1923; Britain, "not wanting to be the lone dissenter [...] accepted the inevitable."[46]

The 1926 Convention to Suppress the Slave Trade and Slavery

The general prohibition against slavery and the slave trade in international law emanates from a wish to consider the issues specifically in regard to Ethiopia. In 1922, Sir Arthur Steel-Maitland, the Delegate from New Zealand submitted two Resolutions to the Assembly of the League of Nations, the first requesting an inquiry into slave-trading in Ethiopia; the second with slavery in Africa, more generally. Ultimately, a single, rather general, resolution was adopted: "to refer to the appropriate Committee the question of the recrudescence of slavery in Africa in order that it be considered and propose the best methods for combating the evil."[47] "This all-embracing resolution," Miers writes, "was intended to disarm suspicions that it was an attack on one country."[48] With Ethiopia's subsequent admission as a Member of the League one year later, the attention of the League of Nations with regard to the issue of slavery turned toward the promotion of an international instrument to end slavery and the slave trade. This call for a treaty flowed from the fact that States had shown little interest in responding to a 1922 questionnaire that had been send out on behalf of the League of Nations by a sub-committee of the Assembly. A year later that sub-committee sought to have the Council of the League "entrust to a competent body the duty of continuing the investigation [of the question of slavery] with a view to obtaining further information on the subject."[49]

45 *Id.*, p. 22.

46 Miers, *Slavery in the Twentieth Century*, *op. cit.* n. 27, p. 79.

47 League of Nations, Motion Proposed by Sir Arthur Steel-Maitland, Delegate for New Zealand, on September 7, 1922, Third Assembly of the League of Nations, 7 September 1922, LofN Doc. 23253 (A/47/1922).

48 Miers, *Slavery in the Twentieth Century*, *op. cit.* n. 27, p. 73.

49 League of Nations, Report of the First Sub-Committee to the Sixth Committee, *Record of the Fourth Assembly, Meetings of the Committees, VI Minutes of the Sixth Committee (Political Questions)*, Annex 10, p. 40. Note that parallel to work of the Assembly, the

As a result, the Council of the League of Nations created, on 14 March 1924, the Temporary Slavery Commission, a body that would exist for only two years but would fundamentally change the emphasis of the League's work in the area of slavery from compiling information, to legislating the international suppression of slavery.[50] The Temporary Slavery Commission, in its final report of 25 July 1925, called on States to consider the "abolition of the legal status of slavery." To that end, it emphasised that the "most important measure for the gradual abolition of slavery is that the status of slavery should no longer be recognised in the eye of the law." Furthermore, the Commission sought to define what it meant by the notion of abolition of the legal status of slavery:

> The 'abolition of the legal status' means that every slave has the right to assert his freedom, without ransom and without going through any formal process of fulfilling any prior condition, by simply leaving his master if he desire to do so. He enjoys and can exercise all the civil rights of a free man – *e.g.*, can sue and be sued in court, can prosecute his master for ill-treatment, and can bequeath and inherit property.[51]

While the Commission gave voice to issues regarding the slave trade, slave-raiding, serfdom, and forced labour in its Report; its most enduring contribution was the call for an international convention on slavery.[52] As Viscount Robert Cecil of Chelwood would later relate, when that Report of the Temporary Slavery Commission was delivered to the Assembly of the League of Nations, the Sixth Committee of the Assembly had picked up on this notion of an

---

Council of the League of Nations instructed the Secretary-General to circulate letters to the League Members "asking them to supply the Council with any information on the existing situation as regards the matter of slavery," which he did in 1922 and 1923. Again, acting at the behest of the Council, the Secretary-General, in 1923, also sought information regarding slavery in "colonial possessions." See League of Nations, Memorandum by the Secretary-General, *The Question of Slavery*, 4 August 1924, LofN Doc. 38385 (A/25/1924).

50 Note that Lugard draws a direct line between slavery in Ethiopia and the establishment of the Temporary Slavery Commission: "The ultimate result – as regards slavery – was the appointment of the present Committee." See League of Nations, Temporary Slavery Commission, *Slavery and Other Systems Restrictive of Liberty*, Memorandum by F.D. Lugard, Annex 3, "Conditions in Abyssinia" May 1925, LofN Doc CTE 36, pp. 1–2.

51 League of Nations, Temporary Slavery Commission, *Report of the Temporary Slavery Commission adopted in the Course of its Second Session, July 13th–25th July*, 1925, 25 July 1925, LofN Doc A.19.1925. VI, p. 3.

52 *Id.*, p. 2.

international instrument and had prepared one for consideration by the Assembly. Viscount Cecil proposed a resolution to the Assembly that the 1925 Draft Convention be sent to Governments and considered with an eye to representatives being given Full Power by the next annual meeting of the Assembly "to sign the Convention with or without alteration."[53]

The 1925 Draft Convention which Viscount Cecil would lay before the Assembly was penned by none other than Sir Frederick Lugard, who had been appointed as a member of the Temporary Slavery Commission. Using the Lugard Draft as a basis, the British Government prepared its own "watered down version of the treaty."[54] That 1925 Draft Protocol was considered by the League of Nations Assembly after having been modified by the "Sixth Committee, with the help of a Sub-Committee and a small Drafting Committee."[55] In presenting the 1925 Draft Convention, Viscount Cecil understood that what had emerged was not as strong as it might otherwise have been, noting to the Assembly that what was on offer was "general principles which might be adopted usefully by all civilized nations as a minimum code in the matter of slavery."[56] By the wording of the Resolution adopted by the Assembly, it was clear that its wish was that States would accept the 1925 Draft Convention in the form it was presented, as far as possible; thus avoiding the need to convene an *ad hoc* conference to negotiate and adopt the instrument. In the course of the subsequent year a number of States made observations in regard to the 1925 Draft Convention and ultimately a revision of its provisions took place within the League of Nations in 1926. For its part, the 1925 Draft Convention was sustained *grosso motto* and found the light of day through its incorporation in the 1926 Convention to Suppress the Slave Trade and Slavery.

Where the actual definition of 'slavery' is concerned, the definition which was adopted in the 1925 British Protocol was modified over the rather short period time between 9 September and 26 September 1925, when the Assembly of the League of Nations adopted the 1925 Draft Convention. As originally conceived by the British Protocol, the definition of slavery read: "is a status in which one person

53 League of Nations, Records of the Sixth Assembly: Text of Debates, *League of Nations Official Journal* (*Special Supplement 33*), Nineteenth Plenary Meeting, 26 September 1925, p. 156.

54 Miers, "Slavery and the Slave Trade," *op. cit.* n. 33, p. 28.

55 League of Nations, Question of Slavery: Report of the Sixth Committee to the Assembly, *League of Nations Official Journal* (*Special Supplement 33*), Annex 29, 26 September 1925, LofN Doc. A.130.1925.VI, p. 435.

56 League of Nations, *Journal of the Sixth Assembly of the League of Nations*, Geneva 1925, No. 3, 9 September 1925, pp. 24–25.

exercises a right of property over another."[57] However, this definition would be forsaken for one proposed by Lord Cecil,[58] when on 22 September, the Drafting Committee having considered the issue proposed the following definition:

> Slavery is the status or condition of a person over whom any or all of the powers attaching to the right of ownership are exercised.[59]

This definition of slavery – unaltered – would find its way into the 1926 Convention to Suppress the Slave Trade and Slavery. Where the *travaux préparatoires* are instructive in regard to the definition of slavery is to be found in a submission made by the Union of South Africa which provides a re-phrasing of the definition of 'slavery', thus providing a supplementary means of interpreting the term as found in the 1926 Convention. Consider the relevant section of the South African submission:

> [...] a person is a slave if any other person can, by law or enforceable custom, claim such property in him as would be claimed if he were an inanimate object;

The result of this enslavement as noted in the Reply of the Union of South Africa was that:

> [...] the natural freedom of will possessed by a person to offer or render his labour or to control the fruits thereof or the consideration therefrom is taken from him.[60]

---

57 *Id.*, p. 25.

58 See League of Nations, Slavery, 24 September 1925, LofN Doc. A.VI/SC1/ Drafting Committee/14. (this document number having been pencilled out and replaced with A.VI/6.1925) as found in Folder R.67.D.46241 entitled *La question de l'esclavage: Discussions, y relatives, de la VIe Assembleé*, 1925. where it reads: "Amendments proposed by Lord Cecil to the text of draft Convention adopted by the Drafting Committee of the Sub-Committee of the VIth Commission (Document A.VI/S.C.I/ Drafting Committee 12 (1))."

59 League of Nations, Sixth Committee, Sub-Committee, Drafting Committee Slavery: Synopsis of the Convention (with handwritten amendments so as to be re-entitled Sixth Committee, Slavery: Synopsis of the Convention), 22 September 1925, LofN Doc. A.VI/ S.C.I/ Drafting Committee/12(1) Revised (this document number having been penciled out and replaced with A.VI/5.1925). As found in Folder R.67.D.46241 entitled *La question de l'esclavage: Discussions, y relatives, de la VIe Assembleé*, 1925.

60 League of Nations, Draft Convention on Slavery, Replies of Governments, Reply from the Government of the Union of South Africa, 22 July 1926, LofN Doc. A.10(a).1926.VI, p. 5; as

One further element in regard to the definition of 'slavery' as developed by the League of Nations might be mentioned. In his Report to the Assembly of the League of Nations in 1926 Viscount Cecil sought, in a rather backdoor-manner to voice the Sixth Committee's understanding of a wider definition of slavery. Speaking in regard to Article 2 – which will be considered shortly – he noted that the emphasis in that Article on "domestic slavery and similar conditions" had been omitted "because it was believed that such conditions came within the definition of slavery contained in the first article and that no further prohibition of them in express terms was necessary." Cecil went on to say that:

> This applies not only to domestic slavery but to all those conditions mentioned by the Temporary Slavery Commission and to which I referred to last year, *i.e.*, "debt slavery," the enslaving of persons disguised as the adoption of children, and the acquisition of girls by purchase disguised as payment of dowry, etc.

To his credit, however, Viscount Cecil did qualify this pronouncement saying that "even if, as is possible, these last practices do not come under the definition of slavery as it is given in Article 1, the Commission is unanimously of the opinion that they must be combated."[61] For their part, States did not recognise this expanded definition of slavery as being imbedded in Article 1 of the 1926 Convention; it would take the signing of the 1956 Supplementary Convention on the Abolition of Slavery, the Slave Trade, and Institutions and Practices Similar to Slavery for this to transpire.

With regard to the definition of the "slave trade," its evolution within the League of Nations was without much difficulty or discussion. It was, as Viscount Cecil noted, "primarily the result of the work of legal experts, and is based on the minimum provisions of existing colonial legislation and on the previous international convention on this subject."[62] Taking the lead from the 1925 British Draft Protocol which sought to indicate the various

---

found in League of Nations, Publications of the League of Nations, VI.B.Slavery.1926, 1–7. Emphasis in the original.

61 League of Nations, Slavery Convention: Report presented to the Assembly by the Sixth Committee, 24 September 1926, 24 September 1926, LofN Doc. A.104.1926.VI, as found in League of Nations, *Publications of the League of Nations*, VI.B.Slavery.1926, VI. B. 5, pp. 1–2.

62 League of Nations, "Question of Slavery: Report of the Sixth Committee to the Assembly," *op. cit.* n. 55, p. 435.

elements of what constituted the slave trade, the Sixth Committee of the Assembly of the League of Nations put forward a definition in September 1925[63] which would ultimately be accepted with very little comment by States and included in the 1926 Convention as the definition of the slave trade. That definition reads:

> The slave trade includes all acts involved in the capture, acquisition or disposal of a person with intent to reduce him to slavery; all acts involved in the acquisition of a slave with a view to selling or exchanging him; all acts of disposal by sale or exchange of a slave acquired with a view to being sold or exchanged, and, in general, every act of trade or transport in slaves.

While the definitions of slavery and the slave trade did not raise much concern with States in the drafting process of the 1926 Convention to Suppress the Slave Trade and Slavery; the provisions of Article 2, which sought to establish the obligations flowing from those definitions elicited more attention. Article 2 of the 1926 Convention reads:

> The High Contracting Parties undertake, each in respect of the territories placed under its sovereignty, jurisdiction, protection, suzerainty or tutelage, so far as they have not already taken the necessary steps:
> (a) To prevent and suppress the slave trade;
> (b) To bring about, progressively and as soon as possible, the complete abolition of slavery in all its forms.

The Haitian Delegation, for instance, sought to move beyond the parameters of simply dealing with slavery and the slave trade by proposing that paragraph (b) read: "To endeavour to bring about as soon as possible the disappearance of all voluntary or involuntary subjections."[64] this proposal, however, was not taken up by the various committees drafting the 1926 Convention. Furthermore, while the Drafting Committee toyed with the inclusion of 'abolition' in

---

63 League of Nations, Question of Slavery: Draft Report Presented to the Sixth Assembly by the Sixth Committee, 23 September 1925, LofN Doc. A.VI/6.1925 as found in Folder R.67.D.46214 entitled *La question de l'esclavage: Discussions, y relatives, de la VIe Assembleé*, 1925, p. 2.

64 League of Nations, Draft Convention on Slavery and Proposed Amendments, LofN Doc. A.VI/S.C.1/1, 10 September 1926; as found in Folder R.77.D.46781 entitled Draft Convention on Slavery: Discussion at the 7th Assembly; 1926.

paragraph (a) of Article 2 to accompany 'prevent and suppress',[65] this was quietly dropped at the level of the Sixth Committee.[66]

Overall, the provisions of Article 2, from the 1925 British Draft Protocol to its inclusion in the 1926 Convention, proposed clearer obligations with regard to the slave trade but more nuanced obligations in regard to slavery. In proposing the 1925 Draft Protocol, Viscount Cecil noted that obligations being sought with regard to slavery were "very cautiously worded."[67] With regard to the actual provisions of Article 2 found in the 1926 Convention, Viscount Cecil sought to explain the cautious nature of the wording of Article 2(b):

> The Sixth Committee was of the opinion that the abolition of slavery could only be successfully brought about with due regard to the maintenance of order and the well-being of the peoples concerned. This accounts for the use of the word "progressively" employed in paragraph (b) for it was recognise that in certain cases in the past the attempt to do away with slavery and other similar conditions is an abrupt manner, although noble in its inspiration, has resulted in unforeseen hardships for the individuals whose conditions it was sought to alleviate, and even in grave social upheavals.

Viscount Cecil continued by saying that it "must be left to the judgement of the Government responsible," as circumstances varied from State to State; and that the Committee was ready to concede that "in certain cases there could be an arrangement whereby freed slaves in possession of all their natural and civil rights might be obliged to continue to serve their former masters for a certain time, but only subject to the obligations and rights consequent upon a labour contract."[68] By way of an overall assessment of Article 2, Cecil concluded that the Sixth Committee "interprets Article 2 as tending to bring about the disappearance from

65 League of Nations, Sixth Committee, Sub Committee 1, Drafting Committee, "Slavery, Synopsis of the Convention," 22 September 1925, LofN Doc. A.VI/S.C.1/Drafting Committee/12(1), p. 2.

66 League of Nations, "Question of Slavery: Draft Report Presented to the Sixth Assembly by the Sixth Committee,", *op. cit.* n. 63, p. 3.

67 League of Nations, Slavery: Draft Resolution and Protocol proposed by the British Government (*continuation*): Statement by Viscount Cecil, *Official Journal, Record of the Sixth Assembly, Meetings of the Committees, Minutes of the Sixth Committee* (*Political Questions*), Special Supplement No. 39, 14 September 1925, p. 14.

68 League of Nations, Slavery Convention: Report presented to the Assembly by the Sixth Committee, 24 September 1926, LofN Doc. A.104.1926.VI, as found in League of Nations, *Publications of the League of Nations*, VI.B.Slavery.1926, VI. B. 5, pp. 1 and 2.

written legislation or from the custom of the country of everything which admits the maintenance by a private individual of rights over another person of the same nature as the rights which an individual can have over things."[69]

Thus, what originally started as a process to investigate slavery in the Ethiopian context developed ultimately into an international instrument governing the suppression of slavery and the slave trade. In bringing 1926 Convention to Suppress the Slave Trade and Slavery into existence, the League of Nations did not abolish slavery or the slave trade *per se*; instead it called upon consenting States to be bound by the Convention to "prevent and suppress the slave trade" and to bring about "progressively and as soon as possible" the "complete abolition of slavery in all its forms." This incremental means of abolishing the slave trade and slavery was to be important in the context of Ethiopia as – although it would not become party to the 1926 Convention during the League era – it took the Convention's lead in seeking to demonstrate from even before it joined the League of Nations that it was actively, though slowly, seeking to abolish both slavery and the slave trade.

Ethiopia, Slavery and the League of Nations

In April 1924, less than a year after having been admitted to the League of Nations, the Regent Ras Tafari provided a Report to the League of Nations in regard to the question of slavery in Ethiopia on behalf of his Government. He emphasised that the suppression of the slave trade could now be considered as the Empire had been consolidated: "Only when the unity of the Empire was attained under the Emperor Menelik II, and the chiefs of the provinces as well as the chiefs of the Kingdom under the suzerainty of the Emperor were definitely subjected to his authority, could the slave trade be effectively suppressed."[70] The Report followed by saying that the "present Government, which adopts energetic and ruthless methods against slave dealers, has succeeded in almost totally suppressing the trade. [...] It may be said that at the present time the slave trade no longer exists in Abyssinia, except in isolated cases which are becoming increasingly rare." With respect to slavery, "immediate abolition does not seem possible, but the Abyssinian Government has issued regulations which will, it is hoped, produce the best results."[71] Those Regulations, issued in

69 *Id.*, pp. 1–2.

70 League of Nations, Report of the Abyssinian Government to the League of Nations on the Question of Slavery, 14 May 1924, LofN Doc. C.209.M.66.1924.VI, p. 1.

71 *Id.*, p. 2.

March 1924 were far reaching as they mandated the emancipation of slaves for the first time in Ethiopian history. However, as historian Richard Pankhurst notes, the new law was "limited in scope, it envisaged the gradual and ultimately complete liberation of all slaves."[72]

Article 1 of the Regulations for the Emancipation of Slaves and their Conditions of Life sought to justify this gradual approach noting that if all slaves were to be freed at once, "they might become thieves, bandits and malefactors, thereby disturbing the public peace. They shall accordingly remain in the hands of their masters." The Regulations then set out the circumstances under which slaves would be set free or considered as being free, such as all children born after 1924 and all other slaves seven years after the death of their master. In addition, it regulated and limited the ability of masters to reclaim runaway slaves; it set out penalties for slave trading; and created slave courts throughout Ethiopia. As Suzanne Miers relates; "on paper, therefore, a significant advance had been made,"[73] although the reality was that slavery and slave trading would persist for some time in Ethiopia. The Regulations, however had an effect beyond the borders of the Empire, as the "Ethiopian reforms of 1924 defused criticism at the TSC"[74] – the Temporary Slavery Commission of the League of Nations. Within the works of the Temporary Slavery Commission, Sir Frederick Lugard had annexed to a general consideration of slavery a specific study of Ethiopia. In that Memorandum, entitled "Conditions in Abyssinia," Lugard note that Ras Tafari "though sincere and eager for reform, has not the means at his command" to suppress issues related to slavery and he noted that "the evidence shows that slavery, slave-dealing and occasional slave-raiding, still exist in Abyssinia." As such, he drew the conclusion that the "conditions of admission to Membership of the League have not therefore been carried out, and in present circumstances there seems little prospect of their fulfilment." Lugard called upon the League to establish a commission of enquiry which would travel to Ethiopia to report on the "existing conditions in regard to slavery and forced labour, and to make recommendations."[75]

72 Pankhurst, *op. cit.* n. 24, p. 114. See also, generally, A.L. Gardiner, "The Law of Slavery in Abyssinia," *Journal of Comparative Legislation and International Law*, Vol. 15, 1933, pp. 189–202.

73 See Miers, "Britain and the Suppression...," *op. cit.* n. 26, p. 257.

74 Miers, "Slavery and the Slave Trade...," *op. cit.* n. 33, p. 25.

75 See League of Nations, Temporary Slavery Commission, *Slavery and Other Systems Restrictive of Liberty*, Memorandum by F.D. Lugard, Annex 3, Conditions in Abyssinia, LofN Doc CTE 36, May 1925, pp. 10–11.

The Temporary Slavery Commission for its part, did not see fit to pursue this line of inquiry. Instead, it suggested, in its 1925 Report, regarding to the legal status of slavery, that:

> The Abyssinian Government could hardly be asked to do more in this respect for the moment. In order, however, to hasten the liberation of slaves so far as circumstances permit, the attention of this Government might be called to certain transitional measures which have been successfully applied in other countries with this object, such as:
> (a) To encourage the principal chiefs in the provinces to set an example by liberating their own slaves [...];
> (b) To register slaves and to liberate those who by a certain date have not been registered. This measure would, it is true involve the recognition of the status of slavery – a status which, however, is still recognised by the Government of Abyssinia;
> (c) On the other hand, to "abolish the legal status of slavery," [...] but with the reservation that the person thus legally freed might be obliged for a fixed period to continue to serve their former master as if they were bound by a contract of labour.[76]

As far as issues of the slave-trade were concerned, the Temporary Slavery Commission supported the Ethiopian call for the colonial Powers which occupied the coastal regions of the Horn of Africa to cooperate and coordinate their activities if the trade in Ethiopia was to ultimately be suppressed. In presenting the Report to the Sixth Committee, the Chairman of the Temporary Slavery Commission, Albrecht Gohr, noted in regard to Ethiopia that "the Committee recognised that the general customs and political situation in that country rendered it very difficult to abolish slavery in one stroke."[77] Yet, it did sound a warning shot across Ethiopia's bow in linking the existence of slavery in Ethiopia to membership, albeit, to application for future membership to the League of Nations: "Further, the Committee suggested that the League of Nations should admit in the future States not Members only when they have

76 League of Nations, Temporary Slavery Commission, *Report of the Temporary Slavery Commission adopted in the Course of its Second Session, July 13th–25th July*, 1925, 25 July 1925, LofN Doc A.19.1925. VI, p. 3.

77 League of Nations, Slavery: Report of the Temporary Slavery Commission, Statement by M. Gohr, Chairman of the Temporary Slavery Commission, *Official Journal, Record of the Sixth Assembly, Meetings of the Committees, Minutes of the Sixth Committee* (*Political Questions*), Special Supplement No. 39, 14 September 1925, p. 11.

gave proof of their desire to abolish slavery. If this abolitions could not take place at once, certain transitional measures were recommended."[78]

As the Temporary Slavery Commission gave way to a move to establish an international instrument in regard to issues of slavery, and a British proposal gave way to the 1925 Draft Convention prepared by the League of Nations; Ethiopia felt compelled – and was the only State to do so – to make a Declaration, which was attached to the minutes of League's Sixth Committee' consideration of the provision of that 1925 Draft Convention:

> Gentlemen, we, the Abyssinian delegation, fully and entirely concur with the lofty humanitarian principles embodied in the Protocol proposed by Viscount Cecil of Chelwood, and together with our eminent colleagues on the Sub-Committee [which drafted the 1925 proposal], we have voted wholeheartedly for the adoption of its fundamental articles.
>
> The dynasty descended from David and Solomon will leave nothing undone to ensure that the Protocol shall be given the widest possible application with the help and grace of God.[79]

Yet, this Declaration rings hollow against Ethiopia's 1926 reply to the League's request to make comments on the substance of the 1925 Draft Convention; as in effect it was reported that the Emperor's "efforts are directed towards ensuring the strictest possible enforcement of [domestic] anti-slavery ordinances," and, as such, "will therefore, not be in a position to furnish this month sufficiently detailed replies indicating among the whole of the text accepted *de plano*, those concerning which some few provisional reservations might possibly have to be made."[80] Ethiopia, however ultimately did not need to make any reservations to the 1926 Convention during the League era, as it would only ratify it in 1969, though it was an original signatory on 25 September 1926.[81]

Despite not being party to the 1926 Convention to Suppress the Slave Trade and Slavery, Ethiopia's dealing with issues regarding slavery remained on the agenda of the League of Nations, in part, as a result of a Resolution adopted by

78 *Id.*, p. 11.

79 League of Nations, Draft Convention on Slavery: Declaration by the Abyssinian Delegate, *Official* Journal, Special Supplement No. 39, Record of the Sixth Assembly, Meetings of the Committees, Minutes of the Sixth Committee (Political Questions), 24 September 1925, p. 32.

80 League of Nations, Draft Convention on Slavery, Replies of Governments, Reply from the Government of Abyssinia, 2 July 1926, LofN Doc. A.10.1926.VI, p. 1; as found in League of Nations, *Publications of the League of Nations*, VI.B.Slavery.1926.

81 See League of Nations, Slavery Convention, 25 September 1926, LofN Doc C.586.M.223.1926. VI, p. 8.

the Assembly on the same day as the signing of the 1926 Convention, that noted: "the League of Nations should continue to interest itself in securing the progressive abolition of slavery and conditions analogous" and thus requested the Council to gather information, not only from the Parties to the 1926 Convention as required by Article 7; but also "any supplementary information which the Members of the League may be disposed spontaneously to furnish with regard to the measures taken by them to this end."[82] In 1927, the Sixth Committee had expressed its hope that Ethiopia would provide information in light of the previous year's Resolution[83] and; indeed, acknowledge receipt of such information, as the Ethiopian Government provided the League of Nation with a Note that included a "nominal" list of individuals who had been freed as a result of the 1924 Ethiopian Regulations and those that had been convicted since its coming into force. As far as the eleven hundred individuals who had been freed was concerned, not only was the number small compared to the two million slaves which the Regent considered to still exist in Ethiopia, but the estimates, it would emerge many years later, were the "equivalent to 'guess'."[84] Nevertheless, the Note concluded by stating that "it should be observed that, despite considerable distances and enormous difficulties, a considerable step forward has been taken on the road of civilisation and human liberty."[85]

While no notable mention of the issue of slavery in regard to Ethiopia was made before the League of Nations between 1927 and 1931; as a result of a League inquiry into issues of slavery in Liberia and fearing such a measure might be imposed on Ethiopia – the former Ras Tafari – now Emperor Haile Selassie I, undertook an action which "successfully disarmed criticism" by the newly established League of Nations' *ad hoc* Committee of Experts on Slavery.[86] "In 1931," historian Suzanne Miers relates, "Haile Selassie was alarmed lest the new League committee might try to send out a commission of inquiry. He feared that the slavery issue might be made a pretext for an attack on Ethiopian independence. Prompted by Lord Lugard (as he had become), the Emperor, in order to forestall

82 League of Nations, Slavery Convention, Resolution adopted by the Assembly at its meeting held on September 25th, 1926, LofN Doc. A.123.1926.VI; as found in League of Nations, *Publications of the League of Nations*, VI.B.Slavery.1926.

83 League of Nations, Slavery Convention, Annual Report by the Council, Report of the Sixth Committee to the Assembly, 17 September 1927, LofN Doc A.74.1927, VI; as found in League of Nations, *Publications of the League of Nations*, VI.B.Slavery.1927.

84 Pankhurst, *op. cit.* n. 24, p. 119.

85 See League of Nations, Slavery Convention, Annual Report by the Council, 15 September 1927, LofN Doc A.37(b).1927.VI, p. 3; as found in League of Nations, *Publications of the League of Nations*, VI.B.Slavery.1927.

86 Miers, "Britain and the Suppression of Slavery...," *op. cit.* n. 26, p. 258.

any League action, asked the [British] antislavery society for help."[87] The Anti-Slavery Society sent a delegation in 1932 headed by Lord Noel-Buxon, who gained a promise from the Emperor that slavery would end within twenty years.[88] This along with the establishment of a new Slavery Department "meant to supervise the slavery laws, register slaves, run the slavery courts, look after freed slaves and run its own police force," was enough to satisfy the Committee of Experts on Slavery which simply provided suggestions to the Ethiopian Government, recognising that "the special situation in Abyssinia shows that it is at present impossible for the Abyssinian Government to abolish slavery by a stroke of the pen and that it is necessary that the Government should only advance by stages."[89] This gradual approach, it should be noted as an aside, was very much in line with the obligations which States that had ratified the 1926 Convention to Suppress the Slave Trade and Slavery had undertaken. Further, the Committee noted that a letter from the Emperor which was forwarded to the Committee by Lord Lugard included proposals "to take measures which forestall some of the recommendations of the Committee."[90] The recommendations which the Committee had made, it should be noted, were hardly intrusive. Supporting the Ethiopian incremental approach to the end of slavery, it noted that:

> The main objective, however, should be to make the Abyssinians themselves realise fully the reprehensible character of slavery and the merit of spontaneous acts of liberation. Though laws may help to transform customs, the laws themselves are only fully applied if, in their conception, they reflect the sentiments of the general mass. It would appear that great progress has been made in this direction.

As such, the Government should seek the clergy's support in setting an example by freeing their slaves, and "for instance," bestowing "rewards on those who voluntarily free their slaves."[91]

---

87 *Id.*

88 Note that while Noel-Buxon was sympathetic to the manner in which Haile Selassie was dealing with the issue of slavery, but in "his efforts to keep up the pressure, he proceeded to sour the relations with tactless talk and articles." Miers, *Slavery in the Twentieth Century*, *op. cit.* n. 27, p. 179. For one such article, see Lord Noel-Buxton, "Slavery in Abyssinia," *International Affairs*, Vol. 11, 1932, pp. 512–526.

89 League of Nations, Slavery, Report of the Committee of Experts on Slavery provided for by the Assembly Resolutoin of September 25th, 1931, 1 September 1932, LofN Doc. C.618.1932.VI, p. 9; as found in League of Nations, *Publications of the League of Nations*, VI.B.Slavery.1932 and 1935.

90 *Id.*, p. 10.

91 *Id.*, p. 9.

By the same token, the permanent body which replaced the *ad hoc* Committee of Experts on Slaves: the Advisory Committee of Experts was rather supportive of Ethiopia's attempts to gradually end slavery, pointing to a further quantitative submission made by the Ethiopian Government in 1934, regarding slaves freed and individuals convicted.[92] While Professor Pankhurst pointed to a number of factors in the economic development of Ethiopia – as it related to the relationship between master and slave – which "accelerated the emancipation process"; which meant that slavery, by "the early thirties, was thus at last beginning to be brought under control";[93] the Ethiopian Governments pointed elsewhere. In its 1934 submission it noted that:

> The opening up in recent years of several motor-tracks radiating from the capital, together with the quartering in many parts of the country of Central Government troops, trained according to the principles of modern military science, will certainly make it easier to stamp out the slave trade, while facilitating the general strict application of the Imperial laws for the liberation of slavers.[94]

In its 1936 Report, the Advisory Committee of Experts simply noted, for the record, the legislation which had been passed to date by the Ethiopian Government in regard to the abolition of slavery by Ethiopia. It did so as events in Ethiopia had fundamentally changed, with the invasion and annexation of Ethiopia by Italy in 1935–1936.

1936 Italian Annexation of Ethiopia

The road to Italian annexation of Ethiopia began in the Ogaden region, at Walwal, on 5 December 1934, when Ethiopian and Italian troops clashed as a result of a dispute over Italian claims to an oasis. By Italian admission; some

92 See League of Nations, Slavery, Report of the Advisory Committee of Experts, 10 April 1935, LofN Doc. C.159.M.113.1935.VI, pp. 9–10; as found in League of Nations, *Publications of the League of Nations*, VI.B.Slavery.1932 and 1935.

93 Pankhurst, *op. cit.* n. 24, p. 123.

94 League of Nations, Slavery, Report of the Advisory Committee of Experts, Annex 7, Communication, dated August 15th, 1934, from the Ethiopian Government to the Secretary-General of the League of Nations, Comprising a Report of the Application of the Ethiopian Laws for the Abolition of Slavery in Ethiopia, 10 April 1935, LofN Doc. C.159.M.113.1935.VI, p. 94; as found in League of Nations, *Publications of the League of Nations*, VI.B.Slavery.1932 and 1935.

years earlier "Wal-Wal and other points along the border were occupied by the Italians, and the Abyssinian Government made no protest,"[95] this despite the assertion by Professor Pitman Potter – who had been one of the arbitrators appointed by Ethiopia to consider the incident – that title by occupation could not have been made effective over the short period of four years, and moreover, that "[a]ll documentary evidence indicates that the frontier in this region [though never demarcated] lay one hundred or more kilometres east of Wal Wal,"[96] that is: well within Ethiopian territory. The Walwal Incident was settled by pacific means; an arbitration panel – which included Potter (later to be a Judge of the International Court of Justice), as well as noted international jurists Geouffre de la Pradelle and Nicolas Politis – determined in September 1935, that responsibility for the confrontation, which left one hundred and sixty dead, could not be imputed to either State.[97] By the time the Walwal Incident was settled, however, the precipitation towards war was already well in advance. Italian stalling tactics before the arbitration panel meant that the dispute, which had mushroomed beyond the simple issue of Walwal, could not be considered by the political organs of the League of Nations as long as it remained in the hands of the arbitrators functioning not on the basis of the Covenant, but on a 1928 Ethio-Italian bilateral treaty of amity.[98] Such delays were in Italy's interest, as it used the interim period to amass troops in East Africa who, in any case, could not be mobilised until the end of the Ethiopian rainy season, which transpired towards the end September 1935.

Ethiopia, as early as March 1935, realising that Italy was moving troops and war materiel to its possessions on the Horn of Africa, asked that the overall dispute be considered by the Council of the League of Nations on the basis of Article 15, with a look to having the League provide a solution to what John Spencer, a former advisor to the Ethiopian Ministry of Foreign Affairs, termed the "threatening military situation in East Africa."[99] For its part, the Council, noting the declared pacific intensions of the parties, differed to on-going arbitration until that panel made its award on 3 September 1935. The Council then established a 'Committee of Five' (France, Poland, Spain, Turkey, and the

95 See Commendatore Luigi Villari, "Abyssinia and Italy," *Journal of Royal African Society*, Vol. 34, 1935, p. 369.

96 Pitman Potter, "The Wal Wal Arbitration," *American Journal of International Law*, Vol. 30, p. 42.

97 See "Italo-Ethiopian Commission of Conciliation and Arbitration: Award of September 3, 1935," *The American Journal of International Law*, Vol. 29, 1935, pp. 690–698.

98 See Alfred Zimmern, "The League's Handling of the Italo-Abyssinian Dispute," *International Affairs*, Vol. 14, 1935, p. 754.

99 John Spencer, "The Italian-Ethiopian Dispute and the League of Nations," *The American Journal of International Law*, Vol. 31, 1937, p. 617.

United Kingdom) which sought to act as a conciliator between the conflicting parties, making quite intrusive recommendations in regard to Ethiopia, calling on it to reorganise various tenets of its government; though it did hold out the possibility for territorial adjustment which would have granted it access to the sea via an Italian port.[100] These suggestions, the Council reported, "were accepted by Ethiopia as a basis of negotiation, but were rejected by Italy."[101] As a result, the Council moved on 26 September to establish a committee of all its members minus Italy (Committee of Thirteen) to report on the larger issue unfolding in East Africa. The previous day, Emperor Haile Sellasie notified the League that his instruction to pull back Ethiopian troops to thirty kilometres from its borders, so as to ensure no incidents might take place and to clearly demonstrate who might well be the aggressor if war was to break out, had now been carried out. On 3 October 1935, Council received notice from Italy that:

> the warlike and aggressive spirit in Ethiopia had succeeded in imposing war against Italy and had found its latest and complete expression in the order for general mobilization announced by the Emperor on September 28. That order stated the Italian Government, represented a direct and immediate threat to the Italian troops with the aggravating circumstances of the creation of a neutral zone [re: the thirty kilometre buffer zone] which, in reality, was only a strategic movement intended to facilitate the assembly and the aggressive preparation of the Ethiopian troops. As a result of the order for general mobilization, the continual and sanguinary aggression to which Italy had been subjected in the last ten years manifestly involved grave and immediate dangers again which it was essential for elementary reasons of security to take action without delay [... has] found itself obliged to authorize the high command in Eritrea to taken the necessary measures of defence.[102]

Italian 'self-defence' had thus commenced.

Italian motivation for attacking Ethiopia can be traced back to a number of factors. The first was manifest in Italy's opening act of war: the symbolic

---

100 Leon Halden, "The Diplomacy of the Ethiopian Crisis," *The Journal of Negro History*, Vol. 22, 1937, p. 183.

101 League of Nations, "Dispute between Ethiopia and Italy: Report of the Council of the League of Nations under Article 15, Paragraph 4, of the Covenant," 5 October 1935, as reproduced in *The American Journal of International Law*, Vol. 30 (Supplement: Official Documents), 1936, p. 14.

102 *Id.*, p. 15.

(though deadly) bombing of Adwa, the site of its humiliating defeat of 1896.[103] In geopolitical terms, Italy saw itself as having been unfairly deprived by the territorial settlement of the First World War, after being promised by France and Great Britain that if they were to benefit territorial at the expense of Germany in Africa, that "equitable compensation, particularly as regards the settlement in her favour of the questions relative to the frontiers of the Italian colonies of Eritrea, Somaliland, and Libya"[104] would be forthcoming – though this never materialised. This grievance resulted in the fact that Italy saw itself as having come "last into the field of colonial expansion and was only able to pick up the scraps."[105] As a result, Italy could not adequately address – the apparent *Zeitgeist* of the era: the need for *Lebensraum*. As the Italian Ambassador, Luigi Villari, was to write in the *Journal of Royal African Society*, Italy "needed expansion more than almost any other country. Her rapidly growing, hard-working and industrious population was limited to a metropolitan area half the size of France [...] it lacked the raw material necessary for industry, and even a proportion of the foodstuffs for feeding the people had to be imported from abroad. [... The] situation was unsatisfactory and unstable, and the necessity for the occupation of colonial territories became ever more urgent."[106]

In a newspaper piece attributed to the Italian Prime Minister, Benito Mussolini, it noted "that slavery exists in Abyssinia…but it is not for that reason that Italy is preparing herself for action… Nor is an essential argument the question of race… Not even civilisation is the object that Italy has in view"; instead the "vital needs of the Italian people" to land was important, but the "decisive" reason for war was "security in East Africa":

> The solution of the problem can only be totalitarian. Any action of expansion or any protectorate must be accomplished by military measures. Italy is the only judge of her security in East Africa. But in military terms, the Italo-Abyssinian problem is simplicity and logic itself. The problem admits of only one solution with Geneva, without Geneva, or against Geneva.[107]

---

103 See, for instance: George Baer, *Test Case: Italy, Ethiopia, and the League of Nations* (1976), p. 156.

104 Halden, *op. cit.*, n. 100, p. 166.

105 SeeVillari *op. cit.*, n. 95, pp. 366–367.

106 *Id.*, p. 367.

107 Halden, *op. cit.*, n. 100, p. 179.

And yet, the notions of civilisation attached to issues of slavery remained a strong element of rhetoric in the Italian justification for war, especially before the League of Nations. A month before the start of their campaign, the Italian Representative had submitted to the Council of the League of Nations a long memorandum which sought to de-legitimise Ethiopia as a less-than-equal State, as unworthy of membership in the League of Nations. Ethiopia, the Memorandum stated "had by her conduct placed herself openly outside the pact of the League of Nations and has made herself unworthy of the trust accorded to her when she was admitted." As a report in *The Times* of London noted:

> The memorandum turns to the alleged violations of the special pledges made by Abyssinia towards the League, especially that regarding the repressions of slavery, the survival of which 'constitutes not only an atrocious offence to civilization and a manifest violation of Article 23 of the Convention, but represent a flagrant violation of the particular obligations assumed by the Abyssinian Government at the time of her admission'. Only if the obligations are observed, adds the memorandum, 'can Abyssinia be sufficiently entitled to remain a member of the League'.[108]

The Italian point of view, however, failed to carry the day; on the 5 October 1935, the Council of the League of Nations established the so-called Committee of Six "to study the situation and report to the Council so as to enable it to take decisions with full knowledge of the matters involved."[109] While the above noted Committee of Thirteen provided a narrative of the dispute between Ethiopia and Italy and made rather banal recommendations in "that any violation of the Covenant should immediately be brought to an end,"[110] the Committee of Six sought to consider whether the war had transpired in violation of the Covenant. The Committee, while noting obligations under the 1928 Pact of Paris (re: Briand-Kellogg Pact), focused on the provisions of Article 12

108 Geneva Correspondent, "Italian Case: Charges against Abyssinia, Memorandum to League," *The Times*, 6 September 1935, p. 7.

109 League of Nations, "Report of the League of Nations Council Committee", 7 October 1935, as reproduced in *The American Journal of International Law*, Vol. 30 (Supplement: Official Documents), 1936, p. 37. The Committee consisted of Chile, Denmark, France, Portugal, Romania and the United Kingdom.

110 League of Nations, "Dispute between Ethiopia and Italy: Report of the Council of the League of Nations under Article 15, Paragraph 4, of the Covenant," 5 October 1935, as reproduced in *The American Journal of International Law*, Vol. 30 (Supplement: Official Documents), 1936, p. 26.

while making reference to Articles 13 and 15 of the Covenant of the League of Nations.[111] It noted that League Members are:

> not entitled, without having first complied with the provisions of Articles 12, 13, and 15, to seek a remedy by war for grievances they consider they have against other members of the League. The adoption by a State of measures of security on its own territory [re: the thirty kilometre buffer zone] and within its international agreements does not authorize another State to consider itself free from its obligations under the Covenant.

As such, the Committee of Six drew the following conclusions: "that the Italian Government has resorted to war in disregard of its covenants under Article 12 of the Covenant of the League of Nations."[112] The Report was agreed to by each of the Members of the Council of the League with the exception of the Italy. The implications of this determination were far-reaching, as the collective security system of the League of Nations required, under Article 16, that should "any Member of the League resort to war in disregard of its covenants under Articles 12, 13 or 15, it shall *ipso facto* be deemed to have committed an act of war against all other Members of the League," mandating trade sanctions and the possibility of military action.

While the Italian campaign persisted in Ethiopia, the Assembly of the League of Nations moved to establish sanctions, agreeing on 18 November 1935 to five proposals with regard to, *inter alia*, financial measures, import and export of goods; and the reversal of a longstanding arms embargo against Ethiopia and the placing of such an embargo on Italy. Further, agreement was reached, in principle, in regard to a petroleum embargo.[113] Yet, the petroleum embargo was never to be, as it was the string which ultimately unravelled the

---

111 Article 12 of the Covenant of the League of Nations reads:

> The Members of the League agree that, if there should arise between them any dispute likely to lead to a rupture they will submit the matter either to arbitration or judicial settlement or to enquiry by the Council, and they agree in no case to resort to war until three months after the award by the arbitrators or the judicial decision, or the report by the Council. In any case under this Article the award of the arbitrators or the judicial decision shall be made within a reasonable time, and the report of the Council shall be made within six months after the submission of the dispute.

112 League of Nations, "Report of the League of Nations Council Committee," 7 October 1935, as reproduced in *The American Journal of International Law*, Vol. 30 (Supplement: Official Documents), 1936, pp. 39 and 40.

113 See *Note on Proposal for the Application of Sanctions against the Italian Government*, in Zimmern, *op. cit.* n. 98, pp. 765–768.

overall sanction regime and caused the abandonment of Ethiopia by the League of Nations. To avoid the oil sanctions – a *causa belli* for Italy – the British and French sought to propose a settlement. The so-called Hoare-Laval Plan was mooted to the Council in December 1935, however, it caused a major uproar when made public, leading to the resignation of both its authors, the British Foreign Secretary and the French Prime Minister, due to the fact that it "confirmed Italian military gains made up to that time, giving Italy parts of Ogaden and Tegre, as well as an economic protectorate over a large part of the rest of Ethiopia."[114] As Historian George Scott noted "Haile Selassie was being called upon to pay a crippling bill for the privilege of being invaded by Italy and protected by the League of Nations."[115] Ethiopia's reaction to the proposal, delivered by the Emperor, was emphatic:

> We desire to state, with all the solemnity and firmness that the situation demands today, that our willingness to facilitate any pacific solution on the basis of the Franco-British proposals would not only be cowardice towards our people, but a betrayal of the League of Nations and of all States that have though up to now they could have confidence in the system of collective security.
>
> Those proposals are, in Ethiopian eyes, a negation and abandonment of the principles upon which the League of Nations was founded. They would consecrate the amputation of Ethiopia's territory and the disappearance of her independence for the benefit of a State that has attacked her [...].[116]

As the proposed petroleum embargo was relegated to a technical committee of the League of Nations in the early months of 1936, it became apparent that not only were oil sanctions not to be implemented, but that the situation in Europe was such that interest in maintaining any sanctions against Italy was waning. Meanwhile Italy was making territorial gains in Ethiopia. John Spencer provides the following pithy narrative of Italian gains in the pages of the *American Journal of International Law*: "During the month of March, 1936, by means of gas attacks on the northern front, the Italian army was able gradually to demoralize the Ethiopian forces, and, by the end of March, to break their resistance so that the gradual advance [...] became, during the month of April, a rout of

114 Zewde, *op. cit.* n. 11, p. 166.

115 George Scott, *The Rise and Fall of the League of Nations* (1973), p. 347.

116 Special Correspondent, "The Emperor's 'No' Reply to Paris Proposals, 'Betrayal of the League'," *The Times*, 17 December 1935, p. 14.

Ethiopian troops."[117] On 3 May 1936, the Emperor fled into exile, two days later, Italian troops occupied Addis Abba; and on the 9 May the Italian Prime Minister, "Mussolini publicly proclaimed the unqualified annexation of Ethiopia and conferred upon King Victor Emmanuel III the title of Emperor of that country."[118] With European Powers turning their attention to the situation in Europe and the rise of an aggressive National Socialist party in Germany, the issue of Ethiopia fell to the wayside, the League in essence accepting a *fait accompli*:

> With regard to the question of the continuation of sanctions, agreement of the delegates was, with the outstanding exception of South Africa, unanimously in favour of the removal of such measures for the reason that military action alone could change the *de facto* situation created in Ethiopia.[119]

On 30 June 1936, above the heckling of Italian journalists, Emperor Haile Sellassie became the first Head of State to address the League of Nations:

> I, Haile Sellassie, Emperor of Ethiopia, am present here today to ask for the impartial justice due to my people and for the help which fifty-two nations had undertaken to extend to it when they affirmed, eight months ago, that a war of aggression, in violation of international law, was being waged against Ethiopia.

The Emperor made a noble but impassioned plea for the respect of the Covenant of the League of Nations and for the territorial integrity of small and weak States, culminating his speech with the following questions:

> I ask the fifty-two nations who have given a promise to the Ethiopian people that they would come to their aid at the time of the aggression against them, in order to prevent the aggressor from defeating them – I ask these fifty-two nations for their support by upholding their promise. What are you willing to do for Ethiopia?
>
> You, Great Powers, who have promised to give guarantees of collective security, lest small nations be extinguished and the fate which has overtaken Ethiopia should befall them as well, have you considered what kind

117 Spencer, *op. cit.* n. 99, p. 630.

118 George Scott, *The Rise and Fall of the League of Nations* (1973), pp. 357–358.

119 Spencer, *op. cit.* n. 99, pp. 637–638.

> of assistance to provide, so that Ethiopia's liberty shall not be destroyed and her territorial integrity shall be respected?
>
> You representatives of the world assembled here! I have come to you to Geneva to carry out the saddest duty that has befallen an Emperor. What answer am I to take back to my people?[120]

The response was, of course, a deafening silence as Ethiopia, though it would retain its membership in League of Nations, would remain under Italian occupation until 1941.

The Italian annexation of Ethiopia meant that ultimately, the issue of slavery stopped being of concern to the League of Nations. This transpired as first, the League was unwilling to recognise the annexation, and thus the Advisory Committee of Experts failed to reproduce those sections related to Ethiopia of the 1936 Italian submission in its Annual Report; and second, that Italy failed to make a further submission in 1937, and withdrew from the League of Nation in 1938. Returning to the 1936 submission of Italy: in occupying Ethiopia, it sought to justify its action retroactively by, *inter alia*, pointing to issues of slavery over territory it now deemed to be part of its Empire. In its submission to the League of Nations Advisory Committee of Experts on issues of Slavery, it pointed to Notes of March and April 1936 it which it announced the "general freeing of slaves in the Ethiopian territories – adjacent to Eritrea and Somaliland – which have been occupied by Italian troops." The Advisory Committee of Experts noted this in its introduction; however, under a procedure which allowed one State to report on issues of slavery in another State, and thus decoupled it from the report which Italy had prepared for the Committee. Yet, despite this unwillingness to recognise the Italian claim to Ethiopia, the Committee surprisingly included in its Report a section of the Italian submission which quoted from the pre-war long memorandum already mentioned which Italy had re-submitted having originally provided it to the League's Council in September 1935 in an attempt to justify its move to conquer Ethiopia. The Advisory Committee of Experts reproduced, without comment, the damning conclusions drawn from the section of the Italian memorandum dealing with the "question of the attitude of Ethiopia to the special engagements assumed by that country towards the League of Nations in regard to slavery":

(a) That Ethiopia recognises slavery as a legal condition;
(b) That raids for the capture of individuals for purposes of slavery are continuing on large scale, especially in the southern and western regions of Ethiopia;

---

120 Sellasie, *op. cit.* n. 22, pp. 311–312.

(c) That the slave trade still persists;
(d) That the Ethiopian Government participates directly in the slave trade by accepting slaves as payment of taxes and allowing detachments of regular troops to capture slaves;
(e) That, in addition to slavery proper, there exists the institution known as 'gebber', to which the population of non-Ethiopians regions are subject and which is a form of servitude akin to slavery;
(f) That the Ethiopian Government taken no account of the recommendations made to it by the Committee of Experts on Slavery, more particularly as regards the abolition of the legal status of slaves, as appears further from the report submitted to the League of Nations in May 1935.[121]

The reproduction of Italy's pre-war claims regarding the attitude of Ethiopia towards the undertaking it had accepted upon entry into the League of Nations was the last words spoken about the issue of slavery within the League of Nations in regard to Ethiopia. A rather sad ending to what may well be considered the saddest episode of the League of Nations – the failure to prevent the annexation of Ethiopia by Italy.

Conclusion

The failure to stop or reverse the Italian annexation of Ethiopia stemmed from an unwillingness of the European Powers of the League of Nations to truly challenge Italy during the mid-1930s, as they sought to avoid war with that Fascist State which was being pushed into the camp of Adolf Hitler of Germany. Ethiopia for its part could be sacrificed as it was considered by those European Powers as less than a member of the League of Nations. This was made evident from its inception when Ethiopia sought to avoid European and League encroachment by seeking admission, in 1923, to the League of Nations; wherein the British Government saw it as being 'unfit' for membership, though it recognised that joining the League might assist Ethiopia in its desire "to raise herself in the scale of civilisation."[122]

The standard of civilisation which was applied in the Ethiopian case was that of the suppression of slavery and the slave trade, which was attached as

121 League of Nations, Slavery, Report of the Advisory Committee of Experts, 15 May 1936, LofN Doc. C.189(1).M.145.1936.VI, p. 7; as found in League of Nations, *Publications of the League of Nations*, VI.B.Slavery.1936.

122 See the British Delegates comments at n. 37.

conditions for its admission to the League of Nations. Requiring Ethiopia to accept the obligations of the 1919 Treaty of St. Germain – the most up-to-date provisions regarding the suppression of the slave trade and slavery – would not, in the words of an Italian delegate, wound its "susceptibilities, since other States, which had arrived at a higher degree of civilisation, had already consented" to such undertakings.[123] Ethiopia, for its part, ultimately decided that it was better to be part of the League than to be a non-Member, despite having to be admitted with reservation. The admission of Ethiopia had unintended consequences for the League of Nations, as it lead to the drafting of what is often considered the first international human rights instrument, the 1926 Convention to Suppress the Slave Trade and Slavery. Despite the fact that the provisions of the 1926 Convention would not apply to Ethiopia during the League era, the Convention acted as a benchmark both as an established definition of slavery and the slave trade, and providing breathing space for Ethiopia in seeking to end slavery and the trade in a progressive manner. This was so as the 1926 Convention did not require the immediate abolition of slavery and the slave trade, but instead called for their gradual disappearance, something which Ethiopia much appreciated and sought to constantly demonstrate to the League through its submissions. For its part, the supervisory bodies of the League, both the Committee of Experts on Slaves and the Advisory Committee of Experts, recognised the progress, however slow, that Ethiopia was making with regard to suppressing slavery and the slave trade.

Ultimately, however, Ethiopia's conditional acceptance as a 'civilised nation' was challenged when Mussolini's Italy developed territorial ambitions in East Africa. Time and again during the dispute between Ethiopia and Italy – the League of Nations through its Committee of Five and the European Powers, by way of the Hoare-Laval Plan, – mediation proposals required that Ethiopian independence be sacrificed to appease Italy. Italian attempts to de-legitimatise Ethiopia in the lead-up to its act of aggression were in large part focused on issues of slavery which resulted in it arguing that Ethiopia openly placed "herself outside the pact of the League of Nations."[124] The criteria of civilisation which mandated Ethiopia's conditional admission to the League of Nations was nowhere made more evident than in the long memorandum placed before the League of Nations by Italy in September 1935:

> The admission of Ethiopia to the League was a political act based on the belief that, through participation in the system of international

123 See n. 44.

124 See n. 108.

> co-operation represented by the League, Ethiopia could be led to make by herself the efforts necessary to approach, even though only gradually, the level of civilisation of the other peoples belonging to the international community. [...] Ethiopia has shown that she does not posses the qualifications necessary to enable her to obtain, through participation in the League, the impulse required to raise herself by voluntary efforts to the level of the other civilised nations. The League would be defeating its own ends and its own mission if it did not take to heart this lesson of experience.[125]

Although the League of Nations did not accept the Italian submission, and despite the personal pleas of the Ethiopian Emperor, the League of Nations was unwilling to carry out its collective security obligations as against a European Power. Despite having labelled Italy the aggressor, European Powers abandoned Ethiopia to its fate, as the geo-politics of Europe meant that the 'civilised nations' concentrated on positioning themselves for the barbary of what would come to be termed: the Second World War.

---

125 League of Nations, "Situation in Ethiopia, Memorandum by the Italian Government dated 4 September 1935, and Documents relating Thereto," 4 September 1935, LoN Doc. C.340.M.171.1935.VI, as found in League of Nations, *Official Journal*, 88th and 89th Council Sessions, Annex 1571, November 1935, p. 1416.

CHAPTER 5

The International Legal Regime of Slavery and Human Exploitation and Its Obfuscation by the Term of Art: 'Slavery-Like Practice'*

Conceptually, focusing on slavery writ large – or better: human exploitation – in three distinct eras provides one with a better understanding of the manner in which the overall legal regime has evolved internationally and the way in which the introduction of the term of art: 'slavery-like practice' has obfuscated the law. This term, introduced in 1966, as a means of viscerally denouncing apartheid, quickly became synonymous, within the United Nations human rights system, with social evils as diverse as incest and female genital mutilation. 'Slavery-like practice' muddied the waters as its use confused the political with the legal not only where 'slavery' as defined by the 1926 Slavery Convention was concerned, but more so with the nomenclature of 'practices similar to slavery', those conventional servitudes noted in the 1956 Supplementary Convention. In so doing, the use of the term 'slavery-like practice' effectively grinded to a halt any evolution which might have transpired with regard to the law of human exploitation. It was only at the start of the twenty-first century, with the enumeration of types of exploitation within the trafficking conventions and the coming into force of the Rome Statute of the International Criminal Court which criminalised enslavement, that the law of human exploitation emerges from the shadows of the term 'slavery-like practice' to become relevant once more.

This study considers the three eras of the abolition of slavery and human exploitation: (i) 1890–1966 – the slave trade, slavery, and servitude in general international law; (ii) 1966–1998 – 'slavery-like practices' and human rights law; and (iii) 1998-present – enslavement and international criminal law. More so, the study focuses on the second era, from 1966–1998, to demonstrate how the United Nations turned from dealing with issues of slavery and human exploitation within a legal paradigm to ridding its legal content and equating the notion of 'slavery-like practice' with any perceived social evil which the

* This chapter first appeared as the following article: Jean Allain "The International Legal Regime of Slavery and Human Exploitation and its Obfuscation by the Term of Art: 'Slavery-Like Practice'," *Cahiers de la recherche en droits fondamentaux*, Vol. 10, 2012, p. 27. Copyright © Presses Universitaires de Caen 2012.

© KONINKLIJKE BRILL NV, LEIDEN, 2015 | DOI 10.1163/9789004279896_007

United Nations' Charter-based system sought to address. The era of 'slavery-like practices' which is now behind us and should be consigned to the dust-bin of history, obfuscated international law and demonstrated a fundamental weakness of the United Nations human rights system which, within the multi-lateral, charter-based system, is at its very core political. It is only with the recent criminalisation of slavery and human exploitation at the international level – manifest in the trafficking conventions and the Statute of the International Criminal Court – where it bumps up against the countervailing right of accused to know the charges against them that the law related to slavery and human exploitation re-emerges as a viable instrument for holding perpetrators accountable and by extension seeking to protecting individuals from nefarious exploitation.

1890–1966 – General International Law

The Slave Trade

The move to address slavery and human exploitation at the international level was first given voice by a declaration at the Congress of Vienna in 1815. Settling the Napoleonic Wars, the European Powers, expressed their wish to "bring to an end a scourge which has for a long time desolated Africa, degraded Europe, and afflicted humanity." In so doing, they declared that they:

> consider the universal abolition of the trade in Negroes to be particularly worthy of their attention, being in conformity with the spirit of the times, and the general principles of our August Sovereigns, who our animated in their sincere desire to work towards the quickest and most effective of measures, by all means at their disposal, and to act, in the use of those means with all zealousness and perseverance which is required of such a grand and beautiful cause.[1]

Despite attempts throughout the era of the Concert of Europe to get agreement on a legal text outlawing the slave trade at sea this was not to be, as a number of maritime powers hesitated in the wake of British dominance of the seas and its zealousness in seeking to outlaw the slave trade by establishing a

1 *Declaration des 8 Cours, relative à l'Abolition Universelle de la Traite des Nègres*, 8 February 1815, 3 *BFSP* 972. The eight Powers were Austria, Britain, France, Prussia, Russia, Portugal, Spain and Sweden.

right to visit ships at sea at variance with established law as rooted in the Grotian notion of the freedom of the seas.[2]

As a result, the United Kingdom turned to building a bilateral network of treaties to suppress the slave trade at sea which ultimately consisted of thirty-one States.[3] In the main, these treaties provided for a mutual right to visit the other flag State's ships on suspicion of involvement in the slave trade, and to the forfeiture by specifically constituted bilateral courts – so-called mixed commissions – of any vessel found to be shipping slaves or having onboard equipment specific to the carrying of slaves.[4] It has been estimated that the various mixed commissions situated on both sides of the Atlantic Ocean were "responsible for the condemnation of over 620 slave vessels and the liberation of nearly 80 000 slaves."[5] By the mid-1860s, the United Kingdom achieved bilaterally what it failed to procure multilaterally: the legal abolition of the slave trade at sea. Universal abolition was given formal recognition by the 1890 General Act of the Brussels Conference which established a maritime zone off the East Coast of Africa wherein European States were granted a limited right to visit so as to suppress the slave trade where it continued to persist.[6]

---

2 See Jean Allain, "Nineteenth Century Law of the Sea and the British Abolition of the Slave Trade," *British Yearbook of International Law 2007*, Vol. 78, 2008, pp. 342–388. [As reproduced in Chapter 2 of this collection.]

3 These thirty-one States included, in chronological order of signature: Portugal, Denmark, France, Spain, Netherlands, Sweden, Buenos Aires, Colombia, Brazil, Mexico, Confederation of Peru, Bolivia, Hanseatic Cities, Tuscany, the two Sicilies, Chile, Venezuela, Uruguay, Haiti, Texas, Austria, Prussia, Russia, The United States of America, Equator, Muscat, Arabs of the Gulf, New Granada, Zanzibar, Egypt. See Robert Phillimore, *Commentaries upon International Law*, 1879, pp. 420–421.

4 Such equipment included open gratings on hatches, spare planks for the creation of a slave-deck, possession of shackles or an overabundance of water and food for needs of the crew on the planned voyage. For an example of an 'equipment clause', see Further Additional Article to the Treaty of 1822 between Great Britain and The Netherlands, for the Prevention of the Traffic in Slaves, 25 January 1823, 10 *British and Foreign State Papers*, Volume 10, p. 559.

For reference to mixed commissions see L. Bethell, "The Mixed Commissions for the Suppression of the Transatlantic Slave Trade in the Nineteenth Century," *Journal of African History*, Vol. 7, 1966, p. 87.

5 J.P. van Niekerk, "British, Portuguese, and American judges in Adderley Street; the international legal background to, and some judicial aspects of, the Cape Town Mixed Commissions for the Suppression of the Transatlantic Slave Trade in the Nineteenth Century (Part 2)," *The Comparative and International Journal of Southern Africa*, Vol. 37(2), 2004, 200.

6 See General Act of the Brussels Conference relative to the African Slave Trade, 2 July 1890, Sir E. Hertslet, *The Map of Africa by Treaty*, Vol. 2, 1967, p. 499.

Susan Miers notes that the Brussels Conference "focused attention on the slavery issue and helped to rally support to the imperialist cause," which was manifest in the scramble by European Powers to appropriate territory on the Africa continent.[7] With this came the move to abolish the slave trade on land and the gradual suppression of the slave trade in Africa. As a result of the First World War and the Treaty of Versailles seeing Germany lose its African colonies; Belgium, France and the United Kingdom sought to abrogation of the 1890 General Act which, beyond the suppression of the slave trade allowed for commercial access to Africa for all. By way of a treaty signed at St. German-en Laye in 1919, the colonial powers effectively reduced the 65 articles of the General Act to the following provision:

> The Signatory Powers exercising sovereign rights or authority in African territories will continue to watch over the preservation of the native populations and to supervise the improvement of the conditions of their moral and material well-being. They will, in particular, endeavour to secure the complete suppression of slavery in all its forms and of the slave trade by land and sea.[8]

As the provision indicates, by the early part of the twentieth-century, State focus had also come to include slavery.

Slavery

The issue of slavery was first considered by the League of Nations in 1922, when a general resolution was passed by the Assembly which "was intended to disarm suspicions that it was an attack" on Ethiopia, a non-Members State of the League which had successfully fought off the Italian colonialism at Adwa in 1893.[9] With the admission of Ethiopia to the League of Nations the following year, focus of League turned to the promotion of an international legal instrument meant to suppress both slavery and the slave trade. In 1924, the Council of the League of Nations created the Temporary Slavery Commission, a body of experts whose work constitutes the intellectual DNA of much of what is found

---

7 Suzanne Miers, *Britain and the Ending of the Slave Trade* (1975), p. 294. For the 'Scramble for Africa' see H. Wesseling, *Divide and Rule: The Partition of Africa 1880–1914* (1996).

8 Paragraph 1, Article 11, *Convention Revising the General Act of Berlin, 26 February 1885, and the General Act and Declaration of Brussels, 2 July 1890*, 10 September 1919.

9 Suzanne Miers, *Slavery in the Twentieth Century: The Evolution of a Global Problem* (2003), p. 73. See also Jean Allain, "Slavery and the League of Nations: Ethiopia as a Civilised Nation," *Journal of the History of International Law*, Vol. 8, 2006, pp. 213–244.

not only in the Slavery Convention negotiated and established in 1926, but also the 1956 Supplementary Convention established by the United Nations.

While the signatories to the St. German-en Laye Convention had endeavoured to "secure the complete suppression of slavery [...] and of the slave trade," the States negotiating the 1926 Slavery Convention where not willing to go so far where slavery was concerned. By way of Article 2 of the 1926 Slavery Convention, States Parties agreed to "suppress and prevent the slave trade," but did not seek to give immediate effect to like obligations with regard to slavery, as they pledged to "bring about, progressively and as soon as possible, the complete abolition of slavery in all its forms."[10] The Convention, recognising that forced labour could develop into conditions analogous to slavery, allowed it to persist for public purposes but sought, though "progressively and as soon as possible," to put an end to the practice. While States Parties committed to undertaking negotiations with the look to once more establishing a general treaty to suppress the slave trade at sea, this provision was still-born as no such instrument ever materialised. Where the slave trade was concerned, however the States parties undertook, at Article 3 to:

> adopt all appropriate measures with a view to preventing and suppressing the embarkation, disembarkation and transport of slaves in their territorial waters and upon all vessels flying their respective flags.

While it can be said that, *lex pasterior legi priori derogate*, the obligation flowing from the 1926 Slavery Convention have been superseded by provisions of contemporary international human rights law, what remains are the normative definitions of slavery and the slave trade as set out in Article 1 of the 1926 Slavery Convention:

1. Slavery is the status or condition of a person over whom any or all of the powers attaching to the right of ownership are exercised.
2. The slave trade includes all acts involved in the capture, acquisition or disposal of a person with intent to reduce him to slavery; all acts involved in the acquisition of a slave with a view to selling or exchanging him; all acts of disposal by sale or exchange of a slave acquired with a view to being sold or exchanged, and, in general, every act of trade or transport in slaves.

---

10 Article 2, Slavery Convention, Geneva, September 25th, 1926, C.586.M.223.1926.VI, 16 October 1926; as found in Publications of the League of Nations, VI.B.Slavery.1926. VI.B.7. As reproduced in Jean Allain, *The Slavery Conventions: The Travaux Préparatoires of the 1926 League of Nations Convention and the 1956 United Nations Convention* (2008), p. 754.

As was noted in the Judgment of the Trial Chamber of the International Criminal Tribunal for the former Yugoslavia in the 2002 *Kunarac et als.* case:

> The customary international law status of these substantive provisions is evinced by the almost universal acceptance of that Convention and the central role that the definition of slavery in particular has come to play in subsequent international law developments in this field.[11]

While the definition of the slave trade has remained uncontested, the definition of 'slavery' has been interpreted in at least three ways. The European Court of Human Rights, in its 2005 *Siliadin* judgment, considered that the definition of slavery in very narrow terms, as applying exclusively in situations of chattel slavery, where a person has *de jure* ownership over another.[12] The Court states:

> [T]his definition corresponds to the "classic" meaning of slavery as it was practiced for centuries. Although the applicant was, in the instant case, clearly deprived of her personal autonomy, the evidence does not suggest that she was held in slavery in the proper sense, in other words that Mr and Mrs B. exercised a genuine right of legal ownership over her, thus reducing her to the status of an "object."

The second interpretation of the term 'slavery' as set out in the 1926 Slavery Convention, was put forward by David Weissbrodt, then Member of the United Nations Sub-Commission on the Promotion and Protection of Human Right, in conjunction with Anti-Slavery International. In their 2000 Report on Contemporary Forms of Slavery the authors content that slavery as defined in the 1926 Slavery Convention goes beyond the written word to also include lesser servitude mentioned by the 1924 Temporary Slavery Commission:

> By referring to "*any* or all of the powers of ownership" in its definition of slavery, and setting forth as its stated purpose the "abolition of slavery in *all* its forms" the Slavery Convention covered not only domestic slavery but also the other forms of slavery listed in the Report of the Temporary Slavery Commission.[13]

---

11 *Prosecutor v. Kunarac, Kovac & Vukovic*, International Criminal Tribunal for the former Yugoslavia, Case Nos. IT-96-23 &-IT-96-23/1-A, Judgment, 12 June 2002, para. 520.

12 See European Court of Human Rights, *Siliadin v France* (Application 73316/01), 26 July 2005, p. 37.

13 See United Nations Sub-Commission on the Promotion and Protection of Human Right, *Contemporary Forms of Slavery: Updated review of the implementation of and follow-up to*

This interpretation, however, cannot be sustained. It is clear that States, in negotiating the content of the 1926 Convention, did *not* intend to widen the scope of 'slavery' by subsuming within the definition lesser servitudes which did not meet the threshold of the "status or condition of a person over whom any or all of the powers attaching to the right of ownership are exercised." The *travaux préparatoires*, bear this out, as the Union of South Africa, in commenting on the 1925 League of Nations Draft Convention, noted that the "Convention as drafted goes somewhat further than seems necessary for the abolition of slavery and the slave trade." Where an early draft of the Convention introduce the concept of 'domestic slavery and similar conditions' beside slavery the Union of South Africa protested saying that either a person was a slave as defined by the proposed Convention or they were not:

> If, [...], they have become domestic slaves or persons in similar conditions in the manner indicated, that can only be because others have acquired a right of property in them, and they are therefore slaves as defined in Article 1.[14]

When the 1926 Slavery Convention was presented to the Assembly of the League of Nations for signature, the Report which accompanies it recognised, though hesitantly, that "these last practices do not come under the definition of slavery as it is given in Article 1."[15] As a result the provision 'domestic slavery and similar conditions' had been deleted from the final provisions of the 1926 Slavery Convention.

The third interpretation of the definition of slavery[16] flows from the *travaux préparatoires*, and has been expressed in part by the High Court of Australia in the 2008 *The Queen v Tang* case wherein it was determined that the definition applies to both *de jure* and *de facto* slavery.[17] The High Court looked to the

---

the conventions on slavery, Working Paper prepared by David Weissbrodt and Anti-Slavery International, UN Doc. E/CN.4/Sub.2/2000/3, 26 May 2000, p. 5. Emphasis in the original.

14 League of Nations, Draft Convention on Slavery, Replies of Governments, Reply from the Government of the Union of South Africa, A.10(a).1926.VI, 22 July 1926, p. 5; as found in League of Nations, Publications of the League of Nations, VI.B.Slavery.1926, VI. B. 3.

15 League of Nations, Slavery Convention: Report presented to the Assembly by the Sixth Committee, LofN Doc. A.104.1926.VI, as found in League of Nations, Publications of the League of Nations, VI.B.Slavery.1926, VI. B. 5, 24 September 1926, p. 1–2.

16 See Jean Allain, "The Definition of Slavery in International Law," *Howard Law Journal*, Vol. 52, 2009, pp. 239–275.

17 See *The Queen v Tang* [2008] HCA 39, 28 August 2008; see also Jean Allain, "The Queen v. Tang: Clarifying the Definition of 'Slavery' in International Law," *Melbourne Journal of*

wording to the first element of the definition of slavery – the phrase 'status or condition' – to make the *de jure/de facto* distinction: status, it noted "is a legal concept," while "the evident purpose of the reference to 'condition' was to cover slavery *de facto* [...]."[18] The High Court then made clear that the definition, unlike the European Court of Human Rights' interpretation did not turn on the "exercised a genuine right of legal ownership," but instead that the "definition turns upon the exercise of power over a person"; and that in *de facto* conditions the "definition was addressing the exercise over a person of powers of the kind that attached to the right of ownership when the legal status was possible."[19] In other words, one could conceive of a *de jure* right of ownership over a person, but also the exercise of the powers which would otherwise be attached to a right of ownership in situations of *de facto* slavery.

In giving content to the scope of the definition of slavery, the High Court makes reference to a 1953 Report, in which the United Nations Secretary-General provides a reading of 'powers attaching to the right of ownership'. The Secretary-General puts forward the following characteristics of such powers attaching to the right of ownership: the ability to purchase or transfer a person; the absolute use of a person, their labour or the ownership of the product of that labour; as well as the indeterminacy or the inheritability of the status or condition of a person held in slavery.[20]

International Law, Vol. 10, 2009, pp. 246–257. [As reproduced in Chapter 19 of this collection.]

18 *The Queen v Tang* [2008] HCA 39, 28 August 2008, p. 12.

19 *Id.*

20 United Nations, Economic and Social Council, *Report of the Secretary-General on Slavery, the Slave Trade, and Other Forms of Servitude*, UN Doc. E/2357, 27 January 1953, p. 36, n. 1. As noted in this report the six powers attaching to the right of ownership read:

1. the individual of servile status may be made the object of a purchase;
2. the master may use the individual of servile status, and in particular his capacity to work, in an absolute manner, without any restriction other than that which might be expressly provided by law;
3. the products of labour of the individual of servile status become the property of the master without any compensation commensurate to the value of the labour;
4. the ownership of the individual of servile status can be transferred to another person;
5. the servile status is permanent, that is to say, it cannot be terminated by the will of the individual subject to it;
6. the servile status is transmitted *ipso facto* to descendants of the individual having such status.

Note also See Jean Allain, "The Definition of Slavery in International Law," *Howard Law Journal*, Vol. 52, 2009, pp. 262–266.

Servitude

In 1948, the United Nations General Assembly adopted the Universal Declaration of Human Rights which notes at Article 4 that "No one shall be held in slavery or servitude."[21] One year later, the General Assembly requested that the Economic and Social Council consider the issue of slavery and, by 1953, requested the UN Secretary-General canvas all States, both Members and non-members of the United Nations, "concerning the desirability of a supplementary convention and its possible contents."[22] Within this process, the United Kingdom put forward a Draft Supplementary Convention on Slavery and *Servitude* as a basis of negotiation. That title of the Convention would give way by the time it was accepted by the Diplomatic Conference of 1956 so as to read: the Supplementary Convention on the Abolition of Slavery, the Slave Trade, and *Institutions and Practices Similar to Slavery*.[23] This shift from considering issues of 'servitude' to issues of 'institutions and practices similar to slavery' was one brought on by the unwillingness by States negotiating the Convention to accept immediate obligations to suppress servitude. Instead, the States Parties negotiating the 1956 Supplementary Convention agreed, like in 1926, that they would "take all practicable and necessary legislative and other measures to bring about progressively and as soon as possible the complete abolition or abandonment" of these institutions and practices.[24]

Despite this, throughout the whole negotiation process and stretching back as far as the 1924 Temporary Slavery Commission, the four institutions and practices enumerated in Article 1 were considered 'servitudes'. These four conventional servitudes, re-branded as 'institutions or practices similar to slavery' are defined in Article 1 in the following terms:

(a) Debt bondage, that is to say, the status or condition arising from a pledge by a debtor of his personal services or of those of a person under his control as security for a debt, if the value of those services as reasonably assessed is not applied towards the liquidation of the debt or the

21 United Nations, General Assembly, Resolution 217 A (III), 10 December 1948.

22 See United Nations, General Assembly, Resolution 278 (III), 13 May 1949.; and United Nations, Economic and Social Council, Resolution 475 (XV), 27 April 1953.

23 United Nations Conference of Plenipotentiaries on a Supplementary Convention on the Abolition of Slavery, the Slave Trade and Institutions and Practices Similar to Slavery, Final Act and Supplementary Convention, 4 September 1956, UN Doc E/CONF.24/23.

24 See Article 1, United Nations Conference of Plenipotentiaries on a Supplementary Convention on the Abolition of Slavery, the Slave Trade and Institutions and Practices Similar to Slavery, Final Act and Supplementary Convention, 4 September 1956, UN Doc E/CONF.24/23.

length and nature of those services are not respectively limited and defined;

(b) Serfdom, that is to say, the condition or status of a tenant who is by law, custom or agreement bound to live and labour on land belonging to another person and to render some determinate service to such other person, whether for reward or not, and is not free to change his status;

(c) Any institution or practice whereby:
 (i) A woman, without the right to refuse, is promised or given in marriage on payment of a consideration in money or in kind to her parents, guardian, family or any other person or group; or
 (ii) The husband of a woman, his family, or his clan, has the right to transfer her to another person for value received or otherwise; or
 (iii) A woman on the death of her husband is liable to be inherited by another person;

(d) Any institution or practice whereby a child or young person under the age of 18 years is delivered by either or both of his natural parents or by his guardian to another person, whether for reward or not, with a view to the exploitation of the child or young person or of his labour.

The four institutions and practices similar to slavery are in essence (re: normatively) conventional servitudes. If one considers the evolution of international human rights law which established under Article 8(2) of the International Covenant on Civil and Political Rights, that: 'No one shall be held in servitude'; it can be argued that nomenclature of 'institutions and practices similar to slavery' can be dropped in favour of recognising these as types of servitudes. To maintain that the obligation of the 1956 Supplementary Convention to move "progressively and as soon as possible" towards "the complete abolition or abandonment" of the four institutions and practices similar to slavery some fifty years after the coming into existence of the 1956 Supplementary Convention and the evolution of human rights law seems dubious at best; and thus, the original understanding of these practices as types of servitude should revert to kind.[25]

Beyond the nature of these four institutions and practices similar to slavery, it should be noted that the 1956 Supplementary Convention creates for States Parties specific obligations, of which the criminalisation of dependency on

25 See Jean Allain, "On the Curious Disappearance of Human Servitude from General International Law," *Journal of the History of International Law*, Vol. 11, 2009, pp. 303–332. [As reproduced in Chapter 14 of this collection.]

slavery or attempt, accessory, conspiracy to enslave or to participate in the slave trade; with such criminalisation for institutions or practices similar to slavery required to take place progressively and as soon as possible. Where servile marriage was concern, Article 2 requires that States Parties "undertake to prescribe, where appropriate, a suitable minimum age of marriage" and to set out State control over the institutions. Further provision are also found within the Convention regarding the slave trade, wherein States Parties are required regarding to suppress the conveying of slaves by via ports, the coast or via airfields. While these obligations remain live for States Parties, it may be said that, like the 1926 Slavery Convention, the most relevant product of the 1956 Supplementary Convention on the Abolition of Slavery, the Slave Trade, and Institutions and Practices Similar to Slavery is its definitions.

1966–1998 – Human Rights Law and 'Slavery-like Practices'

In the aftermath of the negotiation of the 1956 Supplementary Convention monumental changes took place in international relations. For the first ten years of existence of the United Nations, membership was limited by the inability, within the context of the Cold War, of the Soviet Union and the United States of America to agree on a formula which would allowed States, beyond the declared allies of the victors of the Second World War, to accede to the Organisation. In 1955, the log-jam of potential members was resolved, and membership in the United Nations has grown from its original forty-nine to its current one-hundred and ninety-two Member States. The bulk of the new membership resulted from the decolonisation process which ultimately shifted the balance of power from the North to the South within the democratic bodies of the United Nations. This was very much in evidence, with the issue of slavery and human exploitation was concerned, as the legal regime just considered – manifest in the 1926 Slavery Convention and the 1956 Supplementary Convention – would take a backseat for nearly half a century to the political concept of 'slavery-like practices'. By turning to 'slavery-like practices' newly-independent States were given a platform to criticise colonialism, but more so, as a further means of challenging apartheid; while deflecting attention away from "entrenched customs," such as child marriage and widow inheritance which, as Suzanne Miers writes, "they did not consider forms of servitude."[26]

26 Suzanne Miers, *Slavery in the Twentieth Century*, 2003, p. 362.

The Slavery-like Practice of Apartheid

In the direct aftermath of the establishment of the 1956 Supplementary Convention on the Abolition of Slavery, the Slave Trade, and Institutions and Practices Similar to Slavery, no sense of urgency existed within the United Nations to address issues of human exploitation writ large. On an annual basis from 1960 to 1962, the United Nations Economic and Social Council did little more than passed resolutions urging States to adhere to the 1926 and 1956 Conventions.[27] But by 1963, the Council considered that "there exists a need for accurate, comprehensive and up-to-date information of the extent of slavery, the slave trade and institutions and practices similar to slavery still persist today." As such, it requested the UN Secretary-General appoint a special rapporteur,[28] who would bring up to date a study which had been carried out in 1955 by Hans Engen on the extent to which slavery, the slave trade and servitude persisted.[29] The new Special Rapporteur on Slavery, Mohamed Awad, presented his Report in 1966. In that Report, the link between slavery and apartheid was made for the first time as a result of a submission by the Union of Soviet Socialist Republics (Soviet Union) wherein it considered the lack of adherence to the 1956 Supplementary Convention as being "abnormal"; and stated that the "main factors upholding and encouraging slavery at the present time are colonialism, *apartheid* and racism."[30] This wording was reproduced by Awad in the section of his Report related to 'suggestions for possible action by the United Nations in the field of slavery'.[31]

During consideration of Mohamed Awad's *Report on Slavery*, the Social Committee of the UN Economic and Social Council was drawn to the section dealing with suggestions for possible UN action. It was during these – rather contentious – deliberation that the term of art 'slavery-like practice' emerged as the focal point of the drafting of a resolution which would later be forwarded to the Economic and Social Council and later still, on 26 July 1966, pass as Resolution 1126(XLI). It was the representative of the Soviet Union who, while thanking Awad for his work, noted "that slavery was not limited exclusively to the facts mentioned in the report. Apartheid and certain forms of colonial

27 United Nations, United Nations Action in the Field of Human Rights, UN Doc ST/HR/2/Rev.4, 1994, p. 77.

28 United Nations, Economic and Social Council, Resolution 960 (XXXVI) 12 July 1963.

29 See United Nations, Economic and Social Council, Report of the Rapporteur appointed under Council Resolution 525 A (XVII), UN Doc E/2673, 9 February 1955.

30 United Nations, Mohamed Awad, *Report on Slavery*, UN Doc. E/4168/Rev.1, 1966, p. 285. Emphasis in the original.

31 *Id.*, p. 303.

exploitation still found in South Africa and in territories administered by Portugal constituted perhaps one of the most insidious forms of slavery with which the United Nations had to contend."[32]

While it was the Soviet Union that first put forward the claim, it was the Representative of the United Republic of Tanzania, Mr. Waldo Waldron-Ramsey, who took the lead in advocating the link between slavery and apartheid and colonialism throughout the discussion of the Social Committee and was the intellectual engine behind the concept of 'slavery-like practice'. For Waldron-Ramsey, one had to start with the definition of 'slavery'. In his view:

> the policy of apartheid followed by South Africa in its own territory and in South West Africa, by the racist, traitorous and illegal regime in the Colony of Rhodesia and the colonialist methods applied by the Portuguese Government in the so-called Portuguese territories of Mozambique, Angola, and Portuguese Guinea, were flagrant examples of slavery.
>
> It was manifest that the methods traditionally used by the colonialist must be regarded as practices similar to slavery.[33]

Mr Waldron-Ramsey disagreed with Mohamed Awad's proposal that a committee of experts be established to consider issues of slavery, "unless the endeavour was first made to widen the actual definition of slavery."[34]

The Chair of the Social Committee, seeing that a number of delegates wished to go beyond considering the *Report on Slavery* by putting forward specific proposals for dealing with slavery, called for the establishment of a working group to seek agreement on a draft resolution.[35] When the Working Group reported back to the Social Committee, it was clear that agreement could not be reached on the contentious issues of apartheid and colonialism which were being equated to 'practices similar to slavery' – that is, in line with the wording of the 1956 Supplementary Convention. As the note accompanying the draft resolution put forward by the Working Group stated, the "texts on which members of the Working Group were not in agreement are indicated by the use of

32 United Nations, Economic and Social Council, Social Committee, Summary Record of the Five Hundred and Thirty-Fourth Meeting, 6 July 1966, UN Doc E/AC.7/SR.534, 13 December 1966, p. 11.

33 United Nations, Economic and Social Council, Social Committee, Summary Record of the Five Hundred and Thirty-Sixth Meeting, 7 July 1966, UN Doc E/AC.7/SR.536, 14 December 1966, p. 5.

34 *Id.*, p. 6.

35 *Id.*, p. 7.

square brackets." Of these, the third and seventh preambluar paragraphs, as well as paragraph four of the Working Group's Draft Resolution provided a choice between the phrase 'slavery, the slave trade and institutions and practice similar to slavery' or 'slavery, the slave trade and all institutions of *apartheid* and colonialism which form part of the practice of slavery'. Further disagreement was manifest in the Draft Resolution as to what further studies should flow from the Awad's Report. While general agreement existed as to an examination of "the working of laws, regulations and administrative measures" adopted by States to give effect to the 1926 and 1956 Conventions; agreement was not forthcoming to allow for the study of "the practice of apartheid in the Republic of South Africa and the trust territory of South West Africa" or to "study the slave trade and sweated labour which [is obtained] in the Portuguese colonies in Africa."[36]

When the Working Group's Draft Resolution was considered by the Social Committee of the Economic and Social Council, the Representative of Greece spoke to the move to develop an expanded definition of slavery as proposed by Waldron-Ramsey: "if it was desired to widen or restrict the definition of slavery as given in those Conventions [read: 1926 Slavery and 1956 Supplementary Conventions], a new conference of plenipotentiaries should be convened. That was the only proper legal procedure and the procedure advocated by the Tanzanian representative in his draft resolution could not be adopted."[37] For his part, Waldron-Ramsey stated that the definition of slavery "should not give rise to any difficulty." He then provided a definition, saying that slavery "obviously meant the domination of one individual or group of individuals by another." He then continued: "What better example of slavery could be found than the situation at present prevailing on the African continent, in South Africa, Rhodesia and the Portuguese colonies of Mozambique, Angola, and Guinea, not to mention the territory of South-West Africa? Any failure to recognise that would clearly be a denial of the classic definition of slavery."[38]

Waldron-Ramsey did not stop there. Clearly making a political, as opposed to a legal, argument, he stated that he was not going to fathom such 'humbug' by States which sought to abide by the legal definition of slavery:

36 United Nations, Economic and Social Council, Social Committee, Slavery, Draft resolution by the Working Group established by the Social Committee at its 536th Meeting, UN Doc E/AC.7/L.486, 8 July 1966, pp. 2–3.

37 United Nations, Economic and Social Council, Social Committee, Summary Record of the Five Hundred and Thirty-Eight Meeting, 11 July 1966, UN Doc E/AC.7/SR.538, 14 December 1966, p. 4.

38 *Id.*, pp. 4–5.

> The Committee was not asked to go back to the 1926 or 1956 Conventions, to which the Greek representative had referred, but to deal with slavery in 1966. Some delegations interpreted the notion of slavery in a limited technical sense and were endeavouring to restrict its definition to suit their own ends; he was not fooled by their humbug.
>
> They drew attention to the slavery alleged to exist in India and Pakistan where it was supposed to result from traditional debtor-creditor relationships, or in the High Andes of Peru and Bolivia, where it was said to stem from landlord-tenant relationships. In point of fact there was no slavery either in those Asian countries or in Latin America, but slavery undoubtedly existed in the African counties he had mentioned [re: South Africa, Rhodesia, etc.].
>
> Similarly, it had been claimed that forms of slavery were to be found in certain Islamic customs, particularly polygamy. He protested against such allegations which were designed purely to camouflage other motives. Forms of bondage similar to slavery might be said to exist in certain European and American countries particularly in the Anglo-Saxon countries where prostitution and drug addiction were rife, as he remembered from the time when he had practised as a barrister in London.
>
> Nor could the question of racialism be excluded, for it was the direct corollary of slavery. In his opinion, the classic definition of slavery he had given should either be accepted or extended to include all related manifestations of it without exception.[39]

Following this discussions of the definition of slavery by the Tanzanian Representative, the Social Committee decide to suspend consideration of the issue of slavery for a day to allow States to try to gain agreement on a draft resolution. No such agreement was forthcoming, however, as a number of texts emerged which, in essence, marked the split within the Working Group, that is: between those who favoured wording that reflected the 1926 Slavery Convention and 1956 Supplementary Conventions and those which sought to include apartheid and colonialism within the terms of slavery.[40]

---

39 *Id.*, p. 5.

40 See United Nations, Economic and Social Council, Social Committee, Slavery, Canada, Panama, Philippines and Sweden; draft resolution, UN Doc E/AC.7/L.487, 12 July 1966; United Nations, Economic and Social Council, Social Committee, Slavery, Draft Resolution submitted by Algeria, Gabon, Iraq and the United Republic of Tanzania, UN Doc E/AC.7/L.488, 12 July 1966; United Nations, Economic and Social Council, Social Committee,

Speaking in favour of maintain the wording of the 1926 and 1956 Conventions were the representatives of the United States of America and France. The Representative of the United States of America stated that "it seemed to him that a number of delegations represented in the Committee had lost sight of the definition of which the Special Rapporteur [re: Mohamed Awad] had based his study; that definition was, in its turn, based on the definition laid down in the 1926 and 1956 Conventions. He agreed with the representative of Greece that any departure from that definition should be made only after the most careful consideration."[41] The French Representative was rather succinct, simply stating that he "continued to doubt the advisability of the extension of the definition of slavery" contained in the draft resolution supported by most delegations.[42]

Not surprising, the text which would emerge as Economic and Social Council was a compromise. That text, sponsored by Algeria, Gabon, Cameroon, Iran, Iraq, Morocco and the United Republic of Tanzania, did not seek to establish the 'slavery-like practices of apartheid and colonialism' as a stand-alone item beside slavery and the slave trade, but instead sought to place this phrase under the umbrella of slavery and the slave trade. Thus the Resolution notes in the preamble that "action should be taken to put an end to slavery and the slave trade in all their practices and manifestation including the slavery-like practices and aspects of apartheid and colonialism." Likewise, in the operative part of the Draft Resolution, Paragraph 5 reads: "*Decides* to refer the question of slavery and the slave trade in all their practices and manifestations including the slavery-like practices of apartheid and colonialism, to the Commission on Human Rights."[43]

The Representative of Gabon stated that proposed draft resolutions which included reference "to apartheid and colonialism had not been made in order to introduce politics into the debate";[44] and yet, overtly this is what happened

---

Slavery, Draft Resolution submitted by Algeria, Gabon, Iraq and the United Republic of Tanzania, UN Doc E/AC.7/L.488/Rev.1, 13 July 1966; and United Nations, Economic and Social Council, Social Committee, Slavery, Algeria, Gabon, Cameroon, Iran, Iraq, Morocco and the United Republic of Tanzania: draft resolution, UN Doc E/AC.7/L.492, 14 July 1966.

41 United Nations, Economic and Social Council, Social Committee, Summary Record of the Five Hundred and Forty-First Meeting, 15 July 1966, UN Doc E/AC.7/SR.541, 14 December 1966, p. 8.

42 *Id.*, p. 10.

43 United Nations, Economic and Social Council, Social Committee, Slavery, Algeria, Gabon, Cameroon, Iran, Iraq, Morocco and the United Republic of Tanzania: draft resolution, UN Doc E/AC.7/L.492, 14 July 1966.

44 United Nations, Economic and Social Council, Social Committee, Summary Record of the Five Hundred and Forty-First Meeting, 15 July 1966, UN Doc E/AC.7/SR.541, 14 December 1966, p. 4.

when the Representative of Iraq claimed that "some of the institutions and practices referred to in the Convention had disappeared following the accession to independence of the countries in which they had existed, and others would disappear as those countries acquired economic stability." Little time need be spend on the possibility of debt-bondage, serfdom, servile marriage or child exploitation somehow disappeared as a result of independence, but to say that the claim is certainly doubtful. The Representative of Iraq went on to say that both apartheid and colonialism "had been mentioned at the 1956 Conference, but at that time not enough people had been prepared to press for the inclusion in the Convention of a reference to apartheid and colonialism as being institutions and practices similar to slavery."[45] However, this claim is unsustainable as an examination of the record of the 1956 United Nations Conference of Plenipotentiaries on a Supplementary Convention on the Abolition of Slavery, the Slave Trade and Institutions and Practices Similar to Slavery, shows no consideration of the possible inclusion of apartheid or colonialism as practices or institutions similar to slavery. In fact, apartheid was literally not mentioned at all during the Conference; and discussion of colonialism only emerged in a benign manner as a result of the inclusion at Article 12 of the 1956 Supplementary Convention of a 'territorial' or 'colonial' clause.[46]

Despite such considerations the phrase 'the slavery-like practices of apartheid and colonialism' found its place in the lexicon of the United Nations; and considerations of human exploitation went from being exclusively legal – based on the 1926 Slavery Convention (i.e.: slavery and the slave trade) and the 1956 Supplementary Convention (i.e.: institutions and practices similar to slavery) – to being also considered under the rubrics of a term of art 'slavery-like practices'.

The Report of the Social Committee on slavery was forwarded to the Economic and Social Council and considered on 26 July 1966; with the result that Resolution 1126 was adopted, declaring that "slavery in all its forms, the trade in persons, *apartheid* and colonialism should be eradicated."[47] The Economic and Social Committee, for its part, referred "the question of slavery and the slave trade in all their practices and manifestations including the slavery-like practices of apartheid and colonialism, to the Commission on

---

45 *Id.*, p. 6.

46 See Jean Allain, *The Slavery Conventions: The Travaux Préparatoires of the 1926 League of Nations Convention and the 1956 United Nations Convention* (2008), p. 22.

47 See United Nations, Economic and Social Council, Slavery: Report of the Social Committee, UN Doc. E/4244, 19 July 1966, p. 3. For the discussion and vote, see United Nations, Economic and Social Council, *Official Record, 41st Session, 5 July–5 August 1996*, 1439th Meeting, 26 July 1996, p. 154.

Human Rights."[48] The Commission, following suit, handed the issue over to its Sub-Commission on Prevention of Discrimination and Protection of Minorities in 1967 with the mandate to "undertake regular consideration of the question of slavery in all its forms, including the slavery-like practice of apartheid and colonialism."[49] Also in 1967, in the context of dealing with issues of slavery as it relates to the Commission on the Status of Women, the Economic and Social Council affirmed "that the racist policies of apartheid and colonialism constitute slavery-like practices and should be eradicated completely and immediately." However, it went further, stating that it recognised:

> that both the International Slavery Convention of 1926 and the Supplementary Convention of 1956 on the Abolition of Slavery, the Slave Trade and Institutions and Practices Similar to Slavery should be reconsidered in order to embrace the contemporary manifestations of slavery exemplified by apartheid and colonialism.[50]

In 1972, the Economic and Social Council sought to draw attention "to the close relationship between the effects of slavery, apartheid and colonialism" and directed the Sub-Commission to "examine the possibility of the establishment of some form of permanent machinery to give advice on the elimination of slavery [...]."[51] Yet by that time the Sub-Commission proposed a mechanism to deal with issues of slavery, the die had been cast with regard to any legal link between apartheid and slavery. It should be noted that from this time forward the notion of the slavery-like practice of colonialism never gained any true independent footing, instead when 'slavery-like practice' was mention it was primarily in conjunction with apartheid.[52]

The association of apartheid with slavery through the term 'slavery-like practice' would fail to find legal footing. In fact, when States moved, in 1973, to establish a convention to suppress and punish apartheid, even in its earliest

48 United Nations, Economic and Social Council, Resolution 1126 (XLI), 26 July 1966.

49 United Nations, Economic and Social Council, Commission on Human Rights, Resolution 13 (XXII), 21 March 1967.

50 United Nations, Economic and Social Council, Resolution 1232 (XLI), 6 June 1967.

51 United Nations, Economic and Social Council, Resolution 1695 (LII), 2 June 1972.

52 The most substantive consideration of the slavery-like practice of colonialism is found in: United Nations, Economic and Social Council, Commission on Human Rights, Sub-Commission on Prevention of Discrimination and Protection of Minorities, Question of Slavery and the Slave Trade in all their Practices and Manifestations, including the Slavery-Like Practices of Apartheid and Colonialism, *Report submitted by the Special Rapporteur Mr. Mohamed Awad*, UN Doc E/CN.4/Sub.2/AC.2/332, 16 July 1971, pp. 66–76.

draft form, the proposed instrument failed to make this connection.[53] The lack of inclusion of such a provision was made more evident by the fact that the original draft was developed in tandem between Guinea and the Union of Soviet Socialist Republics, the latter having been the vary same State which had put forward the original proposition that apartheid was an 'insidious forms of slavery'. The nearest that original draft came to making a link between slavery and apartheid was the crime of apartheid which was deemed to be "committed for the purpose of establishing and maintaining domination by one racial group of persons over any other racial group of persons and of systematically oppressing them" by, *inter alia*, the "[e]xploition of labour of the members of an oppressed racial group."[54] That provision was later modified at the prompting of wording put forward by Nigeria, Pakistan and the United Republic of Tanzania, which sought to bring into the equation forced labour. As a result, when the 1973 International Convention on the Suppression and Punishment of the Crime of *Apartheid* established, amongst the instances of the crime of apartheid: "Exploitation of the labour of the members of a racial group or groups, in particular by submitting them to forced labour."[55]

Apartheid Unbridled from the Notion of 'Slavery-like Practice'

One year later, the Sub-Commission on Prevention of Discrimination and Protection of Minorities recommended through the Commission of Human Rights, and the Economic and Social Council accepted, the establishment of a five-person Working Group on Slavery, comprised of members of the Sub-Commission. It was here, within the Working Group on Slavery (and its later incarnation as the Working Group on Contemporary Forms of Slavery) that

53 See Annex I, Guinea and Union of Soviet Socialist Republics: draft Convention on the suppression and punishment of the crime of apartheid. As found in United Nations, General Assembly, Elimination of All Forms of Racial Discrimination, Draft Convention on the Suppression and Punishment of the Crime of Apartheid, Note of the Secretary-General, UN Doc A/8768, 14 September 1972.

54 Article 2(e), Annex I, Guinea and Union of Soviet Socialist Republics: draft Convention on the suppression and punishment of the crime of apartheid. As found in United Nations, General Assembly, Elimination of All Forms of Racial Discrimination, Draft Convention on the Suppression and Punishment of the Crime of Apartheid, Note of the Secretary-General, UN Doc A/8768, 14 September 1972.

55 See Article 2(e), International Convention on the Suppression and Punishment of the Crime of *Apartheid*, United Nations, General Assembly, Resolution 3068, 30 November 1973.

Note that as Article 5 of the Slavery Convention makes plain, forced labour can develop "into conditions analogous to slavery" (re: in situations where any or all of the powers attaching to the right of ownership are exercised).

the legal regime of slavery and human exploitation gave way to the political; wherein the Working Group, at its very first session in 1975 made plain that it was not going to be bound by the definition of slavery established by the 1926 Slavery Convention (which, it should be added is reiterated and confirmed in the 1956 Supplementary Convention); instead, while tentatively putting forward two possible broad definitions of slavery, the Working Group was in general agreement "that the definition should be flexible enough to be applicable to any new form of slavery which might emerge in the future and not to limit the scope of investigation of all its possible manifestations."[56]

With this in mind, the Working Group did not hesitate, despite the silence of the newly established Apartheid Convention to equate in direct terms apartheid and slavery. "Apartheid," the Working Group stated, "was considered as the most extended practice of slavery, since the whole population finds itself under the control of a few, through force." With this as a starting point, some Members of the Working Group considered that apartheid and colonialism "were, in themselves, forms of slavery and, therefore the formulation 'slavery-like practices of apartheid and colonialism' should be replaced by the formulation 'the slavery of apartheid and colonialism." For other Members of the Working Group, slavery was found only in some features of apartheid and colonialism.[57] Where the Working Group was in agreement beyond a link between slavery and apartheid was that there was a lack of information and that an in-depth study of the relationship was necessary.

In its 1976 Report, the Working Group on Slavery, in considering the work of the International Commission of Jurists, agreed that a number of penal sanctions applied to terms and conditions of employment found in Southern Rhodesia's 1901 Masters and Servants Act were "akin to slavery."[58] The Working Group on Slavery continuedto shift the goal posts this time determining, in 1977, that "apartheid could be considered a collective form of slavery" and a recommendation that apartheid as a collective form of slavery be considered

56 United Nations, Economic and Social Council, Sub- Commission on Prevention of Discrimination and Protection of Minorities, *Report of the Working Group on Slavery on its First Session*, UN Doc E/CN.4/Sub.2/AC.2/3, 28 August 1975, p. 4.

57 *Id.*, p. 5.

58 United Nations, Economic and Social Council, Commission on Human Rights, Sub-Commission on Prevention of Discrimination and Protection of Minorities, *Report of the Working Group on Slavery on its Second Session*, UN Doc E/CN.4/Sub.2/AC.2/373, 19 August 1976, p. 2.

at its next session.[59] In 1978, on the recommendation of the Working Group on Slavery, the Sub-Commission on Prevention of Discrimination and Protection of Minorities requested the UN Secretary-General "carry out, as a matter of priority, a study of apartheid and colonialism as collective forms of slavery."[60] Having moved from the slavery-like practice to a collective form of slavery saw the further obfuscation of the legal with the political.

The Secretary-General, in his 1980 *Apartheid as a Collective Form of Slavery*, sought to rectify the situation, as he noted that this was "the first report prepared for the United Nations which attempts to spell out the various elements of the apartheid system as a slavery-like practice."[61] In speaking about apartheid, the Secretary-General acknowledged that a general consensus had developed within the international community that apartheid should to be understood as "the dispossession and oppression by the white ruling minority of the entire black population for the purpose of exploiting its labour." Flowing from this general consensus was an attempt to deal with the issue in legal terms:

> apartheid and colonialism in southern Africa are therefore practices similar to slavery and forced labour which rely increasingly on indirect compulsion exercised through discriminatory and repressive legislation, but which have developed out of, and co-exist with, historical forms of direct compulsion.[62]

"This definition," the UN Secretary-General writes, "is clearly broader than the definitions of slavery and slavery-like practices [sic: it should read 'institutions and practices similar to slavery'] and of forced labour contained in the Slavery Convention of 1926, the Supplementary Convention on the Abolition of Slavery, the Slave Trade and Institutions and Practices Similar to Slavery of 1956, and the Forced Labour Convention (No. 29) of 1930." Instead, the

59 United Nations, Economic and Social Council, Commission on Human Rights, Sub-Commission on Prevention of Discrimination and Protection of Minorities, *Report of the Working Group on Slavery on its Third Session*, UN Doc E/CN.4/Sub.2/AC.2/389, 30 August 1977, pp. 4 and 6.

60 United Nations, Economic and Social Council, Sub- Commission on Prevention of Discrimination and Protection of Minorities, *Apartheid as a Collective form of Slavery: Report of the Secretary-General*, UN Doc E/CN.4/Sub.2/449, 18 July 1980, p. 4.

61 United Nations, Economic and Social Council, Commission on Human Rights, Sub-Commission on Prevention of Discrimination and Protection of Minorities, *Apartheid as a Collective Form of Slavery, Report of the Secretary-General*, UN Doc UN Doc E/CN.4/Sub.2/449, 18 July 1980, p. 8.

62 *Id.*, p. 5.

Secretary-General notes, this wider definition "emphasizes the indirect nature of the coercion exercised on the black population and it historical roots in colonial conquest and expropriation."[63]

In essence, the Secretary-General considers the slavery-like practices of apartheid to be exploitation through indirect or structural forced labour. He writes of the "international consensus which holds that apartheid is a slavery-like practice is supported by a variety of recent historical studies which have analysed the development of apartheid as a system of forced labour based on the dispossession and exploitation of the black people of South Africa."[64] As the Secretary-General notes, "apartheid as a slavery-like system relies in the first place on the exercise of control over the conditions under which African labour is made available to white employers."[65] Such control, the Secretary-General reports, includes that of residency (African being confined and forced to relocate to 'bantustans' or reserved lands, and to settle in single-sex hostiles will providing labour in white areas), of movement (pass-cards attached to labour), and of labour (restricted to low-skilled occupations and through a 'colour-bar' to advancement in career). As a result of the limited land available for subsistence farming within the bantustans, along with taxation on each African male, constructed a requirement to provide one's labour; hence through structural elements of the State, collective forced labour was the result of the South African apartheid system.

The Secretary-General concludes his study by saying that apartheid is "not simply a racial discrimination problem," but:

> the essence of apartheid lies in the dispossession of the black population through the imposition of quasi-colonial rule, and in the harnessing of the labour of the vanquished indigenous people through a variety of coercive measures for the profit of white investors, both South African and foreign. The international community has therefore described the apartheid system as a slavery-like practice imposed on an entire collectivity, which can be eradicated only through a complete restructuring of the existing political and economic relationships.[66]

For the first and only time, within the United Nations system, notion of the 'slavery-like practice' of apartheid was given specific consideration. The

63 *Id.*

64 *Id.*, p. 10.

65 *Id.*, p. 18.

66 *Id.*, p. 59.

Secretary-General found the link a rather tenuous one, basing himself on the pronouncement of what he termed the 'policy-making organs of the United Nations' – in other words, pronouncements of the United Nations' political organs. Within these organs, no clear understanding of the term 'slavery-like practice of apartheid' had emerged, instead in considering the various UN reports on apartheid, the Secretary General sought to show that if there was a slavery-like elements to apartheid it lay in a collective, structural, inducement of forced labour on racial grounds.

Having been privy to the interim Report of the Secretary-General in 1979, the Working Group on Slavery determined that "denial of freedom of residence, movement and employment and the denial of the right to organize in order to change the situation" in South Africa was "the essence of apartheid as a slavery-like practice."[67]

While the Secretary-General's Report appeared to right things by establishing apartheid as a slavery-like practice, this was undone shortly thereafter. In 1980, the Economic and Social Council decided to appoint Benjamin Whitaker, as Special Rapporteur to update Mohamed Awad's 1966 *Report on Slavery*. Where apartheid was concerned, Whitaker noted that in general terms that "unjust economic exploitation underlies many of the most serious violations of human rights," he then singled out apartheid, saying that "if a dominant stratum forces others either to work on sub-human terms or to starve, it may be said to be employing a slavery-like practice."[68] However, Whitaker once more brought into the fold the notion of apartheid as collective slavery by noting first that "apartheid is in the opinion of many people the most oppressive manifestation of slavery that exists in the world today." The continuing: "apartheid and colonialism, in many of their effects, are forms of collective or group slavery that fundamentally oppresses the human rights of several million people. A particular virulent evil of its immorality is that the victims are condemned, involuntarily, to their predicament from the day of their birth and without redress."[69]

---

67 United Nations, Economic and Social Council, Commission on Human Rights, Sub-Commission on Prevention of Discrimination and Protection of Minorities, *Question of Slavery and the Slave Trade in all their Practices and Manifestations, including the Slavery-Like Practices of Apartheid and Colonialism, Report of the Working Group on Slavery on its Fifth Session*, UN Doc E/CN.4/Sub.2/AC.2/434, 24 August 1979, p. 9.

68 United Nations, Economic and Social Council, Commission on Human Rights, Sub-Commission on Prevention of Discrimination and Protection of Minorities, *Updating of the Report on Slavery Submitted to the Sub-Commission in 1966, Report of Mr. Benjamin Whitaker, Special Rapporteur*, UN Doc E/CN.4/Sub.2/1982/20, 5 July 1982, p. 7.

69 United Nations, Economic and Social Council, Commission on Human Rights, Sub-Commission on Prevention of Discrimination and Protection of Minorities, *Updating of*

In its 1984 Report, the Working Group on Slavery combined the notions of the slavery-like practice of apartheid and the designation of apartheid as collective slavery by recognised awkwardly "that apartheid is the gravest disregard of human dignity and a collective slavery-like practice."[70] This was followed the following year by a determination by the Working Group that apartheid is the "most evil practice analogous to slavery, which constitutes a crime against humanity."[71] Despite this, the now newly rebranded Working Group on Contemporary Forms of Slavery, in its 1988 Report sought to infer that it was somehow being consisted in its use of terminology by recommending that "apartheid, including the labour practices under apartheid, should continue to be viewed as a collective form of slavery."[72] Despite this continued vacillation as to what nomenclature should be used to link slavery with apartheid, such consideration would become moot as events on the ground would quickly overtake those of the UN Human Rights system.

The fall of the Berlin Wall in 1989 marked the start of the implosion of the Soviet Union and the end of the Cold War which in its wake lead to the end of apartheid South Africa. With the freeing of Nelson Mandela in February 1990 after twenty-seven years of imprisonment the road towards the new, apartheid-free South Africa began in earnest. For the Working Group on Contemporary Forms of Slavery, a new path beckoned, having been laid out in a recommendation to the Commission on Human Rights that with regard to this "item under the agenda, particular emphasis should be given to the

---

the Report on Slavery Submitted to the Sub-Commission in 1966, Report of Mr. Benjamin Whitaker, Special Rapporteur, UN Doc E/CN.4/Sub.2/1982/20, 5 July 1982, p. 11.

70 United Nations, Economic and Social Council, Commission on Human Rights, Sub-Commission on Prevention of Discrimination and Protection of Minorities, Question of Slavery and the Slave Trade in All their Practices and Manifestations, including the Slavery-like Practices of Apartheid and Colonialism, Report of the Working Group on Slavery on its tenth session, UN Doc. E/CN.4/Sub.2/1984/25, 21 August 1985, p. 13.

71 United Nations, Economic and Social Council, Commission on Human Rights, Sub-Commission on Prevention of Discrimination and Protection of Minorities, Report of the Working Group on Slavery on its eleventh session, UN Doc. E/CN.4/Sub.2/1985/25, 15 August 1984, p. 11;

72 United Nations, Economic and Social Council, Commission on Human Rights, Sub-Commission on Prevention of Discrimination and Protection of Minorities, Question of Slavery and the Slave Trade in All their Practices and Manifestations, including the Slavery-like Practices of Apartheid and Colonialism, Report of the Working Group on Contemporary Forms of Slavery on its thirteenth session, UN Doc. E/CN.4/Sub.2/1988/32, 22 August 1988, p. 24.

situation of children and of women under apartheid."[73] This gave way to a recommendation in 1989 that "under this agenda item more attention should be given to in future sessions to the situation of women and children"; that is: dropping the need to consider the issue as linked to apartheid.[74] The following year this recommendation evolved further, speaking of "the situation of vulnerable groups, particularly women and children."[75] No discussions were held under the agenda heading of 'slavery-like practices of apartheid and colonialism' the following year. Despite the fact that the Working Group put forward a recommendation in 1992 to "devote greater attention to ways and means of assisting the victims of apartheid in order to mitigate its consequences,"[76] the line item of the 'slavery-like practices of apartheid and colonialism' was removed from the agenda of the Working Group in 1993.

'Slavery-like Practice' Unbridled from Apartheid

While apartheid came to be unbridled from the notion of 'slavery-like practice' as being, for instance 'akin to slavery', or 'collective form of slavery', etc.; the

---

73 United Nations, Economic and Social Council, Commission on Human Rights, Sub-Commission on Prevention of Discrimination and Protection of Minorities, Question of Slavery and the Slave Trade in All their Practices and Manifestations, including the Slavery-like Practices of Apartheid and Colonialism, Report of the Working Group on Contemporary Forms of Slavery on its thirteenth session, UN Doc. E/CN.4/Sub.2/1988/32, 22 August 1988, p. 24.

74 United Nations, Economic and Social Council, Commission on Human Rights, Sub-Commission on Prevention of Discrimination and Protection of Minorities, Question of Slavery and the Slave Trade in All their Practices and Manifestations, including the Slavery-like Practices of Apartheid and Colonialism, Report of the Working Group on Contemporary Forms of Slavery on its fourteenth session, UN Doc. E/CN.4/Sub.2/1989/39, 28 August 1989, p. 29.

75 United Nations, Economic and Social Council, Commission on Human Rights, Sub-Commission on Prevention of Discrimination and Protection of Minorities, Contemporary Forms of Slavery, Report of the Working Group on Contemporary Forms of Slavery on its fifteenth session, UN Doc. E/CN.4/Sub.2/1990/44, 23 August 1990, p. 23.

76 United Nations, Economic and Social Council, Commission on Human Rights, Sub-Commission on Prevention of Discrimination and Protection of Minorities, Contemporary Forms of Slavery, Report of the Working Group on Contemporary Forms of Slavery on its seventeenth session, UN Doc. E/CN.4/Sub.2/1992/34, 23 June 1992, p. 26. Note also limited discussion in United Nations, Economic and Social Council, Commission on Human Rights, Sub-Commission on the Promotion and Protection of Human Right, *Contemporary Forms of Slavery: Updated review of the implementation of and follow-up to the conventions on slavery – Addendum: Forms of Slavery*, Working Paper prepared by David Weissbrodt and Anti-Slavery International, UN Doc. E/CN.4/Sub.2/2000/3/Add.1, 26 May 2000, p. 22.

very term 'slavery-like practice' also gained an independent existence from its association to apartheid.

This decoupling of 'slavery-like practice' from apartheid and its attachment to other types of human exploitation first transpire in the 1982 Report by Benjamin Whitaker in which he introduce new 'slavery-like practices' for consideration. Under the heading of 'slavery-like practices involving women'. Whitaker examined involuntary marriage and abortion, trafficking in women, exploitation of prostitution, women under apartheid, genital mutilation, sale of women and killing for reasons of dowry. Having extended the term of art beyond its original link to apartheid, the Report confuses the political with the legal, including with types of slavery-like practices, that of servile marriage (re: in Whitaker's words: involuntary marriage) which is covers as a institution or practice similar to slavery found at Article 1(c) of the Supplementary Convention; and the sale of women which would fall within the definition of slavery as set out in the 1926 Slavery Convention.

In 1989, the Working Group on Contemporary Forms of Slavery sensing that term 'slavery-like practice' and its association with apartheid was to become obsolete, appropriated the term as an agenda item. Rather incredibly it substituted the term 'slavery-like practice' for that of 'institutions and practices of slavery' as established by the 1956 Supplementary Convention. Under line item 3 of its 1989 Report, the Working Group maintained a heading for five years which read: "Review of Information Received on the Status and the Implementation of Conventions on Slavery and Slavery-like Practices."[77] This was a monumental shift as from the first substantive agenda set in 1977 until 1988, the Working Group had an agenda item under the heading of "Review of Developments in the Field of Slavery and the Slave Trade in all their Practices and Manifestations." This however gave way as the newly renamed Working Group on Contemporary Forms of Slavery sought to make the distinction between the legal – by providing a line-item on 'slavery and slavery-like practices' meant to consider the 1926 and 1956 Conventions, and a new line-item which included a more encompassing "Review of Developments in other Fields of Contemporary Forms of Slavery," which would come to consider, over time: trafficking in persons, exploitation of prostitutes (in 1989); child

77 See United Nations, Economic and Social Council, Commission on Human Rights, Sub-Commission on Prevention of Discrimination and Protection of Minorities, Question of Slavery and the Slave Trade in All their Practices and Manifestations, including the Slavery-like Practices of Apartheid and Colonialism, Report of the Working Group on Contemporary Forms of Slavery on its fourteenth session, UN Doc. E/CN.4/Sub.2/1989/39, 28 August 1989, p. 1.

pornography, children in armed conflict (1990); child soldiers (1991); removal of organs (1992); incest (1993); migrant workers, sex tourism (1994); illegal adoption (1996); early marriages, detained juveniles (1997).

In 2000, David Weissbrodt of the Sub-Commission and the NGO Anti-Slavery International updated the Awad and Whitaker reports. The 2000 Working Paper also conflated, as the Working Group on Contemporary Forms of Slavery had done before it, the term of law 'institution and practice similar to slavery' and the term of art 'slavery-like practice'. The Weissbrodt – Anti-Slavery International Working Paper stated that "ownership is the common theme existing in all of the conventions concerning the abolition of slavery and slavery-like practices."[78] As such, the 2000 Working Paper gave 'slavery-like practice' an independent meaning from that of apartheid and muddied the waters further by substituting it for the term of law 'institution and practice similar to slavery' as set out in the 1956 Supplementary Conventions.

Here then we see the manner in which a failed attempt in 1966 to have apartheid and colonialism equated to slavery created a new term of art: slavery-like practice. That term, over time, not only lost its meaning but its component parts were detached from each other. Apartheid was no longer a slavery-like practice, it became a collective form of slavery among other variations on the theme. Likewise 'slavery-like practices' having be decoupled from apartheid came to be conflated with the legal term 'institutions and practice similar to slavery'. As a result of the varied and continued loose use of terminology within the United Nations system, the legal terms – 'slavery' and 'institutions and practice similar to slavery' – lost their meaning, obfuscated within a UN Charter-based human rights regime which is, to its very core political.

1998-Present – International Criminal Law

As the twentieth century drew to a close, the international legal regime regarding slavery and human exploitation excised for all intents and purposes in name only. The 1926 Slavery Convention and the 1956 Supplementary Conventions had been surpassed by the UN Charter-based regime's conflation

78 United Nations, Economic and Social Council, Commission on Human Rights, Sub-Commission on the Promotion and Protection of Human Right, *Contemporary Forms of Slavery: Updated review of the implementation of and follow-up to the conventions on slavery*, Working Paper prepared by David Weissbrodt and Anti-Slavery International, UN Doc. E/CN.4/Sub.2/2000/3, 26 May 2000, p. 7. See also paragraph 62 at p. 15 for the same type of conflation.

of 'slavery-like practice' with 'slavery' and 'institutions and practices similar to slavery' so as to render these latter two terms virtually without meaning. That said, the apparent diminution of the legal regime governing slavery and human exploitation has had a reprieve, having been given a new life by the move which manifests itself in the twenty-first century through international criminal law. While the twentieth century saw but one international judgment focused on slavery and human exploitation – the 1905 *Muscat Dhows* case; the twenty-first century has thus far seen decisions by the International Criminal Tribunal for the former Yugoslavia (2002 *Kunarac et als.* case), the European Court of Human Rights (2005 *Siliadin* case), the ECOWAS Community Court of Justice (2008 *Mani v Niger* case); and a consideration by the High Court of Australia of the definition of slavery in international law (2008 *The Queen v Tang*). This new found interest in issues of slavery and human exploitation results from recent international agreements which seek to deal with these issues from the perspective of criminal law – with a focus on those who would enslave – as opposed to the human rights regime and its focus on the victim of a human rights abuse.

The Trafficking Instruments

This renascence of legal issues surrounding slavery and human exploitation was given impetus through the 2000 Palermo Protocol to the United Nations Convention against Transnational Organized Crime. That instrument, the Protocol to Prevent, Suppress and Punish Trafficking in Persons, especially Women and Children, sets out a definition of 'trafficking in persons' wherein various types of human exploitation are noted. It might be added here that the 2005 Council of Europe Convention on Action against Trafficking in Human Beings sets out, in the exact same terms its definition for 'trafficking in human beings' as:

> the recruitment, transportation, transfer, harbouring or receipt of persons, by means of the threat or use of force or other forms of coercion, of abduction, of fraud, of deception, of the abuse of power or of a position of vulnerability or of the giving or receiving of payments or benefits to achieve the consent of a person having control over another person, for the purpose of exploitation. *Exploitation shall include, at a minimum, the exploitation of the prostitution of others or other forms of sexual exploitation, forced labour or services, slavery or practices similar to slavery, servitude or the removal of organs.*[79]

---

79 See Article 3(a), 2000 United Nations Protocol to Prevent, Suppress and Punish Trafficking in Persons, Especially Women; and Children and Article 4(a), 2005 Council of Europe Convention on Action against Trafficking in Human Beings. Emphasis added.

In essence, the trafficking conventions do not seek to suppress human exploitation *per se* as the conventions deal with the crime of trafficking for the *purposes* of exploitation, the crime being the 'recruitment, transportation, transfer, harbouring or receipt of persons' not, for instance, the actual enslavement of a person. What these conventions do, however, is for the most part give voice to the various types of human exploitation which have international instruments attached to them and brings them together for the first time.[80] In a somewhat convoluted manner, the conventions enumerate the most serious types of exploitation as being 'at minimum' what constitutes exploitation. This allows for the possibility of lesser or differing types of exploitation to also fall under the definitional element of exploitation, forming part of what, in law, constitutes 'trafficking in persons'.

The Palermo Protocol is transnational in nature, much like the 1926 Slavery Convention and the 1956 Supplementary Convention, it does not create an international regime, but a transnational one requiring each State Party to act within its jurisdiction. The Protocol requires States to criminalise the conduct established by the definition of trafficking in persons, that is, participating, acting as an accomplice, organising or directing other to trafficking, as well as, where the legal system permits, the crime of attempting to commit.[81] The Protocol further sets out ways in which States Parties are meant to cooperate with each other while requiring each State to strengthen its respective border controls.

The importance of the trafficking conventions to the regime of slavery and human exploitation is found in the fact that these confirm the relevance of the definitions of slavery and institutions and practices similar to slavery as set out in the 1926 Slavery Convention and the 1956 Supplementary Convention on the Abolition of Slavery, the Slave Trade, and Institutions and Practices Similar to Slavery. The *travaux préparatoires* of both the Palermo Protocol and the Council of Europe convention indicate that the diplomats negotiating those instruments had the definitions of slavery as set out in the 1926 Slavery Convention and that of institutions and practices similar to slavery as set out in the 1956 Supplementary Convention in mind when they included these terms in the trafficking conventions.[82]

---

80 See 1949 Convention for the Suppression of the Traffic in Persons and of the Exploitation of the Prostitution of Others; 1930 Forced Labour Convention (ILO No. 29); 1926 Slavery Convention; 1956 Supplementary Convention on the Abolition of Slavery, the Slave Trade, and Institutions and Practices Similar to Slavery; 1966 International Covenant on Civil and Political Rights.

81 See Article 5, 2000 United Nations Protocol to Prevent, Suppress and Punish Trafficking in Persons, Especially Women; and Children.

82 See United Nations, *Travaux Préparatoires* of the Negotiations for the Elaboration of the United Nations Convention against Transnational Organized Crime and the Protocols

Enslavement and the International Criminal Court

If anything, the legacy for international relations of the short Post-Cold War era – that period between the fall of the Berlin Wall in 1989 and the attacks of 11 September 2001 – is the actualisation of a regime of international criminal law. The establishment in 1993 and 1994 of the *ad hoc* criminal tribunals for the former Yugoslavia and for Rwanda followed by hybrid courts and the ultimate negotiation in Rome of the Statute of the International Criminal Court in 1998 means that the twenty-first century is endowed with a system of international criminal justice which may prosecute "the most serious crimes of concern to the international community as a whole."[83]

Amongst these international crimes is the crime against humanity of enslavement and the crime against humanity and war crime of sexual slavery.[84] As the UN Special Rapporteur, Gay McDougall noted with regard to 'sexual slavery, in her Report on *Systematic Rape, Sexual Slavery and Slavery-like Practices during Armed Conflict*, the "term 'sexual' is [...] an adjective to describe a form of slavery, not to denote a separate crime. In all respects and in all circumstances, sexual slavery is slavery."[85] While this acknowledgement that sexual slavery describes a type of slavery; the same could not be said to be true, until recently, with regard to the term 'enslavement'. Before the coming into existence of the 1998 Statute of the International Criminal Court, the legacy of the Nuremburg trials was such that the International Law Commission considered that:

> *Enslavement means establishing or maintaining over persons a status of slavery, servitude or forced labour* contrary to well-established and widely recognized standards of international law, such as: the Slavery Convention (slavery); the Supplementary Convention on the Abolition of Slavery, the

---

thereto, United Nations Publication Sales No. E.06.V.5, 2006; and Council of Europe, Council of Europe Convention on Action against Trafficking in Human Beings and its Explanatory Report, 16.V.2005.

83 Article 5, Statute of the International Criminal Court, UN Doc. A/CONF.183/9, 17 July 1998.

84 See Article 7(1)(c) – Crime against humanity of enslavement; Article 7(1)(g) – Crime against humanity of sexual slavery; Article 8(2)(b)(xxii) – War crime of sexual slavery (international conflict); and Article 8(2)(e)(vi) – War crime of sexual slavery (non-international armed conflict) of the Statute of the International Criminal Court, UN Doc. A/CONF.183/9, 17 July 1998.

85 United Nations, Economic and Social Council, Commission in Human Rights, *Contemporary Forms of Slavery: Systematic rape, sexual slavery and slavery-like practices during armed conflict*, Final report submitted by Ms. Gay J. McDougall, Special Rapporteur, UN Doc. E/CN.4/Sub.2/1998/13, 22 June 1998, para. 30.

> Slave Trade, and Institutions and Practices Similar to Slavery (slavery and servitude); the International Covenant on Civil and Political Rights (slavery and servitude); and ILO Convention No. 29, concerning Forced or Compulsory Labour (forced labour). Enslavement was included as a crime against humanity in the Charter of the Nurnberg Tribunal (art. 6, subpara. (c)), Control Council Law No. 10 (art. II, subpara. (c)), the statute of the International Tribunal for the Former Yugoslavia (art. 5) and the statute of the International Tribunal for Rwanda (art. 3) as well as the Nurnberg Principles (Principle VI) and the 1954 draft Code (art. 2, para. 11).[86]

This understanding, that enslavement included not only slavery, but also servitude and forced labour was acknowledged by the International Criminal Tribunal for the former Yugoslavia in the *Kunarac* case, where the Trial Chamber determined that the definition of enslavement "may be broader than the traditional and sometimes apparently distinct definitions of slavery, the slave trade and servitude or forced or compulsory labour found in other areas of international law."[87]

Despite the fact that the law developed by the International Law Commission and the International Criminal Tribunal for the former Yugoslavia seems to indicate that customary international law considered 'enslavement' to be distinct from 'slavery', as being an umbrella term which included not only slavery, but also lesser servitudes including forced labour, this understanding has not found its way into the Statute of the International Criminal Court. Instead, the Statute defines enslavement as being synonymous with slavery, that is:

> 'Enslavement' means the exercise of any or all of the powers attaching to the right of ownership over a person and includes the exercise of such power in the course of trafficking in persons, in particular women and children[88]

Synonymous, as the first part of the definition of enslavement mirrors the definition of slavery established by the 1926 Slavery Convention; while the second

86 See Article 18, United Nations, General Assembly, International Law Commission, Draft Code of Crimes against the Peace and Security of Mankind with commentaries, *Yearbook of the International Law Commission*, UN Doc. A/51/10 (Volume 2, Part 2), 1996, p. 47. Emphasis added.

87 International Criminal Tribunal for the former Yugoslavia, *Kunarac et als.* (IT-96-23-T &-IT-96-23/1-T) Judgment, 22 February 2001, p. 193.

88 Article 7(2)(c), Rome Statute of the International Criminal Court, UN Doc. A/CONF.183/9, 17 July 1998.

part (re: and includes the exercise of such power in the course of trafficking in persons, in particular women and children) does not extend the definition nor modify it, but simply highlights the fact that enslavement within cases of trafficking also fall within the purview of this provision.[89] Thus, on the basis of a treaty, the Statute of the International Criminal Court narrows 'enslavement' so as to be, in law, 'slavery'; while discarding the perceived customary international law established to date.

That said, it should be acknowledged that the secondary legislation of the International Criminal Court, its Elements of Crimes, which are meant to assist "the Court in the interpretation and application" of these crimes does ultimately mention lesser servitudes.[90] However, the mention of forced labour and lesser servitudes within the Elements of Crimes does not – as will be demonstrated – expanded the definition of enslavement beyond that of 'slavery'. This is so as Article 9(3) of the Statute of the International Criminal Court requires that the "Elements of Crimes [...] be consistent with this Statute."

Turning to the provisions of the Elements of Crimes of the crime of enslavement, Element 1 reads:

> The perpetrator exercised any or all of the powers attaching to the right of ownership over one or more persons, such as by purchasing, selling, lending or bartering such a person or persons, or by imposing on them a similar deprivation of liberty.

At the end of this Element is the footnote which states:

> It is understood that such deprivation of liberty may, in some circumstances, include exacting forced labour or otherwise reducing a person to servile status as defined in the Supplementary Convention on the Abolition of Slavery, the Slave Trade, and Institutions and Practices Similar to Slavery of 1956. It is also understood that the conduct described

---

89 See *Katanga and Chui* case, International Criminal Court, *Amicus Curiae on Observations related to Sexual Slavery submitted by Queen's University Belfast Human Rights Centre*, ICC-01/04-01/07-1257-Anx, 30 June 2009, para. 24. Note that the High Court of Australia has stated that such a formulation as the latter part of the definition of enslavement is "a common drafting technique." See *The Queen v Tang* [2008] HCA 39, 28 August 2008, para. 33.

90 See Article 9(3), Rome Statute of the International Criminal Court, UN Doc. A/CONF.183/9, 17 July 1998.

in this element includes trafficking in persons, in particular women and children.[91]

Prima facie, one might say, via the footnote to Element 1 of the crime against humanity of enslavement that forced labour and the institutions and practices similar to slavery established by the 1956 Supplementary Convention fall within the definition of enslavement and thus expand that notion beyond slavery to included lesser servitudes. This, however, cannot be as the Elements of Crimes must be consistent with the Statue which set the definition of enslavement as mirroring that of slavery as first established by the 1926 Slavery Convention. The manner in which the footnote to Element 1 can be reconciled so as to be consistent with the Statute is to be found through the clause which states that the "deprivation of liberty may, *in some circumstances*, include" the exacting of forced labour or the reduction of a person via the institutions and practices similar to slavery. Those circumstances would have to be when forced labour or debt bondage, serfdom, servile marriage or child exploitation (i.e.: the institutions and practices similar to slavery) manifest powers attaching to the right of slavery and thus slip their definitional moorings to become also – in law – slavery and, as a result, also meet the definition of enslavement as established by the Statute of the International Criminal Court.

The possibility that forced labour and the institutions and practices similar to slavery can also manifest powers attaching to the right of ownership and thus be considered as slavery as well (and enslavement via the Statute of the International Criminal Court) if foreseen in international law. Article 5 of the 1926 Slavery Convention calls on States Parties to take "all necessary measures to prevent compulsory or forced labour from developing into conditions analogous to slavery."[92] In other words, there was a recognition as far back as 1926 that forced labour could degenerate into slavery; that is: forced labour could manifest 'powers attaching to the right of ownership'. Likewise, where the institutions and practices similar to slavery as set out in the 1956 Supplementary

---

91 See Element 1 of the crime against humanity of enslavement, Article 7(1)(c) of the Elements of Crimes, ICC-ASP/1/3(part II-B). 9 September 2002.

Note that Element 1 of the crime against humanity of enslavement is reproduced verbatim, including the footnote, as Element 1 common to the crimes of sexual slavery. See Article 7(1)(g)-2 – Crime against humanity of sexual slavery; Article 8(2)(b)(xxii)-2 – War crime of sexual slavery; and Article 8(2)(e)(vi)-2 – War crime of sexual slavery and the corresponding footnotes 18, 53, and 65.

92 Article 5, Slavery Convention, Geneva, September 25th, 1926, C.586.M.223.1926.VI, 16 October 1926; as found in Publications of the League of Nations, VI.B.Slavery.1926. VI.B.7.

Convention are concerned, that instrument expresses in clear terms that these institutions and practices may also constitute slavery as defined by the 1926 Slavery Convention. Article 1 of the Supplementary Convention, while setting out the four types of servile status (i.e.: debt bondage, serfdom, servile marriage or child exploitation), provides in its introductory paragraph that States Parties "shall take all practicable and necessary legislative and other measures to bring about progressively and as soon as possible the complete abolition or abandonment of [these] institutions and practices." The introductory paragraph then continues, stating that the abolition or abandonment of these institutions and practices should take place *"where they still exist and whether or not they are covered by the definition of slavery contained in article 1 of the Slavery Convention signed at Geneva on 25 September 1926."*[93]

The Elements of Crimes are meant to both assist the Court in "the interpretation and application" of the Statute and be consistent with that Statute.[94] By acknowledging that the lesser servitudes noted in footnote can, *in some circumstances*, manifest powers attaching to the right of ownership means that forced labour and institutions and practices similar to slavery can manifest the elements required to constitute the crime against humanity of enslavement as set out in the Statute of the International Criminal Court.

Conclusion

The advent of the trafficking conventions and the coming into existence of the International Criminal Court in 2002 provides a reprieve for the legal regime of slavery and human exploitation which had lost its way as a result of the introduction of the term of art 'slavery-like practice' during the latter half of the twentieth century. During the first half of the twentieth century, through the height of the colonial era, States within the early years of both the League of Nations and the United Nations established a legal regime governing both slavery and servitude manifest in the 1926 Slavery Convention and the 1956 Supplementary Convention on the Abolition of Slavery, the Slave Trade and Institutions and Practices Similar to Slavery. With the balance of power

93 United Nations Conference of Plenipotentiaries on a Supplementary Convention on the Abolition of Slavery, the Slave Trade and Institutions and Practices Similar to Slavery, Final Act and Supplementary Convention, 4 September 1956, UN Doc E/CONF.24/23. Emphasis added.

94 See Article 9(1) and 9(3), Rome Statute of the International Criminal Court, UN Doc. A/CONF.183/9, 17 July 1998.

shifting in the United Nations from 1966 onwards, newly independent States sought – and ultimately failed – to have apartheid recognised as a 'practice similar to slavery'. Instead a diplomatic compromise was achieved with labelled apartheid with a term of art, that of: 'slavery like-practice'. This term ultimately allow for the evolution of the notion of 'contemporary forms of slavery' to emerge from the United Nations as an umbrella term utilised to define various social ills. Referral back to the legal only took place at the start of the twenty-first century, with the establishment of a definition of trafficking in human beings and the coming into force of the Statute of the International Criminal Court which established the crime against humanity of enslavement. In reverting back to the legal, within a paradigm of criminal law, the law governing slavery appears to have been given a true lease on life as it become a viable instrument for holding perpetrators accountable for enslavement and thus offering protection those enslaved.

PART 2

Challenging the Status Quo

CHAPTER 6

A Review of *Understanding Global Slavery: A Reader* by Kevin Bales*

Berkley: University of California Press, 2005

Contemporary considerations of issues of slavery remain touched by the messianic ambitions which underscored the abolitionist movements of the eighteenth and nineteenth centuries. Professor Kevin Bales, scholar and activist, fails to escape this weight of history in his *Understanding Global Slavery: A Reader*. The book does much to engage and explain modern manifestations of exploitation yet, by riding roughshod over the law, fails to provide a path which would be amenable to those wishing to use the law to end slavery writ large.

Unusual for a reader, which is typically a thematic compilation or acts as a *festschrift*, *Understanding Global Slavery* is a sole-authored thematic collection of Bales previous publications and writings. Following a year after his *Disposable People: New Slavery in the Global Economy* (2004), and coming shortly before his *Ending Slavery – How We Free Today's Slaves* (2007), Bales has established himself as the foremost experts on issues of slavery today. Having given the study of modern manifestation of exploitation under the rubrics of 'slavery' much needed academic rigour, Bales has failed to completely extract himself from an ordained mission to rid the world of wrong. Having left behind a professorship in sociology at the University of Surrey, Roehampton, Bales is now a full-time advocate, the President of 'Free the Slaves', the American-based sister organisation of Anti-Slavery International.

This dichotomy between scholar and activist is manifest throughout *Understanding Global Slavery* which, on the one hand provides sound and well research considerations of issues surrounding slavery, while on the other hand often couches arguments in the rhetoric of virtue and good versus evil. Bales ultimate goal is to end slavery, which he says is not a "problem of apathy or indifference to the continued presence of slavery, but ignorance of it" (p. 4). While acknowledging that there has been a growth of research in the area, Bales notes that "we are in the dark when it comes to the most basic questions of who, how, how many, and where"; yet Bales switches tacks the very next sentence, saying: "These question are crucial not just for the slaves but for all of us.

* This review appeared was originally published as Jean Allain, "Kevin Bales, *Understanding Global Slavery: A Reader*, 2005," *International Journal of Refugee Law*, Vol. 20, 2008, p. 228. Copyright © Oxford University Press, 2008.

For if the path of freedom is not as smooth as we can make it, if it leads only to lives of continued exploitation, then the problem is not solved; it is merely postponed" (p. 5). This passion over academic objectivity is manifest time and again throughout the *Reader*. Bales writes of that a "community that allow slavery in its midst is sick to its core," of the "sickness of slavery" (p. 7), and includes chapters entitled "Slavery and the Human Right to Evil" and "Globalization and Redemption." Those picking up *Understanding Global Slavery* must thus accept that the appeals made in this book are pointed as much at the heart as at the intellect and are foremost a call-to-arms: "Virtually every person wants to live in a world without slavery, but in our fight against slavery our tools are few, our resources scarce, and our knowledge piecemeal. The chapters of the *Reader* aim to "fill in some of the holes" and "to explore some of the fundamental and underlying ideas about slavery in order to help that understanding grow (pp. 7 and 8)."

Bales consider that modern manifestations of slavery differ from traditional, chattel, slavery. He writes that at is "core the attributes of slavery remain the same": control based on violence, subsistence living conditions and ownership of the fruits of labour; yet in three fundament ways things have changed. First, that the "cost of slaves has fallen to an historical low" which, echoing the title of his 2004 book, makes people disposable. Second, a bi-product of a disposable commodity is that slaves are "now held for a shorter length of time" making it more difficult to address the phenomena; and finally, that "today slavery is globalized," the forms of slavery becoming "similar wherever they are located" (p. 9).

In devoting a chapter to legal issues, Bales writes that while slavery has existed since time immemorial, "the form that it has taken and takes today, as well as its definition, has evolved and changed." "My aim" Bales writes "is to generate a more dynamic and universal definition of contemporary slavery from theoretical models and substantive examples" (p. 40). That Chapter 3, co-authored with the Sociologist Peter T. Robbins belies the fact that neither Bales nor Robbins have a strong grasp of international law or even the United Nations system; for they write that "a convention is an agreement between states that is less formal than a treaty" (fn. 12), and the Human Rights Committee is a Sub-organ of the General Assembly (p. 42). Beyond these minor snafus, their consideration of the definition of slavery in international law, based on the 2000 Weissbrodt and Anti-Slavery International Working Paper,[1] is fundamentally flawed. They write that the 1926 Slavery Convention,

---

1 See United Nations Sub-Commission on the Promotion and Protection of Human Right, *Contemporary Forms of Slavery: Updated Review of the Implementation of and Follow-up to the Conventions on Slavery*, Working Paper prepared by David Weissbrodt and Anti-Slavery International, UN Doc. E/CN.4/Sub.2/2000/3, 26 May 2000.

which defines slavery at Article 1 as "the status or condition of a person over whom any or all of the powers attaching to the right of ownership are exercised" when coupled with Article 2 ("abolition of slavery in all its forms") "had the effect of covering not only traditional types of slavery but also the other forms of slavery referred to in the [1924] Report of the Temporary Slavery Commission." This attempt at an expanded definition of slavery fails on three counts. First, the *travaux préparatoires* do not reflect this interpretation; second, I know of no situation whereby an international instrument has been negotiated which, *by inference*, seeking to include in a definition material developed by an expert body two years previous; and finally, that the 'forms of slavery referred to in the Report of the Temporary Slavery Commission' are precisely those which required the negotiation of an additional convention in 1956 to deal to with 'servile status'.[2] They contradict themselves in law by saying that Article 1 of 1956 Convention "extended and broadened the definition of slavery put forward in the 1926 Convention"; as in the very next sentence they write that the "provisions of Article 1 oblige states parties to abolish certain institutions and practices analogous to slavery that create the circumstances of 'servile status'" (p. 47). Finally, Bales and Robbins argue that by 1998, the definition of slavery had returned to its original 1926 version, but with the addition of the practice of trafficking. Again, in law this is not precise and rather misleading, as the definition of enslavement (not slavery) found the Rome Statute does not add trafficking as an additional type of slavery, but the opposite: the Statute acknowledges that slavery is but one possible component part of the definition of trafficking.[3]

2 This interpretation given by Bales and Robbins, in line with the David Weissbrodt and Anti-Slavery International Working Paper, first emerged in the Report of 1930 International Commission of Inquiry into the Existence of Slavery and Forced Labour in the Republic of Liberia. For a critique of this interpretation see my Paper presented at as part of the Guest Lecture Series of the Office of the Prosecutor of International Criminal Court entitled: "The Definition of 'Slavery' in General International Law and the Crime of Enslavement within the Rome Statute," as reproduced in chapter 18 of this volume.

3 Article 7(2)(c) of the 1998 Statute of the International Criminal Court reads:

> Enslavement' means the exercise of any or all of the powers attaching to the right of ownership over a person and includes the exercise of such power in the course of trafficking in persons, in particular women and children.

Article 3(a), 2001 United Nations Protocol to Prevent, Suppress and Punish Trafficking in Persons, Especially Women and Children and Article 4(a), 2005 Council of Europe Convention on Action against Trafficking in Human Beings read:

> 'Trafficking in persons' shall mean the recruitment, transportation, transfer, harbouring or receipt of persons, by means of the threat or use of force or other forms of coercion, of

That said, it should be noted that Bales and Robbins have strong basis for pursuing this ever-expanding definition of slavery:

> If it is defined in a way that includes phenomena across the breadth of social injustice or human rights violations, then the word *slavery* becomes diluted and meaningless. An overly broad approach in turn leads to a diffusion of the effort to eliminate slavery, which means that the resources dedicated to eliminating slavery are spread thinly across many areas, some of which may be less clearly linked to the core types of human bondage (p. 43).

Thus they can reject the legal definition, saying that "enslavement does not require ownership, only control, usually achieved through violence or its threat" and come up with their own definition (based on "three key dimensions: loss of free will, the appropriation of labor power, and the use or threat of violence" (p. 57)), serving their own purpose and distance themselves from any possible international legal remedy for the enslaved.

By way of conclusion, one might ask of the relationship between slavery and refugees. We know that forced migration places people in vulnerable situations, Bales for this part speaks of vulnerability as being the "key to slavery" (p. 10). We also know that people often flee their country of origin in times of war as they are vulnerable to war crimes by invading forces;[4] and, that by crossing an international border illegally, forced migrants are often vulnerable in countries of refuge.[5] Further, though rarely a basis for the determination of refugee status, enslavement clearly constitutes the type of persecution (and slaves the type of social group) meant to be protected by the 1951 Convention, if the other elements of Article 1 of the 1951 Convention are at hand.[6] Finally,

---

abduction, of fraud, of deception, of the abuse of power or of a position of vulnerability or of the giving or receiving of payments or benefits to achieve the consent of a person having control over another person, for the purpose of exploitation. Exploitation shall include, at a minimum, the exploitation of the prostitution of others or other forms of sexual exploitation, forced labour or services, slavery or practices similar to slavery, servitude or the removal of organs.

4 For a finding of enslavement in time of war see International Criminal Tribunal for the former Yugoslavia, *Kunarac et al.* (IT-96-23-T &-IT-96-23/1-T) Judgment, 22 February 2001, p. 192.

5 See European Court of Human Rights, *Siliadin v. France* (Application 73316/01), 26 July 2005, which notes that the taking of Ms. Siliadin's passport and the expiration of her visa was fundamental in creating a state of vulnerability which allow for her exploitation.

6 Consider the *Handbook on Procedures and Criteria for Determining Refugee Status under the 1951 Convention and the 1967 Protocol Relating to the Status of Refugees*, HCR/IP/4/Eng/REV.1,

considering the dicta in the *Barcelona Traction* case indicating that the protection from slavery and other fundamental human rights were of such importance that "all States can be held to have a legal interest in their protection; they are obligations *erga omnes*,"[7] might it not be argued that States and UNHCR have an obligation when making refugees status determinations to, for instance, bring to the attention of the Prosecutor of the International Criminal Court cases where claims involve enslavement?

Professor Kevin Bales, does not profess to be a legal expert, and thus not surprisingly falls short of giving a solid, or even adequate, understanding of the law of slavery, despite his profession of wanting to bring rigour to the domain of the study of slavery. This Review, for its part, has focused, in essence, on one chapter and thus does not truly do justice to *Understanding Global Slavery: A Reader*. If one is interested in issues of modern day slavery and its suppression, Bales is the person to turn to. For the law, look elsewhere.

January 1992, along with the *Guidelines On International Protection: Gender-Related Persecution within the Context of Article 1A(2) of the 1951 Convention and/or Its 1967 Protocol Relating to the Status of Refugees*, HCR/GIP/02/01, 7 May 2002; and the *Guidelines On International Protection: The Application of Article 1A(2) of the 1951 Convention and/or 1967 Protocol Relating to the Status of Refugees to Victims of Trafficking and Persons at Risk of Being Trafficked*, HCR/GIP/06/07, 7 April 2006.

7 *Barcelona Traction, Light and Power Company, Limited*, Judgment, I.C.J. Reports 1970, p. 32.

CHAPTER 7

A Review of *Trafficking in Human Beings: Modern Slavery* by Silvia Scarpa*

New York: Oxford University Press, 2008

Trafficking in Human Beings Modern Slavery is a PhD thesis defended within the Faculty of Political Science of the Sant'Anna School of Advanced Study, an institution associated with the University of Pisa, Italy; Silvia Scarpa is now Lecturer in International Law at Tuscia University of Viterbo and Research Fellow at the Sant'Anna School.

Trafficking in Human Beings: Modern Slavery is a doctrinal study of the contemporary legal and institutional responses to human trafficking manifest in international protection standards for victims. The first chapter considers the definition of trafficking in persons; the second and third chapters, the response to trafficking by the United Nations and other intergovernmental organisations such as the UN High Commissioners for Refugees and the International Labour Organisation. The final two chapters, investigate the regional response to trafficking in Europe by examining the work of the Council of Europe and the European Union.

The thesis of *Trafficking in Human Beings* fundamentally fails to hold and shifts throughout. The author first states that trafficking is a 'slavery-like practice'; then goes on to argue that trafficking in persons is a 'new form of slavery'; later that trafficking equates to the slave trade; and finally moves to say that trafficking in persons amounts to slavery when it meets the definitional criteria of slavery. As a result, the thesis finally settles on the premise which is tantamount to saying: corporal punishment is torture (when it amounts to torture) or driving a car is terrorism (when it is packed with explosives and used in a terrorist attack).

In her introduction, Scarpa spells out the thesis of *Trafficking in Human Beings: Modern Slavery*:

> While slavery and the slave trade were abolished long ago, new and more subtle forms of slavery-like practices are alarmingly on the rise in many

* Originally published as Jean Allain, "Silvia Scarpa, *Trafficking in Human Beings: Modern Slavery*, 2008," *European Journal of International Law*, Vol. 20, 2009, p. 453. Copyright © Oxford University Press, 2009.

 | DOI 10.1163/9789004279896_009

> parts of the world. Among them, in the last decades the international community has focused its attention on trafficking in persons, which must be one of the most worrying phenomena of the XXI century. This book reviews this crime in all its complexity and discusses the many and varied international responses to it since it first appeared as an issue of international concern. Many efforts have been made to fight against trafficking in persons; however, some gaps need to be filled and improvements to the international protection standards of trafficking victims need to be made [at 1].

In more simplified terms, Scarpa's first chapter starts, "This chapter aims to review trafficking in persons as a slavery-like practice of our time" (at 3). The notion of 'slavery-like practice' is not defined by Scarpa, nor does it have much currency internationally, as it is not used in any substantive way, bar one instance, where during the 1990s, the United Nation Sub-Commission on Prevention of Discrimination and Protection of Minorities had a 'Special Rapporteur on Systematic Rape, Sexual Slavery and Slavery-like Practices'. Where Scarpa, picks up the term, is from Weissbrodt and Anti-Slavery International's 2002, *Abolishing Slavery and its Contemporary Forms*, a study prepared for the former UN Working Group on Contemporary Forms of Slavery, which uses the term 'slavery-like practices' to consider not only forms of servitude, but also sex tourism, mail-order brides, apartheid, colonialism, and incest.[1]

Instead of providing a definition of the term, Scarpa gives examples of 'slavery-like practices', juxtaposing them with '*traditional* or *chattel* slavery' saying that in "the last decades, [...] the existence of a variety of *new* slavery-like practices has been proved [sic] as well; among the latter there are: forced labour, the bonded labour/debt bondage practice, forced prostitution and sex slavery, the worst forms of child labour, trafficking in persons, and early and forced marriage" (at 4). It is not clear why Scarpa has chosen these types of exploitation as, though she cites Weissbrodt, she fails to mention the other forms which are discussed in his study, nor does she go on to consider each of these so-called 'slavery-like practices'. Instead, she is content to turn to 'trafficking in persons', not as a new 'slavery-like practice', but now as a 'new form of slavery' (at 4).

Her approach, rather than clarifying, confuses. In law, slavery is defined by the 1926 Slavery Convention as the 'status or condition of a person over whom

1 United Nations, Office of the United Nations High Commissioner for Human Rights, Weissbrodt and Anti-Slavery International, *Abolishing Slavery and Its Contemporary Forms*, UN Doc. HR/PUB/02/4, 2002.

any or all of the powers attaching to the right of ownership are exercised'.[2] That definition remains the contemporary definition of slavery, having been reproduced in substance most recently in the 1998 Rome Statute of the International Criminal Court. Beyond slavery, there is in law, the term, 'institutions or practices similar to slavery', established by the 1956 Supplementary Convention, which sets out four servile statuses; debt bondage, serfdom, as well as specific types of servile marriage and child exploitation.[3] Despite this, Scarpa turns to what she now calls 'new forms of slavery' and identifies trafficking in persons as one such form which has been placed at the 'top of the international agenda'. Yet 'trafficking is persons' cannot, in law, be a new form of slavery. That would require the snake to swallow its own tail. This is so, as the definition of trafficking in persons, as found in the 2000 UN Palermo Protocol and repeated in the 2005 Council of Europe trafficking convention reads as follows:

> 'Trafficking in persons' shall mean the recruitment, transportation, transfer, harbouring or receipt of persons, by means of the threat or use of force or other forms of coercion, of abduction, of fraud, of deception, of the abuse of power or of a position of vulnerability or of the giving or receiving of payments or benefits to achieve the consent of a person having control over another person, for the purpose of exploitation. Exploitation shall include, at a minimum, the exploitation of the prostitution of others or other forms of sexual exploitation, forced labour or services, slavery or practices similar to slavery, servitude or the removal of organs.

These conventions thus include slavery as an example of exploitation to be suppressed. Trafficking in person cannot be a new form of slavery, as slavery is but one example of eight component parts (examples of exploitation) of one of three elements (the means, the method and the purpose) of the definition of trafficking.

If trafficking in persons is indeed a new form of slavery in law, then the other examples of exploitation must also be deemed to be swallowed up by the definition of slavery. Not quite – however – as the definition of trafficking in persons requires "the recruitment, transportation, [etc.] by means of the threat or use of force or other forms of coercion [etc.] for the purpose of exploitation."

---

2 See Jean Allain, "The Definition of Slavery in International Law," *Howard Law Journal*, Vol. 52, 2009 at 239.

3 For a consideration of the Slavery Conventions see: Jean Allain *The Slavery Conventions: The Travaux Préparatoires of the 1926 League of Nations Convention and the 1956 United Nations Convention*, 2008.

Thus, according to Scapa, if all the criteria of the definition of trafficking in persons are met, and the purpose of exploitation is to remove organs or forced labour, this is, in fact and law, slavery. This of course, cannot be. For Scarpa, trafficking in persons is slavery, but this is a faulty argument to premise the thesis upon; it is a non-starter as a foundation and as a result, the rest of the book does not hold up. It also begs the question: why trafficking as a new form of slavery? Why not trafficking as a new form of forced labour or of servitude?

Despite this, Scarpa continues, this time moving to determine that trafficking in persons is the "new slave trade" (at 12). As she does not elaborate on this new designation, but leaves the statement to stand on its own, this might be an opportune time to consider a further weaknesses which this book manifests. Where considerations of the slave trade are concerned, Scarpa's research is revealed to be lacking. She writes that "between 1839 and 1890 more than 300 international agreements were adopted to abolish the slave trade but they were all ineffective" (at 43). This is a thoroughly inaccurate statement. Putting aside the fact that 80,000 slaves were freed on the basis of mixed commissions emanating from these agreements and that the last recorded slave voyage across the Atlantic took place in 1867; it should be understood that such bilateral treaties were not ineffective, but instead so effective that States were, by 1890, willing to move beyond a web of bilateral arrangements to sign the universal 1890 General Act of the Brussels Conference.[4]

Beyond Scarpa's research, her analysis is wanting as, in the following sentence, she notes that the General Act limited the right to visit to vessels of less than 500 tons; Scarpa states that "therefore, no action was possible against [...] those vessels of more than 500 tons." This, however, is a moot point as, by 1890, with the Atlantic slave trade dead; where slaving persisted – on the East Coast of Africa through to the Persian Gulf – it was recognised to be carried out exclusively by small artisan dhows. Therefore, the implication which Scarps seeks to draw: that European States were seeking to exclude their own large ships from being visited simply does not hold water. Scarpa follows this assertion with a statement which is counter-temporal; as she notes that in some cases the right to visit had the "unwanted effect" that slaves were thrown overboard to "avoid any accusation of slave trading." Far from being an issue in the aftermath of the Brussels Conference, the issue of avoiding capture by

4 Why Scarpa uses 1839 as her starting date is unclear, as the first bilateral treaty related to the slave trade dates from 1810 as between the United Kingdom and Portugal. See Jean Allain, "Nineteenth Century Law of the Sea and the British Abolition of the Slave Trade," *British Yearbook of International Law*, Vol. 78, 2008, p. 358. [As reproduced in Chapter 2 of this volume.]

unshipping slaves was settled by 1818, with the introduction into bilateral treaties of so-called 'equipment clauses', which led to forfeiture where the outfitting of a ship included, for instance, shackles or an overabundance of water and food; as these were deemed *prima facie* evidence of involvement in the slave trade.[5]

Returning once more to the shifting thesis of *Trafficking in Human Beings*, Scarpa again moves the goal posts, not in the direction of firming up her thesis, but of undermining it still further. In the second chapter of her book, she discusses the *Kunarac* judgment of the International Criminal Tribunal for the former Yugoslavia, and its *indicia* of 'enslavement'. Having done so, Scarpa now modifies her earlier statement that trafficking in persons is a new form of slavery, to say that "trafficking in persons may be included in the definition of slavery given by the Slavery Convention if the elements listed by the ICTY [...] are met" (at 80). More succinctly, she repeats the assertion: "trafficking in persons can be considered, under certain circumstances, as a form of slavery" (at 81 and 82).

The fundamental flaw with the argument is that for trafficking in persons to exist, one of the following methods has to be present: "recruitment, transportation, transfer, harbouring or receipt of persons," as well as one of the following means must be used "the threat or use of force or other forms of coercion, of abduction, of fraud, of deception, of the abuse of power or of a position of vulnerability or of the giving or receiving of payments or benefits to achieve the consent of a person having control over another person"; and, these methods and means must take place for the purpose of exploitation; of which one of the eight types of exploitation enumerated is 'slavery'. As a result, slavery need not take place, only trafficking for the purposes of slavery. Now, it is conceded that where the elements of the definition of trafficking in persons overlap with the definition of slavery, then the act of trafficking will breach a *jus cogens* norm, but not because it is manifestly an act of trafficking in persons, but because it is slavery. By Scarpa's logic, there would be a *jus cogens* norm prohibiting the use of one's military (if that military is used for an act of aggression) or sailing (when piracy ensues). Put in these terms, little value can be made from arguing, as Scarpa does, that trafficking in persons is considered a *jus cogens* norm, when trafficking amounts to slavery.

Later, Scarpa, makes the same argument in discussing the 2005 European Court of Human Rights case of *Siliadin v. France*. Acknowledging that Article 4 of the European Convention on Human Rights (ECHR), deals with slavery, servitude and forced labour, Scarpa states that "it is evident that trafficking in

5 *Id.* at 358.

person can be considered, depending on the specific circumstances, as falling within either slavery or servitude (or even forced labour). Consequently, protection for trafficking victims is indeed guaranteed by the ECHR, as demonstrated by *Siliadin v. France*" (at 141). Again, here, the protection from trafficking will transpire not on the basis of trafficking having taken place but on the basis of slavery, servitude or forced labour manifesting itself, plus all the elements of trafficking having been present.

Beyond those limitations of *Trafficking in Human Beings: Modern Slavery* is, in large part, descriptive. This is true for the last three chapters of the book which consider the approaches to dealing with trafficking within the context of international and regional (read: European) mechanisms. For instance, in a formalistic manner, Chapter 3 examines the UN human rights treaties and their monitoring bodies, the special procedures, the Statute of the International Criminal Court and the work of the International Labour Organisation, repeating the various provisions and pronouncements without developing an underlying theme, failing to make or sustain an argument. As a conclusion to this Chapter, Scarpa writes, in regard to the institutions considered: "Some of them are very important because they allow for the enhancement of the standards of protection of trafficking victims. Others are currently not able to provide a fundamental contribution but they may become more relevant in the future" (at 134).

Scarpa, is often times prone to giving advice to States throughout the pages of *Trafficking in Human Beings: Modern Slavery*. Without having undertaken any empirical work on trafficking, Scarpa feels well placed to make recommendations with regard to, for instance, the United States Department of State Trafficking in Persons Report, that "future reports explain how the estimates has been calculated, which data are taken into consideration from every region of the world" (at 11). Despite the high standards Scarpa seeks to hold others to, she is willing to base her own consideration of trafficking in human organs on the following: "there are rumours that all around the world an illegal trade in human organs is flourishing" (at 34). Likewise, while willing to be prescriptive with others' work, Scarpa is less so with her own: where early and forced marriage is concerned, she recommends that "specific prevention policies should be adopted in the next few years" without offering any suggestions (at 27).

The issue of trafficking in persons, like any human exploitation, is a serious human rights issue. The international community deems that it has a special obligation to suppress such acts, like others touching on the integrity of the body such as torture and disappearance. Yet, to date, the scholarship on slavery and trafficking has not been worthy of the task. The waters have been so muddied with regard to the issue of slavery and human exploitation that only a sustained effort can seek to turn the tide towards a serious and solid study of the legal areas surrounding issues of trafficking in persons. Silvia Scarpa's *Trafficking in Human Beings: Modern Slavery* does not move knowledge in the domain of trafficking or slavery forward; quite the opposite.

CHAPTER 8

A Case Note of *Hadijatou Mani Koraou v. Republic of Niger**

Community Court of Justice of the Economic Community of West Africa States, 27 October 2008

In October 2008, the ECOWAS Community Court of Justice found the Republic of Niger in violation of the prohibition of slavery as set out in the African Charter on Human and Peoples' Rights.[1] In *Mani v. Niger*, the Court determined that the Nigerien judiciary, in recognizing but failing to denounce the slave status of the plaintiff, had tolerated, if not accepted, a situation in violation of Niger's positive obligation to suppress slavery within its jurisdiction.[2]

ECOWAS – the Economic Community of West African States – was established in 1975[3] to, inter alia, "raise the living standards of its peoples...and contribute to the progress and development of the African Continent." Under the 1993 Revised Treaty, its fifteen member states share a common currency and seek to liberalize trade and remove barriers within the Community "to the free movement of persons, goods, service and capital."[4] The ECOWAS Court emerged as a result of the 1991 Protocol relating to the Community Court of Justice, as the "principal legal organ of the Community." Composed of seven members, the Court was originally, under that Protocol, given jurisdiction to hear disputes between member states and the executive organ of ECOWAS.[5] However, under

* This case note originally appeared as Jean Allain "*Hadijatou Mani Koraou v. Republic of Niger*" 103 *American Journal of International Law* (2009) 311. It is reproduced with permission from the April 2009 issue of the *American Journal of International Law* © 2009 American Society of International Law. All rights reserved.

1 African Charter on Human and Peoples' Rights, June 27, 1981, 21 ILM 58 (1982).

2 Hadijatou Mani Koraou v. La Republic de Niger, Arrêt No. ECW/CCJ/JUD/06/08, para. 11 (ECOWAS Cour de Justice Oct. 27, 2008), available at <http://www.unhcr.org/refworld/docid/491168d42.html>. An unofficial translation into English is available at <http://www.unhcr.org/cgi-bin/texis/vtx/refworld/rwmain?docid=496b41fa2>.

3 *See* Treaty of the Economic Community of West African States, May 28, 1975, 1010 UNTS 17, *reprinted in* 14 ILM 1200 (1975).

4 Revised Treaty of the Economic Community of West African States, July 24, 1993, Art. 3(1), (2), 35 ILM 660 (1996). The fifteen Members of ECOWAS are Benin, Burkina Faso, Cape Verde, Côte d'Ivoire, The Gambia, Ghana, Guinea, Guinea-Bissau, Liberia, Mali, Niger, Nigeria, Senegal, Sierra Leone, and Togo. Mauritania, an original member, withdrew its membership in 2000.

5 *See* Protocol A/P.1/7/91 (1991), Art. 9, 30 ILM 1241 (1991).

 | DOI 10.1163/9789004279896_010

the 1993 Revised Treaty, the ECOWAS Court gained a constitutional mandate to consider issues of human rights by virtue of Article 4, which spells out the fundamental principles that are to be adhered to when pursuing regional economic integration. Among these principles, Article 4(g) calls for the "recognition promotion and protection of human and peoples' rights in accordance with the provisions of the African Charter on Human and Peoples' Rights."

It has been noted that, having introduced this new, 1993 mandate to consider issues of human rights, "the member states of ECOWAS realised the need to create a forum for human rights litigation. Accordingly, the member states agreed to review the 1991 Protocol of the ECOWAS Court to empower the Court to hear cases relating to human rights violations."[6] That review precipitated the adoption of the 2005 Supplementary Protocol relating to the Community Court of Justice, which deleted the provisions touching on jurisdiction and replaced them with a wider remit: the Court has, inter alia, "the jurisdiction to determine case[s] of violation of human rights that occur in any Member State," and individuals have been granted standing to appear before the Court.[7]

The facts of *Mani v. Niger* are as follows. In 1996, at age 12, Hadijatou Mani Koraou was sold for the equivalent of approximately $400 to El Hadj Souleymane Naroua, a 46-year-old tribal chief in her native Niger. She was his *Sadaka*, or "fifth wife"; that is, a female who is taken as a wife but cannot be acknowledged as such under the precepts of Islam. This purchase took place under a practice still current in Niger called *Wahiya*, whereby a young girl is forced into servile status, acting as both domestic servant and concubine. Naroua first had forced sexual relations with Hadijatou Mani when she was twelve years of age. Mani bore Naroua four children during her nine years as *Sadaka*. As the ECOWAS Court relates, Mani "was often the victim of acts of violence on the part of her master, as a result of genuine or supposed rebelliousness."

In August 2005, Naroua manumitted Hadijatou Mani by way of a liberation certificate countersigned by the village chief. Thereafter, a dispute arose as Naroua refused to allow Mani to leave his home, considering her his wife. Having left Naroua's home in February 2006, Mani brought a case before the

---

6 *See* Solomon T. Ebobrah, "A Rights-Protection Goldmine or a Waiting Volcanic Eruption? Competence of, and Access to, the Human Rights Jurisdiction of the ECOWAS Community Court of Justice," Vol. 7 *African Human Rights Law Journal*, 2007, pp. 307, 312–313.

7 *See* Supplementary Protocol A/SP.1/01/05 Amending the Preamble and Articles 1, 2, 9 and 30 of Protocol A/P.1/7/91 Relating to the Community Court of Justice and Article 4 Paragraph 1 of the English Version of the Said Protocol, Art. 3, Jan. 19, 2005, available at <http://www.africancourtcoalition.org/content_files/files/HD14.doc>.

Civil and Customary Law Tribunal of Konni, a city in the Maradi region of South Central Niger, seeking to have her freedom from marriage recognized in law. This freedom appeared to have been obtained by way of a judgment delivered on March 20, 2006, which noted that the Naroua and Mani were never properly married "because there never was payment of the dowry nor a religious ceremony" and as such Mani "remains free to remake her life with the person of her choice" (para. 16). Naroua appealed to the Court of First Instance in Konni and was successful in quashing the tribunal's judgment. However, the decision at first instance was itself quashed in December 2006 as Mani was successful before the judicial chamber of the Supreme Court of Niamey in the capital of Niger. The Supreme Court, which is the highest appellate court in the land, remitted the case back to the Court of First Instance for review.

In the interim, Hadijatou Mani married Ladan Rabo – in response to which, Souleymane Naroua filed a criminal complaint. On May 2, 2007, the criminal division of the Court of First Instance found Mani and her new husband, along with her brother as an accomplice, guilty of bigamy and sentenced them each to six months in jail and a fine of the equivalent of $100. A week later, Mani and her brother were incarcerated; being provisionally released only two months later as a result of an interim order by the Criminal Division of the Court of Appeal in Niamey. Responding to the criminal proceeding against her for bigamy, Hadijatou Mani filed a complaint on May 17, 2007, against Naroua for slavery. She subsequently filed, on December 14, 2007, an application to the ECOWAS Community Court of Justice seeking to have Niger found in violation of the African Charter of Human and Peoples' Rights. The ECOWAS Court merged admissibility questions with the merits and, on October 27, 2008, rendered judgment.[8]

With regard to admissibility, the ECOWAS Court considered whether exhaustion of domestic or local remedies is a general principle of international human rights law. For its part, "the Republic of Niger argued *in limine litis* inadmissibility on the grounds of non-exhaustion of domestic remedies on the one hand, and that the matter brought before the ECOWAS Court of Justice was still pending before domestic courts in Niger" (para. 35). Niger brought forward two normative arguments in favor of promoting the rule of exhaustion of domestic remedies: it allows international courts to decide whether a state is, in fact, protecting human rights; and the international protection of human rights is subsidiary to domestic protection.

8 The ECOWAS Court consisted of three judges: the Honorable Justice Aminata Sanogo Mallé of Mali (presiding), Justices Awa Nana Daboya of Togo and El-Mansour Tall of Senegal.

In answer, the Court noted that while "subsidiarity of human rights protection by international mechanisms is longstanding, this principle has evolved over time. As a result, interpretation of the rule of exhaustion of domestic remedies has been very flexible" (para. 39). To justify this claim, the ECOWAS Court turned to the 1971 European Court of Human Rights judgment in the *Vagrancy* case, which stated that nothing prevented states "from waiving the benefit of the rule of exhaustion of domestic remedies."[9] The Court in *Mani v. Niger* noted that the ECOWAS Community legislation "must have answered that call [to waive the rule] when it decided not to make the rule of exhaustion of domestic remedies a condition of admissibility before the Court. Waiving such a rule applies to all ECOWAS Member States, and the Republic of Niger shall not depart from it" (para. 40). In considering the admissibility requirements of Article 10(d) of its Supplementary Protocol (that an application not be anonymous or pending in another international forum), the Court stated that these provisions fell "within the strict limits of what international practice" required and that as a result "it is not for this Court to add to the Supplementary Protocol conditions that are not provided for by the texts" (para. 53).

Turing to the merits, *Mani v. Niger* – though dealing with issues of discrimination and arbitrary arrest and detention – was primarily focused on the issue of slavery. In its own defense, Niger "acknowledged that slavery survives" but that "the practice had become more discreet and been confined to very narrow social circles" (para. 78). The Court found, however, that there was "no doubt that the applicant, Habijatou Mani Koraou, was held in slavery for nearly nine (09) years in violation of the legal prohibition of this practice" (para. 80). In lieu of pursuing in depth or detail what constitutes "slavery" in law, the ECOWAS Court grounded its decision on "slavery"[10] in the case law of the Nuremberg and Yugoslav tribunals dealing with the international criminal law concept of "enslavement." While acknowledging that "it is true that [enslavement] is among the constitutive elements of the crimes against humanity," the Court declined to consider the issue in that light, saying the "such considerations fall to other international mechanisms, more precisely those having jurisdiction over international criminal law" (para. 89). Despite this statement and the fact that the case was seeking to deal with the responsibility of a state rather than an individual, the ECOWAS Court turned to the case law of criminal tribunals

9 De Wilde ("Vagrancy") v. Belgium, "European Court of Human Rights," 12 *European Convention on Human Rights*, (ser. A) at para. 39 (1971).

10 Slavery is defined in Article 1(1) of the 1926 Slavery Convention, Sept. 25, 1926, 212 UNTS 17, which reads: "Slavery is the status of condition of a person over whom any or all of the powers attaching to the right of ownership are exercised."

on "enslavement." In summarizing some of the facts related to Mani's case, the Court noted that these elements effectively portrayed "the applicant's servile situation and show all of the indicators of the slavery definition contained in Article 1 of the [1926 Slavery] Convention and as interpreted by the International Criminal Tribunal for the former Yugoslavia (ICTY)" (para. 77) in the *Kunarac* case. The ECOWAS Court followed the ICTY in providing an understanding not of slavery, but of "enslavement": "apart from exercising the powers attached to the right of ownership typical of the notion of slavery, it also depends 'on the operation of the factors or indicia of enslavement'." These indicia include the "control of someone's movement, control of physical environment, psychological control, measures taken to prevent or deter escape, force, threat of force or coercion, duration, assertion of exclusivity, subjection to cruel treatment and abuse, control of sexuality and forced labour" (*id.*, quoting *Kunarac*).[11]

The ECOWAS Court then quoted the International Court of Justice in the 1970 *Barcelona Traction* case as stating that "the outlawing of slavery is an obligation *erga omnes* imposed on all State's organs" (para. 81).[12] From this basis, the ECOWAS Court moved to find a violation of the prohibition of slavery – a violation arising out of the positive obligations attributable to the Nigerian judiciary. Of special note here was that the judge of the Court of First Instance of Konni had stated: "the marriage of a free man with a slave woman is lawful, as long as he cannot afford to marry a free woman and if he fears to fall into fornication" (para. 83). From this assertion, the ECOWAS Court determined that it "considers that recognising the slave status of Ms. Hadijatou Mani Koraou without denouncing the situation is a form of acceptance, or at the very least, tolerance of this crime or offence which the Nigerien judge had the obligation to bring a criminal charges or punish those salient elements."

The Court concluded by noting that where the case resulted from the actions of an individual "acting within a claimed customary or individual context," the state's authorities, "be they administrative or judicial," had an obligation to protect – and, as such, incurred responsibility under international law "for all forms of human rights violations of the applicant based on slavery as a result of tolerance, passivity, inaction and abstention by the authorities in the face of such practice" (paras 84–86). As a result, the ECOWAS Community Court of Justice concluded that Niger "had not sufficiently protected the applicant's right against the practice of slavery," awarding Mani approximately $21,500 and expenses.

---

11 Prosecutor v. Kunarac, Nos. IT-96-23 &-IT-96-23/1-A), Judgment, paras 118–119 (June 12, 2002).

12 The original quotation in French reads: "la mise hors la loi de l'esclavage est une obligation *erga omnes* qui s'impose à tous les organs de l'Etat."

With regard to issues of the exhaustion of domestic remedies – the foundation upon which the ECOWAS Court built its determination is rather misleading It misquotes (para. 39) the European Court of Human Right's *Vagrancy* case as saying: "in conformity with the evolution of international practice, there is nothing to prevent States from waiving the benefit of the rule of exhaustion of domestic remedies."[13] Yet, that Court in fact stated:

> [T]here is nothing to prevent States from waiving the benefit of the rule of exhaustion of domestic remedies, the essential aim of which is to protect their national legal order. There exists on this subject a long established international practice from which the Convention has definitely not departed as it refers, in Article 26 [current Article 35], to "the generally recognised rules of international law." (Para. 55)

In speaking of "long established international practice," the European Court was not speaking of a practice of waiving the rule of the exhaustion of domestic remedies, but in line with previous Article 26 (now Article 35), of respecting the applicability of that rule.[14] Better would have been for the ECOWAS Court to consider the jurisprudence of the Inter-American Court of Human Rights; in its very first case, the central question was whether Costa Rica could bring a case directly to the Court by waiving the treaty requirements of admissibility, including the requirement to exhaust local remedies. While the Inter-American Court determined that Costa Rica had to follow the treaty requirements on admissibility, it noted that

---

13 Quoting *De Wilde*, para. 55. In the ECOWAS decision, rendered in French, what is found in quotation marks reads: "conformément à l'évolution de la pratique international, les Etats peuvent bien renouncer au benefit de la régle de l'épuisement des voies de recours internes." What the European Court actually said is:

> rien n'empêche les Etats de renoncer au bénéfice de la règle de l'épuisement des voies de recours internes, qui a pour but essentiel de protéger leur ordre juridique national. Il existe à ce sujet une longue pratique internationale à laquelle la Convention n'a sûrement pas entendu déroger car elle se réfère, en son article 26 [current article 35], aux principes de droit international généralement reconnus.

14 Article 26 of the European Convention for the Protection of Human Rights and Fundamental Freedoms, Nov. 4, 1950, ETS No. 5, 213 UNTS 222, reads: "The Commission may only deal with the matter after all domestic remedies have been exhausted, according to the generally recognized rules of international law, and within a period of six months from the date on which the final decision was taken."

> under the generally recognized principles of international law and international practice, the rule which requires the prior exhaustion of domestic remedies is designed for the benefit of the State, for that rule seeks to excuse the State from having to respond to charges before an international body for acts imputed to it before it has had the opportunity to remedy them by internal means. The requirement is thus considered a means of defense and, as such, waivable, even tacitly.[15]

Where the merits of *Mani* v. *Niger* are concerned, a fundamental critique can be levelled at the ECOWAS Court for transposing of jurisprudence and the definition of "enslavement" from international criminal law onto the international human rights law concept of "slavery." Where "enslavement" is concerned, the ICTY itself stated that "definition may be broader than the traditional and sometimes apparently distinct definitions of either slavery, the slave trade and servitude or forced or compulsory labour found in other areas of international law," but that the trials at Nuremburg had expanded the notion of "enslavement" to "included forced or compulsory labour under enslavement as a crime against humanity."[16]

As this was a clear case of de jure slavery, the ECOWAS Court need not have gone beyond the definition of slavery established by the 1926 Slavery Convention,[17] in conjunction with Article 5 of the African Charter on Human and Peoples' Rights to render judgment.[18] By relying on the case law of international criminal law, the Court cross-pollinated different "species" of international law, thus grafting a genealogy forged in wartime onto international human rights law – which, for its part, has been consistent in maintaining a normative separation between slavery, servitude, and forced labor.[19]

The ECOWAS Court, in moving to consider issues of positive obligation, misquoted once more – this time, the famous statement from the 1970 *Barcelona Traction* case – by stating that "the outlawing of slavery is an obligation *erga*

15 *In re* Gallardo, Inter-American Court of Human Rights (ser. A) No. G 101/81 at para. 26 (July 15, 1981).

16 *Kunarac*, No. IT-96-23/1-T, Judgment, paras 541 (Feb. 22, 2001).

17 *See supra* note 10.

18 Article 5 of the African Charter on Human and Peoples' Rights, *supra* note 1, reads: "Every individual shall have the right to the respect of the dignity inherent in a human being and to the recognition of his legal status. All forms of exploitation and degradation of man particularly slavery, slave trade, torture, cruel, inhuman or degrading punishment and treatment shall be prohibited."

19 *See*, for instance, Article 8 of the International Covenant on Civil and Political Rights, Dec. 19, 1966, 999 UNTS 171.

omnes imposed on all State's organs" (para. 81).[20] For its part, in discussing obligations *erga omnes*, the International Court of Justice stated: "Such obligations derive, for example, in contemporary international law, from the outlawing of acts of aggression, and of genocide, as also from the principles and rules concerning the basic rights of the human person, including protection from slavery and racial discrimination."[21] The ECOWAS Court added the notion of obligation being "imposed on all State's organs" as a means of finding a breach of slavery flowing from positive obligations attributable to the rather incredible pronouncement (noted earlier) of the Court of First Instance of Konni. The ECOWAS Court need not have strained to put words in the mouth of the International Court of Justice, as there is much precedent in international human rights law with regard to positive obligations.[22]

By their pronouncement in *Mani v. Niger*, the judges of the Community Court of Justice appeared to be out of their depth in going beyond the ECOWAS *acquis*, to consider issues of international human rights law. Yet, the manner in which the judges misquoted from both the International Court of Justice and European Court of Human Rights speaks to a more fundamental flaw in the makeup of the ECOWAS Court. *Mani v. Niger* appears to have reached the right outcome in determining that Hadijatou Mani Koraou had been held in slavery; however, it did so at the expense of the law.

---

20 The original quotation, in French, reads: "la mise hors la loi de l'esclavage est une obligation *erga omnes* qui s'impose à tous les organs de l'Etat."

21 *Barcelona Traction, Light and Power Co.*, (Belg. v. Spain), Second Phase, 1970 ICJ Reports 3, para. 34 (Feb. 5).

22 *See, e.g.,* Sandra Fredman, *Human Rights Transformed: Positive Rights and Positive Duties* (2008).

CHAPTER 9

A Case Note of *Rantsev v. Cyprus and Russia**

European Court of Human Rights, 7 January 2010

On 7 January 2010, the European Court of Human Rights rendered judgment in *Rantsev v. Cyprus and Russia*,[1] a case which will be laurelled for revealing the human cost of sex tourism in Europe and the European Court's willingness to take on the issue of trafficking of women. That human cost is brought into sharp relief with the fate of Oxana Rantseva, a 21 year old woman from Russia, who stepped off a plane in Cyprus in 2001 and less than a fortnight later was dead. As important as this case is for taking aim at the exploitive nature of the sex industry and the willingness of States to turn a blind eye to it, *Rantsev* brings with it questions regarding the very ability of the Court to adjudicate over issues emanating from Article 4 of the European Convention on Human Rights (ECHR). With the determination of the Court that obligations emanating from Article 4 of the ECHR come into play because trafficking is based on slavery, the Court reveals itself as not having truly engaged with the legal distinctions which exist between these two concepts. As a result, the Court has further muddied the waters where legal distinction should be made regarding various types of human exploitation be it debt-bondage, forced labour, slavery or servitude.

Trafficking in Cyprus

The *Rantsev* case revealed the Cypriot sex industry for what it is: one which allowed the systemic sexual exploitation of young women from the former Soviet Union by cabaret owners with the knowledge of the Cypriot authorities, if not the very structural assistance of that State. The sexual exploitation of foreign women in Cyprus would not have been brought to light but for the persistence of the applicant in *Rantsev*, the father of the Oxana Rantseva, who sought justice for the death of his daughter in Cyprus, Russia, and ultimately,

* This case note first appear as Jean Allain, "*Rantsev v. Cyprus and Russia*: The European Court of Human Rights and Trafficking as Slavery," *Human Rights Law Review*, Vol. 10, 2010, p. 546; Copyright © Oxford University Press, 2010.

1 *Rantsev v. Cyprus and Russia*, Application no. 25965/04, 7 January 2010.

 | DOI 10.1163/9789004279896_011

at court in Strasbourg. The death of Oxana Rantseva thus acted as a catalyst, moving the Cypriot sex industry out of the shadows.

In 2003, as a result of the death of Oxana Rantseva and 'in light of similar cases which have been brought into publicity [sic] regarding violence or demises of alien women who arrives in Cyprus', the Cypriot Ombudsman took it upon herself to investigate the situation *ex officio*.[2] That investigation centred upon 'artiste' visas. While the Ombudsman's report noted that "the word 'artiste' in Cyprus has become synonymous with 'prostitute'"; the Cypriot artiste visa could not be mistaken for anything but a prostitute visa, as temporary residency and work permits were granted upon satisfactory 'AIDS and other infectious or contagious diseases' tests.[3] The 'artiste' regime, which came into existence in the mid-1970s, was based on immigration and employment laws which saw tens of thousands of alien women come to Cyprus to work in cabarets and night clubs.[4] The Ombudsman's report rings true for those familiar with cases of human trafficking and more so with the role played by the State in creating the super-structure which allowed for exploitation to transpire:

> The majority of the women entering the country to work as artistes come from poor families of the post socialist countries. Most of them are educated.... Few are the real artistes. Usually they are aware that they will be compelled to prostitute themselves. However, they do not always know about the working conditions under which they will exercise this job. There are also cases of alien women who come to Cyprus, having the impression that they will work as waitresses or dancers and that they will only have drinks with clients ('*consommation*'). They are made by force and threats to comply with the real terms of their work....
>
> Alien women who do not succumb to this pressure are forced by their employers to appear at the District Aliens and Immigration Branch to declare their wish to terminate their contract and to leave Cyprus on ostensible grounds.... Consequently, the employers can replace them quickly with other artistes.
>
> The alien artistes from the moment of their entry into the Republic of Cyprus to their departure are under constant surveillance and guard of their employers. After finishing their work, they are not allowed to go wherever they want. There are serious complaints even about cases of artistes who remain locked in their residence place. Moreover, their passports and

2 Ibid., para. 80.

3 Ibid., para. 116.

4 'Approximately 4000 artiste visa are issued each year'. Ibid., para. 96.

> other personal documents are retained by their employers or artistic agents. Those who refuse to obey are punished by means of violence or by being imposed fees which usually consist in deducting percentages of drinks, '*consommation*' or commercial sex. Of course these amounts are included in the contracts signed by the artistes.
>
> Generally, artistes stay at one or zero star hotels, flats or guest-houses situated near or above the cabarets, whose owners are the artistic agents or the cabaret owners. These places are constantly guarded. Three or four women sleep in each room. According to reports given by the Police, many of these buildings are inappropriate and lack sufficient sanitation facilities.
>
> Finally, it is noted that at the point of their arrival in Cyprus alien artistes are charged with debts, for instance with travelling expenses, commissions deducted by the artistic agent who brought them in Cyprus or with commissions deducted by the agent who located them in their country etc. Therefore, they are obliged to work under whichever conditions to pay off at least their debts.[5]

For his part, the Council of Europe Commissioner for Human Rights had visited Cyprus and issued three reports between 2003 and 2008. In the last of these reports, the Commissioner noted: 'In 2008, the island still is a destination country for a large number of women trafficked from the Philippines, Russia, Moldova, Hungary, Ukraine, Greece, Vietnam, Uzbekistan and the Dominican Republic for the purpose of commercial sexual exploitation'. The Commissioner went on to say that a 'paradox certainly exists that while the Cypriot government has made legislative efforts to fight trafficking in human beings and expressed its willingness through their National Action Plan 2005, it continues to issue work permits for so-called cabaret artistes and licences for the cabaret establishments'.[6] As the European Court noted in its judgment in *Rantsev*, there could be 'no doubt that the Cypriot authorities were aware that a substantial number of foreign women, particularly from the former Soviet Union, were being trafficked to Cyprus on artistes visas and, upon arrival, were being sexually exploited by cabaret owners and managers'.[7]

It was into this regime of artistes visas that Oxana Rantseva flew on 5 March 2001. Having been granted a temporary residence and work permit under this scheme, she started work on 16 March but left that employment after three

5 Ibid., para. 85.

6 Ibid., paras 101 and 103.

7 Ibid., para. 295.

days. A week later, in the early hours of 28 March, she was spotted in a discotheque in the Cypriote seaside resort of Limassol. Her previous employer, Marios Athanasiou, was informed and with the assistance of a security guard from his cabaret, took Ms Rantseva to a police station, where she was detained. After looking into the matter for some time, the police officer on duty, having found that as Ms Rantseva was not in Cyprus illegally, was instructed to contact Mr Athanasiou to say that if he did not return to pick Ms Rantseva up, she would be released. Mr Athanasiou collected Ms Rantseva, her passport, and other documents, and brought her to an apartment of one of his male employees at around 5.45 AM, where she was, in the European Court's assessment, placed in a bedroom against 'her own free will'.[8] At 6.30 AM Ms Rantseva was found dead on the street below. The police later found a bedspread looped around the balcony of the fifth-floor apartment. On 29 March a Cypriot autopsy concluded that the injuries she sustained were consistent with the fall which caused her death.

The inquest into the death of Ms Rantseva determined that there 'was no evidence…that suggests criminal liability of a third person for her death'.[9] A later autopsy came to a different conclusion. Conducted in Chelyabink, Russia[10] in May 2001 after Ms Rantseva's body had been repatriated an autopsy was conducted at the behest of her father. This autopsy concluded 'without a doubt' that the injuries sustained 'happened while she was alive' and transpired 'within a very short time period, one after another', just before she died.[11]

The Case before the European Court of Human Rights

In the wake of this second autopsy, Nicolay Rantsev sought to have his daughter's case in Cyprus reopened. However, what followed was a long string of misunderstandings and a lack of cooperation between Russian and Cypriot authorities. In 2004, with little progress taking place on this front, Nicolay Rantsev made an application to the European Court of Human Rights complaining, *inter alia*, of violations of Articles 2 (right to life), 3 (prohibition against torture), 4 (prohibition against exploitation), and 5 (right to liberty). In April 2009, with the case pending before the European Court, Cyprus made a

8 Ibid., para. 316.

9 Ibid., para. 41.

10 Located in Central Asia, north of central Kazakhstan.

11 *Rantsev, supra* n. 1, para. 45.

unilateral declaration acknowledging violations of positive obligations with regard to Articles 2, 3, 4, acting inconsistently with Article 5(1) of the ECHR, and offering to pay €37,000. In its unanimous judgment of 10 January 2010, the First Section of the European Court rejected this unilateral declaration on the basis that the case raised serious allegations and that it was the 'Court's duty to elucidate, safeguard and develop the rules instituted by the Convention' as the case at hand raised 'trafficking issues', which 'the Court has yet to rule on'.[12]

The Court's judgment centred on Article 4. However, it concluded that where Article 2 was concerned, Cyprus had violated its procedural obligations, 'because of the failure to conduct an effective investigation into Ms Rantseva's death'.[13] With regard to Article 5, the Court found in general terms and without enumerating grounds as set out in Article 5(1) 'that the detention of Ms Rantseva at the police station and her subsequent transfer and confinement to the apartment amounted to a deprivation of liberty'. The Court did not deem it necessary to consider the Article 3 complaint separately. As for Russia, the Court held that it had failed in its procedural obligation under Article 4 by failing to assist the Cypriot authorities in investigating 'the recruitment aspect of alleged trafficking' which would in turn 'allow an important part of the trafficking chain to act with impunity'.[14]

Ultimately, the European Court held that the Cyprus must pay €43,150 in costs and non-pecuniary damages while Russia was to pay €2,000 in damages.

Trafficking as Slavery

The European Court saw the *Rantsev* case as one dealing with trafficking and falling under the provisions of Article 4 of the ECHR, which reads:

> 1. No one shall be held in slavery or servitude.
> 2. No one shall be required to perform forced or compulsory labour.
> 3. For the purpose of this article the term 'forced or compulsory labour' shall not include:
>   (a) any work required to be done in the ordinary course of detention imposed according to the provisions of Article 5 of this Convention or during conditional release from such detention;

12 Ibid., para. 200.

13 Ibid., operative para. 5.

14 Ibid., para. 307.

(b) any service of a military character or, in case of conscientious objectors in countries where they are recognised, service exacted instead of compulsory military service;
(c) any service exacted in case of an emergency or calamity threatening the life or well-being of the community;
(d) any work or service which forms part of normal civic obligations.

At a normative level, the European Court's judgment in the *Rantsev* case, raises fundamental questions about the manner in which the Court engages with Article 4. By its own admission, the 'Court is not regularly called upon to consider the application of Article 4'.[15] In fact, but for this and the previous *Siliadin* judgment rendered in 2005,[16] the Court has not truly engaged with the fundamental nature of Article 4; that is: with human exploitation. Instead, as a 1999 book which considered the jurisprudence of the Court up to that point noted: 'The leading case on Article 4 is *Van der Mussels*..., in which a lawyer complained about the obligations to provide free legal assistance to poor clients'.[17] This is hardly the stuff of slavery or forced labour. The lack of engagement of the Court with Article 4 is manifest in the Court's understanding of the very nature of that provision. The Court stated in *Rantsev* that Article 4, like Articles 2 (right to life) and 3 (prohibition against torture), 'enshrines one of the basic values of the democratic societies making up the Council of Europe', and went on to say that Article 4 'makes no provision for exceptions and no derogation from it is permissible under Article 15 § 2 even in the event of a public emergency threatening the life of the nation'.[18] This is factually wrong and a glaring error by the Court. Only Article 4(1), dealing with slavery and servitude, is non-derogable; the obligations under Articles 4(2) and 4(3), relating to forced or compulsory labour, may be derogated from and, as such, are not listed under Article 15(2).

Where Article 4 is concerned, the Court noted that the term 'trafficking' was absent from its provisions. It then considered the general rules of treaty interpretation as set out by Article 31 of the 1969 Vienna Convention on the Law of Treaties (re: ordinary meaning, in context, with a look to the object and purpose of the treaty), and determined that trafficking fell within the purview of Article 4, though it considered 'it unnecessary to identify whether the treatment

---

15 Ibid., para. 279.

16 *Siliadin v France* 43 EHRR 16, paras 91, 92, 98 and 100.

17 Lawson and Schermes (eds), *Leading Cases of the European Court of Human Rights*, 2nd ed (Nijmegen; Ars Aequi Libri, 1999), xx.

18 *Rantsev, supra* n. 1, para. 279.

about which the applicant complains constitutes "slavery", "servitude" or "forced and compulsory labour.""[19] Yet, it should be stated at the outset that, there is an established definition in the law of trafficking, which has been repeated in both the UN 2000 Palermo Protocol and the Council of Europe's 2005 Convention on Action against Trafficking in Human Beings:

> 'Trafficking in human beings' shall mean the recruitment, transportation, transfer, harbouring or receipt of persons, by means of the threat or use of force or other forms of coercion, of abduction, of fraud, of deception, of the abuse of power or of a position of vulnerability or of the giving or receiving of payments or benefits to achieve the consent of a person having control over another person, for the purpose of exploitation. Exploitation shall include, at a minimum, the exploitation of the prostitution of others or other forms of sexual exploitation, forced labour or services, slavery or practices similar to slavery, servitude or the removal of organs.[20]

This definition, developed within a criminal law paradigm, requires three elements to be present before a person is criminally liable for trafficking in human beings. Trafficking requires an individual to be involved in one of the following activities: 'recruitment, transportation, transfer, harbouring or receipt of persons'. This involvement must have taken place by the means 'of the threat or use of force or other forms of coercion, of abduction, of fraud, of deception, of the abuse of power or of a position of vulnerability or of the giving or receiving of payments or benefits to achieve the consent of a person having control over another person'. The methods and the means utilised must then have as their ultimate object: exploitation of the person. The definition then sets out what is to be considered, at minimum, as human exploitation: 'the exploitation of the prostitution of others or other forms of sexual exploitation, forced labour or services, slavery or practices similar to slavery, servitude or the removal of organs'.

Within the European context, the various types of human exploitation enumerated in the European Convention against Trafficking have an established treaty regime attached to each of them. Thus the language of 'the exploitation

---

19 Ibid., para. 282.

20 See Article 3(a), 2001 United Nations Protocol to Prevent, Suppress and Punish Trafficking in Persons, Especially Women and Children and Article 4(a), 2005 Council of Europe Convention on Action against Trafficking in Human Beings. Note that the Palermo Protocol speaks of 'Trafficking in persons' not 'Trafficking in human beings'.

of the prostitution of others' comes directly from the 1949 Convention for the Suppression of the Traffic in Persons and of the Exploitation of the Prostitution of Others; 'forced labour or services' from the 1930 ILO Convention No. 29: Forced Labour Convention; 'slavery or practices similar to slavery and servitude' from the 1926 Slavery Convention and the 1956 Supplementary Convention on the Abolition of Slavery, the Slave Trade, and Institutions and Practices Similar to Slavery; while the 'removal of organs' is governed by the 1997 Council of Europe Convention on Human Rights and Biomedicine. Where the types of exploitation enumerated in Article 4 of the ECHR are concerned – slavery, servitude and forced labour – the European Court has taken its cue for the definition of slavery from the 1926 Convention and of forced labour from the 1930 Convention; while developing its own jurisprudence with regard to servitude.[21]

Regarding the link between Article 4 and trafficking, the Court noted that it is 'appropriate in the present case to examine the extent to which trafficking itself may be considered to run counter to the spirit and purpose of Article 4 of the Convention such as to fall within the scope of the guarantees offered by that Article without the need to assess which of the three types of proscribed conduct [i.e. slavery, servitude and forced labour] are engaged by the particular treatment in the case in question'.[22] That said, it is rather disingenuous for the European Court to say that it 'has had only one occasion to date to consider the extent to which treatment associated with trafficking fell within the scope of that Article (*Siliadin*...)', as the Court itself makes no mention of the issue of trafficking in the substance of that case, despite the applicant having raised the issue.

The European Court determined that it 'considers that trafficking in human beings, by its very nature and aim of exploitation, is based on the exercise of powers attaching to the right of ownership'. It then stated that

> in view of its obligation to interpret the Convention in light of present-day conditions, the Court considers it unnecessary to identify whether the treatment about which the applicant complains constitutes 'slavery', 'servitude' or 'forced and compulsory labour'. Instead, the Court concludes that trafficking itself, within the meaning of Article 3(a) of the

---

21 Note that 'practices similar to slavery' and 'servitude' should be understood as being identical in normative terms. See Allain, "On the Curious Disappearance of Human Servitude from General International Law," *Journal of the History of International Law*, Vol. 11, 2009, p. 303. [As reproduced in Chapter 14 of this volume.]

22 *Rantsev*, *supra* n. 1, para. 290.

> Palermo Protocol and Article 4(a) of the Anti-Trafficking Convention, falls within the scope of Article 4 of the Convention.[23]

The first of these pronouncements raises fundamental concerns regarding the Court's approach to Article 4 and its unwillingness to engage normatively with what it calls the 'three types of proscribed conduct' (slavery, servitude and forced labour). The Court stated that it 'considers that trafficking in human beings, by its very nature and aim of exploitation, is based on the exercise of powers attaching to the right of ownership'.[24] In effect, the Court made a determination that trafficking is based on slavery; as the final phrase – 'exercise of powers attaching to the right of ownership' – is the substance of the definition of slavery as established by the 1926 Slavery Convention, which reads: 'Slavery is the status or condition of a person over whom any or all of the powers attaching to the right of ownership are exercised'. With this pronouncement, the Court excluded from its understanding of trafficking, the elements of 'recruitment, transportation, transfer, harbouring or receipt of persons'; as well as the utilisation of specific means, such as 'the threat or use of force or other forms of coercion, of abduction', etc. Further, the Court excluded the other types of exploitation which could be at play in a case of trafficking, such as 'the exploitation of the prostitution of others or other forms of sexual exploitation, forced labour or services, … practices similar to slavery, servitude or the removal of organs'. In sum, with this pronouncement, the Court rids the content of trafficking of the methods of trafficking, the means of trafficking, and seven of the eight types of human exploitation as set out in the 2000 Palermo Protocol and the Council of Europe's 2005 Convention on Action against Trafficking in Human Beings.[25]

If we replace the phrase 'the exercise of powers attaching to the right of ownership' in the Court's pronouncement with the term 'slavery' it reads: the Court 'considers that trafficking in human beings, by its very nature and aim of exploitation, is based on [slavery]'. How then are we to understand a case where trafficking takes place with the purpose not of slavery, but for the removal of organs; is this slavery? Or, for that matter, what are we to make of the work of the International Labour Organisation with regard to trafficking into forced labour; is such trafficking slavery? This is the reading which the European Court has given to trafficking in *Rantsev*.

---

23 Ibid., paras 281 and 282.

24 Ibid., para 280.

25 This argument is developed further in Allain, "Book Review: Silvia Scarpa, *Trafficking in Human Beings: Modern Slavery*," *European Journal of International Law*, Vol. 20, 2008, p. 453. [As reproduced in Chapter 7 of this volume.]

The High Court of Australia, has taken a very different approach, in the 2008 case of *The Queen v. Tang*.[26] There, the High Court's approach began along similar lines to that of the European Court. But the High Court later discounted this thinking:

> It is unnecessary, and unhelpful, for the resolution of the issues in the present case, to seek to draw boundaries between slavery and cognate concepts such as servitude, peonage, forced labour, or debt bondage. The 1956 Supplementary Convention in Art 1 recognised that some of the institutions and practices it covered might also be covered by the definition of slavery in Art 1 of the 1926 Slavery Convention. To repeat what was said earlier, the various concepts are not all mutually exclusive. Those who engage in the traffic in human beings are unlikely to be so obliging as to arrange their practices to conform to some convenient taxonomy.[27]

That said, the High Court then went on to say: 'It is important not to debase the currency of language...by giving slavery a meaning that extends beyond the limits set by the text, context, and purpose of the 1926 Slavery Convention.... The term "slave" is sometimes used in a metaphorical sense to describe victims of such conditions, but that sense is not of present relevance'.[28] Moving on to consider the meaning given to slavery by the 1926 Slavery convention, the High Court determined that it applied to situations where either *de jure* or *de facto* a person exercised powers over a person which were tantamount to those that a person could exercise over a thing which they owned. By making reference to the work of the UN Secretary General in 1956, the High Court determined that slavery required, either the *de facto* or *de jure*, buying, selling, transferring of a person, or the total control of their labour or the fruits of that labour.[29] In this manner, the High Court, in a criminal case, gave legal certainly to the term 'slavery' as being distinct from forced labour, servitude, etc.

26 [2008] HCA 39.

27 Ibid., para. 29.

28 Ibid., para 32.

29 See Allain, "*The Queen v. Tang*: Clarifying the Definition of 'Slavery' in International Law," *Melbourne Journal of International Law*, Vol. 10, 2009, p. 257 [As reproduced in Chapter 19 of this volume.]. See also: United Nations, Economic and Social Council, Slavery, the Slave Trade, and other forms of Servitude (Report of the Secretary-General), UN Doc. E/2357, 27 January 1953, p. 28.

Turning to the European Court's second pronouncement that trafficking falls within the scope of Article 4 of the ECHR but that it was unnecessary to identify whether the treatment alleged by the applicant fell within 'slavery', 'servitude' or 'forced labour'. In a contradictory manner, the Court did not narrow the scope of application to make trafficking synonymous with slavery, but instead, it expanded the scope of Article 4, beyond its textual boundaries of slavery, servitude and forced labour, to being applicable to any type of exploitation including those others enumerated in the treaty definitions of 'trafficking in human beings' (i.e. exploitation of the prostitution of others or other forms of sexual exploitation and the removal of organs). The Court made a determination that, in light of the present-day conditions, trafficking itself falls within the scope of Article 4 of the ECHR. As a result of these conflicting pronouncements – that on the one hand trafficking equals slavery, and, on the other hand, that, teleologically, trafficking falls within the scope of Article 4 without determining under which provision – the Court has failed to demonstrate or set out a clear understanding of the substance or content of Article 4.

Beyond the possibility that the Court should not have dealt with issues of trafficking at all, as this falls within the competence of the supervisory body of the Council of Europe's 2005 Convention on Action against Trafficking in Human Beings: the Group of Experts on Action against Trafficking in Human Beings or 'GRETA'; the Court having considered trafficking within its remit, should have followed the lead of the trafficking conventions and determined that Article 4 seeks to address human exploitation. Such exploitation – the *purpose* of trafficking, as set out in the definition – is best understood in the context of negative obligations. As a result of *Rantsev*, Member States of the Council of Europe now have an obligation to suppress not only slavery, servitude and forced labour, but any type of human exploitation on their territory. The nexus of such human exploitation to trafficking is best understood (with the proviso that not all human exploitation will take place in the context of trafficking) with regard to positive obligations, of which the *Rantsev* is primarily concerned. The definition of trafficking in persons sets out a blueprint of the activities to be dealt with so as to suppress exploitation. This is a situation in which, through 'the threat or use of force or other forms of coercion, of abduction, of fraud, of deception, of the abuse of power or of a position of vulnerability or of the giving or receiving of payments or benefits to achieve the consent of a person having control over another person' a person is recruited, transported, transferred, harboured or in receipt of persons.

The Court, in *Rantsev*, set out an overall regime incumbent on States to ensure that trafficking does not take place in violation of Article 4:

> The Court considers that the spectrum of safeguards set out in national legislation must be adequate to ensure the practical and effective protection of the rights of victims or potential victims of trafficking. Accordingly, in addition to criminal law measures to punish traffickers, Article 4 requires member States to put in place adequate measures regulating businesses often used as a cover for human trafficking. Furthermore, a State's immigration rules must address relevant concerns relating to encouragement, facilitation or tolerance of trafficking.[30]

Where positive obligations are concerned, the Court notes that operationally, States must demonstrate that where they 'were aware, or ought to have been aware, of circumstances giving rise to a credible suspicion that an identified individual had been, or was at real and immediate risk of being trafficked or exploited', they must remove that individual from the situation of risk or find themselves in violation of Article 4.[31] Procedurally, States must investigate potential cases of trafficking; whereas States of origin or transit have a duty to cooperate effectively in cross-border cases.[32]

With regard to Cyprus, the Court held that its immigration regime of 'artiste' visas 'did not afford to Ms Rantseva practical and effective protection against trafficking and exploitation', and as such a violation of Article 4 had transpired. The Court went on to consider the positive obligations incumbent on Cypriot authorities to take protective measures against trafficking, which they failed to do in the case of Ms Rantseva, thus breaching Article 4. Where Russia is concerned, the Court held that it had failed to fulfil its procedural obligation under Article 4 by not assisting the Cypriot authorities in investigating 'the recruitment aspect of alleged trafficking' which would in turn 'allow an important part of the trafficking chain to act with impunity'.[33]

Conclusion

With its determination in *Rantsev v Cyprus and Russia*, the European Court of Human Rights has further muddied the waters of the normative elements of human exploitation but also muddled the jurisprudence of Article 4. In its 2005 *Siliadin* case, the Court determined that slavery was not at issue, as its:

30 *Rantsev*, *supra* n. 1, para. 283.
31 Ibid., para. 286.
32 Ibid., para. 289.
33 Ibid., para. 307.

> definition corresponds to the 'classic' meaning of slavery as it was practiced for centuries. Although the applicant was, in the instant case, clearly deprived of her personal autonomy, the evidence does not suggest that she was held in slavery in the proper sense, in other words that Mr and Mrs B. exercised a genuine right of legal ownership over her, thus reducing her to the status of an 'object'.[34]

And yet, in *Rantsev*, the Court determined that trafficking was based on the definition of slavery. It will be recalled that the Court stated that it 'considers that trafficking in human beings, by its very nature and aim of exploitation, is based on the exercise of powers attaching to the right of ownership'. As a result, the Court appears to determine that for trafficking to take place a genuine right – a *de jure* right – of legal ownership must be present. This is, of course, a legal impossibility, and thus, following the logic of the development of the Court's jurisprudence regarding Article 4, it must be understood that, legally speaking, trafficking cannot transpire within Europe as there exists no legal right to own a person within the Council of Europe.

Having identified State complicity in trafficking through Cypriote 'artiste' visas, the Court in essence assimilated trafficking to slavery, at the expense of recognising that it was seeking to deal with human exploitation and not 'slavery' in the metaphorical sense. In so doing, it did not engage with the constituent elements of what constitutes trafficking (its methods, means, or the various lesser servitudes than slavery, including debt bondage and forced labour) and thus provided what appears to be a very narrow understanding of trafficking. That said, in a rather contradictory manner, by determining that Article 4 is a vehicle for considering issues of trafficking, the Court appears to have widened the scope of that Article by providing for issues beyond slavery, servitude and forced labour, to be considered within the purview of the ECHR, most obviously with regard to trafficking in persons for the removal of organs.

While *Rantsev* will be used to good effect by the advocates of human rights and those dealing with trafficking or 'modern forms of slavery', in legal terms it is deeply flawed.

---

34 *Siliadin v. France* (2006) 43 EHRR 16, para. 122.

CHAPTER 10

Immanent Critique: International Law and the Dubious Case-Law on Slavery*

The task I have busied myself with over the last seven years or so has been to consider what 'slavery' means in law. The project evolved to now encompass a consideration of human exploitation in all its guises, from its most serious – slavery – to lesser servitudes, be it debt bondage, serfdom or forced labour. The project has been to develop an understanding of the law from the start of the international abolition movement through its modern day manifestations of human exploitation. I would say that the fruits of that labour only truly manifest themselves with the publication of *The Slavery Conventions* in 2008 and the analysis which emerges (and is currently emerging) as a results of a consideration of the drafting history of those 1926 Slavery and 1956 Supplementary Conventions.[1] In the introduction of *The Slavery Conventions* I note that part of the justification for assembling the *travaux préparatoires* of the conventions was the contradictory case-law which had emerged before the European Court of Human Rights and the International Criminal Tribunal for the former Yugoslavia. Since then there have

---

* Paper presented at The Wilberforce Institute for the Study of Slavery and Emancipation (WISE), May 2009.

1 Consider the following: Jean Allain, *The Slavery Conventions: The Travaux Préparatoires of the 1926 League of Nations Convention and the 1956 United Nations Convention*, 2008, p. 821.

Forthcoming: "On the Curious Disappearance of Human Servitude from General International Law," *Journal of the History of International Law*, Vol. 11, 2009, 25 pp; *forthcoming*: "The Definition of Slavery in International Law," *Howard Law Journal*, Vol. 52, 2009, pp. 239–275; "Nineteenth Century Law of the Sea and the British Abolition of the Slave Trade," *British Yearbook of International Law 2007*, Vol. 78, 2008, pp. 342–388; "Slavery and the League of Nations: Ethiopia as a Civilised Nation," *Journal of the History of International Law*, Vol. 8, 2006, pp. 213–244;

Forthcoming: Book Review: Claudia Aradau, *Rethinking Trafficking in Women: Politics out of Security*, 2008, *Journal of Human Rights and Civil Society*, Volume 2, 2009, pp. 4; *forthcoming*: Case Note: *The Queen v. Tang*, [2008] HCA 39, *Melbourne Journal of International Law*, Vol. 10, 2009, 10 pp. *forthcoming*: Book Review: Silvia Scarpa, *Trafficking in Human Beings: Modern Slavery*, 2008, *European Journal of International Law*, Vol. 20, 2009, 5 pp; *forthcoming*: Case Note: *Mani v. Niger*, *American Journal of International Law*, Vol. 103, 2009, 6 pp; and, Book Review: Kevin Bales, *Understanding Global Slavery: A Reader*, 2005; *International Journal of Refugee Law*, Vol. 20, 2008, 228–232.

 | DOI 10.1163/9789004279896_012

been two further cases dealing with slavery, one before the High Court of Australia, the other in front of the Economic Community of West Africa States Community Court of Justice. Within each of these four cases, the jurisprudence appears to play fast and loose with either the law or the facts to reach the policy-oriented ends sought by each of these adjudicative instances.

Jurisprudence of courts is fundamental to establishing the parameters of human exploitation in law, it provides authoritative pronouncements and is considered a subsidiary means of determining the rules of international law.[2] This Paper examines the failings of three of these four cases, along with the determination by a Commission of Inquiry of the International Labour Organisation that forced labour amounts to a peremptory norm of *jus cogens*, so as to consider whether the international jurisprudence on human exploitation can survive an implosion by immanent critique. If the case-law, having been shown to be failings in certain areas, can hold at the core, then its authoritative nature will remain intact though bruised; if not then these finding must be deemed to fail as legal pronouncements and reveal themselves to be politics by other means, lacking a jurisprudential foundation necessary to be deemed international law manifest by what States say the law is. This is so as international law as a species of law, is rather distinct from domestic legal orders, as it is decentralised in nature, requiring law to find its source in the positive expression of States. Through treaties and or their legal practice (re: the State practice and *opinio juris* of international customary law), States are deemed to create international law; whereas international courts (like scholar) are meant to reflect the pronouncements of States as a collective, thus providing a third-party assessment of rules of international law. If they fail to do so, as in the cases to be considered shortly, their pronouncements cannot be said to reflect international law, thus weakening not only the jurisprudential foundation of the institution, but bringing into question the very institutional itself.

Immanent Critique founds its voice in the Frankfurt School of critical social theory, thought its roots are to be found in Hegel and Marx.[3] It is a means of turning the tools of critical thinking of, in this case, law against itself. To consider, not the manner in which the case-law speaks to the issue of slavery, but to ask whether the cases at hand actually meet the requirements – the givens – of the discipline of international law. What this requires is that the pronouncements handed down not be taken at face-value and considered in the social context

---

2 See Article 38(1)(d), Statute of the International Court of Justice, 1945.

3 See Robert Antonio, "Immanent Critique and the Core of Critical Theory: Its Origins and Developments in Hegel, Marx and Contemporary Thought," *British Journal of Sociology*, Vol. 32, 1981, 330.

which they emerged, but that the jurisprudential foundation upon which these judgements are created and developed be examined to ensure they reflect the historical precedent they say they do. For Max Horkheimer, Immanent Critique is to be found in "the dialectic in history which is driven by the contradiction between ideology and reality."[4] In the case at hand, this is manifest in the attempts by courts to bring the law in line with their sense of where the law should be (ideology) as opposed to what the genealogy of the law ought to tell them (reality). Thus, in the cases to follow, the holding courts up to the standards set within international law of what the law should be, an immanent critique demonstrate an inability to "secure their own legitimacy" and without this – as William Butler Yeats would say – 'things fall apart; the centre cannot hold'.[5]

Slavery in International Law

The established definition of slavery in international law is found in the 1926 Slavery Convention wherein it states that "slavery is the status or condition of a person over whom any or all of the powers attaching to the right of ownership are exercised." That definition has withstood the test of time, having been reconsidered in the lead up to the 1956 Supplementary Convention, wherein it was determined by a committee of experts of the United Nations that despite there being a "feeling that perhaps that definition might be improved in the light of modern thinking"; that once they had considered the issue, found "that there is not sufficient reason for discarding or amending the definition of slavery contained in Article 1 of the International Slavery Convention of 1926. It agreed therefore to recommend that this definition should continue to be accepted as an accurate and adequate definition of the term."[6] Likewise the substance of the 1926 definition was included in the 1998 Statute of the International Criminal Court as constituting the definition of enslavement as a crime against humanity.

4 *Id.*, p. 335.

5 Geoff Pearson and Michael Slater, "Getting Public Law Back into Critical Condition: The Rule of Law as a Source of Immanent Critique," *Social & Legal Studies*, Vol. 8, 1999, 285. William Butler Yeats, "*The Second Coming*," 1920.

6 United Nations, Economic and Social Council, Report of the *Ad Hoc* Committee on Slavery (Second Session), UN Doc. E/1988, E/AC.33/13, 4 May 1951, pp. 5–7; as reproduced in Jean Allain, *The Slavery Conventions: The Travaux Préparatoires of the 1926 League of Nations Convention and the 1956 United Nations Convention*, 2008, 494.

Slavery in international law turns on the exercise of 'powers attaching to the right of ownership' as opposed to powers of ownership. That distinction is one which allows for the possibility of making a determination of slavery in cases of de facto slavery. In other words, where a person does not own another in the legal sense, but the exercise powers of ownership of that individual. Where chattel is concerned this is distinction is apparent in property crime. A thief does not own the television he has nicked, but in the eyes of the law he exercise a power of ownership – possession – which would then carry criminal charges. That analogy, it seems to me, does not work as well as the following: Consider a dispute between two individuals over something illegal – a kilo of heroin; either of the two dealers has a legal claim of ownership over the drugs as no judge will give satisfaction if the parties where so unwise as to bring the dispute to court. So would be the case of a dispute between two individuals over a slave, neither party in dispute could have a legal right vindicated as ownership is illegal. Yet in both the case of the heroin and the slave, a judge is well placed in law to find that one or the other exercised the powers attaching to the right of ownership – say possession.

What now follows is a consideration of four pronouncements considered in chronological order, the first is the 1998 Report of the ILO Commission of Inquiry into issues of forced labour in Myanmar. This is followed by three court cases dealing the issues of slavery: the European Court of Human Rights' 2005 *Siliadin v France* case; the 2008 High Court of Australia case *The Queen v Tang*; and the ECOWAS Community Court of Justice's 2008 *Mani v Niger* case.

1998 Report of the ILO Commission of Inquiry into Issues of Forced Labour in Myanmar

As result of more than 30 years of criticism by the International Labour Organisation (ILO), Workers' delegates to the 1996 International Labour Conference brought forward a complaint against the State of Myanmar (Burma) for non-observance of the 1930 Forced Labour Convention. They alleged that Myanmar engaged actively in promoting forced labour "so that it was today an endemic abuse affecting hundreds of thousands of workers who were subjected to the most extreme forms of exploitation."[7] In March 1997, in

---

7 International Labour Organisation, Governing Body, Forced Labour in Myanmar (Burma), Report of the Commission of Inquiry appointed under article 26 of the Constitution of the International Labour Organization to examine the observance by Myanmar of the Forced Labour Convention, 1930 (No. 29), 2 July 1998, para. 100.

accordance with Article 26 of the Constitution of the International Labour Organisation, the ILO's Governing Body established a Commission of Inquiry composed of the former chief justices of Barbados, Sir William Douglas, and India, Prafullachandra Bhagwati, and the Australian Barrister and Member of the ILO Committee of Experts on the Application of Conventions and Recommendation, Robyn Layton.[8] As part of its deliberations, the Commission of Inquiry received written communications from Myanmar and a number of other States, as well as Intergovernmental organisations and Non-governmental labour and human rights organisations; heard witnesses; and visited the region (though not Myanmar as it had refused to receive the Commission).[9]

In Part 4 of its 1998 Report, the Commission of Inquiry, before turning to consider the factual state of Myanmar and its relevant legislation, provided a section on both general international law and the requirements of the Forced Labour Convention. Where international law was concerned, the Commission of Inquiry provided a section entitled "General International Law, including slavery, forced labour and other slavery-like practices."[10] This section is riddled with a number of inaccuracies and deserves a thorough consideration. First it should be noted that slavery and forced labour have established definitions in international law: slavery being defined by the 1926 Slavery Convention as "the status or condition of a person over whom any or all of the powers attaching to the right of ownership are exercised"; will forced labour is defined by the 1930 Forced Labour Convention as: "All work or service which is exacted under menace of any penalty for its non-performance and for which the worker concerned does not offer himself voluntarily."[11] The notion of 'slavery-like practices' is a term of art not of law, it having been introduced when the balance of power shifted within the United Nations from Western States to newly decolonised States in the mid-1960s as a compromise term meant of characterising apartheid and colonialism.[12] The notion of 'slavery-like practices' should not be confused with the legal term "institutions and practices similar to slavery" which connotes those servile statuses established by the 1956 Supplementary

8 See *id.*, paras 1–6.

9 *Id.*, para. 78.

10 *Id.*, see Part IV at 9(a).

11 Article 1(1), 1926 Slavery Convention; and Article 2(1), 1930 Forced Labour Convention (No. 29).

12 See discussions at United Nations, Economic and Social Council, Social Committee, UN Doc E/AC.7/L.486, 8 July 1966, and 11 July 1966, UN Doc E/AC.7/SR.538; as well as the outcome manifest in United Nations, Economic and Social Council, Resolution 1126 (XLI), 26 July 1966.

Convention, that is: debt bondage, serfdom, servile marriage and child exploitation. It is thus counter-temporal (and in legal terms inaccurate) to speak, as the Commission of Inquiry does, in the following terms: "After the First World War, slavery and slavery-like practices were among the first issues addressed by the League of Nations."

In considering the work of the League of Nations, the Commission of Inquiry does well to highlight the fact that the first limitation in international law of forced labour appears in the 1926 Slavery Convention wherein Article 5 requires the States Parties "to take all necessary measures to prevent compulsory or forced labour from developing into conditions analogous to slavery." Yet, the Commission of Inquiry appears to conflate slavery and forced labour. It does so to reach the conclusion "that there exists now in international law a peremptory norm prohibiting any recourse to forced labour and that the right not to be compelled to perform forced or compulsory labour is one of the basic human rights."[13] A peremptory norm, more often referred to in the literature by its Latin term *jus cogens*, is a norm which in a domestic setting would be considered as having strict liability; that is no justification can excuse a violation, and thus no derogation is permitted. A peremptory norm is a custom-based and requires through State practice and *opinio juris* not only that States recognise that a practice would be counter to a legal norm but also that the practice amounts to a legal norm for which no derogation is permitted.[14] The Commission of Inquiry fails to truly provide justification for the apparent leap of faith that forced labour is a peremptory norm, thought it notes the International Court of Justice the protection of persons from slavery – not forced labour – as an obligation *erga omnes* (re: obligations 'towards all'), that is an obligation of such importance that "all States can be held to have a legal interest in its protection." The Commission of Inquiry then states that finally, "any person who violates *this* peremptory norm is guilty of a crime under international law and thus bears individual criminal responsibility." The Commission then continues:

---

13 International Labour Organisation, Governing Body, Forced Labour in Myanmar (Burma), Report of the Commission of Inquiry appointed under article 26 of the Constitution of the International Labour Organization to examine the observance by Myanmar of the Forced Labour Convention, 1930 (No. 29), 2 July 1998, para. 203.

14 See for instance the section entitled "Le double consentement" in A. Gómez Robledo, "Le *ius cogens* international," *Collected Courses of the Hague Academy of International Law*, Vol. 172, 1981, pp. 104–108; and Phillipe Cahier, "Cours général de droit international public," *Collected Courses of the Hague Academy of International Law*, Vol. 195, 1985, 198.

> More specifically, enslavement, which was defined by the International Law Commission as establishing or maintaining over persons a status of slavery, servitude or forced labour contrary to well-established and widely recognized standards of international law, is *also*, if committed in a widespread or systematic manner, a crime against humanity that is punishable under the terms of the statutes setting up the four ad hoc international criminal tribunals established since the Second World War to try those responsible for serious violations of international humanitarian law, as well as under the draft statute for an international criminal court [...].[15]

Here it must be said that 'enslavement' is different in law than 'slavery'. Enslavement is part of international criminal law, it is a crime against humanity. The international criminal law does not know a lesser crime than the *crime against humanity* of enslavement. Thus it is wrong for the Commission of Inquiry to state, with reference to the phrase 'is also', that something less than being committed in a widespread or systematic manner would constitute enslavement. This is rather incidental to the fundamental issue to be taken with the confluence of slavery with enslavement. It states, as noted above, that enslavement was "defined by the International Law Commission as establishing or maintaining over persons a status of slavery, servitude or forced labour." And Yet, the International Law Commission never *defined* enslavement.[16] What is quoted by the Commission of Inquiry is a commentary to the 1996 Draft Code of Crimes against the Peace and Security of Mankind; this Draft Code remains to this day a draft and has, in essence, fallen into abeyance as a result of the establishment of the International Criminal Court.[17] The 1998

---

15 International Labour Organisation, Governing Body, Forced Labour in Myanmar (Burma), Report of the Commission of Inquiry appointed under article 26 of the Constitution of the International Labour Organization to examine the observance by Myanmar of the Forced Labour Convention, 1930 (No. 29), 2 July 1998, para. 204. Emphasis added and citations in the original omitted.

16 Article 18 of the 1996 Draft Code of Crimes against the Peace and Security of Mankind reads:

> A crime against humanity means any of the following acts, when committed in a systematic manner or on a large scale and instigated or directed by a Government or by any organization or group:
>
> [...](d) Enslavement; [...].

17 The moratorium of the Draft Code was foreseen in Jean Allain and John R.W.D. Jones, "A Patchwork of Norms: A Commentary on the 1996 Draft Code of Crimes against the Peace and Security of Mankind," *European Journal of International Law*, Vol. 8, 1997, pp. 100–117. The following is the commentary:

Statute of the International Criminal Court, despite the reference of the Commission of Inquiry to its adoption in draft form of this expanded notion of enslavement to include force labour, establishes that the definition of 'enslavement' is the same as that of 'slavery'.[18] As a result, one cannot say that enslavement today includes forced labour and thus that force labour can piggy-back on slavery so as to constitute a peremptory norm of international law. This of course is with the general caveat that forced labour will always amount to slavery where the powers attaching to the right of ownerships are exercised.

The ILO Commission of Inquiry concluded its consideration of the issue of forced labour in Myanmar by stating that there "is abundant evidence before the Commission showing the pervasive use of forced labour imposed on the civilian population throughout Myanmar by the authorities and the military."[19] Where international law is concerned, it noted that:

> A State which supports, instigates, accepts or tolerates forced labour on its territory commits a wrongful act and engages its responsibility for the violation of a peremptory norm in international law. Whatever may be

---

> Enslavement means establishing or maintaining over persons a status of slavery, servitude or forced labour contrary to well-established and widely recognized standards of international law, such as: the Slavery Convention (slavery); the Supplementary Convention on the Abolition of Slavery, the Slave Trade, and Institutions and Practices Similar to Slavery (slavery and servitude); the International Covenant on Civil and Political Rights (slavery and servitude); and ILO Convention No. 29, concerning Forced or Compulsory Labour (forced labour). Enslavement was included as a crime against humanity in the Charter of the Nurnberg Tribunal (art. 6, subpara. (c)), Control Council Law No. 10 (art. II, subpara. (c)), the statute of the International Tribunal for the Former Yugoslavia (art. 5) and the statute of the International Tribunal for Rwanda (art. 3) as well as the Nurnberg Principles (Principle VI) and the 1954 draft Code (art. 2, para. 11).

See United Nations, General Assembly, International Law Commission, Draft Code of Crimes against the Peace and Security of Mankind with commentaries, *Yearbook of the International Law Commission*, UN Doc. A/51/10 (Volume 2, Part 2), 1996, p. 47.

18 There are a number of caveats here, which I have explored these in detail in the following Conference Paper: Jean Allain, "The Parameters of 'Enslavement' in International Criminal Law," International Symposium on the New Developments of International Criminal Law, China University of Political Science and Law, Beijing, China, 25 April 2009.

19 International Labour Organisation, Governing Body, Forced Labour in Myanmar (Burma), Report of the Commission of Inquiry appointed under article 26 of the Constitution of the International Labour Organization to examine the observance by Myanmar of the Forced Labour Convention, 1930 (No. 29), 2 July 1998, para. 528. Citations in the original omitted.

> the position in national law with regard to the exaction of forced or compulsory labour and the punishment of those responsible for it, any person who violates the prohibition of recourse to forced labour under the Convention is guilty of an international crime that is also, if committed in a widespread or systematic manner, a crime against humanity.[20]

As has been demonstrated above, it is not possible to establish how the Commission of Inquiry came to the determination that forced labour constitutes a peremptory norm in international law. What is certain, however, is that a person who violates the prohibition of forced labour under the Forced Labour Convention cannot be found guilty of an international crime, at least not under the statute of the International Criminal Court, unless forced labour manifests the exercise of powers attaching to the right of ownership. If this was the case, the crime is enslavement, not forced labour.[21]

2005 *Siliadin v France* – European Court of Human Rights

In 2005 the European Court of Human Rights delivered its first case of substance with regard to Article 4 of the 1950 European Convention on Human Rights and human exploitation. Before *Siliadin v France*, it was noted that "the leading case on Article 4 is *Van der Müssele*, in which a lawyer complained about the obligation to provide free legal assistance to poor clients."[22] ...Hardly the stuff of human exploitation. The *Siliadin* case dealt with to a Togolese child exploited as domestic labourer in a private home in France. In this case, the Court found there was a breach of the provisions of Article 4 touching on forced labour and servitude, but found no violation with regard to slavery.

It might first be emphasised that, as opposed to the standalone crime against humanity of 'enslavement' before the International Criminal Court, international human rights law generally and the European Convention specifically

20 International Labour Organisation, Governing Body, Forced Labour in Myanmar (Burma), Report of the Commission of Inquiry appointed under article 26 of the Constitution of the International Labour Organization to examine the observance by Myanmar of the Forced Labour Convention, 1930 (No. 29), 2 July 1998, para. 538. Citations in the original omitted.

21 I would just highlight here that the Commission of Inquiry, having signed off on its Report thankes "Ms. Anne-Marie La Rosa, whose mastery of the principles of international law is matched by unusual clarity of thought and expression."

22 R.A Lawson & H.G. Schermers, *Leading Cases of the European Court of Human Rights*, 1999, p. xx.

knows not only slavery, but also servitude and forced labour.[23] Thus the Court could and did consider the fate of Siliadin on a gradation of exploitation, turning first to forced labour. As has been noted by the Council of Europe, "prohibits forced labour without defining it," yet the drafters of the European Convention used the definition found in the 1930 Forced Labour Convention as "their model."[24] In *Siliadin* determined that with regard to forced labour, that this "brings to mind the idea of physical or mental constraint." What there has to be is work "exacted [...] under the menace of any penalty" and also performed against the will of the person concerned, that is work for which he "has not offered himself voluntarily." The Court continued:

> in the instant case, although the applicant was not threatened by a 'penalty', the fact remains that she was in an equivalent situation in terms of the perceived seriousness of the threat. [...] Accordingly, the Court considers that the first criterion was met, especially since the applicant was a minor at the relevant time, a point which the Court emphasises.
>
> As to whether she performed this work of her own free will, it is clear from the facts of the case that it cannot seriously be maintained that she did. On the contrary, it is evident that she was not given any choice.
>
> In these circumstances, the Court considers that the applicant was, at the least, subjected to forced labour within the meaning of Article 4 of the Convention at a time when she was a minor.[25]

---

23 Article 4 of the European Convention for Protection of Human Rights and Fundamental Freedoms reads:

> No one shall be held in slavery or servitude.
>
> No one shall be required to perform forced or compulsory labour.
>
> For the purpose of this article the term 'forced or compulsory labour' shall not include:
>
> a any work required to be done in the ordinary course of detention imposed according to the provisions of Article 5 of this Convention or during conditional release from such detention;
>
> b any service of a military character or, in case of conscientious objectors in countries where they are recognised, service exacted instead of compulsory military service;
>
> c any service exacted in case of an emergency or calamity threatening the life or well-being of the community;
>
> d any work or service which forms part of normal civic obligations.

24 Council of Europe, Council of Europe Convention on Action against Trafficking in Human Beings and its Explanatory Report, Council of Europe Treaty Series – No. 197, 16 May, 2005, p. 39, paras 89–90.

25 Council of Europe, European Court of Human Rights, *Siliadin v France*, Application 73316/01, 26 July 2005, pp. 38–40.

Turning now to the issue of servitude, while it may be said that the 'practices similar to slavery' established by the 1956 Supplementary Convention constitute the four main types of servitudes in it general international law, the notion of 'servitude' still has currency in international human rights law as it has been given content by reference, primarily, to decisions of the European Court of Human Rights.[26] When considering the notion of servitude as included in the 2005 European anti-Trafficking Convention, the Council of Europe that servitude should be regarded "as having to live and work on another person's property and perform certain services for them, whether paid or unpaid, together with being unable to alter one's condition." The Report goes on to say that servitude "is thus to be regarded as a particular form of slavery, differing from it less in character [...] than in degree. Although it constitutes a state or condition, and is a 'particularly serious form of denial of freedom', [...] it does not have the ownership features characteristic of slavery."[27]

In *Siliadin*, the European Court repeated its earlier finding in the 1980 *Van Droogenbroeck* case, that servitude is "a particularly serious form of denial of freedom." The Court then notes that this may include "in addition to the obligation to provide certain services to another [...] the obligation on the 'serf' to live on the other's property and the impossibility of changing his status." The Court, in *Siliadin*, states that it "follows in the light of the case-law on this issue that for Convention purposes 'servitude' means an obligation to provide one's services that is imposed by the use of coercion, and is to be linked with the concept of 'slavery'." The Court then considered a number of facts in the case, including that Ms. Siwa-Akofa Siliadin having been a minor at the time, had not chosen to work for those who had reduced her to servitude, and that lacking resources she was both "vulnerable and isolated." Her papers having been confiscated and fearing arrest by the police, she was entirely at the mercy of those who were exploiting her. "In those circumstances, the Court concludes that the applicant, a minor at the relevant time, was held in servitude within the meaning of Article 4 of the Convention."[28]

Where slavery is concerned the European Court had the following to say, with reference to the definition of slavery established by the 1926 Convention:

---

26 Consider the forthcoming: Jean Allain, "On the Curious Disappearance of Human Servitude from General International Law," *Journal of the History of International Law*, Vol. 11, 2009, 25 pp. [As reproduced in Chapter 14 of this volume.]

27 Council of Europe, Council of Europe Convention on Action against Trafficking in Human Beings and its Explanatory Report, Council of Europe Treaty Series – No. 197, 16 May, 2005, p. 40, para. 95.

28 *Id.*, pp. 38–40.

> this definition corresponds to the 'classic' meaning of slavery as it was practiced for centuries. Although the applicant was, in the instant case, clearly deprived of her personal autonomy, the evidence does not suggest that she was held in slavery in the proper sense, in other words that Mr and Mrs B. exercised a genuine right of legal ownership over her, thus reducing her to the status of an "object."[29]

Putting aside the fact that the victim, Ms Siwa-Akofa Siliadin, is named, but the perpetrators of this case of human exploitation, 'Mr and Mrs B.', are given anonymity; the case begs the question why is a 'a genuine right of legal ownership' required, that is why *de jure* slavery as opposed to the 'powers attaching to the right of ownership' as set out the 1926 definition which would then include not only *de jure* but also *de facto* slavery? This truly narrow interpretation is not consonant with the negotiation history of the 1926 Slavery Convention or the 1956 Supplementary Convention which again considered the 1926 definition, nor is it in line with an ordinary reading of the provision with reference to the rules of treaty interpretation as set out the 1969 Vienna Convention on the Law of Treaties.[30] That said, it might be emphasised that the European Court is known to have a backlog of tens of thousands of cases and thus little time can be given to carrying out the time of research that I have over the last five or six years which has brought to light an understanding of what that 1926 definition of slavery means in law. Thus, one could say that the European Court simply did not have the time or inclination to undertake a study to get to the heart of what this provision means in law.

If one wishes to put a better gloss on approach of the European Court of Human Rights in *Siliadin* one might say that first historically, Europe has witness, in the 1930s, the legalisation of enslavement manifest in German-run concentration camps;[31] and second, as opposed to international criminal law

---

29 European Court of Human Rights, *Siliadin v France* (Application 73316/01), 26 July 2005, para. 122.

30 For a consideration of the drafting history see: Jean Allain, *The Slavery Conventions: The Travaux Préparatoires of the 1926 League of Nations Convention and the 1956 United Nations Convention*, 2008.

For a consideration of the definition of slavery see: Jean Allain, "The Definition of Slavery in International Law," *Howard Law Journal*, Vol. 52, 2009, pp. 239–275.

Article 31(1) of the Vienna Convention on the Law of Treaties reads: "A treaty shall be interpreted in good faith in accordance with the ordinary meaning to be given to the terms of the treaty in their context and in the light of its object and purpose"....

31 See Michael Bazyler and Roger Alford (eds), *Holocaust Restitution: Perspectives on the Litigation and Its Legacy*, 2006.

which only knows the crime against humanity of 'enslavement', the European Convention provides for the prohibition of both 'slavery' and 'servitude'. As a result, the Court has the luxury of falling back on the notion of 'servitude', much as it has in the past, with regard to Article 3, when it failed to find any State in violation of 'torture' for some forty year, instead deeming all violations of this article as falling under the lesser prohibition on 'inhuman or degrading treatment or punishment'. By using 'servitude' in cases of *de facto* slavery, the European Court has the possibility of holding a State responsible for a breach of Article 4 while reserving the use 'slavery' should the day arise when a European State would seek once more to introduce into law slavery on the Continent.

The argument put forward, however, fails to answer the failings of the European Court to interact, as it should, with the definition of slavery manifest in the 1926 Slavery Convention and is a justification *ex post facto*. By failing to abide by the general rules of treaty interpretation, the very legitimacy of the role of the European Court as an authoritative body delivering pronouncements on the law (at least with regard to Article 4) must be brought into question.

2008 *The Queen v Tang* – High Court of Australia[32]

It should come as little surprise that I agree in long measure with the High Court of Australia's pronouncement in *The Queen v Tang*. The case, dealing a brothel owner who was appealing a ten-year prison sentence for having enslaved Thai prostitutes, was heard on appeal from the Court of Appeal of the Supreme Court of Victoria. The High Court of Australia, in my eyes has put to rest the approach to the definition of slavery which attempts to say that slavery could be manifest even where the powers attached to the right of ownership were not present so as to include lesser servitudes. This approach was first found voice internationally through the 1931 International Commission consider the issue of slavery in Liberia,[33] which although mandated to consider slavery, readily acknowledged that it went further and considered lesser servitudes where "issues of powers attaching to the right of ownership were not manifest," picked up once more in the work of David Weissbrodt for the United Nations.

32 Note that the material used in this section will appear in the forthcoming case note: Jean Allain, *The Queen v. Tang*, *Melbourne Journal of International Law*, Vol. 10, 2009.

33 See *International Commission of Inquiry into the Existence of Slavery and Forced Labour in the Republic of Liberia, Report of the International Commission of Inquiry*, 1931.

In 2007, the Court of Appeal of the Supreme Court of Victoria spelled out these approach in counter-distinction to one I was just starting to make public with regard to the definition of 'slavery' in international law:

> The understanding of the scope of the definition of slavery stated by Jean Allain is at odds with that of David Weissbrodt in his paper commissioned by the Office of the United Nations High Commissioner for Human Rights.[34] Weissbrodt concluded that the definition was intended to include the broader range of practices that had been addressed by the Temporary Slavery Commission of 1924, including debt bondage, serfdom, practices involving restrictions of liberty and personal control analogous to slavery, practices such as acquisition of women and girls in the guise of payment of dowry, and so forth. It was not limited to chattel slavery, but required examination of the degree of restriction and control exercised over the person, rather than concentration on the criterion of ownership.[35]

In that case, the Supreme Court of Victoria concluded that "in final analysis, it is unnecessary to resolve the dispute between Allain and Weissbrodt." However on appeal, in August 2008, the supreme court of Australia – the High Courts of Australia – resolved that dispute in *The Queen v Tang*.[36]

The High Court relying in part of research I had developed in 2007 and published early in 2008 determined that the definition of slavery, as established by the 1926 Slavery Convention, was meant to apply to both *de jure* and *de facto* slavery and manifest when the powers attaching to the right of ownership were exercised.

In April 2008, I was contacted by the Australian Human Rights and Equality Commission which was looking to intervene in the case but was hesitating. They were aware of my forthcoming *The Slavery Conventions*, asking for a copy. As it was, the book had not yet come out but I forwarded the proofs which I had received a fortnight earlier. The Commission did in fact intervene and the High Court went on to cite my *travaux préparatoires* and other working papers as a basis of their determination.

---

34 See David Weissbrodt and Anti-Slavery International, *Abolishing Slavery and its Contemporary Forms*, Economic and Social Council Resolution 2001/282, UN Doc HR/Pub/02/04, 2002.

35 Supreme Court of Victoria (Court of Appeal), *Queen v Wei Tang*, [2007] VSCA 134, 2 July 2007, para. 36.

36 See Jean Allain, *The Slavery Conventions: The Travaux Préparatoires of the 1926 League of Nations Convention and the 1956 United Nations Convention*, 2008.

In writing for the majority, Chief Justice Murray Gleeson noted that the "travaux préparatoires of the 1926 Slavery Convention are not especially illuminating as to the meaning of Art 1"; yet, "certain observations may be made as to the text and context, including the purpose, of the Convention."[37] Three such observations led the majority of the Court to conclude that the 1926 definition found in Slavery Convention applies to both *de jure* and *de facto* slavery. First, Gleeson CJ noted that for many States, including Australia, which became party to the Convention in 1926, the legal status of slavery no longer existed. Second, that the aim of the Convention was to bring about the same situation universally. Third, that the phrase 'status or condition', found within the 1926 definition makes the distinction between *de jure* ("Status is a legal concept."); and, taking into consideration the first and second observations made, "the evident purpose of the reference to "condition" was to cover slavery *de facto* [...]."[38] The High Court then stated that the "definition turns upon the exercise of the power over a person"; and that in *de facto* conditions the "definition was addressing the exercise over a person of powers of the kind that attached to the right of ownership when the legal status was possible." The High Court then went on to consider what should be understood by such powers which are manifest when ownership is legal.

What I would like to take issue with in this case is the first of the observations upon which the High Court based its findings on the meaning of the definition of slavery; that: "in 1926, in the case of many of the parties to the Convention, including Australia, the legal status of slavery did not exist, and legal ownership by one person of another was impossible."[39] While this statement is factually accurate, it does not reflect the 'context' which the High Court refers to as being the motivation of States for establishing the 1926 Slavery Convention. The aim of the Convention was, as its Preamble states, to continue the work started with the limitation place on the slave trade in Berlin in 1885 and at Brussels in 1990 with a look to "securing the complete suppression of slavery in all its forms and of the slave trade by land and sea." The Convention was very much a piece of colonial legislation, wherein for instance, the first draft of the Article dealing with forced labour read in part that where States were required to use such labour, "they will take all necessary precautions, particularly where the labourers belong to the less advanced races, to prevent conditions analogous to these of slavery from resulting from such employment."[40] Likewise, Portugal considers that the forbidding of forced labour sent the

37 *The Queen v Tang* [2008] HCA 39, 28 August 2008, p. 12.

38 *Id.*, p. 12.

39 *The Queen v Tang* [2008] HCA 39, 28 August 2008, p. 12. Footnote in the original omitted.

40 See League of Nations, Annex I: Slavery: Draft Resolution and Protocol, Official Journal: Record of the Sixth Assembly, Meetings of the Committees, Minutes of the Sixth Committee

wrong message to the indigenous populations of the colonies, as it suggests "to the native races that its prohibitions implies for them a right to idleness"; and that this was counter to their "well-being and their development."[41]

As a result the object and purpose was to put to an end slavery, be it *de jure* or *de facto* in colonial territories and those States not currently a Member of the League of Nations.[42] There was no sense that the 1926 Slavery Convention would be applicable to the parties negotiating it on their metropolitan territory. It is only now, in the twenty-first century, with the end of the decolonisation process that States such as Australia accept that there is a positive obligation to deal with 'retail' acts of slavery carried out for private gain and that *de facto* slavery is very much alive in modern societies and in need of suppression. While it is counterfactual to imply that the motivation for drafting the Convention was to acknowledge the possibility of the suppression of *de facto* slavery in metropolitan areas of colonial States, as *The Queen v Tang* indicates, the 1926 definition of slavery has proven itself not only resilient, having been scrutinised in the lead up to its inclusion in the 1956 Supplementary Convention and the 1998 Statute of the International Criminal Court, but to have come into its own as a standard which now applies universally in an era where de jure slavery no longer exists. Or does it…as we know turn to consider:

2008 *Mani v Niger* – ECOWAS Community Court of Justice[43]

In October 2008, the Economic Community of West African States (ECOWAS) Community Court of Justice made a determination in *Hadijatou Mani Koraou*

(Political Questions) Special Supplement No. 39, 14 September 1925, p. 41; as reproduced in Jean Allain, *The Slavery Conventions: The Travaux Préparatoires of the 1926 League of Nations Convention and the 1956 United Nations Convention*, 2008, p. 102.

41 See 5 League of Nations, Note Submitted to the First Sub-Committee of the Sixth Committee by the Portuguese Delegate, General Freire d'Andrade, A.VI/S.C.1/2.1925, 11 September 1925, as found in Folder R.67.D.46214 entitled *La question de l'esclavage: Discussions, y relatives, de la VIe Assembleé*, 1925, p. 5; as reproduced in Jean Allain, *The Slavery Conventions: The Travaux Préparatoires of the 1926 League of Nations Convention and the 1956 United Nations Convention*, 2008, p. 105.

42 Note the case of Ethiopia which joined the League of Nations in 1923 so as to avoid scrutiny by colonial States. See Jean Allain, "Slavery and the League of Nations: Ethiopia as a Civilised Nation," *Journal of the History of International Law*, Vol. 8, 2006, pp. 213–244. [As reproduced in Chapter 4 of this volume.]

43 Note that the material used in this section will appear in the forthcoming case note: Jean Allain, *Mani* v. *Niger*, *American Journal of International Law*, Vol. 103, 2009. [As reproduced in Chapter 8 of this volume.]

v. The Republic of Niger (hereafter *Mani v Niger*) that State had failed to protect Hadijatou Mani from the prohibition of twenty-first century *de jure* slavery. At age twelve Mani was sold into slavery, and gave birth to four children during her nine years of enslavement. In August 2005, Mani received a liberation certificate countersigned by the village chief and sought to have her supposed marriage recognised as void by the local courts, this was successful at first instance but failed originally on appeal. When the case was still being considered within the Niger legal system, it was seized by the ECOWAS Court for consideration. The Community Court found that there was "no doubt that the applicant, Habijatou Mani Koraou, was held in slavery for nearly nine years in violation of the legal prohibition of this practice."[44]

The ECOWAS Community Court of Justice is first and foremost a court meant to deal with issues of economic integration. In *Mani v Niger* it proved itself ill-equipped to deal with issues of human rights and provides a judgment which is flawed in a number of respects, most obviously where it misquoted previous court judgements so as to reach the desired outcome in this case.

A fundamental critique which can be levelled at the ECOWAS Court is first the transposing of jurisprudence of 'enslavement' in customary international criminal law onto the international human rights law concept of 'slavery'.[45] Where 'enslavement' is concerned, the International Criminal Tribunal for the former Yugoslavia itself has stated that "definition may be broader than the traditional and sometimes apparently distinct definitions of either slavery, the slave trade and servitude or forced or compulsory labour found in other areas of international law," but that the trials at Nuremburg, had expanded the notion of 'enslavement' to "included forced or compulsory labour under enslavement as a crime against humanity."[46] As this was a clear case of *de jure* slavery, the ECOWAS Court need not have gone beyond the definition of slavery established by the 1926 Slavery Convention, in conjunction with Article 5 of the African Charter on Human and Peoples' Rights to render judgment.[47] By

44 *Dame Hadijatou Mani Koraou contre La Republic de Niger*, La Cour de Justice de la Communauté Economique des Etats de l'Afrique de l'Ouest, Arret No. ECW/CCJ/JUD/06/08, 27 Octobre 2008, at para. 80. Item in parenthesis (re: '09') omitted.

45 Jean Allain, "The Parameters of 'Enslavement' in International Criminal Law," International Symposium on the New Developments of International Criminal Law, China University of Political Science and Law, Beijing, China, 25 April 2009.

46 *Kunarac et als.*, International Criminal Tribunal for the former Yugoslavia (IT-96-23 &-IT-96-23/1-A) Judgment, 12 June 2002, pp. 191 and 193.

47 Article 5 of the African Charter on Human and Peoples' Rights reads: "Every individual shall have the right to the respect of the dignity inherent in a human being and to the recognition of his legal status. All forms of exploitation and degradation of man particularly

relying on the case-law of international criminal law, the Court cross-pollinated different 'species' of international law, thus grafting a genealogy forged in wartime onto international human rights law which, for its part, has been consistent in keeping a normative separation between slavery, servitude and forced labour intact.[48]

As serious a flaw as this may be in the reasoning of the ECOWAS Community Court of Justice, there appears to be no precedent for what is to follow: a case of a court wilfully misquoting jurisprudents so as to reach a desired outcome. Here I choose my words carefully, as such a charge must be substantiated. I say wilful, as the ECOWAS Community Court of Justice misquotes on two occasion. First it misquotes the European Court of Human Right's *Vagrancy* case as saying: "in conformity with the evolution of international practice, there is nothing to prevent States from waiving the benefit of the rule of exhaustion of domestic remedies."[49] Yet, that Court in fact stated:

> there is nothing to prevent States from waiving the benefit of the rule of exhaustion of domestic remedies, the essential aim of which is to protect their national legal order. There exists on this subject a long established international practice from which the Convention has definitely not departed as it refers, in Article 26 (art. 26), to 'the generally recognised rules of international law'.[50]

---

slavery, slave trade, torture, cruel, inhuman or degrading punishment and treatment shall be prohibited."

48 See for instance, Article 8, International Covenant on Civil and Political Rights, 1966 and the already considered Article 4 of the European Convention for Protection of Human Rights and Fundamental Freedoms.

49 *De Wilde, Ooms and Versyp* ('Vagrancy') v. Belgium, European Court of Human Rights, Application nos. 2832/66; 2835/66; 2899/66 (18 June 1971) at para. 39. In the ECOWAS decision, rendered in French, what is found in quotation marks reads: "conformément à l'évolution de la pratique international, les Etats peuvent bien renouncer au benefit de la régle de l'épuisement des voies de recours internes." What the European Court actually said is:

> rien n'empêche les Etats de renoncer au bénéfice de la règle de l'épuisement des voies de recours internes, qui a pour but essentiel de protéger leur ordre juridique national. Il existe à ce sujet une longue pratique internationale à laquelle la Convention n'a sûrement pas entendu déroger car elle se réfère, en son article 26 (art. 26), aux principes de droit international généralement reconnus.

Article 26, European Convention on Human Rights, 4 November 1950, reads: "The Commission may only deal with the matter after all domestic remedies have been exhausted, according to the generally recognized rules of international law, and within a period of six months from the date on which the final decision was taken."

50 *Id.*, at para. 55.

The ECOWAS Community Court of Justice seeks to imply that there is a tradition of waving the rule of exhaustion of local remedies before being able to access an international court, when in fact European Court, in speaking of "long established international practice," was not speaking of a practice of waiving the rule of the exhaustion of domestic remedies, but in respecting the applicability of that rule.

The second instance of the ECOWAS Community Court of Justice misquoting, is when it considered the notion of Niger having a positive obligation to ensure that when an individual like Mani appeared before a judge, that their status as slave be denounced and that those involved be sanctioned by criminal law. Here the Community Court of Justice misquoted the famous *dicta* of the 1970 *Barcelona Traction* case, saying that "the outlawing of slavery is an obligation *erga omnes* imposed on all State's organs."[51] The International Court of Justice, for its part says nothing of the sort. In discussing obligations *erga omnes*, the International Court stated that such "obligations derive, for example, in contemporary international law, from the outlawing of acts of aggression, and of genocide, as also from the principles and rules concerning the basic rights of the human person, including protection from slavery and racial discrimination."[52] The ECOWAS Court added the notion of obligation being 'imposed on all State's organs' as a means of finding a breach of slavery flowing from positive obligations attributable to the rather incredible pronouncement of the judge of the Court of First Instance of Konni "the marriage of a free man with a slave woman is lawful, as long as he cannot afford to marry a free woman and if he fears to fall into fornication...."[53] The reality is that the ECOWAS Community Court of Justice need not have strained to put words in the month of the International Court of Justice, as there is much precedent in international human right law with regard to positive obligations.[54]

By their pronouncement in *Mani* v. Niger, the judges of the Community Court of Justice bring the very legitimacy of their Court into question. They were clearly out of their depth in going beyond the ECOWAS *acquis*, to consider issues of international human rights law. Yet, the manner in which the judges misquoted from both the International Court of Justice and European Court of

51 *Mani* v. *Niger*, *supra* at para. 81. The original quotation, in French, reads: "la mise hors la loi de l'esclavage est une obligation *erga omnes* qui s'impose à tous les organs de l'Etat."

52 *Case concerning the Barcelona Traction, Light and Power Company, Limited*, International Court of Justice, 5 February 1970, p. 32.

53 *Mani* v. *Niger*, *supra* at para. 83.

54 See for instance Sandra Fredman, *Human Rights Transformed: Positive Rights and Positive Duties*, 2008.

Human Rights speaks to a more fundamental flaw in the make-up of the ECOWAS Court.

Conclusion

Having considered these four cases, I wish to consider if the jurisprudence survives an Immanent Critique. When I started considering the issue, I thought this might be a vein of research which would produce nuggets of gold. Having considered the issue, while the vein is rich, it is not truly worth pursuing any longer. Here is a case of having sought to push the study of human exploitation further, but have gained mixed results. Where the European Court of Human Rights is concerned in the *Siliadin v France*, one can criticise the Court, but its fundamental legitimacy is not brought into question, it has not sought to reach its conclusion at the expense of the fundamental precepts of international law or human rights law; it has simply sought to plot a course consonant with a Europe which is not truly interested in dealing with human exploitation and has reserved itself the possibility to use 'slavery' in situations where *de jure* slavery might once more appear within a Council of Europe State. It does so, however, in ignorance of the legislative history of the Slavery Conventions, something it was not privy to in 2005. Likewise, the High Court of Australia in the 2008 *The Queen v Tang* is, it appears to me to be on quite solid ground; where it diverges to some extent is to give emphasis to those States which, in 1926, had already abolished slavery as a justification for determining that dealing with *de facto* slavery was at the heart of the negotiation process. I have sought to show that this is not truly accurate. While that element of the judgment is not critical to the Court's findings of *de facto* slavery, it is a rather novel interpretation of the historical record.

Where an Immanent Critique is successful, it seems to me is in the two other cases of the 1998 ILO Commission of Inquiry into forced labour in Myanmar and its pronouncement that forced labour constitutes a peremptory norm of international law; and the handling of international human rights law in 2008, by the ECOWAS Community Court of Justice in the *Mani v Niger*. In both cases, the determinations marshal the law to reach objectives at the expense of the law itself. For the ILO to speak of the International Law Commission 'defining' enslavement does not withstand scrutiny of the record; ultimately, because the Draft Code of Crimes against the Peace and Security of Mankind have fallen into abeyance. And, yet the fact that the ILO shifts from consider Myanmar's Responsibility to individual criminal responsibility and from slavery to 'enslavement' defies the legal logic but meets its objective of finding forced labour as being a *jus cogens* norms, when in fact it is only slavery that should be considered as such. In *Mani v Niger*, the charge is even more severe, and the Court of Justice's legitimacy, it seems to me, cannot withstand a critique which turns on the Court's very use of material to back its claim that *de jure* slavery was manifest. The pity here is that the Court need not have used the case-law of the European Court of Human Rights or the International Court of Justice; yet in doing so it showed itself to be unequal to the task.

CHAPTER 11

Review of *The Slave Trade and the Origins of International Human Rights Law* by Jenny S. Martinez*

New York: Oxford University Press, 2012

Should the genealogy of international human rights law predate both the Nuremberg trials and the UN Charter by some 150 years and trace its origins to the nineteenth-century suppression of the slave trade at sea? Jenny S. Martinez, the Warren Christopher Professor in the Practice of International Law and Diplomacy at Stanford Law School, believes so.

In *The Slave Trade and the Origins of International Human Rights Law*, Martinez links the abolition of the slave trade in the nineteenth century to contemporary international human rights. By pushing back the genesis of international human rights law to this earlier period, she shows how the United Kingdom, a dominant state, was able to use selective gunboat diplomacy to create a sea change: what had been considered legitimate commerce at the end of the Napoleonic Wars in 1815 was, by the Brussels Conference of 1890,[1] an odious trafficking of human chattel. Consequently, "close examination of the history of the abolition of the slave trade should cause international legal scholars to rethink the relationship between power, ideas, and international legal institutions" (p. 165).

While Martinez puts forward lessons to be learned and thus provides much food for thought, the main contribution of *The Slave Trade* is its historical research into the courts of mixed commission established to determine the fate of ships seized that were suspected of involvement in the slave trade. In the evocative opening chapter, Martinez uses the tale of the 1822 capture of

* This review originally appeared as Jean Allain "Jenny Martinez, *The Slave Trade and the Origins of International Human Rights Law*," *American Journal of International Law*, Vol. 107, 2012, p. 109. It is reproduced with permission from the October 2012 issue of the *American Journal of International Law* © 2012 American Society of International Law. All rights reserved.

1 The Brussels Conference of 1890 produced the Convention Relative to the Slave Trade and Importation into Africa of Firearms, Ammunition and Spirituous Liquors General Act for the Repression of African Slave Trade, July 2, 1890, 27 Stat. 886 [hereinafter Brussels Convention]. The United States was one of the treaty signatories.

 | DOI 10.1163/9789004279896_013

Portuguese slavers by Captain Henry Leeke of the British Navy and their subsequent two-month journey to be adjudicated in Sierra Leone as a means of setting out the regime of bilateral treaties that allowed naval ships to suppress the slave trade through the "right to visit" ships suspected of involvement in the slave trade and the courts of mixed commission to decide the fate of seized ships and crews. Martinez even shares the story of one of the more than 80,000 slaves who were freed as a result of these bilateral courts. Adjai, a slave boy who was released from the Portuguese slave ship, would be reunited with Leeke some forty-two years later at Canterbury Cathedral when Adjai[2] was ordained as the first African bishop of the Anglican Church.

In the two chapters that follow, *The Slave Trade* charts a course along various legal markers to reach the courts of mixed commission. Chapter 2 describes late eighteenth-century Britain as setting the tone for the abolition of slavery due in great part to its supremacy of the seas, which was confirmed at the Battle of Trafalgar in 1805. As a result of its military might, Britain was able to move its antislavery stance onto the international agenda. During the Napoleonic Wars from 1803 to 1815, with no country able to challenge it at sea, the British Navy not only stepped up its right to visit any ship at sea to search for contraband but also invoked a natural-right-based "right to visit" to suppress the slave trade. Such visits and the resulting seizure of American sailors led, in part, to the War of 1812. In the subsequent peace treaty, the 1814 Treaty of Ghent,[3] both countries pledged that they would abolish the slave trade as "the traffic in slaves is irreconcilable with the principles of humanity and justice"[4] (p. 30). Unfortunately, as Martinez notes, "[T]he treaty did not include particular mechanisms for enforcing this promise" (*ibid.*).

In Chapter 3, she characterizes the United States during the early part of the nineteenth century as "an ambivalent foe" to the slave trade (p. 38). Although the United States criminalized the slave trade, due to its own antebellum tensions it remained aloof to the growing regime of bilateral treaties concluded by the United Kingdom to allow for a right to visit ships to suppress the slave trade at sea. Yet, in 1820, the US Congress defined piracy as either involving robbery at sea or participation in the slave trade at sea; US citizens were to face the death

2 At the time of his baptism in 1825, Adjai took the name Samuel (Adjai) Crowther.

3 Treaty of Peace and Amity, US–UK, Dec. 24, 1814, 8 Stat. 218 [hereinafter Treaty of Ghent].

4 Article 10 of the Treaty of Ghent provides in full: "Whereas the Traffic in Slaves is irreconcilable with the principles of humanity and Justice, and whereas both His Majesty and the United States are desirous of continuing their efforts to promote its entire abolition, it is hereby agreed that both the contracting parties shall use their best endeavours to accomplish so desirable an object."

penalty if found guilty. Despite the United Kingdom's continued pressure on the United States to ratify a bilateral treaty allowing for the mutual right to visit ships to suppress the slave trade, the US response was the 1823 Monroe Doctrine, which in part asserted disentanglement from European affairs. Secretary of State John Quincy Adams was at pains to acknowledge that while both the United Kingdom and the United States had assimilated the slave trade to piracy, their actions did not create universal jurisdiction over the slave trade: "[T]he distinction between piracy by the law of nations and piracy by statute... [was that] while the former subjects the transgressor guilty of it to the jurisdiction of any and every country into which he may be brought, ...the latter forms a part of the municipal code of the country where it is enacted and can be tried only by its own courts" (p. 61).[5] While the United States pledged to hold its citizens to account for the slave trade at sea (and one individual was hanged for the offense in 1862), the United Kingdom, in contrast, signed bilateral treaties with the Netherlands, Portugal, and Spain to establish courts of mixed commission.

The epicenter of these courts was Freetown, Sierra Leone – the British West African colony – as the bilateral treaties required that each party establish a court under its own jurisdiction. The British, for their part, rolled their courts into one location, while others were established in Suriname, Rio de Janeiro, and Havana. These courts were followed in 1826 by an Anglo-Brazilian court (based in Freetown and a post-independent Rio de Janeiro) and in 1842 with an Anglo-Portuguese court (based in Freetown, Luanda, Boa Vista, Spanish Town, and Cape Town). Martinez's strength as a legal historian comes to the fore here. She lays out the numbers of cases (500), ships seized (225), and persons freed (more than 80,000). Of this last figure, Martinez rightly explains that "[i]n sheer human impact, no other international court has directly affected so many individuals" (p. 85).

Likewise, she demonstrates the influence of these courts at the height of naval operations when "an average of one out of every five or six vessels known to have been engaged in the transatlantic trade was brought for trial in the courts of mixed commission, with the highest annual percentage occurring in 1835 when some 39 percent of known slave ship voyages that departed that year ended up in the mixed courts" (p. 80). Beyond the direct impact of tens of thousands freed by the court proceedings, Martinez speaks to the further impact of sea patrols and mixed commissions as "some underwriters began including clauses in their insurance policies exempting from insurance ships seized under the [bilateral] treaties" (p. 83).

---

5 Quoting 7 John Quincy Adams, *The Writings of John Quincy Adams* 501–02 (Worthington Chancey Ford ed., 1917) (statement of Adams to Viscount Stratford Canning).

Between 1837 and 1862, the United States agreed in principle to the suppression of the slave trade, though it held, above all, to the Grotian concept that the seas were open to all, with jurisdiction remaining the exclusive domain of the flag state. In exercising its own jurisdiction, the US Navy seized 105 American-flagged ships during this period. The United States eventually joined in the international antislavery efforts, agreeing in 1862 to establish courts of mixed commission in Sierra Leone, New York, and Cape Town, though these courts never heard a case.

Does the history of the courts of mixed commission justify the claim that they were the antecedent of international human rights law? The question might be better framed as, "Why have those writing about the evolution of international human rights law not harked back to the courts of mixed commission and the suppression of the slave trade at sea?" The answer, it seems to me, may be found in what transpired between the end of the slave trade at sea and Nuremberg.

In *The Slave Trade*, Martinez seeks to explain the origins of universal jurisdiction and, in Chapter 6, entitled "*Hostis Humani Generis*: Enemies of Mankind," she writes: "The link between slave trading and piracy, and between slave trading and universal jurisdiction, has not been entirely forgotten in international law, but unfortunately it has often been misunderstood. This chapter seeks to clarify that link" (p. 115). Pointing to the US Alien Tort Statute, originally enacted in 1789, and noting the more recent *Filártiga v. Peña-Irala* case, decided in 1980, which stated that "for the purpose of civil liability, the torturer has become – like the pirate and slave trader before him – *hostis humani generis*, an enemy of all mankind"[6] (p. 116), Martinez points out that "the treatment of pirates and slave traders under international law [is often] cited as the main precedents for the contemporary doctrine of universal jurisdiction" (*ibid.*).

Working through the evidence, however, Martinez notes that, despite "a number of countries... [having] declared the slave trade piracy by treaty, it was apparently not enough to persuade some commentators in the mid-nineteenth century that slave trading was piracy by the law of nations" (p. 130). Moreover, towards the latter half of the century, "[o]thers, particularly American writers, continued to maintain that the slave trade was not piracy under the law of nations" (p. 133). Ultimately, she concludes:

> Attempts to subject the slave trade to universal jurisdiction by declaring it piracy foreshadowed this development [that sovereignty is semipermeable where violations of international human right law are concerned],

6 *Filártiga v. Peña-Irala*, 630 F.2d 876, 890 (2d Cir. 1980).

> but [these attempts] were not entirely successful. The seed of the idea was planted in the nineteenth-century actions against the slave trade, but it was not until Nuremberg that the barrier [of sovereignty] would be shattered (pp. 138–139).

Through the equating of the slave trade to piracy as *hostis humani generis* and the discussion of universal jurisdiction, Martinez seeks to show that the seeds of international human rights law are to be found in a realization that such antislavery efforts demonstrated that states "could legitimately be concerned with the welfare of individual persons in other states and could covenant with one another to protect the rights of those individuals" (p. 139). Here is one of the thought provoking elements of *The Slave Trade*: if we date international human rights law to the time of the suppression of the slave trade, then its emergence is drawn from the same normative pool as the US Declaration of Independence, and the natural rights that "inspired and informed the American Revolution" (p. 160) also influenced international law:

> The same philosophers who posited the existence of a natural law that encompassed unalienable rights also saw the law of nations as part of that fabric of natural law transcending nation-states. During the nineteenth century, the United States and other nations agreed that they could voluntarily consent to make the behavior of their citizens on their ships the concern of other nations (*ibid.*)

From Martinez's vantage point, the seeds of international human rights law were planted during the era of the abolition of the slave trade and bore fruit from Nuremberg onwards.

Yet, another historical narrative serves as a counterargument against this proposition. That narrative starts from a fundamental basis: the slave trade was never recognized as being equated to piracy in international law, as being *hostis humani generis*, or as having attached to it universal jurisdiction. These three elements are, of course, interrelated: by declaring slave traders to be enemies of mankind – like pirates – meant that anybody could act to suppress them, resulting in universal jurisdiction. The problem with this narrative is that it fails to provide an accurate picture of the final abolition of the slave trade. Martinez provides an account of the end of the slave trade that appears to be almost an afterthought in Chapter 7, as it is merely eight pages in length and is silent on both the outcome of the Brussels Conference of 1890[7] and the

7 Brussels Convention, *supra* note 1.

role that France played in the latter half of the nineteenth century with regard to the slave trade at sea.

The outcome of the Brussels Conference was the Brussels Convention, the first international legal instrument to circumscribe the slave trade. Far from equating the slave trade at sea to piracy, being *hostis humani generis*, or establishing universal jurisdiction, the Convention allowed for the right to visit – and to search ships and to detain slavers – but only in a specific maritime zone off Eastern Africa and into the Red Sea and the Persian Gulf, while being only applicable to "native vessels" of limited tonnage, that is the vessels of the local inhabitants.[8] Even these restrictions on maritime commerce were too much for France; it attached a reservation to certain provisions, opting out of the regime of suppression of the slave trade at sea. The fact that France never accepted that naval ships of one state could stop and visit ships of another state to suppress the slave trade, coupled with other states, including the United States, denying that any such right could exist short of a formal treaty, meant that an international custom that might have granted universal jurisdiction for such suppression never emerged.

The death knell marking the end of the international slave trade at sea was sounded in 1905 by the *Muscat Dhows* case before the Permanent Court of Arbitration. In that case, the court determined that, due to the very limited obligations that France had undertaken at the Brussels Conference, vessels from modern-day Oman could only benefit from the protection and use of the French flag in the Indian Ocean.[9] As a result, the award of the Permanent Court meant that the last flag under which the slave trade could persist within the maritime zones established by the 1890 Brussels Conference would end at the death of the vessels' designated captains or destruction of the vessels themselves.

This historical narrative also reaches well into the twentieth century, as the United Kingdom tenaciously held on to its desire to assimilate the slave trade to piracy. However, such interests were considered and rejected both in 1926 during the negotiation of the Slavery Convention and in 1956 during the negotiations of the Supplementary Convention on the Abolition of Slavery, the Slave Trade, and Institutions and Practices Similar to Slavery.[10] The International

8 *Ibid.*, Arts. XXI, XXIII, XXXI.

9 Muscat Dhows Case (Fr. v. Gr. Brit.), Hague Ct. Rep. (Scott) 93 (Perm. Ct. Arb. 1905); *see also* Jean Allain, "Nineteenth Century Law of the Sea and the British Abolition of the Slave Trade," *British Year Book of International Law*, 2008, p. 342. [As reproduced in Chapter 2 of this volume.]

10 Convention to Suppress the Slave Trade and Slavery, Sept. 25, 1926, 212 UNTS 17; Supplementary Convention on the Abolition of Slavery, the Slave Trade, and Institutions and Practices Similar to Slavery, Apr. 30, 1956, 266 UNTS 3.

Law Commission, for its part, set out the existing law in the lead-up to the 1958 Convention on the High Seas:

> States were not prepared to go nearly so far in the case of the slave trade as in the case of piracy. In the one case [relating to the slave trade] they had limited the right of approach to specified zones, but not in the other [relating to piracy]. [The Special Rapporteur] did not think that the two questions could be lumped together, unless the law governing the slave trade were substantially widened, in which case the Commission would no longer be codifying existing law.[11]

Contemporary international law reflects these differences between piracy and the slave trade. While Article 105 of the 1982 Law of the Sea Convention allows any state vessel to seize a pirate ship, Article 110 dealing with the slave trade, by contrast, reinforces the rights of flag states. Under Article 110, the boarding of a ship suspected of being engaged in the slave trade is open to all states, but such a visit may only proceed so as to ascertain the fraudulent use of a flag, not actually to suppress the slave trade, which is a right falling exclusively within the jurisdiction of the flag state.[12]

When the historical narrative that has just been laid out is coupled with the following doubts to which Martinez points as to why scholars have been unwilling to regard the slave trade as the genesis of international human rights law, her line of argument regarding the starting point of international human rights law being pushed back 150 years has diminishing returns:

> Perhaps the shameful complicity of so many nation-states in the institution of slavery makes this story less appealing than the Nuremberg narrative, which conveniently attributes responsibility for the Holocaust to a handful of individuals from a losing nation (Germany). The British abolitionist discourse contains embarrassing overtones of the "white man's burden" and the controversial history of colonialism extended for a hundred years after the abolition of slavery. For scholars in the United States, perhaps America's problematic (but eerily familiar) role as the reluctant outsider in the antislavery regime is less appealing than its starring turn

11 Regime of the High Seas, para. 76, in *Yearbook of the International Law Commission*, Vol. 1, 1951, p. 346, 350, UN Doc. A/CN.4/SR.123, available at http://untreaty.un.org/ilc/documentation/english/a_cn4_sr123.pdf.

12 United Nations Convention on the Law of the Sea, 1982, Arts. 105, 110, 1833 UNTS 396; *see also* Jean Allain, *Slavery In International Law: Of Human Exploitation and Trafficking*, 2012, 98–104.

> at Nuremberg with Justice Jackson's eloquent speeches as chief prosecutor (pp. 154–155).

Ultimately, Martinez has brought to light and engaged with a very interesting, if not well-known, area of international law, and, for this achievement, she should be commended. Likewise, she is to be applauded for raising thought-provoking issues in seeking to call attention to the place of courts of mixed commission and the abolition of the slave trade at sea in the evolution of human rights law. Her historical account is compelling. Only time will tell if it will become part of the discourse that would have international human rights law trace its history back to a time when countries cooperated to free more than 80,000 human beings.

CHAPTER 12

Review of *Colonialism, Slavery, Reparations and Trade: Remedying the Past?* Edited by Fernne Brennan and John Packer*

Adingdon: Routledge, 2012

Colonialism, Slavery, Reparations and Trade can be seen as a microcosm of the standard of research and discourse surrounding the issue of reparations touching on the transatlantic slave trade. This collection is a window on to a world of pseudo-academic writing, where established facts are of little concern and a particular reading of history is mobilised to justify a particular argument. If not for a couple of contributors coming to the rescue and providing an opportunity to discuss the malaise at the heart of reparations debates, there would be little left worth reviewing.

The driving force behind this collection is Fernne Brennan, a Senior Lecturer in the School of Law at the University of Essex who, by her own admission, has "one great passion – slave trade reparations – by which I mean reparations for the legacy of the slave trade" (p. 196). Her approach to the issue of reparations appears to be quantitative rather than qualitative, as she writes:

> To tackle the underlying cause of racial discrimination we must locate it in institutional racism, a racism whose bed was first made by the slave trade and slavery. As more and more people write about these problems the more it can be prophesised that the pen, being mightier than the sword, will make a dent in the all too familiar refusal to believe, accept responsibility, apologise and make restitution for a tragedy that we have *all* lived through and continue so to do (p. 206; emphasis in the original.).

Colonialism, Slavery, Reparations and Trade takes this approach and despite providing 252 pages of material on the matter, very little emerges of quality, in the sense of adding new insights or making arguments based on historical facts or sound legal analysis.

---

* Originally published as Jean Allain, "Colonialism, Slavery, Reparations and Trade: Remedying the Past? 2012," in Brennan Fernne and John Packer (eds.), *Irish Yearbook of International Law*, (2012) 7, 305. Copyright © Hart Publishing, 2014.

 | DOI 10.1163/9789004279896_014

At the level of editing, the collection is missing both a coherent introduction which sets out the overall aim of the book and a theme which ties the various contributions to something original to be said about entrenched debates surrounding reparations resulting from the transatlantic slave-trade (for considerations regarding these debates see Alfred Brophy, *Reparations Pro & Con*, OUP, 2006 and the more recently the 2012 Special Issue of *Social & Legal Studies*: "Repairing Historical Wrongs" edited Gerry Johnstone and Joel Quirk). From this perspective, it is not clear why 'colonialism' and 'trade' are given special status in the title, as these are touched upon in a limited manner in the contributions, and are discussed no more than numerous other topics.

The four-page introduction consists of, in the main, a description of the content of the various contributions. Where the rationale for the collection is set out is in the top and tail of the Introduction where we learn that chapters emerge from a November 2008 Conference. Brennan and Packer write: "How to obtain reparations for the legacy of the transatlantic slave trade is the main theme of this book." While there is an acknowledgment that there is no consensus on issues of reparations today, there is a sense that there "is still room to manoeuvre" (p. xv). With this in mind, the Editors of *Colonialism, Slavery, Reparations and Trade*, while acknowledging that there is a "strong debate" over reparation claims for the transatlantic slave trade, seek to "mould matters" by "dealing with some of the issues and try to provide solutions," with the acknowledgment that "this is only the beginning of a long road" (p. xviii). Yet, beyond this, there is no coherent narrative which sets out to contextualise this collection within the rather larger pool of writings related to reparations, nor is there a sense of what 'issues' will be dealt with and what 'solutions' will be forthcoming.

For Brennan, much depends on the lead Chapter, written by a PhD candidate. This, in and of itself, need not be a bad thing, but Norma Wittmann's chapter demonstrates a lack of expertise in both international law and the history of the transatlantic slave trade. While Wittmann is willing to utilise international law when it serves her purpose (that during the era of the transatlantic slave-trade, African States had international legal personality), she is quick to dismiss it with regard to the slave trade. Wittman argues that it is an "allegation (presented as a fact) that transatlantic slavery [sic]would have been 'legal' in its time" (p. 3). She goes on to say that "the historically-documented legal facts indicate that transatlantic slavery [sic] was illicit" (p. 4). It might also be noted here that another contributor, Marcus Goffee, an LLM Candidate, who made his presentation on behalf of the Jamaican Rastafari Community, sings from the same hymn book, as he "argues that chattel slavery of this sort and on the scale conducted by the major European nations states over four centuries was not legal at the time, despite it not being expressly illegal according to the West European Westphalian conceptualisation of international law" (p. 226).

Little space need be given to refute a claim that few would endorse beyond the ignorant and the polemic. From time immemorial, slavery was recognised as being contrary to natural law, but a part of *jus gentium*, manifest in the enslavement of prisoners of war rather than putting them to death (See Allain, *Slavery in International Law*, 2013, pp. 12–13). While it is true that the transatlantic slave-trade was different in *form*, as it industrialised what had transpired before it; but it has remained the same in *substance* from before recorded time up to the present. From the historical perspective, Wittmann denies that slavery was part of the fabric of African life before Europeans commenced the transatlantic slave-trade (p. 9: "The concept and reality of African 'slavery' instead coincided with the meaning of the term 'servile labour' or 'serfdom'"). She also speaks of African collaborators, painting the depopulation of more than 12.5 million Africans as being the result of – and here she quotes the well-respected professor of world history Patrick Manning – "a few greedy or opportunistic persons" (pp. 14–15). Yet, in reading Manning in context, he makes plain in his *Slavery and African Life*, that as a result of the fragmentation of the Continent, African traders in slaves were always available and empires came and went, built on the riches gained from supplying prisoners of war from the interior to become slaves on the coast. In other words, the industrial scale of the transatlantic slave-trade, required an industrial level commitment by African leaders to make war and supply captives.

Brennan and Packer repeat Wittmann's assertions discussing her chapter in the Introduction, but also challenge a dedicated piece of research by Dinah Shelton, one of the foremost legal experts on remedies and recent President of the Inter-American Human Rights Commission. In considering the jurisprudence to emerge from the United States regarding claims for past mass human rights violations, Shelton notes a number of limitations to success including statutes of limitations and non-retroactivity of law. To this Brennan and Packer add: "we will have already seen in Wittmann's chapter that the latter can be swept away and as for the former it has previously been argued that reparations for the slave trade should not be subject to the Statute of Limitations" (p. xvii – The previous argument cited, which is apparently enough to place in doubt a fundamental pillar of criminal justice is a 2000 word blog-post by a former provincial court judge from Kamloops, British Columbia.). In this manner the two fundamental legal obstacles which stand in way of reparations for the transatlantic slave-trade are set to the side; and with it very little serious discussion is to be found in *Colonialism, Slavery, Reparations and Trade*, but for the pieces by Shelton, Kate Bracegridle and Sheila Dziobon.

Instead, this edited collection provides vanity pieces: Lord Anthony Gifford noting that he knows very little about reparations ("I was not an expert in international law" p. 79), having been approached to write a brief by the Jamaican High Commissioner to Nigeria ("who defended Jomo Kenyatta in the 1950s," p. 77); his knowledge of the issue of reparations having come from the British Member of Parliament for Tottenham ("the most radical and outspoken of the four Black MPs elected in 1987," p. 78); while the "catalyst for awaking the concept of reparations in Africa itself was supplied by another larger-than-life individual, Chief Moshood Abiola of Nigeria" (p. 78), the politician whose apparent victory in the presidential race was annulled in a coup by General Sani Abacha. So moved by the issue of reparations was Gifford that he decided, despite being "an absentee member of the House of Lords" since moving to Jamaica, to raise the question in the House of Lords where he noted that a fellow Lord said that "I spoke in the tradition of Thomas Clarkson and William Wilberforce" (p. 90).

Likewise, the inclusion of His Excellency Ambassador Kwesi Quartey, Ghana's Ambassador to Ethiopia and Permanent Representative to the African Union, has clearly had little more to do with his position, rather than the level of his scholarship, as his contribution is ill-informed and anecdotal in the main. Quartey sets the tone for the level of scholarship and his approach by starting his contribution in the following manner:

> Many of us have tended to believe that the transatlantic slave trade which took place between 1450 and 1807 when it was abolished by the British parliament was perhaps a series of sporadic events carried out by a few bad people. (p. 125)

First, the transatlantic slave-trade did not end with its abolition by the British Parliament, as Westminster could not dictate international law to other sovereign powers involved in the slave-trade (See Allain, 78 (2008) "Nineteenth Century Law of the Sea and the British Abolition of the Slave Trade," *British Yearbook of International Law* 342; and Allain, *Slavery in International Law*, 2013, pp. 57–104). By setting the end of the slave-trade in 1807, Quartey fails to acknowledge the nearly three million Africans enslaved between 1807 and 1866. (See http://www.slavevoyages.org; which notes that 2,893,466 slaves were embarked during this period of time.) Further, no serious commentator would say that the slave-trade was "a series of sporadic events carried out by a few bad people" in light of the historical study of the transatlantic slave-trade over the last forty-years which, in many ways has been the primary area of study of history departments in the United States of America and beyond.

Of the other contributors, the recommendations put forward for addressing the issues of reparations make no sense "One possible beginning here would be a rethink by the IMF, the World Bank (e.g., to cancel all debts), and those 'aid' givers who pay high salaries to endless numbers of 'advisors' who then recommend the purchase of what are not the best materials or expertise, but what is available from their own countries" (Sherwood p. 34); or set out a path based on the Declaration on the Right to Development, which by Rohan Kariyawasam's own admission, is not "a legally binding instrument, has suffered from a lack of implementation and the political will required for international cooperation" (p. 59).

Redemption within *Colonialism, Slavery, Reparations and Trade* as previously noted, is found in three contributions. Kate Bracegridle considers the English law of restitution as an approach to transatlantic slave-trade reparations with specific reference to unjust enrichment. For Bracegridle, the English context is such that the statute of limitation is "not the most significant problem [...] which would form the basis of a claim of restitution for historical slavery." Instead, the bigger hurdle would be attempts at a general classification of descendants of slaves and the "disparity in wealth between Black and White people in the West [...] into a very precise legal concept such as unjust enrichment and various torts" (p. 161).

For Sheila Dziobon, the contribution considers English law beyond *Somerset v Stewart* which held that English common law did not permit slavery on British soil. Her conclusions of the jurisprudence touching on slaves and the slave-trade from 1729 to 1807, is that the judiciary were part of the landed gentry and as such they reflected the interests of the elite including support for transatlantic slave-trade. Despite the abolitionist movement which ultimately led to 1807, Dziobon makes plain that judicial enlightenment only transpired after the judicial hero of *Somerset*, Lord Mansfield left the bench.

For her part, Dinah Shelton considers the record of reparations claims made in courts of law in the United States and concludes that "the synergies produced by activism, litigation and legislation have produced the greatest success in a direct relationship with how recent the events are to be presented" (p. 99). Quoting from a preliminary determination in the 1995 circuit court case of *Cato v United States*, related to two groups who sought damages for having been enslaved and subsequent discrimination, Shelton makes the point that the path to reparations is not through the law, but by political accommodation:

> While plaintiff may be justified in seeking redress for past and present injustices, it is not within the jurisdiction of this Court to grant the requested relief. The legislature, rather than the judiciary, is the appropriate forum for plaintiff's grievances. (p. 100–101)

Shelton provides conclusions which speak to the realities of the legal landscape: that "even where the claims lack a firm legal foundation, experience thus far suggests that reparations may still take place via the political process." She continues saying that "demands for reparations will probably only succeed with political pressure and strong, cohesive support from the victims themselves" (p. 113).

Colonialism, Slavery, Reparations and Trade hurts the case for reparations as it provides an incoherent reading of the objects, aims, and outcomes which could then be fostered as a unified approach to claims for repairing the historical wrong which is the transatlantic slave-trade. But for the contributions of Shelton, Bracegridle and Dziobon, the Editors (Brennan and Packer) have provided a collection which lacks academic rigour.

CHAPTER 13

No Effective Trafficking Definition Exists: Domestic Implementation of the Palermo Protocol*

When we speak across international borders we speak different languages. So, is a lesson to be learned from considering the definition of trafficking in persons as it has been incorporated in the domestic legal order of the vast majority of countries of the world? While the United Nations established a definition of trafficking in persons in 2000,[1] the mechanism meant to give voice to the suppression of such traffic is transnational rather than international in nature. As a result, it is for each State to decide, once they have consented to be bound by the 2000 UN Palermo Protocol,[2] not only the extent to which they will adopt provisions meant to prevent, suppress, and punish trafficking in persons, but more fundamentally, how each State will decide what constitutes 'trafficking in persons' within their own national jurisdiction. What emerges from examining the manner in which the Palermo Protocol has been incorporated into the legal order of various countries is that the very regime of trafficking in persons is fundamentally flawed. This is so, as the Palermo Protocol is first and foremost an instrument related to cooperation amongst national law enforcement agencies seeking to suppress the trafficking in persons by organized crime groups across international borders.[3] Yet, in

* This chapter appears originally as Jean Allain, "No Effective Trafficking Definition Exists: Domestic Implementation of the Palermo Protocol," *Albany Government Law Review*, Vol. 7, 2014, p. 111. Copyright © *Albany Government Law* Review 2014.

1 Protocol to Prevent, Suppress and Punish Trafficking in Persons, Especially Women and Children, Supplementing the United Nations Convention against Transnational Organized Crime, art. 3, 344, Nov. 15, 2000, 2237 UNTS 319, http://treaties.un.org/doc/publication/UNTS/Volume%202237/v2237.pdf [hereinafter Protocol for Trafficking in Persons].

2 *Id.* at 343. *See The Palermo Protocol*, Palermo Protocol, http://www.palermoprotocol.com/general/the-palermo-protocol (last visited Sept. 25, 2013) (explaining that the Protocol to Prevent, Suppress and Punish Trafficking in Persons, Especially Women and Children is usually referred to as the Palermo Protocol).

3 *See generally id.* (explaining that "despite the existence of a variety of international instruments…there is no universal instrument that addresses all aspects of trafficking in persons," alluding to the responsibility of each State to define the term as they see fit).

© KONINKLIJKE BRILL NV, LEIDEN, 2015 | DOI 10.1163/9789004279896_015

their attempt to end this transnational crime, States speak to each other in different languages: both literally, but also figuratively. Figuratively, as their jurisdictions are not truly compatible with each other, when they speak of 'trafficking', they are mainly speaking about different things.

This Article considers the overall regime established by the 2000 Palermo Protocol to demonstrate the manner in which the law of trafficking has come to be incorporated into the domestic legal order of States. In doing so, and with special reference to the definition of trafficking, it shows the limited ability of States to actually carry out their avowed wish to suppress trafficking in persons. Because their jurisdiction over what is termed 'trafficking' is different, the ability for the origin, transit and/or destination countries to 'join-up' is rendered unworkable by, for instance, extradition treaties that require crimes to be common to both jurisdictions or the application of extraterritorial jurisdiction when what is deemed a crime in one jurisdiction is not so in another. Thus, in a very short period of time, legislators around the world have created, under the banner of 'trafficking', an international regime which, through its implementation in the domestic sphere, has fractured its potential effectiveness.[4]

The Transnational Law of Trafficking

On the 15th of November, 2000, the United Nations General Assembly adopted the United Nations Convention against Transnational Organized Crime, which was meant "[t]o promote cooperation among States Parties" in order to "to prevent and combat trafficking in persons" more effectively.[5] Along with that Convention are three protocols – additional instruments meant to supplement the original – which cover trafficking in persons, smuggling, and illicit firearms, which were also opened for signature.[6] The trafficking in

4 *See* Anthony M. DeStefano, The War on Human Trafficking: U.S. Policy Assessed 26–27 (2007) (discussing the conflict between States who desired to abolish prostitution as a part of this directive and the States that would not sign if such language was added, leading to a compromise that excluded defining "*exploitation of prostitution of others* and *other forms of sexual exploitation*").

5 Protocol for Trafficking in Persons, *supra* note 1, at 343–344.

6 *See id.*; Protocol against the Smuggling of Migrants by Land, Sea and Air, Supplementing the United Nations Convention against Transnational Organized Crime, Nov. 15, 2000, 2241 UNTS 450, 507–508, http://treaties.un.org/doc/publication/UNTS/Volume%202241/v2241.pdf. *See also* Protocol against the Illicit Manufacturing of and Trafficking in Firearms, Their Parts and

persons protocol is entitled the "Protocol to Prevent, Suppress and Punish Trafficking in Persons, Especially Women and Children, Supplementing the United Nations Convention Against Transnational Organized Crime."[7] So as to emphasize the quest to challenge organized crime, the UN originally opened the Conventions and its Protocols for signature in Palermo, Italy, the heartland of the Sicilian mafia.[8] Since then, the anti-trafficking protocol has come to be known as the Palermo Protocol.[9]

The starting point for understanding the obligations which flow from the Palermo Protocol is its relationship to the UN Convention against Transnational Organized Crime, as both of these instruments are to be "interpreted together."[10] States consenting to the Convention have an obligation to criminalize the involvement in an organized criminal group, laundering the proceeds of crime, corruption, and in obstruction of justice where the offense is transnational in nature.[11] By an "offence [that] is transnational in nature," what is meant is that either "[i]t is committed in more than one State," or when committed in one State, it "has substantial effects in another," or "substantial part of its preparation, planning, direction or control takes place in another State," or again, it "involves an organized criminal group that engages in criminal activities in more than one State."[12] By reading the Convention in conjunction with Palermo Protocol, it becomes clear that this Protocol is not exclusively applicable to situations where a person is trafficked across an international border, but in fact can be trafficked internally – that is to say the victim may be moved solely within one State, while the crime by contrast may be "transnational in nature" if, for instance, it "involves an organized criminal group that engages in criminal activities in more than one State."[13]

Components and Ammunition, Supplementing the United Nations Convention Against Transnational Organized Crime, May 31, 2001, 2326 UNTS 208.

7 Protocol for Trafficking in Persons, *supra* note 1.

8 DeStefano, *supra* note 4, at 27–28.

9 *See The Palermo Protocol*, *supra* note 2.

10 United Nations Convention against Transnational Organized Crime, art. 37, Nov. 15, 2000, 2225 UNTS 209, [hereinafter United Nations Convention]. *See also* Protocol for Trafficking in Persons, *supra* note 1, at 343.

11 United Nations Convention, *supra* note 10, at 275 ("organized criminal group" is defined by the Convention in the following terms: "a structured group of three or more persons, existing for a period of time and acting in concert with the aim of committing one or more serious crimes or offences established in accordance with this Convention, in order to obtain, directly or indirectly, a financial or other material benefit").

12 *Id.* at 276.

13 *Id.*

While laundering, corruption and obstruction of justice are tangential to an understanding of 'trafficking in persons', the concept of an 'organized criminal group' as set out in the Convention is fundamental. An "[o]rganized criminal group" has a specific definition applicable both to the Convention and to the Protocols:

> 'Organized criminal group' shall mean a structured group of three or more persons, existing for a period of time and acting in concert with the aim of committing one or more serious crimes or offences established in accordance with this Convention, in order to obtain, directly or indirectly, a financial or other material benefit.[14]

As this is often overlooked by commentators considering instances of trafficking in persons, it should be understood that such an "organized criminal group" is not merely the sum of those who came into contact with a person as they were trafficked. Instead it must be a "[s]tructured group" where the notion of a 'structured group' is defined in the Convention as a "group that is not randomly formed for the immediate commission of an offence."[15] In other words, an organized criminal group is more than simply those that conspire or commit a crime. Rather, such a group needs to have cohesion, acting over time, and with the aim of committing a serious crime, though it "does not need to have formally defined roles for its members, continuity of its membership or a developed structure."[16] In criminalizing the involvement in an organized criminal group, the Convention requires States to adopt legislation which ensures that there is a juridical space in which activities in and around such a group is made illegal.[17] That space includes activities touching on those who agree to commit, as well as those that take active part in the committing of a serious crime. An active part in the committing of a serious crime, for the Convention, includes the following activities: "[o]rganizing, directing, aiding, abetting, facilitating or counselling…," as well as other activities which knowingly contribute to the aim of the crime.[18]

---

14 *Id.* at 275.

15 *Id.*

16 *See id.* ("'Structured group' shall mean a group that is not randomly formed for the immediate commission of an offence and that does not need to have formally defined roles for its members, continuity of its membership or a developed structure.")

17 *Id.* at 276–277.

18 United Nations Convention, *supra* note 10, at 276–277.

The Palermo Protocol supplements the UN Convention against Transnational Organized Crime. Beyond criminalizing involvement in organized criminal groups, money laundering, corruption, and obstruction of justice, a State has the authority to criminalize trafficking in persons within their own domestic legal systems.[19] Trafficking in persons is defined, for the purposes of the Protocol, as follows:

> 'Trafficking in persons' shall mean the recruitment, transportation, transfer, harbouring or receipt of persons, by means of the threat or use of force or other forms of coercion, of abduction, of fraud, of deception, of the abuse of power or of a position of vulnerability or of the giving or receiving of payments or benefits to achieve the consent of a person having control over another person, for the purpose of exploitation. Exploitation shall include, at a minimum, the exploitation of the prostitution of others or other forms of sexual exploitation, forced labour or services, slavery or practices similar to slavery, servitude or the removal of organs.[20]

When interpreting the Protocol together with the UN Convention, the crime meant to be prescribed at the domestic level is one in which – in essence – a number of people are working together to move an individual against his or her will or knowledge so as to exploit that person.[21]

While the definition of 'trafficking in persons' has been considered in depth,[22] that definition is somewhat moot, as despite being established at the international level, its true application takes place at the domestic level, where oftentimes unique readings of trafficking have been promulgated by various States that are a party to the Palermo Protocol.

At the international level, I have just noted that the definition is 'some what moot' as there is, in fact, limited scope to give voice to its criminalization internationally. That scope is to be found in the Rome Statute of the International Criminal Court, which establishes the crime against humanity of "[e]nslavement."[23] This crime is defined as "the exercise of any or all of the

19 *Id.* at 276–279. *See also* Protocol for Trafficking in Persons, *supra* note 1, at 344 (*stating* "The offences established in accordance with article 5 of this Protocol shall be regarded as offences established in accordance with the Convention" and criminalising "[t]rafficking in persons" as defined in Article 3(a)).

20 Protocol for Trafficking in Persons, *supra* note 1, at 344.

21 *Id.* at 344.

22 *See, e.g.*, Anne T. Gallagher, The International Law of Human Trafficking 24 (2010).

23 Rome Statute of the International Criminal Court, UN Doc. A/CONF.183/9, at art. 7(1)(c) (July 17, 1998) [hereinafter Rome Statute].

powers attaching to the right of ownership over a person and includes the exercise of such power in the *course of trafficking in persons, in particular women and children*."[24] While the jurisdiction of the Court does not criminalize trafficking in persons *per se*, it does, by reference to the phrase just highlighted, utilize the language of what would come to be the official title of the Palermo Protocol, bringing the possible application of this instrument into the orbit of international judicial consideration.

The Palermo Protocol, like the UN Convention against Transnational Organized Crime, is transnational in nature. While the Convention provides its own reading of what constitutes a transnational crime, it might be helpful to think of the notion of transnational more generally. Transnational denotes the involvement of a number of nations; however, this understanding could also be applied to the concept of international. The distinction is to be found in the fact that the *international* concept is applicable to systems where international institutions are a central pillar, whereas in the *transnational* concept, the systems function in a purely anarchical fashion, devoid of a central authority.[25] Thus, a transnational instrument is one which sets out a framework for acting that is meant to create half-bridges, which will then connect when other States follow suit. Think of transnational instruments as those red connectors for *Hot Wheels* sets which link up States on specific issues.

Within the context where the crime of trafficking in persons is transnational in nature, issues with regard to which State has the power to act is fundamental. In law, determining the power to act is known as jurisdiction. While the Convention pays perfunctory acknowledgment to the need for State Parties to carry out their obligations "in a manner consistent with the principles of sovereign equality and territorial integrity,"[26] negotiators needed to devote some energy to developing the other provision of Article 4 which, on its face, simply affirms the application of sovereignty, stating "[n]othing in this Convention entitles a State Party to undertake in the territory of another State the exercise

---

24 Rome Statute, *supra* note 23, at art. 7(2)(c) (emphasis added). Note the same phrase is also mentioned in footnote 11 to Article 7(1)(c) of the Elements of Crimes, Crime against Humanity of Enslavement. Assembly of States Parties to the Rome Statute of the International Criminal Court, Sept. 3–10, 2002, UN Doc. ICC-ASP/1/3.

25 *See generally* Stephen J. Kobrin, "Globalization, Transnational Corporations and the Future of Global Governance," in Andreas Georg Scherer and Guido Palazzo (eds.), *Handbook of Research on Global Corporate Citizenship*, 2008, pp. 249–250, 252.

26 UN Office on Drugs & Crime, *Mechanism for the Review of Implementation of the United Nations Convention against Corruption – Basic Documents* 15 (March 2011), http://www.unodc.org/documents/treaties/UNCAC/Publications/ReviewMechanism-BasicDocuments/Mechanism_for_the_Review_of_Implementation_-_Basic_Documents_-_E.pdf.

of jurisdiction and performance of functions that are reserved exclusively for the authorities of that other State by its domestic law."[27] Yet, States felt compelled to add this provision, and, with regard to transnational criminal law, the issue of jurisdiction is fundamental while sovereignty is primal. In setting out its jurisdiction provisions, the UN Convention is quite clear in establishing that only States have the power to assert jurisdiction over offenses committed on their territory or on vessels flying that State's flag.[28] Beyond that, any jurisdictional basis for acting would require assistance of other States. So, while the "Convention does not exclude the exercise of any criminal jurisdiction established by a State Party in accordance with its domestic law," it requires that such jurisdiction be established "[w]ithout prejudice to norms of general international law," foremost amongst these being respect for the sovereignty of States.[29]

Elsewhere, the Convention provides the possibility for establishing greater jurisdiction with the proviso that such extensions of power to act are subject to Article 4, as the provisions mention a paragraph earlier related to sovereignty and the exercise of jurisdiction being the purview of a State and its domestic law.[30] With this as a preamble requirement, States *may* establish jurisdiction over offenses committed by nationals or stateless persons who are habitual residents of that State.[31] Further, States may establish jurisdiction touching on certain elements of money laundering, as well as with regard to issues involving organized criminal groups where a certain activity is "committed outside its territory with a view to the commission of [a serious crime] within its territory."[32]

This then is the context in which one should understand the parameters of trafficking in persons, as established by the Palermo Protocol, when read in tandem with the United Nations Convention against Transnational Organized Crime. Had the regime established to govern trafficking in persons been a truly international one, an oversight body would have been established – say a treaty monitoring body or an international court. Yet, much more would have been required, as the very essence of the agreements which set the foundation for suppressing the crime of trafficking in persons is one which is focused on the domestic rather than the international legal order. All things being equal, this

27 United Nations Convention, *supra* note 10, at 276.

28 *Id.* at 283.

29 *Id.* at 284.

30 *Id.* at 283.

31 *Id.*

32 *Id.*

should not have caused issues, as the vast majority of multilateral treaties in force today are transnational rather than international in nature.[33] Yet, what has led to the fragmentation of our understanding of trafficking is specific to its definition.

Domestic Implementation of 'Trafficking in Persons'

The definition of trafficking in persons, as set out in the Palermo Protocol, was an unstated invitation to legislators around the world to modify its provisions.[34] This is so as the definition is a flawed piece of drafting. The provisions of the Palermo Protocol were always destined to be incorporated into domestic legislation; this is the essence of both it and the Convention – that the State parties adopt legislation, which establishes trafficking as a criminal offense. Yet the definition, as set out in the Palermo Protocol is, in the main, three sets of categories: "recruitment, transportation, transfer, harbouring"; "of coercion, of abduction, of fraud, of deception"; and forced labour, slavery, servitude, removal of organs.[35] For the members of legislatures around the world, this raised more questions than it answered as the Protocol off-loaded the need to define these various terms to domestic legislators.[36] The invitation was further extended by the fact that the category of types of exploitation was left open-ended by the phrase "[e]xploitation shall include, ..."[37] As a result, it was left to each country to determine what type of exploitation it would seek to suppress

33 *See* United Nations, Treaty Handbook 33 (2012), http://treaties.un.org/doc/source/publications/THB/English.pdf.

34 Protocol for Trafficking in Persons, *supra* note 1, at 344 (It will be recalled that the definition speaks in essence of: *the movement of a person* – "the recruitment, transportation, transfer, harbouring or receipt of persons..."; *against their will* – "by means of the threat or use of force or other forms of coercion, of abduction, of fraud, of deception, of the abuse of power or of a position of vulnerability..."; *so as to exploit that person* – "for the purpose of exploitation. Exploitation shall include, at a minimum, the exploitation of the prostitution of others or other forms of sexual exploitation, forced labour or services, slavery or practices similar to slavery, servitude or the removal of organs").

35 *Id.* at 344.

36 *See generally* UN Office on Drugs and Crime, *Travaux Préparatoires of the Negotiations for the Elaboration of the United Nations Convention Against Transnational Organized Crime and the Protocols Thereto*, Notes by the Secretariat (October 4–15, 2006), 339–40, www.unodc.org/pdf/ctoccop_2006/04-60074_ebook-e.pdf (providing no guidance as to what the various terms in the definition mean).

37 Protocol for Trafficking in Persons, *supra* note 1, at 344.

in the context where the very term "exploitation" was ill understood and nowhere defined in law.

How then did legislators around the world incorporate the definition of trafficking in persons into their domestic legal orders? As a backdrop, it might be emphasized that we have entered a "neo-abolitionist" era as a result of the Palermo Protocol, which has led in a very short period of time to many States incorporating anti-trafficking provisions into their domestic legal order.[38] This, in the main, is the result of the emphasis, which the United States of America has placed on the issue of trafficking as part of its foreign policy. The United States has taken on the primary role as anti-trafficking advocate internationally through its development of an annual Trafficking in Persons Report, which is backed by coercive legislation developed by the U.S. Congress and has precipitated a proliferation of domestic anti-trafficking laws.[39] As the International Organization of Migration notes, combating "human trafficking has become an increasingly important political priority for many governments around the world."[40] This is so, in large part, because by virtue of the William Wilberforce Trafficking Victims Protection Re-authorization Act of 2008, the U.S. Congress makes it "the policy of the United States not to provide non-humanitarian, nontrade-related foreign assistance to any government that...does not comply with minimum standards for the elimination of trafficking...."[41] Thus, by

38 Jean Allain & Kevin Bales, *Slavery and Its Definition, Global Dialogue*, Vol. 14, No. 2, (2012), *available at* http://www.worlddialogue.org/content.php?id=529. *See also*, Liana Sun Wyler, Cong. Research Serv., R42497, Trafficking in Persons: International Dimensions and Foreign Policy Issues for Congress 2 (2013), http://www.fas.org/sgp/crs/row/R42497.pdf.

39 Susan W. Tiefenbrun, "The Domestic and International Impact of the U.S. Victims of Trafficking Protection Act of 2000: Does Law Deter Crime?" *Loyola University Chicago International Law Review* Vol. 2, 2004–2005, pp. 193, 199–200, 204, 207.

40 "Data and Research on Human Trafficking: A Global Survey," *International Organization for Migration*, Vol. 43 (1/2), at 6 (2005), www.iom.int/jahia/webdav/site/myjahiasite/.../data_res_human.pdf.

41 Victims of Trafficking and Violence Protection Act of 2000, Pub. L. No. 106–386, 114 Stat. 1480, at § 110 (2006), codified at 22 U.S.C. § 7107(a) (2006). *See also*, Victims of Trafficking and Violence Protection Act of 2000, Pub. L. No. 106–386, 114 Stat. 1480, at § 108(a) (2006); 22 U.S.C. § 7106(a) (2006), which spells out those minimum standards for the elimination of trafficking as follows:

(1) The government of the country should prohibit severe forms of trafficking in persons and punish acts of such trafficking.

(2) For the knowing commission of any act of sex trafficking involving force, fraud, coercion, or in which the victim of sex trafficking is a child incapable of giving meaningful consent, or of trafficking which includes rape or kidnapping or which causes a death,

threatening to withdraw financial support (both American and its support before the IMF and World Bank), measuring States against its own minimum standards, and placing States that fail to meet these standards on 'watch-lists', the United States has forced countries to take trafficking seriously.

Giving voice to issues of trafficking has meant that States incorporated various elements of the Palermo Protocol into their domestic legal order. That instrument, it should be acknowledged, is not an international human rights law treaty, but a transnational criminal law convention, as it supplements the 2000 UN Convention against Transnational Organized Crime.[42] While this is formally so, the Palermo Protocol is also in substance very much an instrument of criminal law as opposed to human rights law. In other words, the emphasis of the Protocol is with regards to perpetrators of the crime rather than the victim. While the Protocol mandates the criminalization of trafficking in persons: "[States] shall adopt such legislative and other measures"; it leaves it to States "[i]n appropriate cases and to the extent possible," to protect, not the victims, but their "privacy and identity."[43] It is left to each State then to "consider implementing measures to provide for the physical, psychological and social recovery of victims of trafficking in persons," rather than actually providing for such recovery.[44]

Perhaps the best indication that the Palermo Protocol is not a human rights instrument is the fact that in 2005, the Council of Europe felt compelled to adopt its own Convention on Action against Trafficking in Human Beings, so as to include binding human rights obligations.[45] Much as the failure in the infancy of the United Nations to provide for a legal instrument dealing with

---

the government of the country should prescribe punishment commensurate with that for grave crimes, such as forcible sexual assault.

(3) For the knowing commission of any act of a severe form of trafficking in persons, the government of the country should prescribe punishment that is sufficiently stringent to deter and that adequately reflects the heinous nature of the offense.

(4) The government of the country should make serious and sustained efforts to eliminate severe forms of trafficking in persons.

42 *United Nations Convention against Transnational Organized Crime and the Protocols Thereto*, United Nations Office on Drugs and Crime, http://www.unodc.org/unodc/treaties/CTOC/ (last visited Sept. 10, 2013).

43 Protocol for Trafficking in Persons, *supra* note 1, at 344–345.

44 *Id.* at 345.

45 *Council of Europe Convention on Action against Trafficking in Human Beings and its Explanatory Report*, C.E.T.S. No. 197, at 27, 31 (2005), *www.conventions.coe.int/Treaty/EN/Treaties/Word/197.doc.*

human rights led to the non-binding 1948 Universal Declaration of Human Rights being adopted by the General Assembly, prompting European States in 1950 to create the binding human rights obligation manifest in the European Convention of Human Rights,[46] so too has the failure to provide adequate human rights protection in the 2000 Palermo Protocol led to the 2005 Council of Europe Convention.

When moving to incorporate "trafficking" into the domestic legal order, State legislators have not sought to simply transpose the Palermo definition verbatim into their legislation. Instead, in many instances, they have opened the definition to the domestic process in which the legislators crafted their own understanding of what constitutes "trafficking."[47] This was well within their right, as a 2009 Model Law against Trafficking in Persons prepared by the United Nations makes plain that "the general provisions and the definitions... are not mandated by the Protocol *per se*."[48] As we shall now see, very few States have incorporated the actual definition of trafficking in persons found in the Palermo Protocol, often they have set out what is in essence a variation on the theme, but in other instances they have provided a unique reading of what constitutes the criminal offense of trafficking in persons.

The case of Moldova is indicative of States with unique readings of trafficking, wherein the Palermo Protocol definition is used as a benchmark from which to build in new understandings of what constitutes trafficking.[49] In the main, States have left the means and methods elements of the definition in place and focused on expanding the purpose element of the definition – that is to say, expanding the types of exploitation to be covered under the heading of trafficking. Moldova has taken on board the widest understanding of exploitation amongst States with anti-trafficking legislation in place. Its provision establishes that exploitation includes:

46 Jonathan L. Black-Branch, "Observing and Enforcing Human Rights under the Council of Europe: The Creation of a Permanent European Court of Human Rights, *Buffalo Journal of International Law*, Vol. 3, 1996, pp. 1, 3–8.

47 Maggy Lee, *Trafficking and Global Crime Control* 16, 19, 28 (2011).

48 *Model Law against Trafficking in Persons,* United Nations Office on Drugs and Crime (2009), http://www.unodc.org/documents/human-trafficking/UNODC_Model_Law_on_Trafficking_in_Persons.pdf.

49 Protocol for Trafficking in Persons, *supra* note 1, at 344. *See also,* Privind Prevenirea şi Combaterea Traficului de Fiinţe Umane [hereinafter Laws on Preventing and Combating Trafficking in Human Beings], No. 241-XVI of 20 Oct. 2005, art. 2(1) (Rep. of Mold.), http://www.hsph.harvard.edu/population/trafficking/moldova.traf.05.pdf.

(a) compelling to perform work or services, by use of force, threats or other forms of coercion, in violation of the legal provisions connected to labour conditions, remuneration, health and security;
(b) slavery, use of certain practices similar to slavery, or resorting to other ways of deprivation of liberty;
(c) compelling to engage in prostitution, to participate in pornographic performances, with a view to the production, distribution and any introduction into circulation of such performances, the acquisition, sale or possession of pornographic material, or practicing other forms of sexual exploitation;
(d) compelling harvesting of organs or tissues for transplantation or collection of other component parts of the human body;
(e) using a woman as a surrogate mother or for reproductive purposes;
(f) abuse of child's rights with a view to illegal adoption;
(g) use in armed conflicts or in illegal military formations;
(h) use in criminal activities;
(i) compelling to engage in begging;
(j) sale to another person;
(k) compelling to engage in other activities that violate fundamental human rights and freedoms.[50]

Having provided the Moldovan examples of a very far reaching provision, which establishes a number of other instances which constitute exploitation and thus modifies the Palermo Protocol understanding of trafficking, consideration now turns to various other readings, which States have given in their domestic legislation to the notion of trafficking in persons. It might be emphasized at this point, that legislation is drafted in the official language of States in question. Thus, the vast majority of the following definitions has been translated into English and thus should be treated with caution.

In the first instance, it might be emphasized that a small number of States such as the Bahamas,[51] Liberia,[52] and the Philippines[53] have legislation which

50 Law on Preventing and Combating Trafficking in Human Beings, *supra* note 49, at art. 2(3).

51 Trafficking in Persons (Prevention and Suppression), Ch. 106, pt. 1(2) (2007) (Bah.), http://laws.bahamas.gov.bs/cms/images/LEGISLATION/PRINCIPAL/2007/2007-0027/TraffickinginPersonsPreventionandSuppressionAct_1.pdf.

52 An Act to Ban Trafficking in Persons within the Republic of Liberia, art. 1 §§ 100, 102 (2005) (Liberia), https://www.unodc.org/tldb/showDocument.do?documentUid=7975&country=LIR&language=ENG.

53 Anti-Trafficking in Persons Act of 2003, Rep. Act No. 9208, § 3(a) (2003)(Phil.), http://www1.umn.edu/humanrts/research/Philippines/RA%209208%20-%20Anti-Trafficking%20Law.pdf.

mirrors the definition as established in the Palermo Protocol. And yet, even in this case, what constitutes trafficking is not guaranteed to be the same. The legislation of the Bahamas is instructive. If one mines deeper than the actual definition of trafficking in persons which is promulgated in the Bahamas', The Trafficking in Persons (Prevention and Suppression) Act,[54] and consider the various provisions that make up that definition which are in turn defined (abuse of a position of vulnerability, coercion, exploitation, forced labor, illicit removal of organs, practices similar to slavery, servitude, and sexual exploitation),[55] it becomes clear that even in situations where the Palermo Protocol definition of trafficking in persons is reproduced, it does not necessarily mean the same thing or constitute the same crime. In the case of the Bahamas, this is most evident with regard to its definition of sexual exploitation. While the 2009 UN Model Law provides a definition which reads:

> 'Sexual exploitation' shall mean the obtaining of financial or other benefits through the involvement of another person in prostitution, sexual servitude or other kinds of sexual services, including pornographic acts or the production of pornographic materials.[56]

The 2008 Act of the Bahamas goes beyond prostitution and pornography by setting out a unique provision dealing with "any other sexual activity."[57] It criminalizes, in the context of trafficking for sexual exploitation, "any other sexual activity" which results from "being subjected to threat, coercion, abduction, ...force, abuse of authority, or fraud."[58]

However, it goes further. The 2008 Act criminalizes, as does Jamaican legislation,[59] the trafficking in persons for sexual exploitation where a person is recruited, transported, etc., but then compelled to participate in any other sexual activity – beyond prostitution or pornography – "as a result of being subjected to...the effects of narcotic drugs."[60] While it might be recognized that such a provision is aimed at the use of narcotic drugs as a means of establishing control over a person with the aim of sexual exploitation, the provision

---

54 The Trafficking in Persons (Prevention and Suppression) Act, (Bah.).

55 *Id.* at § 2.

56 Model Law against Trafficking in Persons, *supra* note 48.

57 The Trafficking in Persons (Prevention and Suppression) Act, § 2 (Bah).

58 *Id.*

59 The Trafficking in Persons (Prevention, Suppression and Punishment) Act, § 2.1 (2007) (Jam.).

60 The Trafficking in Persons (Prevention and Suppression) Act, § 2 (Bah.).

could be interpreted in a manner which expands the reach of its application much further. As the 2008 Act deems that trafficking may transpire where a person assists another person engaged in transporting any person in the Bahamas,[61] the marginal case of two people meeting at a bar, sharing a tablet of Ecstasy, and leaving to the privacy of a house to engage in "any other sexual activity," would meet the threshold of trafficking. Such activity might include consensual sexual intercourse, but an activity as innocuous as kissing in this context would also constitute a form of sexual activity. In such a scenario, not only would the person who drove the vehicle be committing the crime of trafficking in persons, but if the couple had decided to hale a taxi, the legislation would deem the taxi driver a trafficker. While the *mens rea* would be absent for the taxi driver, for either party to this new romance, the threshold of trafficking in persons, as established in the Bahamas, would be met.

Beyond exploitation resulting from being subject to the effects of narcotic drugs, there are a great number of varied acts which have been deemed as exploitation by State parties to the Palermo Protocol. Such legislation has established that the following are forms of exploitation and thus fall under the more general heading of trafficking in persons: begging;[62] illegal adoption;[63]

61 *Id.*

62 States which have begging as part of their definition of exploitation include: (1) Columbia, Act 985 of 2005-Human Trafficking 1/16, art. 3 § 188A (Colom.), *available at* http://qub.ac.uk/slavery/?page=countries&category=6&country=37; (2) Costa Rica, Penal Code Law No. 4573, art. 172 (1970)(Costa Rica), *available at* http://www.qub.ac.uk/slavery/?page=countries&country=40&category=6; (3) Egypt, The People's Assembly Law No. 64 of 2010 (Combating Human Trafficking), art. 2 (Egypt), *available at* http://qub.ac.uk/slavery/?page=countries&country=53&category=2; (4) Haiti, Bill to Combat against Trafficking in Persons, art. 11 § 1.3.1 (Haiti), *available at* http://www.qub.ac.uk/slavery/?page=countries&country=73&category=1; (5) Italy, Act Aug. 11, 2003, n. 228, in G.U. Aug. 23, 2003, n. 195 (It.), *available at* http://www.qub.ac.uk/slavery/?page=countries&country=83&category=4; (6) Moldova, Law on Preventing and Combating Trafficking in Human Beings No. 241-XVI of 20 Oct. 2005, art. 2 (Rep. of Mold.); (7) Poland, The Police Act, art. 115 § 22 (2010)(Pol.), *available at* http://www.qub.ac.uk/slavery/?page=countries&category=8&country=135; (8) Saudi Arabia, Anti-Human Trafficking Law Issued by the Council of Ministers' Resolution No. 244 dated 20.7.1430 AH and Royal Approval No. M/40 dated 21.7.1430 AH and circulated by the Minister of Justice under No. 13/T13733 dated 25.8.1430 AH, art. 2 (Saudi Arabia), *available at* http://www.qub.ac.uk/slavery/?page=countries&country=149&category=3; and (9) Thailand, The Anti-Trafficking in Persons Act B.E. 2551, § 4 (2008)(Thai.), *available at* http://www.qub.ac.uk/slavery/?page=countries&country=169&category=4.

63 The following States have legislative provisions which deem illegal adoptions as constituting exploitation: (1) Costa Rica, Penal Code Law No. 4573, art. 172 (Costa Rica); (2) Dominican Republic, Law No. 137–03 Smuggling on of Migrants and Trafficking, § 1(a) (2003)

servile or forced marriage;[64] pornography;[65] sex tourism;[66] surrogacy;[67] and one or more of the removal of the following: blood, cells, organs, tissues, or body parts.[68]

(Dom. Rep.), *available at* http://www.qub.ac.uk/slavery/?page=countries&category=6&country=51; (3) El Salvador, Penal Code Legislative Decree NO. 1030, art. 367–B (1997) (El Sal.), *available at* http://www.qub.ac.uk/slavery/?page=countries&country=54&category=1; (4) Equatorial Guinea, Law No. 1/2004 of Sept. 14, 2004 on the Smuggling of Migrants and Trafficking in Persons, art. 1 (Eq. Guinea), *available at* http://www.qub.ac.uk/slavery/?page=countries&country=55&cateogry=4; (5) Kyrgyzstan, The Kyrgyz Republic Criminal Code, art. 124(8) (1997), *available at* http://www.qub.ac.uk/slavery/?page=countries&category=9&country=91; (6) Macedonia, Republic of Macedonia Criminal Code, art. 418-(a)(1) (1996), *available at* http://www.qub.ac.uk/slavery/?page=countries&country=170&category=1; (7) Madagascar, Penal Code Law No. 2007–038, art. 333 (2008) (Madagascar), *available at* http://www.qub.ac.uk/slavery/?page=countries&category=9&country=101; (8) Moldova, Law on Preventing and Combating Trafficking in Human Beings No. 241-XVI of 20 Oct. 2005, art. 2(3)(Rep. of Mold.); (9) Nicaragua, Penal Code Law No. 641 of Nov. 13, 2007, art. 182 (Nicar.), *available at* http://www.qub.ac.uk/slavery/?page=countries&category=9&country=123; (10) Pakistan, Act XLV of 1860, Pak. Penal Code, § 361 (Pak.), *available at* http://www.qub.ac.uk/slavery/?page=countries&category=9&country=128; (11) Tajikistan, Criminal Code of the Republic of Tajikistan, art. 172, *available at* http://www.qub.ac.uk/slavery/?page=countries&category=9&country=168; (12) Ukraine, Criminal Code of Ukraine, art. 149 (2001), *available at* http://www.refworld.org/docid/4c4573142.html; (13) Venezuela, Organic Law on the Right of Women to a Life Free of Violence, art. 56 (Venez.), *available at* http://www.qub.ac.uk/slavery/?page=countries&category=0&country=188.

64 The following States have provisions designating servile or forced marriage as a type of exploitation: (1) Columbia, Act 985 of 2005- Human Trafficking 1/16, art. 3 § 188A (Colom.); (2) Costa Rica, Penal Code Law No. 4573, art. 172 (Costa Rica); (3) Dominican Republic, Law No. 137–03 Smuggling on of Migrants and Trafficking, § 1(a)(Dom. Rep.); (4) El Salvador, Penal Code Legislative Decree No. 1030, art. 367-B (El Sal.); (5) Equatorial Guinea, Law No. 1/2004 of Sept. 14, 2004 on the Smuggling of Migrants and Trafficking in Persons, art. 1 (Eq. Guinea); (6) Haiti, Bill to Combat against Trafficking in Persons, art. 11 § 1.3.1 (Haiti); (7) Kenya, The Counter Trafficking in Persons Bill, (2010) Cap. 8 § 24 (Kenya), *available at* http://www.qub.ac.uk/slavery/?page=countries&country=88&category=6; (8) Macedonia, Republic of Macedonia Criminal Code, art. 418-(a)(1); (9) Mauritius, Combating of Trafficking in Persons Act 2009, § 4 (Mauritius), *available at* http://www.qub.ac.uk/slavery/?page=countries&country=6&country=109; (10) New Zealand, Section 208 of the Crimes Act of 1961, as substituted by Section 9 of the Crimes Amendment Act 2005 (N.Z.), *available at* http://www.qub.ac.uk/slavery/?page=countries&category=6&country=122.

65 The following are states that have specifically determined that pornography is a type of exploitation: (1) Dominican Republic, Law No. 137–03 Smuggling on of Migrants and

Beyond these examples of States providing new types of exploitation, which fall under the general banner of trafficking in persons, the European Union (EU) has, for its twenty-eight member States, established that "the exploitation of criminal activities" is also included in its reading of exploitation.[69] Like the EU, a number of States have provided an all-encompassing provision under the banner of exploitation, which establishes that trafficking in persons will transpire where the first two elements of trafficking are present, the *method* and the *means,* and where the *purpose* of trafficking is any illegal activity. Thus, Antigua and Barbuda speak of precisely this "any illegal activity."[70] Azerbaijan

---

Trafficking, § 1(a)(Dom. Rep.); (2) Equatorial Guinea, Law No. 1/2004 of Sept. 14, 2004 on the Smuggling of Migrants and Trafficking in Persons, art. 1 (Eq. Guinea); (3) Haiti, Bill to Combat against Trafficking in Persons, art. 11 § 1.3.1 (Haiti); (4) Macedonia, Republic of Macedonia Criminal Code, art. 418-(a)(1); (5) Mozambique, Law Nr. 6/2008, art. 11 (Mozam.), *available at* http://www.qub.ac.uk/slavery/?page=countries&country=116&category=7; (6) Peru, Criminal Code Law No. 28251, art. 182 (2004)(Peru), *available at* http://www.qub.ac.uk/slavery/?page=countries&country=133&category=1; (7) Poland, The Police Act, art. 115 § 22 (Pol.); (8) Tajikistan, The Law of the Republic of Tajikistan on Fight Against Human Trafficking, ch. 1, art. 1, *available at* http://www.qub.ac.uk/slavery/?page=countries&category=2&country=168; (9) Thailand, The Anti-Trafficking in Persons Act B.E. 2551, § 4 (Thai.).

66 The two States that have determined that sex tourism is a form of exploitation are: (1) Bolivia, Trafficking and Trafficking in Persons and Other Related Offences Law of 18 Jan. 2006, art. 281 (Bol.), *available at* http://www.qub.ac.uk/slavery/?page=countries&category=2&country=21; (2) Colombia, Act 985 of 2005-Human Trafficking 1/16, art. 3 § 188A (Colom.).

67 Both Azerbaijan and Moldova have deemed the surrogacy as being exploitative. Criminal Code of the Azerbaijan Republic, art. 108–1 (Azerbaijan), *available at* http://www.qub.ac.uk/slavery/?page=countries&category=2&country=11; Law on Preventing and Combating Trafficking in Human Beings No. 241-XVI of 20 Oct. 2005, art. 2(3) (Rep. of Mold.).

68 The following States have deemed exploitation to include the removal of elements of the body: (1) Egypt, The People's Assembly Law No. 64 of 2010 (Combating Human Trafficking), art. 2 (Egypt); (2) Indonesia, Law of the Republic of Indonesia No. 21 of 2001 About Combating Crime of the Trade by the Grace of God Almighty President of the Republic of Indonesia, art. 1, *available at* http://www.qub.ac.uk/slavery/?page=countries&category=8&country=78; (3) Kenya, The Counter Trafficking in persons Bill, (2010) Cap. 8 § 24 (Kenya); (4) Poland, The Police Act, art. 115 § 22 (Pol.); (5) Slovenia, Criminal Code of the Republic of Slovenia, art. 387 (a)(1) (2005)(Slovn.), *available at* http://www.qub.ac.uk/slavery/?page=countries&cateogry=8&country=156.

69 Council Directive 2011/36/EU, art. 2, Offences Concerning Trafficking in Human Beings, 2011 O.J. (L 101) 6, http://eur-lex.europa.eu/LexUriServ/LexUriServ.do?uri=OJ:L:2011:101:001:0011:EN:PDF, [hereinafter Council Directive].

70 The Trafficking in Persons (Prevention) Act, 2010, No. 12 of 2010, pt, I, § 2, at 9 (Ant. & Barb.), http://laws.gov.ag/acts/2010/a2010-6.pdf.

uses the language of the "recruitment for unlawful activities (including criminal activities)";[71] Georgia uses "involvement of a person in criminal or other anti-societal conduct";[72] Kyrgyzstan, the shorter "involvement of a person in criminal activities";[73] while Laos is even less wordy, speaking of "for other unlawful purposes."[74] For its part, Luxembourg speaks in terms of "to commit that person of a crime or offense against their will,"[75] while Moldova criminalizes trafficking in persons in the context of exploitation, which is understood to include the use of a person "in criminal activities."[76] For Sri Lanka, the net is thrown quite wide, as exploitation relates to "any other act which constitutes an offence under any law."[77] Tajikistan, for its part, criminalizes "engaging in sexual or criminal activity" in the context of trafficking,[78] while Ukraine speaks of simply "engagement in criminal activities."[79]

With the inclusion of various States deeming that any and all criminal activity, when carried out against one's will or knowledge, that is, using the Palermo Protocol definition: "by means of the threat or use of force or other forms of coercion, of abduction, of fraud, of deception,"[80] when coupled with the movement of a person, constitutes trafficking in persons. It may be appropriate to consider what in fact, and in law, exploitation actually is. Nowhere in the law related to trafficking in persons is "exploitation" defined. Instead, domestic legislation takes the lead of the Palermo Protocol in providing examples of

---

71 Law of the Republic of Azerbaijan on Trafficking in Persons, ch. I, art. 1, § 1.0.2 (2005), *available at* http://www.refworld.org/docid/4417f1214.html.

72 Law of Georgia on Combating Human Trafficking, ch. I, art. 3(d) (2006), http://www.lexis-nexis.com/documents/pdf/20081027094649_large.pdf.

73 The Kyrgyz Republic Criminal Code, art. 124(8).

74 Laos Penal Code, ch.6, art. 134 (2006), http://www.protectionproject.org/wp-content/uploads/2010/09/Laos_Penal-Code-TiP_2005.pdf.

75 Loi du 13 Mars 2009 Relative à la Traite des Êtres Humains [Act of 13 March 2009 on Trafficking in Human Beings], art. 3(4) (Lux.), http://www.protectionproject.org/wp-content/uploads/2010/09/Luxembourg_TIP-Law_2009-French.pdf, *translated by* Google Translate.

76 Law on Preventing and Combating Trafficking in Human Beings No. 241-XVI of 20 Oct. 2005, art. 2(3)(h).

77 Penal Code (Amendment) Act, No. 16 of 2006, §360c.(1)(b) (Sri Lanka), http://www.documents.gov.lk/Acts/2006/Penal%20Code%20(Amend)%20Act%2016%202006/PL%20000608%20(E)%20Penal%20Code%20Act%20No.%2016%20of%202006.pdf.

78 The Law of the Republic of Tajikistan on Fight Against Human Trafficking (2004), Ch. 1, art. 1(a).

79 Criminal Code of Ukraine, art. 149(1).

80 Protocol for Trafficking in Persons, *supra* note 1, at 344.

what constitutes exploitation. Thus, in the law under consideration, exploitation is, at the international level, categorical rather than conceptual.

Where thought has been given to the notion of exploitation, the most in-depth consideration has taken place in Alan Wertheimer's 1996 philosophical study, Exploitation.[81] For Wertheimer, "[a]t the most general level, A exploits B when A takes unfair advantage of B."[82] In The Definition of Slavery in International Law, I have applied Wertheimer's consideration of exploitation in the legal context of trafficking in persons by establishing that, in seeking to understand the term, we should consider that unfair advantage be deemed the legal threshold.[83] In other words, taking unfair advantage of a person transpires when the person is compelled "by means of the threat or use of force or other forms of coercion, of abduction, of fraud, of deception," to be party to an illegal activity.[84] Thus, a person is exploited when they work as a prostitute while under the menace of violence, but so too a grocery clerk, forced to take less than minimum wage as a result of a threat of losing her job. In this reading of exploitation, the activity undertaken is not the most important activity; what stands out is the means by which the person is compelled to undertake that activity. Force, fraud, and deception are then the main elements, which speak to a situation where a person takes unfair advantage of another. Marx would consider that all workers are exploited in a capitalist system as a result of profit going to employers;[85] but this threshold does not assist in determining, in the law of trafficking in persons, what constitutes exploitation. The law should be the standard for determining what constitutes exploitation; it is legislators around the world who are to determine what constitutes "unfair advantage."

With this in mind, the approach of the European Union and other states, in establishing exploitation in the context of any and all criminal activity, speaks to the notion of exploitation evolving through its incorporation – at least in European domestic legal order – from being a set of categories to being, in fact and law, a concept. Instead of delineating what constitutes instances of exploitation – slavery, forced labor, etc. – as has been done at the international

---

81 Alan Wertheimer, Exploitation (1996).

82 *Id.* at 10.

83 *See generally* Jean Allain, *The Definition of Slavery in International Law*, 52 How. L.J. 239, 273–75 (2009).

84 Wertheimer, *supra* note 81; Protocol for Trafficking in Persons, *supra* note 1, at 344.

85 *See* Karl Marx & Frederick Engels, *The Communist Manifesto* 18 (Samuel Moore trans., Marxist Internet Archive 2010) (1848), http://www.marxists.org/archive/marx/works/download/pdf/Manifesto.pdf.

level, in various states noted above, exploitation is understood as constituting any and all illegal activities in which a person, against his or her will or knowledge, (forced, fraud, deception, etc.) is compelled to perform.[86] When this is coupled with the process of moving a person – "recruitment, transportation, transfer, harbouring or receipt of persons," including the exchange or transfer of control over those persons,[87] – it will amount to trafficking.

Where states have not moved to this conceptual model of embracing that all criminal activities could constitute trafficking, if the two elements – the means and the methods – are at play, we witness the introduction of specific examples of what constitutes exploitation in various pieces of domestic legislation.

In the Australian context, while the Criminal Code provides for 'trafficking in persons' within the Palermo Protocol meaning of that term, it goes on to add to those provisions by creating a unique reading of the term, and thus determining that trafficking in persons is tantamount to forced smuggling. That is, trafficking in persons includes the use of force or threats to obtain a person's compliance in his or her entering into Australia.[88] Further examples of unique acts deemed exploitation found in the legislation of specific states include Azerbaijan: "bio-medical research on a person";[89] Bolivia: "farm labor";[90] Bulgaria: "debauchery";[91] Mauritania: "unpaid work";[92] Oman: "sexual assault";[93] and Pakistan: "purpose of exploitative entertainment," wherein exploitative entertainment is defined as "all activities in connection

86 *See* Inter-Parliamentary Union & UN Office on Drugs & Crime, *Combating Trafficking in Persons: A Handbook for Parliamentarians*, at 12–15, UN Sales No. E.09.V.5 (2009), [Hereinafter Combating Trafficking in Persons Handbook].

87 Protocol for Trafficking in Persons, *supra* note 1, at 344 ("'Trafficking in persons' shall mean the recruitment, transportation, transfer, harbouring or receipt of persons, by means of the threat or use of force or other forms of coercion, of abduction, of fraud, of deception…for the purpose of exploitation."). *See also* Combating Trafficking In Persons Handbook, *supra* note 86, at 12–14.

88 *Criminal Code Act 1995*, § 271.2 (Austl.).

89 Law of the Republic of Azerbaijan on Trafficking in Persons, ch. I, art. 1, § 1.0.2 (2005).

90 Trafficking and Trafficking in Persons and Other Related Offences Law of 18 Jan. 2006, art. 281(f) (Bol.).

91 Закон за борба с трафика на хора [Combating Trafficking in Human Beings Act], § 1 (2003) (Bulg.), http://www.hsph.harvard.edu/population/trafficking/bulgaria.traf.03.pdf.

92 Presidency of the Republic Justice Honor Fraternity Act No. 025/2003/ On Suppression of Trafficking in Persons, art. 1 (Mauritania), *available at* http://qub.ac.uk/slavery/?page=countries&category=1&country=108.

93 Combating Trafficking In Persons, art. 1 (2008)(Oman), http://www.ilo.org/dyn/natlex/docs/MONOGRAPH/81766/88931/F1239239215/OMN81766.pdf.

with human sports or sexual practices or sex and related abusive practices."[94] Macedonia has determined that exploitation includes "forced fertilization."[95] Moldova includes a somewhat unique catchall provision, determining that exploitation includes compelling to engage "in other activities that violate fundamental human rights and freedoms."[96] South Africa deems that "the impregnation of a female person against her will for the purpose of selling her child when the child is born," is to be considered a form of exploitation;[97] while the Ukraine has a number of unique provisions which it deems to constitute exploitation: "to experiment on a person without its consent," "forced pregnancy."[98] Within its definition of trafficking, Uruguay also has a residual clause, which, beyond enumerated types of exploitation, criminalizes "any activity that undermines human dignity."[99]

A number of states have also sought to include, in their legislation on trafficking in persons, issues around armed conflict. Thus, Kenya determines that exploitation also includes "forcible or fraudulent use of any human being to take part in armed conflict";[100] whereas Kyrgyzstani, Tajikistani and Ukraine legislation all speak of using a person in armed conflict.[101] Sierra Leone makes plain the relationship it is seeking to criminalize: "exploitation during armed conflicts";[102] while Norway is more concerned with it citizens fighting for foreign powers: "war service in a foreign country."[103]

---

94 Prevention and Control of Human Trafficking Ordinance (2002), art. 2–3 (Pak.), *available at* http://qub.ac.uk/slavery/?page=countries&category=1&country=128.

95 Republic of Macedonia Criminal Code, art. 418-a1 (1996).

96 Laws on Preventing and Combating Trafficking in Human Beings, No. 241-XVI of 20 Oct. 2005, art. 2(3)(k). *But see also* Romania, which includes within its meaning of exploitation a provision which reads, "engaging in other such activities that violate fundamental human rights and liberties." Law on the Prevention and Combat of Trafficking in Human Beings, art. 2 § 2(e), (Rom.), *available at* http://www.hsph.harvard.edu/population/trafficking/romania.traf.01.htm.

97 Prevention and Combating of Trafficking in Persons Act, 2013, Act 7 (GG)(S. Afr.).

98 Criminal Code of Ukraine, art. 149.

99 Law No. 18,250 Diario Oficial de la Republica Oriental del Uruguay [Migration-Standards], § 2, art. 78 (2998)(2008)(Uru.), *available at* http://www.qub.ac.uk/slavery/?page=countries&category=4&country=185.

100 The Counter Trafficking in Persons Bill, Cap. 8 § 24(e).

101 The Kyrgyz Republic Criminal Code, art. 124(8)(1997); The Law of the Republic of Tajikistan on Fight Against Human Trafficking, ch. 1, art. 1(a)(2004); Criminal Code of Ukraine, art. 149 (2001).

102 The Anti-Human Trafficking Act, pt. II, 2(3)(h) (2005)(Sierra Leone), http://www.sierra-leone.org/Laws/2005-7p.pdf.

103 General Civil Penal Code, ch. 21, § 224 (2005)(Nor.), http://www.ub.uio.no/ujur/ulovdata/lov-19020522-010-eng.pdf.

Legislators around the world have taken up the unstated invitation, provided by the Palermo Protocol, to define trafficking in persons, opening up the definition to their legislative process. Having considered the legislation of all States that have introduced provisions into their domestic law related to trafficking, it can be stated as fact that, at the domestic level, no two definitions of trafficking in persons are identical. While a number of States have variations on the theme regarding the methods and the means elements of the Palermo Protocol, a much larger proportion of States have promulgated different readings of exploitation by including various acts that are deemed exploitive in their domestic legal order.

As a result, no generalization can be proffered when speaking of 'trafficking in persons'. Instead, the near totality of obligation flowing from the Palermo Protocol, or any other obligation related to trafficking in persons, will be dependent on the manner in which individual States have incorporated the notion of 'trafficking in persons' into their domestic law. The overwhelming approach of States has been to take what was conceived as a transnational regime, meant to interrupt organized criminal groups from creating an industry out of the trafficking in persons, and, instead, with the ratification of the Palermo Protocol, create an approach focused on activities solely within their borders, further defining the notion of 'trafficking in persons' in ways that are sometimes unique, but oftentimes idiosyncratic.[104]

The Transnational Law of Trafficking after Domestic Implementation

As a result of the manner in which States have implemented the Palermo Protocol, the various understandings of what constitutes 'trafficking in persons' means that coordinating actions meant to prevent, suppress, and punish trafficking in persons must be considered on a bilateral basis, not an international or transnational basis.[105]

The focus here is to ask the question: Can States effectively cooperate in addressing the transnational crime of trafficking in persons, as a result of domestic implementation which has trafficking in persons defined differently

104 *See* Michelle Madden Dempsey *et al.*, "Defining Sex Trafficking in International and Domestic Law: Mind the Gaps," *Emory International Law Review*, Vol. 26, 2012, pp. 137, 138–42, 145–147.

105 Protocol for Trafficking in Persons, *supra* note 1, at art. 346–347 (Providing that the domestic laws of individual states must be respected during the investigation and prosecution of international human trafficking offenses).

in each country? The UN Convention against Transnational Organized Crime makes plain that "the description of the offences established in accordance with this Convention...[are] reserved to the domestic law of a State Party..." and "such offences shall be prosecuted and punished in accordance with that law."[106] Thus, each reading of 'trafficking in persons' developed by a country is to be the basis of interaction between States, making sure that each reading of the definition being undertaken is in accordance with domestic law.

Let us now turn to a specific situation to demonstrate the extent to which the implementation of the Palermo Protocol has strayed away from the initial intent of the drafters during the diplomatic conference where the UN Convention against Transnational Organized Crime and the Palermo Protocol were developed. The United Kingdom of Great Britain and Northern Ireland (UK) have not passed any specific statutes pertaining to the criminalization of trafficking in persons, or sought to specifically implement the UN Convention or the Palermo Protocol. Instead, incorporation in the domestic legal order in the UK has taken place through the amending of two pieces of legislation: the Asylum and Immigration (Treatment of Claimants, etc.) Act 2004 and the Sexual Offences Act 2003.[107] Under the Asylum and Immigration Act, a person is exploited when they have been a victim of slavery or forced labor, in line with the European Human Rights Convention, or involved in commercial dealings where "force, threats, or deception" are at play,[108] violating the Human Organ Transplants Act 1989.[109] In the context of that legislation, a person is involved in trafficking if they facilitate the arrival into, travel within,

106 United Nations Convention, *supra* note 10, at 280.

107 Asylum and Immigration (Treatment of Claimants, etc.) Act, 2004, c. 19, §§ 1, 4 (U.K.), http://www.legislation.gov.uk/ukpga/2004/19/pdfs/ukpga_20040019_en.pdf [Hereinafter Asylum and Immigration Act]; Sexual Offences Act, 2003, c. 42, §§ 57–59 (U.K.), *available at* http://www.legislation.gov.uk/ukpga/2003/42/contents. *See also* Home Office & Scottish Executive, UK Action Plan on Tackling Human Trafficking, (2007), at 15–17.

108 Asylum and Immigration Act, at § 4.

109 *Id. See also* Human Organ Transplants Act, 1989, c. 31, § 1(1) (U.K.), http://www.legislation.gov.uk/ukpga/1989/31/pdfs/ukpga_19890031_en.pdf.

(1) A person is guilty of an offence if in Great Britain he –

(a) makes or receives any payment for the supply of, or for an offer to supply, an organ which has been or is to be removed from a dead or living person and is intended to be transplanted into another person whether in Great Britain or elsewhere;

(b) seeks to find a person willing to supply for payment such an organ as is mentioned in paragraph (a) above or offers to supply such an organ for payment;

(c) initiates or negotiates any arrangement involving the making of any payment for the supply of, or for an offer to supply, such an organ; or

or departure from the UK, a victim or possible victim of exploitation.[110] With regard to the Asylum and Immigration (Treatment of Claimants, etc.) Act 2004, victims are to be understood as being involved in international transit, as the legislation speaks of them as "passenger[s]," as in "[a] person commits an offence if he arranges or facilitates the arrival in the United Kingdom of an individual (the 'passenger') and (a) he intends to exploit the passenger."[111]

The Sexual Offences Act 2003 also criminalizes the trafficking into, within, or out of the UK;[112] however, it criminalizes this movement in conjunction with various crimes of a sexual nature, including rape, sexual assault, child sex offenses, and exploitation of prostitution.[113] What is absent from the Sexual Offences Act 2003, but is found in the Asylum and Immigration (Treatment of Claimants, etc.) Act 2004, is the need for a movement to transpire as a result of "force, threats or deception."[114] As a result, in the UK, the 'trafficking of a person' for sexual exploitation misses the linchpin of the Palermo Protocol, namely that such criminality transpired against the will or wishes of the victim. Thus, in the UK, the offenses under the Asylum and Immigration (Treatment of Claimants, etc.) Act 2004 are in line with the three elements of trafficking in persons, as defined in the of Palermo Protocol – the *method*, the *means*, and the *purpose* – however, crimes under the Sexual Offences Act 2003 are trafficking in name only, as they lack the *means* element, "force, threats or deception,"[115] of the crime of trafficking in persons. As a result, the Sexual Offences Act 2003 establishes that trafficking for sexual exploitation in the UK is simply the movement of a person in the context of a sexual offense.

In the UK, the extent to which the notion of trafficking in persons has been diluted from its original international intent is made most evident in the actual application of domestic legislation in the first case heard in Northern Ireland.[116]

(d) takes part in the management or control of a body of persons corporate or unincorporate whose activities consist of or include the initiation or negotiation of such arrangements.

110 Asylum and Immigration Act, at § 4(1–3).

111 *Id.* at § 4(1).

112 Sexual Offences Act, at §§ 57–59.

113 *Id.* at §§ 1–15, 51–54, 57–59.

114 Asylum and Immigration Act, at § 4(4)(c).

115 *Id.*

116 *Queen v. Matyas Pis*, [2012] NICC 14 [pp. 1, 3] (Ir.). It should be noted that in Northern Ireland, for jurisdictional reasons, certain UK legislation was promulgated by way of a separate order. While the Asylum and Immigration (Treatment of Claimants, etc) Act 2004 is applicable in Northern Ireland by virtue of UK-wide legislation, the Sexual Offences Act 2003 was, in light of the suspension of the activities of Northern Ireland

In the 2012 *Queen v Matya Pis* case, the individual was jailed for little more than having booked air tickets, picking up two sex workers at the airport in Dublin, Ireland, and bringing them north across the virtual border into the UK to an apartment in Belfast, Northern Ireland.[117]

Judge Burgess of the Belfast Crown Court noted: "[a]lthough there is no indication that [the two women] were brought into the United Kingdom or required to work in prostitution against their will, they are still victims of sexual offences."[118] He goes on to say:

> The agreed facts of this case, to which I will turn shortly, confirm that there is no allegation of coercion and corruption of unwilling victims which marks cases at the higher end of the sentencing range for these offences. However I want to take this opportunity to make it very clear that anyone who is brought before the courts in Northern Ireland for offences of this nature can, other than in exceptional circumstances, expect a custodial sentence. That sentence will be heavier for those who coerce their victims, who use violence against them, who sexually assault and degrade them and who placed them in fear for their own or their loved ones' lives.[119]

Clearly in this context, there is a distinction between the crime of trafficking in the UK, for which Mr. Pis is found guilty, and the notion of trafficking in persons found in the Palermo Protocol, which requires the "threat or use of force or other forms of coercion, of abduction, of fraud, of deception, of the abuse of power or of a position of vulnerability or of the giving or receiving of payments or benefits to achieve the consent of a person having control over another person" to be at play for the offense of trafficking in persons to be present.[120] In other words, Mr. Pis would be innocent of any charges under the Palermo Protocol.

Assembly, brought into force by way of the Sexual Offences (Northern Ireland) Order 2008. Much, as in the United States, where the divisions of powers means that the Federal Government and the State Governments have constitutionally entrenched exclusive jurisdiction over certain legislative areas; so too in the UK, where Northern Ireland, Scotland and Wales have certain devolved powers. Asylum and Immigration Act, at § 4; Sexual Offences (Northern Ireland) Order, 2008, S.I. 2008/1769, art. 76–78, http://www.legislation.gov.uk/nisi/2008/1769/pdfs/uksi_20081769_en.pdf.

117 *Queen v. Matyas Pis*, [2012] NICC 14 [p. 6] (Ir.).

118 *Id.* at p. 2.

119 *Id.* at p. 5.

120 Protocol for Trafficking in Persons, *supra* note 1, at 344.

Further, the *raison d'être* of the international criminalization of trafficking – the suppression of organized crime – appears lost in the domestic implementation of the Palermo Protocol in the UK, as among the agreed statement of facts in this case was an acknowledgement by the prosecution that Mr. Pis was "not part of any criminal gang operating in Northern Ireland."[121] Instead, Mr. Pis was found guilty of trafficking for sexual exploitation because "[h]e actively recruited Hungarian woman to come to the United Kingdom to work as prostitutes" and, once in the UK, his "role was limited to introducing the women to others who would place them in brothels."[122]

While it is the UK's sovereign prerogative to define trafficking as it wishes, the issue lies with the coordination of transnational obligations in a context where the UK can establish that anybody involved in moving a sex worker into, within, or out of the UK, has committed the crime of trafficking.[123] Such coordination is relevant with regard to both extradition and extra-territorial jurisdiction.

Extradition refers to international cooperation in the handing over of an individual facing criminal charges in another State.[124] A cornerstone of extradition is the notion of "dual" or "dual criminality," or that the offense be punishable in both the requesting State and the prospective surrendering State.[125] Article 16 of the 2000 UN Convention against Transnational Organized Crime makes this plain, as extradition may only take place with regard to "the offences covered by this Convention...provided that the offence for which extradition is sought is punishable under the domestic law of both the requesting State Party

121 *See Queen v. Matyas Pis*, [2012] NICC 14 [p. 7(e)] (Ir.).

122 *Id.* at 29.

123 Asylum and Immigration Act, at § 4. It should be emphasized that the reach of what is termed 'trafficking' in the UK goes beyond prostitution, as it also falls within the context of trafficking for sexual exploitation. This crime consists of moving a victim of an offence, defined under the Sexual Offences Act of 2003, into, within, or out of the UK. Such offences include child sex offences, incest, rape, voyeurism, etc. Sexual Offenses Act, at §§ 1, 5–29, 57–60, 64–71.

124 *Extradition Definition,* Merriam-Webster Dictionary, http://www.merriam-webster.com/dictionary/extradition (last visited Sept. 20, 2013).

125 UN Human Rights: Office of the High Comm'r for Human Rights, Recommended Principles and Guidelines on Human Rights and Human Trafficking, at 205, UN Doc. HR/PUB/10/2, UN Sales No. E.10.XIV.1 (2010) (despite the fundamental character of dual criminality to protect the rights of the accused in an extradition hearing, the report considers that the rights of the accused may well get in the way of putting people in prison. "The principle of dual criminality," the author of the commentary writes, "can have the effect of obstructing prosecutions").

and the requested State Party."[126] For Anne Gallagher, the "principle of dual criminality provides an additional, compelling reason for States to criminalize trafficking as it has been defined by international law."[127] Yet this pronouncement, made in 2010, is somewhat disingenuous. Tantamount to closing the stable door after the horse has bolted, the definition of trafficking in persons has been considered to be incorporated into the domestic legal order, but less than a handful of the 157 states that are a party to the Palermo Protocol have "criminalize[d] trafficking as it has been defined by international law."[128] Instead, the practice of trafficking in persons has been fractured.

The incorporation of an understanding of 'trafficking in persons' into the domestic order of States in a multifaceted manner is fractured because the ability to extradite individuals is not predicated on the fact that the requesting and potential sending states have legislation in place that allows for the extradition of individuals accused of trafficking in persons. Instead, such extraditions will depend on whether both states have criminalized the actual act, which has transpired within their respective legislation. As was noted in the Pinochet case, relating to the request by Spain to extradite the former Head of State of Chile from the United Kingdom, it was noted that "the most important requirement is that the conduct complained of must constitute a crime under the law both of Spain and of the United Kingdom. This is known as the double criminality rule."[129] In the context of the UK, this was considered more in depth in Government of Canada v. Aronson, where it was stated that "[i]t is axiomatic that a person charged with a crime is entitled to know not only the offence with which he is charged…but also to have particulars of the conduct which it is alleged constitutes the offence."[130] In the United States, the Supreme Court has established that the substance is more important than the form, or name given to the crime. In Heilbronn v. Kendall, the Court said:

---

126 United Nations Convention, *supra* note 10, at 284.

127 Gallagher, *supra* note 22, at 405.

128 *Protocol to Prevent, Supress and Punish Trafficking in Persons, Especially Women and Children, Supplementing the United Nations Convention against Transnational Organized Crime,* United Nations, http://treaties.un.org/doc/Publication/MTDSG/Volume%20II/Chapter%20XVIII/XVIII-12-a.en.pdf (last visited Oct. 1, 2013). *See generally,* Anne Gallagher & Nicole Karlebach, Prosecution of Trafficking in Persons Cases: Integrating A Human Rights-Based Approach in the Administration of Criminal Justice 5.

129 *Regina v. Bow Street Metropolitan Stipendiary Magistrate and Others, Ex parte* Pinochet Ugarte (No.3) [1999], 1 A.C. 147 (H.L.) [189] (appeal taken from Eng.).

130 *Gov't of Can. et al. v. Aronson,* [1989] 1 A.C. 579 (H.L.) [594] (appeal taken from Eng.).

> The law does not require that the name by which the crime is described in the two countries shall be the same, nor that the scope of the liability shall be coextensive, or, in other respects, the same in the two countries. It is enough if the particular act charged is criminal in both jurisdictions.[131]

Later in the decision "[t]he fact that a particular act is classified differently or that different requirements of proof are applicable in the two countries does not defeat extradition."[132] As a result, not only may extradition take place where the same act is criminalized under different headings, but the reverse also holds; extradition will not take place where the crime under the same heading in both countries does not incorporate the particular act under consideration as criminal.

Having provided the example of the British legislature which incorporates its United Nations obligations regarding trafficking, it becomes obvious, in light of the survey conducted in the previous section regarding the definition of trafficking in persons, as implemented in the domestic jurisdiction of the states that are a party to the Palermo Protocol, that any request for extradition related to trafficking, either made or received, should not automatically be granted. Beyond the formal issues of jurisdiction required for any extradition hearing, the substance of what is being termed trafficking will have to be scrutinized to ensure that, in fact and in law, what is termed trafficking in one jurisdiction is, in substance, also criminalized in the other jurisdiction. This ensures that the double criminality obligation fundamental to extradition is met.

Beyond issues of extradition, the fact that States that are a party to the Palermo Protocol have implemented a multi-varied understanding of what constitutes trafficking in persons limits the effectiveness of the transnational elements of the fight against trafficking, where issues of extra-territorial jurisdiction are brought into play. Here, the issue is much more critical than with regard to extradition. As in situations of extra-territorial jurisdiction, a State is unilaterally establishing jurisdiction over an act which has transpired in another State. This may also go as far as establishing jurisdiction where the crime has transpired in a foreign state, and the individual suspected of committing this crime is a national of that foreign state. In such a situation, the challenge to sovereignty over one's territory and one's nation is acute. For the issue at hand, this is most evident with the enactment of the 2011

131 *Heilbronn v. Kendall*, 775 F. Supp. 1020, 1025 (W.D. Mich. 1991) (quoting Collins v. Loisel, 259 U.S. 309, 312 (1922)).

132 *Id.*

European Union Directive on Preventing and Combating Trafficking in Human Beings and Protecting its Victims, which allows the twenty-eight members of the European Union[133] to establish jurisdiction over the crime of trafficking beyond their respective borders.[134] While it would ordinarily be considered that a State has exclusive jurisdiction within its territory, the sovereign equality of States denies the possibility of invoking jurisdiction within the borders of another State, with extra-territorial jurisdiction being the exception.

The 2011 EU Directive does exactly this, as it allows States to establish "jurisdiction over the offences...committed outside its territory."[135] Such jurisdiction could be invoked if the crime was committed in State *A*, while the individual committing the crime of trafficking, or the victim of the crime of trafficking, is a national or habitual resident of State *B*. In such a case, despite the crime having taken place in State *A*, State *B* could establish jurisdiction over the matter as a result of the involvement of one of its habitual residents, or one of its citizens in the crime of trafficking.[136] While the possibility to invoke extra-territorial jurisdiction exists for European Union States as a result of the 2011 EU Directive, it might be noted that the 2009 UN Model Law against Trafficking in Persons already called for such extra-territorial jurisdiction to be included in trafficking legislation.[137]

Once again, this time in the context of seeking to invoke extra-territorial jurisdiction over the crime of trafficking in persons, success will hinge on how trafficking in persons is defined in both the State seeking to invoke extra-territorial jurisdiction, with regard to one of its nationals or habitual residents, and the State on whose territory the offense transpired. While elements of those definitions may be common to both states in question, this cannot be presumed. Thus, while Kenya will hold that a national has committed the crime of trafficking as defined under its extra-territorial jurisdiction in persons, if the national moved a victim to, for instance, Moldova, and coerced that person into a forced marriage,[138] this would not constitute the crime of

133 *Member Countries of the European Union,* European Union, http://europa.eu/about-eu/countries/member-countries/index_en.htm (last visited Oct. 10, 2013).

134 *See generally,* Council Directive, *supra* note 69, at art. 10.

135 *Id.*

136 Extra Territorial Jurisdiction in the European Union: A Study of Laws and Practice in the 27 Member States of the European Union 13 (2010) (A number of EU States now exercise extra-territorial jurisdiction in relation to crimes under international law. Examples of Member States which exercise extra-territorial jurisdiction are: Belgium, Denmark, France and Germany). *Id.* at 78, 110, 131, 138.

137 *Model Law against Trafficking in Persons, supra* note 48, at 27.

138 The Counter Trafficking in Persons Bill, at pt. II, § 3(1), pt. VI, § 25.

trafficking under its legislation, as forced marriage is not included as a type of exploitation.[139] As a result, Moldova would have no obligation, stemming from its trafficking legislation, to cooperate in an investigation to assist the victim (victim, that is, from a Kenyan perspective) or to repatriate or extradite the Kenyan national.

A second scenario, more theoretical in nature, will assist in driving the point home. Consider once more the case of the United Kingdom where trafficking in persons is defined, in the context of sexual exploitation, as the simple movement of a sex worker, void of any type of "force, threats or deception."[140] If the United Kingdom was to apply – it has not – what is termed in law the "passive personality" principle,[141] and established in its legislation extra-territorial jurisdiction over offenses committed against one of its nationals or habitual residents, far-reaching implications for other States would be created. UK legislation regards the trafficking in persons, the assisting of a prostitute who is a UK national outside of the UK, as a criminal act. In the Netherlands, where sex workers are legal, the same act would amount to nothing more than assisting a EU citizen in exercising his or her right to work within the Union. One could go further by examining the 2011 EU Directive, which not only criminalizes the act of trafficking in persons, but also the act of "aiding and abetting," which would throw a much larger net over the application of the UK conception of trafficking in persons.[142] If the UK sex worker were traveling to Amsterdam, having been provided a license to establish a brothel, would the municipality be liable for trafficking in persons? Would the Mayor of Amsterdam, whose city provided the license, the Attorney General of the Netherlands, who maintained the legislation allowing prostitution, or the

139 *Id.* at pt. II, §3.

140 Asylum and Immigration Act, at § 4(4)(c).

141 Vicki Trapalis, "Comment, *Extraterritorial Jurisdiction: A Step Towards Eradicating the Trafficking of Women into Greece for Forced Prostitution*," *Golden Gate University Law Review*, Vol.32, 2002, pp. 207, 231–32 (defining passive personality principle). The passive personality principle emerges only after the Cold War, through its development before the Yugoslav and Rwanda Tribunals and the creation of the International Criminal Court, and then comes to be accepted as part of international relations. The Judges write: "The contemporary trends, reflecting international relations as they stand at the beginning of the new century, are striking… Passive personality jurisdiction, for so long regarded as controversial…today meets with relatively little opposition…" *See Arrest Warrant of 11 April 2000* (Dem. Rep. of the Congo v. Bel.), 2002 I.C.J. 63, 70, 76–77 (Joint and Separate Opinions of Judges Higgins, Koojimans, and Buergenthal), http://www.icj-cij.org/docket/files/121/8136.pdf.

142 Council Directive, *supra* note 69, at art. 3.

former Queen of the Netherlands having signed the law into existence,[143] be complicit in aiding and abetting the crime of trafficking in persons as understood from the UK perspective?

Conclusion

The regime of trafficking in persons, conceptualized in the 2000 Palermo Protocol, is flawed, as its operationalization has been fractured by the incorporation of the UN Convention against Transnational Organized Crime and the anti-trafficking Protocol in the domestic legal order. This study has shown how States, during their domestic legislating processes, have developed a large range of very diverse readings of what constitutes 'trafficking in persons'. As a result, when we speak about trafficking in persons across borders, we are, in essence, speaking in different languages.

The fundamental flaw of the regime of trafficking in persons is manifest in this: the system meant to facilitate the prevention, suppression, and punishment of trafficking through transnational cooperation cannot do so because the States have created different variations of what constitutes trafficking. These variations mean that points of interaction and possible cooperation amongst States do not necessarily mesh. This is most evident with regard to issues of extradition where the double criminality principle comes into play, as well as questions surrounding the application of extra-territorial jurisdiction. While there is much in common within the definitions of trafficking in persons, as incorporated into domestic legislation worldwide, there is also enough variation within those provisions as to limit the very effectiveness of the regime envisioned in the Palermo Protocol. As a result, it is imprudent to generalize about 'trafficking in persons'. Instead, there should be a realization that when we use the language of 'trafficking in persons' we mean different things, depending on the country we are dealing with.

---

143 *See generally* Dutch Ministry of Foreign Affairs, Dutch Policy on Prostitution 3–6 (2012), http://www.minbuza.nl/binaries/content/assets/minbuza/en/import/en/you_and_the_netherlands/about_the_netherlands/ethical_issues/faq-prostitutie-pdf--engels.pdf-2012.pdf (laying out how the act was implemented and how the act is enforced).

PART 3

Servitude and Forced Labour

CHAPTER 14

On the Curious Disappearance of Human Servitude from General International Law*

Hindsight is a great thing, that the Universal Declaration of Human Rights paved the way for the Covenants and, in their wake, international and regional human rights law standards is today a given; but in 1956, during the negotiations of the Supplementary Slavery Convention, it was not. The Covenants were still in embryonic form and where they were concerned "it was considered that there was apparently no intention of taking further action."[1] Yet during those 1956 negotiations, despite the possibility of no human rights treaties ever seeing the light of day, the Universal Declaration was the elephant in the room. It forced States negotiating the Supplementary Convention to move to expunge the term 'servitude' from the operative provisions of an instrument meant to deal with that exact issue. This was because a number of States where unwilling to go as far as the 1948 Declaration which pledged that "no one shall be held in slavery or servitude"; as the 1956 Supplementary Convention simply requires States to take all practicable measures to bring about "progressively and as soon as possible the complete abolition or abandonment" of servitudes specified in that Convention.

This study considers the drafting history of Article 4 of the Universal Declaration of Human Rights and its impact on the negotiations of the 1956 Supplementary Convention on the Abolition of Slavery, the Slave Trade and *Institutions and Practices Similar to Slavery*. The latter instrument, it bares noting, was originally drafted in 1954 as: the Draft Supplementary Convention on Slavery and *Servitude*.[2] The unwillingness of States to abolish servitude

* This chapter was first published as Jean Allain, "On the Curious Disappearance of Human Servitude from General International Law," *Journal of the History of International Law*, Vol. 11, 2009, p. 303. Copyright © Brill |Nijhoff, 2009.

1 See United Nations, Economic and Social Council, United Nations Conference of Plenipotentiaries on a Supplementary Convention on the Abolition of Slavery, the Slave Trade and Institutions and Practices Similar to Slavery, Summary Record of the Fourth Meeting, 15 August 1956, UN Doc. E/CONF.24/SR.4, 11 November 1958, p. 9.

2 See United Nations, Economic and Social Council, The Draft Supplementary Convention of Slavery and Servitude Submitted by the Government of the United Kingdom and Comments Thereon (Memorandum by the Secretary-General), UN Doc. E/AC.43/L.1, 2 December 1955, p. 1. Emphasis added.

 | DOI 10.1163/9789004279896_016

outright in 1956, led to a fragmentation of international law, which is reflected today in both the 2001 United Nations and 2005 Council of European instruments related to human trafficking – which reproduce the same definition of 'trafficking in persons' and enumerate various types of exploitation to be suppressed. Amongst those types of exploitation are including both *practices similar to slavery* and *servitude*. Yet, 'practices similar to slavery' are no different than 'servitude' in their nature, but in law they have been divided, with the former forming part of general international law as manifest in the 1956 Supplementary Convention, the latter in international human rights law as 'servitude' left undefined. Thus *practices similar to slavery* are those four conventional servitudes established in general international law in 1956: debt-bondage, serfdom, forced marriage, and child exploitation; while *servitude* has not been defined by an international instrument though it has been given content in large measure through the pronouncement of bodies supervising human rights treaties.

Of Slavery and Servitude

Servitude should be understood as human exploitation falling short of slavery. That is to say, such exploitation which does not manifest powers which would normally be associated with ownership, whether *de jure* or *de facto*.[3] The definition of slavery established by the 1926 Slavery Convention and accepted as such in international law speaks of the 'status or condition of a person over which any or all of the powers attaching to the right of ownership are excised'. Such powers, the UN Secretary General of the United Nations noted in 1953 are to be considered as the purchase, transfer or inheritance of a person; or the absolute control over a person, their labour or the product of that labour. Finally the Secretary-General he noted that such powers attaching to the right of ownership were manifest when the end of the status or conditions was indeterminate for the enslaved.[4] The 1956 Supplementary Convention while establishing conventional servitudes, acknowledges this link between slavery and servitude, by determining that certain institutions and practises similar to slavery should be abolished "progressively and as soon as possible the complete

3 For the application of the 1926 definition of slavery to both *de facto* and *de jure* slavery, see *The Queen v Tang*, High Court of Australia, [2008] HCA 39, 28 August 2008; and Jean Allain, "The Definition of Slavery in International Law," *Howard Law Journal*, Vol. 52, 2009, p. 239.

4 See United Nations, Economic and Social Council, Slavery, the Slave Trade, and other forms of Servitude (Report of the Secretary-General), UN Doc. E/2357, 27 January 1953, p. 28.

abolition or abandonment of the following institutions and practices, where they still exist and whether or not they are covered by the definition of slavery contained in Article 1 of the Slavery Convention signed at Geneva on 25 September 1926." That is to say: whether or not these servitudes would also be considered slavery as manifesting powers attaching to the right of ownership.

As early as 1924, a League of Nations expert committee on slavery, the Temporary Slavery Commission, considered human exploitation writ large. They did so by giving an expansive definition of slavery which included forced labour and various servitudes. During the negotiation of the 1926 Convention, this expansive understanding of slavery was rejected by States in favour of one which turned on the powers attaching to the right of ownership. Thus, in his Report to the Assembly of the League of Nations on the 1925 Draft Convention, the Rapporteur, Viscount Cecil of Chelwood, considered the notion of 'domestic slavery and similar conditions' which, he explained, "include all forms of 'debt slavery', the enslaving of persons disguised as the adoption of children, and the acquisition of girls by purchase disguised as payment of dowry, etc. as mention in the report of the Temporary Slavery Commission."[5] However, after having received comments by States, Cecil reported back to the Assembly in 1926 and modified his language to make plain that there was only one type of 'slavery' – wherein the powers attaching to the right of ownership were exercised. Viscount Cecil acknowledged that these lesser servitudes did not amount to slavery:

> Even if, as is possible, these last practices [debt bondage, serfdom, forced marriage and child exploitation] do not come under the definition of slavery as it is given in Article 1, the [Temporary Slavery] Commission is unanimously of the opinion that they must be combated. In a more general way, it interprets Article 2 as tending to bring about the disappearance from written legislation or from the custom of the country of everything which admits the maintenance by a private individual of rights over another person of the same nature as the rights which an individual can have over things.[6]

5 League of Nations, Annex: Draft Convention, League of Nations Official Journal (Special Supplement 33) Records of the Sixth Assembly: Text of Debates, 26 September 1925, p. 439.

6 League of Nations, Slavery Convention: Report presented to the Assembly by the Sixth Committee, A.104.1926.VI, as found in League of Nations, Publications of the League of Nations, VI.B.Slavery.1926, VI. B. 5, 24 September 1926, pp. 1–2.

In other words, Viscount Cecil recognised that 'slavery in all it forms' required the demonstration of a power attaching to the right of ownership to be exercised over an individual as established by the definition of slavery in Article 1.

This distinction between slavery and servitudes was noted by the League of Nations Committee of Experts on Slavery in 1936 when it considered the issue of serfdom and emphasised that one must make a distinction between slavery as defined in the convention and other forms of exploitation:

> It is important, however, to keep the fundamental distinction clearly in mind, and to realise that the status of 'serfdom' is a condition 'analogous to slavery' rather than a condition of actual slavery, and that the question whether it amounts to 'slavery' within the definition of the Slavery Convention must depend upon the facts connected with each of the various systems of 'serfdom'.[7]

The Committee of Experts on Slavery was more explicit in regard to its considerations of debt slavery, noting that:

> the conditions in which the debt-slave lives are often of the nature that repayment is an impossibility and the debtor is therefore a slave for life. Even worse than this may sometimes happen, for in some systems there are cases in which the debt is 'hereditary' and, after the death of the debtor, it is transmitted to the children and children's children. It is right, perhaps, that one should realise quite clearly that the system – *whatever form it may take in different countries – is not 'slavery' within the definition set forth in Article 1 of the 1926 Convention, unless any or all the powers attaching to the right of ownership are exercised by the master.*[8]

Having examined the distinction between slavery and servitude, consideration now turns to the drafting of the 1948 Universal Declaration of Human Rights and the 1956 Supplementary Convention to demonstrate how the notion of servitude fragmented to also become 'practices similar to slavery'.

---

7 League of Nations, Slavery: Report of the Advisory Committee of Experts, Third (Extraordinary) Meeting of the Advisory Committee, C.189(I). M.145.1936, VI, 13–14 April 1936, p. 27.

8 *Id.*, pp. 24–25. Emphasis added.

Drafting Article 4 of the Universal Declaration on Human Rights

In 1947, at its first session, the United Nations Commission on Human Rights delegated to a *ad hoc* Drafting Committee the formulation of a preliminary draft of an international bill of human rights.[9] Included in that Draft Outline of an International Bill of Rights was Article 8 which reads:

> Slavery and compulsory labour are inconsistent with the dignity of man and therefore prohibited by this Bill of Rights. But a man may be required to perform his just share of any public service that is equally incumbent upon all, and his right to a livelihood is conditioned by his duty to work. Involuntary servitude many also be imposed as part of a punishment pronounced by a court of law.[10]

Commenting on this proposal, the United Kingdom sought a more succinct formulation which focused exclusively on slavery ("No form of slavery shall be permitted")[11] When the Drafting Committee turned to consider each of the provisions of the Draft Outline of an International Bill of Rights so as to get "a general idea as to the substance to be included in each provisions," René Cassin proposed – and it was accepted – that compulsory labour, servitude, and inhuman exploitation should be added to the provision prohibiting slavery.[12]

Shortly thereafter, a consensus emerged within the Drafting Committee that the International Bill of Rights "would have greater unity if drawn up by one person"; with Cassin given that task. Cassin suggested that the provision in question "be expanded rather than shortened," and proposed that slavery be "prohibited in all its forms." Eleanor Roosevelt of the United States of America following this lead suggested that the article under consideration

9 See United Nations, Economic and Social Council, Commission on Human Rights, Drafting Committee, Memorandum on Historical Background of the Committee, UN Doc. E/CN.4/AC.1/2, 29 May 1947.

10 United Nations, Economic and Social Council, Commission on Human Rights, Drafting Committee, Draft Outline of an International Bill of Rights, UN Doc. E/CN.4/AC.1/3, 4 June 1947, p. 4.

11 United Nations, Economic and Social Council, Commission on Human Rights, Drafting Committee, International Bill of Rights: Document Outline, Texts, United Kingdom Draft International Bill of Human Rights, UN Doc. E/CN.4/AC.1/3/Add.3, 10 June 1947, p. 4.

12 See United Nations, Economic and Social Council, Commission on Human Rights, Drafting Committee, Summary Record of the Fourth Meeting, 12 June 1947, UN Doc. E/CN.4/AC.1/3/SR.4, 13 June 1947, pp. 2 and 3.

should read: "Slavery, which is inconsistent with the dignity of man, is prohibited under all its forms."[13]

During the second session of the Commission on Human Rights in late 1947, the United States proposed a new form for the article, one which read: "No one shall be held in slavery or involuntary servitude. No one shall be subject to torture, or to cruel or inhuman punishment or indignity."[14] In May 1948, the Drafting Committee of the Commission on Human Rights considered the provisions, of what was now forming part of a Draft International Declaration on Human Rights, wherein Mrs. Roosevelt proposed the following provision: "Everyone is entitled to freedom from slavery and servitude in any form. Their practice is a challenge to the conscience of the world." This proposal elicited a number of comments, but what emerged from the Drafting Committee was a very succinct provision which now read: 'Slavery in all its forms shall be prohibited'.[15] When, in June 1948, this provision was considered by the Commission on Human Rights, the Chinese Representative, Mr. Chang, proposed the following be substituted for the Drafting Committee's proposal: "No one shall be held in slavery or in voluntary servitude or be subject to torture or to cruel or inhuman punishment or indignity."[16] But a joint the India-United Kingdom proposal sought the inclusion of only the first part of that proposal: 'No one shall be held in slavery or in voluntary servitude',[17] which gained support of the Commission and was adopted by nine votes to three with three abstentions and was thus included in the 1948 Draft International Declaration of Human

13 United Nations, Economic and Social Council, Commission on Human Rights, Drafting Committee, Summary Record of the Thirteenth Meeting, 20 June 1947, UN Doc. E/CN.4/AC.1/3/SR.13, 8 July 1947, p. 2.

14 See Article 5, United Nations, Economic and Social Council, Commission on Human Rights, Proposal for a Declaration of Human Rights submitted by the Representative of the United States on the Commission on Human Rights, UN Doc. E/CN.4/36, 26 November 1947, p. 2.

15 United Nations, Economic and Social Council, Commission on Human Rights, Drafting Committee (Second Session), Summary Record of the Thirty-Sixth Meeting, 17 May 1948, UN Doc. E/CN.4/AC.1/SR.36, 19 May 1948, p. 5.

See also the United Nations, Economic and Social Council, Commission on Human Rights (Second Session), Report of the Drafting Committee to the Commission on Human Rights, UN Doc. E/CN.4/95, 21 May 1948, p. 5.

16 United Nations, Economic and Social Council, Commission on Human Rights (Third Session), China: Amendments to the Draft International Declaration on Human Rights, UN Doc. E/CN.4/102, 27 May 1948, p. 3.

17 United Nations, Economic and Social Council, Commission on Human Rights (Third Session), India and the United Kingdom: Proposed Amendments to the Draft International Declaration on Human Rights, UN Doc. E/CN.4/99, 24 May 1948, p. 2.

Rights. The Draft Declaration was forwarded to the Economic and Social Council, which in turn forward it to the General Assembly. On 24 September 1948, the Assembly referred the matter to its Third Committee (Social, Humanitarian and Cultural Questions) which considered the provision touching on slavery and servitude (Article 4) on 21 October 1948.

The first issue of substance considered by the Third Committee was with regard to the notion of 'involuntary' servitude, as the Costa Rican Representative, Mr. Cañas, asked "for an explanation of the difference between the English and French texts of Article 4, pointing out that the English text stated: 'No one shall be held in…involuntary servitude', while the French text said: *Nul ne sera…tenu en servitude*. The adjective 'involuntary', used in English, was not to be found in the French text." Was it, Mr. Cañas asked, a case of the text not being authentic. The French Representative, Mr. Grumbach, assured him that it was not, as "word 'servitude' alone seemed to be the only way of expressing precisely what Article 4 should state." The British Representative, Mrs. Corbet, for her part "explained that the English word 'servitude' described the situation of a person who performed services, whether voluntarily or involuntarily. It was therefore necessary to add the adjective 'involuntary' in the English text."[18] The India Representative, Mr. Habib was also in favour of keeping the adjective, noting that "he hoped that the word 'involuntary' would be retained, as the term 'voluntary servitude' was its current use in India to describe a particular type of military or labour contract."[19]

Mrs. Corbet's understanding of servitude was countered by Mr. Watt, the Representative from Australia, who noted that after "consulting the Oxford Dictionary, he had come to the conclusion that it would be wiser to omit the word 'involuntary' before 'servitude' in the English text."[20] Mr. Demchenko of the Ukrainian Soviet Socialist Republic for his part stated that "he felt that the retention of the word 'involuntary' […] might provide an escape clause, as slave owners would be able to evade the provisions of the declaration by saying that their slaves had entered into servitude voluntarily."[21] When put to a vote the deletion of the word 'involuntary' was adopted by a rather slender vote of seventeen in favour, fifteen opposed, with four abstentions.[22] What emerged

18 United Nations, General Assembly, Official Records of the Third Session of the General Assembly, Part I, Third Committee, Summary Record of Meetings, 21 September – 8 December, Agenda Item 33: Draft International Declaration of Human Rights, One Hundred and Ninth Meeting, 21 October 1948, Volume 2 A, p. 212.

19 *Id.*, p. 216.

20 *Id.*

21 *Id.*

22 *Id.*, p. 222.

thus from the work of Third Committee was the provision which would ultimately be adopted by the General Assembly by thirty-two votes in favour, six opposed, with three abstentions as a new version of Article 4. The United Nations General Assembly in passing Resolution 217 A(III), on 10 December 1948, adopted the Universal Declaration of Human Rights, which thus includes the following Article 4: "No one shall be held in slavery or servitude; slavery and the slave trade shall be prohibited in all their forms."

Drafting the 1956 Supplementary Convention

In 1949, the United Nations General Assembly requested that the Economic and Social Council study the problem of slavery;[23] which in turn instructed the UN Secretary-General to appoint an *ad hoc* committee to, *inter alia*: "survey the field of slavery and other institutions or customs resembling slavery."[24] The 1950–51 *Ad Hoc* Committee on Slavery considered the 1926 Convention adequate for dealing with slavery, as one of its members noted "the 1926 Convention did not seem to have come in for any drastic criticism and that no one had showed conclusively why it should be replaced by a new convention."[25] In its 1951 Report, the *Ad Hoc* Committee on Slavery called for "the preparation and adoption of an international convention supplementary to the Slavery Convention of 1926," stating that: "Such a supplementary convention, in its view, should affirm the Slavery Convention of 1926 as a whole, and should be more precise than that instrument in defining the exact forms of servitude dealt with."

The *Ad Hoc* Committee on Slavery recommended a number of principles be embodied within a supplementary convention, and that States should endeavour to "undertake to abolish, at the earliest possible date, the following institutions and practices analogous to slavery or resembling slavery in some of their effects, in so far as they are not already covered by the Article 1 of the International Slavery Convention of 1926": debt bondage, serfdom, interminable labour pledges, forced marriage, and transferring of children to exploitation.[26] Finally,

---

23 United Nations, General Assembly, Resolution 278 (III), 13 May 1949.

24 United Nations, Economic and Social Council, Resolution 238(IX), 20 July 1949.

25 United Nations Economic and Social Council, *Ad Hoc* Committee on Slavery, First Session: Summary Record of the Twenty-Seventh Meeting, UN Doc. E/AC.33/SR.27, 21 March 1950, p. 5.

26 United Nations, Economic and Social Council, Report of the *Ad Hoc* Committee on Slavery (Second Session), UN Doc E/1998, E/AC.33/13, 4 May 1951, p. 19.

the *Ad Hoc* Committee prepared a draft Resolution for the Economic and Social Council which embodied these, and other, recommendations and proposed that a drafting committee be established to "prepare the draft of a supplementary international convention on slavery and other forms of servitude."[27]

The Economic and Social Council, for its part, having considered the Draft Resolution prepared by the *Ad Hoc* Committee on Slavery noted that it was unable to deal with the Recommendations as "the material is not at present in such a form as to allow the Council to act upon"[28] The Secretary-General, reported back to the Economic and Social Council in 1953 and, as a result, the Secretary-General was requested to "consult the governments of all States, both Members and non-members of the United Nations, concerning the desirability of a supplementary convention and its possible contents."[29] As part of those consultations of 1954, the United Kingdom submitted a draft of a supplementary convention which was used as a basis for negotiating what would become not a convention on slavery and servitude but the 1956 Supplementary Convention on the Abolition of Slavery, the Slave Trade, and Institutions and Practices Similar to Slavery.

The Obligations of the Convention

Article 1 of the 1956 Supplementary Convention on the Abolition of Slavery, the Slave Trade and Institutions and Practices Similar to Slavery sets out four types of servitudes which are to be abolished progressively and as soon as possible. These conventional servitudes, are not considered formally as 'servitudes'; instead they are grouped under the heading of 'institutions and practices similar to slavery', while 'a persons of servile status' is defined in the Supplementary Convention as a "person in the condition or status resulting from any of the institutions or practices mentioned in Article 1 of this Convention."[30] Yet as originally conceived, the Convention was meant to deal with slavery and servitude, not 'institutions and practices similar to slavery' nor 'servile status'. How did this change come to pass? The answer can be reduced to the following: the

27 *Id.*, p. 31.

28 United Nations, Economic and Social Council, Resolution 388(XIII), 10 September 1951.

29 United Nations, Economic and Social Council, Resolution 475 (XV), 27 April 1953.

30 See United Nations, Economic and Social Council, United Nations Conference of Plenipotentiaries on a Supplementary Convention on the Abolition of Slavery, the Slave Trade and Institutions and Practices Similar to Slavery, Final Act and Supplementary Convention, 4 September 1956, UN Doc E/CONF.24/23.

States negotiating the 1956 Supplementary Convention were unwilling to go as far as the 1948 Universal Declaration of Human Rights which called stated that 'no one shall be held in servitude'. Instead, they wished to act "progressively and as soon as possible" to abolition of servitude. As a result, and so as not to be seen as back-tracking on their pleadge that no one should be held in servitude, States avoided using the term 'servitude' in the 1956 Supplementary Convention, instead calling debt-bondage, serfdom, forced marriage, child exploitation 'institutions or practices similar to slavery'.

The *chapeau* of Article 1 – that is: the introductory provision of that Article – spells out the obligations which States undertake with regard to institutions and practices similar to slavery that each "of the States Parties to this Convention shall take all practicable and necessary legislative and other measures to bring about progressively and as soon as possible the complete abolition or abandonment of the following institutions and practices [...]".[31] The phrase "progressively and as soon as possible" was a reproduction of the obligation found in the 1926 Slavery Convention as attached to the abolition of slavery. Although a number of States and Non-governmental Organisations sought in 1955 and 1956, to have the clause "progressively and as soon as possible" removed in favour of provisions establishing the immediate suppression of institutions and practices under consideration, this was not to be. What stands out here is the approach of the leading anti-slavery organisation, the London-based Anti-Slavery Society which was in favour of retaining a gradualist approach. The Anti-Slavery Society justified its stance, saying that in one region of the world where chattel slavery still existed the rulers were "sympathetic to the abolition of the legal status of slavery but that they are in advance of public opinion."[32] This rather State-centric position allowed the British Government the diplomatic room to fight off challenges from those who wanted a convention which abolished servitudes forthwith. Thus the British Government, during the 1956 UN Conference negotiating the Supplementary Convention, turned to the Anti-Slavery Society position to justify its own:

---

31 United Nations, Economic and Social Council, United Nations Conference of Plenipotentiaries on a Supplementary Convention on the Abolition of Slavery, the Slave Trade and Institutions and Practices Similar to Slavery, Final Act and Supplementary Convention, 4 September 1956, UN Doc E/CONF.24/23.

32 United Nations, Economic and Social Council, The Draft Supplementary Convention of Slavery and Servitude Submitted by the Government of the United Kingdom and Comments Thereon (Memorandum by the Secretary-General), UN Doc E/AC.43/L.1, 2 December 1955, p. 21.

> The situation faced by a government in trying to eradicate the practices mentioned in the draft supplementary convention would require it to move step by step, as it would be dealing with long-established customs which could not be abolished overnight. He drew attention, in that connexion, to the communication submitted by the Anti-Slavery Society of the United Kingdom to the Drafting Committee. The Society's zeal for abolishing slavery in all its forms was well-known, and it had informed the Drafting Committee that, in its opinion the words 'progressively' and 'as soon as possible' should be retained as they had been used in the 1926 Slavery Convention. In support of its opinion the Society had quoted a passage from an article entitled 'Slavery in all its forms' by Lord Lugard, member of the League of Nations Temporary Slavery Commission, which had been published in January 1933. In that article Lord Lugard had emphasized that in countries where from time immemorial slavery had existed as an integral part of the structure of society it was obvious that a decree of compulsory emancipation would result in social chaos. He had further stated that masters who had acquired their slaves under the pre-existing secular law and religious sanction could not without injustice be suddenly deprived of their legal property and be reduced to poverty. Slaves unaccustomed to fend for themselves would starve or turn to theft and the woman to prostitution. The aged and sick would perish.
>
> The United Kingdom delegation could therefore not support any move to delete the word 'progressively'[…].[33]

Other States fell in line, China, for one noting that it had been "allayed by the statements" of the United Kingdom and the Anti-Slavery Society. The Representative of the Netherlands followed suit saying that the sudden abolition of servitudes "might disrupt the social and economic life of the country concerned";[34] while Australia considered that abolition of forced marriages would affect the "stability of marriage and family organization."[35]

Such gradualist arguments, though they were successful, did not go unchallenged. Mr. Lopez , the Representative of the Philippines, noted, rather caustically that:

---

33 United Nations, Economic and Social Council, United Nations Conference of Plenipotentiaries on a Supplementary Convention on the Abolition of Slavery, the Slave Trade and Institutions and Practices Similar to Slavery, Summary Record of the Fourth Meeting, 15 August 1956, UN Doc E/CONF.24/SR.4, 11 November 1958, pp. 5–6. Citation in the original deleted.

34 *Id.*, p. 6.

35 *Id.*, p. 3.

> while he appreciated the humanitarian motives which had prompted the delegations of the United Kingdom, Australia, Netherlands [etc.] to insist on the retention of the word 'progressively', he must point out that, as those who know the relationship of ruler and ruled from the other side were aware, the argument that reforms should be introduced slowly and gradually had sometimes been used in the past to retard progress, perhaps even against the will of the administrating authorities concerned. Slowness to act in destroying backward tribal practices had in fact prolonged those practices and maintained the rule of ignorance and superstition. Insistence on the need for progressive action must not operate against the interests of the backward peoples themselves. An administering authority might conceivably base its refusal to put an end to such institutions as serfdom on the grounds that it must act progressively.[36]

That said, it was the Egyptian Representative, Mr. Abdel-Ghani, who made the link between the obligations which were being proposed during the negotiations of this Supplementary Convention and the pronouncement of Article 4 of the Universal Declaration, as he pointed out "that the practices covered by the Convention were condemned by the Universal Declaration on Human Rights, Article 4 of which required the prohibition of slavery and the slave trade in all their forms." He went on to argue that

> Since, however the Declaration was not binding, but represented a standard to be applied by all States, he would refer to the draft covenants on human rights. The main difference between the two draft covenants – the draft covenant on political and civil rights and the draft covenant on education, social, and cultural rights – was that the former was to come into force immediately while the aims of the latter were to be achieved gradually. The article of the covenant relating to slavery had been place in the covenant on political and civil rights, and the supplementary draft convention should convey the same need for urgency.
>
> The covenants on human rights were of course still in the drafting stage, but so was the supplementary convention on slavery. Consequently, they were all on the same basis, and as far as slavery was concerned it would be better to adopt the treatment advocated in the covenants.[37]

---

36 *Id.*, pp. 9–10.

37 United Nations, Economic and Social Council, United Nations Conference of Plenipotentiaries on a Supplementary Convention on the Abolition of Slavery, the Slave

Mr. Giraud, the Representative of France, disagreed with that position, calling for wider participation at the expense of more expansive obligations:

> The Conference had not been called in order to define an ideal or recommend general objectives; that had been done with the Universal Declaration of Human Rights. Its purpose was to conclude a convention and do everything possible for its acceptance by a large number of States and after that for its effective application.
>
> The covenants on human rights, which the Egyptian representative had mentioned as a model, were still merely drafts, on which there was apparently no intention of taking further action. The Conference desired a better fate for the convention which it was preparing, and for that reason it should eschew rigid formulae which would preclude the accession of many States.[38]

As for the four 'institutions and practices similar to slavery' found in Article 1, it was acknowledged during the negotiation process that these were in fact 'servitudes' and were considered as such until the negotiation process of the 1956 Supplementary Convention and legal considerations forced the nomenclature to change to 'institutions and practices similar to slavery'. But for Article 4 of the Universal Declaration, these servitudes would have been labelled as such.

In essence, the definitions of these four 'institutions and practices similar to slavery' are technical in nature and thus what had been drafted by the 1950–51 Economic and Social Council expert group, the *Ad Hoc* Committee on Slavery, was picked up by the British in their 1954 Draft Convention and did not meet with substantive changes throughout the negotiation process.

Debt Bondage

With regard to the first of these 'institutions and practices similar to slavery', the British Government, in putting forward its 1954 Draft Convention, quoted with approval the *Ad Hoc* Committee on Slavery with regard to debt bondage:

> the practice of debt bondage, which is the status or condition arising from a pledge by a debt of his personal services, or those of a third person under his control, where those services do not count towards payment of

Trade and Institutions and Practices Similar to Slavery, Summary Record of the Fourth Meeting, 15 August 1956, UN Doc E/CONF.24/SR.4, 11 November 1958, pp. 10–11.

38 *Id.*, p. 9.

> the debt, or are undefined as regards the nature and length of the services to be preformed, or force the person pledged to submit to conditions that do not allow such person to exercise the rights normally enjoyed by ordinary individuals within the framework of local custom.[39]

The *Ad Hoc* Committee on Slavery was clear that debt bondage might "arise in one of two ways: either an individual, owing a debt to another individual, pledges his personal services in payment of the debt; or he pledges the services of a third person under his control."

> However, the Committee did not feel that the resulting status or condition alone constituted a form of servitude; it agreed that there must also be present a general denial or disregard of the principle that an individual should be treated as a person rather than as a thing, and considered as an end in himself and not only as a means to the purpose of someone else. It therefore agreed that the presence of one or more of the following conditions was necessary to bring debt bondage within the Committee's concept of servitude;
>
> (a) if the service rendered by the bondsman or the pawn do not count toward the payment of the debt;
> (b) if the nature and length of the services to be performed by the bondsman or the pawn are not defined; or
> (c) if the bondsman or the pawn submits to conditions that do not allow the person pledged to exercise the rights enjoyed by ordinary individuals with the framework of local social customs.[40]

Thus, the approach of the United Kingdom to debt bondage, which was not challenged throughout the drafting process of the 1956 Supplementary Convention was that of the 1950–51 Economic and Social Council *Ad Hoc* Committee on Slavery, which recognised that debt bondage 'constituted a form of servitude'.

Serfdom

Likewise, with regard to serfdom, the second enumerated institution or practice similar to slavery found in the 1956 Supplementary Convention, the United

39 United Nations, Economic and Social Council, Report of the *Ad Hoc* Committee on Slavery (Second Session), UN Doc. E/1988, E/AC.33/13, 4 May 1951, p. 19.

40 *Id.*, pp. 8–9.

Kingdom once more took the lead of the *Ad Hoc* Committee on Slavery. Again, those negotiating the 1956 Supplementary Convention did not challenge in any substantive manner the provisions put forward by the *Ad Hoc* Committee. For that Committee,

> the legal status of serfdom, and the practice whereby an individual is by law (including customary law), custom, or agreement, attached to agricultural or pastoral land and cannot change his status or freely dispose of the produce of his labour, whether or not he may be required to perform, without compensation, duties for the landowner.[41]

The Committee stated that "it felt that such a condition constitutes a form of servitude that should be abolished."[42]

Servile Marriage

Where forced marriage – the third institution or practice similar to slavery – was concerned, again the position of the 1950–51 *Ad Hoc* Committee was never challenged during the drafting process of the 1956 Supplementary Convention. That position was that "it would consider as a form of servitude the practice whereby a woman is given in marriage, without the right to refuse, at a price or under conditions which given to the husband, to his clan or family, a right of disposal over her or over her children and permit her exploitation for the advantage of others."[43]

Child Exploitation

Finally, where the fourth institution or practice similar to slavery, child exploitation, was concerned, the Committee felt that "a status or condition of servitude existed only when the conditions of the transfer were such as to permit the exploitation of the child regardless of its welfare."[44]

Although Article 1 of the 1956 Supplementary Convention spells out four institutions or practices similar to slavery, as originally conceived by the experts who developed their definitions, these were indeed servitudes. Yet the very notion of 'servitude' does not feature in the substantive elements of the Supplementary Convention; at least not in its final form. However, with

---

41 United Nations, Economic and Social Council, Report of the *Ad Hoc* Committee on Slavery (Second Session), UN Doc E/1988, E/AC.33/13, 4 May 1951, p. 20.

42 *Id.*, p. 11.

43 *Id.*, pp. 9–10.

44 *Id.*, p. 10.

regard to a further obligation under the Convention related to the criminal offences, the term 'servitude' survived until the diplomatic conference which finalised the 1956 Supplementary Convention.

As originally conceived the provisions of Article 6 the 1956 Supplementary Convention, related to criminal offences, used the term 'servitude' within its provisions. Both the 1954 British Draft Convention, and the 1956 Draft Convention prepared by an Economic and Social Council committee required States to make it an offence to induce "another person to give himself" or a dependent "into slavery or any other form of servitude." During the United Nations Conference of Plenipotentiaries on a Supplementary Convention on the Abolition of Slavery, the Slave Trade and Institutions and Practices similar to Slavery, Mr. Phan-Trong-Nhien, the Representative from Vietnam proposed that "for the sake of consistency with the title of the draft Convention as adopted by the 1956 *ad hoc* Committee, the words 'any other form of servitude'" should be replaced by the phrase "institutions and practices similar to slavery."[45] In response, the French Representative agreed that with the Vietnamese proposal, as the words 'any other form of servitude' "seemed to introduce a new concept into the Convention." Mr. Giraud continued:

> if the expression 'institutions and practices similar to slavery', which was terminologically more suitable, were adopted, allowance would have obviously to be made for the fact that that penalties foreseen by Article [6] could only be applied is so far as they institutions and practices mentioned in Article 1 became illegal in a country party to the convention.[46]

This theme was picked up by the Belgian Representative, Mr. Somerhausen who "pointed to an inconsistency between Article 1" and the provisions dealing with criminal offences as Article 1 required the progressive abolition, while the provisions of what would become Article 6 of the Supplementary Convention "did not allow for any lapse of time. This meant that the States Parties would [...] be under an immediate duty to punish persons who induced others to submit to practices similar to slavery, whereas under the particular

45 United Nations, Economic and Social Council, United Nations Conference of Plenipotentiaries on a Supplementary Convention on the Abolition of Slavery, the Slave Trade and Institutions and Practices Similar to Slavery, Summary Record of the Ninth Meeting, 21 August 1956, UN Doc E/CONF.24/SR.9, 13 November 1958, p. 3. Citation in the original omitted.

46 *Id.*, p. 4.

municipal law such acts would not yet be punishable offences."[47] What it also meant was that States consenting to the 1956 Supplementary Convention would be under an obligation to criminalise enslavement forthwith.

As there was some questions as to whether Articles 1 and 6 were contradictory, the Conference called on the Representative of the UN Legal Division, Mr. Schachter, to consider the issue. The Legal Advisor answered in the affirmative, stating that:

> The inconsistency arose only in connexion with the phrase 'or any other form of servitude'. The difficulty might be obviated by dividing Article [6] into two paragraphs, in the first of which slavery would be required to be made a criminal offence immediately, while in the second the provisions of the first paragraph would be made subject to the provisions of the introductory paragraph of Article 1.[48]

The President of the diplomatic Conference, then asked Mr. Schachter to submit a working draft on what a new, two paragraph, Article 6 might look like. That Working Paper,[49] though modified to some extent, came to be incorporated in the 1956 Supplementary Convention as the following – void of the term servitude:

1. The act of enslaving another person or of inducing another person to give himself or a person dependent upon him into slavery, or of attempting these acts, or being accessory thereto, or being a party to a conspiracy to accomplish any such acts, shall be a criminal offence under the laws of the States Parties to this Convention and persons convicted thereof shall be liable to punishment.
2. Subject to the provisions of the introductory paragraph of Article 1 of this Convention, the provisions of paragraph 1 of the present article shall also

47 *Id.*, p. 6.

48 United Nations, Economic and Social Council, United Nations Conference of Plenipotentiaries on a Supplementary Convention on the Abolition of Slavery, the Slave Trade and Institutions and Practices Similar to Slavery, Summary Record of the Tenth Meeting, 21 August 1956, UN Doc E/CONF.24/SR.10, 14 November 1958, p. 6.

49 United Nations, Economic and Social Council, United Nations Conference of Plenipotentiaries on a Supplementary Convention on the Abolition of Slavery, the Slave Trade and Institutions and Practices Similar to Slavery, Article 5 (Working paper prepared by the Secretariat at the request of the President), UN Doc E/CONF.24/L.19, 21 August 1956.

> apply to the act of inducing another person to place himself or a person dependent upon him into the servile status resulting from any of the institutions or practices mentioned in Article 1, to any attempt to perform such acts, to bring accessory thereto, and to being a party to a conspiracy to accomplish any such acts.[50]

The Suppressing of 'Servitude'

The suppression of the term 'servitude' as manifest in Article 6 which has just been recounted also took place with regard to other provisions of what would become the 1956 Supplementary Convention on the Abolition of Slavery, the Slave Trade and Institutions and Practices Similar to Slavery. As originally conceived by the United Kingdom in 1954, the convention was meant to deal with slavery and servitude. This was manifest in its Draft Convention, which was used as the basis of negotiations of the Supplementary Convention, and was entitled the *Draft Supplementary Convention on Slavery and Servitude.*[51] From April 1954 to April 1955 the UN Economic and Social Council requested comments from States on this British Draft Convention. In 1955, the Council established the *ad hoc* Committee on the Drafting of a Supplementary Convention on Slavery and Servitude, consisting of ten Member States of the Council, which was meant to, using the 1954 British Draft Convention as its basis, prepare a UN draft convention. Emerging from the discussions of the *ad hoc* Drafting Committee was a move away from using the term 'servitude' in the title. It did so, for reasons which appeared to be related the drafting of a legal instrument in a number of authentic languages. It was the Representative of the Soviet Union who noted that the title of the Convention "presented a linguistic difficulty" as slavery and servitude were covered by the same word in Russian, while his counterpart from Egypt noted that 'servitude' corresponded to 'serfdom' in Arabic. Mr. Nikolaev, the Representative of the Union of Soviet Socialist Republics, stated that as "the 1926 Convention spoke only of slavery, it

---

50 United Nations, Economic and Social Council, United Nations Conference of Plenipotentiaries on a Supplementary Convention on the Abolition of Slavery, the Slave Trade and Institutions and Practices Similar to Slavery, Final Act and Supplementary Convention, 4 September 1956, UN Doc E/CONF.24/23.

51 United Nations, Economic and Social Council, The Draft Supplementary Convention of Slavery and Servitude Submitted by the Government of the United Kingdom and Comments Thereon (Memorandum by the Secretary-General), UN Doc E/AC.43/L.1, 2 December 1955, p. 1.

might be logical, especially in view of the linguistic difficulty, to delete the reference to servitude from the title."

Yet, the Russian speaking representative of Yugoslavia, Mr. Bozovic, let the cat out of the bag stating "that Russian text of Article 4 of the Universal Declaration of Human Rights successfully drew a distinction between slavery and servitude."[52] This was followed by the Representative of Turkey, Mr. Benler, who stated, rather facetiously, that "Russian and Arabic were such developed vehicles of thought that it should surely be possible to convey the necessary shades of meaning" as between slavery and servitude.[53] The British Representative, Mr. Scott-Fox, for his part pointed to Article 4 of the Universal Declaration saying that it proclaimed "that 'no one shall be held in slavery or servitude'. There was therefore a valid precedent for the use of the term 'servitude'" in the title of convention.[54] For his part, the Chairman of the Drafting Committee, Mr. Cutts from Australia, noted that "the purpose of including servitude as well as slavery in the title had been to emphasize that the convention covered certain institutions and practices, such as those referred to in Article 1 which were not slavery in the strict sense."[55]

At the following meeting of the Drafting Committee, Mr. Nikolaev stuck to his guns, stating that as the "word 'servitude' had no equivalent in Russian, it would have to be translated by a paraphrase which either would unduly enlarge its meaning or else would be identical with a definition of slavery and would therefore be redundant." He then proposed two solutions, the first was to delete the term 'servitude' from the title, the second, was to title the convention, the '*Supplementary Convention on the Abolition of Slavery, the Slave Trade and Institutions and Practices Similar to Slavery*'.[56] As the British Representative noted, the first solution was not really a solution at all, as "the convention covered something more than slavery." For his part, the Yugoslav Representative was willing to accommodate the Russian proposal saying that the wording proposed by the Soviet Union was "more in conformity with the Committee's terms of reference" and thus should be accepted.

---

52 United Nations, Economic and Social Council, Committee on the Drafting of a Supplementary Convention on Slavery and Servitude, Summary Record of the Eight Meeting, 20 January 1956 UN Doc. E/AC.43/SR.8, 17 February 1956, p. 3.

53 *Id.*, p. 4.

54 *Id.*, p. 7.

55 *Id.*, p. 3.

56 United Nations, Economic and Social Council, Committee on the Drafting of a Supplementary Convention on Slavery and Servitude, Summary Record of the Ninth Meeting, 23 January 1956 UN Doc. E/AC.43/SR.9, 17 February 1956, p. 3.

The title of the Draft Convention, "as amended by the USSR, was adopted unanimously."[57]

The move by the Mr. Nikolaev to seek to change the title of the Draft Convention is not too difficult to discern. The Representative of the Union of Soviet Socialist Republics was not averse to the title put forward in the 1954 British Draft, that is: Draft Supplementary Convention on Slavery and Servitude; instead he sought to avoid the ramifications of a new title being put forward by the United Kingdom as part of a proposal to revise the title and the preamble. The new title being proposed was very much in line with the pronouncement of the Universal Declaration, as it read: "The Draft Convention on the *Abolition* of Slavery and Servitude."[58] During the discussions of the Drafting Committee, Mr. Nikolaev had prefaced his move to seek changes to the title of the Convention on the grounds of linguistic difficulties by saying that these linguistic difficulties emerged from the revised draft of the preamble and title put forward by the United Kingdom.[59] As the only change to the title was the inclusion of the term 'abolition', it is clear that it was not a linguistic difficult as between slavery and servitude which prompted the intervention but an issue of obligations which were to flow from the establishment of such a Supplementary Convention.

After it became clear what was at stake, both the Russian and Egyptian representative sought to expunge the term 'servitude' from the Convention fearing that, in line with Article 4 of the Universal Declaration, States would be required to abolish servitude forthwith; and not with the luxury of moving 'progressively and as soon as possible' toward abolition of servitudes. That attempt to rid the term 'servitude' from the content of the Supplementary Convention was not, it might be said, completely successful. This is so, as the only mention of 'servitude' to survive the drafting process and appear in the 1956 Supplementary Convention is to be found in the preamble by way of reference to the provisions of Article 4 of the Universal Declaration:

---

57 *Id.*, p. 4. Note that although discussions regarding the title took place, and proposals were made, during the 1956 the United Nations Conference of Plenipotentiaries, no changes were made to the title of the 1956 Supplementary Convention on the Abolition of Slavery, the Slave Trade and Institutions and Practices Similar to Slavery.

58 United Nations, Economic and Social Council, Committee on the Drafting of a Supplementary Convention on Slavery and Servitude, United Kingdom: Proposed title and preamble of the Draft Convention on the Abolition of Slavery and Servitude (E/2540/Add.4), UN Doc. E/AC.43/L.18, 19 January 1956. Emphasis added.

59 United Nations, Economic and Social Council, Committee on the Drafting of a Supplementary Convention on Slavery and Servitude, Summary Record of the Eight Meeting, 20 January 1956 UN Doc. E/AC.43/SR.8, 17 February 1956, p. 3.

> *Considering* that the Universal Declaration of Human Rights, proclaimed by the General Assembly of the United Nations as a common standard of achievement for all peoples and all nations, states that no one shall be held in slavery or servitude and that slavery and the slave trade shall be prohibited in all their forms;

As originally drafted in the 1954 British Draft Convention, the provision stated: "*Considering* that Article 4 of the Universal Declaration of Human Rights proclaims as one of the aims of the United Nations that no one shall be held in slavery or servitude."[60] The Egyptian Representative, Mr. Abdel-Ghani, "suggested the deletion of the reference to Article 4 because the Universal Declaration in fact contained several references to slavery and similar practices." This erroneous statement was dealt with in a most diplomatic fashion; taking a literal interpretation of Mr. Abdel-Ghani's words, the British Representative did not agree to the deletion of the paragraph, instead Mr. Scott-Fox simply "agreed that the words 'in Article 4' could be deleted."[61] Mr. Nikolaev thought the provision which mentioned servitude that ultimately found its way into the 1956 Convention was a "sweeping statement [...] which would appear to endorse all the aims mentioned in the Universal Declaration of Human Rights. It was only necessary to refer to one of those aims – one with which his Government was fully in agreement: the abolition of slavery and similar practices." Mr. Scott-Fox was unwilling to part with the reproduction of the provisions of Article 4 of the Universal Declaration, though at the same time sought to allay the fears of Mr. Nikolaev: "It is misleading to suggest," Mr. Scott-Fox said "that the Universal Declaration of Human Rights, in proclaiming that no one shall be held in slavery or servitude and that slavery and slave trade were prohibited in all their forms, was stating anything more than a general aim."[62]

Mr. Nikolaev, having failed to remove the reference to servitude as manifest in Article 4 of the Universal Declaration then turned his attention to the fourth paragraph of the preamble which had been revised by the British delegation during the discussions of the *ad hoc* Committee on the Drafting of a

---

60 See United Nations, Economic and Social Council, Slavery: Consultations Concerning the Desirability of a Supplementary Convention on Slavery and its Possible Contents, UN Doc E/2540/Add.4, 12 April 1954.

61 United Nations, Economic and Social Council, Committee on the Drafting of a Supplementary Convention on Slavery and Servitude, Summary Record of the Eight Meeting, 20 January 1956 UN Doc. E/AC.43/SR.8, 17 February 1956, p. 4.

62 *Id.*, p. 8.

Supplementary Convention on Slavery and Servitude to read: "*Being aware* slavery has not yet been eliminated in all parts of the world and that other forms of servitude of a similar nature still exist."[63] The Soviet Representative noted that this provision was "not consistent with existing world conditions" and, as a result, proposed the following text as an amendment: "Being aware, however, that slavery and institutions and practices associated therewith have not yet been eliminated in all parts of the world."[64] For his part, the French Representative, Mr. Giraud, moved to establish consistency in the text and said that the "preamble should employ the same expression as the title of the convention. He proposed that the use of the phrase 'Slavery and similar practices throughout'." That "the terminology used in the preamble should be that of the title of the convention" was agreed to by the British Representative, who put forward the following proposal, which was accepted and retained through the subsequent drafting process to appear in the preamble of the 1956 Supplementary Convention as: "Being aware, however, that slavery, the slave trade and practices similar to slavery have not yet been eliminated in all parts of the world."[65]

The shift from 'servitude' to 'institutions and practices similar to slavery' as a means of avoiding the obligation to abolition servitude in line with the Universal Declaration looked to have been successful during the negotiation which transpired under the auspices of the Economic and Social Council's Committee on the Drafting of a Supplementary Convention on Slavery and Servitude in early 1956; however, the term 'servitude' reared its ugly head once more in late 1956, at the United Nations Conference of Plenipotentiaries on a Supplementary Convention on the Abolition of Slavery, the Slave Trade and Institutions and Practices Similar to Slavery, where the question was raised as to whether the term 'servitude', as it appeared in the preamble, should be defined.[66]

---

63 United Nations, Economic and Social Council, Committee on the Drafting of a Supplementary Convention on Slavery and Servitude, United Kingdom: Proposed title and preamble of the Draft Convention on the Abolition of Slavery and Servitude (E/2540/Add.4), UN Doc. E/AC.43/L.18, 19 January 1956.

64 United Nations, Economic and Social Council, Committee on the Drafting of a Supplementary Convention on Slavery and Servitude, Summary Record of the Eight Meeting, 20 January 1956 UN Doc. E/AC.43/SR.8, 17 February 1956, p. 8.

65 *Id.*, p. 9.

66 See United Nations, Economic and Social Council, United Nations Conference of Plenipotentiaries on a Supplementary Convention on the Abolition of Slavery, the Slave Trade and Institutions and Practices Similar to Slavery, Summary Record of the Twentieth Meeting, 30 August 1956, UN Doc E/CONF.24/SR.20, 20 November 1958, p. 3.

This prompted Mr. Sommehausen, the Representative of Belgium, to say that:

> The legal terms used in the articles should be clear so that they would not give rise to controversy; but the expressions used in the preamble were used in their ordinary meaning, and hence did not have to be defined. If the word 'servitude' was thought to require definition, he would propose that it be deleted rather than a new definition be inserted in Article [7].[67]

Mr. Jafri, the Representative of India, who had broached the question, responded saying that "there was no hard and fast rule for defining words which appeared only in the preamble," but that he did "not think that a separate definition was necessary in the case at issue as the paragraph was in essence a quotation from the Universal Declaration of Human Rights and the word 'servitude' was used in that same sense as it was in the Declaration."[68]

Despite this, a move to establish a definition of 'servitude' was undertaken during the diplomatic conference, though that definition did not find its way into the final text. The introduction and then exclusion of a definition of 'servitude' transpired not as a result of the discussions touching on the preamble, but on those touching on the notion of 'a persons of servile status', a term which would ultimately be included in the Supplementary Convention. In 1951, the *Ad Hoc* Committee on Slavery established by the United Nations Economic and Social Council sought to make the distinction between slavery and the slave trade on the one hand and servitude on the other. The Committee, after considering the 'definitions of slavery' and the 'slave trade' went on to say that "it was questionable whether these definitions embrace all the types of servile status the abolition of which, in its opinion, should be promoted by the United Nations." It continued:

> It took note of information received from many sources which indicated that other forms of servitude, in addition to slavery and the slave trade, existed to a considerable extent in many portions of the world. When it attempted to define these forms of servitude, it discovered that a great deal of confusion had arisen because different names were applied to

---

67 *Id.*

68 United Nations, Economic and Social Council, United Nations Conference of Plenipotentiaries on a Supplementary Convention on the Abolition of Slavery, the Slave Trade and Institutions and Practices Similar to Slavery, Summary Record of the Twentieth Meeting, 31 August 1956, UN Doc E/CONF.24/SR.21, 20 November 1958, p. 2.

> these practices in different regions of the world, and even in different countries. It therefore discarded the existing nomenclature for the time being, and instead attempted to describe these forms of servitude be reference to their particular characteristics.[69]

While the Committee went on to define debt bondage, serfdom, various forms of forced marriage and the exploitation of children, it did not consider the term to be used for those who became subject to such exploitation. The notion of 'a person of servile status' would emerge during the 1956 diplomatic Conference negotiating the Supplementary Convention. It was within this context that a definition of 'servitude' was mooted. The genesis of the definition of 'a person of servile status' is to be found in an article of the 1954 British Draft Convention dealing with mutilation or branding, which read, in "a country where the abolition of servile status is not yet complete, any person who mutilates, brands or otherwise marks another person to indicate that status, and any person accessory to such an act, shall be guilty of a criminal offence and liable to punishment."[70] The United Nations Secretary-General in considering this provision suggested that "the relevant provision of Article 3 might be reworded in such a way as to replace the phrase 'servile status':

> In a country where the abolition of slavery or of the institutions or practices mentioned in Article 1 of the Convention is not yet complete, any person who mutilates, brands or otherwise marks another person to indicate that status of slavery or the condition arising from either of those institutions or practices, and any person accessory to such an act, shall be guilty of a criminal offence and liable to punishment".[71]

During the meeting of the Economic and Social Council's *ad hoc* Committee on the Drafting of a Supplementary Convention on Slavery and Servitude in 1956, the French Representative put forward the Secretary-General's suggestion,

---

69 United Nations, Economic and Social Council, Report of the *Ad Hoc* Committee on Slavery (Second Session), UN Doc E/1988, E/AC.33/13, 4 May 1951, p. 8.

70 See United Nations, Economic and Social Council, Slavery: Consultations Concerning the Desirability of a Supplementary Convention on Slavery and its Possible Contents, UN Doc E/2540/Add.4, 12 April 1954.

71 United Nations, Economic and Social Council, The Draft Supplementary Convention of Slavery and Servitude Submitted by the Government of the United Kingdom and Comments Thereon (Memorandum by the Secretary-General), UN Doc E/AC.43/L.1, 2 December 1955, p. 32.

saying "that it was somewhat confusing to use the term 'servile status' to refer collectively to slavery and to analogous institutions."[72] Despite this, the revised text, in line with Secretary-General's suggestions, was adopted unanimously by the Drafting Committee,[73] which read:

> In this Article 'person of servile status' means any slave or any person who has a servile status resulting from any of the institutions or practices mentioned in Article 1 of this Convention.[74]

At the United Nations Conference of Plenipotentiaries in 1956, it was suggested that the provision regarding persons of servile status be decoupled from the provisions dealing with mutilation or branding and be incorporated in a stand-alone article of definitions.[75] This was followed by a proposal by Pakistan which sought to define servitude. It read in part:

> For the purpose of the present Convention, the following definitions are agreed upon:
> [...]
> (c) *Person of servile status* means any slave or any person who has a servile status resulting from any of the institutions or practices mentioned in Article 3 [present Article 2] of this Convention;
> (d) *Servitude* is the status of a slave or of a person of servile status; [...][76]

---

72 United Nations, Economic and Social Council, Committee on the Drafting of a Supplementary Convention on Slavery and Servitude, Summary Record of the Twelve Meeting, 24 January 1956, UN Doc. E/AC.43/SR.12, 20 February 1956, p. 9.

73 See United Nations, Economic and Social Council, Committee on the Drafting of a Supplementary Convention on Slavery and Servitude, Summary Record of the Fourteenth Meeting, 25 January 1956, UN Doc. E/AC.43/SR.14, 29 February 1956, p. 3.

74 United Nations, Economic and Social Council, Committee on the Drafting of a Supplementary Convention on Slavery and Servitude, United Kingdom of Great Britain and Northern Ireland: Suggested redraft of Article 5, UN Doc. E/AC.43/L.31/Rev.1, 25 January 1956.

75 See United Nations, Economic and Social Council, United Nations Conference of Plenipotentiaries on a Supplementary Convention on the Abolition of Slavery, the Slave Trade and Institutions and Practices Similar to Slavery, Portugal: Amendments to Articles 3 and 4 and Proposal for a New Article, UN Doc E/CONF.24/L.14, 21 August 1956.

76 United Nations, Economic and Social Council, United Nations Conference of Plenipotentiaries on a Supplementary Convention on the Abolition of Slavery, the Slave Trade and Institutions and Practices Similar to Slavery, Pakistan: Proposal for a New Article, UN Doc E/CONF.24/L.31, 28 August 1956.

However, objections were quickly raised to the term 'servitude'. Mr. Jay, the Canadian Representative, stated that "the word 'servitude' no longer appeared in the draft articles adopted at the first reading, so that paragraph (d) might be omitted."[77] Mr. Jafri, the Representative of Pakistan acknowledged this saying that "the word 'servitude' had been used in paragraph (d) to cover both slavery and the institutions and practices similar to slavery defined in Article 1 of the draft supplementary convention. If, however, the word 'servitude' no longer appeared in the final draft of the other articles, the paragraph might well be deleted." It was, however, left to a drafting committee working on the overall provisions of, what would become Article 7 incorporating definitions to "revise the Pakistan text and report back to the Conference."[78] At the next meeting, the *ad hoc* Drafting Committee on Definitions made its recommendations which included the following: that the Conference adopted a text which included the following provisions touching on servile status:

> With regard to the definition of 'servile status', the Drafting Committee had decided that the definition should be confined to the narrow meaning of that term and had rejected that suggestion made by the Pakistan delegation at an earlier meeting that it should also include slavery.
>
> The Drafting Committee had also decided to omit the definition of 'servitude' since the word no longer appeared in any article of the draft supplementary convention.[79]

What thus emerged from the Conference to be incorporated into Article 7, beyond the definitions of slavery and the slave trade as established by the 1926 Slavery Convention, was a definition of 'A person of servile status', which "means a person in the condition or status resulting from any of the institutions or practices mentioned in Article 1 of this Convention."[80]

---

77 United Nations, Economic and Social Council, United Nations Conference of Plenipotentiaries on a Supplementary Convention on the Abolition of Slavery, the Slave Trade and Institutions and Practices Similar to Slavery, Summary Record of the Eighteenth Meeting, 29 August 1956, UN Doc E/CONF.24/SR.18, 19 November 1958, p. 11.

78 *Id.*, p. 12. The Committee consisted of representatives of Belgium, Cuba, France, Pakistan and Portugal.

79 United Nations, Economic and Social Council, United Nations Conference of Plenipotentiaries on a Supplementary Convention on the Abolition of Slavery, the Slave Trade and Institutions and Practices Similar to Slavery, Summary Record of the Nineteenth Meeting, 29 August 1956, UN Doc E/CONF.24/SR.19, 19 November 1958, p. 17.

80 United Nations, Economic and Social Council, United Nations Conference of Plenipotentiaries on a Supplementary Convention on the Abolition of Slavery, the Slave Trade

Conclusion

In 1956, international human rights law did not exist. Yet, it was the 1948 Universal Declaration of Human Rights which loomed large in the considerations of those drafting the 1956 Supplementary Convention. Article 4 of the Universal Declaration, which set as a common standard of achievement that no one shall be held in servitude created an awkward situation for those drafting an instrument that sought to abolish servitude but who were only willing to move toward its outlawing 'progressively and as soon as possible'. The solution was to expunge the very term of 'servitude' from a convention which was originally conceived as the Draft Supplementary Convention on Slavery and *Servitude*, but came into force as the 1956 Supplementary Convention on the Abolition of Slavery, the Slave Trade and *Institutions and Practices Similar to Slavery*.

This study has considered the drafting history of Article 4 of the Universal Declaration of Human Rights and its impact on the negotiations of the 1956 Supplementary Convention on the Abolition of Slavery, the Slave Trade and Institutions and Practices Similar to Slavery. The penny dropped when the United Kingdom proposed that the instrument be called The Draft Convention on the *Abolition* of Slavery and Servitude. From this point onwards the Representative of the Soviet Union sought to ensure that there was a clear break between the Universal Declaration conception of servitude which required immediate abolition and something new: 'institutions and practices similar to slavery' which could be outlawed progressively and as soon as possible.

As it turned out, the primary task was to get agreement on the title, which Mr. Nikolaev achieved during a session of the 1956 Economic and Social Council's Committee on the Drafting of a Supplementary Convention on Slavery and Servitude, wherein his proposed title: *Supplementary Convention on the Abolition of Slavery, the Slave Trade and Institutions and Practices Similar to Slavery*, was adopted. Thereafter, it was rather easy 'for the sake of consistency', to expunge the term 'servitude' from the Convention; but for the gentle reminder which remains in the preamble, that the Universal Declaration holds that no one should be held in servitude.

The unwillingness of States to abolish servitude outright in 1956, lead to the concept of 'servitude' being manifest in public international law through the 1956 Supplementary Convention as 'institutions and practices similar to

---

and Institutions and Practices Similar to Slavery, Final Act and Supplementary Convention, 4 September 1956, UN Doc E/CONF.24/23.

slavery'; and in international human rights law as servitude, with as its source the Universal Declaration of Human Rights' Article 4. This fragmentation of the concept of servitude as between the 1956 Supplementary Convention and international human rights law is recognised in the both the 2001 United Nations and 2005 Council of European instruments related to human trafficking, where examples of exploitation including both 'practices similar to slavery' and 'servitude'.

What this study has sought to show is that this fragmentation resulted, not from the normative understanding of the concept, but from the obligations which might flow from its suppression. As such, where, in contemporary situations, issues of human exploitation are at issue, judges should not hesitate to apply the normative understanding of the law, be it on the basis of general international law in the 1956 Supplementary Convention and its institutions and practices similar to slavery or on the basis of international human rights law and its notion of servitude.

CHAPTER 15

Sham Adoption: The DNA of a Conventional Servitude

The 1956 Supplementary Convention sets out four conventional servitudes. The Convention itself categorises the first two servitudes as 'Debt Bondage' and 'Serfdom', but fails to label the two which follow. While the third servitude has come to be recognised under the term of art 'Servile Marriage', the final provision has yet to settle on a fixed term. *Mea cupla*: I have created some confusion by terming these provisions in my 2008 *The Slavery Conventions* as 'Child Exploitation' and referring to the same provisions under the heading of 'Child Trafficking' in my 2013 *Slavery in International Law*.

This chapter sets out the DNA of that conventional servitude and demonstrates that the fourth conventional servitude found within the 1956 Supplementary Convention should be given the common designation of 'sham adoption', a term utilised within the negotiation process as early as 1926. As will become clear, the provisions related to sham adoption found in the 1956 Convention are rather obscure or ambiguous, as a result international law prescribes recourse to the preparatory work so as to determine their meaning. In considering the legislative history set out in this chapter, it is evident that these provisions are meant to apply specifically to adoptions which were detrimental to the welfare of the child.

To bring this understanding into the Twenty-First Century would be to consider the specific provisions related to sham adoption to apply – whether *de jure* or *de facto* – where they transpired against the touchstone of the Convention on the Right of the Child, that is: against the best interest of the child.

Before consideration the legislative history, it is worthwhile settling out the provisions related to sham adoption. The 1956 Supplementary Convention on the Abolition of Slavery, the Slave Trade and Institutions and Practices Similar to Slavery sets out, at Article 1, four so-called 'institutions and practices similar to slavery' or what are often referred to in the literature in abbreviated form as 'practices similar to slavery'. I have shown elsewhere that these should, in fact, and in law, be understood as, and thus termed as: conventional servitudes. Article 1 of the 1956 Convention recognised that these servitudes should be complete abolished or abandoned whether or not such practices fell under the 1956 Convention as servitudes or where such practice were in fact, and thus in

 | DOI 10.1163/9789004279896_017

law, "covered by the definition of slavery contained in article 1 of the Slavery Convention." Beyond debt bondage, serfdom, servile marriage, the provision related to sham adoption read:

> Any institution or practice whereby a child or young person under the age of 18 years is delivered by either or both of his natural parents or by his guardian to another person, whether for reward or not, with a view to the exploitation of the child or young person or of his labour.

While I have also demonstrated elsewhere that, by their very definitions, both serfdom and the servile marriages are slavery in law, as those definitions as written constitute the exercise of a powers attaching to the right of ownership, this does not hold with regard to debt bondage nor sham adoption. Here then, we consider the DNA of sham adoption.[1]

During the League of Nations Era

The genesis of suppression of sham adoption in international law develops tangentially from the desire to abolition slavery and the slave trade during the early years of the League of Nations. The issue of slavery was rather easy to confront for the League of Nations, as a dichotomy existed between the League Members as being 'civilised nations' where slavery did not exist and the 'uncivilised nations' those not considered worthy of admission to the League, where slavery persisted and where the fight could be taken.[2] In 1922, the Assembly of the League of Nations decided "to refer to the appropriate Committee the question of the recurrence of slavery in Africa in order that it be considered and propose the best methods for combating the evil."[3] One year later, a subcommittee of the Assembly having received little feedback on a questionnaire sent to States dealing with issues of slavery, sought to have the Council of the

1 See Jean Allain, *Slavery in International Law: Of Human Exploitation and Trafficking*, 2013, pp. 143–203.

2 See Jean Allain, "Slavery and the League of Nations: Ethiopia as a Civilised Nation," *Journal of the History of International Law*, Vol. 8, 2006, pp. 213–244. [As reproduced in Chapter 4 of this volume.]

3 League of Nations, Motion Proposed by Sir Arthur Steel-Maitland, Delegate for New Zealand, on 7 September 1922, Third Assembly of the League of Nations, 7 September 1922, LofN Doc. 23253 (A/47/1922).

League "entrust to a competent body the duty of continuing the investigation [of the question of slavery] with a view to obtaining further information on the subject."[4]

As a result, the Council of the League of Nations created, on 14 March 1924, the Temporary Slavery Commission, a body that would exist for only two years but would fundamentally change the emphasis of the League's work in the area of slavery from seeking to compile information to establishing legal standards for the suppression of both slavery and the slave trade – but not servitudes.

The Temporary Slavery Commission, in its final report of 1925, considered the issue of the 'enslaving of persons disguised as the adoption of children', focusing on practices which persisted in Africa and Asia. In Africa, the Report, reflecting the colonial language of the day stated that:

> households in which there are no children – or in which the children have grown up – are [...] generally eager to procure children to act as household drudges. Care must therefore be taken when freed-slave or other children are place with native families to see that they are not practically enslaved – a possibility the more likely as they are held in native opinion to be of the slave status.

With regard to Asia, the Commission simply highlighted the existence of a "system of procuring children for so-called 'adoption' [...] as, for instance, in China, Hong-Kong, and the Straits Settlements under the name *Mui Tsai*."[5]

In its 1925 Report, the Temporary Slavery Commission recommended that an international instrument be prepared which would *inter alia*, "confer on domestic courts the jurisdiction necessary to repress child enslavement, be it through adoption or other means."[6] As consideration was given to the drafting of what would become the 1926 Slavery Convention, the issue of lesser servitudes than slavery emerged. It had been proposed that States not only suppress the slave trade, but to "bring about progressively and as soon as possible the

4 League of Nations, Report of the First Sub-Committee to the Sixth Committee, Record of the Fourth Assembly, Meetings of the Committees, VI Minutes of the Sixth Committee (Political Questions), Annex 10, p. 40.

5 League of Nations, Temporary Slavery Commission, Report of the Temporary Slavery Commission adopted in the Course of its Second Session, 13–25 July 1925, A.19.1925. VI, 25 July 1925, p. 8.

6 League of Nations, Temporary Slavery Commission, Letter from the Chairman of the Commission to the President of the Council, A.19.1925. VI, 25 July 1925, p. 2.

disappearance of slavery in every form, notably in the case of domestic slavery and similar conditions."[7] When the Rapporteur in charge of the draft process reported to the Assembly of the League of Nations, he stated that the notion of 'similar conditions' was meant to "include all forms of debt slavery, the enslaving of persons disguised as the adoption of children, and the acquisition of girls by purchase disguised as payment of dowry, etc. as mention in the report of the Temporary Slavery Commission."[8] The Rapporteur stated that such similar conditions "approach very close to and are, in fact a form of slavery, but are not usually included in the simple term slavery."[9] For its part, Germany, in seeking to include lesser servitudes into the 1926 Convention, utilised the term *sham adoption* for the first time. The German Delegate propose a new subparagraph, saying that a number of 'conditions resembling slavery' existed and these could be addressed by accepting the following amendment: "To endeavour, as far as possible, to bring about the disappearance of conditions of servitude resembling slavery, *e.g.*, debt slavery, sham adoption, childhood marriage, traffic in women, etc."[10]

Yet, the inclusion of 'the enslaving of persons disguised as the adoption of children' as a 'similar condition' or a 'condition resembling slavery' did not find its way into the 1926 Slavery Convention. Having negotiated a Draft Convention in early 1926, the League of Nations requested comments from States as to the content of what was being proposed. The Union of South Africa responded, saying that the proposal to include the phrase 'notably in the case of domestic slavery and similar conditions' extended the scope of the Draft Convention by going beyond abolition of slavery and the slave trade, as a result moved that this clause be deleted. South Africa made the argument that either individuals are a slave as defined by Article 1(1) – that is: 'a person over whom any or all of the powers attaching to the right of ownership are exercised' – or they are not. Thus, if individuals "become domestic slaves or persons in similar conditions [...] that can only be because others have acquired a right of property in them,

7 League of Nations, Annex: Draft Convention, League of Nations Official Journal (Special Supplement 33) Records of the Sixth Assembly: Text of Debates, 26 September 1925, p. 439.

8 League of Nations, Question of Slavery: Report of the Sixth Committee; Resolution, League of Nations Official Journal (Special Supplement 33) Records of the Sixth Assembly: Text of Debates, Nineteenth Plenary Meeting, 26 September 1925, p. 156. Emphasis added.

9 *Id.*, p. 156.

10 League of Nations, Draft Convention on Slavery and Proposed Amendments, A.VI/ S.C.1/1, 10 September 1926; as found in Folder R.77.D.46781 entitled Draft Convention on Slavery: Discussion at the 7th Assembly; 1926.

and they are therefore slaves as defined in Article 1."[11] If not, then such 'similar conditions' would not amount to slavery and thus should be excluded from the definition of slavery.

Using the approach of the Union of South African then, with regard to discussions of the Temporary Slavery Commission on the enslaving of children disguised as adoption, it is clear that such enslavement would meet the threshold of the definition of slavery found in Article 1 and would therefore be considered as 'slavery'; not the lesser 'domestic slavery and similar conditions'. The reverse also being true, that if a false adoption did not create a slave of a child, then it did not meet the threshold of the definition of slavery as per Article 1.

With a limited number of States becoming party to the 1926 Slavery Convention in the direct aftermath of its coming in to force, it was felt by some delegations that the Temporary Slavery Commission should be revived. Hesitation by other Members of the League of Nations, however, meant that it took until 1931 for agreement to be reached on the newly formed *ad hoc* Committee of Experts on Slavery. The reports of the Committee of Experts followed the same format as that of the Temporary Slavery Commission, so that the issue of enslavement disguised as adoption once more found itself on the international agenda. The Committee of Experts reported that as of 1931, "adoption was a current practice in the Far East and Oceania, but appears to be less common in Africa." The Committee turned its attention China where it was alleged that "adoption is frequently deprived of its true character in such a way as to amount to real enslavement" and that this may be the distinction between true adoption and *Mui Tsai*.[12]

However, the Committee noted that it was not in a position to "contest or to confirm these assertions," but did give further consideration to the system of *Mui Tsai* under the heading of slave-dealing:

---

11 League of Nations, Draft Convention on Slavery, Replies of Governments, Reply from the Government of the Union of South Africa, A.10(a).1926.VI, 22 July 1926, p. 5; as found in League of Nations, Publications of the League of Nations, VI.B. Slavery.1926, VI.B.3.

12 League of Nations, Slavery: Report of the Committee of Experts on Slavery provided by the Assembly Resolution of 25 September 1931, C. 618.1932. VI, 1 September 1932, p. 17.

Note that The Committee reported that the *Mui Tsai* system was:

> not confined to the territories under the sovereignty of the Chinese Republic; it is also practiced in the European Concession in China and, in particular, in the International Concessions of Shanghai and Kulangsu, as well as at Hong-Kong, the Straits Settlements and the Malay States, both Federated and Unfederated, and in Borneo.

See League of Nations, Slavery: Report of the Committee of Experts on Slavery provided by the Assembly Resolution of 25 September 1931, C. 618.1932. VI, 1 September 1932, p. 16.

> While it is certain that a large number of children, especially females – who, if they are not really adopted, are known as 'Mui Tsai' – are placed by their parents with others persons, generally in return for a money payment to the parents and the obligation to support the child, the nature of the contract and the rights which it confers on the person with whom the children are place are not very clear. Some regard it as a real sale of the child. The lot of such children, they add, is particularly wretched, since apart from being neglected and overworked, which alone entails the cruellest bodily suffering, they are often, it would appear, victims of the depraved instincts of their employers, or of person with whom the latter bring them into contact, and sometimes also of acts of revolting cruelty.[13]

The Chinese delegation contested this understanding and it appeared that there was a genuine divergence of opinion on the nature of *Mui Tsai*. This led the Committee of Experts on Slavery to "wonder whether this difference of opinion is not due to a misunderstanding. May it not be the case that, side by side with the *Mui Tsai* system there is a clandestine traffic in young girls in China, as in other countries, for the purposed of prostitution?"[14] If this were the case, then parents, in sending their daughters to the city, were having their confidence – and daughters – abused by having them placed in brothels.

The *ad hoc* Committee of Experts on Slavery was replaced in 1934 by permanent Advisory Committee of Experts on Slavery which, in 1935, once more considered the *Mui Tsai* system. Like in the 1932 Report, the Advisory Committee of Experts on Slavery dealt with the issue under the heading of slave-dealing and took the opportunity to summarised the difference of opinion expressed Committee of Experts on Slavery in the following terms:

> in the opinion of some, a *Mui Tsai* is really sold, other consider that the master of the *Mui Tsai* only acquires the right of receiving services in proportion to her age and capabilities in return for the obligations to feed and educate her and sometimes to pay in advances a certain sum to her parents.[15]

The Advisory Committee, like its predecessor, did not feel it had enough information to make a determination as to nature of *Mui Tsai* system, however, it

---

13 *Id.*, p. 15.

14 *Id.*, p. 16.

15 League of Nations, Slavery: Report of the Advisory Committee of Experts, Second Session of the Committee, C.159. M.113.1935.VI, 10 April 1935, p. 15.

took issue with the statement made a Chinese Delegate to the Sixth Committee of the Assembly which "shows that a master does not possess an absolute right of ownership over the *Mui Tsai* but that his relationship is rather that of a guardian towards a minor." "Consequently," the Committee noted "the master has rights over the *Mui Tsai*, not completely alien to the right of ownership." As a result, the Advisory Committee of Experts on Slavery called on the Chinese Government to provide it with "precise information which will enable it to form an exact idea of the nature of the rights which, under Chinese law, the master acquires over the Mui Tsai."[16] The Advisory Committee then continued:

> In the Committee's eyes, if the master had any right of ownership or an actual right of pledge over the child, the radical suppression of this legal system would be essential and should be undertaken without delay.
>
> It would be different if the actual legal situation was that of a kind of delegation by the parents of the exercise of their paternal authority over the child and of their obligations towards it. In such a case the Committee would not regard this system as contrary to human liberty; it would doubtless be open to criticism – but from another point of view – should that delegation of authority not be revocable *ad nudum* [re: lost of rights upon transfer] on the part of the parents and especially should the Mui Tsai's master have a right to keep her as long as the sum paid in advance to the parents, or owing by the latter to the creditor, had not be refunded in whole or in part.
>
> While, however, the Committee does not in any respect regard as slavery the delegation by parents of their paternal authority to third parties, it is nevertheless of opinion that such delegation may actually give rise to many grave abuses on the part of unscrupulous persons, when such powers are delegated to them, and that measures are required to prevent those abuses.[17]

In its 1936 Report, the Advisory Committee of Experts on Slavery received some information from the Chinese delegation to the League of Nations including the fact that new regulations had come into force in January 1936 which prohibited the keeping of *Mui Tsai*. The Committee reported that for those *Mui Tsai* who had not attained the age of consent, they were to be "returned to their families or entrusted to local relief homes," and if they had

16 *Id.*, p. 15.

17 *Id.*, p. 15.

researched the age of consent, they were to be liberated, with the possibility of then being employed by their former masters.[18] This was followed, in 1937 Report by a consideration by the Committee of the very term *Mui Tsai* which the China noted had been used in its legislation due to its common appearance in League material. For its part, the Committee noted that the term *Mui Tsai* "may be translated as 'Little Sister' is a colloquial or slang expression in the Cantonese dialect"; but that the "correct official expression in the mandarin dialect is *Nu Pi* or *Pi Nu* and that both expressions are accurately translated as 'slave-girl'."[19]

In the final Report of the Advisory Committee of Experts on Slavery, presented in 1938, the Committee explained how *Mui Tsai* functioned:

> Under this system, young girls are transferred by their parents to other persons for employment in domestic service until they reach an age when they can marry. When they are married, they are under no further obligation to their employers. In almost every case some money is paid in consideration of the transfer. Occasionally, it happens that a child is transferred as a free gift. Sometimes there is an intermediary or broker, who takes the child from the parents and later transfers her to the employer. In some cases, the child or young girl is definitely sold: in other cases, the parties to the transaction regard the money payment as a consideration for the transfer of the child's service in domestic employment.[20]

In seeking to make suggestions as to how to remedy the *Mui Tsai* system, the Committee was at pains to emphasise that it was not stepping beyond its mandate of considering issues of slavery:

> When a girl is only a victim of a transfer, and not necessarily a 'slave', she does not come under the Committee's notice. Often she is both a 'slave' and a victim of a transfer. This is the point which the Committee wishes to establish. It is one of the greatest importance, for it sets in its proper perspective the special problem of the 'girl-slave', with the far larger problem of the 'transferred child'. The Committee is not in a position at present to

18 League of Nations, Slavery, Report of the Advisory Committee of Experts, Third (Extraordinary) Session of the Committee, C.189(I).M.145.1936, VI, 15 May 1936, p. 26.

19 League of Nations, Slavery: Report of the Advisory Committee of Experts, Fourth Session of the Committee, C.188. M.173.1937. VI, 19 April 1937, p. 15.

20 League of Nations, Slavery: Report of the Advisory Committee of Experts, Fifth (Extraordinary) Session of the Committee, C.112. M.98.1938. VI, 5 April 1938, p. 11.

> do more than enunciate a proposition, which will require the most careful consideration.[21]

That proposition, was based on the practice of the British Straits Settlements Government (re: modern day Malaysia and Singapore), that such practice should be outlawed, "whether the child has been transferred for adoption, or quasi-adoption, whether she is a ward, a servant, a labourer under 'contract' or whether she is destined to become a prostitute," with the emphasis being made as to the age of the child and whether the transfer was made via the proper authorities.[22]

Thus, as we shall see, the provisions which would make their way into the 1956 Supplementary Convention where meant to apply to transfer of children, which is wider in scope than 'girl-slave', wherein "the child has been transferred for adoption, or quasi-adoption." As we shall see as we consider the United Nations era, the emphasis of such sham adoptions, is predicated on such transfers where it goes against the welfare of the child.

The United Nations Era

In a 1949 Resolution, the United Nations Economic and Social Council instructed the Secretary-General to appoint an *ad hoc* committee to, *inter alia*, "survey the field of slavery and other institutions and customs resembling slavery."[23] In setting out the terms of reference of the *Ad Hoc* Committee on Slavery, the Secretary-General noted that the "question as to what are the institutions or customs resembling slavery is one of great complexity." The Secretary-General then asked the Committee, in undertaking its survey, to consider whether such institutions or customs resembling slavery should be included in "a new convention on slavery."[24] Where child exploitation was concerned, *Ad Hoc* Committee on Slavery recommended, in 1951, that the abolition of "the practice whereby a child is transferred by its parents or guardians

21 League of Nations, Slavery: Report of the Advisory Committee of Experts, Fifth (Extraordinary) Session of the Committee, C.112. M.98.1938. VI, 5 April 1938, p. 15.

22 *Id.*, p. 15.

23 United Nations, Economic and Social Council, Resolution 238(IX), 20 July 1949.

24 United Nations, Economic and Social Council, Notes on the Terms of Reference of the Ad Hoc Committee on Slavery (Memorandum submitted by the Secretary-General), UN Doc. E/AC.33/4, 3 February 1950, pp. 3 and 6.

to a third party on payment or under conditions permitting the exploitation of the child regardless of its welfare."[25] The Committee explained its inclusion of these provisions in the following manner:

> The Committee next turned to the practice, particularly prevalent in the Far East, which in some localities is know as *mui tsai*. This involves the sale of a child's working capacity and usually takes the form of the transfer of a small child, usually a girl, for employment as a domestic servant by means of an adoption procedure, sometimes fraudulent. The custom has been known to exist under other names in other regions of the world, including parts of Africa. The Committee recognized that in many cases an element of servitude may not be involved. Often the parents of the child affect such a transfer in what they believe to be the best interests of the child. The Committee therefore felt that a status or condition of servitude existed only when the conditions of the transfer were such as to permit the exploitation of the child regardless of its welfare. The Committee was aware of the fact that in many areas there has been a great deal of recent legislation on this subject, and that some of the laws have integrated these measures in such a way with other measures for the protection of children as to make them particularly effective. It expressed the hope that similar legislation might be considered favourably by the governments of those countries in whose territories the practice exists.[26]

In 1954, the United Kingdom, responding to the consultation process undertaken by the United Nations Secretary-General with a look to establishing supplementary convention, by putting forward a draft convention which included the following provisions on through sham adoption:

> any institution or practice whereby a child or young person is delivered by either or both his natural parents or his guardian to another person, whether for reward or note, under conditions which permit that person to exploit the child or young person or his or her labour; except that this

25 Economic and Social Council, Report of the *Ad Hoc* Committee on Slavery (Second Session), UN Doc E/1988, E/AC.33/13, 4 May 1951, p. 20.

26 Economic and Social Council, Slavery: Consultations Concerning the Desirability of a Supplementary Convention on Slavery and its Possible Contents, UN Doc E/2540/Add.4, 12 April 1954, p. 10.

> Article shall not be construed so as to prohibit or hinder bona fide adoptions intended to promote the welfare of children or young persons.[27]

In making reference to the pronouncement of the *Ad Hoc* Committee on Slavery, the United Kingdom provided comments which it noted applied to the provisions it put forward on sham adoption, but also those related to servile marriage spelled out in Article 1(c) of its Draft Convention:

> Her Majesty's Government are firmly convinced of the necessity of abolishing as early as possible the practices whereby the persons of women and children are disposed of without their consent. It is however their view, based on experience, that attempts to abolish long established customs and practices of any kind, including such practices as these, can only lead to the disintegration of the local social structures unless they are carried out gradually, with extensive educational preparations and with full regard to the wishes and feelings of the local inhabitants. They therefore believe that the proposed convention should provide that the contracting parties should undertaken all practical measures, including legislation where appropriate, to bring the institutions or practices defined to an end progressively and as sooner as possible.[28]

With regard to the issue of the exploitation of children through adoption, the United Nations Secretary-General, in a Memorandum collating the comments made on the 1954 British Draft Convention, noted that the Haiti acknowledged that such practice, by which children of 'peasants' were by custom often 'adopted' by 'townspeople', but stated that laws had been put in place to prevent "malpractices." The Haitian Government concluded that, as a result of such laws, it had no objection to the adoption of the draft, "subject to drafting changes."[29]

---

27 *Id.*, p. 3.

28 Economic and Social Council, Committee on the Drafting of a Supplementary Convention on Slavery and Servitude, Summary Record of the Third Meeting, 17 January 1956, UN Doc. E/AC.43/SR.3, 9 February 1956, p. 3.

29 Economic and Social Council, The Draft Supplementary Convention of Slavery and Servitude Submitted by the Government of the United Kingdom and Comments Thereon (Memorandum by the Secretary-General), UN Doc E/AC.43/L.1, 2 December 1955, pp. 24–25. Note the issue of restavèk in Haiti considered contemporaneously in the *Report of the Special Rapporteur on Contemporary Forms of Slavery, including its Causes and Consequences, Gulnara Shahinian*, Addendum: Mission to Haiti, UN Doc. A/HRC/12/21/Add.1, 4 September 2009.

Turning to the substance of the proposal article, the International Organizations Committee of the International Labour Organization noted that "it was for consideration whether the last phrase, 'except that this Article shall not be construed so as to prohibit or hinder *bona fide* adoption intended to promote the welfare of children and young persons' should be retained." The ILO Committee continued:

> If the phrase were retained, the effect might well be that contrary to that intended that it might condone many adoptions, still practiced, which were contrary to long-term interest of the child or young person. It could be argued that the adoption of children of impoverished parents who had not the means to feed them properly was in the interest of those children, even though the ultimate purpose of the adoption was to exploit their labour or their persons. During the Committee's discussion of this point it was observed that there were two risks to be faced: that *bona fide* adoption might be hindered if the phrase in question were omitted, and that if the phrase were retained children or young persons might be laid open to the unfortunate consequences of adoption which were not *bona fide*.[30]

To this, the British Representative "considered that the two risks mentioned above should be weighed up rather in connexion with a general consideration of the protection of children than in connexion with consideration of an international instrument on slavery, the slave trade and other forms of servitude." Wherein the ILO Committee simply suggested that notice should be taken of the following:

(i) to the apprehension which existed of the possibilities of abuse resulting from the wording proposed by the United Kingdom on this point;
(ii) to the suggestion that the competent national authorities might be made responsible for determining whether the adoption was really *bona fide* or not; and
(iii) to the fact that there were some countries in which adoption did not exist as an institution.[31]

---

30 Economic and Social Council, The Draft Supplementary Convention of Slavery and Servitude Submitted by the Government of the United Kingdom and Comments Thereon (Memorandum by the Secretary-General), UN Doc E/AC.43/L.1, 2 December 1955, p. 25.

31 *Id.*, pp. 25–26.

In general terms, non-governmental bodies were in favour of the British Draft Article, but sough modification. The St. Joan's International Social and Political Alliance thought that "the exception in the second half of the paragraph is unnecessary and would tend to weaken the force of the prohibition in the first half." Should that exception in the second half be retained, the Alliance suggested, the following should be added: "provided that these are under legal safeguards." The Anti-Slavery Society provided a further suggestion stating that the "words 'legal adoption' should be replaced by *bon fide* adoptions."[32] For its part, the International Abolitionist Federation suggested the deletion of the passage 'except that this Article shall not be construed so as to prohibit or hinder *bona fide* adoptions intended to promote the welfare of children or young persons' as "it unnecessarily weakens the text."[33] The Federation considered it "necessary to combat all exploitation of this type without exception, particularly as the victims are defenceless minors placed in the charge of adults. It gives as an example the case of the *mui-tsai*, who are exploited in this way by the persons to whom they are committed, being trained for prostitution."[34] Finally, one State provided a comment, the Government of Pakistan suggested that the phrase "or freely dispose of the produce of his labour" be added to the end of the provision.[35]

When, in 1956, an *ad hoc* Committee on the Drafting of a Supplementary Convention on Slavery and Servitude established by the Economic and Social Council considered the provisions on sham adoptions, the Member of the Committee from the United Kingdom, proposed that reference to "bona fide adoptions" might be deleted as it could "lead to difficulties. If the phrase were

---

32 *Id.*, p. 26. Note that the International Bureau for the Suppression of Traffic in Persons fully supported these proposed amendments. See Economic and Social Council, The Draft Supplementary Convention of Slavery and Servitude Submitted by the Government of the United Kingdom and Comments Thereon (Memorandum by the Secretary-General) Addendum, UN Doc E/AC.43/L.1/Add.1, 4 January 1956, p. 2.

33 Economic and Social Council, The Draft Supplementary Convention of Slavery and Servitude Submitted by the Government of the United Kingdom and Comments Thereon (Memorandum by the Secretary-General) Addendum, UN Doc E/AC.43/L.1/Add.1, 4 January 1956, p. 2.

34 *Id.*

35 Economic and Social Council, The Draft Supplementary Convention of Slavery and Servitude Submitted by the Government of the United Kingdom and Comments Thereon (Memorandum by the Secretary-General) Addendum, UN Doc E/AC.43/L.1/Add.2, 25 January 1956.

retained, the effect might be contrary to the one intended."[36] The Netherlands Representative was in agreement, stating that the "exception would tend to weaken the force of the prohibition in the first half of the paragraph."[37] Thus, the Committee agreed to remove the reference to 'bona fide adoptions'.[38]

With regard to a second proposal put forward by the United Kingdom, which reads: replace "the words 'under conditions which permit that person to exploit a child or young person or his or her labour' with the words 'for the purpose of exploiting, in a manner detrimental to his or her welfare, the child or young person, or his or her labour'."[39] The British Representative noted that the term 'to exploit' had two meanings: "In the sense in which it was used in many political textbooks it implied the inequitable treatment of workers. As used in such expressions as 'to exploit natural resources', it also had a favourable connotation. His amendment aimed at leaving the door open for the employment of child actors and musicians."[40] The Member from the Union of Soviet Socialist Republics (Soviet Union) opposed this amendment saying its "language suggested that exploitation was permissible so long as it could be considered as not detrimental to the welfare of the child or young person concerned." The Soviet Member continued:

> The original United Kingdom text (E/2540/Add.4) employed the term 'to exploit', the meaning of which was perfectly clear: no one spoke of exploitation for beneficial purposes. The case of a child actor or musician working under a contract signed by his parent with a film company or other institution was very far removed from those cases which the draft supplementary convention was intended to cover, namely the exploitation of practices resembling slavery. It was concerned with a mass problem, not with isolated cases involving child actors.[41]

---

36 Economic and Social Council, Committee on the Drafting of a Supplementary Convention on Slavery and Servitude, Summary Record of the Third Meeting, 17 January 1956, UN Doc. E/AC.43/SR.3, 9 February 1956, p. 10. Emphasis in the original.

37 *Id.*, 9 February 1956, p. 11.

38 See Economic and Social Council, Committee on the Drafting of a Supplementary Convention on Slavery and Servitude, Summary Record of the Twelfth Meeting, 24 February 1956, UN Doc. E/AC.43/SR.12, 20 February 1956, p. 6.

39 Economic and Social Council, Committee on the Drafting of a Supplementary Convention on Slavery and Servitude, Turkey: Amendment to Article 1 of the Draft Convention on the Abolition of Slavery and Servitude (E/2540/Add.4), UN Doc. E/AC.43/L.19, 19 January 1956.

40 See Economic and Social Council, Committee on the Drafting of a Supplementary Convention on Slavery and Servitude, Summary Record of the Twelfth Meeting, 24 January 1956, UN Doc. E/AC.43/SR.12, 20 February 1956, p. 6.

41 *Id.*, p. 7.

For his part, the French Representative stated "that in French the phrase 'to exploit a person' always had an evil connotation," and suggested the following phrase: "to utilize the labour of the child or young person in a manner detrimental…".[42] The Indian Representative, "said that a stigma always attached to the exploitation of an individual." He accordingly proposed that the text should read "employing in a manner detrimental to his or her welfare."[43] At this point, the Chairman noted that there was agreement amongst Committee members that "the article was not intended to prevent legitimate employment of a child in a manner not detrimental to his or her welfare, but rather to prevent practices of actual exploitation."[44] He suggested that the original text be retained and an explanatory paragraph be included in the Report of the *Ad Hoc* Committee. This proposal was not immediately taken up, as the French Representative noted his support for the Indian amendment, while the Representative from the Soviet Union asked that any decision on that proposal be delay until the next meeting "in view of the linguistic difficulties involved" in regard to the substituting of the words 'to employ' for 'to exploit'.[45] This was agreed to by the Committee.

At the following meeting the Soviet Member of the Committee on the Drafting of a Supplementary Convention on Slavery and Servitude stated that he maintained his view that the amendment proposed by the United Kingdom "in effect condoned the exploitation of child labour":

> While the original text had provided for the complete abolition of that practice, the amendment qualified that abolition, making it contingent upon the child, or his or her labour, being exploited in a manner detrimental to his or her welfare. No indication was given as to what would constitute detrimental exploitation. Substitution of the word "employing" for "exploiting," as had been suggested, would not change the position in the slightest. The Soviet delegation was therefore opposed to the amendment which, in effect, legalized exploitation.[46]

The United Kingdom Member of the drafting Committee responded, saying that he felt that,

---

42 *Id.*

43 *Id.*

44 *Id.*, p. 8.

45 *Id.*

46 Economic and Social Council, Committee on the Drafting of a Supplementary Convention on Slavery and Servitude, Summary Record of the Thirteenth Meeting, 25 January 1956, UN Doc. E/AC.43/SR.13, 27 February 1956, pp. 3–4.

> despite appearance, there was no substantial difference between the views of the United Kingdom and the Soviet delegations. Both favoured the abolition of child labour. As a conciliatory gesture, he was prepared to delete the words "in a manner detrimental to his or her welfare" from his amendment on the understanding that the interpretation his delegation placed on the paragraph remained unchanged and that this would be made clear in the Committee's report.
>
> Nothing would be gained by substituting the word "employing" for "exploiting" since the former, unlike the latter, failed to imply that the child worked primarily for the benefit of another person.[47]

Beyond the issue of exploitation, a third proposal was put forward by the Member from India, who suggested that the term 'minor' should supersede 'young person', to which the French Representative stated that the "term 'child' and 'adolescent' were physiological terms, but of a universal nature, whereas the term 'minor' was a legal one which varied from one country to another."[48] The Representative of the United Kingdom, for his part, noted that "under Moslem law a minor was a child who had not attained the age of puberty. The use of the term might subsequently introduce an unwarranted limitation into the provision. He would favour the retention of 'young person', which, at least in English law, signified a child between the ages of fourteen and seventeen."[49] The Soviet Representative stated that he "preferred the term 'minor'. The concept of a 'child or young person' was biological rather than legal and the text gave no indication of the exact meaning of the expression. The concept of minority, on the other hand, had a strict legal connotation under most systems."[50] The French Member added that "although the term 'minor' admittedly had a strict juridical meaning, the age-limit of legal minority varied from one country to another. The expression 'child or young person' might be preferable, as it gave a reasonable indication of the category of the individuals whom the provision was designed to protect."[51] Further discussion ensued with the British Representative believing that it "would be difficult a legal term which

47 *Id.*, p. 4.

48 Economic and Social Council, Committee on the Drafting of a Supplementary Convention on Slavery and Servitude, Summary Record of the Third Meeting, 17 January 1956, UN Doc. E/AC.43/SR.3, 9 February 1956, p. 11.

49 Economic and Social Council, Committee on the Drafting of a Supplementary Convention on Slavery and Servitude, Summary Record of the Twelfth Meeting, 24 January 1956, UN Doc. E/AC.43/SR.12, 20 February 1956, p. 4.

50 *Id.*, p. 4.

51 *Id.*, p. 4.

had a uniform significance to all countries. The expression used in the draft was elastic and adequate to all circumstances. He would, however be willing to consider alternative proposals, if the expression 'young person' gave rise to difficulties." The Chairman of the Committee "pointed out that the term 'minor' might render the provision applicable only to children who had not attained a specific age. Such a limitation would be inconsistent with the purpose of the convention, which was intended to apply to all adolescents."

The apparent impasse was broken by an intervention by the Representative of the International Labour Organisation who stated "that international labour conventions spoke of 'children and young persons'." The texts often defined the former as under fourteen and the latter under eighteen. The French Member believed that this example should be followed, "he therefore, formally propose that 'a child or young person' should be changed to 'a person under the age of eighteen years'." To this, the British Member stated that "there might be some doubt whether a child was a 'person'," which prompted some discussion, with a proposal by the Member from Yugoslavia, that the "wording 'child or young person under the age of eighteen'" being accepted.[52] The provisions related to sham adoption where then adopted by the *ad hoc* Committee on the Drafting of a Supplementary Convention on Slavery and Servitude, in the following terms:

> Any institution or practice whereby a child or young person under the age of 18 years is delivered by either or both his natural parents or his guardian to another person, whether for reward or not, for the purpose of exploiting the child or young person, or his or her labour.[53]

When these provisions where then considered at the 1956 United Nations Conference of Plenipotentiaries on a Supplementary Convention on the Abolition of Slavery, the Slave Trade and Institutions and Practices Similar to Slavery, the Representative of China, voiced concern over the phrase 'the age of 18 years', as he stated that different countries had different ages of majority and, "consequently expressions such as 'minor' and 'of legal age' were too imprecise. On the other hand, it was unsatisfactory to specify the age of eighteen years, because in many countries persons, whether male or female, could be legally

52 *Id.*, pp. 5–6.

53 Economic and Social Council, Draft Supplementary Convention on the Abolition of Slavery, the Slave Trade and Institutions and Practices Similar to Slavery, UN Doc. 2824, Annex I, 15 February 1956.

married under that age."[54] The Representative from the United Kingdom, for his part explained that much discussion on this very subject had taken place in the meetings of the *ad hoc* drafting Committee, and expressions "such as 'minor', 'young person' and 'adolescent' had all been considered, and in the end it had been decided that it would be better to lay down a definite age-limit since all other expressions were susceptible of different interpretations."[55]

The Representative of the Netherlands for her part suggested, with the Representative of China in agreement, "that the word 'exploiting' should be clarified by the addition of the phrase 'in a manner detrimental to his or her welfare'."[56] When, this proposed amendment was opened for consideration by the Conference, the Canadian Representative stated "that the term 'exploiting' itself implied an act detrimental to welfare. The Netherlands amendment seemed unnecessary but might be acceptable if the word 'employing' was substituted for 'exploiting'." The Representative of the Netherlands, Ms Lunsingh-Meijer, responded saying "that she had submitted the amendment merely to make it quite clear that 'exploitation' was used to imply something detrimental. There should be no risk of the term being construed as simply 'employing'."

The Cuba Representative pointed out that the term 'exploiter' in Spanish "was always pejorative"; wherein, French Representative stated that in French, the term "had two meanings, only one of which was pejorative." To this the Belgium Representative stated "that the word 'exploiter' in its neutral meaning could apply only to things, whereas it always had a pejorative sense when applied to persons. Hence, as applied to a child, the term could not be understood as meaning the mere use of the services of a child with no harm to the child. There was therefore no justification for the Netherlands delegation's proposal." The Soviet Representative for his part did not believe the Dutch proposal moving things forward, as he:

> could not accept any form of words implying that parents or guardians might deliver to another person (whether for reward or not), the labour of a child or adolescent, even if partly in the child's own interest. The exploitation of persons under age, and, especially, of children, was repugnant to the civilized conscience, for it was harmful to their health. The

54 Economic and Social Council, United Nations Conference of Plenipotentiaries on a Supplementary Convention on the Abolition of Slavery, the Slave Trade and Institutions and Practices Similar to Slavery, Summary Record of the Fourth Meeting, 15 August 1956, UN Doc E/CONF.24/SR.4, 11 November 1958, p. 8.

55 *Id.*

56 *Id.*, p. 6.

> amendment proposed by the Netherlands delegation did not improve the draft convention as it might lead to the disguisement of certain institutions that were akin to slavery.

The British Representative followed his Soviet counterpart saying that this point had been discussed at some length by the Economic and Social Council's *ad hoc* drafting Committee, and that there had been a difference of opinion which had been dealt with by all members having agreed to the intended purpose of the provisions put forward:

> The United Kingdom and other delegations had argued that there was a shade of meaning in the term 'exploiting' which was not necessarily detrimental, but in the interest of compromise had agreed to the use of the term on the ground that the commoner acceptance was the pejorative one. The Netherlands amendment was not, therefore, strictly necessary, but it made the meaning clearer and he would therefore support it.

With the Soviet Representative saying that "meaning of 'exploiting' is the context – the exploiting of a child or young person – was quite clear," the Representative of the Netherlands stated "that the consensus was obviously that the term 'exploiting' meant in a manner detrimental to welfare," and as such she would withdraw where proposed amendment.[57] As a result, the United Nations Conference of Plenipotentiaries on a Supplementary Convention on the Abolition of Slavery, the Slave Trade and Institutions and Practices Similar to Slavery adopted the provisions on sham adoption unaltered in substance from those prepared by the Economic and Social Council's *ad hoc* drafting Committee. The provisions which appear as Article 1(d) of the 1956 Supplementary Convention read:

> Any institution or practice whereby a child or young person under the age of 18 years is delivered by either or both of his natural parents or by his guardian to another person, whether for reward or not, with a view to the exploitation of the child or young person or of his labour.[58]

57 Economic and Social Council, United Nations Conference of Plenipotentiaries on a Supplementary Convention on the Abolition of Slavery, the Slave Trade and Institutions and Practices Similar to Slavery, Summary Record of the Fifth Meeting, 16 August 1956, UN Doc E/CONF.24/SR.5, 11 November 1958, pp. 3–4.

58 See United Nations Conference of Plenipotentiaries on a Supplementary Convention on the Abolition of Slavery, the Slave Trade and Institutions and Practices Similar to Slavery, Final Act and Supplementary Convention, 4 September 1956, UN Doc E/CONF.24/23.

Conclusion

The fourth conventional servitude set out in the 1956 Supplementary Convention on the Abolition of Slavery, the Slave Trade and Institutions and Practices Similar to Slavery has yet to settle on a fixed term. The genealogy set out above demonstrates that when Article 1(d) of the 1956 Supplementary Convention speaks of a child being 'delivered', it was a term which the negotiators settle upon when seeking to express the transfer of a child for adoption or quasi-adoption. Further, the understanding that such adoptions were in fact a shame was manifest in the agreement that such transfers where they took place would be against the welfare of the child.

This chapter sets out the DNA of the fourth conventional servitude set out in 1956 Supplementary Convention, and designates it as 'sham adoption', a term of art meant to capture the essence – the object and purpose – of the provision, by reference to its negotiation history. Where work remains to be done is with regard to bring this provisions into the Twenty-First Century by measuring it against the touchstone of the Convention on the Right of the Child: best interest of the child; as well as its relationship to the 1993 Hague Convention on the Protection of Children and Co-operation in respect to Inter-Country Adoption.

CHAPTER 16

Exploitation and Labour in International Law*

Free labour is the product of law. It is only through the establishment of domestic and international regulation that a person can assert their right to free choice of employment. While it is common to think of labour in binary terms as being either free or coerced, in fact a continuum exists which allows one to consider the various limitations which are put on free labour moving it from a situation of benefit, towards one of exploitation resulting from increasing degrees of coercion. The introduction of the legal concept of 'exploitation' into the international anti-trafficking conventions provides the opportunity to consider the role that law plays in ensuring that labour distances itself from exploitive practices. While these conventions seek to criminalise the sharp end of the stick: trafficking for the purposes of forced labour; international law has developed standards which deal with labour exploitation through a continuum which first establishes minimum labour standards; then creates positive duties of international human rights law requiring States to establish the legal infrastructure to ensure that exploitation in both the public and private sectors does not amount to violation of a worker's human rights. While leaving it to States to determine how best to ensure that worker's rights – as human rights – are protected, this protection is ordinarily manifest in a State's administrative law, its regulations of industry, but also goes as far a criminalising certain labour practices.

This Working Paper considers the various examples of exploitation laid down by the trafficking conventions while acknowledging that these are, 'at minimum', the types of exploitation which exist. This acknowledgment opens the possibility for considering the continuum of coercion which moves from free labour to exploitation; to abuse through servile situations including forced labour; and finally, to the most extreme type of coercion manifest as enslavement; and the manner in which international law addresses such exploitation. The advent of a market economy and globalisation has created new challenges where labour exploitation is concerned. While international legal norms, by their very nature, have typically escaped private actors, international labour standards have set the benchmark for decent work and a marker for questioning whether employers are in fact being exploitative. During much of the twentieth century, international law dealing with forced

* Working Paper originally drafted in 2008 for the International Labour Organisation.

 | DOI 10.1163/9789004279896_018

labour, servitude, and slavery sought to address exploitation by States; yet today it is recognised that exploitation takes place primarily at the hands of non-State actors. International law is well placed to deal with private individuals and companies where they are exploiting workers, as international human rights law has, at the dawn of the twenty-first century, come to encompass not only the obligation of States not to exploit, but also the duty – a so-called 'positive' duty – to ensure that exploitation does not take place within their jurisdiction. A failure to protect a worker's human right is ultimately backed internationally by criminal sanctions where exploitation reaches the threshold of enslavement. In such an extreme case, the policy-maker has two options, either to address the exploitive behaviour so as to ensure it does not recur; or second, face the possibility of standing in the dock for failing to take adequate positive steps to suppress such exploitation.

What is being witnessing at the advent of the twenty-first century is an international order prepared to take human exploitation seriously. International law now has at its disposal the tools to seek to suppress exploitation, even of the mildness forms. Through top-down pressure States are required to end exploitive labour practices: international criminal law remains the ultimate threat: if international labour standards are not meet and exploitation develops into servile labour then international human rights law can be invoked; if servile labour develops into slavery then international criminal law can come into play. Thus, if used effectively, the criminal law buttresses human rights law which, in turn, strengthens international labour standards, so as to distance labour from exploitation.

The Legal Conception of Exploitation

The very concept of 'exploitation' in international law manifests itself in two manners, exploitation of a thing which is promoted in certain instances; and exploitation of a human being which, for the most part, is outlawed. Where exploitation is allowed in international law, for instance, is most evident with maritime environment, wherein the 1982 United Nations Convention on the Law of the Sea allows for, and regulates, "economic exploitation" of both living and non-living natural resources.[1] As was noted during the negotiations of the 1956 Supplementary Convention on the Abolition of Slavery, the Slave Trade, and Institutions and Practices Similar to Slavery, dealing with the exploitation of children as an institution and practice similar to slavery, the term 'to exploit'

1 United Nations Convention on the Law of the Sea, 1982.

can have two meanings: "In the sense in which it was used in many political textbooks it implied the inequitable treatment of workers. As used in such expressions as 'to exploit natural resources', it also had a favourable connotation.[2] Towards the end of that negotiation process, reference was made once more to the dual nature of exploitation, wherein a State Representative noted that it had been "argued that there was a shade of meaning in the term 'exploiting' which was not necessarily detrimental, but in the interest of compromise [his Delegation] had agreed to the use of the term on the ground that the commoner acceptance was the pejorative one." That pejorative notion of exploitation was accepted by consensus by the negotiators of the 1956 Supplementary Convention as being in "a manner detrimental to welfare" of a child.[3]

For its part, the Oxford English Dictionary defines exploitation as "the action of turning to account for selfish purposes, using for one's own profit."[4] In legal terms, the notion of exploitation is not defined internationally, but appears as a new legal concept in the definition of 'trafficking in persons', as found in identical terms in the 2000 UN 'Palermo' Protocol on Trafficking in Persons[5] and the 2005 Council of Europe Convention on Trafficking in Human Beings[6] as:

> "Trafficking in persons" shall mean the recruitment, transportation, transfer, harbouring or receipt of persons, by means of the threat or use of force or other forms of coercion, of abduction, of fraud, of deception, of the abuse of power or of a position of vulnerability or of the giving or receiving of payments or benefits to achieve the consent of a person having control over another person, for the purpose of exploitation. *Exploitation shall include, at a minimum, the exploitation of the prostitution of others or other forms of sexual exploitation, forced labour or services, slavery or practices similar to slavery, servitude or the removal of organs.*

---

2 United Nations, Economic and Social Council, Committee on the Drafting of a Supplementary Convention on Slavery and Servitude, Summary Record of the Twelfth Meeting, 24 January 1956, UN Doc. E/AC.43/SR.12, 20 February 1956, p. 6.

3 United Nations, Economic and Social Council, United Nations Conference of Plenipotentiaries on a Supplementary Convention on the Abolition of Slavery, the Slave Trade and Institutions and Practices Similar to Slavery, Summary Record of the Fifth Meeting, 16 August 1956, UN Doc E/CONF.24/SR.5, 11 November 1958, p. 4.

4 *Oxford English Dictionary*, 2nd Edition, 1989, Online Edition.

5 Protocol to Prevent, Suppress and Punish Trafficking in Persons, Especially Women and Children, Supplementing the United Nations Convention Against Transnational Organized Crime, 2000.

6 Council of Europe Convention on Action against Trafficking in Human Beings, 2005.

While consideration will be given to these various types of exploitation in more detail later, what is important to note at this junctures is that these types of exploitation have a pedigree in international law, they are, by and large, defined by previous international treaties and thus have established definitions in law. Yet, the inclusion of the phrase 'at a minimum' means that 'exploitation' goes further than those types of exploitation enumerated in the trafficking conventions. This Working Paper demonstrates that exploitation is best understood as manifesting itself when coercion is used as a means of compelling labour. While a continuum of coercion may mean that a worker has to decide between disagreeable alternatives; international law legislates so as to ensure that the worker need not choose under duress the lesser of two evils. It does this through the standards it establishes responding to this continuum via labour law, human rights law and, ultimately, criminal law.

Traditionally, Western historians have argued that free labour was synonymous with wage labour and the move away from medieval labour systems manifest in indentured servitudes such as serfdom was the norm rather than the exception. Yet, in the 1990s, such assumptions were challenged as the work of labour historians showed that labour systems were best understood on a continuum from free to coerced work as opposed to being in binary opposition. By today's standards, what would have been termed free labour as late as the nineteenth century would be deemed unfree and, by its very nature, exploitive. Thus, in the 1800s, indenture servitude was considered free labour as employees freely consented to a contract which committed them to working for a set number of years. What, by today's standards, makes that relationship a coercive one was that the State, through its criminal law, ensured that the terms of the contract would be respected no matter the treatment of employees, by physically returning those who ran away from such contracts, by legislating to add additional days to a contract to make up those lost to illness, and by allowing employers to administer corporal punishment.[7] While free markets emerged in the nineteenth century, what would have been termed 'free labour' during this period was hardly free by today's standards, as nonpecuniary pressures were used to create a form of 'coerced contractual labour'. The move away from this type of contractual labour emerges as a result of legal labour standards – statutory legislation – which regulate industry, limiting the freedom of the employer to, for instance, contract above a maximum set of working hours or minimum amount of pay. It should be understood that it is the State, through its law, that arbitrates between employee and employer in

7 Robert Steinfeld, *The Invention of Free Labour: The Employment Relations in English & American Law and Culture, 1350–1870*, 1991, p. 7.

establishing a subjective line between what is deemed free labour and what is to be considered coerced.

At its most abstract, any labour can be understood as being either voluntary or coerced. Beyond being physically compelled to work, coerced labour can best be understood as a "situation in which the compelled party is offered a choice between disagreeable alternatives and chooses the lesser of two evils."[8] Again, in rather abstract terms, coercion can been deemed to exist where a person is required to choose between living on the street or taking up unpleasant work. Yet by contemporary standards, such a choice between two disagreeable alternatives would not be deemed, in law, coerced labour. The determination as to what is considered coercive and what is to be considered free labour is "a judgment about what kinds of coercive pressures are legitimate and illegitimate in labour relations."[9] Today, this determination is based on the rather nebulous term of 'exploitation', which seeks to address coercive labour in its most extreme forms – forced labour, slavery, servitude – through criminal law, while allowing States the leeway to legislate to ensure that labour practices do not degenerate into these types of exploitation primarily through labour legislation in line with international labour standards and international human rights law. On the continuum of coercion then, it will be recognised that a failure to meet international labour standards will be considered exploitative, but such exploitation will not necessary constitute a human rights violation or a criminal matter but will be dealt with through labour law. A benchmark for seeking to understand what exploitation means in law, can be drawn from the commonalities of the types of exploitation noted in the recently established trafficking conventions.

In its 2001 Judgment in the *Kunarac* case, the Trial Chamber of the International Criminal Tribunal for the Former Yugoslavia considered four types of exploitation, forced labour, slavery, the practices similar to slavery, and servitude, as its basis for 'enslavement' and deduced from the following indicators common to these forms of exploitation:

> elements of control and ownership; the restriction or control of an individual's autonomy, freedom of choice or freedom of movement; and, often, the accruing of some gain to the perpetrator. The consent or free will of the victim is absent. It is often rendered impossible or irrelevant by, for example, the threat or use of force or other forms of coercion; the fear of violence, deception or false promises; the abuse of power; the victim's

8 Robert Steinfeld, *Coercion, Contract and Free Labour in the Nineteenth Century*, 2001, p. 14.

9 *Id.*, p. 16.

> position of vulnerability; detention or captivity, psychological oppression or socio-economic conditions.[10]

Two elements emerging from this consideration are control and lack of consent. Considering the types of exploitation noted in the trafficking conventions, it is clear that the issue of *control* is common to the various types of exploitation established (but for the different 'species' of the removal of organs). That control, whether it be of the person or their labour, is present to varying degrees in the exploitation of the prostitution of others or other forms of sexual exploitation, in forced labour, in slavery, in practices similar to slavery and in servitude. At its most extreme that control over the person or their labour will be complete and exhibit the powers which would normally be attached to ownership. The enslaved, having lost autonomy is now treated as a thing, to be used at the complete discretion of another.

Where *lack of consent* is concerned there is a direct correlation to the issue of control and the shift from personal autonomy to being compelled to do something against one's will. For the Yugoslav Tribunal, like the trafficking conventions, this lack of consent results from coercion, deception, or the abuse of power or of a position of vulnerability; These means of inducing consent – and maintaining control – are central to understanding the common characteristics of what constitutes exploitation. While they are constituted within the trafficking conventions as the means of placing somebody in a position to be trafficked; it must also be recognised that through coercion – as manifest in most of the means outlined in the definition of 'trafficking in person' in these conventions – individuals are often maintained in exploitive situations. The means found in the conventions can be assimilated under two headings: coercion and deception. While deception will include fraud; coercion should be understood as including the other means listed in the trafficking conventions: the threat or use of force, abduction, control over another person and the abuse of power or of a position of vulnerability.

A special word should be given to this concept 'of the abuse [...] of a position of vulnerability' as a coercive means of facilitating trafficking spelled out in the conventions. Rohit Malpani in a previous Working Paper of the Special Action Programme to Combat Forced Labour does well to show how, by the abusing of a position of vulnerability, through coercion, a person exerts psychological control over another.[11] As the Interpretative Note of the drafter of

---

10 United Nations, Security Council, International Criminal Tribunal for the former Yugoslavia, *Kunarac et als.* (IT-96-23 &-IT-96-23/1-A) Judgment, 12 June 2002, p. 193.

11 Rohit Malpani, *Legal Aspects of Trafficking for Forced Labour Puposes in Europe*, ILO Doc. Declaration/WP/48/2006, 2006.

the Palermo Protocol notes, the "reference to the abuse of a position of vulnerability is understood to refer to any situation in which the person involved has no real and acceptable alternative but to submit to the abuse involved."[12] Malpani writes that coercion in such situations will be successful as a result of either "some innate characteristic of the victim (physical or mental deficiency, ill health, or youth)" or the situation in which the a person will find themselves in, such as resulting from the taking of identification documents or their inability to speak a language foreign to them.

As for the notion of coercion itself, it is interesting to note that Pakistan defines coercion so as to, in essence, incorporate all the means through which a person will be induced into exploitation as spelled out by the trafficking conventions. Its 2002 legislation defines coercion as "the use of force, violence, physical restraint, deception, fraud, or acts or circumstances not necessarily including physical force but calculated to have the same effect, such as the credible threat of force or of infliction of serious harm."[13]

The Danish Criminal Code speaks of unlawful coercion as being perpetrated by any person who:

(1) by violence or under threat of violence, of substantial damage to property, of the deprivation of liberty or of a false accusation of having committed a punishable act or dishonourable conduct or of revealing matters appertaining to someone's private affairs, forces any person to do, suffer or omit to do anything; or who

(2) under threat of denouncing or revealing a punishable act or of making true accusations of dishonourable conduct, forces any person to do, suffer or omit to do anything, provided such coercion is not deemed to be duly justified by virtue of the circumstances to which the threat relates [...].[14]

Likewise, Georgia provides a definition of coercion within its legislation which reads "Illegal restriction of a person's freedom of action, i.e. his/her physical or mental coercion to perform or note to perform a particular action the performance of or abstinence from which is his/her rights or coercion to experience

---

12 United Nations Office on Drugs and Crime, *Travaux Préparatoires of the Negotiations for the Elaboration of the United Nations Convention against Transnational Organized Crime and the Protocols Thereto*, 2006, p. 347.

13 Article 2(d), Islamic Republic of Pakistan, *Prevention and Control of Human Trafficking Ordinance*, 2002.

14 Section 260, Kingdom of Denmark, *Criminal Code: Consolidation Act No. 909*, 27 September 2005.

pressure upon oneself against one's own will [...]."[15] The United States' legislation defines coercion by giving three examples, "threats of serious harm to or physical restraint against any person; any scheme, [...] intended to cause a person to believe that failure to perform an act would result in serious harm to or physical restraint against any person; or the abuse or threatened abuse of the legal process."[16]

For its part, German legislation makes a distinction between trafficking for the purposes of sexual exploitation and trafficking for the purposes of the "exploitation of workers," and establishes a link between exploitation and coercion by establishing that:

> Whoever exploits another person through a coercive situation or the helplessness that is associated with their stay in a foreign country to induce them into slavery, serfdom, or debt bondage, or to take up or continue work with him or a third party under working conditions that are strikingly disproportionate to the working conditions of other workers who perform the same or a comparable activity, shall be punished with imprisonment from six months to ten years. [...][17]

For the Republic of Tajikistan, its trafficking legislation establishes that the form of coercion will reflect the type of exploitation which takes place, thus

(a) forcible physical coercion and (or) with the use of strong drug, alcohol, medicines;
(b) economical coercion in the form of debt bondage or other material dependence including slavery or conditions similar to slavery;
(c) psychological coercion by blackmailing, fraud, deceiving or threat of violation;
(d) legal dependence in connection with adoption or guardianship or in connection to marriage without the purpose of establishing a family.

---

15 Article 50, Republic of Georgia, *Criminal Code*, "22 July 1999 (as amended 16 April, 2003). See also Article 139, The former Yugoslav Republic of Macedonia, *Criminal Code*, 23 July 1996 (as amended, 23 March, 2004); and Montenegro which defines coercion as "Anyone who by use of force or threat compels someone to do or not to do something or to endure something [...]." Article 165, Criminal Code, Number 13 of 2004.

16 Section 103(2) United States of America, *Victims of Trafficking and Violence Protection Act of 2000*, 28 October 2000.

17 Section 233, Federal Republic of Germany, *Criminal Code*, 15 August 1998 (as amended, 16 August 2005).

Such coercion may result in a number of exploitative activities such as the removal of organs, domestic and agricultural labour, sexual exploitation, or use for military activities.[18]

This emphasis on coercion – recalling that we are speaking of coercion writ large as including the threat or use of force, abduction, where a person has control over another – which manifest itself in the legislation of a various of States appears to be at the heart of the phenomena of trafficking where issues of forced labour are concerned. Having conducted a review of the literature in the area of labour exploitation, a Report commissioned by the United Kingdom Home Office notes that coercion (along with deception) "are the fundamental elements of trafficking and are used to control and exploit victims." Such coercion is achieved through debt-bondage, the withholding of identification documents, physical and psychological abuse, threat of reporting to the authorities and overall dependency on the perpetrator."[19] Where migrants in the United Kingdom are concerned a study found that beyond physical and sexual violence and threats of violence, coercion was manifest in "threats and intimidation based on immigration status, blackmailing, and confiscation of identity documents or withholding payments. The use of these forms of coercion is made more effective if the migrant is dependent on an agent or employer, either because of incurred debts or the restriction of work permits."[20] The Dutch National Rapporteur on Trafficking in Human Beings, in considering exploitation beyond the sex industry noted that coercion, as an indicator of possible exploitative situations was manifest where there was "(threats of) physical violence against the employee; (threats of) reporting the employee's illegal residence status, putting unacceptable pressure on the employee in some other way."[21]

Both in the legislation in place and with regard to the reality on the ground, the notion of coercion is recognised as playing a fundamental role in the trafficking for purposes of forced labour and, it should be said, plays a necessary role in maintain an individual in a situation where forced labour can be exploited. The control established over a person through coercion leads to a relationship where the benefit incurred by one emerge as a result of an inability by the other to break the (real or perceived) bond of exploitation. Where forced labour is concerned, coercion should be understood as the 'menace of

18 Article 5, Republic of Tajikistan, *Decree of Majlisi Milli of the Republic of Tajikistan on the Fight against Human Trafficking*, 8 July 2004.

19 Samantha Dowling, Karen Moreton, Leila Wright, *Trafficking for the Purpose of Labour Exploitation: A Literature Review*, Home Office Online Report 10/07, 2007, p. 8.

20 Bridget Anderson and Ben Rogaly, *Forced Labour and Migration to the uk*, 2005, p. 36.

21 Dutch National Rapporteur on Trafficking in Human Beings, *Trafficking in Human Beings: Fifth Annual Report of the Dutch National Rapporteur*, 2007, p. 153.

any penalty' which vitiates the ability to freely consent to exploitive work. Thus not only are the coercive means within the definition of trafficking in persons the way in which one will be trafficked, but they are also the means of keeping a person in a state of forced labour: the means are the menace in forced labour. The threat or menace of coercion allows forced labour, like other types of exploitation, to continue beyond the trafficking stage to the exploitation itself.

International Labour Law

Exploitation of workers takes place where sub-standard working conditions exist. In seeking to establish where the minimum threshold is wherein labour becomes exploitive, recourse should be made to the international labour standards developed by the International Labour Organisation (ILO). When an employer fails to meet international labour standards established by States as reflected in ILO conventions and recommendations, it can be said that they are being exploitive of their labour force. But exploitation should not be understood as being a synonymous with criminal activity, much less for 'forced labour'. In isolation, violations of international labour standards may be considered exploitive, but such breaches are typically dealt with as labour infractions. Give a choice, the disagreeable alternatives of working below minimum wage or not working at all, an individual will often choose the lesser of two evils. But such an infraction of a labour code often times does not reach the threshold of a criminal law, but is dealt with through administrative sanction, requiring, for instance, the reimbursement of back-wages and the payment of a fine. Where international labour standards are concerned, it is the antithesis which is worth highlighting: if employers are meeting the ILO standards, then their labour practices are not explosive *ipso facto*.

International labour standards seek to ensure a decent work environment and have, at their core, the principles established in eight fundament conventions which were highlighted in the ILO's 1998 Declaration on Fundamental Principles and Rights at Work.[22] These eight instruments touch on the following areas of labour relations: freedom of association and the effective

22 The eight Convention are:

Freedom of Association and Protection of the Right to Organise Convention, 1948 (No. 87); Right to Organise and Collective Bargaining Convention, 1949 (No. 98); Forced Labour Convention, 1930 (No. 29); Abolition of Forced Labour Convention, 1957 (No. 105); Minimum Age Convention, 1973 (No. 138); Worst Forms of Child Labour Convention, 1999 (No. 182); Equal Remuneration Convention, 1951 (No. 100); and Discrimination (Employment and Occupation) Convention, 1958 (No. 111).

recognition of the right to collective bargaining; the elimination of all forms of forced or compulsory labour; the effective abolition of child labour; and the elimination of discrimination in respect of employment and occupation. Beyond this hardcore, international labour standards include ILO conventions and recommendations which deal with labour inspection and administration, wages, working hours, occupational safety and health promotion, employment security, social security, employment policy, social policy, vocational guidance and training, maternity protection, plus protection to specific categories of workers, including seafarers, fishers, dockworkers, migrant workers and indigenous peoples. These instruments "aim to guarantee a minimal universal threshold of protection for workers."[23] They do so by acknowledging that States are at various levels of economic development and seek to establish frameworks or regimes to be incorporated into domestic law as a baseline for ensuring the protection of workers, decent work and adequate standards in the workplace.

The front-line of action for dealing with issues of exploitation in the workplace is labour inspection.[24] Labour inspection has been central to the mandate of the International Labour Organisation as reflected in Article 427(9) the Treaty of Versailles, which called on States establishing the Organisation to make provision "for a system of inspection, [...] in order to ensure the enforcement of laws and regulations for the protection of the employed." Upholding international labour standards through a regime of labour inspection is established by the ILO through a number of instruments modelled on the 1947 Labour Inspection Convention.[25] That Convention, which is ratified by 138

---

23 International Labour Conference, *Labour Inspection*, General Survey of the reports concerning the Labour Inspection Convention, 1947 (No. 81), and the Protocol of 1995 to the Labour Inspection Convention, 1947, and the Labour Inspection Recommendation, 1947 (No. 81), the Labour Inspection (Mining and Transport) Recommendation, 1947 (No. 82), the Labour Inspection (Agriculture) Convention, 1969 (No. 129), and the Labour Inspection (Agriculture) Recommendation, 1969 (No. 133), Report III (Part 1B), Report of the Committee of Experts on the Application of Conventions and Recommendations, Ninety-fifth Session, 2006, p. 3.

24 As the ILO Committee of Experts notes:

> Because of their free access to workplaces and special relationship with employers and workers, labour inspectors are potentially the public officials in the best position to identify situations that might call for legal and legislative solutions aimed at improving protection at work.

See International Labour Conference, *Labour Inspection, id.*, p. 45.

25 See also the Protocol of 1995 to the Labour Inspection Convention, 1947 (P. 81), the Labour Inspection (Agriculture) Convention, 1969 (No. 129), the Labour Inspection (Seafarers) Convention, 1996, (No. 178); along with the Labour Inspection Recommendation, 1947 (No. 81), the Labour Inspection (Mining and Transport) Recommendation, 1947 (No. 82),

States, requires that each State Party "maintain a system of labour inspection" in the industrial and commercial workplaces,[26] so as:

> to secure the enforcement of the legal provisions relating to conditions of work and the protection of workers while engaged in their work, such as provisions relating to hours, wages, safety, health and welfare, the employment of children and young persons, and other connected matters, in so far as such provisions are enforceable by labour inspectors.[27]

The system is also meant "to bring to the notice of the competent authority defects or abuses not specifically covered by existing legal provisions." The Labour Inspection Convention provides that labour inspectors are to be empowered to remedy defects "which they may have reasonable cause to believe constitute a threat to the health or safety of the workers." In so doing they may turn to judicial or administrative authorities to secure, by legal means, the protection of workers. Article 17 of the Convention provides discretion to the labour inspector as to whether to give a warning or advice[28] to an employer which is in violation or has neglected to observe labour standards, but can either recommend, or where the domestic system permits, institute legal proceeding against such institutions by way of an administrative injunction or criminal law. In making a determination as to what course should be followed, the Committee of Experts has stated that "decisions are based on criteria such as the nature of the contravention, the circumstances under which it is committed, the attitude of the person responsible with regard to his legal obligations, repeat offences, the consequences of the contravention and

---

the Labour Inspection (Agriculture) Recommendation, 1969 (No. 133), and the Labour Inspection (Seafarers) Recommendation, 1996 (No. 185).

26 Article 1, Labour Inspection Convention, 1947 (No. 81). Note that, as of October 2008, the 1995 Protocol had been ratified by 11 States and seeks to extend the reach of the Labour Inspection Convention from the industrial and commercial workplace to "essential national (federal) government administration; the armed services, whether military or civilian personnel; the police and other public security services; and prison services, whether prison staff or prisoners when performing work."
Note that Article 25(1) of the Convention allows for the possibility of States Party to exclude commercial workplaces from consideration.

27 Article 3, Labour Inspection Convention, 1947 (No. 81).

28 As the ILO Committee of Experts notes, the discretion as to whether to give a warning, advice, or a recommend or the institute legal proceeding": implies that inspection staff have the necessary capacity for judgement to be able to distinguish between serious or repeated wilful non-compliance, culpable negligence or flagrant ill will, which call for a penalty, and an involuntary or minor violation, which may lead to a mere warning."
See International Labour Office, *Labour Inspection*, op. cit., n. 23, p. 93.

the risks that it entails, correct conduct or misconduct, the age of the enterprise, the resources of the employer, etc. Consequently, whenever an inspector considers that advice or warnings are no longer sufficient, he must have the power of recourse to legal proceedings."[29]

In its 2008 General Report, the Committee of Experts emphasised cooperation "between the labour inspection services and the justice system is necessary to ensure the enforcement of legal provisions relating to conditions of work and the protection of workers in cases where the other means of action of the labour inspectorate, such as advice, notifications and warnings, have not been effective."[30] Before turning to consider the legal enforcement of labour standards, a word might be said about inspectors and the use of non-legal means of gaining compliance with international labour standards.

Belgium has instituted a health and safety charter as between prime contractors and subcontracts wherein its inspectorate will certify that an applicant has not been the subject "of a definitive conviction, an administrative fine or a work stoppage order relating to circumstances occurring during the previous three years." [...] This certificate enhancing the company's image "through its positioning as a decent, reliable enterprise investing in the safety and health of workers. It can use the charter logo on its correspondence, bid documents, etc."[31] Beyond this innovative approach to preventing labour violations, consideration should be given to the use by labour inspectors of advice, notification and warnings. The ILO Committee of Experts notes that "competent and experienced inspectors are aware of the value of advice and warnings as incentives for the proper application of legal requirements. Generally, it is enough to make a follow-up visit after giving the employer a time limit within which to take remedial action."[32]

In most situations, inspectors will "rely on advice and persuasion before instituting or recommending proceedings"; but for situations where there is "wilful or serious non-compliance, culpable negligence or flagrant ill will" more is required.[33] In such situations, the "effectiveness of the binding measures taken by the labour inspectorate depends to a large extent on the manner in which the judicial authorities deal with cases referred to them by, or at the

29 International Labour Office, International Labour Conference, General Report of the Committee of Experts on the Application of Conventions and Recommendations, Report III (Part 1A), Nineteen-seventhly Session, 2008, p. 449.

30 *Id.*, p. 422.

31 *Id.*, p. 445.

32 International Labour Office, International Labour Conference, *Labour Inspection*, op. cit., n. 23, p. 93.

33 *Id.*, p. 94.

recommendation of labour inspectors."[34] The effectiveness of this measure is brought into sharp relief by the Ibero-American Confederation of Labour Inspectors, when they noted that in Paraguay "the violations that are detected do not give rise to the imposition of the penalties established by the law and that inspectors are principally engaged in conciliation functions. As a result, the authority and impartiality which are necessary in their relations with employers and workers are seriously prejudiced."[35] The Committee of Experts, for its part calls for cooperation between labour inspection services and the justice system in the form of legislation which would establish:

(i) cases in which the representative of the public prosecutor may either issue a prior warning to the entity responsible for a violation or, within a reasonable period, refer reports of violations by labour inspectors to the competent court;
(ii) cases in which labour inspectors may seek a judicial ruling to give injunctions or administrative fines executory force; and
(iii) cases in which interim daily penalties for non-compliance may be imposed until the measures ordered by the labour inspector have been given effect.[36]

In its 2006 General Survey on Labour Inspection, the Committee noted that:

> It is essential for the credibility and effectiveness of systems for the protection of workers for violations to be identified by national legislation and for the proceedings instituted or recommended by labour inspectors against employers guilty of violations to be sufficiently dissuasive and to make employers in general aware of the risks they run if they fail to meet their obligations. In order to be credible, it is important for penalties to be defined in proportion to the nature and gravity of the offence.[37]

Typically, the manner in which States deal with infractions of their domestic labour codes is either by way of administrative sanctions including fines or through criminal law. While criminal law issues will be considered later – as

---

34 International Labour Office, General Report of the Committee of Experts on the Application of Conventions and Recommendations, op. cit., n. 29, p. 442.

35 *Id.*, p. 481.

36 *Id.*, p. 442.

37 International Labour Office, International Labour Conference, *Labour Inspection*, op. cit., n. 23, p. 96.

the Working Paper moves along the continuum of coercion – where fines are concerned, the Committee of Experts has called on the Dominican Republic to "ensure that a method is devised to review the amount of the fines imposed so that they maintain their dissuasive purpose despite any monetary fluctuations and that these penalties are effectively enforced."[38] In its General Survey, the Committee stated that it "would be regrettable in every respect if employers preferred to pay fines as a less costly alternative to taking the measures necessary to ensure compliance with the legal provisions on working conditions."[39] Such was the case until recently in Uruguay where International Trade Union Confederation stated that in general "it is less costly for enterprises to pay off fines than to put an end to the violations, in particular on temporary construction sites."[40]

The amount of fines and the way in which such fines are determine varies greatly among States, in Cambodia, Kazakhstan and Venezuela, fines are based on multiples of the daily reference wage, while in Guatemala "inspectors are empowered to impose penalties ranging from 2 to 12 times the minimum wage, depending on the gravity of the offence."[41] In Brazil where the State has also allow for moral damages to be sought in instances of what it terms 'slave labour', the Government has noted that this, along with large fines, has been a "highly effective since they undermine the economic advantages of using slave labour."[42]

Where recalcitrant or recitative employers are concerned, Belgium appears once again to take a novel approach, determining that the extra burden placed on the inspectorate by repeat visits should be borne by the employer. As the Committee of Experts relates, for the Belgium Government, "it is also morally unjustifiable that this additional capacity should be paid for by the community. Offenders should consequently be made to pay for additional inspections resulting from their unsocial attitude."[43]

Beyond fines, administrative injunctions include the revoking of operating licences, suspension of operations, and closing of an enterprise are typical

38 International Labour Office, General Report of the Committee of Experts on the Application of Conventions and Recommendations, op. cit., n. 29, p. 457.

39 International Labour Office, *Labour Inspection*, op. cit., n. 23, p. 96.

40 International Labour Office, General Report of the Committee of Experts on the Application of Conventions and Recommendations, op. cit., n. 29, p. 494.

41 International Labour Office, *Labour Inspection*, op. cit., n. 23, p. 97.

42 International Labour Office, General Report of the Committee of Experts on the Application of Conventions and Recommendations, op. cit., n. 29, p. 201.

43 *Id.*, p. 445.

remedies of breaches of labour infractions. The closing of operations is not uncommon, especially where exploitation is severe: after the death, in 2006, of six Bolivians who had been trafficked to Argentina for the purposes of forced labour, a "programme of inspections was ordered, which resulted in the closure of 30 of the 54 workshops inspected because of the appalling working conditions."[44] In the Guatemalan context administrative action are deemed essential by the International Trade Union Confederation, as "the judicial authority intervenes only in the event of refusal to execute the sanction."[45]

With regard to what in Brazil is termed 'slave labour', a bill has been for some time before the federal legislature which would allow for the expropriation without compensation of properties of those found to be using such labour. The Committee of Experts considers that this Bill "would make it possible to impose truly dissuasive penalties on the owners of such establishments." Also in the Brazil context, since 2005, those convicted of having used 'slave labour' have had their names placed on a 'Register of Employers', which then precludes them from receiving "financial assistance, grants or public credit' from the State (a legislative bill is also under consideration which would exclude those on the Register from participating in public tenders), while the Brazilian Banking Federation has decided that it will "dissuade its associates from granting credit to those on the Register.

Exploitation then begins where international labour standards are not met. While the types of exploitation enumerated in the trafficking conventions are governed by international human rights law and international criminal law, international labour standards seek to govern exploitation of a lesser degree, as found on the continuum of coercion where illegitimate labour practices are not deemed in law to require more than administrative responses. Yet, it is possible to create top-down pressure by evoking international human rights law where the State fails to ensure that international labour standards are respected, resulting in exploitation of the type named in the trafficking conventions. This is rather acute, as the Committee of Experts noted in 2006 that in many countries penalties prescribed for punishing those in violation of labour law "are only rarely imposed and that an effective enforcement procedure is generally conducted only if the violation resulted in serious harm to health or safely."[46] Attention, thus turns to positive obligations and international human rights law.

---

44 *Id.*, p. 192.

45 *Id.*, p. 464.

46 International Labour Office, International Labour Conference, *Labour Inspection*, op. cit., n. 23, p. 98.

International Human Rights Law

Having considered international labour standards as the benchmark for determining whether or not a practice is exploitive; it is now time to turn to international human rights law and those practices that are deemed exploitive as noted in the trafficking conventions, so as to consider not only their scope, but the remedies which are attached to their violation. Where remedies are concern, international human rights law has progressed to the point where States recognise that they have an obligation to ensure that rights are protected; in other words, not only is the State not to violation human rights, but that the State also have an obligation – a positive obligation – not to allow private persons or companies to violate person's human rights.[47] As the UN Human Rights Committee has noted, "failing to take appropriate measures or to exercise due diligence to prevent, punish, investigate or redress the harm caused by such acts by private persons or entities" would constitute a violation of international human rights law as manifest in the Covenant on Civil and Political Rights (ICCPR).[48]

Such positive obligations of international human rights law create downward pressure, requiring States to have in place a system of protection of workers which seeks to *prevent* exploitive labour practices from reaching the threshold of a human rights violation, to *punish* those who are committing such violations of human rights, to *investigate* with a look to ensuring that such violations do not take place again, and to *redress the harm* caused. In this manner, international human rights law leaves it to States to address the issue, but acts as oversight, should the State fail to abide by its obligations. It does this through the regime of State Responsibly which acknowledges that where a State is in violation of the law, it must provide reparations. Such reparations may entail simple satisfaction – an apology for a moral harm with the promise that such an infraction will not take place in the future; *restituto in integrum* – the obligation to return the situation as far as possible to what it was prior to the violation; and compensation. While the European Court of Human Rights provided for compensation as the basis of its awards; the Inter-American Court of Human Rights has been more creative is seeking to repair the damage made

---

47 See generally, Sandra Fredman, *Human Rights Transformed: Positive Rights and Positive Duties*, 2008; and Alastair Mowbray, *The Development of Positive Obligations under the European Convention on Human Rights by the European Court of Human Rights*, 2004.

48 United Nations, Human Rights Committee *Nature of the General Legal Obligation Imposed on States Parties to the Covenant* (General Comment No. 31), UN Doc. CCPR/C/21/Rev.1/Add.13, 26 May 2004, para. 8.

by human rights violations. This has included orders by the Court to remedy defects in domestic law so as to ensure that those making human rights claims have access to justice; and 'rehabilitative services' in the guise of "educational, medical or similar services or scholarships to survivors and affected family members" of human rights abuses. Further, the Inter-American Court has provide satisfaction by way of symbolic measures, by ordering that States name a "street, school, plaza, [or] memorial" for those victim of human rights violations.[49]

Before turning to the scope of the practices deemed exploitive by the trafficking conventions; these, it should be recalled, are: 'the exploitation of the prostitution of others or other forms of sexual exploitation, forced labour or services, slavery or practices similar to slavery, servitude or the removal of organs'. Of these, forced labour, servitude and slavery have currency in international human rights law and are often grouped together, such as with Article 8 of the ICCPR, Article 6 of the American Convention on Human Rights, and Article 4 of the European Convention for the Protection of Human Rights and Fundamental Freedoms. With regard to the latter, in the *Siliadin* case – which will be considered later in more detail – the Court held that "in accordance with contemporary norms and trends in this field, the member States' positive obligations under Article 4 of the Convention must be seen as requiring the penalisation and effective prosecution of any act aimed at maintaining a person in such a situation [read: forced labour, servitude or slavery]."[50] The Court went on to determine that "limiting compliance with Article 4 of the Convention only to direct action by the State authorities would be inconsistent with the international instruments specifically concerned with this issue and would amount to rendering it ineffective."[51] As such, the Court determined that there existed a positive obligation "to adopt criminal-law provisions which penalise the practices referred to in Article 4 and to apply them in practice. Failure to do so would amount to a violation of international human right law.

As we turn to consider the actual scope of the specific types of exploitation innumerate in the definition of 'trafficking in persons' as found in the 2000 UN 'Palermo' Protocol on Trafficking in Persons and the 2005 Council of Europe

49 Douglas Cassel, "The Expanding Scope and Impact of Reparations Awarded by the Inter-American Court of Human Rights, Feyter, Parmentier, Bossuyt, Lemmes (eds.) *Out of the Ashes: Reparations for Victimes of Groos and Systematic Human Rights Violations*, 2005, p. 204.

50 Council of Europe, European Court of Human Rights, *Siliadin v France* (Application 73316/01), 26 July 2005, para. 112.

51 *Id.*, para. 89.

Convention on Trafficking in Human Beings, it is worth emphasising that the failure to utilise criminal law to suppress the most severe types of exploitation while amount to a violation of international human rights law; while international human rights standards mandate the suppression of forced labour, slavery and servitude as exploitative practices which in their cumulative effects or by their very nature violation of international labour standards. Consideration now turns to the scope of forced labour, servitude and slavery as various forms of exploitation set out in the trafficking convention though forming part of international human rights law.

Forced Labour or Services

The starting point for considering issues of forced labour is the Treaty of Versailles and the establishment of the Mandates system under the auspices of the League of Nations. The Covenant of the League of Nations required that Member States holding Mandates "secure and maintain fair and humane conditions of labour"; while a number of Mandates prohibited "all forms of forced or compulsory labour, except for essential public works and services."[52] The move towards establishing a grander, more general prohibition against forced labour resulted from the League of Nations placing the issue of slavery on its agenda starting in 1922.[53] In 1924, the League established the Temporary Slavery Commission which included as a member, Harold Grimshaw, Representative of the International Labour Organisation, who would write that on

> the whole where the measures taken to abolish slavery and the slave trade have [been] effectively enforced, they have resulted in the gradual disappearance of these evils, but that on the other hand the servile forms of labour which have frequently replaced slave conditions have in some cases led to effects as disastrous, or even more disastrous than those of slavery itself.[54]

The Temporary Slavery Commission called for an international convention on slavery which would include the "prohibition of forced or compulsory labour,

52 International Labour Office, International Labour Conference, *Forced Labour: Report and Draft Questionnaire*, Twelve Session, 1929, p. 8.

53 For a consideration of slavery during the League of Nations era see Jean Allain, "Slavery and the League of Nations: Ethiopia as a Civilised Nation," *Journal of the History of International Law*, Vol. 8, 2006, pp. 213–244; see also Suzanne Miers, *Slavery in the Twentieth Century*, 2003.

54 League of Nations, Temporary Slavery Commission, Memorandum by Mr. H.A. Grimshaw, (Representative of the International Labour Organisation) on the Question of Slavery, CTE 31, 15 April 1925, p. 110.

except for essential public works and services and in return for adequate remuneration."[55]

The Assembly of the League of Nations moved on the Commission's call for a convention with the British Government presenting a Draft Protocol in 1925 that included the following provision which, while recognising "the grave evils that may result from the employment of forced labour," admitted the possibility of using such labour for essential public works, though requiring – pejoratively – that "all necessary precautions, particularly where the labourers belong to the less advanced races, to prevent conditions analogous to those of slavery from resulting from such employment."[56] The provisions on forced labour proved to be the most contentious during the negotiations of what would become the 1926 Slavery Convention, as it was recognised that, as opposed to slavery which was outlawed by League Members, all States possessed the ability "to require forced or compulsory labour on the part of its citizens."[57] One State's representative went so far as to called for the removal of the forced labour from consideration seeing it as sending the wrong message to the indigenous populations of the colonies, as it suggested "that its prohibitions implies for them a right to idleness."[58] Yet, provisions related to forced labour did make their way into the 1926 Slavery Convention.

During the negotiation process, a proposal was accepted to add to the words 'or compulsory' to those of 'forced labour', as it was pointed out that a distinction could be made between forced labour "which might mean that which the courts may condemn certain criminals under common law" and compulsory labour which was more in tune with work for public purposes.[59] The Draft Convention prepared by the League of Nations in 1925 was criticized as it

55 League of Nations, Temporary Slavery Commission, Letter from the Chairman of the Commission to the President of the Council and Report of the Commission, 1925, A.19.1925. VI, 25 July 1925, p. 2.

56 League of Nations, Annex I: Slavery: Draft Resolution and Protocol, Official Journal: Record of the Sixth Assembly, Meetings of the Committees, Minutes of the Sixth Committee (Political Questions) Special Supplement No. 39, 14 September 1925, p. 41.

57 League of Nations, Sixth Committee, Question of Slavery: Report of the Sixth Committee: Resolution, League of Nations Official Journal (Special Supplement 33) Records of the Sixth Assembly: Text of Debates, Nineteenth Plenary Meeting, 26 September 1925, p. 157.

58 League of Nations, Sixth Committee, Note Submitted to the First Sub-Committee of the Sixth Committee by General Freire d'Andrade, A.VI/S.C.1/2.1925, 11 September 1925, p. 3; as found in Folder R.67.D.46214 entitled *La question de l'esclavage: Discussions, y relatives, de la VIe Assembleé*, 1925, p. 3.

59 League of Nations, Sixth Committee, Amendments proposed by the Portuguese Delegation to the Draft Protocol submitted by Viscount Cecil, A.VI/S.C.1/3.1925, 11 September 1925, as found in *id.*, p. 5.

required States to take measures “to prevent conditions analogous to those of slavery from resulting from compulsory or forced labour.”[60] The Draft Convention, it was pointed out,

> wishes to bind the signatories to interference with certain industrial and economic conditions, for […] they are to take all necessary measures to prevent not only ‘slavery’ but *conditions analogous to those of slavery* resulting from forced or compulsory labour. Now forced or compulsory labour is either slavery or it is not. Either the person compelling another to such labour does so because he has for the time being the right of property in him, or the person doing the labour unwillingly does so because he fears that a worse thing may befall him. In the first case it is slavery, because the compeller has a proprietary right in respect of the compelled. In the latter case there is some element of choice or consent on the part of the compelled.[61]

As a result, the provisions were modified so as not to require States to deal with ‘conditions analogous to slavery’ which resulted from forced labour, but instead to take measures to ensure that forced labour did not degenerate into conditions tantamount to slavery. This distinction between slavery and forced labour is fundamental and will be returned to shortly. However, what is important to note with regard to the negotiating of the 1926 Slavery Convention is that a number of proposals to amend the provisions on forced labour were mooted, but to no avail. As a result, the Rapporteur in charge of the drafting process put forward the following principles which would come to form the basis of the provisions found in the 1926 Slavery Convention:

- Forced labour should generally speaking be only for essential public services.
- Forced labour may be admitted for services not of a public nature for exceptional reasons.
- Forced labour must never be allowed to degenerate into slavery and must be adequately rewarded.[62]

---

60 League of Nations, Annex: Draft Convention, League of Nations Official Journal (Special Supplement 33) Records of the Sixth Assembly: Text of Debates, 26 September 1925, p. 439.

61 League of Nations, Draft Convention on Slavery, Replies of Governments, Reply from the Government of the Union of South Africa, A.10(a).1926.VI, 22 July 1926, p. 6; as found in League of Nations, Publications of the League of Nations, VI.B.Slavery, 1926.VI.B.3. Emphasis in the original.

62 League of Nations, Sixth Committee, First Sub-Committee, Article 3, Draft Protocol, Article 3, Principles laid down by Viscount Cecil, A.VI/S.C.1/Drafting Committee/7, as

Using this as a basis, the following provisions were accepted as Article 5 of the 1926 Slavery Convention:

> The High Contracting Parties recognise that recourse to compulsory or forced labour may have grave consequences and undertake, each in respect of the territories placed under its sovereignty, jurisdiction, protection, suzerainty or tutelage, to take all necessary measures to prevent compulsory or forced labour from developing into conditions analogous to slavery.

It is agreed that:

(1) Subject to the transitional provisions laid down in paragraph (2) below, compulsory or forced labour may only be exacted for public purposes.
(2) In territories in which compulsory or forced labour for other than public purposes still survives, the High Contracting Parties shall endeavour progressively and as soon as possible to put an end to the practice. So long as such forced or compulsory labour exists, this labour shall invariably be of an exceptional character, shall always receive adequate remuneration, and shall not involve the removal of the labourers from their usual place of residence.
(3) In all cases, the responsibility for any recourse to compulsory or forced labour shall rest with the competent central authorities of the territory concerned.

In presenting the 1926 Slavery Convention to the Assembly of the League of Nations, the Rapporteur noted that it "represents a definite attempt to deal with the question of forced labour in a general international agreement. This alone marks progress of considerable importance."[63] Further, it was reported that the provision on forced labour made clear "that forced labour for private purposes ought to come to an end as soon as possible,"[64] while

---

found in Folder R.67.D.46214 entitled *La question de l'esclavage: Discussions, y relatives, de la VIe Assembleé*, 1925.

63 League of Nations, Slavery Convention: Report presented to the Assembly by the Sixth Committee, A.104.1926.VI, as found in League of Nations, Publications of the League of Nations, VI.B.Slavery 1926, VI. B. 5, 24 September 1926, p. 3.

64 League of Nations, Slavery Convention: Report of the Sixth Committee: Resolution, League of Nations Official Journal (Special Supplement 44) Records of the Seventh Ordinary Assembly: Text of Debates, Seventeenth Plenary Meeting, 25 September 1926, p. 132.

those touching on public purposes should not be resorted to unless States were compelled."[65]

With regard to the provisions of Article 5(2), relating to forced labour for private ends, it was considered that States had gone as far as they could "in regulating forced labour"; it was judged by the negotiators "that to do more would be to go beyond our province."[66] While States were unwilling to place provisions within the 1926 Slavery Convention regulating forced labour for public ends, they did pass an Assembly resolution to that end, which stated that "forced labour for public purposes is sometimes necessary," but that as "as a general rule, it should not be resorted to unless it is impossible to obtain voluntary labour and that it should receive adequate remuneration."[67] As it was deemed, during the negotiation process, that it was not the providence of those negotiating to regulate forced labour, to whom did that task fall? The Assembly passed a second resolution requesting the International Labour Office to take over the issue of forced labour generally, and especially where it might develop into conditions analogous to slavery:

> Taking note of the work undertaken by the International Labour Office in conformity with the mission entrusted to it and within the limits of its constitution;
>
> Considering that these studies naturally include the problem of forced labour;
>
> Requests the Council to inform the Governing Body of the International Labour Office of the adoption of the Slavery Convention, and to draw its attention to the importance of the work undertaken by the Office with a view to studying the best means of preventing forced or compulsory labour from developing into conditions analogous to slavery."[68]

65 League of Nations, Slavery Convention, Resolutions adopted by the Assembly at its meeting held on September 25th, 1926, A.123.1926.VI, 25 September 1926, as found in League of Nations, Publications of the League of Nations, VI.B.Slavery.1926.

66 League of Nations, Slavery Convention: Report of the Sixth Committee: Resolution, League of Nations Official Journal (Special Supplement 44) Records of the Seventh Ordinary Assembly: Text of Debates, Seventeenth Plenary Meeting, 25 September 1926, p. 132.

67 League of Nations, Slavery Convention, Resolutions adopted by the Assembly at its meeting held on September 25th, 1926, A.123.1926.VI, 25 September 1926, as found in League of Nations, Publications of the League of Nations, VI.B.Slavery.1926.

68 League of Nations, Slavery Convention: Report of the Sixth Committee: Resolution, League of Nations Official Journal (Special Supplement 44) Records of the Seventh Ordinary Assembly: Text of Debates, Seventeenth Plenary Meeting, 25 September 1926, p. 132.

In so doing, an artificial distinction was created between forced labour and other types of servile status, as the International Labour Organisation was given the task of dealing with forced labour while the League of Nations and later the United Nations would deal with other types of exploitation.

In 1927, the Governing Body of the International Labour Office placed the issue of forced labour on the agenda for the 1929 General Conference of the International Labour Organisation (ILO) and, as the question was "one which affects for the most part, though not exclusively, the working conditions of subject peoples" under colonialism, created a Committee of Experts on Native Labour to consider the issue.[69] The International Labour Office in conjunction with the Committee of Experts determined that, from the legislation in force domestically and the opinions of experts, principles could be deduced which would allow for the regulation of forced labour where it still existed "with the triple object of removing from it any conditions which still render it 'analogous to slavery', of avoiding the evils associated with it, and of providing for its abolition."[70] These principles, it was concluded, were such that they could be included in a convention on forced labour.

In 1930, the Conference of the International Labour Organisation adopted the Forced Labour Convention (ILO Convention Number 29), though for the Workers' Members of the Committee of Forced Labour, which had been involved in the drafting process, what was being negotiated appeared, though it professed to have the aim of suppressing forced labour, in fact, tended "towards a kind of codification of forced labour."[71] While requiring States to suppress the use of forced or compulsory labour in all forms within the shortest possible period, the Forced Labour Convention established a transition period, where, for public purposes, as an exceptional measure, forced or compulsory labour was allowed, through regulated by the guarantees which make up the bulk of provision of the Convention. Thus, for example, only able-bodied males of between eighteen and forty-five could be used for no more than sixty days a year, working for the same hours and pay as prevailing for voluntary work. But for the definition of 'forced and compulsory labour' found at Article 2 which reads: "All work or service which is exacted under menace of any penalty for its non-performance and for which the worker concerned does not

---

69 International Labour Conference, 12th Session, Item III, *Forced Labour: Report and Draft Questionnaire*, 1929, p. 1.

70 *Id.*, p. 263.

71 International Labour Conference, 14th Session, Item I, Minority Report of the Workers Members of the Committee on Forced Labour, *Forced Labour*, 1930, p. 46.

offer himself voluntarily"; not much remains of the 1930 Forced Labour Convention.[72]

In 2007, the ILO's Committee of Experts on the Application of Conventions and Recommendations determined "that the use of any form of forced or compulsory labour falling within the scope of the Convention as defined by Article 2 may no longer be justified by invoking observance" of the transitional provisions; that is Articles 1(2) and 3-24. In other words, but for Article 25 which requires that illegal exaction of forced or compulsory labour shall be punished as a penal offence," the definition itself at Article 2, and the final provisions related to the ratification and denunciation, all other provisions of the 1930 Forced Labour Convention are to be considered not applicable, or dead-letter law. This is so, as the Committee of Experts relates: "since the Convention adopted in 1930 calls for the suppression of forced labour within the shortest possible period, it appears to be no longer possible to invoke these transitional provisions to the detriment of its main purpose. For a State to now be seen to rely on these transitional provisions would appear to disregard their transitional function and contradict the spirit of the Convention."[73]

In 1957, the Abolition of Forced Labour Convention (ILO Convention Number 105), was adopted, supplementing the 1930 Forced Labour Convention. While the 1930 Convention is mean to suppress all forms of forced labour, the 1957 Abolition of Forced Labour Convention seeks to highlight specific types of forced labour and require States to "take effective measures to secure the immediate and complete abolition" of such practices.[74] These types include forced labour as a means of political coercion, labour discipline, or discrimination; as a method of mobilising labour for economic development; or as punishment for participating in industrial action. In essence, the 1957 Convention seeks to protect certain workers rights regarding freedom of expression and rights of association and assembly; as opposed to the 1930 Convention which focused "on forms of forced labour for economic purposes."[75] Just as the 1930

72 Article 2, Forced Labour Convention, 1930 (No. 29).

73 International Labour Conference, *Eradication of Forced Labour*, General Survey concerning Forced Labour Convention, 1930 (No. 29), and the Abolition of Forced Labour Convention, 1957 (No. 105), Item III, Report of the Committee of Experts on the Application of Conventions and Recommendations, 2007, p. 6.

74 Abolition of Forced Labour Convention, 1957, (no. 105).

75 International Labour Conference, *Eradication of Forced Labour*, General Survey concerning Forced Labour Convention, 1930 (No. 29), and the Abolition of Forced Labour Convention, 1957 (No. 105), Item III, Report of the Committee of Experts on the Application of Conventions and Recommendations, 2007, pp. 81 and 91.

Convention was meant to focus on labour in the colonies and sought to eliminate forced labour within that context, the 1957 Convention was, in essence, focused on the type of forced labour practices by wartime totalitarian States and within the Socialist camp of the Cold War. With the demise of colonialism and the end of the Cold War, the driving force behind these types of forced labour, with notable exceptions, receded.[76]

One final element to the notion of forced labour is worth noting, the 1999 Worst Forms of Child Labour Convention (ILO Convention Number 182), establishes that one such worst form of child labour includes the forced or compulsory labour of children, but adds that this includes "forced or compulsory recruitment of children for use in armed conflict."[77]

Returning to consider the definition of forced labour, it bears repeating that the concept is defined as: *All work or service which is exacted under menace of any penalty for its non-performance and for which the worker concerned does not offer himself voluntarily*. This definition was put forward during the negotiations of the 1930 Forced Labour Convention and was considered by a tri-party Committee on Forced Labour which rejected a proposed amendment as "being possibly too wide," that the definition include the words 'or obligation' after 'penalty'; however, the same Committee was unanimous in holding that 'penalty' was not to be interpreted "in a strict sense to mean punishment inflicted by a court of justice," but instead that it was to mean "any penalty or punishment, inflicted by a persons or body whatever."[78] In the Report to 1930 International Labour Conference, the Worker's Group proposed a further amendment, seeking to include after the words 'under the menace of any penalty' the words, 'or the loss of any rights or privileges'. This proposal was however withdrawn "after it had been shown that the expression 'under the menace of penalty' would cover the contingencies which the amendment contemplated."[79]

---

76 For forced labour in a colonial setting, note the International Labour Conference, *Report of the Committee of Experts on the Application of Conventions and Recommendations*, Report III (Part IV), 46th Session, 1962, p. 194; where the Committee states that recourse to forced labour for economic purposes "has progressively diminished in a large number of countries, and even disappeared, under the influence of movement of thought, international standards, the gradual political emancipation of people and the general progress which had taken place in the economic and social sphere." For forced labour during the Cold War, consider S. Swianiewicz, *Forced Labour and Economic Development: An Enquiry into the Experience of Soviet Industrialization*, 1965.

77 Worst Forms of Child Labour Convention, 1999 (No. 182).

78 International Labour Conference, 14th Session, Item I, Report of the Committee on Forced Labour to the Twelfth Session of the Conference, *Forced Labour*, 1930, p. 11.

79 *Id.*, p. 691.

During the presentation of that Report of the Committee on Forced Labour to the 1930 General Conference, the Rapporteur noted that with regard to the definition of forced labour "it was right that this Article should be of a very sweeping character and that we should include everything we could in the terms of the definition; but this has the inevitable disadvantage that we cannot make so broad and sweeping a definition without subsequently making certain exceptions."[80] These exceptions, which remain to this day part of the overall definition of forced labour, as accepted in law, are:

(a) Any work or service exacted in virtue of compulsory military service laws for work of a purely military character;
(b) Any work or service which forms part of the normal civic obligations of the citizens of a fully self-governing country;
(c) Any work or service exacted from any person as a consequence of a conviction in a court of law, provided that the said work or service is carried out under the supervision and control of a public authority and that the said person is not hired to or placed at the disposal of private individuals, companies or associations;
(d) Any work or service exacted in cases of emergency, that is to say, in the event of war or of a calamity or threatened calamity, such as fire, flood, famine, earthquake, violent epidemic or epizootic diseases, invasion by animal, insect or vegetable pests, and in general any circumstance that would endanger the existence or the well-being of the whole or part of the population;
(e) Minor communal services of a kind which, being performed by the members of the community in the direct interest of the said community, can therefore be considered as normal civic obligations incumbent upon the members of the community, provided that the members of the community or their direct representatives shall have the right to be consulted in regard to the need for such services.[81]

---

80 International Labour Conference, 14th Session, Volume I – First and Second Part, Proceedings, Fifteenth Sitting, 25 June 1930, 1930 p. 269.

81 Article 2, Forced Labour Convention, 1930 (No. 29). The Rapporteur in presenting the draft Convention to the Conference noted that the "exceptions we have given generally speaking, fall into five divisions":

> We have decided that the definition of compulsory labour cannot include work exacted in virtue of compulsory military service laws, for the work of a purely military character. [...]
>
> Our second exception refers to the normal ci34.016 ptvic obligation of a self-governing community. [...] we did not want to interfere with the obligation of a citizen to serve

Where the elements of the definition of forced labour are concerned, turning first to the notion of a 'menace of a penalty'. A menace of a penalty – the means by which a person is held in a situation of forced labour[82] – was considered in the 2007 Report of the Committee of Experts on the Application of the Conventions and Recommendations which turned to examples of loss of rights or privileges which would constitute a 'menace of any penalty' within the 1930 definition:

> where persons who refuse to perform voluntary labour may lose certain rights, advantages or privileges, in a situation when such rights, privileges or other benefits (e.g. promotion, transfer, access to new employment, the acquisition of certain consumer goods, housing or participation in

---

on a jury, with his obligation to help to put out a conflagration, and many instances of this nature. It is with a view to such cases that this exception has been included.

Our third exception was penal labour. We felt that prisoners under sentence and labouring under the terms of their sentence did not represent the kind of forced labour contemplated, and that therefore such labour should be exempted.

Then we made an exception with regard to emergencies. We followed the principle *salus poluli suprema lex*; in case of emergency every man must play his part and must do whatever he is called upon to do to meet the emergency. It is perfectly certain that that will actually happen, and I do not think that the exception to the definition of forced labour is framed in too comprehensive terms.

Then came an exception which presented some difficulty; that is the last exception which removes from the definition of forced labour 'minor communal services'. We were not thinking of Europe, but of small native communities with their own history, their own traditions, their own habits, which very often have made it a practice that they should do a certain amount of work together for themselves and for one another. We did not want to interfere with that; on the other hand, we wanted to be sure that we were not making our exceptions too wide. We therefore all of us accepted – I think gladly – an amendment which was proposed by the Workers' Group, to provide that services of this kind should have the benefit of the exception only if the community had the right to express their own opinion upon it. In other words, we accepted the purely democratic principle. We will not appeal to what I might call the conservative principle of custom, practice, previous habit; we will appeal to the will of the people of the community. If they feel that what they are doing is for the common good, for the sake of one another, we do not call it forced labour at all. That which you are forced to do only by the constraints of your own sense of a communal duty is not a form of labour which we wish to interfere.

International Labour Conference, 14th Session, Volume I – First and Second Part, Proceedings, Fifteenth Sitting, 25 June 1930, 1930 pp. 269–270.

82 International Labour Conference, 93rd Session, Report of the Director-General: *Global Report under the Follow-up to the ilo Declaration on Fundamental Principles and Rights at Work*, Report I (B), 2005, 6.

> university programmes) depend on the merits that have been accumulated and noted in the worker's work book.[83]

In 2008, the Committee of Experts noted in the case of Algeria, that where, upon completing a course in higher education as person was required to provide from one to four years of civic service in order to be able to "obtain employment or exercise a trade," such persons "discharge this service under a menace because, in the event of refusal, they are denied access to any professional self-employed activity or to any employment in the private sector, as a result of which civic service falls within the concept of compulsory labour within the meaning of Article 2(1) of the Convention."[84] Likewise, the Committee of Experts noted that in Guatemala where public sector employees faced the termination of their contracts if they refused to work hours beyond the normal work day and where certain companies set excessive production targets so as to have employees work "excess of the ordinary hours of the working day in order to earn a survival wage," these consisted of work imposed under a menace of a penalty. The Committee continues:

> in both cases the common denominator is the imposition of work or a service and the worker has the possibility to "free her or himself" from such imposition only by leaving the job or accepting dismissal as a sanction for refusing to perform such work. In theory, workers have the choice of not working beyond normal working hours, but their choice is not real in practice in view of their need to earn, at least, the minimal wage and to retain their employment, or for both reasons. The Committee considered that in such cases the work or service is imposed under the menace of a penalty.[85]

As for the element of 'voluntary offer' of labour, this should be understood as being the requirement of consent.[86] The Committee of Experts, in considering

---

83 International Labour Conference, *Eradication of Forced Labour*, General Survey concerning Forced Labour Convention, 1930 (No. 29), and the Abolition of Forced Labour Convention, 1957 (No. 105), Item III, Report of the Committee of Experts on the Application of Conventions and Recommendations, 2007, p. 20.

84 International Labour Office, International Labour Conference, General Report of the Committee of Experts on the Application of Conventions and Recommendations, Report III (Part 1A), Nineteen-seventhly Session, 2008, p. 189.

85 *Id.*, p. 211.

86 International Labour Conference, 93rd Session, Report of the Director-General: *Global Report under the Follow-up to the ilo Declaration on Fundamental Principles and Rights at Work*, Report I (B), 2005, 6.

the element of 'voluntary offer', found that such a freedom must be understood as being prescribed by law, that is: "account must be taken of the legislative and practical framework which guarantees or limits that freedom." Beyond such statutory constraints, "indirect coercion interfering with a worker's freedom to 'offer himself voluntarily' may result [...] from an employer's practice, e.g. where migrant workers are induced by deceit, false promises and retention of identity documents or forced to remain at the disposal of an employer; such practices represent a clear violation of the Convention."[87] A worker's freedom to offer himself voluntarily, mandates that "the workers' right to free choice of employment remains inalienable" and, as such, "statutory provisions preventing termination of employment of indefinite duration (or very long duration) upon notice of reasonable length is to turn a contractual relationship based on the will of the parties into service by compulsion of law, and is thus incompatible with the Convention." Likewise, the requirement "to serve beyond the expiry of a contract of fixed duration" would be incompatible.[88]

Beyond the understanding of forced labour within the International Labour Organisation, the prohibition of forced labour within international human rights instruments and was introduced into that corpus by way of the Universal Declaration of Human Rights as a right as opposed to a prohibition; that is the right "to free choice of employment."[89] This, despite early consideration which saw proposals which read "slavery and compulsory labour are inconsistent with the dignity of man and therefore prohibited by this Bill of Rights"[90] and "compulsory labour is obnoxious to the dignity of man and should not be resorted to except in the case of war or other emergency threatening the life or well-being of the community or in the case of punishment of persons sentenced by a competent court in due process of law,"[91] being mooted, but ultimately not accepted for inclusion in the Declaration.

---

87 International Labour Conference, *Eradication of Forced Labour*, General Survey concerning Forced Labour Convention, 1930 (No. 29), and the Abolition of Forced Labour Convention, 1957 (No. 105), Item III, Report of the Committee of Experts on the Application of Conventions and Recommendations, 2007, p. 20.

88 International Labour Conference, *Eradication of Forced Labour*, General Survey concerning Forced Labour Convention, 1930 (No. 29), and the Abolition of Forced Labour Convention, 1957 (No. 105), Item III, Report of the Committee of Experts on the Application of Conventions and Recommendations, 2007, p. 20.

89 See Article 22, Universal Declaration of Human Rights, 1948.

90 United Nations, Economic and Social Council, Commission on Human Rights, Drafting Committee, Draft Outline of an International Bill of Rights, UN Doc. E/CN.4/AC.1/3, 4 June 1947, p. 4.

91 United Nations, Economic and Social Council, Commission on Human Rights (Second Session), Summary Record of the Thirty-Seventh Meeting, UN Doc. E/CN.4/SR.37, 13 December 1947, pp. 5 and 6.

The International Covenant on Civil and Political Rights provides at Article 8(3) that "No one shall be required to perform forced or compulsory labour," then proceeds to provide various exceptions which build on those of the 1930 Forced Labour Convention.[92] The supervisory body of that instrument, the Human Rights Committee has said little with regard to forced labour, but has noted positive obligations flowing from the provisions of the Covenant dealing with forced labour:

> The Committee urges the State party to enforce laws prohibiting forced labour, child labour and child prostitution and to implement programmes to prevent and combat such human rights abuses. In addition, the Committee exhorts the State party to establish more effective supervisory mechanisms to ensure compliance with the provisions of national legislation and relevant international standards. It is imperative that persons who are responsible for, or who directly profit from, forced labour, child labour and child prostitution, be severely punished under law.[93]

At the regional level, the European Court has developed jurisprudence regarding forced labour which the Explanatory Report of Council of Europe's trafficking convention points to, stating that Article 4 of the European Convention on Human Rights "prohibits forced labour without defining it," yet the drafters of the European Convention used the definition found in the Forced Labour

---

92 Article 8(3) of the International Covenant of Civil and Political Rights reads:
(a) No one shall be required to perform forced or compulsory labour;
(b) Paragraph 3 (a) [re: inhuman or degrading treatment or punishment] shall not be held to preclude, in countries where imprisonment with hard labour may be imposed as a punishment for a crime, the performance of hard labour in pursuance of a sentence to such punishment by a competent court.
(c) For the purpose of this paragraph the term 'forced or compulsory labour' shall not include:
   (i) Any work or service, not referred to in sub-paragraph (b), normally required of a person who is under detention in consequence of a lawful order of a court, or of a person during conditional release from such detention;
   (ii) Any service of a military character and, in countries where conscientious objection is recognized, any national service required by law of conscientious objectors;
   (iii) Any service exacted in cases of emergency or calamity threatening the life or well-being of the community;
   (iv) Any work or service which forms part of normal civil obligations.

93 United Nations, Human Rights Committee, Concluding Observations of the Human Rights Committee: Brazil. UN Doc. CCPR/C/79/Add.66, 24 July 1996, para. 336.

Convention as "their model."[94] The European Court has stated that "the concept of compulsory or forced labour cannot be understood solely in terms of the literal meaning of the words." That, instead, having reference to ILO conventions and resolutions there emerged certain elements which were reasonable to use when interpreting the provisions of the European Convention touching on forced labour: "first, that the work or service is performed by the worker against his will and, secondly, that the requirement that the work or service is performed is unjust or oppressive or the work or service itself involves unavoidable hardship."[95] In the case of *Siliadin v France*, the Court had the opportunity, in considered the case of a Togolese child exploited for domestic labour in France, and determined that with regard to forced labour, that this "brings to mind the idea of physical or mental constraint": "What there has to be is work "exacted [...] under the menace of any penalty" and also performed against the will of the person concerned, that is work for which he "has not offered himself voluntarily."

> The Court notes that, in the instant case, although the applicant was not threatened by a 'penalty', the fact remains that she was in an equivalent situation in terms of the perceived seriousness of the threat.
>
> She was an adolescent girl in a foreign land, unlawfully present in French territory and in fear of arrest by the police. Indeed, Mr and Mrs B. nurtured that fear and led her to believe that her status would be regularised.
>
> Accordingly, the Court considers that the first criterion was met, especially since the applicant was a minor at the relevant time, a point which the Court emphasises.
>
> As to whether she performed this work of her own free will, it is clear from the facts of the case that it cannot seriously be maintained that she did. On the contrary, it is evident that she was not given any choice.
>
> In these circumstances, the Court considers that the applicant was, at the least, subjected to forced labour within the meaning of Article 4 of the Convention at a time when she was a minor.[96]

94 Council of Europe, Council of Europe Convention on Action against Trafficking in Human Beings and its Explanatory Report, Council of Europe Treaty Series – No. 197, 16 May, 2005, p. 39, paras 89–90.

95 Council of Europe, European Court of Human Rights, *X. v. Federal Republic of Germany*, Application 4653/70, 1 April 1974.

96 Council of Europe, European Court of Human Rights, *Siliadin v France*, Application 73316/01, 26 July 2005, pp. 38–40.

Finally, the European Court has had the opportunity, in *Van der Müssele v. Belgium*, to consider the notion of 'forced services', as it stated that it is "true that the English word 'labour' is often used in the narrow sense of manual work, but it also bears the broad meaning of the French word 'travail' and it is the latter that should be adopted in the present context."[97] With this in mind the Explanatory Report of Council of Europe's trafficking convention states that words forced labour, "as used in Article 4 ECHR [European Convention of Human Rights], were to be given a broad meaning and encompassed the concept of forced services. From the standpoint of the ECHR, therefore, there is no distinction to be made between the two concepts."[98] Where the trafficking conventions are concerned, of course, this is not an issue as they speak of 'forced labour or services'.

Servitude (Practices Similar to Slavery)

It may be said that the term 'practices similar to slavery' as found in the trafficking conventions has colonised the area once inhabited by 'servitude'. As a result of the 1956 Supplementary on the Abolition of Slavery, the Slave Trade, and Institutions and Practices Similar to Slavery, 'servitude' no longer exists within general international law, instead having found a home within international human rights law. The term 'practices similar to slavery', for its part, should be understood as conventional servitudes established by the 1956 Supplementary Convention. Previous to 1956, the international community had dealt with debt bondage, serfdom, forced marriage and child exploitation under the rubric of 'servitude' as far back as the Temporary Slavery Commission in 1924. Yet as a result of the Universal Declaration of Human Rights, which proclaimed that "No one shall be held in slavery or servitude […]";[99] negotiators of the 1956 Convention found themselves in a difficult situation as they sought to deal with the abolition of servitude, only "progressively and as soon as possible."[100] To work their way out of this situation, the negotiators of the

---

97 Council of Europe, European Court of Human Rights, *Van der Müssele v. Belgium*, Application. 8919/80, 23 November 1983, p. 15.

98 Council of Europe, Council of Europe Convention on Action against Trafficking in Human Beings and its Explanatory Report, Council of Europe Treaty Series – No. 197, 16 May, 2005, p. 39, para. 92

99 See United Nations, General Assembly, Universal Declaration of Human Rights, Resolution 217 A(III), 10 December 1948, Article 4.

100 See Article 1, United Nations, Economic and Social Council, Slavery: Draft Supplementary Convention on the Abolition of Slavery, the Slave Trade, and Institutions and Practices Similar to Slavery: Report of the Committee appointed by Resolution 564 (XIX), 7 April 1955, UN Doc. E/2824, 15 February 1956, p. 20.

1956 Supplementary Convention moved to systematically expunge the term 'servitude' from its substantive provisions, replacing the term 'servitude' with 'institutions and practices similar to slavery'.

Thus, 'practices similar to slavery' are debt bondage, serfdom, forced marriage and child exploitation as defined by Article 1 of the 1956 Supplementary Convention on the Abolition of Slavery, the Slave Trade, and Institutions and Practices Similar to Slavery. Turn now to the various practices similar to slavery established by the 1956 Supplementary Convention; debt bondage is defined as:

> the status or condition arising from a pledge by a debtor of his personal services or of those of a person under his control as security for a debt, if the value of those services as reasonably assessed is not applied towards the liquidation of the debt or the length and nature of those services are not respectively limited and defined;[101]

In proposing that debt bondage be abolished, the United Nations 1951 *Ad Hoc* Committee on Slavery noted that debt bondage could manifest itself in two ways; "either an individual, owing a debt to another individual, pledges his personal services in payment of the debt; or he pledges the services of a third person under his control." Yet, the Committee did not consider that this "alone constituted a form of servitude," what was also required was a "general denial or disregard of the principle that an individual should be treated as a person rather than as a thing."

It therefore agreed that the presence of one or more of the following conditions was necessary to bring debt bondage within the Committee's concept of servitude:

(a) if the service rendered by the bondsman or the pawn do not count toward the payment of the debt;
(b) if the nature and length of the services to be performed by the bondsman or the pawn are not defined; or
(c) if the bondsman or the pawn submits to conditions that do not allow the person pledged to exercise the rights enjoyed by ordinary individuals with the framework of local social customs.[102]

---

101 United Nations Conference of Plenipotentiaries on a Supplementary Convention on the Abolition of Slavery, the Slave Trade and Institutions and Practices Similar to Slavery, Final Act and Supplementary Convention, 4 September 1956, UN Doc E/CONF.24/23.

102 United Nations, Economic and Social Council, Report of the *Ad Hoc* Committee on Slavery (Second Session), UN Doc E/1988, E/AC.33/13, 4 May 1951, pp. 8–9.

While the final conditions did not find its way into the definition of debt bondage accepted by States in the 1956 Supplementary Convention, the first two did. When considering the Draft Supplementary Convention in early 1956, the Egyptian member of the drafting committee asked if the first part – i.e.: 'the status or condition arising from a pledge by a debtor of his personal services or those of a third person under his control as a security for a debt' – "was a definition of debt bondage," while the second part – 'here the value of those services rendered is not applied towards the liquidation of the debt and the person pledged has to serve the creditor until the debt is repaid' – "was a qualification of that definition"? This was not so, according to the sponsor of the text and the chair of the drafting committee, both of whom "thought that the whole paragraph was a definition of debt bondage. Where the conditions specified in the second part were not fulfilled, the situation was perfectly legitimate."[103]

The second type of a practice similar to slavery is serfdom which is defined as:

> the condition or status of a tenant who is by law, custom or agreement bound to live and labour on land belonging to another person and to render some determinate service to such other person, whether for reward or not, and is not free to change his status.[104]

It was again the 1951 UN *Ad Hoc* Committee on Slavery which, in recommending serfdom be included in a supplementary convention which noted that this practice still existed wherein "an individual is attached to agricultural or pastoral land and cannot change his status or freely dispose of the produce of his labour. The attachment might be effected either by law (including customary law), custom, or agreement. In some cases the individual may be required to perform duties for the landowner without compensation."[105] As will be noted, the notion of being freely able to dispose of the produce of one's labour was dropped from the definitions despite an attempt by the Pakistani negotiator to have such a provision appear in the final text. The Representative of Pakistan argued that a:

103 United Nations, Economic and Social Council, Committee on the Drafting of a Supplementary Convention on Slavery and Servitude, Summary Record of the Eleventh Meeting, 20 January 1956, UN Doc. E/AC.43/SR.11, 24 February 1956, pp. 6 and 7.

104 United Nations Conference of Plenipotentiaries on a Supplementary Convention on the Abolition of Slavery, the Slave Trade and Institutions and Practices Similar to Slavery, Final Act and Supplementary Convention, 4 September 1956, UN Doc E/CONF.24/23.

105 *Id.*, p. 11.

> condition in which a tenant was bound to labour on the land and to give the produce of his labour to a landlord or other person without any choice in the matter did appropriately fall within the meaning of the term serfdom. According to the present, somewhat loose, definition of serfdom, the condition in which A entered into an agreement with B to live and labour on the latter's land and to render him service for wages was serfdom provided only that A was not free to change his status. Serfdom started where in the case of tenant and a landlord the former was not free to change his status. If that conception was enlarged, a condition where a tenant was bound to work on the landlord's land having no freedom to dispose of a crop which had been cultivated by him was akin to the condition of serfdom contemplated in the convention."[106]

This argument however did not hold sway, as the International Labour Organisation's representative noted that the proposal would bring into question the system of share-cropping and that the "ILO would regard such a system as an aspect of abnormally low standards of labour rather than of slavery."[107] The French Representative added, that tenant farmers and *métayers* "could not be regarded as a form of slavery, since – apart from contractual obligations of limited duration – both were free to change their status."[108]

The third type of institutions of practice similar to slavery covered by Article 1 of the Supplementary Convention on the Abolition of Slavery, the Slave Trade, and Institutions and Practices Similar to Slavery is forced marriage, which was meant to cover marriages steeped in social custom. The provision of Article 1(c) seeks to abolish:

Any institution or practice whereby:

(i) A woman, without the right to refuse, is promised or given in marriage on payment of a consideration in money or in kind to her parents, guardian, family or any other person or group; or
(ii) The husband of a woman, his family, or his clan, has the right to transfer her to another person for value received or otherwise; or

106 United Nations, Economic and Social Council, United Nations Conference of Plenipotentiaries on a Supplementary Convention on the Abolition of Slavery, the Slave Trade and Institutions and Practices Similar to Slavery, Summary Record of the Twenty-First Meeting, 31 August 1956, UN Doc E/CONF.24/SR.21, 20 November 1958, pp. 6–7.
107 *Id.*, p. 7.
108 *Id.*

(iii) A woman on the death of her husband is liable to be inherited by another person.[109]

The 1951 UN *Ad Hoc* Committee on Slavery noted that where the payment of bride-price was tokenistic or ritualistic it was not concerned, however, it was not willing to accept "any practice which placed a women in a servile status."

> It found ample evidence that in certain parts of the world the bride-to-be is regarded as the property of her father, or that at least his right is recognized to dispose of her in marriage; and that as a widow she is regarded as part of the heritable property of her husband and as such passes to the person who inherits the property on his death. Children of the marriage in such cases are also often at the disposal of their late father's heir. It was the presence of one or more of these elements which in the opinion of the Committee brought the practice of payments of bride-price within the scope of its study. [...] The Committee decided, therefore, that it would consider as a form of servitude the practice whereby a women is given in marriage [...].[110]

The final type of institutions of practice similar to slavery is found at Article 1(d) 1956 Supplementary Convention; it touches on the exploitation of children and reads:

> Any institution or practice whereby a child or young person under the age of 18 years is delivered by either or both of his natural parents or by his guardian to another person, whether for reward or not, with a view to the exploitation of the child or young person or of his labour.[111]

In considering the issue, the 1951 UN *Ad Hoc* Committee on Slavery pointed to the practice known as '*mui tsai*' in Asia, noting that it involves the sale of a child's working capacity and usually takes the form of the transfer of a small child, usually a girl, for employment as a domestic servant by means of an

109 United Nations Conference of Plenipotentiaries on a Supplementary Convention on the Abolition of Slavery, the Slave Trade and Institutions and Practices Similar to Slavery, Final Act and Supplementary Convention, 4 September 1956, UN Doc E/CONF.24/23.

110 United Nations, Economic and Social Council, Report of the *Ad Hoc* Committee on Slavery (Second Session), UN Doc E/1988, E/AC.33/13, 4 May 1951, pp. 9–10.

111 United Nations Conference of Plenipotentiaries on a Supplementary Convention on the Abolition of Slavery, the Slave Trade and Institutions and Practices Similar to Slavery, Final Act and Supplementary Convention, 4 September 1956, UN Doc E/CONF.24/23.

adoption procedure, sometimes fraudulent. The custom has been known to exist under other names in other regions of the world, including parts of Africa." The Committee recognised that in many cases issues of servitude were not at issue as parents had the best interests of the child at heart; the "Committee therefore felt that a status or condition of servitude existed only when the conditions of the transfer were such as to permit the exploitation of the child regardless of its welfare."[112] For its part, the Interpretative Notes of the Palermo Protocol adds some substance to this provision noting that "where illegal adoption amounts to a practice similar to slavery as defined in article 1, paragraph (d), of the Supplementary Convention on the Abolition of Slavery, the Slave Trade, and Institutions and Practices Similar to Slavery, will also fall within the scope of the Protocol."[113] Paragraph (d) speaks of when a child is delivered by a parent or guardian for reward with "a view to the exploitation of the child or young person or their labour."

While it is accurate to say that practices similar to slavery have taken over from 'servitude' it general international law, the notion of 'servitude' still has currency in international human rights law as it has been given content by reference, primarily, to decisions by adjudicative organs related to human rights. In international human rights law, the provisions flowing from the Universal Declaration are those of Article 8(2) of the International Covenant on Civil and Political Rights, which states that "No one shall be held in servitude." While the Human Rights Committee has yet to comment on the substance of that provision, the monitoring bodies of the Council of Europe have. As the Explanatory Report of the Trafficking Convention notes, the former European Commission of Human Rights regarded servitude "as having to live and work on another person's property and perform certain services for them, whether paid or unpaid, together with being unable to alter one's condition." The Report goes on to say that servitude "is thus to be regarded as a particular form of slavery, differing from it less in character [...] than in degree. Although it constitutes a state or condition, and is a 'particularly serious form of denial

112 *Id.*, p. 10.

113 See General Assembly, Report of the Ad Hoc Committee on the Elaboration of a Convention against Transnational Organized Crime on the work of its First to Eleventh Sessions, Addendum: Interpretative notes for the official records (*travaux préparatoires*) of the negotiation of the United Nations Convention against Transnational Organized Crime and the Protocols thereto, A/55/383/Add.1, 3 November 2000, p. 12.
The same provisions, *mutatis mutandis*, are found in Council of Europe, Council of Europe Convention on Action against Trafficking in Human Beings and its Explanatory Report, Council of Europe Treaty Series – No. 197, 16 May, 2005, p. 39, para. 93.

of freedom', [...] it does not have the ownership features characteristic of slavery."[114]

It must be said that this explanation is lacking in certain regards, as there is an internal inconsistency in the pronouncement: if servitude is a 'particular form of slavery' then it must meet the threshold of the definition of slavery. However, the Explanatory Report goes on to say that 'it does not have the ownership features characteristic of slavery'. That said, it is clear that the European Court of Human Rights in its 2005 *Siliadin* case, has taken a novel approach to issues of slavery and servitude. This approach might result from two factors, first historically, Europe has witness, in the 1930s, the legalisation of enslavement manifest in German-run concentration camps;[115] second, as opposed to international criminal law which only knows the crime of 'enslavement', the European Convention provides for the prohibition of 'servitude' along with 'slavery' under its jurisdiction. These two factors might explain the European Court of Human Rights' approach toward slavery and servitude, wherein it has determined that for slavery to exist one must have "exercised a genuine right of legal ownership" over a person, reducing them "to the status of an 'object'."[116] Having determined that in the European context 'slavery' means legal enslavement, the Court has reserved the concept should the day arise when a European State seek once mare to introduce into law slavery on the Continent. This the Court can do as it has the luxury of falling back on the notion of 'servitude', much as it has in the past, with regard to Article 3, when it failed to find any State in violation of 'torture' for some forty year, instead deeming all violations of this article as falling under the lesser prohibition on 'inhuman or degrading treatment or punishment'.

In *Siliadin*, the European Court of Human Rights repeated its earlier finding in the 1980 *Van Droogenbroeck* case, that servitude is "a particularly serious form of denial of freedom." The European Court notes that this may include "in addition to the obligation to provide certain services to another [...] the obligation on the 'serf' to live on the other's property and the impossibility of changing his status." The Court, in *Siliadin*, states that it "follows in the light of the case-law on this issue that for Convention purposes 'servitude' means an

114 Council of Europe, Council of Europe Convention on Action against Trafficking in Human Beings and its Explanatory Report, Council of Europe Treaty Series – No. 197, 16 May, 2005, p. 40, para. 95.

115 See Michael Bazyler and Roger Alford (eds.), *Holocaust Restitution: Prespectives on the Litigation and its Legacy*, 2006.

116 Council of Europe, European Court of Human Rights, *Siliadin v France* (Application 73316/01), 26 July 2005, p. 39.

obligation to provide one's services that is imposed by the use of coercion, and is to be linked with the concept of 'slavery'." The Court then considered a number of facts in the case, including that Ms. Siwa-Akofa Siliadin having been a minor at the time, had not chosen to work for those who had reduced her to servitude, and that lacking resources, she was both "vulnerable and isolated," her papers having been confiscated and fearing arrest by the police, she was entirely at the mercy of those who were exploiting her. "In those circumstances, the Court concludes that the applicant, a minor at the relevant time, was held in servitude within the meaning of Article 4 of the Convention."[117]

Slavery

Turing now to slavery, it is accepted in law that the definition of slavery is that found in the 1926 Slavery Convention. While the European Court of Human Rights has decided that this definition hinges on establishing "a genuine right of legal ownership" over the victim;[118] this understanding is at variance with the International Criminal Tribunal for the former Yugoslavia which determined "that the law does not know of a 'right of ownership over a person'. Article 1(1) of the 1926 Slavery Convention speaks more guardedly 'of a person over whom any or all of the powers attaching to the right of ownership are exercised'. That language is to be preferred."[119]

Indeed, that language is preferred; the definition in essence relates to not only the *de jure* status of slavery, but the *de facto* condition of slavery. In international law if, in interpreting a treaty provision – such as the definition of slavery – "the meaning is ambiguous or obscure,"[120] then recourse may be had to the legislative history to confirm the meaning as it was understood by those negotiating the provision. As a result of conflicting interpretation by these two judicial instances, renewed interest in the legislative history has emerged, which has resulted in the preparation of the *travaux préparatoires* of the slavery conventions.[121] The preparatory works of those convention confirms the approach taken by the Yugoslav Tribunal, that slavery defined in international law is not restricted to legal ownership – a status which exists nowhere

117 *Id.*, pp. 38–40.

118 *Id.*

119 United Nations, Security Council, International Criminal Tribunal for the former Yugoslavia, *Kunarac et als.* (IT-96-23 &-IT-96-23/1-A) Judgment, 12 June 2002, paras 117–119.

120 See Article 32,Vienna Convention on the Law of Treaties, 1969.

121 See Jean Allain, *The Slavery Conventions: The* Travaux Préparatoires *of the 1926 League of Nations Convention and the 1956 United Nations Convention*, 2008.

today – but to a situation where one individual exercises powers over another which are akin to, or attach themselves to, a right of ownership. To use the analogy of illegal drugs, in a dispute over heroin neither criminal party can claim a right of ownership to be vindicated in a court of law; yet the authorities may arrest the parties and establish that one or the other exercised powers attaching to the right of ownership, in their case: possession. While the drug dealer did not 'own', *de jure*, the heroin, he did exercise *de facto* possession, a power which attaches to ownership despite the fact that ownership is not possible in law.

What then are these 'powers attaching to the right of ownership'? In 1953, the United Nations Secretary-General turned his attention to this issue and explained that the 'powers attached to the right of ownership' were the purchase; transfer; and absolute control over a person, in particular their labour and the product of that labour. Further, he noted that the end of the condition of slavery was one which was seen by the slave as being indeterminate; and finally that the status or condition of slavery could be inherited.[122] This understanding that the definition of slavery encompasses both *de jure* and *de facto* acts of enslavement was recognised during the League of Nations era, when in 1936, the Committee of Experts on Slavery considered the notion of 'debt' slavery, stating that no matter the form it might take in any States, it "is not 'slavery' within the definition set forth in Article 1 of the 1926 Convention, unless any or all the powers attaching to the right of ownership are exercised by the master."[123]

During the move toward establishing the 1956 Supplementary Convention on the Abolition of Slavery, the Slave Trade, and Institutions and Practices Similar to Slavery, doubts were raised as to whether such a supplementary convention was necessary. The UN Secretary-General himself seemed against the move towards establishing a new convention, acknowledging that some members of the 1951 *Ad Hoc* Committee on Slavery considered that debt bondage, forced marriage, and child exploitation, already fell within the 1926 definition of slavery and that for his part,

> It would appear from a study of the International Slavery Convention of 1926, and of the preparatory work leading to its adoption, that the obligations of

---

122 See United Nations Economic and Social Council, Slavery, the Slave Trade, and other forms of Servitude (Report of the Secretary-General), UN Doc. E/2357, 27 January 1953.

123 League of Nations, Slavery: Report of the Advisory Committee of Experts, Third (Extraordinary) Meeting of the Advisory Committee, C.189(I). M.145.1936, VI, 13–14 April 1936, pp. 24–25.

> the Parties therefore extended to all institutions or practices, whether or not designated as 'slavery', provided that, as stated in Article 1 of the Convention, 'any or all of the powers attaching to the right of ownership are exercised' over a person in these institutions or practices.[124]

Thus, even if it was, for example, termed 'debt bondage', in law, if a power attached to the right of ownership was manifest, it is deemed 'slavery'. The Anti-Slavery Society, the former incarnation of Anti-Slavery International, recognised as much[125] when its proposal was accepted that States recognise that the 1956 Supplementary Convention should seek to abolish various servitudes "where they still exist and whether or not they are covered by the definition of slavery contained in article 1 of the Slavery Convention."[126]

International Criminal Law

It is recognised in international law that slavery is the most severe type of exploitation established along the continuum of coercion. As a result, where slavery and the other forms of exploitation are concerned, a hierarchy in international law exists and though a practice may be tantamount to forced labour, to serfdom, or to debt bondage; if it meets a certain threshold it will also be deemed slavery in law. This hierarchy is recognised as, for instance, the 1926 Slavery Convention speaks of preventing "compulsory or forced labour from developing into conditions analogous to slavery," while the 1956 Supplementary Convention, moves to abolish servitudes, "where they still exist and whether or not they are covered by the definition of slavery contained in article 1 of the Slavery Convention." Furthermore, in international criminal law, sexual exploitation, forced labour, practices-similar to slavery, or servitude are not international crimes *per se*, but may be considered as such if they meet the threshold of 'enslavement' in law. This is separate from the issue of criminalisation at the domestic level, wherein there is a

---

124 See United Nations, Economic and Social Council, Slavery, the Slave Trade, and other forms of Servitude (Report of the Secretary-General), UN Doc. E/2357, 27 January 1953, p. 23.

125 See United Nations, Economic and Social Council, The Draft Supplementary Convention of Slavery and Servitude Submitted by the Government of the United Kingdom and Comments Thereon (Memorandum by the Secretary-General), UN Doc. E/AC.43/L.1, 2 December 1955, pp. 21–22.

126 See Article 1, Supplementary Convention on the Abolition of Slavery, the Slave Trade, and Institutions and Practices Similar to Slavery, 1956, p. 22.

requirement, emanating from a number of international treaties, to criminalise in the domestic order most types of exploitation mentioned in the trafficking conventions. The trafficking conventions, for their part, mandate that States criminalise the conduct of trafficking in persons, thus requiring parties to these conventions to criminalise not exploitation, but "the recruitment, transportation, transfer, harbouring or receipt of persons, by means of the threat or use of force or other forms of coercion [...] for the purpose of exploitation."

Enslavement as an International Crime

As noted an established hierarchy with slavery at the pinnacle of human exploitation is acknowledged within the 1926 Slavery Convention and the 1956 Supplementary Convention as well as the Council of Europe which acknowledges the difference between slavery and servitude being one of degree rather than character. In the case of the 1926 and 1956 Conventions, there is an acknowledgment that lesser servitudes may amount to slavery. In law, how is this to be determined? Referring back to the earlier discussion of slavery, if forced labour or services, institutions or practices similar to slavery, or servitude, whatever the terminology used to describe a practice, be it debt bondage or forced marriage, manifests any or all of the powers attaching to the right of ownership, then such examples of exploitation are in law also 'slavery'. That is not to say that these exploitive practices are not, for instance, forced labour or servitude, but that they have also met the higher threshold of slavery and thus can be considered for prosecution as such.

It might thus be worthwhile to examine what slavery is, by considering in greater depth the 'powers attaching to the right of ownership' which allow for a distinction to be made between slavery and lesser forms of exploitation. In 2008, the Australian Human Rights and Equality Commission intervened in a case in the High Courts of Australia, regarding a brothel owner who was appealing a ten-year prison sentence for having enslaved Thai prostitutes, seeking to speak to the definition of slavery in international law. The Commissions "list of the factors that might indicate that a power attaching to a right of ownership has been exercised" is as follows:

(a) The partial or total destruction of the juridical personality of the victim.
(b) Some restriction or control of an individual's autonomy, freedom of choice or freedom of movement.
(c) The control of matters relating to an individual's sexual activity.
(d) The psychological control or oppression of the individual.
(e) The control or partial control of an individual's personal belongings.

(f) The measures taken to prevent or deter a person from escape.
(h) The absence of informed consent or the fact that consent has been rendered irrelevant by the use offeree or coercion, the use of deception or false promises or the abuse of power in the context of the relationship where the individual over whom the power is exercised is in a position of vulnerability.
(i) The threat or use offeree or other forms of coercion.
(j) The use of, or the fear of the use of, violence including, for example, the cruel treatment or abuse of an individual.
(k) The quality of the relationship between the accused and the person over whom the powers are exercised, including any abuse of power, the person's vulnerability, the person's socio-economic situation and the duration of the relationship.
(m) The exaction of forced or compulsory labour or service, often without remuneration and often, though not necessarily, involving physical hardship, sex, prostitution and human trafficking.[127]

This approach appears to go too far, as it escapes the link to ownership, either *de facto* or *de jure*, which is the basis of the definition of slavery. By introducing issues such as the oppression of the individual, of deception and abuse of power creating a situation of vulnerability, and of cruel treatment or abuse, the Commission has over-stretched the notion of slavery beyond the judicial horizons of what could provide for legal certainty. This assessment is borne out in the judgement of that case, where the High Courts of Australia in *The Queen v Tang*, determined that a more measured consideration of those 'powers attaching to the right of ownership', was developed by the United Nations Secretary-General in 1953,[128] wherein he stated that these powers include the following:

1. the individual of servile status may be made the object of a purchase;
2. the master may use the individual of servile status, and in particular his capacity to work, in an absolute manner, without any restriction other than that which might be expressly provided by law;

127 See Australian Human Rights and Equality Commission, Submission in Support of the Application for Leave to Intervened and Submission on the Appeal, *Commonwealth Director of Public Prosecution v Wei Tang*, High Court of Australia, Melbourne, 5 May 2008, p. 15. Footnotes excluded.

128 See The High Courts of Australia, *The Queen v Tang* [2008] HCA 39, 28 August 2008, M5/2008, p. 13, para. 26.

3. the products of labour of the individual of servile status become the property of the master without any compensation commensurate to the value of the labour;
4. the ownership of the individual of servile status can be transferred to another person;
5. the servile status is permanent, that is to say, it cannot be terminated by the will of the individual subject to it;
6. the servile status is transmitted *ipso facto* to descendants of the individual having such status.[129]

The first and fourth of these characteristics, that is: a person who finds him or herself being made the object of purchase or transfer would, thus, be in the status or condition of slavery.[130] Put this way, it becomes clear that being made the object of purchase or transfer, if this were legal, would create in the individual the status of a slave and create for the master a right of ownership over the individual; whereas if a person is made the object of purchase or transfer where no such selling or transfer is possible in law, it creates for the individual the *condition* of slavery and manifests, for the recipient, an exercise of a power attached to the right of ownership, though not a *right of ownership* able to be vindicated in a court of law.

The second of the UN Secretary-General's six characteristics of the powers attaching to the right of ownership turns on the ability to exploit another: "the master may use the individual of servile status, and in particular his capacity to work, in an absolute manner, without any restriction other than that which might be expressly provided by law." Here the apparent contradiction between being able to use an individual in 'an absolute manner' as against 'without any restriction other than that which might be expressly provided by law' is solved by reference to an earlier discussion by the Secretary-General regarding Roman

129 See United Nations, Economic and Social Council, Slavery, the Slave Trade, and other forms of Servitude (Report of the Secretary-General), UN Doc. E/2357, 27 January 1953, p. 28.

130 It should be noted that the use of the phrase 'servile status' by the Secretary-General predates the use of the term as defined in Article 7(2) of the 1956 Convention: "'A person of servile status' means a person in the condition or status resulting from any of the institutions or practices mentioned in article 1 of this Convention," with the institutions and practices in Article 1 being debt bondage, serfdom, forced or sham marriages and exploitation of children via adoptions. Thus, the definition as set out in Article 7(2) of the 1956 Convention of 'a person of servile status' is not applicable here as being retrospective; instead, 'servile status' should be understood as being synonymous with the status or condition wherein, if one of the six characteristics of the Secretary-General is attached, a power of the right of ownership would be exercised, and thus slavery would be manifest.

Law where he noted that the "authority of the master over the slave was subjected successively to more and more limitations; but even though it was restricted, the master never had towards his slave the obligations that an employer has today towards his servant or employee."[131] As *de jure* slavery no longer exists, an overarching prohibition exists and thus restrictions existing in law no longer hold. Despite this, or as a result, the 'master' in using the individual and their labour 'in an absolute manner', would be acting outside the law. The third of the Secretary-General's characteristics, follows closely from the second, as 'the products of labour of the individual of servile status become the property of the master without any compensation commensurate to the value of the labour'. Here, whether having the status of a slave or being in the condition of slavery remains irrelevant to the fact that the master would benefit from exercising the power attaching to the right of ownership with regard to the fruits of one's labour. The 1926 submission of the Union of South Africa of the draft of the Slavery Convention, picks up on this point:

> That definition puts as the test of slavery the status or condition of a person over whom all or any of the powers attaching to the right of *ownership* are exercised. In other words, a person is a slave if any other person can, by law or enforceable custom, claim such property in him as would be claimed if he were an inanimate object; and thus the natural freedom of will possessed by a person to offer or render his labour or to control the fruits thereof or the consideration therefrom is taken from him.[132]

Having already considered the fourth of the Secretary-General's six characteristics, consideration now turns to the fifth: "the servile status is permanent, that is to say, it cannot be terminated by the will of the individual subject to it." The discussion by the Secretary-General deals with an assertion made in 1926 by the Union of South Africa that the definition of slavery "also seems to imply a *permanent* status or condition of a person whose natural freedom is taken away, for from the proprietary interest of the other person in the person to whom that status attaches is implied a right of disposal of sale, gift or exchange."[133] But

---

131 United Nations, Economic and Social Council, Slavery, the Slave Trade, and other forms of Servitude (Report of the Secretary-General), UN Doc. E/2357, 27 January 1953, p. 29.

132 League of Nations, Draft Convention on Slavery, Replies of Governments, Reply from the Government of the Union of South Africa, A.10(a).1926.VI, 22 July 1926, p. 5; as found in Publications of the League of Nations, VI.B.Slavery, 1926.VI.B.3. Emphasis in the original.

133 *Id.* The temporal issue of whether slavery had to be permanent in nature also arose in the considerations of 1930 the International Commission of Inquiry into the Existence of Slavery and Forced Labour in the Republic of Liberia. 8 September 1930, at p. 14.

here one sees that the Secretary-General is not concerned so much with there being a permanent status or condition which would last until the enslaved dies but, instead, that the status or condition "cannot be terminated by the will of the individual subject to it," and thus an indefinite status or condition exists, as far as the enslaved is concerned.

The final characterisation of a power attached to the right of ownership which the Secretary-General mentions is that 'the servile status is transmitted *ipso facto* to descendants of the individual having such status'. Little need be said about this power as for instance with regard to debt-bondage, the condition of slavery often manifests itself through the inheritance of debt, and, as such, it is, like the other UN Secretary-General's characteristics, an authoritative description of a manifestation of the exercise of a power attaching to the right of ownership and thus 'slavery' as established by international law.

Coming back to the distinction between slavery and other types of human exploitation; it is important to understand the hierarchy which has developed, which deems slavery to occupy the terrain wherein *de jure* or *de facto* rights of ownership are manifest and lesser forms of exploitation where such powers attaching to the right of ownership are not present. This is rather important as, in international criminal law there exists the crime of 'enslavement', most prominent in the 1998 Statute of the International Criminal Court, but no crime of forced labour, practices similar to slavery, or servitude *per se*.

The Statute of the International Criminal Court establishes enslavement as a crime against humanity; and sexual slavery as both a crime against humanity and a war crime. Enslavement is defined as "the exercise of any or all of the powers attaching to the right of ownership over a person and includes the exercise of such power in the course of trafficking in persons, in particular women and children."[134] Here then there is an acknowledgement of slavery being an example of exploitation manifest in the trafficking conventions. But, there is more to the story than that. The International Criminal Court has secondary legislation which seeks to provide further understanding to the meaning of the crimes under its jurisdiction: the Elements of the Crimes.[135] Where enslavement is concerned, the Elements of the Crimes elaborates on this definition by noting, in part, that it should be recognised that the perpetrator will have "exercised any or all of the powers attaching to the right of ownership over one or more persons, such as by purchasing, selling, lending or bartering

134 Article 7(2)(c), Statute of the International Criminal Court, 1988.

135 See Assembly of States Parties to the Rome Statute of the International Criminal Court, "Elements of the Crimes," ICC-ASP/1/3, 3–10 September 2002, pp. 108–155.

such a person or persons, or by imposing on them a similar deprivation of liberty." Attached to this, detailing of the crime of enslavement, is a footnote which reads:

> It is understood that such deprivation of liberty may, in some circumstances, include exacting forced labour or otherwise reducing a person to a servile status as defined in the Supplementary Convention on the Abolition of Slavery, the Slave Trade, and Institutions and Practices Similar to Slavery of 1956. It is also understood that the conduct described in this element includes trafficking in persons, in particular women and children.[136]

The Elements of the Crimes, thus recognise that forced labour, practices similar to slavery or the exploitive practices manifest in the trafficking conventions, may 'in some circumstances' fall under the heading of the crime of enslavement. Those circumstances would be when these examples of exploitation rise to the level where they manifest any or all of the powers attaching to the right of ownership.

i Forced Labour or Services

While Article 25 of 1930 Forced Labour Convention requires that the "illegal exaction of forced or compulsory labour shall be punishable as a penal offence" and that States Party are required to ensure that the penalties imposed by law are really adequate and are strictly enforced"; it may be said that forced labour is not an international crime *per se*. Instead, only when forced labour degenerates – or through the continuum of coercion – moves to manifest powers attaching to the right of ownership will it be considered that forced labour is deemed 'slavery' in international law and thus an international crime. Recalling that the definition of forced labour is *all work or service which is exacted under menace of any penalty for its non-performance and for which the worker concerned does not offer himself voluntarily*. If we then consider once more the powers attaching to the right of ownership as put forward by the United Nations Secretary-General in 1953, in light of this definition, two such powers become relevant. Forced labour would be tantamount to 'slavery' in law when one's capacity to work was controlled, in an absolute manner, by another; or

136 *Id.*, p. 117. Note that, for sexual slavery, the Elements of the Crimes repeat verbatim the elements of enslavement but add that the "perpetrator caused such person or persons to engage in one or more acts of a sexual nature." The footnote is also repeated verbatim.

when the produce of one's labour becomes the property of the another "without any compensation commensurate to the value of the labour."[137] In international criminal law, such situations being manifest would allow for the prosecution of forced labour as 'enslavement'; situations falling short of that would be considered forced labour. This understanding of the relationship of forced labour to slavery was spelled out both before the International Criminal Tribunal for the former Yugoslavia and the Special Court for Sierra Leone. The Special Court noted that the Yugoslav Tribunal – in the *Krnojelac* case regarding prisoners of war – required its Prosecutor to establish that forced labour constituted enslavement by demonstrating that "the Accused forced the detainees to work, that he exercised any or all of the powers attaching to the right of ownership over them, and that he exercised those powers intentionally."[138]

ii Practices Similar to Slavery (and Servitude)

During the negotiations of both the 1926 and 1956 slavery conventions, it was clear that servitude was a lesser form of exploitation than slavery; that is: where the elements of *de facto* or *de jure* ownership were not present. Further, as a result of the 1956 Supplementary Convention, 'servitude' was displaced by the conventional servitudes of debt bondage, serfdom, forced marriage, and child exploitation know as 'practices similar to slavery'.[139] What is thus left for the term 'servitude' in international law is the covering of these same-said servile forms of debt bondage, serfdom, forced marriage, and child exploitation for States which are not party to the 1956 Convention,[140] plus any further customary elaboration, manifest through State practice and *opinio juris*, of the term accepted by States.

It is worth repeating that the 1956 Supplementary Convention on the Abolition of Slavery, the Slave Trade, and Institutions and Practices Similar to Slavery, which sets out institutions or practice similar to slavery, establishes

---

137 See United Nations Economic and Social Council, Slavery, the Slave Trade, and other forms of Servitude (Report of the Secretary-General), UN Doc. E/2357, 27 January 1953, p. 28.

138 Special Court of Sierra Leone, *Prosecutor v. Brima, Kamara, and Kanu*, SCSL-04-16-T, 20 June 2007, p. 230.

139 The term 'servile status', used within the Elements of the Crimes tracks the language of the 1956 Convention, wherein Article 7(b) provides a definition of 'A person of servile status' which "means a person in the condition or status resulting from any of the institutions or practices mentioned in article 1 of this Convention," those institutions or practices being debt bondage, serfdom, forced marriage, and child exploitation.

140 This would cover approximately seventy States, as there were, as of 1 January 2008, one hundred and twenty-two States party to the 1956 Supplementary Convention.

that debt bondage, serfdom, forced marriage, and child exploitation, are to be abolished "where they still exist and whether or not they are covered by the definition of slavery contained in article 1 of the Slavery Convention." In other words, if debt bondage, serfdom, forced marriage, or child exploitation manifest any or all of the powers attaching to the right of ownership, they can also be considered as 'slavery' in law for the purposes of prosecution. But if they lack the element of *de facto* or *de jure* ownership, they are still to be considered and dealt with exclusively under the heading of 'practices similar to slavery'. Thus debt bondage, serfdom, forced marriage, and child exploitation *as defined by the 1956 Supplementary Convention* are to be understood as 'practices similar to slavery' where manifestations of ownership, either *de jure* or *de facto*, are not present. This very premise, however, was questioned by some members of the expert group leading up the 1956 Supplementary Convention: the 1951 *Ad Hoc* Committee on Slavery – which considered that debt bondage, forced marriage and child exploitation fell exclusively within the definition of slavery and could not but manifest powers either *de jure* or *de facto* of ownership; though this opinion did not forestall the move towards establishing the 1956 Supplementary Convention.[141]

iii Trafficking in Persons

The Elements of the Crimes of the International Criminal Court note that beyond forced labour and servile status (re: practices similar to slavery), that trafficking in persons may, where the powers attaching to the right of ownership are present, constitute enslavement. This crime would thus be the "the recruitment, transportation, transfer, harbouring or receipt of persons, by means of the threat or use of force or other forms of coercion, of abduction, of fraud, of deception, of the abuse of power or of a position of vulnerability or of the giving or receiving of payments or benefits to achieve the consent of a person having control over another person, for the purpose of exploitation," where the purpose of exploitation would reach the threshold of exhibition powers which are attached to the right of ownership. Having considered forced labour and practices similar to slavery (including servitude), it is worthwhile to turn to the other examples of exploitation set out in the trafficking conventions to consider them, with an eye to these types of exploitation manifesting the powers attaching to the right of ownership, and thus being deemed 'enslavement' for the purposes of international criminal law.

---

141 See United Nations Economic and Social Council, Slavery, the Slave Trade, and other forms of Servitude (Report of the Secretary-General), UN Doc. E/2357, 27 January 1953, p. 23.

Conclusion

Sir Moses Finley reminds us that, from the perspective of universal history, it is coercive labour and not free labour which has been the norm.[142] It has only towards the end of the nineteenth century that law seeks to regulate labour relations in a manner which nears the notion of free labour. Yet labour in abstract terms may always be understood as existing on a continuum of coercion wherein workers at one end of the spectrum is forced to decide between working or a life of destitution. In the contemporary market system, such a decision however is not deemed to be the type of coercion which should be regulated. Where coercion is considered illegitimate is to be found within a band of the continuum of coercion which is regulated by law. Law outlaws exploitive labour and thus creates free labour. The notion of free labour, however, is subjective: what might be deemed a wage which is exploitive in one State will be above the minimum wage in another and consonant with that State's economic development.

This Working Paper has demonstrated that exploitation is best understood as coercion used to compel labour. Within the exploitive band of continuum of coercion, the worker is called upon to decide between two disagreeable alternatives. For its part, international law seeks to ensure that a worker is free from these alternatives, by prescribing international legal standards which address coercion practices amounting to human exploitation. It does this first by recourse to international labour standards; where such standards are not respected, international human rights law will take over, wherein there is a positive obligation by States to ensure that forced labour, servitude and slavery do not take place within their jurisdiction. Failure to respect international human rights obligations will incur the responsibility of the State, but will also, where exploitation meets the threshold of demonstrating powers attached to the right of ownership, it will also create individual criminal responsibility.

This top-down pressure created by international law see the International Criminal Court as the ultimate bulwark against those that would promote exploitive labour. If a person in a position of authority, either in the public sector or in the private sectors, allows labour to develop into slavery to take place and fails to "take all necessary and reasonable measures within his or her powers to prevent or repress" the "or to submit the matter to the competent authorities for investigation and prosecution" they may be held individually responsible for an international criminal.[143] Thus, it is in the interest of those

142 See Brent Shaw (ed.), Moses Finley, *Ancient Slavery and Modern Ideology*, 1998, p. 299.

143 Article 28 (b)(iii), Statute of the International Criminal Court, 17 July 1998.

in positions of authority to ensure that labour standards are effective so that servile labour does not manifest powers which could be considered as attaching themselves to the right of ownership and those meet the threshold of enslavement as an international crime.

Yet, exploitive labour practices need not wait till an employer manifests powers which would normally be attached to ownership before acting. International law has created a regime of positive obligation under international law which requires States to act in a pro-active manner to suppress servile labour. Through international human rights law, therefore, the State is called upon to not only regulate the public sector, but also the private sector, as failure to do so would incur that State's responsibility. The manner in which that regulation will take place within each State will depend on its stage of economic develop; however international labour standards require that regimes be put in place to ensure that, at minimum, whether it be pay, work hours, or dangerous conditions, that exploitation of workers does not take place.

PART 4

Slavery

CHAPTER 17

A Legal Consideration 'Slavery' in Light of the *Travaux Préparatoires* of the 1926 Convention*

While the issue of contemporary slavery persists, and Professor Kevin Bales estimates that there are 27 million people currently held in slavery;[1] it remains true that we simply do not know how many people fit the legal definition of slavery, primarily because there has yet to appear any thorough legal analysis which examines the issue in. At the start of the Twenty-First Century, the need to establish the precise definition of slavery has become acute, as the establishment of the International Criminal Court in 2002 allows for the prosecution of individuals for the crime against humanity of enslavement and sexual slavery; and sexual slavery as a war crime. Yet, as Professor Suzanne Miers has noted in her 2003 *Slavery in the Twentieth Century*, the common connotation of the term 'slavery', as manifest in its use by the United Nations Working Group on Contemporary Forms of Slavery is such that it "covers such a wide range of practices" so as to render it "virtually meaningless."[2] Professor Bales' estimates are important at the level of providing us with a sense of the enormity of the problem of exploitation; but if we are going to end 'slavery', we must understand its legal parameters, the obligations which States have undertaken in this regard and devise strategies for holding States and individuals to account with regard to the specific crime of enslavement.

This Paper establishes the parameters of slavery within the confines of the 1926 League of Nations Convention on the Suppression of the Slave Trade and Slavery. Acknowledging that the definition of 'slavery' *per se* has not evolved since 1926; the current study does not seek to consider the expansion of forms of servitude which have been outlawed either by 1956 UN Convention or human rights instruments, while accepting that these types of exploitation,

---

* Paper presented at the Twenty-First Century Slavery: Issues and Responses Conference, The Wilberforce Institute for the Study of Slavery and Emancipation (WISE), November 2006.

1 See Kevin Bales, *Disposable People: New Slavery in the Global Economy*, 1999, p. 8. Note that Bales himself makes plain that, based on his own (non-legal) definition of slavery it is very difficult to establish the number of slaves beyond "rough estimates based on aggregation" of available sources broken down by country. See Kevin Bales, "The Challenge of Measuring Slavery," *Understanding Global Slavery: A Reader*, 2005, p. 103.

2 Suzanne Miers, *Slavery in the Twentieth Century*, 2003, p. 453.

 | DOI 10.1163/9789004279896_019

like trafficking, can slip into slavery, if a condition of ownership emerges. Instead, this Paper considers the Preparatory Works of the 1926 Convention which have been assembled for the first time, so as to demonstrate the legal parameters of the term 'slavery'; and to show that, in fact, the term in law must be construed narrowly. That while the term 'slavery' has been used as an umbrella to cover so-called 'contemporary forms of slavery', it should be understood that the term 'slavery' – proper – has a very specific meaning in law, as the Preparatory Works of the 1926 Convention make plain.

Preparatory Works or *Travaux Préparatoires* have a special place in international legal circles and, with regard to 'slavery', are of fundamental importance as they establish the legal parameters of what is meant by slavery and what is entailed by a determination of 'slavery' in law. The general importance of a *Travaux Préparatoires* is found in the 1969 Vienna Convention on the Law of Treaties. That Convention lays out the rules which govern written agreements between States. The Vienna Convention notes at Article 32 that in seeking to interpret a treaty, if its meaning is "ambiguous or obscure" or one's *prima facia* understanding is "manifestly absurd or unreasonable," you may turn to "supplementary means of interpretation, including the preparatory works of the treaty [...] in order to confirm the meaning." The importance of the *Travaux Préparatoires* of the 1926 Convention is given added weight because so little actual interpretation of the treaty has taken place. This, however, may well change – and should change – as in 1998, the Statute of the International Criminal Court established that the act of 'enslavement' constituted an international crime. Thus, for the first time in the history of the anti-slavery movement there is the possibility to hold an individual – internationally – criminally responsible for slavery. Further, the knock-on effect is that if you do not wish to have your citizens tried internationally for the crime of enslavement, you must try them yourself domestically. This forces States to take seriously possible cases of enslavement or face the prospect of being embarrassed internationally for failing to act. Thus the establishment of the International Criminal Court should be understood as arguably, the most important development in the anti-slavery movement since the 1926 Convention itself.[3]

3 The Preparatory Works of the 1926 Convention have never been considered because, until recently, they have not yet been assembled. Yet, over the course of a number of visits to the Archives of the League of Nations in Geneva, I have established the paper-trail which explains the manner in which each of the provisions of the 1926 Convention came into being.

The most valuable preparatory material garnered from the Archives allowing for a reconstruction of the drafting process of the 1926 Convention to Suppress the Slave Trade and Slavery includes the 1925 British Draft Protocol and Viscount Cecil of Chelwood's Report of 9 September 1925 to the Assembly of the League of Nations considering the Protocol's

The *Travaux Préparatoires* and the Definition of Slavery

The provisions of the 1926 Convention to Suppress the Slave Trade and Slavery materialise as result of the work of the League of Nations' Temporary Slavery Commission in 1924 and a British initiative manifest in a Draft Protocol put forward in early September 1925. That 1925 Draft Protocol was thoroughly amended and adopted by the Assembly of the League of Nations in late September 1925 as a Draft Convention. This Draft Convention, was then considered by States and modified so as to ultimately emerge as the 1926 Convention to Suppress the Slave Trade and Slavery opened for signature on 25 September 1926. The starting point for considering the drafting of the provision defining slavery is Article 1 of the 1925 British Draft Protocol which, taken in its entirety, defined both slavery and the slave trade. With regard to slavery, the Article 1 reads:

> For the purpose of the present Protocol, [...] slavery are defined as follows:
>
> Slavery is a status in which one person exercises a right of property over another [...].[4]

---

provisions. With regard to the period between 9 September and the adoption of the 1925 Draft Convention on 26 September, 1925, the Archives have a near complete set of the working papers of the Sub-Committee and the Drafting Committee of the Sixth Committee of the League of Nations, as well as the Reports of the Drafting Committee, Sub-Committee and the Sixth Committee. Unfortunately, no minutes were recorded during the deliberations of the Sub-Committee and Drafting Committee in 1925, so that any insights gained as to why changes transpired at this stage are only to be gleamed from the second Report which Viscount Cecil presented to the Assembly on behalf of the Sixth Committee: his Report of 26 September 1925.

During the calendar year between the adoption of the 1925 Draft Convention in 1925 and the adoption of the 1926 Convention to Suppress the Slave Trade and Slavery; the most valuable documents of the Preparatory Works are the replies by States to the Assembly's request for comment on the 1925 Draft Convention. Beyond this, the work of the Sub-Committee and the Legal Section of the League of Nations in August and September 1926 are of relevance and most important with regard to the final provisions (re: Articles 9 to 12) of the 1926 Convention. Finally, the 1926 Report of the Sixth Committee, once more presented by Viscount Cecil, introducing the various provisions of the 1926 Convention to Suppress the Slave Trade and Slavery and his oral report to the Assembly as found in the minutes, are of significant importance to the generation of the *Travaux Préparatoires* of the 1926 Convention.

4 League of Nations, Journal of the Sixth Assembly of the League of Nations, Geneva 1925, No. 3, 9 September 1925, p. 25.

Viscount Cecil of Chelwood – the British Delegate to the League of Nations who played *the* fundamental role in bringing about the 1926 Convention to Suppress the Slave Trade and Slavery as he acted as Rapporteur throughout the drafting process – noted, in presenting the 1925 British Draft Proposal to the Assembly of the League of Nations, that Article 1 "merely defined 'the slave trade' and 'slavery'" and that "he did not think that any objection would be raised."[5] Yet, as we shall see, this was not so, as the transition from the 1925 Draft Protocol proposed by Great Britain to the 1925 League of Nations Draft Convention marked an overall change to the wording of the provision. In doing so, however, it should be emphasised that the fundamental element of slavery – ownership of one individual by another – remained at the heart of the definition throughout the drafting process.

When the Drafting Committee established by the League of Nations to consider the provisions of the 1925 Draft Protocol met, it expanded the definition of slavery from "a status in which one person exercises a right of property over another," to:

> *Slavery* is the status of a person over whom another person or group of persons exercises the power attaching to proprietorship; or in the holding of a pledge or who is complied to serve such other person or group of persons for an undetermined time.[6]

The development of the definition came as a result of a draft which Albrecht Gohr, the Chair of the Temporary Slavery Commission, had proposed. That Proposal, used as a working document by the Drafting Committee was later to be amended in the following manner, first by the Drafting Committee itself:

> *Slavery* is the status of a person over whom another person or group of persons exercises the power attaching to ~~ownership~~ [proprietorship]; or is the ~~possession~~ [holding] of a pledge or who is complied to serve

---

5 League of Nations, Slavery: Draft Resolution and Protocol proposed by the British Government (*continuation*): Statement by Viscount Cecil, Official Journal, Record of the Sixth Assembly, Meetings of the Committees, Minutes of the Sixth Committee (Political Questions), Special Supplement No. 39, 14 September 1925, p. 14.

6 League of Nations, Slavery: Draft Protocol Text proposed by M.Gohr (as amended), LofN Doc. A.VI/S.C.1/5, 9 September 1925; as found in Folder R.67.D.46214 entitled *La question de l'esclavage: Discussions, y relatives, de la VIe Assembleé*, 1925.

> such other person or group of persons for an undetermined ~~period~~ [time].[7]

Then by a Sub-Committee:

> *Slavery* is the status of a person over whom another person or group of persons exercises the power attaching to proprietorship; ~~or is the holding of a pledge or who is complied to serve such other person or group of persons for an undetermined time.~~[8]

So as to read:

> *Slavery* is the status of a person over whom another person or group of persons exercises the powers attached to proprietorship.[9]

However, this definition would be forsaken for one proposed by Viscount Cecil[10] when, on 22 September, the Drafting Committee, having once more considered the issue proposed the following definition:

> Slavery is the status or condition of a person over whom any or all of the powers attaching to the right of ownership are exercised.[11]

---

7 League of Nations, Slavery: Draft Protocol Text proposed by M.Gohr (with handwritten amendments), LofN Doc. A.VI/S.C.1/5.1926, 9 September 1925; as found in Folder R.67.D.46214 entitled *La question de l'esclavage: Discussions, y relatives, de la VIe Assembleé*, 1925.

8 League of Nations, Slavery: Draft Protocol Text adopted by Sub-Committee of the VIth Commission on 17th of September 1925 (with handwritten amendments) LofN Doc. A.VI/S.C.1/8.1926 as found in Folder R.67.D.46214 entitled *La question de l'esclavage: Discussions, y relatives, de la VIe Assembleé*, 1925.

9 League of Nations, Slavery: Draft Protocol Text adopted by Sub-Committee of the VIth Commission on 17th of September 1925 LofN Doc. A.VI/S.C.1/8.1926 as found in Folder R.67.D.46214 entitled *La question de l'esclavage: Discussions, y relatives, de la VIe Assembleé*, 1925.

10 See League of Nations, Slavery, LofN Doc. A.VI/SC1/ Drafting Committee/14. (this document number having been pencilled out and replaced with A.VI/6.1925), 24 September 1925; as found in Folder R.67.D.46214 entitled *La question de l'esclavage: Discussions, y relatives, de la VIe Assembleé*, 1925. where it reads: "Amendments proposed by Lord Cecil to the text of draft Convention adopted by the Drafting Committee of the Sub-Committee of the VIth Commission (Document A.VI/S.C.I/ Drafting Committee 12 (1))."

11 League of Nations, Sixth Committee, Sub-Committee, Drafting Committee Slavery: Synopsis of the Convention (with handwritten amendments so as to be re-entitled

Thus, it was through this drafting process that the definition of slavery was established as it is this definition that finds its way, unaltered, into the 1926 Convention to Suppress the Slave Trade and Slavery as Article 1(1):

> Slavery is the status or condition of a person over whom any or all of the powers attaching to the right of ownership are exercised.

The Archives of the League of Nations reveals little in regard to the substance of the provisions of the definition of slavery as it evolved from the British Draft Protocol to the 1925 League of Nations Draft Convention. An unexplained gap emerges as to why the definition presented by Gohr, which was considered and later modified, was subsequently replaced by the provision put forward by Viscount Cecil. Likewise, the very definition put forward by Viscount Cecil is nowhere justified or elaborated upon in the archival material. As such, while the drafting process of the 1925 League of Nations Draft Convention provides limited insights into the manner in which the provisions which are found in the 1926 Convention to Suppress the Slave Trade and Slavery came into existence, they do not assist in our understanding of State appreciation of Article 1. Instead, the value of the *Travaux Préparatoires* must lie not in the discussions of the drafters working within the inter-governmental League of Nations but, ultimately, with the manner in which States reacted to provisions put forward. Thus, it is what follows that gives juridical weight to the *Travaux Préparatoires*.

The definition of 'slavery' having been agreed to in the 1925 Draft Convention, it was now left to States to comment. Three States did so: Belgium, Germany, and the Union of South Africa. For Belgium, it considered that the "definition given does not appear to the Belgium Colonial authorities to be strictly accurate. They consider that the fact that any or all of the powers attaching to the right of ownership are exercised over a person does not necessarily mean that that person is a slave."[12] Where Belgium considered the definition too wide, Germany considered the definition too narrow, making plain first that it "is exceptionally difficult to define slavery, inasmuch as the legal conception of civilised States and those of the African natives do not

Sixth Committee, Slavery: Synopsis of the Convention), LofN Doc. A.VI/S.C.I/ Drafting Committee/12(1) Revised (this document number having been pencilled out and replaced with A.VI/5.1925, 22 September 1925); as found in Folder R.67.D.46214 entitled *La question de l'esclavage: Discussions, y relatives, de la VIe Assembleé*, 1925.

12 League of Nations, Draft Convention on Slavery, Replies of Governments, Reply from the Government of Belgium, LofN Doc. A.10(a).1926.VI, 22 July 1926, p. 1; as found in League of Nations, Publications of the League of Nations, VI.B.Slavery, 1926.VI.B.3.

completely coincide"[13] Germany, then went on to say that the definition is precisely that: "too narrow, since prisoners of war derived from ancient tribal feuds are not bought, and according to the laws of many tribes, may not be sold, although they constitute a very important class of the un-free population." As a result of this consideration, Germany put forward a proposed amendment to the definition of slavery as presented in Article 1 of the 1925 Draft Convention. While acknowledging the appropriate nature of Article 1 as it stood, that is to say, with regard to the primacy of the element of ownership, it went on to say: "it might be made clearer by adding the words 'under private law' after the word 'exercised', so that:

> Article 1, Section 1 would then read as follows:
>
> 'Slavery is the status of a person over whom any or all of the powers attaching to the right of ownership are exercised, under private law, by some other person or group of persons'.[14]

As for South Africa, it made a rather lengthy submission wherein it elaborated on its understanding of the term 'slavery':

> No exception can be taken to the definition of 'slavery' [...] contained in Article 1. That definition puts as the test of slavery the status or condition of a person over whom all or any of the powers attaching to the right of *ownership* are exercised. In other words, a person is a slave if any other person can, by law or enforceable custom, claim such property in him as would be claimed if he were an inanimate object; and thus the natural freedom of will possessed by a person to offer or render his labour or to control the fruits thereof or the consideration therefrom is taken from him. The term also seems to imply a *permanent* status or condition of a person whose natural freedom is taken away, for from the proprietary interest of the other person in the person to whom that status attaches is implied a right of disposal of sale, gift or exchange.[15]

---

13 League of Nations, Draft Convention on Slavery, Replies of Governments, Reply from the Government of Germany, LofN Doc. A.10(a).1926.VI, 22 July 1926, p. 3; as found in League of Nations, Publications of the League of Nations, VI.B.Slavery, 1926.VI.B.3.

14 *Id.*

15 League of Nations, Draft Convention on Slavery, Replies of Governments, Reply from the Government of the Union of South Africa, LofN Doc. A.10(a).1926.VI, 22 July 1926, p. 5; as found in League of Nations, Publications of the League of Nations, VI.B.Slavery, 1926. VI.B.3. Emphasis in the original.

Further, in discussing the issue of forced labour (in regard to Article 5 of the 1925 Draft Convention), the Union of South Africa sought to make the distinction between it and slavery: "In the first case it is slavery, because the compeller has a proprietary right in respect of the compelled. In the latter case there is some element of choice or consent on the part of the compelled."[16] Thus, for South Africa, the test of whether or not a person was a slave revolved around ownership.

While the German proposed amendment was not taken on board, nor were its, nor Belgium's comments considered fundamental enough to change the definition as found in the 1925 Draft Convention; the South African intervention does give scope to one's understanding of the provisions of what became Article 1(1) of the 1926 Convention to Suppress the Slave Trade and Slavery. In seeking to gain an understanding of the provisions of Article 1, so as to make a larger argument, the submission by the Union of South Africa provides a rewording of the Article, thus, providing a supplementary means of interpreting the term 'slavery' as found in the 1926 Convention. It is thus worth reproducing here once again the relevant section of the South African Reply to the request by the Assembly of the League of Nations to comment on the 1925 Draft Convention:

> a person is a slave if any other person can, by law or enforceable custom, claim such property in him as would be claimed if he were an inanimate object;

The result of this enslavement as noted in the Reply of the Union of South Africa, as provided by the South African High Commissioner, Jacobus Smit, was that:

> the natural freedom of will possessed by a person to offer or render his labour or to control the fruits thereof or the consideration therefrom is taken from him.

Providing further understanding of the parameters of the definition of slavery as put forward in the 1925 Draft and accepted as such in the 1926 Convention, in regard its *ratione tempori* and to the implication to be drawn from the fundamental element of ownership are as follows:

16 League of Nations, Draft Convention on Slavery, Replies of Governments, Reply from the Government of the Union of South Africa, LofN Doc. A.10(a).1926.VI, 22 July 1926, p. 5; as found in League of Nations, Publications of the League of Nations, VI.B.Slavery, 1926. VI.B.3. See *supra*. Article 1(1).

> The term also seems to imply a *permanent* status or condition of a person whose natural freedom is taken away, for from the proprietary interest of the other person in the person to whom that status attaches is implied a right of disposal of sale, gift or exchange.[17]

This then is the added significance of having examined the records of the Preparatory Works leading to the creation of the definition of slavery as established by the 1926 Convention to Suppress the Slave Trade and Slavery.

Contemporary Understanding of Slavery in Light of the *Travaux Préparatoires*

Having developed the *Travaux Préparatoires* and its relevance with regard to the definition of slavery, a firm foundation has been created to examine contemporary scholarship in regard to 'slavery'. Consideration turns to the most authoritative pronouncement on slavery developed thus far during the Twenty-First Century, the United Nations Sub-Commission of Human Rights' Working Paper prepared by Professor David Weissbrodt and Anti-Slavery International entitled *Contemporary Forms of Slavery: Update review of the implementation of and follow-up to the conventions on slavery*. This May 2000 study requested by the United Nations Working Group on Contemporary Forms of Slavery sought the preparation of "a comprehensive review of existing treaty and customary law covering all the traditional and contemporary slavery-related practices and relevant monitoring mechanisms" and was meant to provide an update of the previous studies by members of the UN Sub-Committee, the 1966 Awad and the 1984 Whitaker Reports.[18]

---

17 League of Nations, Draft Convention on Slavery, Replies of Governments, Reply from the Government of the Union of South Africa, LofN Doc. A.10(a).1926.VI, 22 July 1926, p. 5; as found in League of Nations, Publications of the League of Nations, VI.B.Slavery.1926, 1–7. Emphasis in the original.

Note that beyond State pronouncements on the 1925 Draft Convention, the legal Committee of the Assembly of the League of Nations, having taken into consideration the work of the committees drafting the 1926 Convention, considered the obligations flowing from having established a definition of slavery and provided its own interpretation of the term 'slavery': "the maintenance by a private individual of rights over another person of the same nature as the rights which an individual can have over things." See *id.*

18 United Nations Sub-Commission on the Promotion and Protection of Human Right, *Contemporary Forms of Slavery: Updated Review of the Implementation of and follow-up to*

In considering the definition of slavery, the Weissbrodt and Anti-Slavery International Report seeks to expand the definition of 'slavery' so as to consider it as a *concept*, thereby creating an umbrella under which 'various forms of slavery' can seek shelter. The Report states:

> In order for the United Nations or any other international body to carry out a mandate concerned with slavery effectively, it is necessary to develop an international consensus on what practices are included within the concept of slavery.[19]

It then points to the findings of the Temporary Slavery Commission in 1924 which included in its Report discussions of "Practices restrictive of the liberty of the person, or tending to acquire control of the person in conditions analogous to slavery," as examples:

> 1. (c) Slavery or serfdom (domestic or predial);
> 2. Practices restrictive of the liberty of the person, or tending to acquire control ofthe person in conditions analogous to slavery, as for example:
>   (a) Acquisition of girls by purchase disguised as payment of dowry, it beingunderstood that this does not refer to normal marriage customs;
>   (b) Adoption of children, of either sex, with a view to their virtualenslavement, or the ultimate disposal of their persons;
>   (c) All forms of pledging or reducing to servitude of persons for debt or otherreason... [and]
> 4. System of compulsory labour, public or private, paid or unpaid.

The Weissbrodt and Anti-Slavery International Report then goes on to say:

> By referring to "any or all of the powers of ownership" in its definition of slavery, and setting forth as its stated purpose the "abolition of slavery in all its forms" the Slavery Convention covered not only domestic slavery but also the other forms of slavery listed in the Report of the Temporary Slavery Commission.[20]

---

the Conventions on Slavery, Working Paper prepared by David Weissbrodt and Anti-Slavery International, UN Doc. E/CN.4/Sub.2/2000/3, 26 May 2000, p. 3.

19 *Id.*, p. 4.

20 *Id.*, p. 5. Emphasis in the original.

This argument, however must be rejected. It is clear that States, in negotiating the content of the 1926 Convention, did *not* intend to widen the scope of 'slavery' by subsuming within it other items which went beyond the "status or condition of a person over whom any or all of the powers attaching to the right of ownership are exercised." Likewise, having considered the *Travaux Préparatoires*, it is factually inaccurate to say that "the Slavery Convention covered not only domestic slavery but also the other forms of slavery listed in the Report of the Temporary Slavery Commission." In fact, the Drafting Committee and States which made comments did not accept this possibility, instead maintaining the requirement of ownership as being fundamental to slavery.

While the Preparatory Works do not explain what is meant by "any or all of the powers of ownership," they do go into detail with regard to what is meant by "abolition of slavery in all its forms." This phrase is part of Article 2(b) of 1926 Convention which sets out the obligation flowing from the definitions in Article 1; it requires that "High Contracting Parties undertake, each in respect of the territories placed under its sovereignty, jurisdiction, protection, suzerainty or tutelage, so far as they have not already taken the necessary steps: [...] (b) To bring about, progressively and as soon as possible, the complete abolition of slavery in all its forms." As originally proposed by Great Britain in its 1925 Draft Protocol, a distinction was made between slavery and "domestic and other slavery."[21] As Viscount Cecil of Chelwood noted in presenting the 1925 British Draft Protocol, the British Government "recognized that, with regard to domestic slavery, a very difficult question arose, and therefore [as opposed to slavery] all that they could ask States to agree to was the desirability of getting rid of domestic slavery, and to do so as and when the opportunity offered."[22]

The provisions of what would become Article 2(b) of the 1926 Convention as originally presented by Great Britain were amended by the League of Nations in their 1925 Draft Convention to read: "To bring about progressively and as soon as possible the disappearance of slavery in every form, *notably*

21 Article 2(b) of the 1925 British Draft Protocol reads:

> Provide for the eventual emancipation of all slaves in their respective territories, and also for as speedy an elimination of domestic and other slavery as social conditions will allow.

League of Nations, Journal of the Sixth Assembly of the League of Nations, Geneva 1925, No. 3, 9 September 1925, p. 25.

22 League of Nations, Slavery: Draft Resolution and Protocol proposed by the British Government (*continuation*): Statement by Viscount Cecil, Official Journal, Record of the Sixth Assembly, Meetings of the Committees, Minutes of the Sixth Committee (Political Questions), Special Supplement No. 39, 14 September 1925, p. 14.

in the case of domestic slavery and similar conditions."[23] In his Report to the Assembly of the League of Nations on the 1925 League of Nations Draft Convention, Viscount Cecil considered the notion of 'domestic slavery and similar conditions' which he noted was meant to "include all forms of 'debt slavery', the enslaving of persons disguised as the adoption of children, and the acquisition of girls by purchase disguised as payment of dowry, etc. as mention in the report of the Temporary Slavery Commission."[24] Viscount Cecil noted in 1925 that such similar conditions "approach very close to and are, in fact a form of slavery, but are not usually included in the simple term slavery. With respect to all those, we [re: the Drafting Committee] ask for their abolition, we ask all the nations to agree to their abolition, which will be carried out, as all reform must necessarily be carried out, as progressively as may be possible, and as soon as possible."[25]

Viscount Cecil, did not however, report that the Belgium Delegate had proposed that the provisions of Article 2(b) remove the distinction between 'slavery' and 'domestic slavery' so that it would simply read: "to bring about progressively the disappearance of slavery in every form."[26] In fact, in a rather contradictory manner, Viscount Cecil himself opposed this change, noting that he "would be sorry to see this alteration; he thought the terms 'domestic slavery and similar conditions' were usually understood as distinct from slavery, though they might possibly be considered as a form of slavery. M. Gohr, Chairman of the Temporary Slavery Commission had also thought that it was desirable to have some reference to domestic slavery in this article."[27] As a result of this intervention, the Belgium Delegate withdrew his proposal. Thus, at the end of the drafting process in 1925, it was rather unclear as to whether there was a distinction to be made between 'slavery' proper and 'domestic slavery and similar conditions'. Yet, this was not the last word with regard to the phrase 'domestic slavery and similar conditions', as it would once more come

23 League of Nations, Annex: Draft Convention, League of Nations Official Journal (Special Supplement 33) Records of the Sixth Assembly: Text of Debates, 26 September 1925, p. 439. Emphasis added.

24 *Id.*

25 League of Nations, Question of Slavery: Report of the Sixth Committee; Resolution, League of Nations Official Journal (Special Supplement 33) Records of the Sixth Assembly: Text of Debates, Nineteenth Plenary Meeting, 26 September 1925, p. 156.

26 League of Nations, Slavery: Examination of the Report of the Sub-Committee and of the Draft Convention, Official Journal, Special Supplement No. 39, Record of the Sixth Assembly, Meetings of the Committees, Minutes of the Sixth Committee (Political Questions), 24 September 1925, p. 28.

27 *Id.*

under scrutiny during the drafting process of the 1926 Convention where it would, ultimately, be omitted.

In providing comments on the 1925 League of Nations Draft Convention, the Union of South Africa observed that the proposed "Convention as drafted goes somewhat further than seems necessary for the abolition of slavery and the slave trade."[28] The argument put forward revolved around the final clause of sub-paragraph (b): "notably in the case of domestic slavery and similar conditions," which the Union considered as an attempt to extend the definition of slavery as spelled out in Article 1 of the Draft Convention. It pointed out that in the comments provided by the Sixth Committee that 'domestic slavery and similar conditions' is to be understood as "'debt slavery', the enslaving of persons disguised as the adoption of children, and the acquisition of girls by purchase disguised as payment of dowry;" and went on to raise the following legal issue which speaks to the element of ownership being central to the definition of slavery:

> Now either such persons are *sui juris* [re: a separate category] or they are not. If they are *sui juris*, they can only become subject to domestic slavery or similar conditions by a voluntary act, and the essential element of slavery is absent. If they are not *sui juris*, they can only be subject to domestic slavery or similar conditions by the acts of those who by law are their guardians, and it is no more than a form of paternal power. If, further, they have become domestic slaves or persons in similar conditions in the manner indicated, that can only be because others have acquired a right of property in them, and they are therefore slaves as defined in Article 1.

The South African observation continued:

> There seems no reason, then, to differentiate them from the person in a condition of slavery defined in that article. If, on the other hand, no right of property in them exists, the scope of the draft Convention seems to be extended to compel the signatories to undertake to interfere in social customs. It would seem to be desirable that these social customs which signatories are to undertake to interfere with should be more clearly defined.

---

28 League of Nations, Draft Convention on Slavery, Replies of Governments, Reply from the Government of the Union of South Africa, LofN Doc. A.10(a).1926.VI, 22 July 1926, p. 5; as found in League of Nations, Publications of the League of Nations, VI.B.Slavery.1926, VI. B. 3.

In concluding, the Union of South Africa requested that "the provisions of Article 2(b) [...] should be deleted or considerably modified or clarified."[29]

Germany for its part, proposed that this distinction between 'slavery' and 'domestic slavery' should be done away with, and that instead sub-paragraph (b) should simply read: "to abolish slavery in all its forms."[30] Its basis for making this proposal was that it appeared that States were backtracking on what had been agreed to at Saint Germain-en-Laye in 1919, which Germany noted: "was concluded seven years ago and whose signatories undertake to assure the complete suppression of slavery in all its forms, [which] seemingly goes further than the present proposal."[31] Germany then proposed a new sub-paragraph, saying that a number of "conditions resembling slavery" existed and as such the notion of servitude could be addressed by accepting the following amendment:

> To endeavour, as far as possible, to bring about the disappearance of conditions of servitude resembling slavery, *e.g.* debt slavery, sham adoption, childhood marriage, traffic in women, etc.[32]

This proposal, like the one made by the Delegate of Haiti ("To endeavour to bring about as soon as possible the disappearance of all voluntary or involuntary subjections")[33] was not taken up by the Sixth Committee. Thus, there was an unwillingness to include mention of servitude in the Convention. Yet, the provisions of sub-paragraph (b) were in fact modified as Viscount Cecil, for his part, reported to the Assembly of the League of Nations in 1926:

> A slight change has been made in the drafting of sub-paragraph (b) of this article, the words "notably in the case of domestic slavery and similar conditions" being now omitted. This modification was made because it was believed that such conditions came within the definition of slavery

---

29 *Id.*

30 League of Nations, Draft Convention on Slavery, Replies of Governments, Reply from the Government of Germany, LofN Doc. A.10(a).1926.VI, 22 July 1926, p. 4; as found in League of Nations, Publications of the League of Nations, VI.B.Slavery.1926, VI. B. 3.

31 *Id.*

32 *Id.*

33 League of Nations, Draft Convention on Slavery and Proposed Amendments, LofN Doc. A.VI/S.C.1/1, 10 September 1926; as found in Folder R.77.D.46781 entitled Draft Convention on Slavery: Discussion at the 7th Assembly; 1926.

> contained in the first article and that no further prohibition of them in express terms was necessary.[34]

Viscount Cecil then went on to enumerate these types of domestic slavery and similar conditions as "all those conditions mentioned by the Temporary Slavery Commission and to which I referred to last year, *i.e.*, "debt slavery," the enslaving of persons disguised as the adoption of children, and the acquisition of girls by purchase disguised as payment of dowry, etc." Yet Viscount Cecil here is not quoting the Temporary Slavery Commission verbatim, instead he has re-termed the items so as to included elements of ownership within them. So instead of quoting from the Temporary Slavery Commission Report of 1924 as the Weissbrodt and Anti-Slavery International Report does, and pointing to all "forms of pledging or reducing to servitude of persons for debt or other reason," Viscount Cecil speaks of "debt slavery;" instead of using the language of the Temporary Slavery Commission: "considering conditions analogous to slavery, as for example:" the adoption "of children, [...] with a view to their virtual enslavement" or the acquisition "of girls by purchase disguised as payment of dowry," the Cecil Report speaks of the "enslaving of persons disguised as adoption of children and the acquisition of girls by purchase disguised as payment of dowry." Finally, in line with the observations made by the Union of South Africa and Germany, Viscount Cecil did make plain that the requirement of ownership had to be present:

> Even if, as is possible, these last practices do not come under the definition of slavery as it is given in Article 1, the [Temporary Slavery] Commission is unanimously of the opinion that they must be combated. In a more general way, it interprets Article 2 as tending to bring about the disappearance from written legislation or from the custom of the country of everything which admits the maintenance by a private individual of rights over another person of the same nature as the rights which an individual can have over things.[35]

In other words, Viscount Cecil accepted that 'slavery in all it forms' required the demonstration of the power of ownership over an individual as established by the definition of slavery in Article 1 and conceded as much in his 1926 Report

34 League of Nations, Slavery Convention: Report presented to the Assembly by the Sixth Committee, LofN Doc. A.104.1926.VI, as found in League of Nations, Publications of the League of Nations, VI.B.Slavery.1926, VI. B. 5, 24 September 1926, p. 1.

35 *Id.*, pp. 1–2.

to the Assembly. As the German proposed amendment to Article 2 pointed out, such institutions as the Temporary Slavery Commission had highlighted as being 'domestic slavery' were in fact "conditions of servitude resembling slavery," not slavery.[36] This dichotomy between slavery and servitude was not addressed by the 1926 Convention; instead *servitude* – that wider umbrella of forms of 'slavery' put forward by Weissbrodt and Anti-Slavery International Report – was only legally suppressed with the coming into force of the 1956 Supplementary Convention on the Abolition of Slavery, the Slave Trade, and Institutions and Practices Similar to Slavery. Or put differently, had serfdom, forced marriage, child adoption, or debt bondage been subsumed within the definition of Article 1 of the 1926 Convention, *per se*, there would not have been a need to establish the 1956 Convention. While the 1956 Convention acknowledges that these instances of servitude could metamorphosis into slavery if the power of ownership over an individual was present, it sought to band servitudal practices "whether or not they are covered by the definition of slavery contained in Article 1 of the Slavery Convention signed at Geneva on 25 September 1926."

Further issue should be taken with the presentation by the Weissbrodt and Anti-Slavery International Report of the definition of slavery. Turing once more to the argument that:

> By referring to "<u>any</u> or all of the powers of ownership" in its definition of slavery, and setting forth as its stated purpose the "abolition of slavery in <u>all</u> its forms" the Slavery Convention covered not only domestic slavery but also the other forms of slavery listed in the Report of the Temporary Slavery Commission;[37]

The Report provides, as means of clarifying Article 2(b) of the 1926 Convention, the following quotation of the "report to the Sixth Committee of the League of Nations Assembly in 1926" in a footnote:

> that the words "notably in the case of domestic slavery and similar conditions" were being omitted on the grounds that "such conditions come within the definition of slavery contained in the first article and that no further prohibition of them in express terms was necessary. This provision applies not only to domestic slavery but to all those conditions mentioned by the Temporary Slavery Commission…i.e. debt slavery, the

36 *Id.*

37 *Id.*, p. 24, f.n. 14.

> enslaving of persons disguised as adoption of children and the acquisition of girls by purchase disguised as payment of dowry"[38]

The Weissbrodt and Anti-Slavery International Report goes no further, yet the passage, as noted earlier, continues by stating that:

> Even if, as is possible, these last practices do not come under the definition of slavery as it is given in Article 1, the Commission is unanimously of the opinion that they must be combated. In a more general way, it interprets Article 2 as tending to bring about the disappearance from written legislation or from the custom of the country of everything which admits the maintenance by a private individual of rights over another person of the same nature as the rights which an individual can have over things.[39]

Thus the omission in the Weissbrodt and Anti-Slavery International Report fails to point to the fact that (1) it was possible that "domestic slavery and similar conditions" did not come under the definition of slavery; (2) that this was a *voeu* or wish of the Temporary Slavery Commission, not a binding obligation on States or the express wish of States commenting on the provision; and, (3) that the obligation to suppress slavery was in regard to "everything which admits the maintenance by a private individual of rights over another person of the same nature as the rights which an individual can have over things:" that is, as defined in Article 1(2) but nothing more, or less, than that.

Thus far, this section has considered the argument put forward in the Weissbrodt and Anti-Slavery International Report that "the Slavery Convention covered not only domestic slavery but also the other forms of slavery listed in the Report of the Temporary Slavery Commission," and sought to demonstrate how the Preparatory Works of the 1926 Convention fail to substantiate this claim. The *Travaux Préparatoires*, as noted earlier are considered by the 1969 Geneva Convention on the Law of Treaties as a supplementary means of interpretation. To consider the general rules of treaty interpretation one must turn

38 *Id.*, p. 5. Emphasis in the original.

39 The Weissbrodt and Anti-Slavery International Report quotes this passage from the "Report of the Temporary Slavery Commission to the Council of the League of Nations (A.17.1924.VI.B), 1924, quoted in The Suppression of slavery: Memorandum submitted by the Secretary General to the Ad Hoc Committee on Slavery, 1951, para. 22." see p. 24, f.n. 13. Note that I have here retained the format as it appears in the source quoted by Weissbrodt and Anti-Slavery International.

to Article 31 of the Vienna Convention, which notes that a "treaty shall be interpreted in good faith in accordance with the ordinary meaning to be given to the terms of the treaty in their context and in the light of its object and purpose." These four elements – good faith, ordinary meaning, in context, and in light of the object and purpose of the treaty – are the DNA of treaty interpretation. Leaving aside good faith, which turns to the motivation of a party interpreting a treaty; the ordinary meaning of slavery as defined in the 1926 League of Nations Convention on the Suppression of the Slave Trade and Slavery establishes a status turning on ownership of one by another ("Slavery is the status or condition of a person over whom any or all of the powers attaching to the right of ownership are exercised."). The drafting process of Article 1 by the League of Nations in 1925 makes this clear, as it sought to get the element of ownership into an agreeable format for consideration by States. Further, the section of the *Travaux Préparatoires* touching on Article 2(b) makes plain that there was agreement amongst States that 'slavery' did not include "conditions of servitude resembling slavery," but focused on this notion of slavery as ownership. Though Viscount Cecil sought to include servitudal items in the provisions of Article 1 he made plain that he was doing so where they had slipped into 'slavery'.

With regard to the element of 'in context' in treaty interpretation, an understanding of Article must be considered in reference to the analysis which has thus far been provided in regard to Article 2(b) of the 1926 Convention. Beyond this Article 31 of the Vienna Convention on the Law of Treaties goes on to say that in interpreting one "shall take into account:"

(a) any subsequent agreement between the parties regarding the interpretation of the treaty or the application of its provisions;
(b) any subsequent practice in the application of the treaty which establishes the agreement of the parties regarding its interpretation;
(c) any relevant rules of international law applicable in the relations between the parties.

Since the coming into force of the 1926 Convention, there has been no subsequent agreement, practice, or relevant rules of international law which might assist in giving context to the definition of slavery as noted in Article 1(1) of the League of Nations Convention. For its part, the Weissbrodt and Anti-Slavery International Report notes that the "United Nations has made various restatements of the definition but in the international legal context the definition has not been altered substantially since 1926." For my part, I would remove the modifier 'substantially' and say that the definition has not been altered since

1926. Finally, with regard to considering 'context' in treaty interpretation, one could take into consideration "A special meaning shall be given to a term if it is established that the parties so intended." Here it is clear that the parties to the 1926 Convention on the Suppression of the Slave Trade and Slavery did not make their intensions known that there was a 'special meaning' to be attached to the term 'slavery' beyond that accepted as Article 1(1). The work of the Temporary Slavery Commission two years before the conclusion of the 1926 Convention is irrelevant both *ratione temporis* but more importantly *ratione personae* to the interpretation of the Convention. Thus the contextual element of treaty interpretation as noted in the Vienna Convention precludes the fundamental approach taken in the Weissbrodt and Anti-Slavery International Report; that is: States, having defined a term in law, have agreed, though not expressly in the provisions of the treaty, to a tacit expansion of that definition on the basis of a study conducted two-years previous to the conclusion of the 1926 Convention.

The final element of treaty interpretation is that "treaty shall be interpreted [...] in the light of its object and purpose." The Weissbrodt and Anti-Slavery International Report claims that the "stated purpose" of the 1926 Convention is the "abolition of slavery in all its forms," yet the Convention sets a lower ambition, in that it speaks in the Preamble not of the abolition of slavery and the slave trade but of its *suppression*:

> Whereas the signatories of the Convention of Saint-Germain-en-Laye of 1919, to revise the General Act of Berlin of 1885, and the General Act and Declaration of Brussels of 1890, affirmed their *intention of securing the complete suppression of slavery in all its forms and of the slave trade by land and sea.*

Further, with regard to the slave trade, the obligations which Parties have undertaken is to "prevent and suppress," not abolish; while with regard to slavery the Convention reads: "to bring about, progressively and as soon as possible, the complete abolition of slavery in all its forms." Despite this, the issue of the object and purpose of 1926 Convention can not be taken in isolation and must form the alchemy of treaty interpretation by also mixing with the three other elements of Article 31(1) of the 1969 Vienna Convention to reflect both the States' intention in drafting the instrument and any evolution which has transpired since the mid-1920s that might modify the stated intension of the parties to define slavery with regard to ownership as "the status or condition of a person over whom any or all of the powers attaching to the right of ownership are exercised." This, to my knowledge, has not taken place.

Conclusion

By developing and considering the *Travaux Préparatoires* of the 1926 Convention on the Suppression of the Slave Trade and Slavery, this paper establishes the a legal of what 'slavery' means in international law. In so doing, it has provided the first building block in seeking to hold a State or an individual accountable for enslavement on the international plane. This is of vital importance as the issue of enslavement has now been established as an international crime for which individuals may stand accused before the International Criminal Court. The definition of slavery as noted in Article 1(1) of the 1926 Convention as "the status or condition of a person over whom any or all of the powers attaching to the right of ownership are exercised" remains the established definition in law. The Preparatory Works of the Convention, both in the manner in which the Drafting Committee sought to define slavery in 1925, and with reference to the comments made by the Representatives of Germany, Union of South Africa, along with Viscount Cecil of Chelwood, demonstrates that the issue of ownership is the *sine qua non* of the definition of slavery in law. While the definition of slavery in law has been shown to be a narrow one, it is one which is, for instance commensurate with the finding of the European Court of Human Rights when it considered for the first time in 2005 a true case of severe exploitation and determined that it amounted to servitude because the element of ownership was not part of the equation.[40] Yet, this is what 'slavery' means in law. That is not to say that forms of servitude, be it forced or bonded labour or serfdom, can not be considered slavery – if issues of ownership can be demonstrated; or be used to hold States responsible for human rights violations. It does however mean that such violation of international law would be on the basis of violations of the norm of servitude and not slavery and, for instance, would not entail individual criminal responsibility before the International Criminal Court. If anything, what this paper has sought to show is that the term 'slavery' has a very specific connotation in international law; the fact that attempts have been made to expand its ambit must be considered as falling beyond the express wishes and dictates of States, which are, at the end of the day, the entities which determine, interpret and apply international law. We may not like it, but there it is. This Paper presents the parameters within which advocates must work, if they wish to combat slavery (as opposed to servitude) using the tools available to them by virtue of in international law.

40 See *Siliadin v France* (Application 73316/01) 26 July 2005.

CHAPTER 18

The Definition of 'Slavery' in General International Law and the Crime of Enslavement within the Rome Statute*

For more than two hundred years, the antislavery movement has had a monopoly on what 'slavery' means. Over the last eighty years, this has meant that the definition of 'slavery' in law has lived in the shadowlands of disuse resulting from the anti-slavery movement's messianic ambitions to rid the world of human exploitation. Yet, this ambition has meant that 'slavery' as propagated by the anti-slavery movement has become an ever-growing phenomena, so that for instance, the UN Working Group on Contemporary Forms of Slavery has examined issues such as apartheid, colonialism and incest, under the guise of slavery.[1] In proportion to slavery's growth in breadth, has been its diminishing legal worth, to the extent that the leading academic (and President of the NGO Free the Slaves) in the field, Kevin Bales, has discarded the legal definition for his own, one based on "three key dimensions: loss of free will, the appropriation of labor power, and the use or threat of violence";[2] and a recent study on Modern Slavery in the United Kingdom defined it as "severe economic exploitation; the lack of a human rights framework; and control of one person over another by the prospect or reality of violence."[3] The anti-slavery ownership of the term slavery, however, no longer holds true, as 'slavery' in the twenty-first century comes up against a countervailing human right: the right of an accused to "be informed promptly and in detail of the nature, cause and

* Paper presented at the Guest Lecture Series of the Office of the Prosecutor, International Criminal Court, 26 April 2007.

1 United Nations Sub-Commission on the Promotion and Protection of Human Right, *Contemporary Forms of Slavery: Updated review of the implementation of and follow-up to the conventions on slavery: Addendum – Forms of Slavery*, UN Doc. E/CN.4/Sub.2/2000/3/Add.1, 26 May 2000.

2 See Kevin Bales, "'No One Shall be Held in Slavery or Servitude': A Critical Analysis of International Slavery Agreements and Concepts of Slavery," *Understanding Global Slavery*, 2005, p. 57.

3 Gary Graig, Aline Gaus, Mick Wilkinson, Klara Skrivankova and Aidan McQuade, *Contemporary Slavery in the uk: Overview and Key Issues* (Joseph Rowntree Foundation, 2007), p. 12.

 | DOI 10.1163/9789004279896_020

content of the charge" of enslavement before the International Criminal Court.[4]

The coming into existence of the International Criminal Court in 2002 and the right of the accused to know the content of the charge of enslavement requires a precise understanding of what 'slavery' means in general international law and what the parameters of 'enslavement' are within international criminal law. Emerging from the shadowlands then is the 1926 League of Nations definition which remains – much to the chagrin of advocates of the end of exploitation – the agreed-upon definition of slavery in international law. That definition, which is repeated in the 1956 United Nations slavery convention also finds its way into the 'legislation' of the International Criminal Court. The 1926 definition, found at Article 1(a) of the 1926 Convention to Suppress the Slave Trade and Slavery, reads:

> Slavery is the status or condition of a person over whom any or all of the powers attaching to the right of ownership are exercised.

That definition is added to under Article 7(a) of the 1956 Supplementary Convention on the Abolition of Slavery, the Slave Trade, and Institutions and Practices Similar to Slavery as follows:

> "Slavery" means, as defined in the Slavery Convention of 1926, the status or condition of a person over whom any or all of the powers attaching to the right of ownership are exercised, and "slave" means a person in such condition or status.

Finally, under the Rome Statute, 'enslavement' is deemed a crime against humanity under Article 7(1)(c) and defined at Article 7(2)(c) as:

> "Enslavement" means the exercise of any or all of the powers attaching to the right of ownership over a person and includes the exercise of such power in the course of trafficking in persons, in particular women and children.

What remains consistent in each of these definitions is the phrase: "the powers attaching to the right of ownership." The notion of 'ownership' thus appears to be the *sine qua non* of slavery in international law – yet this is not an accurate reading of the phrase. This paper considers the evolution of the definition

4 See Article 67(1)(a), Rome Statue of the International Criminal Court, 17 June 1998.

of slavery as it emerges in 1926 and reiterated in 1956 as a means to understand its parameters while giving special attention to the phrase 'any or all of the powers attaching to the right of ownership' – *as opposed to 'ownership'*. This is done so as to give *content* and *context* to the notion of enslavement before the International Criminal Court and thus provide for the possibility of actually holding an individual internationally criminally responsible for this crime against humanity. What emerges from this consideration of the legal definition of slavery is an understanding which does not diverge significantly from what Professor Bales or other anti-slavery advocates put forward as their understanding that of slavery but channels such an understanding away from meaningless hyperbole manifest in the UN Working Group towards a definition which can be relied upon in a court of law and used to find persons guilty of enslavement. It should be said that the anti-slavery movement has misinterpreted the definition of slavery, having picked up on a vein of interpretation which has channelled the understanding of slavery away from its legal definition towards one which has done a disservice to the anti-slavery movement. From the preparation of the 1926 definition onwards, attempts have been made to obfuscate the term 'slavery' and to distance its legal definition from a definition that might well be attached to any type of exploitation. Individuals interested in ending exploitation in the guise of forced, bonded, or indentured labour or sexual exploitation muddied the waters of what was meant by 'slavery' and sought to intimate that 'slavery' persisted beyond the 1926 Convention definition, even where the 'powers attaching to the right of ownership' were not at issue. In so doing, they forced the legal definition of slavery into a shadowland of disuse where it retained its normative value among States but hibernated as an anti-slavery tool for repression or advocacy against exploitation. This paper seeks to redress the balance by demonstrating that the legal definition goes further in advancing an anti-slavery agenda as it is wide enough to be accepted by advocates while opening a new vista, one which can be used to hold individuals criminally responsible for enslavement, whether *de jure* or *de facto*.

Drafting the 1926 Definition of Slavery

The 1926 definition of slavery emerged as a result of the dynamics between anti-slavery advocates and colonial States, members of the League of Nations, in the period between 1924 and 1926. While the 1924 Temporary Slavery Commission, composed of independent experts had proposed the establishment of an international convention meant to suppress slavery in all it forms;

a 1925 draft convention narrowed its application, for instance, away from forced labour; and limited its obligations, i.e. to bring about, *progressively and as soon as possible*, the complete abolition of slavery in all its forms, thus allowing for the 1926 Convention to be acceptable to States. While the Members of the Temporary Slavery Commission had sought a wide definition of 'slavery' encompassing all types of exploitation, it was clear that Members of the League of Nations – and primarily States which retained the use of various forms of exploitive labour in their colonies – wanted to deal, in essence, with the end of legal slavery. As the French Member of the Temporary Slavery Commission, Maurice Delafousse, wrote in private correspondence to his British counterpart, Lord Frederick Lugard, "I was, like you, rather surprised at the line adopted [...] regarding the Slavery Convention. As the matter has been agreed to, much does not remain of the work of the Temporary Commission, expect your idea of an international convention."[5]

Instead of these independent experts, it fell to Viscount Cecil of Chelwood, the son of former British Prime Minister Salisbury and winner of the Nobel Peace Prize, to act as Rapporteur and usher a draft towards acceptance by States as the 1926 Convention. It was he who, on 22 September 1925, proposed[6] a definition which would ultimately become Article 1(a) of the 1926 Convention:

> Slavery is the status or condition of a person over whom any or all of the powers attaching to the right of ownership are exercised.[7]

More importantly for this study, was Viscount Cecil's deftly drafted Report accompanying the proposed 1926 Convention, which appeared to allow for the abolition of slavery in all its forms yet, in fact, clearly established that the

5 See Delafouss to Lugard, 16 November 1925, Papers of Baron Lugard of Abinger, Box 102/1, Folio 31, Rhodes House Library, Oxford. Translated from the French.

6 See League of Nations, Slavery, LofN Doc. A.VI/SC1/ Drafting Committee/14. (this document number having been pencilled out and replaced with A.VI/6.1925), 24 September 1925; as found in Folder R.67.D.46214 entitled *La question de l'esclavage: Discussions, y relatives, de la VIe Assembleé*, 1925. where it reads: "Amendments proposed by Lord Cecil to the text of draft Convention adopted by the Drafting Committee of the Sub-Committee of the VIth Commission (Document A.VI/S.C.I/ Drafting Committee 12 (1))."

7 League of Nations, Sixth Committee, Sub-Committee, Drafting Committee Slavery: Synopsis of the Convention (with handwritten amendments so as to be re-entitled Sixth Committee, Slavery: Synopsis of the Convention), LofN Doc. A.VI/S.C.I/ Drafting Committee/12(1) Revised (this document number having been pencilled out and replaced with A.VI/5.1925, 22 September 1925); as found in Folder R.67.D.46214 entitled *La question de l'esclavage: Discussions, y relatives, de la VIe Assembleé*, 1925.

'powers attaching to the right of ownership' were required for slavery to exist. It is from this Report that advocates of an expanded understanding of slavery have sought to justify their claims.

While the discussion leading to the establishment of a definition of slavery do not explain what is meant by 'any or all of the powers attaching to the right of ownership', the *travaux prépratoires* do go into detail with regard to the notion of the 'abolition of slavery in all its forms'. This phrase is part of Article 2(b) of 1926 Convention which sets out the obligation flowing from the definitions in Article 1. It requires that 'High Contracting Parties undertake, each in respect of the territories placed under its sovereignty, jurisdiction, protection, suzerainty or tutelage, so far as they have not already taken the necessary steps: [...] (b) To bring about, progressively and as soon as possible, the complete abolition *of slavery in all its forms*'. But as proposed in 1925, the draft Article 2(b) read:

> To bring about progressively and as soon as possible the disappearance of slavery in every form, notably in the case *of domestic slavery and similar conditions*.[8]

In his Report to the Assembly of the League of Nations on the 1925 Draft Convention, Viscount Cecil considered the notion of 'domestic slavery and similar conditions' which he noted was meant to "include all forms of 'debt slavery', the enslaving of persons disguised as the adoption of children, and the acquisition of girls by purchase disguised as payment of dowry, etc. as mention in the report of the Temporary Slavery Commission."[9] However, in the intervening year, when this time reporting to the Assembly of the League of Nations on the 1926 Convention, Viscount Cecil took into consideration the comments made by States and modified his language to make plain that there was but one

---

8 League of Nations, Annex: Draft Convention, League of Nations Official Journal (Special Supplement 33) Records of the Sixth Assembly: Text of Debates, 26 September 1925, p. 439. Emphasis added.

9 *Id.*

Viscount Cecil noted in 1925 that such similar conditions "approach very close to and are, in fact a form of slavery, but are not usually included in the simple term slavery. With respect to all those, we [re: the Drafting Committee] ask for their abolition, we ask all the nations to agree to their abolition, which will be carried out, as all reform must necessarily be carried out, as progressively as may be possible, and as soon as possible." See League of Nations, Question of Slavery: Report of the Sixth Committee; Resolution, League of Nations Official Journal (Special Supplement 33) Records of the Sixth Assembly: Text of Debates, Nineteenth Plenary Meeting, 26 September 1925, p. 156.

type of 'slavery' – where the powers attaching to the right of ownership are exercised. While mentioning the work of the Temporary Slavery Commission once more, Chelwood rephrased the manifestation of exploitation so as to include the term 'slavery' where it had been absent in the Report of the Temporary Slavery Commission. Viscount Cecil enumerated the types of domestic slavery and similar conditions as "all those conditions mentioned by the Temporary Slavery Commission and to which I referred to last year."[10] Yet Viscount Cecil speaks of "debt *slavery*" where the Temporary Slavery Commission spoke of "forms of pledging or reducing to servitude of persons for debt or other reason." Instead of using the language of the Commission, "considering conditions analogous to slavery, as for example," the adoption "of children, [...] with a view to their virtual enslavement" or the acquisition "of girls by purchase disguised as payment of dowry," Viscount Cecil's 1926 Report speaks of the "*enslaving* of persons disguised as adoption of children and the acquisition of girls by purchase disguised as payment of dowry."[11] Furthermore, Viscount Cecil sought to reaffirm the link between slavery and the powers attached to the right of ownership, as he noted that:

> Even if, as is possible, these last practices do not come under the definition of slavery as it is given in Article 1, the [drafting] Commission is unanimously of the opinion that they must be combated. In a more general way, it interprets Article 2 as tending to bring about the disappearance from written legislation or from the custom of the country of everything which admits the maintenance by a private individual of rights over another person of the same nature as the rights which an individual can have over things.[12]

In other words, Viscount Cecil recognised that 'slavery in all it forms' required the demonstration of a power attached to the right of ownership to be exercised over an individual as established by the definition of slavery in Article 1.

The modification of the 1925 draft of the convention so as expunge the term 'domestic and other slavery' was brought about as a result of comments made by States which sought to ensure that only slavery as defined by Article 1(a) was included in the Convention and that other types of exploitation would be

10 League of Nations, Slavery Convention: Report presented to the Assembly by the Sixth Committee, LofN Doc. A.104.1926.VI, as found in League of Nations, Publications of the League of Nations, VI.B.Slavery.1926, VI. B. 5, 24 September 1926, p. 1.

11 *Id.* Emphasis added.

12 *Id.*, pp. 1–2.

excluded. This precise point was made by the Union of South Africa, when it commented that the 1925 draft "Convention as drafted goes somewhat further than seems necessary for the abolition of slavery [...]."[13]

> That definition puts as the test of slavery the status or condition of a person over whom all or any of the powers attaching to the right of *ownership* are exercised. In other words, a person is a slave if any other person can, by law or enforceable custom, claim such property in him as would be claimed if he were an inanimate object; and thus the natural freedom of will possessed by a person to offer or render his labour or to control the fruits thereof or the consideration therefrom is taken from him.[14]

The South African comment continues:

> If the draft Convention had merely proceed to impose on the contracting parties the duty to prevent within their community any person being in a condition of slavery as defined in Article 1 [...] there would be little criticism to offer upon the draft. But in Article 2(b), the draft Convention desires to bring about the disappearance not only of slavery as defined in Article 1 but to bring about *progressively* the disappearance of what is called "*domestic* slavery and similar conditions." It is obviously therefore desired to extend the definitions given in Article 1 (which makes property or rights of ownership the test) to conditions wherein no property of one person in another is recognised by law – such as the relationship by custom of heads of families to persons related to them by consanguinity or marriage or to person who are deemed by adoption to be places in such relationships. This seem to go beyond the object of the draft Convention as set out in the Preamble. If it does not go beyond those objects, there seems no reason why the so-called domestic slavery should not be included in the definition of Article 1. The argument seems to be that the so-called domestic slavery can only be brought to an end *progressively*; and thus admittedly the draft Convention is asking the signatories to the Convention to interfere as opportunity presents itself in the social conditions and custom of the people forming their communities. It is even uncertain as to what would thus be suppressed because to 'domestic slavery' is added 'or

---

13 League of Nations, Draft Convention on Slavery, Replies of Governments, Reply from the Government of the Union of South Africa, LofN Doc. A.10(a).1926.VI, 22 July 1926, p. 5; as found in League of Nations, Publications of the League of Nations, VI.B.Slavery.1926, VI. B. 3.

14 *Id.* Emphasis in the original.

> similar condition' – an expression by which, it is explained, is meant all forms of "debt slavery," enslaving of persons disguised as adoption of children, and the acquisition of girls by purchase disguised as payment of dowry.

Having noted this, the submission by the Union of South Africa turned to legal analysis:

> Now either such persons are *sui juris* [re: a separate category] or they are not. If they are *sui juris*, they can only become subject to domestic slavery or similar conditions by a voluntary act, and the essential element of slavery is absent. If they are not *sui juris*, they can only be subject to domestic slavery or similar conditions by the acts of those who by law are their guardians, and it is no more than a form of paternal power. If, further, they have become domestic slaves or persons in similar conditions in the manner indicated, that can only be because others have acquired a right of property in them, and they are therefore slaves as defined in Article 1. There seems no reason, then, to differentiate them from the person in a condition of slavery defined in that article. If, on the other hand, no right of property in them exists, the scope of the draft Convention seems to be extended to compel the signatories to undertake to interfere in social customs.[15]

Beyond these comments, which were at the heart of the suppression of the phrase 'domestic slavery and similar conditions', two failed attempts by States seeking to expand the definition of slavery beyond manifestations of the powers attached to the right of ownership transpired. Germany proposed a new sub-paragraph creating for States the obligation to suppress types of servitude. The German proposal read:

> To endeavour, as far as possible, to bring about the disappearance of conditions of servitude resembling slavery, *e.g.* debt slavery, sham adoption, childhood marriage, traffic in women, etc.[16]

This proposal, like the one made by the Delegate of Haiti ("To endeavour to bring about as soon as possible the disappearance of all voluntary or

---

15 *Id.*, p. 6. Emphasis in the original.

16 League of Nations, Draft Convention on Slavery, Replies of Governments, Reply from the Government of Germany, LofN Doc. A.10(a).1926.VI, 22 July 1926, p. 4.

involuntary subjections")[17] was not taken up by the Sixth Committee or later by the Assembly. Thus, there was an unwillingness to include servitude in the Convention. For his part, Viscount Cecil reported to the Assembly of the League of Nations in 1926 that "the words 'notably in the case of domestic slavery and similar conditions' [were] being now omitted. This modification was made because it was believed that such conditions came within the definition of slavery contained in the first article and that no further prohibition of them in express terms was necessary."[18]

The argument being put forward here is that without this background the 1926 Report to the Assembly of the League of Nations by Viscount Cecil of Chelwood appears to be ambiguous on the definition of slavery, yet it is not. Viscount Cecil did not seek to give voice to a wider the definition of slavery. That 'domestic slavery and similar conditions' was omitted was a result of the understanding that where so-called 'domestic slavery and similar conditions' manifested powers attaching to the right of ownership, they fell into the definition of slavery as established by Article 1(a) of the 1926 Convention. If the did not, such exploitation was not covered by the Convention. Thus, Viscount Cecil is clear: despite the wishes of the Temporary Slavery Commission, which sought to outlaw 'domestic slavery and similar conditions'; that 'slavery' is manifest only where 'any or all of the powers attaching to the right of ownership are exercised'.

During the 1930s, a schism emerged between those within the League of Nations who used the Article 1(a) definition of slavery and those who sought to advocate against exploitation, the latter of whom misrepresented Viscount Cecil's remarks as giving licence to also include, within the definition of slavery, the types of servitude mentioned in the 1924 Report of the Temporary Slavery Commission, even where powers attached to the right of ownership were not exercised.[19] Turing to the former, in 1936 the League of Nations Committee of Experts on Slavery considered the issue of serfdom and emphasised that one must make a distinction between slavery as defined in the convention and other forms of exploitation:

17 League of Nations, Draft Convention on Slavery and Proposed Amendments, LofN Doc. A.VI/S.C.1/1, 10 September 1926; as found in Folder R.77.D.46781 entitled Draft Convention on Slavery: Discussion at the 7th Assembly; 1926.

18 League of Nations, Slavery Convention: Report presented to the Assembly by the Sixth Committee, LofN Doc. A.104.1926.VI, as found in League of Nations, Publications of the League of Nations, VI.B.Slavery.1926, VI. B. 5, 24 September 1926, p. 1.

19 That schism emerged as a result of the Report of the 1930 International Commission of Inquiry into the Existence of Slavery and Forced Labour in the Republic of Liberia which truncated Viscount Cecil's 1926 Report to read:

It is important, however, to keep the fundamental distinction clearly in mind, and to realise that the status of 'serfdom' is a condition 'analogous to slavery' rather than a condition of actual slavery, and that the question whether it amounts to 'slavery' within the definition of the Slavery

---

> The Report of the Assembly Committee responsible for drafting of the convention has explained that reference to domestic slavery and similar conditions was omitted 'because it was believed that such conditions came within the definition of slavery contained in the first article and that no further prohibition of them in express terms was necessary. This applies not only to domestic slavery but to all those conditions mentioned by the Temporary Slavery Commission i.e., debt slavery, enslaving of persons disguised as payment of dowry, etc'.

And no more, giving the impression that all such conditions were covered by the 1926 Convention. This type of use of Chelwood's Report is of contemporary significance as it is repeated in United Nations Sub-Commission on the Promotion and Protection of Human Right, *Contemporary Forms of Slavery: Updated review of the implementation of and follow-up to the conventions on slavery*, Working Paper prepared by David Weissbrodt and Anti-Slavery International, UN Doc. E/CN.4/Sub.2/2000/3, 26 May 2000. Note my critique of that Paper in Jean Allain, "A Legal Consideration 'Slavery' in Light of the Travaux Préparatoires of the 1926 Convention," Paper presented at the Wilberforce Institute, Hull, 23 November 2006 available on-line by Googling: Allain, Slavery. In that Working Paper, it was stated at p. 5 that:

> By referring to "any or all of the powers of ownership" in its definition of slavery, and setting forth as its stated purpose the "abolition of slavery in all its forms" the Slavery Convention covered not only domestic slavery but also the other forms of slavery listed in the Report of the Temporary Slavery Commission.

To which the following footnote was added:

> The report to the Sixth Committee of the League of Nations Assembly in 1926 also clarified, in relation to article 2 (b) of the final text of the Slavery Convention, that the words "notably in the case of domestic slavery and similar conditions" were being omitted on the grounds that "such conditions come within the definition of slavery contained in the first article and that no further prohibition of them in express terms was necessary. This provision applies not only to domestic slavery but to all those conditions mentioned by the Temporary Slavery Commission…i.e. debt slavery, the enslaving of persons disguised as adoption of children and the acquisition of girls by purchase disguised as payment of dowry."

Thus from both these considerations of the definition of slavery is the omitted what Viscount Cecil went on to say:

> Even if, as is possible, these last practices do not come under the definition of slavery as it is given in Article 1, the Commission is unanimously of the opinion that they must be combated. In a more general way, it interprets Article 2 as tending to bring about the disappearance from written legislation or from the custom of the country of everything which admits the maintenance by a private individual of rights over another person of the same nature as the rights which an individual can have over things.

> Convention must depend upon the facts connected with each of the various systems of 'serfdom'.[20]

The Committee of Experts on Slavery was more explicit in regard to its considerations of debt slavery, noting that at least theoretically:

> debt slavery is only a temporary form, for the assumption is that the slavery ends as soon as the debt is repaid. In practice, however, the conditions in which the debt-slave lives are often of the nature that repayment is an impossibility and the debtor is therefore a slave for life. Even worse than this may sometimes happen, for in some systems there are cases in which the debt is 'hereditary' and, after the death of the debtor, it is transmitted to the children and children's children. It is right, perhaps, that one should realise quite clearly that the system – *whatever form it may take in different countries – is not 'slavery' within the definition set forth in Article 1 of the 1926 Convention, unless any or all the powers attaching to the right of ownership are exercised by the master.*[21]

Taking these examples into consideration, it is clear that ten years after the establishment of the 1926 Convention, the expert body established to consider issues of slavery was of the view that the definition of slavery confined to the parameters of Article 1(a). Thus, the powers attached to the right of ownership remained the *sine quo non* of slavery.

The Powers Attached to the Right of Ownership

Consideration now turns to the United Nations era, not to consider the divergence between the legal definition of slavery and the ever-expanding notion of slavery, but instead, to examine the most significant pronouncement regarding

---

See League of Nations, Slavery Convention: Report presented to the Assembly by the Sixth Committee, LofN Doc. A.104.1926.VI, as found in League of Nations, Publications of the League of Nations, VI.B.Slavery.1926, VI. B. 5, 24 September 1926, p. 1.

20 League of Nations, Slavery: Report of the Advisory Committee of Experts, Third (Extraordinary) Meeting of the Advisory Committee, LofN Doc. C.189(I). M.145.1936, VI,13–14 April 1936, p. 27.

21 League of Nations, Slavery: Report of the Advisory Committee of Experts, Third (Extraordinary) Meeting of the Advisory Committee, LofN Doc. C.189(I). M.145.1936, VI,13–14 April 1936, pp. 24–25. Emphasis added.

the legal definition of slavery as the starting point for an examination of what constitutes 'any or all of the powers attaching to the right of ownership'. In 1949 the United Nations General Assembly requested that the Economic and Social Council study the problem of slavery.[22] As a result, the Economic and Social Council, by way of a resolution, instructed the UN Secretary-General to appoint an *ad hoc* committee to, *inter alia*, "suggest methods of attacking" issues of slavery and servitude.[23] With regard to this point, the Secretary-General suggested that the newly established 1950 *Ad Hoc* Committee on Slavery might propose a new convention:

> Should the Committee find that the substantive provisions of the Slavery Convention of 1926 are no longer adequate in the light of the present situation, it might consider the possibility and desirability of proposing a new convention on slavery. Several questions may be raised and studied with respect to the substantive provisions of the 1926 Convention. For instance:
>
> (a) Is the definition of slavery in Article 1 of the Convention satisfactory? [...][24]

To that end, the *Ad Hoc* Committee expressed the view in its first Report that:

> certain modifications of the International Slavery Convention of 1926 appeared to be necessary and that it might prove desirable to draft a new convention broader in scope, or alternatively, to draw up an instrument supplementary to the existing Convention.[25]

By the time the *Ad Hoc* Committee on Slavery produced its second Report in 1951, it called for "the preparation and adoption of an international convention supplementary to the Slavery Convention of 1926," which "should be more precise than that instrument in defining the exact forms of servitude

22 General Assembly, Resolution 278 (III), 13 May 1949.

23 Economic and Social Council, Resolution 238(IX), 20 July 1949.

24 Economic and Social Council, Notes on the Terms of Reference of the Ad Hoc Committee on Slavery (Memorandum submitted by the Secretary-General), UN Doc. E/AC.33/4, 3 February 1950, pp. 3–4.

25 United Nations Economic and Social Council, Report of the First Session of the *Ad Hoc* Committee on Slavery to the Economic and Social Council, UN Doc E/AC.33/9, 27 March 1950, p. 11.

dealt with."[26] The United Nations Economic and Social Council, for its part, having considered the Draft Resolution prepared by the *Ad Hoc* Committee on Slavery noted that it was unable to deal with the Recommendations, as "the material is not at present in such a form as to allow the Council to act upon," and called on the Secretary-General to report back to it "indicating what action the United Nations and specialized agencies could most appropriately take in order to achieve the elimination of slavery, the slave trade and forms of servitude resembling slavery in their effects."[27]

The Secretary-General reported back to the Economic and Social Council in 1953, stating that the *Ad Hoc* Committee had envisioned an instrument which covered the subject matter of the 1926 Convention and "certain other institutions and practices" and would "be in operation side by side with that Convention."[28] The Secretary-General also considered the definition of slavery as found in the 1926 Convention. He, started by once more noting Viscount Cecil's Report on the 1926 Convention and cited the relevant text in full:

> In this interpretation the Rapporteur stated that reference to domestic slavery and similar conditions was omitted:
>
> > because it was believed that such conditions came within the definition of slavery contained in the first article and that no further prohibition of them in express terms was necessary. This applies not only to domestic slavery but to all those conditions mentioned by the Temporary Slavery Commission…i.e., 'debt slavery', the enslaving of persons disguised as the adoption of children, and the acquisition of girls by purchase disguised as payment of dowry, etc. Even if, as is possible, these last practices do not come under the definition of slavery as it is given in Article 1, the Commission is unanimously of the opinion that they must be combated. In a more general way, it interprets Article 2 as tending to bring about the disappearance from written legislation or from the custom of the country of everything which admits the maintenance by a private individual of rights over another person of the same nature as the rights which an individual can have over things.
>
> It would appear from a study of the International Slavery Convention of 1926, and of the preparatory work leading to its adoption, that the obligations of

26 United Nations Economic and Social Council, Report of the *Ad Hoc* Committee on Slavery (Second Session), UN Doc E/AC.33/13, 4 May 1951, pp. 16–17.

27 Economic and Social Council, Resolution 388(XIII), 10 September 1951.

28 United Nations Economic and Social Council, Slavery, the Slave Trade, and other forms of Servitude (Report of the Secretary-General), UN Doc. E/2357, 27 January 1953, p. 40.

> the Parties therefore extended to all institutions or practices, whether or not designated as 'slavery', provided that, as stated in Article 1 of the Convention, 'any or all of the powers attaching to the right of ownership are exercised' over a person in these institutions or practices.

The Secretary-General, then turned, by way of an extended footnote at the end of the paragraph, to consider the meaning of the phrase 'any or all of the powers attaching to the right of ownership are exercised'. According to the Secretary-General, one "does not find in the *travaux préparatoires* of the International Slavery Convention of 1926 any precise indication of the meaning of the 'power attaching to the right of ownership' to which the drafters of that Convention intended to refer, or of the legal system by which they were guided." The Secretary-General then continued:

> In the absence of such an indication, it may reasonably be assumed that the basic concept which they had in mind was that of the authority of the master over the slave in Roman law, the '*dominica potestas*'. This authority was of an absolute nature, comparable to the rights of ownership, which included the right to acquire, to use, or to dispose of a thing or of an animal or of its fruits or offspring. By virtue of this right, in its most general form the master could utilise the services of the slave in his house or on his land. The children of the slave also belonged to the master, and he could sell them separately from their mother and father. As a result of the evolution of Roman law, the authority of the master over the slave was subjected successively to more and more limitations; but even though it was restricted, the master never had towards his slave the obligations that an employer has today towards his servant or employee.[29]

To justify this interpretation, the Secretary-General pointed to the submission of the Union of South Africa, saying that this "seems to have been the guiding concept in Geneva, as is apparent from the following quotation of a government communication to the League of Nations in 1926:"

> a person is a slave if any other person can, by law or enforceable custom, claim such property in him as would be claimed if he were an inanimate

29 *Id.*, p. 27. It may be noted that the notion of '*dominicia potestas*' appears to come from the 1910 study entitled *Slavery as an Industrial System* by H.J. Nieboer wherein he seeks to establish a working definition for his study: See H.J. Nieboer, *Slavery as an Industrial System*, 1910, pp. 8–9.

> object; and thus the natural freedom of will possessed by a person to offer or render his labour or to control the fruits thereof or the consideration therefrom is taken from him. The term also seems to imply a *permanent* status or condition of a person whose natural freedom is taken away, for from the proprietary interest of the other person in the person to whom that status attaches is implied a right of disposal of sale, gift or exchange.[30]

Turning to the Roman Law, in his classic 1908 text *The Roman Law of Slavery*, W.W. Buckland considered the laws applicable to slaves during the Roman era. Interestingly, much of the book deals with the slave as a man and the law applicable to a slave as a person, while only one chapter is devoted to the slave as a thing, that is chattel slavery. This is so because the essence of slave laws since time immemorial has been the inability to treat slaves exclusively as property and, thus, to recognise in them their humanity. With regard to Roman Law, it should first be noted that slavery as an institution persists though it was recognised as being against natural law. The institution was allowed to persisted as against this *Ius Naturale* as the *Ius Gentium* (the Law of Nations) deemed that captives in war, instead of being put to death, forfeited their lives to their captors and thus became enslaved.[31] From this flowed the Roman Law notion of the individual as *res* – a thing or an object – which can be owned, and thus was chattel. This notion of chattel – 'goods' – the personal property of another, is the fundamental basis for slavery in Roman Law. As Buckland writes, the "slave, like any other chattel, might be the subject of all ordinary transactions."[32] But what were these transactions, and did they differ where slaves were concerned?

Ownership is a rather elusive concept. A social construct, it is typically understood as a priorital right over something. As A.M. Honoré puts it; "those legal rights, duties and other incidents which apply, in the ordinary case, to the person who has the greatest interest in a thing admitted by a mature legal system."[33] That 'greatest interest' thus does not mean that an individual has a sovereign or absolute right over a thing but, rather, the ability to enjoy and dispose of the thing "provided that one abstains from any use forbidden by statute or

30 *Id.*, p. 28.

31 W.W. Buckland, *The Roman Law of Slavery: The Condition of the Slave in Private Law Ausgustas to Justinian*, 1908, p. 1. Beyond enslavement as a prisoner of war, one could become a slave under Roman Law by two further means, by birth, or through the civil law: by selling yourself or your offspring, or through debt or serious crime.

32 *Id.*, p. 11.

33 A.M. Honoré, "Ownership," in A.G. Guest (ed), *Oxford Essays in Jurisprudence*, 1961, p. 105.

subordinate legislation."[34] Thus ownership entails rights, but those rights are often termed not as absolute but as right vis-à-vis others where one holds the best claim to a thing. Moving beyond the common characterisation of ownership as constituting a 'bundle of rights', Honoré lists what he calls the eleven 'standard incidents' of ownership, of which the majority are rights, but some are also obligations. These incidents are:

(1) The right to posses;
(2) The right to use;
(3) The right to manage;
(4) The right to the income of the thing;
(5) The right to the capital;
(6) The right to security;
(7) The right or incidents of transmissibility;
(8) The right or incidents of absence of the term;
(9) The prohibition of harmful use;
(10) Liability to execution; and
(11) Incident of residuarity.[35]

Thus, it is within these parameters that one may speak of ownership. With regard to slavery, ownership meant the ability to posses and use a slave, to compel and gain from the slave's labour, but also to buy, sell, or even destroy a slave, though even under Roman Law the killing of a slave was criminal as was their use as gladiators...that is, without the consent of a magistrate.[36] Likewise under Louis XIV's 1685 *Code Noir*, an owner could only put to death a fugitive slave after s/he had been caught thee times:

> The fugitive slave who has been on the run for one month from the day his master reported him to the police, shall have his ears cut off and shall be branded with a *fleur de lys* on one shoulder. If he commits the same infraction for another month, again counting from the day he is reported, he shall have his hamstring cut and be branded with a *fleur de lys* on the other shoulder. The third time, he shall be put to death.[37]

Having sketched out what ownership means, focus now shifts to the definition of slavery as 'a status or condition of a person over which any or all of the powers attaching to the right of ownership are exercised'. This phrase should be

34 *Id.*, p. 110.

35 *Id.*, p. 113.

36 David Johnston, *Roman Law in Context*, 1999, p. 42.

37 Article 38, Le Code Noir, Edict of the King: On the subject of the Policy regarding the Islands of French America, March 1685.

broken down into its component parts to demonstrate that where slavery is concerned the issue is *not* about the legal right of ownership – i.e. the legal right to, for instance, buy, sell, or possess a person and, upon challenge, to have such a right vindicated in a court of law – but about the powers attached to the right of ownership. The difference between the two is the difference between slavery *de jure* and slavery *de facto*.

The argument flows as follows: had Members of the League of Nations wished to outlaw only the legal status of slavery their definition would not have had to be as elaborate as the 1926 conventional definition. Instead, removing two elements from the definition, it could have read: *Slavery is a person over whom any or all of the right*[s] *of ownership are exercised.* This definition would have been sufficient to have established that an individual could have been considered to be a slave if another person had proprietary rights over him or her. Yet the definition of Article 1(a) of the 1926 Convention is more elaborate.

Reintroducing the first of the expunged clauses produces the following elaboration of the definition: *Slavery is the **status or condition** of a person over whom any or all of the right*[s] *of ownership are exercised.* What, then, is meant by the phrase 'status or condition'? With regard to the word 'status', while the *Oxford English Dictionary* speaks of social status or financial status, it also defines status as it relates to law:

> The legal standing or position of a person as determined by his membership of some class of persons legally enjoying certain rights or subject to certain limitations; condition in respect, e.g., of liberty or servitude, marriage or celibacy, infancy or majority.[38]

Flowing from this definition, the *Dictionary* also notes the ability to transfer such status and the ability to use the term "in application of things," using as an example the following taken from the 6 November 1914 edition of the *Daily News*: "The Sultan of Turkey not having ratified the Convention relating to the status of enemy merchant vessels." While one cannot infer from this that the inclusion of the term 'status' in a legal definition mandates that the term be used in its legal sense, the lead up to the drafting of the 1926 Convention makes plain that the drafters were using the term in the legal sense. In 1925, in its Final Report, the Temporary Slavery Commission noted that the "most important measure for the gradual abolition of slavery is that the status of slavery should

38 *Oxford English Dictionary*, 1989; on-line edition.

no longer be recognised in the eye of the law" and went so far as to define what it meant by the abolition of the legal status of slavery:

> The "abolition of the legal status" means that every slave has the right to assert his freedom, without ransom and without going through any formal process of fulfilling any prior condition, by simply leaving his master if he desire to do so. He enjoys and can exercise all the civil rights of a free man – *e.g.*, can sue and be sued in court, can prosecute his master for ill-treatment, and can bequeath and inherit property.[39]

While this definition was not taken up during the drafting process which led to the 1926 Convention, the Temporary Slavery Commission's suggestion that the "abolition of the legal status of slavery" might form part of a proposed instrument was clearly integrated into the definition of slavery in Article 1(a).

In the definition of slavery, the notion of 'status' is juxtaposed with the term 'condition' by the conjunction 'or'. 'Condition', as a noun, is defined, *inter alia*, in the *Oxford English Dictionary* as a "mode of being, state, position, nature." The most pertinent example given under this heading is a "characteristic, property, attribute, quality (of men or things)." As opposed to the term 'status', the definition in law provided in the *Oxford English Dictionary* of 'condition' does not apply in the context of the definition of slavery, which definition reads: "In a legal instrument, e.g. a will, or contract, a provision on which its legal force or effect is made to depend," i.e. "Something demanded or required as a prerequisite to the granting or performance of something else; a provision, a stipulation." With regard to the *travaux préparatoires* and the 1926 Convention, the term 'condition' was used during the negotiations of the Convention as part of the phrase 'domestic slavery and similar conditions' which, it will be recalled, was excluded from the substance of the Convention but was recognised as being subsumed within the definition of Slavery during the negotiation process, were the powers of the right of ownership were exercised. While referring to the types of exploitation that the Temporary Slavery Commission had wished to see in the Convention, Viscount Cecil conceded that, while such conditions might not always come under the definition in Article 1, it was clear that the obligation manifest in Article 2 – "To bring about, progressively and as soon as possible, the complete abolition of slavery in all its forms" – touched on two elements, namely the bringing about of the disappearance from

39 League of Nations, Temporary Slavery Commission, Report of the Temporary Slavery Commission adopted in the Course of its Second Session, July 13th-25th July, 1925, LofN Doc A.19.1925. VI, 25 July 1925, p. 3.

"written legislation" and "the custom of a country" of those items which admit "the maintenance by a private individual of rights over another person of the same nature as the rights which an individual can have over things."[40]

From the forgone textual interpretation, it may be said that the phrase 'status or condition' seeks to distinguish between slavery *de jure* and slavery *de facto*, whereby slavery as 'status' is a recognition of slavery in law; and slavery as 'condition' is to be understood as slavery in fact. This interpretation is confirmed first by the dichotomy put forward by Viscount Cecil between the suppression of slavery in law: 'written legislation' and in fact: 'the custom of a country'. It is also manifest in the 1926 submission of the Union of South Africa to the League of Nations' request for comment on the draft Convention, when that State reworded the definition including the phrase 'status or condition' to read: "In other words, a person is a slave if any other person can, *by law or enforceable custom*, claim such property in him as would be claimed if he were an inanimate object."[41]

Building on this understanding and reintroducing the second expunged phrase and thus completing the definition as found in the 1926 Convention, gives the following reading: *Slavery is the status or condition of a person over whom any or all of* ***the powers attaching to*** *the right of ownership are exercised.* By 'powers attaching to the right of ownership' as opposed to 'right of ownership' the definition implies that one would have the powers of ownership but for the fact that the right of ownership cannot be vindicated in law. In other words, exercising the 'powers attaching to the right of ownership' should be understood as meaning that the enslavement of a person does not mean the possession of a legal right of ownership over the individual (such a claim could find no remedy in modern day law) *but the powers attached to such rights* but for the fact that ownership is illegal. To use an analogy, the powers attached to the right of ownership are the powers that manifest themselves say, when two drug dealers have a dispute over a kilo of heroin. Neither can have their claim dealt with in a court of law, but one or the other will exercise the powers attached to the right of ownership, for example, possession; thus what would amount to a right of ownership but for the fact that it is illegal to own, or possess, heroin.

---

40 League of Nations, Slavery Convention: Report presented to the Assembly by the Sixth Committee, LofN Doc. A.104.1926.VI, as found in League of Nations, Publications of the League of Nations, VI.B.Slavery.1926, VI. B. 5, 24 September 1926, p. 2. Emphasis added.

41 League of Nations, Draft Convention on Slavery, Replies of Governments, Reply from the Government of the Union of South Africa, LofN Doc. A.10(a).1926.VI, 22 July 1926, p. 5. Emphasis added.

To buttress this argument, consider Article 33(4) of the Vienna Convention on the Law of Treaties,[42] which mandates that where there is a difference in meaning between the authentic texts of a treaty, the meaning which is best reconciled with the object and purpose of the treaty is to be adopted – the notion of 'powers attaching to' comes into play. In the only other language in which the text was authenticated in – French – the phrase 'powers attaching to' appears as '*les attributs*', which can be translated into English in the literal sense of 'attributes' of the right of ownership. Thus we are not speaking of a right of ownership, but exercising the attributes of the right of ownership without exercising the legal right of ownership. Thus, these three elements, the difference between status and condition, the notion of the 'powers attaching to the right of ownership' versus the right of ownership; and the use of the term '*les attributs*' in the French text, all point towards a definition of slavery that includes both *de jure* and *de facto* enslavement.

The Secretary-General's 1953 Memorandum, after examining the Roman Law nature of the 1926 definition of slavery, turns to consider "the characteristics of the various powers attaching to the 'right of ownership'." As such, the Secretary-General spells out what should be understood not as the right of ownership where it touches upon slavery, but rather, the exercise of the powers attached to the right of ownership:

1. the individual of servile status may be made the object of a purchase;
2. the master may use the individual of servile status, and in particular his capacity to work, in an absolute manner, without any restriction other than that which might be expressly provided by law;
3. the products of labour of the individual of servile status become the property of the master without any compensation commensurate to the value of the labour;
4. the ownership of the individual of servile status can be transferred to another person;

42 Article 33 – Interpretation of treaties authenticated in two or more languages of the 1969 Vienna Convention of the Law of Treaties reads:

> 1. When a treaty has been authenticated in two or more languages, the text is equally authoritative in each language,
>
> [...]
>
> 4. Except where a particular text prevails in accordance with paragraph 1, when a comparison of the authentic texts discloses a difference of meaning which the application of articles 31 and 32 does not remove, the meaning which best reconciles the texts, having regard to the object and purpose of the treaty, shall be adopted.

5. the servile status is permanent, that is to say, it cannot be terminated by the will of the individual subject to it;
6. the servile status is transmitted *ipso facto* to descendants of the individual having such status.[43]

Thus, when these characteristics of the various powers attached to the right of ownership are considered in light of the overall definition of slavery – that is to say "the status or condition of a person over whom any or all of the powers attaching to the right of ownership are exercise" – what emerges are elements which, taken separately or together, constitute slavery in law.

Turning to each of the six characteristics of the powers attached to the right of ownership put forward by the UN Secretary-General, it should first be noted that the use of 'servile status' by the Secretary-General predates the use of the term as noted in Article 7(2) of the 1956 Convention: "'A person of servile status' means a person in the condition or status resulting from any of the institutions or practices mentioned in article 1 of this Convention," with the institutions and practices in Article 1 being debt bondage, serfdom, forced or sham marriages and exploitation of children via adoptions. Thus, the definition as set out in Article 7(2) of the 1956 Convention of 'a person of servile status' is not applicable here, as being retrospective, but instead, 'servile status' should be understood as being synonymous with the status or condition wherein, if one of the six characteristics of the Secretary-General is attached, a power of the right of ownership would be exercised, and thus slavery would be manifest. Turning to the first and fourth of the Secretary-General's six characteristics, a person who finds him or herself being made the object of purchase or transfer would, thus, be in the status or condition of slavery. Put this way, it becomes clear that being made the object of purchase or transfer, if this were legal, would create in the individual the status of a slave and create for the master a right of ownership over the individual, whereas if a person is made the object of purchase or transfer where no such selling or transfer is possible in law it creates for the individual the *condition* of slavery and manifests, for the recipient, an exercise of a power attached to the right of ownership, though not a right of ownership able to be vindicated in a court of law.

The second of the UN Secretary-General's six characteristics of the powers attaching to the right of ownership turns on the ability to exploit another: "the master may use the individual of servile status, and in particular his capacity to work, in an absolute manner, without any restriction other than that which

43 United Nations Economic and Social Council, Slavery, the Slave Trade, and other forms of Servitude (Report of the Secretary-General), UN Doc. E/2357, 27 January 1953, p. 28.

might be expressly provided by law." Here the apparent contradiction between being able to use an individual in 'an absolute manner' as against 'without any restriction other than that which might be expressly provided by law' is solved by returning to the earlier discussion which the Secretary-General had with regard to Roman Law where he noted that the "authority of the master over the slave was subjected successively to more and more limitations; but even though it was restricted, the master never had towards his slave the obligations that an employer has today towards his servant or employee."[44] Of course in a state of *de facto* slavery, due to its overall illegal nature, there would be no restrictions expressly provided by law but, instead, an overarching prohibition. Despite this, or as a result, the 'master' would be able to use the individual and their labour 'in an absolute manner'. The third of the Secretary-General's characteristics, follows closely on from the second, as 'the products of labour of the individual of servile status become the property of the master without any compensation commensurate to the value of the labour'. Here whether having the status of slavery or being in the condition of slavery remains irrelevant to the fact that the master would benefit from exercising the power attached to the right of ownership with regard to the fruits of one's labour. The 1926 submission of the Union of South Africa, it may be recalled, picked up on this precise point:

> That definition puts as the test of slavery the status or condition of a person over whom all or any of the powers attaching to the right of *ownership* are exercised. In other words, a person is a slave if any other person can, by law or enforceable custom, claim such property in him as would be claimed if he were an inanimate object; and thus the natural freedom of will possessed by a person to offer or render his labour or to control the fruits thereof or the consideration therefrom is taken from him.[45]

Having already considered the fourth of the Secretary-General's sixcharacteristics of the powers attaching to the right of ownership, consideration now turns to the fifth: "the servile status is permanent, that is to say, it cannot be terminated by the will of the individual subject to it." The discussion by the Secretary-General deals with an assertion made in 1926 by Union of South Africa that the

44 *Id.*, p. 29.

45 League of Nations, Draft Convention on Slavery, Replies of Governments, Reply from the Government of the Union of South Africa, LofN Doc. A.10(a).1926.VI, 22 July 1926, p. 5; as found in League of Nations, Publications of the League of Nations, VI.B.Slavery, 1926. VI.B.3. Emphasis in the original.

definition of slavery "also seems to imply a *permanent* status or condition of a person whose natural freedom is taken away, for from the proprietary interest of the other person in the person to whom that status attaches is implied a right of disposal of sale, gift or exchange."[46] But here one sees that the Secretary-General is not concerned as much with there being a permanent status or condition which would last until the slave dies but, instead, that status or condition "cannot be terminated by the will of the individual subject to it," thus an indefinite status or condition.

The final characterisation of a power attached to the right of ownership which the Secretary-General mentions is that 'the servile status is transmitted *ipso facto* to descendants of the individual having such status'. Little need be said about this power except that, unlike Honoré's "right or incidents of transmissibility," such a power looks also to be *ipso facto* illegal and thus as a legal status it might no longer exist. Yet, for instances in the area of debt-bondage, the 'condition' of slavery manifests itself through the inheritance of debt, and, as such, it remains, like the other UN Secretary-General's characteristics, an authoritative description of a manifestation of the exercise of a power attached to the right of ownership, and thus slavery.

It should be noted that the 1953 Memorandum by the Secretary-General argued against the need for a further international instrument regulating lesser forms of exploitation than slavery as defined in the 1926 Convention, the Secretary-General writing:

> an examination of the institutions or practices described by the *ad hoc* Committee on Slavery [re: debt-bondage serfdom, forced marriage and child exploitation] indicates that in the main these institutions or practices are covered by the undertaking contained in Article 2(b) of the International Slavery Convention of 1926, interpreted in the light of the definition of slavery contained in Article 1 (1) of the same Convention.[47]

The 1956 Convention concretely manifests of the fact that States did not agree with the Secretary-General's Memorandum and thus moved to establish a supplementary Convention. This, however, does not detract for the Secretary-General's analysis in his 1953 Memorandum because the 1956 Convention

46 *Id.* The temporal issue of whether slavery had to be permanent in nature also arose in the considerations of 1930 the International Commission of Inquiry into the Existence of Slavery and Forced Labour in the Republic of Liberia. 8 September 1930 at. 14.

47 United Nations Economic and Social Council, Slavery, the Slave Trade, and other forms of Servitude (Report of the Secretary-General), UN Doc. E/2357, 27 January 1953, p. 29.

accepts that the institutions and practices it seeks to abolition may well be covered by the 1926 definition, yet seeks to abolish them even if they do not fall within the 1926 definition of slavery.

What emerged as the 1956 Supplementary Convention on the Abolition of Slavery, the Slave Trade, and Institutions and Practices Similar to Slavery was first put forward for consideration as a 1954 Draft Convention penned by the United Kingdom. Article 1 of that British Draft Convention, which set out various forms of servile status (i.e.: debt bondage, serfdom, sham marriages, and exploitation children) opened with the following paragraph:

> All practicable and necessary measures, including legislation where appropriate, shall be taken to bring about, progressively and as soon as possible, the complete abolition or abandonment of the following institutions and practices, where they still exist.[48]

A 1956 *Ad Hoc* Drafting Committee of the Economic and Social Council established to draft the 1956 Convention, turned to consider the 1954 British Draft Convention. In its Report to Economic and Social Council, the Drafting Committee noted that:

> The representative of the United Kingdom proposed[49] to insert at the end of the introductory paragraph the phrase, "and whether or not they are covered by the definition of slavery contained in Article 1 of the Slavery Convention of 25 September 1926." He explained that the proposal was in line with the suggestion of The Anti-Slavery Society.[50]
>
> The representative of India and Australia agreed that the amendment was necessary and that it would help to clarify the text.

48 See Economic and Social Council, The Draft Supplementary Convention of Slavery and Servitude Submitted by the Government of the United Kingdom and Comments Thereon (Memorandum by the Secretary-General), UN Doc E/AC.43/L.1, 2 December 1955, p. 24.

49 See Economic and Social Council, Committee on the Drafting of a Supplementary Convention on Slavery and Servitude, United Kingdom: Amendment to Article 1 of the Draft Convention on the Abolition of Slavery and Servitude (E/2540/Add.4), UN Doc. E/AC.43/L.2, 16 January 1956.

50 See Economic and Social Council, Committee on the Drafting of a Supplementary Convention on Slavery and Servitude, United Kingdom: Amendment to Article 1 of the Draft Convention on the Abolition of Slavery and Servitude (E/2540/Add.4), UN Doc. E/AC.43/L.10, 17 January 1956.

> The Committee unanimously adopted the amendment at the 11th meeting.[51]

The suggested proposal was further adopted during the 1956 Conference of Plenipotentiaries on a Supplementary Convention on the Abolition of Slavery, the Slave Trade and Institutions and Practices Similar to Slavery, such that the first paragraph of Article 1 of the 1956 Convention reads:

> Each of the States Parties to this Convention shall take all practicable and necessary legislative and other measures to bring about progressively and as soon as possible the complete abolition or abandonment of the following institutions and practices, where they still exist and whether or not they are covered by the definition of slavery contained in article 1 of the Slavery Convention signed at Geneva on 25 September 1926.[52]

Thus the 1956 Convention should be understood as dealing with various servile statuses where there are no powers attached to the right of ownership. Thus, this Convention supplements the 1926 Convention by dealing with institutions and practices which do not meet that threshold.

The Crime of Enslavement within the Rome Statute

In contrast to what has been discussed thus far, what follows, with regard to the crime of enslavement within the Statute of the International Criminal

---

See the proposal of The Anti-Slavery Society at Economic and Social Council, The Draft Supplementary Convention of Slavery and Servitude Submitted by the Government of the United Kingdom and Comments Thereon (Memorandum by the Secretary-General), UN Doc E/AC.43/L.1, 2 December 1955, pp. 21–22. In his Memorandum, the Secretary-General when on to explained that the proposal by the Anti-Slavery Society was being put forward as the "possibility of differing opinions as to the precise scope of these definitions would thus be recognized" *id.*, p. 22.

51 Economic and Social Council, Slavery: Draft Supplementary Convention on the Abolition of Slavery, the Slave Trade, and Institutions and Practices Similar to Slavery: Report of the Committee appointed by Resolution 564 (XIX), 7 April 1955, UN Doc E/2824, 15 February 1956, p. 20.

52 Article 1 of the 1956 Convention was adopted during the Sixth Meeting of the Conference, sss Economic and Social Council, United Nations Conference of Plenipotentiaries on a Supplementary Convention on the Abolition of Slavery, the Slave Trade and Institutions and Practices Similar to Slavery, Summary Record of the Sixth Meeting, 16 August 1956, UN Doc E/CONF.24/SR.6, 11 November 1958, p. 3.

Court, must be considered as tentative, as an in depth consideration of enslavement in the evolution of international criminal law has yet to be taken, likewise, for the legislative history of the negotiations leading to, and transpiring in, Rome in 1998. Furthermore, what follows should be understood as applying *mutates mutandis* to the term 'slavery' as it is manifest in 'sexual slavery', both as a crime against humanity and as a war crime.

As note earlier, 'enslavement' is deemed a crime against humanity under Article 7(1)(c) of the Rome Statute and defined at Article 7(2)(c) as:

> "Enslavement" means the exercise of any or all of the powers attaching to the right of ownership over a person and includes the exercise of such power in the course of trafficking in persons, in particular women and children.

What is interesting here is the extension of the definition to include the 'exercise of such power in the course of trafficking in persons, in particular women and children'. This need not detain us, as the international definition of 'trafficking in persons' as found in the 2001 United Nations Palermo Protocol (and reproduced in the 2005 Council of Europe Convention) reads:

> 'Trafficking in persons' shall mean the recruitment, transportation, transfer, harbouring or receipt of persons, by means of the threat or use of force or other forms of coercion, of abduction, of fraud, of deception, of the abuse of power or of a position of vulnerability or of the giving or receiving of payments or benefits to achieve the consent of a person having control over another person, for the purpose of exploitation. Exploitation shall include, at a minimum, the exploitation of the prostitution of others or other forms of sexual exploitation, forced labour or services, slavery or practices similar to slavery, servitude or the removal of organs.[53]

Thus, imbedded in the definition of 'trafficking in persons' is the term 'slavery', a manifestation of enslavement, which despite meeting the other elements of the definition 'trafficking in persons'[54] constitutes not 'trafficking in persons' but 'enslavement' before the International Criminal Court.

---

53 See Article 3(a), 2001 United Nations Protocol to Prevent, Suppress and Punish Trafficking in Persons, Especially Women and Children and Article 4(a), 2005 Council of Europe Convention on Action against Trafficking in Human Beings.

54 Read: the *actions* – 'the recruitment, transportation, transfer, harbouring or receipt of persons' or the *means* – 'the threat or use of force or other forms of coercion, of abduction,

In the secondary legislation of the International Criminal Court – the Elements of the Crimes – the crime of enslavement is elaborated upon at its corresponding Article 7(1)(c):

1. The perpetrator exercised any or all of the powers attaching to the right of ownership over one or more persons, such as by purchasing, selling, lending or bartering such a person or persons, or by imposing on them a similar deprivation of liberty.
2. The conduct was committed as part of a widespread or systematic attack directed against a civilian population.
3. The perpetrator knew that the conduct was part of or intended the conduct to be part of a widespread or systematic attack directed against a civilian population.

In adopting the Elements of the Crimes as drafted by the Preparatory Commission, the Assembly of State Parties expanded the understanding of 'enslavement' by not only itemising the types of powers attached to the right of ownership which a perpetrator might exercise – which track those noted by the Secretary-General in his 1953 Memorandum (i.e. 'purchasing, selling, lending or bartering such a person') –, but also including the phrase 'imposing on them a similar deprivation of liberty'. At the end of Article 7(1)(c)(1), a footnote is added which elaborates on what should be understood by this phrase:

> It is understood that such deprivation of liberty may, in some circumstances, include exacting forced labour or otherwise reducing a person to a servile status as defined in the Supplementary Convention on the Abolition of Slavery, the Slave Trade, and Institutions and Practices Similar to Slavery of 1956. It is also understood that the conduct described in this element includes trafficking in persons, in particular women and children.

Excluding the final sentence of this footnote which has been addressed above, the inclusion of the 'purchasing, selling, lending or bartering such a person' adds credence to the analysis undertaken above with regard to slavery in general international law, that is to say that 'slavery', like 'enslavement' is to be understood as not only being manifest in *de jure* slavery but also in *de facto*

---

of fraud, of deception, of the abuse of power or of a position of vulnerability or of the giving or receiving of payments or benefits to achieve the consent of a person having control over another person, for the purpose of exploitation'.

slavery. Thus, it should be understood that the Elements of the Crimes with regard to enslavement truly reflect the evolution of the fundamental elements of slavery in general international law, namely the exercise of 'any or all of the powers attaching to the right of ownership'.

Before considering the jurisprudence of the International Criminal Tribunal for the former Yugoslavia, which it can be said, confirms the understanding of 'slavery' within international criminal law, attention should be given to the European Court of Human Rights' very narrow interpretation in its only significant consideration of the issue, the 2005 *Siliadin* case. As opposed to international criminal law, where exploitation is manifest only in the crime of slavery, within international human rights law servitude and slavery often go hand-in-hand as they appear in the same article in the 1948 Universal Declaration of Human Rights, the 1966 International Covenants on Civil and Political Rights and, with regard to the case at hand, the 1950 European Convention for the Protection of Human Right and Fundamental Freedoms. In *Siliadin*, the Court found that there was a case of forced labour and servitude in violation of Article 4, but it was unwilling to find that there had been a breach of the provision related to slavery, despite depending on the 1926 conventional definition:

> It notes that this definition corresponds to the "classic" meaning of slavery as it was practiced for centuries. Although the applicant was, in the instant case, clearly deprived of her personal autonomy, the evidence does not suggest that she was held in slavery in the proper sense, in other words that Mr and Mrs B. exercised a genuine right of legal ownership over her, thus reducing her to the status of an "object."[55]

The rationale of the judges here plays not on the powers attached to the right of ownership but on the requirement of demonstrating 'a genuine right of legal ownership'. This truly narrow interpretation of the provisions of Article 1(a) of the 1926 Convention, does not reflect a consideration of the *travaux préparatoires* and may well be a manifestation – maybe the first – of the fragmentation of international law. Thus, that there are two diverging streams of interpretation in international law, between slavery in international human rights law – or at least within the context of the Council of Europe – which can be juxtaposed to 'servitude' and thus raises the threshold for meeting a determination of slavery as requiring a 'genuine right of legal ownership'. It should be

55 European Court of Human Rights, *Siliadin v France* (Application 73316/01), 26 July 2005, para. 122.

said, however, that this interpretation is at odds with the evolution of the term 'slavery' in general international law. Thus, *Siliadin* need not detain us, in part because it reflects a European context in which the 1950 Convention was drafted in the wake of atrocities of the Second World War which included the legal use of slave labour; and thus within a European context to use 'servitude' for *de facto* slavery, allows the term 'slavery' to be keep in reserve for situations mirroring the 1930s and the rise of exploitative policies instituted by the likes of the National Socialist Party in Germany, as manifest in *de jure* enslavement.

More importantly, *Siliadin* need not detain us as the International Criminal Tribunal for the former Yugoslavia (ICTY) has pronounced itself on 'enslavement' as a crime against humanity and has made determinations which are clearly in tune with the understanding of 'slavery' in general international law as presented here. In the *Kunarac* case, the Trial Chamber made a determination, having survey international human rights law, international humanitarian law, the work of the International Law Commission, and the jurisprudence of the Tokyo and Nuremburg tribunals; that at the time of the offences under consideration, "enslavement as a crime against humanity in customary international law consisted of the exercise of any or all of the powers attaching to the right of ownership over a person."[56] The Trial Chamber noted that while this definition "may be broader than the traditional and sometimes apparently distinct definitions of slavery, the slave trade and servitude or forced or compulsory labour found in other areas of international law," it pointed to the case-law of the Second World War and the work of the International Law Commission as supporting its conclusion.

The Trial Chamber went on to say:

> Under this definition, indications of enslavement include elements of control and ownership; the restriction or control of an individual's autonomy, freedom of choice or freedom of movement; and, often, the accruing of some gain to the perpetrator. The consent or free will of the victim is absent. It is often rendered impossible or irrelevant by, for example, the threat or use of force or other forms of coercion; the fear of violence, deception or false promises; the abuse of power; the victim's position of vulnerability; detention or captivity, psychological oppression or socio -economic conditions. Further indications of enslavement include exploitation; the exaction of forced or compulsory labour or service, often without remuneration and often, though not necessarily, involving physical hardship; sex; prostitution; and human trafficking.

---

56 International Criminal Tribunal for the former Yugoslavia, *Kunarac et als.* (IT-96-23-T &-IT-96-23/1-T) Judgment, 22 February 2001, p. 192.

The Trial Chamber continued:

> With respect to forced or compulsory labour or service, international law, including some of the provisions of Geneva Convention IV and the Additional Protocols, make clear that not all labour or service by protected persons, including civilians, in armed conflicts, is prohibited – strict conditions are, however, set for such labour or service. The 'acquisition' or 'disposal' of someone for monetary or other compensation, is not a requirement for enslavement. Doing so, however, is a prime example of the exercise of the right of ownership over someone. The duration of the suspected exercise of powers attaching to the right of ownership is another factor that may be considered when determining whether someone was enslaved; however, its importance in any given case will depend on the existence of other indications of enslavement. Detaining or keeping someone in captivity, without more, would, depending on the circumstances of a case, usually not constitute enslavement.

The Trial Chamber then concluded by noting that it was in general agreement with the factors adduced by the Prosecutor in the case:

> The Trial Chamber is therefore in general agreement with the factors put forward by the Prosecutor, to be taken into consideration in determining whether enslavement was committed. These are the control of someone's movement, control of physical environment, psychological control, measures taken to prevent or deter escape, force, threat of force or coercion, duration, assertion of exclusivity, subjection to cruel treatment and abuse, control of sexuality and forced labour. The Prosecutor also submitted that the mere ability to buy, sell, trade or inherit a person or his or her labours or services could be a relevant factor. The Trial Chamber considers that the *mere ability* to do so is insufficient, such actions actually occurring could be a relevant factor.[57]

For its part, the Appeals Chamber accepted "the chief thesis of the Trial Chamber that the traditional concept of slavery, as defined in the 1926 Slavery Convention and often referred to as 'chattel slavery', has evolved to encompass various contemporary forms of slavery which are also based on the exercise of any or all of the powers attaching to the right of ownership."[58] It went on to say:

---

57 *Id.*, pp. 193–194. Footnote references have been omitted.

58 International Criminal Tribunal for the former Yugoslavia, *Kunarac et als.* (IT-96-23 &-IT-96-23/1-A) Judgment, 12 June 2002, para. 117.

> In the case of these various contemporary forms of slavery, the victim is not subject to the exercise of the more extreme rights of ownership associated with 'chattel slavery', but in all cases, as a result of the exercise of any or all of the powers attaching to the right of ownership, there is some destruction of the juridical personality; the destruction is greater in the case of 'chattel slavery' but the difference is one of degree.

The Appeals Chamber did in fact consider the 1926 definition of slavery, drawing the same conclusions as emerge from the above study of the *travaux préparatoires*:

> The Appeals Chamber will however observe that the law does not know of a 'right of ownership over a person'. Article 1(1) of the 1926 Slavery Convention speaks more guardedly 'of a person over whom any or all of the powers attaching to the right of ownership are exercised'. That language is to be preferred.
>
> The Appeals Chamber considers that the question whether a particular phenomenon is a form of enslavement will depend on the operation of the factors or indicia of enslavement identified by the Trial Chamber. These factors include the "control of someone's movement, control of physical environment, psychological control, measures taken to prevent or deter escape, force, threat of force or coercion, duration, assertion of exclusivity, subjection to cruel treatment and abuse, control of sexuality and forced labour." Consequently, it is not possible exhaustively to enumerate all of the contemporary forms of slavery which are comprehended in the expansion of the original idea; this Judgement is limited to the case in hand.[59]

The Appeals Chamber turned to the "Appellants' contention that lack of resistance or the absence of a clear and constant lack of consent during the entire time of the detention can be interpreted as a sign of consent." The Appeals Chamber, for its part, did "not accept the premise that lack of consent is an element of the crime since, in its view, enslavement flows from claimed rights of ownership;"

> accordingly, lack of consent does not have to be proved by the Prosecutor as an element of the crime. However, consent may be relevant from an evidential point of view as going to the question whether the Prosecutor has established the element of the crime relating to the exercise by the

---

59 *Id.*, paras 118–119.

> accused of any or all of the powers attaching to the right of ownership. In this respect, the Appeals Chamber considers that circumstances which render it impossible to express consent may be sufficient to presume the absence of consent. In the view of the Appeals Chamber, the circumstances in this case were of this kind.

The ICTY Appeals Chamber continued:

> The Appellants contend that another element of the crime of enslavement requires the victims to be enslaved for an indefinite or at least for a prolonged period of time. The Trial Chamber found that the duration of the detention is another factor that can be considered but that its importance will depend on the existence of other indications of enslavement. The Appeals Chamber upholds this finding and observes that the duration of the enslavement is not an element of the crime. The question turns on the quality of the relationship between the accused and the victim. A number of factors determine that quality. One of them is the duration of the relationship. The Appeals Chamber considers that the period of time, which is appropriate, will depend on the particular circumstances of each case.

Finally, the Appeals Chamber turned to the issue of *mens rea* with regard to the enslavement, where it concurred with the Trial Chamber "that the required *mens rea* consists of the intentional exercise of a power attaching to the right of ownership. It is not required to prove that the accused intended to detain the victims under constant control for a prolonged period of time in order to use them for sexual acts."[60] The Appeals Chamber then concluded that it was "of the opinion that the Trial Chamber's definition of the crime of enslavement is not too broad and reflects customary international law at the time when the alleged crimes were committed."

Conclusion

It appears clear from the foregoing, that the evolution of the crime of enslavement has stayed true to the understanding of the definition of 'slavery' as

60 *Id.*, para. 122. The Appeals Chamber continued: Aside from the foregoing, the Appeals Chamber considers it appropriate in the circumstances of this case to emphasise the citation by the Trial Chamber of the following excerpt from the *Pohl* case:

established in the 1926 Convention. Although advocates, such as Professor Kevin Bales, have discarded that definition of slavery, this should be understood in the light of the fact that very little to no effort has gone in to understanding what the 'status or condition of a person over whom any or all of the powers attaching to the right of ownership are exercised' actually means but for the recent pronouncement of the Yugoslav Tribunal. While sending the 1926 definition to the shadowland of disuse, advocates from the 1930 International Commission of Inquiry in Liberia to the 2000 Working Paper prepared by David Weissbrodt and Anti-Slavery International for the UN Sub-Commission on the Promotion and Protection of Human Right have hung their hat on an expanded understanding of the definition. This has come about as a result of a misreading of Viscount Cecil of Chelwood's 1926 Report to the League of Nations,[61] which has lead to interpreting the term 'slavery' as being so all-encompassing as to render it meaningless in law. What this Paper has sought to do is to consider the definition of Article 1(a) of the 1926 Convention in-depth, and to demonstrate that a legal interpretation of the term 'slavery' get one not only as far, but arguable further, than either Bales academic definition (loss of free will, the appropriation of labour power, and the use or threat of violence) or the ever expanding definition used within a number of United Nation *fora*.

Having considered the drafting history of the 1926 and the 1956 Conventions with regard to pronouncement made as to the phrase 'powers attaching to the right of ownership', this Paper has shown that the definition of Article 1(a) as encompasses not only *de jure*, but *de facto*, slavery; it also bring with it, out of the shadowlands, six characteristics which the United Nations Secretary-General put forward in his 1953 Memorandum as being powers attached to the

> Slavery may exist even without torture. Slaves may be well fed, well clothed, and comfortably housed, but they are still slaves if without lawful process they are deprived of their freedom by forceful restraint. We might eliminate all proof of ill-treatment, overlook the starvation, beatings, and other barbarous acts, but the admitted fact of slavery – compulsory uncompensated labour – would still remain. There is no such thing as benevolent slavery. Involuntary servitude, even if tempered by humane treatment, is still slavery.

The passage speaks of slavery; it applies equally to enslavement.

61 See United Nations Sub-Commission on the Promotion and Protection of Human Right, *Contemporary Forms of Slavery: Updated review of the implementation of and follow-up to the conventions on slavery*, Working Paper prepared by David Weissbrodt and Anti-Slavery International, UN Doc. E/CN.4/Sub.2/2000/3, 26 May 2000. Note my critique of that Paper in Jean Allain, "A Legal Consideration 'Slavery' in Light of the Travaux Préparatoires of the 1926 Convention," Paper presented at the Wilberforce Institute, Hull, 23 November 2006 available on line by Googling: Allain, Slavery.

right of ownership. The fundamental argument of this Paper is as follows: that to *exercise the right of ownership* over an individual is fundamentally different than *exercising powers attached to the right of ownership.* Using the analogy of a dispute over illegal drugs, it becomes clear that while no right of ownership – to be remedied in a court of law – exists, the powers attached to the right of ownership do exist for one or the other of the heroin dealers. Thus, like the dealer, the 'master' of a *de facto* slave possesses a right of ownership over his or her 'property' but for the fact that such a legal right does not exist as it can not be vindicated in law. In essence, both the dealer and the master exercise powers attached to the rights of ownership over their illegal 'property', but do not exercise any legal rights of ownership. If the argument being put forward is correct, then it creates a true avenue in international criminal law for the prosecution of individuals involved in enslavement, while giving advocates a wide enough berth to use the definition of slavery found in the 1926 Convention to combat what they term 'contemporary forms of slavery'.

This in-depth study of 'slavery' in general international law, though the European Court of Human Rights has taken a different tact, is consistent with the interpretation of 'enslavement' as a crime against humanity as it has developed in international criminal law. The Trial and Appeals Chamber in the *Kunarac* case have done well to, in essence, interpret 'any or all of the powers attaching to the right of ownership' in good faith, within its ordinary meaning, in context, and with a look to the object and purpose of its Statute. As has been demonstrated, despite the attempts of the anti-slavery movement to expand that definition, and the European Court to restrict it; the *travaux réparatoires* of the 1926 and 1956 Conventions confirm the approach taken by the ICTY and within the Rome Statute and the Elements of the Crimes, as to the definition of 'slavery' and by extensions 'enslavement' as a crime against humanity. Despite these anti-slavery and European Court countervailing forces at work, the International Criminal Court would be well grounded, in law, to retain the interpretation of enslavement as put forward by the ICTY; as any doubt as to the meaning of 'any or all of the powers attaching to the right of ownership', as being 'ambiguous or obscure' (to use the language of Article 31 of the Vienna Convention on the Law of Treaties) can no longer said to be so, in light of a thorough consideration of the *travaux préparatoires*.

CHAPTER 19

Case Note of *The Queen v. Tang*[*]

High Court of Australia, 28 August 2008

The twenty-first century has witnessed a renaissance of court cases dealing with slavery. In the wake of the establishment of the 2000 UN Palermo Protocol[1] and the 2005 Council of Europe[2] conventions on human trafficking, which establish 'slavery' as a type of exploitation to be suppressed; and the coming into existence of the International Criminal Court in 2002 with jurisdiction over the crime of enslavement,[3] there has been three noteworthy decisions which shed light on the term 'slavery' in international law. Beyond the 2002 Appeals Decision in the *Kunarac et als.* case before the International Criminal Tribunal for the former Yugoslavia[4] and the 2005 *Siliadin v France* before the European Court of Human Rights;[5] the Australian High Court in its August 2008 case, *The Queen v Tang*, brought some much needed rigour to the issue of the parameters of what constitutes 'slavery' both in the Australian context, but also in international law.

The decision by the High Court of Australia is welcome, as the Yugoslav Tribunal and the European Court of Human Rights come to diverging conclusions as to what constitutes 'slavery' in law. For the European Court, the 1926 Slavery Convention definition, which reads: 'Slavery is the status or condition of a person over whom any or all of the powers attaching to the right of ownership are exercised', "corresponds to the 'classic' meaning of slavery as it was practiced for centuries" and thus failed, in *Siliadin*, to find that the victim "was held in slavery in the proper sense, in other words that [the perpetrators] exercised a genuine right of legal ownership over her, thus reducing her to the

---

* This chapter first appeared as Jean Allain "*The Queen v. Tang*: Clarifying the Definition of Slavery in International Law," *Melbourne Journal of International Law*, Vol. 10, 2009, p. 246. Copyright © Melbourne Journal of International Law 2009.

1 See Article 3(a), 2000 United Nations Protocol to Prevent, Suppress and Punish Trafficking in Persons, Especially Women and Children.

2 See Article 4(a), 2005 Council of Europe Convention on Action against Trafficking in Human Beings.

3 See Articles 7(1)(c) and 7(2)(c), 1998 Statute of the International Criminal Court.

4 United Nations, Security Council, International Criminal Tribunal for the former Yugoslavia, *Kunarac et als.* (IT-96-23 &-IT-96-23/1-A) Judgment, 12 June 2002.

5 Council of Europe, European Court of Human Rights, *Siliadin v France* (Application 73316/01), 26 July 2005.

© KONINKLIJKE BRILL NV, LEIDEN, 2015 | DOI 10.1163/9789004279896_021

status of an 'object'."[6] Though it must be said, in the case at hand, the Court did find France in violation of Article 4 of the European Convention of Human Rights, but for lesser types of human exploitation, that of forced labour and of servitude.

By contrast, the Appeals Chamber of the International Criminal Tribunal for the former Yugoslavia, observed that: "the law does not know of a 'right of ownership over a person'. Article 1(1) of the 1926 Slavery Convention speaks more guardedly 'of a person over whom any or all of the powers attaching to the right of ownership are exercised'. That language is to be preferred." The Appeals Chamber went on to say that in the case of contemporary forms of slavery, "the victim is not subject to the exercise of the more extreme rights of ownership associated with 'chattel slavery', but in all cases, as a result of the exercise of any or all of the powers attaching to the right of ownership, there is some destruction of the juridical personality; the destruction is greater in the case of 'chattel slavery' but the difference is one of degree."[7]

In light of the conflicting case-law, the High Court of Australia provides a thorough analysis of the definition of slavery. As opposed to the European Court of Human Rights, the High Court found that the 1926 definition includes both *de jure* and *de facto* slavery; though it did not go as far as the Yugoslav Tribunal in accepting that *de facto* slavery included elements which did not manifest powers normally associated with a right of ownership.

Facts

Wei Tang, the Respondent before the High Court, was originally tried in the County Court of Victoria, along with another accused in April 2005. The jury, in that case, found the co-defendant not guilty but could not reach a verdict where Tang was concerned. Having been retried on 3 June 2006, Tang was found guilty on five counts of possessing slaves and five counts of using slaves in relation to five women of Thai nationality used as prostitutes in a brothel in 2002 and 2003. The women, who had worked in the sex industry at home, had come to Australia voluntarily to work as prostitutes. They were escorted during their flight and upon arrival were "treated as being 'owned' by those who procured their passage," with a sum of $20,000 having been used to 'purchase' each woman.[8] The amount which the women were to pay back was set at $45,000

6 *Id.*, para. 122.

7 *Kunarac et als.*, *op. cit.* n. 4, paras 117–119.

8 *The Queen v Tang* [2008] HCA 39, 28 August 2008, pp. 7 and 8.

(this included the purchase price of $20,000, plus airfare and living expenses while working off the debt); this was to be achieved by working six days a week and reducing their debt by $50 for each customer serviced. When the brothel, Club 417, in the Fitzroy neighbourhood of Melbourne, was raided in May 2003, two of the women had worked off their debt, but remained as prostitutes. The High Court summarises the facts thus:

> each complainant was to work in the respondent's brothel [...], serving up to 900 customers over a period of four to six months. The complainants earned nothing in cash while under contract except that, by working on the seventh, 'free', day each week, they could keep the $50 per customer that would, during the rest of the week, go to offset their contract debts.[9]

The trial judge noted that the women were vulnerable upon arriving in Australia, it having been established that the women spoke no English, had little to no money, knew nobody and were not aware of either the terms of their debt or their expectant living conditions. They were required to keep hidden to avoid the immigration authorities and their passports and return tickets were kept by Wei Tang. The High Court noted that the five women "were well-provisioned, fed, and provided for" and "were not kept under lock and key;" though the trial judge noted that they were "effectively restricted to the premises." For the women who had paid off their debt, the restrictions were lifted, passports and tickets returned and free choice of work hours and accommodations granted.[10]

The trial and verdict was heard on appeal by the Court of Appeal of the Supreme Court of Victoria in 2007, wherein Judge Eames J.A. for the Court noted that while the original "verdict was not unsafe and unsatisfactory [...] this Court could not be satisfied beyond reasonable doubt of the guilt of the applicant."[11] The Court of Appeal accepted that the directions to the jury had been inadequate. As a result, the Court determined that leave to appeal be granted and as a result, that the convictions and sentence be quashed. The Prosecutor appealed the case to the High Court of Australia, with Tang making a cross-appeal on three grounds, the first two dealing with the meaning and constitutional validity of the section of the Australian *Criminal Code Act* 1995 which speaks of 'a person who [...] possesses a slave [...]'; the third ground

9 *Id.*, p. 9.
10 *Id.*, p. 10.
11 See *The Queen v. Wei Tang* [2007] VSCA 134, 27 June 2007, pp. 64–65.

being the directions to the jury. The High Court, with the Attorney-General and the Human Rights and Equal Opportunity Commission as interveners, rendered judgment on 28 August 2008, Chief Justice Gleeson writing for the majority.

On Slavery

The charges against Tang stemmed from Section 270.3(1) of the Australian *Criminal Code Act* 1995 which establishes that "a person who, whether within or outside Australia, intentionally: (a) possesses a slave or exercises over a slave any of the other powers attaching to the right of ownership" [...] or "(c) enters into any commercial transaction involving a slave [...]; is guilty of an offence;" the penalty being twenty-five years imprisonment. The definition of 'slavery' as found in Section 270.1 of the Code differs in two ways from the definition found in the 1926 Slavery Convention, first the 1926 Convention speaks of the 'status or condition' whereas the Section 270.1 definition mentions only the 'condition' of slavery. Second, the *Criminal Code* definition adds a final clause, so as it read in its entirety:

> For the purposes of this Division, slavery is the condition of a person over whom any or all of the powers attaching to the right of ownership are exercised, *including where such a condition results from a debt or contract made by the person.*[12]

On cross-appeal to the High Court, Tang first argued that the Court of Appeal had erred in holding that provisions of Sections 270.1 and 270.3(1)(a) were within the Australia's legislative power. The second grounds for cross-appeal were that:

> the Court of Appeal erred in holding that the offences created by s 270.3(1)(a) extended to the behaviour alleged in the present case and that they were not confined to situations akin to 'chattel slavery' or in which the complainant is notionally owned by the accused or another at the relevant time.

Both these grounds centred on what 'slavery' means in law, and it is to that question that the High Court turned. Noting that the definition found in

12 Emphasis added.

Section 270.1 derives from the definition found at Article 1(1) of the 1926 Slavery Convention and is repeated – in essence – in the 1956 Supplementary Convention and most recently in the 1998 Rome Statute of the International Criminal Court, Gleeson C.J. noted that the "travaux préparatoires of the 1926 Slavery Convention are not especially illuminating as to the meaning of Art 1;" yet, "certain observations may be made as to the text and context, including the purpose, of the Convention."[13]

Three such observations led the majority of the Court to conclude that the 1926 definition found in Slavery Convention applies to both *de jure* and *de facto* slavery. First, Gleeson C.J. notes that for many States, including Australia, which became party to the Convention in 1926, the legal status of slavery no longer existed. Second, that the aim of the Convention was to bring about the same situation universally. Third, that the phrase 'status or condition', found within the 1926 definition makes the distinction between *de jure* ("Status is a legal concept."); and, taking into consideration the first and second observations made, "the evident purpose of the reference to "condition" was to cover slavery *de facto* [...]."[14]

The High Court made one final observation: that the "definition turns upon the exercise of power over a person;" and that in *de facto* conditions the "definition was addressing the exercise over a person of powers of the kind that attached to the right of ownership when the legal status was possible." The High Court then went on to consider what should be understood by such powers which are manifest when ownership is legal.

At this point, the High Court did not take on board the more expansive understanding of the 'powers which attach to the right of ownership' which were put forward by the Human Rights and Equality Commission. The Commission, as Intervener, having laid out its understanding of the law on slavery which depended heavily on the *Kunarac et als.* case, identified "a (non-exhaustive) list of the factors that might indicate that a power attaching to a right of ownership has been exercised." That list reads:

(a) The partial or total destruction of the juridical personality of the victim.
(b) Some restriction or control of an individual's autonomy, freedom of choice or freedom of movement.
(c) The control of matters relating to an individual's sexual activity.
(d) The psychological control or oppression of the individual.
(e) The control or partial control of an individual's personal belongings.

---

13 *The Queen v Tang* [2008] HCA 39, 28 August 2008, p. 12.

14 *Id.*, p. 12.

(f) The measures taken to prevent or deter a person from escape.
(g) The absence of informed consent or the fact that consent has been rendered irrelevant by the use offeree or coercion, the use of deception or false promises or the abuse of power in the context of the relationship where the individual over whom the power is exercised is in a position of vulnerability.
(h) The threat or use offeree or other forms of coercion.
(i) The use of, or the fear of the use of, violence including, for example, the cruel treatment or abuse of an individual.
(j) The quality of the relationship between the accused and the person over whom the powers are exercised, including any abuse of power, the person's vulnerability, the person's socio-economic situation and the duration of the relationship.
(k) The exaction of forced or compulsory labour or service, often without remuneration and often, though not necessarily, involving physical hardship, sex, prostitution and human trafficking.[15]

By introducing issues such as the oppression of the individual, of deception and abuse of power creating a situation of vulnerability, and of cruel treatment or abuse, the Commission appeared to go beyond issues of powers reflecting ownership and over-stretched the understanding of slavery beyond the judicial horizons of what the High Court was prepared to accept.

Instead, the High Court based itself on a consideration of the powers attaching to the right of ownership made by the United Nations Secretary General in 1953. As the 1926 definition speaks of '*any or all*' of the powers attaching to the right of ownership, Gleeson C.J. mentions those powers relevant to the case, including:

> the capacity to make a person an object of purchase, the capacity to use a person and a person's labour in a substantially unrestricted manner, and an entitlement to the fruits of the person's labour without compensation commensurate to the value of the labour. Each of those powers is of relevance in the present case.[16]

---

15 See Australian Human Rights and Equality Commission, Submission in Support of the Application for Leave to Intervened and Submission on the Appeal, *Commonwealth Director of Public Prosecution v Wei Tang*, High Court of Australia, Melbourne, 5 May 2008, p. 15. Footnotes excluded.

16 The three final powers noted by the UN Secretary General, but not mentioned by Gleeson CJ, are:

Chief Justice Gleeson ended his consideration of the first grounds of cross-appeal by noting that:

> On the evidence it was open to the jury to conclude that each of the complainants was made an object of purchase (although in the case of one of them the purchaser was not the respondent); that, for the duration of the contracts, the owners had a capacity to use the complainants and the complainants' labour in a substantially unrestricted manner; and that the owners were entitled to the fruits of the complainants' labour without commensurate compensation.

Turning to the second ground for cross-appeal, wherein Tang argued that the Court of Appeal erred in determining that offences established by Section 270.3(1)(a) (read: 'possesses a slave or exercises over a slave any of the other powers attaching to the right of ownership'.) extends "to the behaviour alleged in the present case and that they were not confined to situations akin to 'chattel slavery' or in which the complainant is notionally owned by the accused or another at the relevant time." Gleeson C.J., for the majority of the High Court, stated that from what had been said in previous paragraphs it was clear that chattel slavery "falls within the definition [...] but it would be inconsistent [...] to read the definition as limited to that form of slavery."[17] The High Court turned to the *Kunarac* case before the Yugoslav Tribunal[18] to buttress its understanding that slavery goes beyond that of treating a person as chattel, noting that "enslavement as a crime against humanity in customary international law consisted of the exercise of any or all of the powers attaching to the right of ownership over a person."[19] Gleeson C.J. then noted that it was "unnecessary and unhelpful" in the present case "to draw boundaries between slavery and cognate "concepts such as servitude, peonage, forced labour, or debt

4) the ownership of the individual of servile status can be transferred to another person;
5) the servile status is permanent, that is to say, it cannot be terminated by the will of the individual subject to it;
6) the servile status is transmitted *ipso facto* to descendants of the individual having such status.

See United Nations, Economic and Social Council, Slavery, the Slave Trade, and other forms of Servitude (Report of the Secretary-General), UN Doc. E/2357, 27 January 1953, p. 28 as found in Jean Allain, *The Slavery Conventions: The Travaux Préparatoires of the 1926 League of Nations Convention and the 1956 United Nations Convention*, 2008, p. 497.

17 *The Queen v Tang* [2008] HCA 39, 28 August 2008, p. 13.

18 See *Kunarac et als., op. cit.* n. 4.

19 *The Queen v Tang* [2008] HCA 39, 28 August 2008, p. 14.

bondage." Instead the Chief Justice noted that the concepts where not mutually exclusive, that the 1956 Supplementary Convention recognised the possibility that servitudes could slip into slavery where they manifest powers attaching to the right of ownership and that those "who engage in the traffic in human beings are unlikely to be so obliging as to arrange their practices to conform to some convenient taxonomy."[20]

The High Court then turned to European Court of Human Rights decision in *Siliadin v France*,[21] finding it unhelpful, noting that the Court "referred briefly and dismissively to the possibility that the applicant was a slave within the meaning of Art 1 of the 1926 Slavery Convention." Gleeson C.J., seeking to distance that case from the one at hand, stated that while this was understandable in the context of that case, it was to "be noted that the Court did not refer to the definition's reference to condition in the alternative to status, or to powers as well as rights, or to the words 'any or all'."[22] Chief Justice Gleeson, referring to the European Court's decision that no 'genuine right of legal ownership' was manifest, stated that, on the assumption that slave owning was illegal in France, no such exercise of a genuine right of ownership was possible and that this was "self-evident." He continued: "but it would not have been a complete answer if there had been a serious issue of slavery in the case."[23] The Chief Justice followed this by giving the High Court's assessment of the concept of slavery as defined by the 1926 Slavery Convention:

> It is important not to debase the currency of language, or to banalise crimes against humanity, by giving slavery a meaning that extends beyond the limits set by the text, context, and purpose of the 1926 Slavery Convention. In particular it is important to recognise that harsh and exploitative conditions of labour do not of themselves amount to slavery. The term 'slave' is sometimes used in a metaphorical sense to describe victims of such conditions, but that sense is not of present relevance. Some of the factors identified as relevant in *Kunarac*, such as control of movement and control of physical environment, involve questions of degree. An employer normally has some degree of control over the movements, or work environment, of an employee. Furthermore, geographical and other circumstances may limit an employee's freedom of movement. Powers of

---

20 *Id.*, p. 15.

21 Council of Europe, European Court of Human Rights, *Siliadin v France* (Application 73316/01), 26 July 2005.

22 *The Queen v Tang* [2008] HCA 39, 28 August 2008, p. 15.

23 *Id.*, p. 16.

> control, in the context of an issue of slavery, are powers of the kind and degree that would attach to a right of ownership if such a right were legally possible, not powers of a kind that are no more than an incident of harsh employment, either generally or at a particular time or place.[24]

The majority opinion in *Tang* then shifted from the international to the Australian context, stating that Section 270.1 speaks only of 'condition' not 'status', noting that the legal status of slavery does not exist in Australia, and thus the Australian law "is concerned with *de facto* slavery" and consequently, "the reference to powers attaching to the right of ownership, which are exercised over a person in a condition described as slavery, is a reference to powers of such a nature and extent that they are attributes of effective (although not legal, for that is impossible) ownership."[25] Secondly, the concluding words of the definition in s 270.1 ("including where such a condition results from a debt or contract made by the person") do not alter the meaning of the preceding words because it is only where "such a condition" (that is, the condition earlier described in terms of the 1926 Slavery Convention) results that the words of inclusion apply. The words following "including," therefore, do not extend the operation of the previous words but make it plain that a condition that results from a debt or a contract is not, on that account alone, to be excluded from the definition, provided it would otherwise be covered by it. As a result of this and a consideration of the phrase 'including where such a condition results from a debt or contract made by the person', the High Court determined that:

> the definition of 'slavery' in s 270.1 falls within the definition in Art 1 of the 1926 Slavery Convention, and the relevant provisions of Div 270 are reasonably capable of being considered appropriate and adapted to give effect to Australia's obligations under that Convention. They are sustained by the external affairs power. They are not limited to chattel slavery.[26]

With this, Gleeson C.J. turned to consider the 2007 decision of the Court of Appeal of the Supreme Court of Victoria which, in turn regarded as the "critical issues" at trial: that of "character of the exercise of the power by the accused over the victim."[27] Having given voice to the opinion of the Court of Appeal expressed by Eames J.A., and noting that it was right for that Court to be

24 *Id.*

25 *Id.*

26 *Id.*, p. 17; footnote omitted.

27 *Id.*, p. 18.

"concerned about a problem presented by s 270.3(1)(a), at least in a borderline case" as to "how is a jury to distinguish between slavery, on the one hand, and harsh and exploitative conditions of labour, on the other?" Gleeson C.J., for the High Court, answers the question:

> The answer to that, in a given case, may be found in the nature and extent of the powers exercised over a complainant. In particular, a capacity to deal with a complainant as a commodity, an object of sale and purchase, may be a powerful indication that a case falls on one side of the line. So also may the exercise of powers of control over movement which extend well beyond powers exercised even in the most exploitative of employment circumstances, and absence or extreme inadequacy of payment for services. The answer, however, is not to be found in the need for reflection by an accused person upon the source of the powers that are being exercised. Indeed, it is probably only in a rare case that there would be any evidence of such consideration.[28]

The High Court went on to conclude that:

> In this case, the critical powers the exercise of which was disclosed (or the exercise of which a jury reasonably might find disclosed) by the evidence were the power to make the complainants an object of purchase, the capacity, for the duration of the contracts, to use the complainants and their labour in a substantially unrestricted manner, the power to control and restrict their movements, and the power to use their services without commensurate compensation. As to the last three powers, their extent, as well as their nature, was relevant. As to the first, it was capable of being regarded by a jury as the key to an understanding of the condition of the complainants. The evidence could be understood as showing that they had been bought and paid for, and that their commodification explained the conditions of control and exploitation under which they were living and working.
>
> It was not necessary for the prosecution to establish that the respondent had any knowledge or belief concerning the source of the powers exercised over the complainants, although it is interesting to note that, in deciding to order a new trial, the Court of Appeal evidently took the view that the evidence was capable of satisfying a jury, beyond reasonable

28 *Id.*, p. 20.

> doubt, of the existence of the knowledge or belief that the Court of Appeal considered necessary.[29]

With this the High Court concluded its consideration of the second grounds of cross-appeal. Gleeson C.J. gave little time to the third grounds for cross-appeal; that the Court of Appeal had "erred in failing to hold that the verdicts are unreasonable or cannot be supported having regard to the evidence." The Chief Justice noted that "there was cogent evidence of the intentional exercise of powers of such a nature and extent that they could reasonably be regarded as resulting in the condition of slavery" and as such the Court of Appeal made no error in principle."[30]

The High Court of Australia then ordered, having accepted the cross-appeals, that the first two grounds be "treated as instituted, heard instanter, and dismissed" and the third be refused. It then ordered that the appeal against conviction of Tang be dismissed and returned the case to the Court of Appeal for consideration of sentencing.

Concurrent Opinions

While all Justices concurred in large part with the opinion of Gleeson C.J., two Justice, Kirby and Haynes also wrote in-depth opinions. Kirby J agreed with Gleeson C.J., but for the fact that he believed that a re-trial should take place on the basis that – what is termed in the Australian context – 'a miscarriage of trial' had taken place. This miscarriage resulted from the jury having failed to be explained in accurate and clear terms, where the fault element of intention manifested itself in all of the ingredients of the offence of slavery.[31] Kirby J notes that the Trial Chamber found itself in a novel position where slavery was concerned, as pointed out by the Court of Appeal: "the trial judge had the misfortune to be the first judge in Australia called on to devise directions for these novel offences."[32] The issue for Kirby J was one of 'intention', as a basis for determining whether violations of the provisions of Section 270.3 had taken place. In conclusion, Kirby J notes that where the issue of intention is concerned, there was "very confusing directions […] presented to the jury by the trial judge."[33]

29 *Id.*, p. 22.
30 *Id.*
31 *Id.*, p. 56.
32 *Id.*, p. 42.
33 *Id.*, p. 56.

In constructing his opinion, Kirby J devotes a section to the 'Conformability with international law', and sees the issue of slavery in the same light as the Court of Appeal, as having an interpretation which is "more consonant" with the 1926 Slavery Convention and "the extremely grave international crime that 'slavery', so expressed, involves."[34] For Kirby J, the fact that slavery is a *jus cogens* norm and is non–derogable, requires that it be defined "very carefully and precisely." As a result, Kirby J states that "the crimes provided by s 270.3(1) are reserved to indisputably serious offences containing a substantial, not trivial, intention element."[35]

The concurring opinion of Haynes J, takes no issue with the Order put forward by Gleeson C.J. in his majority opinion. Instead, Haynes wishes to consider the terms 'slavery' and 'slave' as used in the Australian *Criminal Code Act* 1995. For Haynes J, the substance of the definition of slavery found in the 1926 Slavery Convention (powers attaching to the right of ownership) can be rephrased as "the powers that an owner would have over another person, if the law recognised the right to own that other, would be powers whose exercise would not depend upon the assent of the person over whom the powers are exercised."[36] By bringing into the equation the 'assent of the person', Haynes develops his argument on the "antithesis of slavery" by putting forward the following proposition: "whether the person concerned was deprived of freedom of choice in some relevant respect and, if so, what it was that deprived the person of choice." As Haynes J later notes, "[a]sking what freedom a person had may shed light on whether that person was a slave."[37] Haynes J then concludes by considering the trial transcript and determining that the evidence allows for the conclusion that each of five women were indeed held as slaves, that each was used and possessed "as an item of property at the disposal of those who had bought the complainant regardless of *any* wish she might have."[38]

Conclusion

Beyond the judgments of the European Court of Human Rights and the International Tribunal for the former Yugoslavia, the 28 August 2008 decision by the High Court of Australia in *The Queen v. Tang* provides the most rigorous

34 *Id.*, p. 49.
35 *Id.*
36 *Id.*, p. 60.
37 *Id.*, p. 65.
38 *Id.*, Emphasis in the original.

assessment of what 'slavery' means in international law. Gleeson C.J. consideration of the case of *Siliadin v France* rendered by European Court of Human Rights takes little away from that pronouncement which fails to engage with the basis of the definition of slavery, as 'powers attaching to the right of ownership'. Where the *Kunarac et als.* case, before the International Criminal Tribunal for the former Yugoslavia, is concerned, the majority Judgment by the High Court does well to state that "some of the factors identified as relevant in *Kunarac* [...] involve questions of control," but Gleeson C.J. distances himself from the rather liberal interpretation given to the definition of slavery by the Yugoslav judgment by stating that the "[p]owers of control, in the context of an issue of slavery, are powers of the kind and degree that would attach to a right of ownership if such a right were legally possible, not powers of a kind that are no more than an incident of harsh employment, either generally or at a particular time or place."[39]

The decision by the High Court of Australia, penned by its Chief Justice Murray Gleeson, and delivered on the day before his constitutionally mandated retirement from the Court, brings into focus a renewed interest in the legal definition of slavery. Where the issue of slavery in international law is concerned, the twentieth century can be characterised as dealing with slavery as a human rights issue. By comparison, the twenty-first century, with the inclusion of slavery in the United Nations and Council of Europe human trafficking conventions, and enslavement within the Statute of the International Criminal Court, shifts the focus to the criminal law. The very expansive notion of slavery which Suzanne Miers noted in her 2003 *Slavery in the Twentieth Century*, rendered the term "virtually meaningless;"[40] yet in the twenty-first century this cannot persist, as the human right prohibiting slavery comes up against the countervailing human right of the accused right to know the charges against him or her. Let us hope that *The Queen v. Tang* receives the attention it deserves beyond the shores of Australia, as the High Court has provided the most far-reaching and cogent examination to date of the definition of 'slavery' as established in international law.

39 *Id.*, p. 16.

40 Suzanne Miers, *Slavery in the Twentieth Century*, 2003, p. 453.

CHAPTER 20

When Forced Marriage is Slavery*

My research has sought to establish – in law – the parameters around different types of human exploitation, so as to give them legal certainty in a court of law. The underlying premise of my research has been that the term 'slavery' has been over-utilised and expanded, dare I say for propaganda purposes, as a means of describing various social ills at the expense of the legal meaning and, ultimately, prosecutions. Thus, my inclination is to say, in legal terms, that forced marriage is not slavery…and yet….

Where issues of human exploitation are concerned the law is under-developed. The contribution law can make at this point and time are foundational: simply setting out an understanding in law of what constitutes and where to draw the parameters around various types of exploitation still needs to be undertaken. Forced marriage is a case-in-point as it appears to me – especially in times of armed conflict – that in substance it is not in any way a 'marriage', either in a formal or substantive sense. To my way of thinking we should look not to the form – that is: what it is called – but to the substance: that is, in fact, what is transpiring; and then ask what legal definition this activity falls under.

In law, the notion of 'forced marriage', as such is not defined. Its most recent expression within the United Nations system is to be found in the 1979 Convention on the Elimination of All Forms of Discrimination against Women (CEDAW), which considers the issue through the lens of discrimination at its Article 16:

> 1. States Parties shall take all appropriate measures to eliminate discrimination against women in all matters relating to marriage and family relations and in particular shall ensure, on a basis of equality of men and women:
>   (a) The same right to enter into marriage;
>   (b) The same right freely to choose a spouse and to enter into marriage only with their free and full consent;

* Paper presented both at Special Court for Sierra Leone, at International Conference on Forced Marriage in Conflict Situations, as "International Law and Forced Marriage as Exploitation," February 2011, and at Harvard Law School as "When Marriage is Slavery: International Law from Geneva to Freetown," March 2011.

 | DOI 10.1163/9789004279896_022

Thus, the issue is defined not negatively as victimised by forced marriage, but in the positive as a right to choose, to consent.[1]

I would like to argue that we should conceptualise the type of crime which transpires in times of armed conflict which has been termed 'forced marriage' as something else altogether. There is, it seems to me, a distinction to be made between 'forced marriage' in times of peace and 'forced marriage' in times of armed conflict. That forced marriage in times of peace typically transpires on the basis of ancient custom or practice; there is typically a wedding which takes place, which despite the legal obligation by States to allow for entry into marriage only with "free and full consent," the bride is coerced either individually, familially or communally into marriage. Though, if one were to set out to determine the locus of the 'forced' element, it would typically be the family and within the family, the parents. Or put another way, consent is removed from the bride and taken by another, typically the parents. As originally conceived this was the type of 'forced marriage' which was meant to be suppressed by provisions such as CEDAW. The genealogy of these provisions includes the 1962 Convention on Consent to Marriage, Minimum Age for Marriage and Registration of Marriages which, in its preamble, speaks of "abolishing such customs, ancient laws and practices" so as to ensure "complete freedom in the choice of a spouse."[2] Where the issue of consent is concerned – that is: as opposed to what would thus constitute forced marriage – a 1955 Report regarding Pride Price in Eastern colonial Nigeria recommended that where 'native marriages' were concerned "a reappraisal is necessary of the fact that a women has a right to a say in the choice of her future partner in life. Consent should lie with the girl and the part played by the parents should be limited to giving advice."[3] In other words, as originally conceived the suppression of forced

---

1 See United Nations, Report of the Secretary General, *Forced Marriage of the Girl Child*, UN Doc. E/CN.6/2008/4, p. 3; which notes: "In recent years, the issue of forced marriage, that is to say, the case where the free and full consent of at least one of the parties to a marriage is lacking, has gained the attention of the international community."

2 The provisions reads in full:

> Reaffirming that all States, including those which have or assume responsibility for the administration of Non-Self-Governing and Trust Territories until their achievement of independence, should take all appropriate measures with a view to abolishing such customs, ancient laws and practices by ensuring, inter alia, complete freedom in the choice of a spouse, eliminating completely child marriages and the betrothal of young girls before the age of puberty, establishing appropriate penalties where necessary and establishing a civil or other register in which all marriages will be recorded.

3 Recommendation Number 7, Report of the Committee on Pride Price, Eastern Region Nigeria, 1955, p. 49.

marriage was meant to end practices where consent lay within the family but beyond the bride. It would seem to me this is what forced marriage is and what should continue to be understood by the term of forced marriage.

This is in contradistinction to what is transpiring in times of armed conflict, were forced marriage typically transpires in situations where the 'spouse' and the 'bride' are unknown to each other but are brought together through an act of violence visited upon the community or the family. No wedding takes place, no issue of consent at the level of the individual, the family, or the community is sought or given.[4] From this perspective, I would disagree with both the Trial and Appeals Chamber of the Special Court of Sierra Leone as to what transpired in Sierra Leone with regard to the taking of 'rebel wives'; I don't believe that in substance it should have been recognised as sexual slavery or described as a conjugal partnership. With regard to the Trial Chamber determination in *Brima* like the Appeals Chamber, I disagree that the 'sexual' element defines the crime. That said, if you remove the sexual element of sexual slavery, what remains?…you kind of see where I'm going.

Likewise, I disagree with the Appeals Chamber that "forced marriage describes a situation in which the perpetrator […] compels a person by force, threat of force, or coercion to serve as a conjugal partner resulting in severe suffering, or physical, mental or psychological injury to the victim."[5] I believe that the Appeals Chamber fell into the trap of dealing with the form rather than the substance of the crime. In so doing, it has allowed the perpetrators to set the agenda by defining what transpired as marriage. By speaking of a 'conjugal partner' the Appeals Chamber is accepting the perspective of the perpetrator and does a disservice both to the institution of marriage, but more so to the victim who is further disempowered, as a veneer of legitimacy is painted over the crime. The international community recognises that the institution of marriage is worth of protection: in the language of the ICCPR: that it is the "right of men and women of marriageable age to marry and to found a family;" and that the "family is the natural and fundamental group unit of society and is entitled to protection by society and the State."[6] By labelling this crime as 'marriage' we fail in the requirement of the State and society to protect the institution of marriage.

---

4 See Partly Dissenting Opinion of Justice Doherty on Count 7 (Sexual Slavery) and Count 8 ('Forced Marriages'), *Alex Tamba Brima et als.* Judgment, Trial Chamber, Special Court for Sierra Leone, SCSL-2004-16-T, 20 June 2007, paras 26–29, p. 586.

5 *Alex Tamba Brima et als.* Judgment, Appeals Chamber, Special Court for Sierra Leone, SCSL-2004-16-A, 22 February 2008, p. 66.

6 Articles 23(2) and (1), 1966 International Covenant on Civil and Political Rights.

It would seem to me that the crime as it transpires in times of armed conflict more readily fits into category which is manifest in the legal conventions meant to suppress slavery and servitudes: the 1926 Slavery Convention and the 1956 Supplementary Convention. The 1956 Supplementary Convention on the Abolition of Slavery, the Slave Trade, and Institutions and Practices Similar to Slavery, while defining the servitudes of debt bondage, serfdom, and child exploitation also outlines the institution or practice of servile marriages.[7] Article 1(c) of the 1956 Supplementary Convention calls for the suppression of:

> Any institution or practice whereby:
>
> (i) A woman, without the right to refuse, is promised or given in marriage on payment of a consideration in money or in kind to her parents, guardian, family or any other person or group; or
> (ii) The husband of a woman, his family, or his clan, has the right to transfer her to another person for value received or otherwise; or
> (iii) A woman on the death of her husband is liable to be inherited by another person;

While debt bondage, serfdom, child exploitation, and servile marriages are deemed to be servitudes within the 1956 Supplementary Convention, they may also be deemed slavery if, in substance, the institution or practice is covered by "the definition of slavery contained in Article 1 of the Slavery Convention." In other words – and this is borne out in the negotiation history of the 1956 Convention – it may be that some of these conventional servitudes are in fact also slavery. While this may not be true for debt bondage, serfdom, or child exploitation; the substance of the institutions or practices of servile marriage, as set out in Article 1(c), are such that they must always be recognised as meeting the threshold of slavery. This is so, as in the purchase of a bride, the transfer of a wife, or the inheritance of a widow is to be found the exercise of a 'power attaching to the right of ownership' as set out in the 1926 definition of slavery. While these powers may manifest themselves in servile marriages, a more fundamental power will also be present…that of 'possession', which will be considered shortly.

Before going on to consider the 1926 definition of slavery, one final element is worth noting about the 1956 Convention. It is the source of a development of

---

7 That these four institutions or practices should be understood as servitudes see: Jean Allain, "On the Curious Disappearance of Human Servitude from General International Law," *Journal of the History of International Law*, Vol. 11, 2009, pp. 303–332.

the genealogy of attempts to suppress forced marriage in international law. The drafters of the Convention introduced in its Article 2, provisions meant to assist in bringing an end servile marriages, as defined in Article 1(c), by encouraging that consent to marriage be made in public before a civil or religious authority, that marriages be registered, and that a minimum age of marriage should be established. While there was an attempt to be prescriptive in setting out a minimum age, it was acknowledged that the 1956 Convention was not the place for "writing law in relation to marriage."[8] Instead, the Conference negotiating of the Supplementary Convention made the following recommendation:

> Recommends to the Economic and Social Council to consider the appropriateness of having undertaken a study of the question of marriage, with the object of drawing attention to the desirability of free consent of both parties to a marriage and of the establishment of a minimum age for marriage, preferably of not less than 14 years.[9]

That Recommendation, and the subsequent work of the United Nations Economic and Social Council, led to the 1962 Convention on Consent to Marriage, Minimum Age for Marriage and Registration of Marriages.

Turning now to the acknowledge definition of slavery in international law, which is found in the 1926 Slavery Convention, and reads: 'the status or condition of a person over whom any or all of the powers attaching to the right of ownership are exercised'.[10] This definition is worth unpacking as we seek to understand its applicability to situations which have been termed 'forced marriage' in times of armed conflict, but in substance amount to enslavement. As was made plain in the 2008 judgement by the highest court in Australia, the 1926 definition is applicable not only where one person legally owns another – this

---

8 Economic and Social Council, United Nations Conference of Plenipotentiaries on a Supplementary Convention on the Abolition of Slavery, the Slave Trade and Institutions and Practices Similar to Slavery, Summary Record of the Twenty-second Meeting, 31 August 1956, UN Doc E/CONF.24/SR.22, 20 November 1958, p. 5. For context see: Jean Allain, *The Slavery Conventions: The Travaux Préparatoires of the 1926 League of Nations Convention and the 1956 United Nations Convention*, 2008, p. 349.

9 See Economic and Social Council, United Nations Conference of Plenipotentiaries on a Supplementary Convention on the Abolition of Slavery, the Slave Trade and Institutions and Practices Similar to Slavery, Portugal: Draft resolution, UN Doc E/CONF.24/L.45/Rev.1, 3 September 1956.

10 See Jean Allain, "The Definition of Slavery in International Law," 52 *Howard Law Journal*, 2009, p. 239.

conjures up images of the Transatlantic slave trade and people in chains[11] – but also in cases where a person exercises what would normally be the powers of ownership in a *de facto* manner.[12] There has yet to emerge a true consensus as to what the definition means as a number of interpretations have been utilised over the years. However, it appears that with the pressure to ensure the rights of the accused in criminal trials that a cogent understanding of the definition is starting to take hold.

That understanding emerges from a consideration of the negotiation history which brought the 1926 definition into existence as well as a contemporary attempt to understand what constitutes the exercise of those 'powers attaching to the right of ownership'. In other words, what does it mean to own a person? It means that you control a person in the same way you would possess a thing. This gets to the heart of why we abhor slavery, because it is a significant denial of the autonomy of another, of their liberty to make fundamental decisions about who and what they are, about their ability to act, through self-determination, in setting for themselves a life course, including whether or not and who they marry. It is in this significant diminution of autonomy, over a period of time which is for that person indeterminate, which renders the relationship, in substance, slavery.

A person having gained control over another tantamount to possession – typically through force, deception or coercion – may then treat that person as one would treat a thing owned. That is, by exercising other powers normally understood as attaching to ownership, such as buying or selling that person (this will also include exchanging, giving as a gift, or bartering a person) or using that person in the sense of gaining benefit, be it sexual services or through their labour. Where a person exercises control tantamount to possession, they will also be able to manage and make money from the use of that person, or give them away as inheritance. Having 'broken' another human being and taking control over them like a thing possessed, the 'master' will profit through economic gain or another type of benefit.

This understanding of slavery as defined in the 1926 Slavery Convention, it seems to me does well to provide legal certain as to what is, in substance, slavery and what is not. What transpired in the process of enslavement: was the

11 It should be noted that as recently as 2003 the criminal code of Niger recognised slavery *de jure* as it stated that "the marriage of a free man with a slave woman is lawful, as long as he cannot afford to marry a free woman and if he fears to fall into fornication." See *Hadijatou Mani Koraou v Niger*, The Court of Justice of the Economic Community of West African States, ECW/CCJ/JUD/06/08, 27 October 2008, para. 83.

12 See *The Queen v Tang*, [2008] HCA 39, 28 August 2008.

person forced, deceived or coerced? Once enslaved, was the person controlled; their personal autonomy diminished to the extent that they were treated like a thing possessed? Being possessed was that person bought or sold, were they used or managed, or was money made from their use of management?

To assist in seeking to understand what was happening in substance in the case of 'rebel wives' in the *Brima* case, let me put forward the following hypothetical: what if instead of a woman or girl, the heterosexual male military officer had abducted a young male, say age 12, and proceeds to force that child to undertake activities as noted by the Trial Chamber in *Brima*; so "carry the rebel's possessions as they moved from one location to the next, cook for him and wash his clothes."[13] Does this constitute forced marriage? What is missing? Rape? Is this the defining element of 'forced marriage' then: non-consensual intercourse? But this is rather odd: are we then saying that marriage is defined in intercourse; forced marriage by rape? Surely marriage is more than sex and forced marriage more than rape. In the case of the military officer and the boy, there is "no intent to assume a marital or quasi-marital status" over the boy. And yet, the same is true in the case of the women and girls in the *Brima* case, where the Trial Chamber noted that there was "no intent to assume a marital or quasi-marital status"; and continued "in the sense of establishing mutual obligations inherent in a husband wife relationship."[14]

Consider also cases of enslavement of domestic workers. Typical of such cases is the requirement to cook, clean and do laundry, to do anything demanded under threat of violence and where autonomy, including sexual autonomy, is forfeited.[15] Is this any different from the lived experience of 'rebel wives'? I also wish to raise the question as to the parallel, if any as between 'rebel wives' and concubines.

In a 2005 Research Paper, Michael Scharf and Suzanne Mattler considered the viability of forced marriage as a new crime against humanity before the Special Court for Sierra Leone. In that Paper, they argued that "the personal liberty of a 'wife' in a forced marriage is similarly constrained" as it is in a case of slavery, "but the constraint is accomplished not through attachment of right of ownership, but through the enforced, non consensual attachment of the

---

13 *Alex Tamba Brima et als.* Judgment, Trial Chamber, Special Court for Sierra Leone, SCSL-2004-16-T, 20 June 2007, para. 711, p. 219.

14 *Id.*, p. 219.

15 For instance: in the United States' context, see: *Swarna v. AlAwadi*, 622 F.3d 123, 133 (2d Cir. 2010); or *United States v Djoumessi*, 538 F.3d 547, 550–51 (6th Cir. 2008).

right and privileges of marriage."[16] They go on to say that to "classify these crimes as 'enslavement' alone is an inexact description of the crime at best and misleading at worst."

> In the crime of enslavement, as in sexual slavery, the perpetrator's control over the victim comes from attaching of the right of ownership to the victim, while in forced marriages the perpetrator obtains control over the victim by attaching the obligations of a spouse to the victim. The victim of forced marriage is bound not only by the force exerted over her by the perpetrator but by the shift in legal, social, and religious rights and status arising from marriage.

I disagree. For their part, Scharf and Mattler conclude by stating that; "Enslavement lacks the specificity necessary to accurately describe the crime of forced marriage and would inevitably lead to confusion as to how the perpetrator maintained control over the victim."[17]

I believe this analysis to be wrong. While I accept that "enslavement lacks the specificity necessary to accurately describe the crime of forced marriage;" I do believe it is a fundamental element of the crime. Further, I believe that, as marriage is a protected institution, the notion of forced marriage should be a distinct crime in international criminal law. That forced marriage constitutes more than enslavement as the *meas rea* includes, *inter alia*, the perpetrator's non-consensual hosting of the mantel of spouse and/or marriage onto the victim.

The enslavement element, it seems to me is manifest in the near total diminution of autonomy of the victim. The exercise of the power of ownership is not manifest in the buying or selling of the victim, but it is present in the notion of 'possession'. More so in times of armed conflict, where the legal regime has broken down; the ability of soldiers, as was the case in Sierra Leone, to kidnap and make of their victims 'rebel wives' was to control them as a thing owed. While they could have bought or sold their victims and in cases did transfer, exchange, or give these women as gifts, fundamentally they had the power to do so – but instead they simply used their violently acquired possession. Instead, having established control tantamount to possession, military men

16 Michael Scharf and Suzanne Mattler, *Forced Marriage: Exploring the Viability of the Special Court for Sierra Leone's New Crime against Humanity*, Case Research Paper Series in Legal Studies, Working Paper 05–35, October 2005, pp. 18–19.

17 Michael Scharf and Suzanne Mattler, *Forced Marriage: Exploring the Viability of the Special Court for Sierra Leone's New Crime against Humanity*, Case Research Paper Series in Legal Studies, Working Paper 05–35, October 2005, p. 20.

used these women to gain benefit from their service (sexual and otherwise) and labour – this under the mantel of a fraudulent marriage. Thus, for me, the notion of 'forced marriage' in times of armed conflict is linked in fundamental terms to slavery; yet, like 'sexual slavery' the crime of 'forced marriage' has distinct characteristics: primarily, the perpetrator's non-consensual hosting of the mantel of spouse and/or marriage onto the victim.

If this analysis be correct, it leaves me in a pickle. For me forced marriage in times of armed conflict is distinguishable from forced marriage in times of peace where consent is present (thought misplaced in a fiduciary) in what Scharf and Mattler are willing to label as 'arranged marriages'.

If the distinction holds then international criminal law appears to have a gap as 'enslavement' within the Statute of the International Criminal Court is a crime against humanity, but not a war crime (thought sexual slavery is deemed a war crime, as well as a crime against humanity). In real terms, this means that 'forced marriage' would need to transpire on an 'industrial' level as "committed as part of a widespread or systematic attack directed against any civilian population;" as opposed to at the 'artisan' level of a war crime with the lesser threshold of being "part of a place or policy or a part of a large-scale commission of such a crime." What is rather interesting to me – though beyond the scope of the research of this paper – is that the prohibition against slavery has been recognised, through "State practice" as an established "norm of customary international law applicable in both international and non-international armed conflict;"[18] and yet, it is not included as a war crime within the Statute of the International Criminal Court – why?

By way of conclusion, I wonder if we should allow this crime to be labelled marriage – be servile, forced or otherwise? If so, does this not speak against the type of labelling and hierarchy which has been at the heart of the feminist critique both in law and beyond?

---

18 See Rule 94: Slavery and the Slave Trade in all their Forms are Prohibited; in Jean Marie Henckaerts and Louise Doswald-Beck, *Customary International Humanitarian Law*, Volume I: Rules, 2005, p. 327.

CHAPTER 21

Property Law and the Definition of Slavery*

Jean Allain and Robin Hickey

In the afterglow of the 2008 bicentennial commemoration of the British abolition of the slave trade in its colonies, the United Kingdom has been reminded repeatedly that slavery persists to this day. As then Prime Minister Tony Blair noted in the lead up to the bicentenary, 'we also need, while reflecting on the past, to acknowledge the unspeakable cruelty that persists in the form of modern day slavery'.[1] Since then we have seen the introduction of provisions dealing with slavery, servitude and forced or compulsory labour in the Coroners and Justice Act 2009; and in 2011, the Home Secretary launched *Human Trafficking: The Government's Strategy*, meant to address organised crime networks seeking to move people into the United Kingdom to exploit them by way of the crimes set out in the Coroners and Justice Act.

It might seem curious that, having left behind the slave trade in the age of Sail, indeed, having led that abolitionist movement, and having determined in 1772 it was 'a soil whose air is deemed too pure for slaves to breathe in it', the United Kingdom should now find itself for the first time having actually to legislate against slavery.[2] While this is curious indeed, more pressing from a legal perspective is that we do not have a clear understanding in law of what the term 'slavery' actually means. It is generally accepted that the legal definition of slavery is provided by Article 1(1) of the 1926 League of Nations Slavery Convention, which reads: 'slavery is the status or condition of a person over whom any or all of the powers attaching to the right of ownership are exercised'. However, as we show here, in recent times the term 'slavery' has been the subject of misinterpretation to the extent that it has been rendered so wide as to be effectively meaningless. Our aim is to reclaim the legal definition as one with a core settled meaning which has demonstrable relevance to contemporary practice. To make this argument, we use property law perspectives to explain the conception of ownership invoked by Article 1, and to articulate its

* This Chapter first appeared as Jean Allain and Robin Hickey "Property and the Definition of Slavery" (2012) 61 *International and Comparative Law Quarterly* 915, Copyright © British Institute of International and Comparative Law 2012. Robin Hickey, Senior Lecturer, Durham Law School. [now at Queen's University, Belfast.]

1 T. Blair, Times Online, 'Tony Blair's Statement on the Slave Trade in Full', November 27, 2006.

2 Somerset v Stewart, Lofft 1, 98 ER 500, 14 May 1772.

 | DOI 10.1163/9789004279896_023

continuing relevance to the modern world. We argue specifically that it entails a substantive as opposed to a formal understanding of slavery, such that slavery will exist today in any case where the provisions of Article 1 can be satisfied on the facts.

The Problem of Interpreting the Definition of Slavery

In law, the base line for understanding slavery is the definition set out in Article 1(1) of the 1926 Slavery Convention. The Vienna Convention on the Law of Treaties notes that in seeking to interpret a provision, account should be taken, *inter alia,* of 'any subsequent agreement between the parties regarding the interpretation of the treaty or the application of its provisions'.[3] In the case of Article 1 of the 1926 Convention, subsequent agreements confirm its status as the authoritative source on what counts as slavery in law.[4] Thus, prior to the 1956 Supplementary Convention on the Abolition of Slavery, the Slave Trade, and Institutions and Practices Similar to Slavery, the question of the adequacy of the 1926 definition was raised by the *Ad Hoc* Committee on Slavery, an United Nations expert body established to consider the overall issue of slavery. Its determination was that there was 'not sufficient reason for discarding or amending the definition of slavery contained in Article 1 of the International Slavery Convention of 1926'. The Committee therefore recommended that 'this definition should continue to be accepted as an accurate and adequate definition of the term'.[5] That recommendation was carried throughout the process which ultimately saw the inclusion of the 1926 definition of slavery as a provision of the 1956 Supplementary Convention.[6] Likewise, in the process which

3 Article 31(3)(a), Vienna Convention on the Law of Treaties, 1969.

4 This point bears some emphasis, because generally examples abound of League of Nations era treaties which are no longer applicable, whether in virtue of having been over-ridden by more up-to-date agreements (such as the Covenant of the League of Nations being superseded by the Charter of the United Nations), or because some of their elements have become dead-letter law, desuetude brought on by a lack of use (such as those transitional provisions of the 1930 Forced Labour Convention [Articles 3–24], which have been declared to be no longer applicable, the window of their possible application now considered closed. See International Labour Organisation, Report of the Committee of Experts on the Application of the Conventions and Recommendations, Eradication of Forced Labour, 2007, p. 6.

5 Economic and Social Council, Report of the Ad Hoc Committee on Slavery (Second Session), UN Doc E/1988, E/AC.33/13, 4 May 1951, p. 7.

6 See Article 7(a), Supplementary Convention on the Abolition of Slavery, the Slave Trade, and Institutions and Practices Similar to Slavery, 1956; which reads:

ultimately saw the establishment of the International Criminal Court in 2002, the issue of the definition of the crime against humanity of 'enslavement' was open for discussion. During the deliberations of the Preparatory Committee on the Establishment of an International Criminal Court in 1996, it was noted that some 'delegations expressed the view that enslavement required further clarification based on the relevant legal instruments'.[7] Although never explicitly stated in the negotiations leading to the 1998 Statute of the International Criminal Court, States, having given themselves the option to re-work the definition, decided to leave the substance of the 1926 definition of intact.[8] Thus, later agreements show that 'the status or condition of a person over whom any or all of the powers attaching to the right of ownership are exercised', is established as the contemporary, legal definition of slavery.

If the locus of the legal definition of slavery can easily be settled, the question of how the provisions of Article 1 are to be interpreted has proved much more controversial. A general problem has been that the use of the term 'slavery' has often been appropriated to give visceral emphasis to incidents and issues which go far beyond the parameters of the definition or any plain reading of its text. Certainly this has happened in sensationalist newspaper reports, but it also figures in legal scholarship on slavery. For example, Jane Kim has argued that rape should be equated with slavery for legal purposes, since 'rape victims, at the time of their assault and perhaps forward are subject to the domination and degradation by [sic.] another person'.[9] The use of Kim's piece is illustrative of a general interpretative malaise in defining slavery, and usefully points to others who have written about, as Kim puts it, 'less institutive forms of violence as constituting slavery', citing: child abuse, child soldiering, domestic violence, forced prostitution, mail-order brides, prohibited abortions, and sexual harassment in housing.[10] And less one be left with the

---

'Slavery' means, as defined in the Slavery Convention of 1926, the status or condition of a person over whom any or all of the powers attaching to the right of ownership are exercised, and 'slave' means a person in such condition or status.

7 United Nations, General Assembly, Preparatory Committee on the Establishment of an International Criminal Court, Summary of the Proceedings of the Preparatory Committee during the Period 25 March–12 April 1996, UN Doc. A/AC.249/1, 7 May 1996, p. 64.

8 See Article 7(2)(c), Rome Statute of the International Criminal Court, 1998, which reads: 'Enslavement' means the exercise of any or all of the powers attaching to the right of ownership over a person and includes the exercise of such power in the course of trafficking in persons, in particular women and children.

9 See J. Kim, 'Taking Rape Seriously: Rape as Slavery' (2012) 35 *Harvard Journal of Law and Gender* 294.

10 *Id.*, 293.

impression that such equating of slavery is the exclusive domain of American law reviews, it should be emphasised that such comparisons are in good company. During much of 1990s, the United Nations' Working Group on Contemporary Forms of Slavery (the *de facto* guardian of the 1926 and 1956 Conventions) considered the following issues as falling under its rather expansive mandate: child pornography, children in armed conflict (1990); child soldiers (1991); removal of organs (1992); incest (1993); migrant workers, sex tourism (1994); illegal adoption (1996); and, early marriages and detained juveniles (1997).[11]

This desire to interpret so widely the legal definition of slavery stems from a failure of States to prosecute and try individuals for enslavement during much of the twentieth century. Into this vacuum came parties, both NGOs and Governments, which oftentimes had a vested interest in expanding the notion of slavery – thus diluting the legal definition – so as to benefit from the a visceral call to end a particular practice. The result has been ambiguity in the legal definition, but also ambivalence in the value or usefulness of that definition. This dilemma is evident even in Suzanne Miers's leading text on issues of slavery during the Twentieth Century. On the one hand, in considering slavery, Miers notes that the UN 'Working Group was using the term to cover such a wide range of practices as to be virtually meaningless' and goes on to press the need for a new definition, declaring that only 'a new clear definition in international law could untangle the morass, set clear standards, and allow governments to prosecute offenders, and victims to seek redress through the courts'.[12] On the other hand, for Miers, the requirement for a 'new clear definition' of slavery is predicated on the welcome fact that by 'widening the definition of slavery to include "all its forms," it marked the beginning of the attack on a wide range of exploitive practices, and was the first step in an ever-expanding definition, as more and more practices came to be described as "analogous" to slavery'.[13]

Yet, if we return to the actual definition of slavery, the phrase 'all its forms' is not found. Instead of considering the actual definition, Miers follows a well-trotted precedent of interpretation which goes beyond the definition of slavery as set out in Article 1 of the 1926 Convention, and instead reads into the definition other elements of the 1926 Convention to allow for an

11 See the reports of the Working Group on Contemporary Forms of Slavery (UN Doc: E/CN.4) at the website of the UN High Commissioner for Human Rights; http://ap.ohchr.org/Documents/gmainec.aspx.

12 S Miers, *Slavery in the Twentieth Century*, (Walnut Creek, CA: Alta Mira Press, 2003) 453.

13 *Id.*, 130.

ever-expanding notion of slavery. For the sake of clarity: it is not the 1926 definition of slavery which has caused an ever-widening concept of slavery to emerge, but a specific interpretation, by non-legal entities, that has gone beyond the definition as set out in Article 1 of the 1926 Slavery Convention. The genesis of this line of interpretation of the definition of slavery starts with the 1930 International Commission of Inquiry meant to look into whether or not slavery or forced labour existed in Liberia.[14] The International Commission felt constrained in its inquiries as its remit fell to 'whether slavery as defined in the anti-slavery convention in fact exists in the Republic'. As such, beyond slavery itself, the Commission noted, the 1926 Convention did not allow for a consideration of lesser servitudes, as 'in its present form it leaves little room for distinguishing between degrees of restrictive freedom'. Having failed to find slavery, the International Commission of Inquiry moved to justify a wider understanding of slavery so as to be able to investigate forced labour which was then persisting in Liberia. As a result the International Commission provided a novel interpretation of slavery by going beyond the definition and noting that there were 'two important provisos' found in the 1926 Slavery Convention: 'to bring about...as soon as possible the complete abolition of slavery in all its forms' and 'to take all necessary measures to prevent compulsory and forced labour from developing into conditions analogous to slavery'.[15] With this in mind, the International Commission redrew its mandate, stating that 'in the interest of achieving the objective of the convention "to bring about the abolition of slavery in all its forms," it has decided to group its evidence which shall be the basis of its findings under the following divisions: A. Common slavery [... and] B. Oppressive practices restrictive of the freedom of persons, constituting conditions analogous to slavery and tending to acquire the status of common or classic slavery'.[16]

We will see shortly that this interpretation of the 1926 Convention by the International Commission of Inquiry was dubious at best, resting in part on a misreading of the Report which accompanied the tabling of the Convention before the League of Nations in 1926;[17] but it certainly did gain credence as an accepted understanding of slavery throughout the Twentieth Century. This is

14 Report of the International Commission of Inquiry into the Existence of Slavery and Forced Labour in the Republic of Liberia. 8 September 1930; Publication of the Department of State, United States Government Printing Office, 1931.

15 *Id.*, p. 14. Emphasis added.

16 *Id.*, p. 15.

17 See J. Allain, 'The Definition of Slavery in International Law' (2009) 52 *Howard Law Journal* 249–251.

most evident in the 2000 Working Paper of the now defunct UN Sub-Commission of Human Rights, written by David Weissbrodt and Anti-Slavery International, which turned to this notion of abolition of slavery in *all its forms* to anchor its understanding of the definition of slavery. The Working Paper argues that by 'referring to "*any* or all of the powers of ownership" in its definition of slavery, and setting forth as its stated purpose the "abolition of slavery in *all* its forms" the Slavery Convention covered not only domestic slavery but also the other forms of slavery listed in the Report of the Temporary Slavery Commission'.[18] As such, for Weissbrodt, the 1926 definition of slavery includes so-called 'other forms of slavery' such as serfdom and debt bondage.[19] Such an interpretation originally found a footing in the United Nations from mid-1960s onwards, and gained momentum as a consequence of a concerted effort to expand the definition of slavery so as to include apartheid.[20] In this climate, an interpretation like that utilised by Weissbrodt met the political objective of the United Nations, but, as with the International Commission of Inquiry, fails to appreciate the legal definition of slavery.

On legal grounds this expansive interpretation of the definition of slavery simply does not hold. It is clear that States, in negotiating the content of the 1926 Convention, did not intend to widen the scope of slavery by reading into it other types of exploitation which failed to meet the threshold of the exercise of 'any or all of the powers attaching to the right of ownership'.[21] In presenting the Convention to the Assembly of the League of Nations for its adoption, the Rapporteur noted that provisions which would have included lesser servitudes had been excluded as a result of comments received back from States, it being understood that if certain practices met the threshold of the definition of slavery, they came within the preview of the Convention, and yet 'if these last practices do not come under the definition of slavery as is given in Article 1, the

---

18 United Nations Sub-Commission on the Promotion and Protection of Human Rights, Contemporary Forms of Slavery: Updated review of the implementation of and follow-up to the conventions on slavery, Working Paper prepared by David Weissbrodt and Anti-Slavery International, UN Doc. E/CN.4/Sub.2/2000/3, 26 May 2000, p. 5. Emphasis in the original quotation.

19 For the various servitudes, see *id.*, p. 5.

20 See United Nations, Economic and Social Council, Social Committee, Summary Record of the Five Hundred and Thirty-Sixth Meeting, 7 July 1966, UN Doc E/AC.7/SR.536, 14 December 1966; and United Nations, Economic and Social Council, Resolution 1126 (XLI), 26 July 1966.

21 See J. Allain, *The Slavery Conventions: The* Travaux Préparatoires *of the 1926 League of Nations Convention and the 1956 United Nations Convention*, (The Hague: Martinus Nijhoff, 2008), 50–60.

[Temporary Slavery] Commission is unanimously of the opinion that they must be combated'.[22] And combated they were, though only later, in 1956, by the United Nations which brought into being a Supplementary Convention to addresses specifically those servitudes mentioned by Weissbrodt, as developed by the Temporary Slavery Commission.

With the United Nations supporting a diluted notion of slavery and a failure of case-law to emerge during the Twentieth Century, the dawn of the Twenty-First Century has seen renewed emphasis on the Article 1 definition in two important respects. First, in 2000 came the signing of the Palermo Protocol, the United Nations instrument related to trafficking which set out a definition for trafficking in persons which explicitly mentioned slavery. This was followed, in 2002, by the coming into force of the Statute of the International Criminal Court which established the crime against humanity of 'enslavement'. The crime was defined, in substance, in the same terms as slavery, as: 'the exercise of any or all of the powers attaching to the right of ownership over a person and includes the exercise of such power in the course of trafficking in persons, in particular women and children'.

We might suppose then, that recent years would have seen some interpretative consensus on the definition of slavery around the terms of the 1926 Convention, but the opportunities occasioned by 2000 and 2002 proved to be very much a false dawn. In fact the result in legal contexts has been an even more blurred understanding of what counts as slavery. This is well illustrated by the first two international judgments to appear at the start of the new Millenium, which interpret the provisions of the 1926 definition and come to diametrically opposite understanding of what slavery means. In 2003, the Appeals Chamber of the Yugoslav Tribunal, in the *Kunarac* case – related to detention centres in the region of Foca, Bosnia and Herzegovina, where women where enslaved in what were in essence rape camps – sustained 'the chief thesis of the Trial Chamber that the traditional concept of slavery, as defined in the 1926 Slavery Convention [...] has evolved to encompass various contemporary forms of slavery which are also based on the exercise of any or all of the powers attaching to the right of ownership'.[23] The Appeals Chamber of the International Criminal Tribunal for the former Yugoslavia went on to say "that the law does not know of a 'right of ownership over a person." Article 1(1)

22 League of Nations, Slavery Convention: Report presented to the Assembly by the Sixth Committee, A.104.1926.VI, as found in League of Nations, Publications of the League of Nations, VI.B.Slavery.1926, VI.B.5, 24 September 1926, p. 2.

23 International Criminal Tribunal for the former Yugoslavia, *Kunarac et als.* (IT-96-23 &-IT-96-23/1-A) Judgment, 12 June 2002, para. 117.

of the 1926 Slavery Convention speaks more guardedly "of a person over whom any or all of the powers attaching to the right of ownership are exercised." That language is to be preferred'.[24] This determination is to be contrasted with that of the European Court of Human Rights which, in 2005, considered that the 1926 definition was only applicable where there was a *de jure* right of ownership over a person. In the *Siliadin* case, which dealt with the fate of a Togolese girl who was held in servitude as a live-in domestic worker in Paris, the European Court stated that the definition of slavery 'corresponds to the "classic" meaning of slavery as it was practiced for centuries. Although the applicant was, in the instant case, clearly deprived of her personal autonomy, the evidence does not suggest that she was held in slavery in the proper sense, in other words that [the perpetrators] exercised a genuine right of legal ownership over her, thus reducing her to the status of an "object"'.[25]

In an effort to resolve this kind of interpretative deadlock, many have turned to the foremost expert on contemporary slavery, Kevin Bales. His sociologically-based understanding of slavery pervades recent legal discourse, and is taken to provide a normative basis for modern slavery. Thus, for instance, in a 2009 *Human Rights Quarterly* piece entitled 'Defining Contemporary Forms of Slavery: Updating a Venerable NGO', Claude Welch states that 'international actors have struggled to find an adequate definition of "slavery"'. Under the heading 'Forging a New Definition of 'Slavery', Welch juxtaposes what he terms the '"New" forms of slavery manifest in the servitudes set out in the 1956 Supplementary Convention with "Kevin Bales' New Slavery"'.[26] In so doing, Welch seeks to argue that the 1926 and 1956 Conventions fail to adequately address contemporary forms of slavery, and he ends his consideration by stating that 'the struggle to eradicate *all forms* of slavery [...] continues'.[27] As for Bales's understanding of slavery, it has the benefit of clearly setting out markers which allow for individuals to identify the sociological attributes of slavery.

---

24 *Id.*, paras 118–119.

25 European Court of Human Rights, *Siliadin v France* (Application 73316/01), 26 July 2005, para. 122.

26 C. Welch, 'Defining Contemporary Forms of Slavery: Updating a Venerable NGO' (2009) 31 *Human Rights Quarterly* 97–98. Consider also N. McGeehan, 'Misunderstood and Neglected: The Marginalisation of slavery in International Law', (2011) 15 *The International Journal of Human Rights* 436. This piece demonstrated the level of confusion in the literature as the author argues first, that slavery 'is related exclusively to ownership, and therefore only applicable to chattel slavery'; but concludes by stating that it is a 'fallacious notion that slavery relates to ownership'. See 442 and 457.

27 *Id.*, Welch. 97–98.

In his 2009 *The Slave Next Door*, Bales along with co-author Ron Soodalter, states that:

> Slavery has been defined in various ways, but there are three essential criteria from knowing if someone is a slave. The first is the complete control of one person by another, through the use of violence – both physical and psychological. The second – hard labour for little or no pay – clearly applies as well. [...] The third criterion is economic exploitation – making a profit for the slaveholder.[28]

This conception is very helpful, but it does not follow, as Welch suggests, that the 1926 definition fails to address contemporary forms of slavery. Indeed, our argument in the next section will be exactly the contrary.

As we begin to make this argument, it is worth noting first that, since *Kunarac*, in four notable instances the cases of the past few years have shown a trend towards accepting that the 1926 definition has contemporary relevance. In the 2007 *Brima* case before the Special Court for Sierra Leone; in 2008, the ECOWAS Community Court of Justice found Niger, in *Mani Karoau*, in violation of prohibition against slavery as set out in the African Charter on Human and Peoples' Right; also in 2008, the High Court of Australia in *Tang*, confirmed a violation of the provision of the Australian Criminal Code which incorporates the 1926 definition; and finally in 2010, the European Court of Human Rights, in *Rantsev*, moved away from its earlier pronouncement in *Siliadin*.[29]

As for the European Court of Human Rights, while it repeated its determination from the *Siliadin* case, it turned also to *Kunarac*, stating that the Yugoslav Tribunal had 'concluded that the traditional concept of "slavery" has evolved to encompass various contemporary forms of slavery based on the exercise of any or all of the powers attaching to the right of ownership'. It followed this by leaving behind the notion that the definition of slavery was applicable only in *de jure* situations, finding 'that trafficking in human beings, by its very nature and aim of exploitation, is based on the exercise of powers attaching to the

---

28 K. Bales and R. Soodalter, *The Slave Next Door: Human Trafficking and Slavery in America Today* (Berkeley: University of California Press, 2009), 13.

29 See *Brima et als.*, Special Court for Sierra Leone, Trial Chamber, SCSL-2004-16-T, 20 June 2007, paras 744–747; which relates to the enslavement of men as a means of extracting forced labour in alluvial diamond fields. *Hadijatou Mani Koraou v. Niger,* ECOWAS Community Court of Justice, ECW/CCJ/JUD/06/08, 27 October 2008; which relates to the enslavement of a female from childhood onwards under the pretext of marriage. *The Queen v Tang*, High Court of Australia, [2008] HCA 39, 28 August 2008; and, *Rantsev v Cyprus and Russia*, Application no. 25965/04, 7 January 2010.

right of ownership'.[30] While this acknowledgment by the European Court of Human Rights is welcomed, the most thorough consideration of the 1926 definition in these four determinations is found in *Tang*, a decision of the High Court of Australia (the Australian supreme court).

In *Tang*, the High Court found, on appeal, a Melbourne brothel owner guilty of five counts of possessing a slave and five counts of 'intentionally exercising over a slave a power attaching to the right of ownership, namely the power to use'.[31] In turning to its consideration of slavery, the Court dismantled the 1926 definition by first considering the distinction between 'status or condition'. The Court stated that: 'Status is a legal concept'. With regard to 'condition', the Court determined that 'the evident purpose of the reference to "condition" was to cover slavery *de facto* as well as *de jure*'. It went on to explain the application of the 1926 definition to *de facto* situations, stating that:

> In its application to the *de facto* condition, as distinct from the *de jure* status, of slavery, the definition was addressing the exercise over a person of powers of the kind that attached to the right of ownership when the legal status was possible; not necessarily all of those powers, but any or all of them.[32]

The Court then turned to consider what those 'powers attaching to the right of ownership' might constitute, and pointed to a 1953 Memorandum by the United Nations Secretary-General. Speaking specifically to the powers set out by the Secretary-General,[33] the High Court determined that 'on the evidence it

30 *Rantsev v Cyprus and Russia*, Application no. 25965/04, 7 January 2010, paras 276; 280 and 281. See J. Allain, 'Rantsev v. Cyprus and Russia: The European Court of Human Rights and Trafficking as Slavery', 10 (2010) *Human Rights Law Review* 546–557. [As reproduced in Chapter 9 of this volume.]

31 *The Queen v Tang*, High Court of Australia, [2008] HCA 39, 28 August 2008, para. 2.

32 *Id.*, paras, 25 and 26.

33 The powers attaching to the right of ownership set out by the United Nations Secretary-General in: United Nations, Economic and Social Council, Report of the Secretary-General on Slavery, the Slave Trade, and Other Forms of Servitude, UN Doc. E/2357, 27 January 1953, p. 36, n. 1; read:

1. the individual of servile status may be made the object of a purchase;
2. the master may use the individual of servile status, and in particular his capacity to work, in an absolute manner, without any restriction other than that which might be expressly provided by law;
3. the products of labour of the individual of servile status become the property of the master without any compensation commensurate to the value of the labour;

was open to the jury to conclude that each of the complainants was made an object of purchase [...]; that, for the duration of the contracts, the owners had a capacity to use the complainants and the complainants' labour in a substantially unrestricted manner; and that the owners were entitled to the fruits of the complainants' labour without commensurate compensation'.[34]

This approach of the Court in *Tang*, according to which the determination as to whether slavery exists is made through analysis of facts amounting to the exercise of 'powers attaching to the right of ownership', is in keeping with a plain reading of the 1926 definition, and also brings to that definition the substance necessary to give it workable contemporary relevance.

What we lack, so far, is a theoretical basis for this definition, one which can explain its normative underpinnings and its practical operation, and so convince courts, commentators, and anyone interested in ideas of slavery, that in Article 1 we have a useful authoritative reference point which is not so wide as to render the very notion of slavery meaningless. In explaining its approach in *Tang*, the High Court did not feel compelled to go beyond the pronouncement of United Nations Secretary-General; but that determination is more than fifty-years old and sets out examples of 'powers attaching to the right of ownership' without seeking to give an overall understanding of that construct. The construct, though, is very familiar to property lawyers. Indeed, much of our jurisprudence on ownership relies on exactly the same differentiation between the legal right 'ownership' and the various powers and privileges which might be consequent on that right. Accordingly, to seek to understand the parameters of what constitutes slavery in a contemporary context, we find ourselves in unusual and slightly counterintuitive position of arguing that reference to property perspectives can bring clarity and purchase to the definition of slavery in a world which has long since abolished private property rights in respect of persons. This contention we make in the next section before arguing further that, as rendered by property perspectives, the 1926 definition provides a powerful way forward for identifying and prosecuting modern cases of slavery.

---

4. the ownership of the individual of servile status can be transferred to another person;
5. the servile status is permanent, that is to say, it cannot be terminated by the will of the individual subject to it;
6. the servile status is transmitted ipso facto to descendants of the individual having such status.

34 *The Queen v Tang*, High Court of Australia, [2008] HCA 39, 28 August 2008, para. 26.

Applying Property Perspectives to the Definition of Slavery

In seeking to understand and explain ownership, jurists old and new have laid their emphasis on what the owner of something is entitled to have, do or expect in respect of that thing. Formulations vary, but it is fairly uncontroversial to suggest that the owner of a tangible thing might possess and use her thing; she might make decisions about how it can be used by others; she might enjoy income produced by the thing, sell it to realise its capital value, or simply give it away, including to those who survive her as her heirs. We might also say that she is entitled to a certain measure of security. We would not expect her thing to be taken from her without cause, whether by a fellow citizen or the government; and correlatively we would expect her ownership to endure until such time as she decided to stop being the owner, whether by transferring the thing away, or by consuming or destroying it altogether.[35]

Thinking about ownership in this way, we build up a picture of an 'owner' as the person in charge of a given resource. We see very clearly her freedom in controlling the thing in question, or, as it has been put recently, in 'setting the agenda' for the use of the thing.[36] This picture is helpful, and we can use it instrumentally to explain the meaning of Article 1. Specifically, without necessarily agreeing with details of any single formulation of the content of ownership, or committing ourselves irrevocably to an overarching conception of property,[37] we can engage such property narrative to substantiate the kinds of

35 The best known and most influential explanation of ownership in these terms is an essay by Tony Honoré first published in 1961, where the kinds of activities described above are distilled to eleven 'incidents' of ownership: AM Honoré, 'Ownership' in AG Guest (ed), *Oxford Essays in Jurisprudence* (Oxford, OUP 1961). Honoré's work has informed later scholarship on property, and is generally accepted as a departure point in conceptualising ownership see: LC Becker, *Property Rights: Philosophic Foundations* (Boston, Routlege & Kegan Paul 1977, repr 1983) 7, 18; J Waldron, *The Right to Private Property* (Oxford, Clarendon Press 1988), 27–28, 49; SR Munzer, *A Theory of Property* (Cambridge, CUP 1990), 22–27; JE Penner, 'The Bundle of Rights Picture of Property' (1995–6) 43 UCLA Law Rev 711; and see JW Harris, *Property and Justice* (Oxford, OUP 1996) 125–30.

36 L. Katz, 'Exclusion and Exclusivity in Property Law' 58 (2008) University of Toronto Law Journal 275.

37 Specifically we want to avoid the impression that in engaging the explanatory value of an incidents-based description of ownership we are committed to a bundle of rights account of property. Generally substantive description of the standard case of ownership may be consistent with a theoretical position which contends, in contradistinction to bundle of rights accounts, that property does not lack coherent conceptual unity. Consider for example: JE Penner, 'The Bundle of Rights Picture of Property' (1995–6) 43 UCLA *Law Rev* 711, esp 731–733, and 754ff, treating Honoré's account as a 'elaboration' of the entitlements

exploitation against which Article 1 sets it face. So we dwell for a moment on the various rights, powers, liberties or immunities which might be exercised by the owner of something tangible.[38] This will lay the foundation for a crucial claim made in the next section, which very closely resonates with the reasoning of the High Court in *Tang*: it remains possible today for the same kinds of control to be exercised in respect of human beings, even though we have abolished property in persons.

The most basic feature of ownership is possession.[39] If some person *A* is owner of some thing, she is entitled to have it, and to demand that others do not interfere with her control of it, at least not without her permission. To safeguard *A*'s position, and specifically to restrain such interferences with her possession, legal systems recognise that everyone else in the world is under a legal duty not to interfere with *A*'s control of the thing.[40] *A* has access to courts and to formal legal mechanisms to enforce this duty, and ultimately she might bring proceedings against a specific defendant, say *B*, accused of some act of interference.[41] So *A* might sue *B* for return of the thing or its value, and have a judgment against *B* enforced by the appropriate authorities. In lawyerly language, *A* has a *claim-right* against *B*, as will she also have a claim-right against anyone else who breaches the duty not to interfere with her use of the thing.

The potential for this kind of claim-right is one of the defining characteristics of private law ownership.[42] In this respect, in law ownership operates negatively, preserving a sphere of freedom for *A* in dealing with a resource by

---

entailed by the 'right to exclusive use', which latter is argued to provide the core conceptual base of property.

38 For the subdivision of all jural relations (of which the content of ownership is but one example) into rights, liberties, powers and immunities, see W.N. Hohfeld, 'Some Fundamental Legal Conceptions as Applied in Judicial Reasoning' (1913–14) 23 *Yale Law Journal* 16.

39 Honoré says a right to possess is 'the foundation on which the whole superstructure of ownership rests': op. cit. n. 35, 113.

40 J Penner, *The Idea of Property in Law* (Oxford: Clarendon Press, 1997); B McFarlane, *The Structure of Property Law* (Oxford: Hart Publishing, 2008), 22–23.

41 *Id.*, Penner, 24; J.W. Harris, *Property and Justice* (Oxford: OUP, 1996), 24–26.

42 Indeed, on one theoretical view commonly-held by property scholars, the whole content of ownership consists in the proposition that A has a right to exclude everyone else from the resource in question. See for example McFarlane, op. cit., n. 40, 22–23. For an overview of the theoretical position which emphasises the right to exclude as the basis of ownership, see L Katz, op. cit., n. 36, 279–285, and the discussions cited there.

keeping others from interfering with her control.[43] Beyond this negative safeguard, the content of *A*'s sphere of freedom is not precisely defined, nor is it achieved by an exactly enumerated list of privileges. *A* might continue to possess her thing or make whatever use of it she likes just because she is free to do so.[44] So if *A* is the owner of a bike, we say *A* has a *liberty* to ride her bike, to paint it, lock it up, display it an as ornament, and put it to all manner of other possible uses. Correlatively to this liberty, no one else in the world has the right (*B* has *no right*) to prevent *A* from engaging in the any of these uses, nor any claim to make the decisions in her stead.

If possession and use are secured by claim-rights and liberties, other features of ownership are manifested in the implementation of legal constructions properly called *powers*. In law a *power* generally refers to the ability of the holder to bring about changes in the legal relations prevailing between herself and others. In the context of ownership there are some obvious examples. An owner has the power to licence what would otherwise be a trespass. By giving *B* permission to ride her bike, *A* can amend the legal relations prevailing between herself and *B* such that *B* breaches no duty of non-interference with the bike by taking it for a spin. *A* can also change the relations more permanently. She has the power to transfer her thing to *B*, by giving or selling it, in consequence of which the rest of the world now owes a duty of non-interference to *B* rather than *A*.

Some features of ownership consist in *immunities*, that is, in the absence of powers in others to disrupt *A*'s ownership of her thing or it to an end. One manifestation of this is that generally ownership is considered to be of potentially limitless duration, such that it will not (normally) come to an end (or 'determine') on the occurrence of some future event (as is the case with some other kinds of property interests, for example, leases of land). Another good example is provided by rules against unjustified expropriation. This immunity preserves a private sphere of autonomy in dealing with assets, and ensures that *A* might safely make plans for her life on the basis that her given allocation of things will not be disturbed without some due process (such as the procedures for bankruptcy, execution for debt, justified compulsory acquisition). In the

43 Penner, op. cit., n. 40, 103; and J. Penner, 'Ownership, Co-ownership, and the Justification of Property Rights', in T. Endicott et al (eds.), *Properties of Law: Essays in Honour of Jim Harris*, Oxford: OUP, 2006, 167–168.

44 There might (and almost certainly will) be outside limits to this freedom. So A might commit a civil or criminal wrong if, say, she allows her thing to cause nuisance or physical harm to her neighbour. In this sense legal systems will always fix the boundaries of permissible uses, but within those parameters, there is freedom, not regulation.

same way, it ensures that, apart from the operation of such process, transfer or alienation of ownership occurs only with the consent of the present owner, and again this preserves the autonomy of the owner as director of a particular resource.

Private law ownership of human beings is today a 'legal impossibility',[45] but the discussion above will allow us to be precise about the technical effect of this abolition, and consequentially will offer a warning: notwithstanding the technical absence of property rights, it remains possible for the same kinds of control to pertain in respect of persons in ways which continue to be objectionable. First, the abolition of property in respect of human beings means obviously that some person (the slave-holder: call him *SH*) is no longer permitted to hold a legally enforceable claim-right in respect of another person under his control (call that other *S*), and correspondingly no court will entertain litigation in respect of interferences with a person-controlled. Recall, though, that the broad function of claim rights was to preserve a sphere of freedom in using the thing in question. In abolishing claim-rights in respect of persons, we do not necessarily do enough to disrupt these spheres of freedom. For sure, we can say that those freedoms are no longer guaranteed by law, in that law no longer demarcates and preserves a realm of liberty-in-dealing with persons in the manner achieved negatively through the operation of claim-rights. In other words, we can say that the law will no longer protect *SH*'s use of *S*. We can point further to the fact that, strictly, *SH* can never now have a liberty to use *S*, because *S* will have countervailing rights to resist use and interference with her person (for example, through the civil law dealing with assault, battery and false imprisonment). But nonetheless, in the general circumstances of exploitation, and notwithstanding the legal protection available in theory to *S* and the absence of any such protection for *SH*, it remains possible in fact for one person to exercise over another sufficiently close analogues of the liberty-of-dealing associated with ownership. So *SH* might continue to control and use *S* by exploiting her services or labour, as where she is used for sexual gratification or to provide domestic services. *S* might be moved from one place to another; her ties to a particular culture, society or religion may be severed against her will; her means of access to state support or authority may be curtailed. And eventually, when her purpose is exhausted, she might be disposed or discarded,

---

45 *The Queen v. Tang*, [2008] HCA 39, para. 20 (Gleeson C.J.). For a rare exception, see: Hadijatou Mani Koraou v. La Republic de Niger, Judgment No. ECW/CCJ/JUD/06/08, Economic Community of West Africa States Community Court of Justice, October 27, 2008; noted J. Allain, 'Hadijatou Mani Koraou v. Republic of Niger', (2009) 109 *The American Journal of International Law* 311. [As reproduced in Chapter 8 of this volume.]

as a thing no longer worth keeping. These circumstances which might be occasioned by *SH*, whilst they cannot formally be regarded as flowing from the exercise of any liberty associated with ownership, are nevertheless sufficiently similar, and in many respects exactly the same, as consequences which may follow from *de jure* ownership.

Something similar obtains in the case of powers. Where ownership of persons has been abolished, *SH* does not have, say, the power to licence what would otherwise be a trespass, but there will be sufficiently close factual analogues. This is very clearly so in the case of sex slavery, and also in slavery for labour, where *SH* might, for example, direct a manager to discipline workers with force or physical threats, or 'lend' to another the services of *S* for a period of time.[46] In the same way, while *SH* certainly cannot sell *S* to *another*, and cannot in that sense bring about any formal change in the legal relations prevailing between *that person* and the rest of the world in respect of *S*, we will easily find real examples of people being traded for money, or otherwise made the subject of a transaction.[47] Similarly, while *SH* lacks the power to bequeath *S* to anyone, nonetheless there will remain local customs, procedures and practices which will serve to bring about the transfer of control of a person to an heir or successor, as where a woman, on the death of her husband, is deemed to be inherited by another person; or where on the death of a person, a subordinate status passes from her to a member of a successive generation.

De facto manifestations of liberties and powers to use, manage, profit from, and discard a person seem fairly central examples of the kinds of control of persons that we might find in the modern world, but the immunities associated with ownership have resonance here too. As to the potentially limitless duration of ownership, one of the cardinal features of slavery is that, from the perspective of the slave, the control she experiences is indefinite, and it is outwith her will to bring it to an end.[48] As to security of holding, whilst at first glance it seems difficult to transfer this incident of ownership to the context of persons,[49] again we are likely to find sufficiently close factual analogues. In particular, since expropriation of property is often considered to be politically

46 As in European Court of Human Rights, *Siliadin v France* (Application 73316/01), 26 July 2005.

47 See *The Queen v Tang*, High Court of Australia, [2008] HCA 39, 28 August 2008, para. 26.

48 See United Nations, Economic and Social Council, Report of the Secretary-General on Slavery, the Slave Trade, and Other Forms of Servitude, UN Doc. E/2357, 27 January 1953, p. 36, n. 1.

49 If it is usually the case that sovereign States will not recognise that one person might hold a private property right in respect of another person, correlatively we are unlikely to find a regime which expressly secures such relations from expropriation.

legitimate within well defined terms (as in the cases of bankruptcy or compulsory acquisition by the state), practically there will be instances of States operating to disrupt exploitative relationships of control (forced labour markets, prostitution rings) which can operate as analogies to cases of justified expropriation, and in so doing highlight the persistence of modern *de facto* control relations. Moreover, where a state government does not take steps to disrupt such activities, arguably this serves to create *de facto* security of holdings in respect of persons, reinforcing the security of such illegitimate relations.

Accepting generally that the phenomena of ownership might persist in this way allows us effectively to endorse the decision of the High Court of Australia in *Tang*, by observing that the *de jure* abolition of formal slavery relations offers no guarantee against their persistence in fact. Moreover, it brings normative purchase to the Article 1 definition, since very clearly the exercise in fact of these kinds of control in respect of a person cuts to the heart of the objection to slavery. Slavery is wrong when the fundamental assumption of our political philosophy articulates the basic freedom and equality of persons. In objecting to slavery, we object principally to the subjection of one person to another, to the inroads on the freedom of that person that come when she is controlled or used in ways inconsistent with her choosing and inimical to her plans for life. It follows that any enquiry to the existence of slavery should be concerned first with the real, factual existence of such constraints. As Hayne J. put it in *Tang*, the concern should be to identify 'a state of affairs in which there is the complete subjection of' one person by another.[50] A focus on the phenomena of ownership helps with this because *de facto* exercise of the powers attaching to ownership in respect of a person serves to indicate real restrictions on that person's freedom.

Perhaps another way of expressing all of this is to say that there is no very great gulf between legal and factual senses of ownership. Ownership is concerned with control. Where the objects of control are ordinary objects of property rights (bikes, cars, horses, coats) the great majority of the owner's exercises of control will nevertheless occur without the specific intervention of the law. Ultimately the owner can call on the law to affirm her position vis-a-vis the thing by taking legal proceedings against an interferer, but most of her actions will be factual exercises of a liberty to control, or invocations of powers to alter existing legal relations. All things considered, this position is not so far removed from contemporary cases involving the subjection of persons. In the modern world it remains possible to exercise exactly the same kinds of control in respect of a person, to behave as if exercising a power and create the factual

50 *The Queen v Tang*, High Court of Australia, [2008] HCA 39, 28 August 2008, para. 148.

consequences of so doing. Since such exercises of control remain objectionable, it makes sense to continue to refer to the language of ownership in identifying slavery, as much the greater part of ownership's import continues to have resonance in the slavery context.

Identifying Modern Cases of Slavery

Accordingly, the 1926 definition of slavery is useful and important because it opens up a substantive understanding of modern slavery. Invoking the conception of ownership discussed above, it points us away from the necessity of formal slavery relations towards the substance of the problem: exploitative relationships where one person is controlled by another as if she were a thing. In so doing, it correlates the legal definition of slavery with our principal objections to slavery as a social institution, removing the need for any wider understanding of slavery which goes beyond a plain text reading of its provisions, whilst at the same time engaging in a systematic way the concern to address modern forms of subjection which count as slavery. Thus, Article 1 has demonstrable contemporary relevance, and fully deserves its status as the starting point for any enquiry as to whether a given practice should be considered slavery. To help courts and prosecutors (or anyone else interested) to proceed from here and identify modern cases of slavery, we can usefully make two further interrelated observations on the text of the 1926 definition, and then unpack a little more what it means to exercise 'the powers attaching to the right of ownership' in respect of a human being.

First, it will not have escaped the keen reader that Article 1 speaks in terms of '*powers* attaching to' ownership, whereas we have seen that ownership employs a broader range of legal constructs only some of which can accurately be considered as powers. We think it is not necessary to read Article 1 literally and restrictively as being concerned only with the exercise of *powers* or their factual equivalents, as opposed to factual equivalents of the wider phenomena of ownership (claim-rights, liberties and immunities). It might be enough to convince on this point that the legal discourse which conceives of legal rights in these constitutive elements of claim-rights, liberties, powers, and immunities was still very novel in the 1920s,[51] at the time when Article 1 was drafted, and nowhere near as well established as the general conceptual enterprise of understanding ownership in terms of what the owner was entitled to do or

51 W.N. Hohfeld, 'Some Fundamental Legal Conceptions as Applied in Judicial Reasoning' (1913–14) 23 *Yale Law Journal* 16, continued (1916–17) 26 *Yale Law Journal* 710.

expect.[52] More significantly though, as we have tried to show above, and as the Court made clear in *Tang*, the point about slavery is that it results in the total subjection of one person to another. Powers are not the only incidents of ownership which if exercised *de facto* will contribute to subjection. Liberties of possession and use also figure prominently. Indeed, if we take possession to mean the maintenance of effective control, we must take possession as an essential, foundational aspect of the kind of subjection envisaged in *Tang*. So we cannot, and need not confine Article 1 to a strict reading of *power*. For sure that definition embraces analogues of some behaviours correctly thought of as the exercise of a power, but it also embraces the exercise of liberties, and analogues of immunities too. As such, we should read the phrase 'powers attaching to the right of ownership' only as engaging a general conceptual tool which seeks to understand ownership in terms of its incidents, and not in any narrower sense.

Secondly, the 1926 definition recites that the exercise of 'any or all' of the 'powers attaching' indicates the presence of a slavery relation. It would seem to follow on a literal reading that whenever we observe in practice the exercise of *any* one incident of ownership in respect of a person, this serves to indicate that slavery exists. However, this will often be insufficient or problematic. To take a trivial and obvious example, employers routinely expect to make decisions about the tasks and activities of their employees, and might reasonably expect to be entitled to the profits of their labour, subject to payment of a (fair) wage; but only with invective would we refer to the employment relation as slavery, and certainly we would not mean it to fall within the scope of Article 1 of the 1926 Convention. Similarly a government might detain or restrict the movements of identified individuals, and at least some of the time we can recognise these practices as being in pursuit of legitimate goals. At first blush, then, it does not look to be enough in identifying slavery that we point to the existence of *any* of the powers attaching to the right of ownership, though that seems to be what a literal reading of Article 1(1) intends. We need to find something more general to say about the effect of the incidents of ownership in the slavery context that can help us distinguish sound manifestations from unsound ones, and so explain why Article 1 adopts the language of 'any or all'.

When jurists approach the matter of elucidating and explaining ownership, they do so in the context of a background understanding that ownership

---

52 See generally: W. Markby, *Elements of Law* (Oxford: Clarendon Press, 6th edn 1905), paras 307, 309, 314; O.W. Holmes Jnr., *The Common Law* (Boston, MA: Little Brown, 1881), 245; F. Pollock and R.S. Wright, *An Essay on Possession in the Common Law* (Oxford: Clarendon Press, 1888), 22, 93.

implies a particular relation of control (this explains why possession is considered the foundational incident of ownership). For Roman lawyers, the owner was *dominus*, master of the thing owned,[53] and similarly, when Blackstone spoke of 'property', he supposed a despotic relation of control between person and thing.[54] More recently, as we saw earlier, Larissa Katz has referred to the owner as 'the exclusive agenda-setter for the owned thing'.[55] This is a particularly helpful conception because it carries the idea of the owner's empowerment to deal with and make decisions about the thing, and also of the thing's subjection to the will of the owner. That subjection need not be total: others might have a part to play in determining the use of a thing on particular occasions;[56] but ultimately the owner is the person calling the shots, the person who gets to manipulate and control the resource to meet his own ends.

It seems to follow that, when we seek to identify slavery, we should look for manifestations of the powers attaching to ownership which occur against the background of this kind of control relationship between persons. This entails, at a minimum, that slavery occurs where one person controls another as he would control a thing possessed; or to put it more shortly, that slavery entails control of a person tantamount to possession. This understanding resonates with the conception of ownership engaged by Article 1, but also provides descriptive and normative explanations for the 'any or all' criterion. Descriptively, control will almost certainly be a factual pre-requisite for any *de facto* exercise of the powers attaching to ownership. A person can only be sold, lent, used or discarded if first she is within the realm of control of the seller, user, lender or discarder. Absent the presence of such control, it would largely be meaningless to speak of *SH* entering into any kind of transaction in respect of *S*, or putting her to any use: such things just would not be possible in fact. Further, if *SH* must first control *S* tantamount to possessing her, we imbue with normative significance any exercise of a power attaching to the right of ownership in respect of *S*. Selling, using, lending or discarding *S* testifies to *SH*'s

---

53 In a legal dispute over a thing, a claimant would allege he was dominus ex iure Quiritium (owner by Quiritiary right), the Quiritiary law being the ancient civil law of Rome: see B Nicholas, *An Introduction to Roman Law* (Oxford: Clarendon Press, 1962), pp. 63 (fn 1), 101.

54 E Christian (ed), *Commentaries on the Laws of England by Sir William Blackstone* (London: Cadell & Davies, 15th edn 1809), Book 2, Ch 1.

55 L Katz, op. cit, n. 36, 275.

56 Katz makes this same observation in the case of things subject to private law ownership, where others sometimes have property rights which are not inconsistent with the rights of the owner, but which nevertheless will contribute to determination of how the thing is to be used: for example, a right of way over particular land: *id.*, 294–295.

control, and to *S*'s subjection. It is on the wrongness of these that we premise our objection to slavery.

If slavery entails control tantamount to possession, an important corollary is that it will not necessarily constitute slavery where one person exercises any one incidental power of ownership in circumstances where such control is absent. This accounts, for example, for the situation where the employer makes routine management decisions about her worker; but it might also explain more difficult situations, where though there has been some control exercised in a manner which is exploitive, yet this control amounts to something less than possession and thus is not slavery but, say, forced labour. An example of such an instance would be the case of a textile employer exacting forced labour but not controlling other elements of a worker's life, thus failing short of the threshold of control tantamount to possession.[57]

Having established the significance of control as being foundational to slavery, in that it makes possible the *de facto* exercise of further powers attaching to ownership and articulates our objection to the same, the next step is to be more specific about how such exercises might manifest themselves in situations of modern slavery. Both the United Nations Secretary-General and the legislation of the International Criminal Court provide certain examples but, as yet, no systematic attention has been directed to the question of what would constitute exercise of such powers against a human being.[58] Perhaps the most intuitive exercise of such a power would be in the *buying or selling of a person*.[59] In such a transaction, as in other similar transfers of a person, be it through exchange, barter or gift, it becomes obvious that the foundational element of possession is required for slavery to be present. It is only through such

57 For more on this difference between slavery and forced, see further below.

58 For the examples set out by the United Nations Secretary-General see op. cit. n. 33; with regard to the International Criminal Court, the secondary legislation of the Court, its Elements of the Crime touching on enslavement states that the 'The perpetrator exercised any or all of the powers attaching to the right of ownership over one or more persons, such as by purchasing, selling, lending or bartering such a person or persons, or by imposing on them a similar deprivation of liberty'. See International Criminal Court, Assembly of States Parties, Elements of the Crimes, ICC-ASP/1/3, 9 September 2002, p. 117. Emphasis added.

59 See *Hadijatou Mani Koraou v. La Republic de Niger*, Judgment No. ECW/CCJ/JUD/06/08, Economic Community of West Africa States Community Court of Justice, October 27, 2008, para. 8 which reads: 'In 1996, while she was only twelve (12) years old, the applicant, Mrs. Hadijatou Mani Koraou, of the Bouzou custom was sold to the tribe chief, Mr. El Hadj Souleymane Naroua, of the Haoussa custom, aged 46 years old, for two hundred and forty thousand (240.000) CFA francs'.

control, often established through violence or coercion, that a person is made amenable to being the subject of a transaction. Once a person has become the subject of a transaction, that transaction will generate manifold facts which can testify to the existence of slavery, from the revenues and funds associated with any exchange, which approximate to the realisation of *S*'s capital value as a thing, to the physical changes in *S*'s custody and any force applied to bring them about.

Less intuitive, though very present in contemporary practice is the *transferring of a person to an heir or successor*, in situations which constitute slavery. Most evident are cases of inheritance, where a woman, on the death of her husband, is deemed to be inherited by the family of the former husband.[60] This practice is more common than descent-based slavery, which we will still find in Mauritania or Niger, where there continue to be instances of the conveying of a slave to a successive generation, such as from a father to his son.[61] In the case of inheritance, as in the case of the purchasing of a person, the expectation is that benefit will be derived from the service or labour of a slave.

This same benefit underlies our next point as it is easy to suppose, given control tantamount to possession, that a person can still be *used* as if she was a thing, and in such *use of a person* we see an analogue of the function of ownership. This will be manifest where a person is used for sexual gratification, or to provide a service or labour for little or no pay. Such was the case, for instance, in Sierra Leone where, during the 1991–2002 Civil War, when women were abducted and designated as 'bush wives' by the soldiers who took possession of them and forced them under threat of death to cook, clean, and porter.[62]

---

60 See Federation of Women Lawyers – Kenya (FIDA-Kenya) and the International Women's Human Rights Clinic, Kenyan Laws and Harmful Customs Curtail Women's Equal Enjoyment of ICESCR Rights, Submission to the Kenyan Government's Initial Report under the United Nations Committee on Economic, Social, and Cultural Rights, 2008; and Human Rights Watch, Double Standards: Women's Property Rights Violations in Kenya, 2003, p. 12.

61 See United Nations, Human Rights Council, Mission to Mauritania, Report of the Special Rapporteur on Contemporary Forms of Slavery, including its Causes and Consequences, Gulnara Shahinian, UN Doc. A/HRC/15/20/Add.2, 24 August 2010; and Anti-Slavery International and Association Timidira, Slavery in Niger; Historical, Legal, and Contemporary Perspectives, G K Abdelkader (ed.), 2004.

62 See *Brima et als.* case, Special Court for Sierra Leone, Appeals Chamber, Judgment, SCSL-2004-16-A, 22 February 2008, pp. 66–67; where the Appeals Chamber constituted such 'forceful abduction and use of women and girls as forced conjugal partners', as the crime against humanity of 'forced marriage'.

Managing of the use of a person will constitute exercise of a power attaching to the right of ownership amounting to slavery, where the background relationship of control tantamount to possession is present, as where, for example, the day-to-day management of so-called 'captive communities' within Bolivian cattle ranches is delegated by the owner of such estates to over-seers/manager.[63] At a more abstract level, such management of the use of a person will also be manifest in certain steps taken to consolidate control tantamount to possession. Examples include the imposition of a new place of residence, language, or religion, or forcing marriage so as to sever previous social bonds.

In like manner, *profiting from the use of a person* constitutes exercise of a power attaching to the right of ownership, given a background relationship of control tantamount to possession. Such profit might be gained through mortgaging a person, lending her out for profit, or using her as collateral: indeed, in principle, it may include making money or deriving any other kind of income or benefit from her use in any way whatsoever. We can draw a practical example from an instance of an agricultural worker in a situation of slavery, where the profit from the picking of a crop is taken by another, whether in the form of unpaid wages or money derived from the selling of the harvest.[64]

Closely associated with the concept of use would be the power to dispose of one's property. This leads us to suggest that a further exercise of a power attaching to the right of ownership would be manifest in the mistreatment or neglect of that person, inasmuch as it shows that she is being treated as a disposable person.[65] Any such *disposal, mistreatment or neglect of a person* will fall within the parameters of slavery where control tantamount to possession is present. In such instances, mistreatment or neglect leads to the physical or psychological exhaustion of a person, and ultimately may lead to her destruction if it persists. Such mistreatment might be either calculated or indiscriminate, and would impose such demands as to severely curtail the capacity of her body to sustain itself or function effectively. Examples of situations of slavery would be

63 See Organization of American States, Inter-American Commission on Human Rights, *Captive Communities: Situation of the Guaraní Indigenous People and Contemporary Forms of Slavery in the Bolivian Chaco*, 24 December 2009, OEA/Ser.L/V/II, Doc. 58, 24 December 2009.

64 See Florida Farm Labour Slavery Prosecutions, 1997–2010, in Coalition of Immokalee Workers, Slavery in the Fields and Food We Eat; at http://www.sfalliance.org/resources/10SlaveryinFields.pdf.

65 See K. Bales, *Disposable People: New Slavery in the Global Economy*, (Berkeley: University of California Press, 1999).

cases where children are, after a certain period in a mine or begging on the street, no longer deemed effective and are thus abandoned.[66]

Finally, as we said earlier, immunity from expropriation, or 'security of holding' is normally associated with ownership. Generally this means that a State has no power to interfere with private property, but sometimes it will be permitted so to act where prescribed by law, in situations of public interest. In the context of modern slavery, we will find analogies to such permissive disruption of property rights, which can serve to remind us of the persistence of slavery relations. A good example can be found in the jurisprudence of the European Court of Human Rights, which accepts that States of the Council of Europe have a number of far-reaching positive obligations to disrupt property relationships in persons, of which the minimum, which is accepted by all States, is simply to bring about the end of either the status or the condition of a person over whom any or all of the powers attaching to the right of ownership are exercised.[67]

It is thus possible to construct the exercise of powers attaching to the right of ownership in respect of a person. They include (though we do not intend this list to be exhaustive) buying or selling a person; transferring a person to an heir or successor; using a person; managing the use of a person; profiting from the use of a person; disposal, mistreatment or neglect of a person; and as analogous to the immunity from expropriation, the States' positive obligation to bring about, by various means, the cessation of slavery. Control tantamount to possession is a minimum condition for their exercise, but given such control, the exercise of any or all of these powers speaks to the condition of slavery, and thus, possession, as a basic feature of ownership, serves to identify slavery in practice.[68]

---

66 See United Nations, Human Rights Council, Report on Child Slavery in the Artisanal Mining and Quarrying Sector; Report of the Special Rapporteur on Contemporary Forms of Slavery, including its Causes and Consequences, Gulnara Shahinian, UN Doc. A/HRC/18/30, 4 July 2011; Anti-Slavery International, Begging for Change: Research findings and recommendations on forced child begging in Albania/Greece, India and Senegal, 2009; and Human Rights Watch, Off the Backs of the Children: Forced Begging and Other Abuses against Talibés in Senegal, 2010.

67 See *Siliadin v France* (Application 73316/01), 26 July 2005; and *Rantsev v Cyprus and Russia*, Application no. 25965/04, 7 January 2010; as well as H. Cullen, 'Siliadin v France: Positive Obligations under Article 4 of the European Convention on Human Rights', (2006) 6 *Human Rights Law Review* 585 and R. O'Connell, 'Realising Political Equality: The European Court of Human Rights and Positive Obligations in a Democracy', (2010) 61 *Northern Ireland Legal Quarterly* 263.

68 See generally the Bellagio-Harvard Guidelines on the Legal Parameters of Slavery, in J Allain (ed), *The Legal Parameters of Slavery: From the Historic to the Contemporary* (OUP, 2012). [See Appendix 6 of this volume.]

It is no answer to say that formal relations of slavery have been abolished and with them the notion that private property rights might obtain in respect of human beings; because it is remains possible for subjection to persist in fact. Accordingly, attention must be directed not to the technical exercise of any power but rather to the occurrence of facts analogous to those produced by the exercise of power, like the fact that *SH* received a sum of money from *B* in exchange for delivering *S* into the control of the *B*. In other words, we must move beyond the form of slavery and look to the substance. In our view, this is the vision and understanding of slavery which is entailed by the conception of ownership employed in Article 1. It is encouraging to note in this conclusion that, in 1953, the United Nations Secretary-General was attuned to making such a distinction between form and substance, stating that the 1926 Slavery Convention extends to 'all institutions or practices, whether or not designated as 'slavery', provided that, as stated in Article 1 of the Convention, 'any or all of the powers attaching to the right of ownership are exercised' over a person in these institutions or practice'.[69]

Notice that, in this sense, the definition in Article 1 is expansive rather than restrictive, and appropriately configured to address the changing circumstances of modern slavery. It is targeted against all forms of exploitation which satisfy the crucial requirement for slavery: that a person is being controlled as if she were a thing possessed. This is the core meaning of slavery, and in postulating such a core, Article 1 avoids the pitfalls of the spiralling interpretations of slavery that have characterised much of the discourse from the League of Nations era on through much of the Twentieth Century.

It follows that whether or not slavery exists in practice in a given case will hinge on a factual determination that there has been *de facto* exercise of one or more of the powers attaching to the right of ownership in circumstances where control tantamount to possession is present. The High Court in *Tang* adopted such a substantive approach, and prosecutors and courts considering future cases of slavery should take its lead, using the rhetoric of 'powers attaching to the right of ownership' to scrutinise the factual circumstances of subjugation. Where any or all of these powers is exercised in circumstances of control tantamount to possession, slavery exists. Where such control is not present, even though the behaviours in view are exploitative and certainly wrong, yet they are not slavery, inasmuch as they fail to exhibit the core meaning of slavery. Importantly, this accounts for a distinction between slavery and those lesser servitudes also recognised by international law, such as forced labour, and the

---

69 United Nations, Economic and Social Council, Report of the Secretary-General on Slavery, the Slave Trade, and Other Forms of Servitude, UN Doc. E/2357, 17 January 1953, p. 27.

1956 Supplementary Convention's 'institutions and practices similar to slavery', namely, debt bondage, serfdom, servile marriage, and child exploitation. While in principle, a particular circumstance of exploitation might justify a finding of slavery or a finding of one of these lesser servitudes, the appropriate manner to proceed is to address the substance of the situation rather than the form, by asking whether there has been *de facto* exercise of any or all of the powers attaching to the right of ownership.[70] Where this inquiry is answered affirmatively in circumstances disclosing control tantamount to possession, the more serious condition of slavery is present. Where the inquiry brings a negative response, prosecutors and courts can appropriately move to consider the legal definition of the lesser servitude which corresponds to the particular circumstance in question.

In this respect, consider the difference between slavery and the lesser servitude of forced labour. The 1926 Convention, for its part, recognises that forced or compulsory labour can develop 'into conditions analogous to slavery'. As such, forced labour, while meeting its legal definition as set out in the 1930 Forced Labour Convention ('all work or service which is exacted from any person under the menace of any penalty and for which the said person has not offered himself voluntarily') may also amount to slavery in law, if such labour transpires in a situation where the powers attaching to the right of ownership are exercised. Just as the intentional infliction of serious harm upon a person may constitute both assault and, if death ensues, murder, so the circumstances of forced labour will amount to slavery when the critical element of the latter is present on the facts. In a situation where a clerk is forced to accept less than minimum wage under threat of dismissal, this constitutes forced labour; however the threshold of control would have to be much higher for such an instance to constitute slavery. As we have sought to demonstrate through our reading of the 1926 definition, that threshold would be where a person exercises control tantamount to possession.

Conclusion

Article 1 of the 1926 Slavery Convention has long been accepted as the authoritative source on what counts as slavery in law, but subsequent interpretations

70 The 1926 Convention recognises that forced labour can develop 'into conditions analogous to slavery'. The 1956 Supplementary Convention recognises that institutions and practices similar to slavery may be 'covered by the definition of slavery contained in article 1 of the Slavery Convention of 1926'.

of its provisions, premised on agenda-driven desires to bring modern forms of exploitation within the purview of slavery, have lacked consistency and resulted in large measures of confusion. The chief shortcoming has been a failure to engage at all with the ownership construct employed by the text of Article 1. Our purpose in bringing forward a theoretical analysis of the definition of slavery, viewed through the lens of this property paradigm, has been to explain the normative underpinnings of Article 1 and its practical operation, so as to deliver a definition of slavery with a core settled meaning and demonstrable contemporary relevance.

The task for States is to bring this machinery to bear on the behaviours and practices of modern subjugation. Courts should be alive to the import of Article 1 when determining whether slavery exists in a given case, and in its provisions they have a clear structure for how to proceed when making determinations of this kind. For the rest of us, Article 1 should serve as a reminder that, whilst formal slavery relations have long since been abolished, and in that sense 'legal slavery' is no longer possible, international law is not neutral on the matter. Slavery still exists in law where any or all of the powers attaching to the right of ownership are exercised in respect of a person subject to control tantamount to possession. Slavery still exists in law where a person is controlled as if she were a thing.

CHAPTER 22

Slavery and Its Definition*

Jean Allain and Kevin Bales

Had the abolitionists of the past, the likes of Abraham Lincoln or William Wilberforce been able to see into the Twenty-First Century, what might have struck them as very strange was that while we had come far in ending slavery and suppressing human exploitation, we seem to have lost sight of what the term 'slavery' means. This, despite the fact that for more than eighty-five years there has been a consensus in international law as to the legal definition of slavery. Likewise, despite having an established definition of slavery in law at the international level and the majority of States having constitutional or legislative provisions prohibiting slavery in their domestic legal order, very little action has been taken to prosecute individuals for enslaving another person – until recently. We say 'until recently', as it can be said that we are currently living through a 'neo-abolition era', one that goes beyond its historical predecessor which focused on ending legal slavery; to a contemporary movement meant to end slavery in fact. Distinctive parallels between abolition of old and the current, neo-abolitionist, movement exist. Just as Quaker social activism and Anglican evangelicalism laid the foundation for the British abolitionist campaign which ultimately lead to the abolition of legal slavery; so too should we acknowledge the parallel roles of human rights activism (still including Quakers) on one hand and the 'Religious Right' in the United States of America on the other hand and their joint influence on the American Congress in passing the 2000 *Victims of Trafficking and Violence Protection Act*.[1] Likewise, just as British dominance of the seas during the Nineteenth Century allowed it to end of the slave trade; so too has the current dominance of the United States allowed it, through legislation dealing with trafficking, to force other countries to get serious about prosecuting cases of slavery.[2]

---

* This article first appeared in as Jean Allain and Kevin Bales, "Slavery and its Definition," 14 *Global Dialogue* (2012) 1. Reproduced with permission, Copyright © Global Dialogue 2012. Kevin Bales is Professor of Contemporary Slavery, Wilberforce Institute for the Study of Slavery and Emancipation, University of Hull, and co-founder *Free the Slaves*.

1 See Christopher Leslie Brown, Moral Capital, 2006; and Ronald Weitzer, "The Social Construction of Sex Trafficking: Ideology and Institutionalization of a Moral Crusade," Politics Society, Volume 35, 2007, pp. 447–475.

2 See Jean Allain, "Nineteenth Century Law of the Sea and the British Abolition of the Slave Trade," *British Yearbook of International Law*, Vol. 78, 2008, pp. 342–388 [As reproduced as

 | DOI 10.1163/9789004279896_024

The dominant position which the United States of America holds in both soft and hard power has allowed it, through informal empire, to require States to pass legislation that criminalises the movement of persons through coercion, fraud, or deceit, with the intent of exploiting them. In the most recent manifestation of the 2000 Victims of Trafficking Act, the *William Wilberforce Trafficking Victims Protection Re-authorization Act of 2008* makes it "the policy of the United States not to provide non-humanitarian, non-trade related foreign assistance to any government that (1) does not comply with minimum standards for the elimination of trafficking; and (2) is not making significant efforts to bring itself into compliance with such standards."[3] These minimum standards relate to legislating criminal liability for those involved in trafficking in persons and require that the State "should make serious and sustained efforts to eliminate severe forms of trafficking in persons."[4] Thus, in the case of trafficking, the United States is requiring other countries to go beyond legislation to actual suppression.

Before continuing, it should be made plain that trafficking is not in itself slavery, but a process by which slavery can be achieved. However, the moves of the United States to suppress trafficking have a knock-on effect which touches on slavery. This is so because the trafficking legislation which has emanated from the US Congress is modelled upon, and an off-shoot of, the United Nations' 2000 Palermo Protocol – the Protocol to Prevent, Suppress and Punish Trafficking in Persons, especially Women and Children. The Palermo Protocol,

---

Chapter 2 of this volume.]; and Section 110, United States, Department of State, *Victims of Trafficking and Violence Protection Act*, 28 October 2000.

3 Section 110, United States, Department of State, *Victims of Trafficking and Violence Protection Act*, 28 October 2000.

4 Section 108(a), United States, Department of State, *Victims of Trafficking and Violence Protection Act* spells out those minimum standards for the elimination of trafficking as follows:

(1) The government of the country should prohibit severe forms of trafficking in persons and punish acts of such trafficking.

(2) For the knowing commission of any act of sex trafficking involving force, fraud, coercion, or in which the victim of sex trafficking is a child incapable of giving meaningful consent, or of trafficking which includes rape or kidnapping or which causes a death, the government of the country should prescribe punishment commensurate with that for grave crimes, such as forcible sexual assault.

(3) For the knowing commission of any act of a severe form of trafficking in persons, the government of the country should prescribe punishment that is sufficiently stringent to deter and that adequately reflects the heinous nature of the offense.

(4) The government of the country should make serious and sustained efforts to eliminate severe forms of trafficking in persons.

for its part, sets out a definition of trafficking that establishes a crime related to a chain of movement of a person into situations of 'exploitation', as a result of violence or other means. The Palermo Protocol gives examples of the types of exploitation that are meant to be addressed; these include forced labour, servitude, and, most important for our consideration: slavery.[5] As a result, if countries are meant to suppress trafficking where it involves slavery, it is rather difficult to turn a blind eye to cases of slavery on their territory that do not involved trafficking, in the sense of this chain of movement.

The other influence that the United States has had on the emergence of the neo-abolitionist era is rather more equivocal as it relates to the crime against humanity of enslavement within the jurisdiction of the International Criminal Court. While the United States remains hostile to becoming party to the Court, it has also utilised it instrumentally, allowing the United Nations Security Council to act against the leadership of both Sudan and Libya. Where the international crime of enslavement is concerned, what places us on firmer ground with regard to United States' influence is its leading role in creating the *ad hoc* criminal tribunals for the former Yugoslavia and Rwanda which acted as precursors; and thus cleared the way for the establishment of the International Criminal Court.[6] For many of the one hundred and twenty States that have signed up to the International Criminal Court, this has meant the introduction of domestic legislation developed to ensure that the Court can function in a complementary fashion within the domestic legal order. Part of that legislation inevitably addressed the crimes under the jurisdiction of the International Criminal Court and for a number of States, including Burundi, Malta, Niger and Romania, they have, for instance, incorporated 'enslavement' into their domestic legislation.

5 Article 3(a), Protocol to Prevent, Suppress and Punish Trafficking in Persons, Especially Women and Children, 15 November 2000 reads:

> 'Trafficking in persons' shall mean the recruitment, transportation, transfer, harbouring or receipt of persons, by means of the threat or use of force or other forms of coercion, of abduction, of fraud, of deception, of the abuse of power or of a position of vulnerability or of the giving or receiving of payments or benefits to achieve the consent of a person having control over another person, for the purpose of exploitation. Exploitation shall include, at a minimum, the exploitation of the prostitution of others or other forms of sexual exploitation, forced labour or services, slavery or practices similar to slavery, servitude or the removal of organs.

6 See John Cerone, "Dynamic Equilibrium: The Evolution of US Attitudes toward International Criminal Courts and Tribunals," *The European Journal of International Law*, Volume 18, 2007, p. 288.

These are the dynamics at play that have brought slavery back into legal focus in the context of the early Twenty-First Century. Yet, today, the very term 'slavery' and its contours are contested despite the fact that an international definition of slavery was established in 1926, was confirmed in 1956, and was replicated in substance as the definition of enslavement included in the 1998 Statue of the International Criminal Court. However, it may also be said that the legal contours of slavery remain contested not necessarily despite the 1926 definition of slavery, but because of it. This is so as the definition looks rather opaque at first glance:

> Slavery is the status or condition of a person over whom any or all of the powers attaching to the right of ownership are exercised.

One's first impression might be that of ownership; that a person needs to own another for slavery to be said to exist. But this is not so.

As the Australian equivalent of the United States Supreme Court made clear in its 2008 *Tang* case, the definition has contemporary relevance in situations where a person does not legally own another, as they did in days of old. What the High Court of Australia determined was that while the 1926 definition applied in *de jure* situations – that is: where a person legally owns another – it also applied in *de facto* situations where a person exercised the powers attaching to the right of ownership instead of exercising the right of ownership over a person. In other words, that a person could be in a condition of slavery without legal ownership, if it could be shown that they were treated like a slave in fact, if not in law. Let us provide some examples to illuminate this *de jure-de facto* difference.

Consider the case of a bigamist. In a majority of countries it is illegal for a married person to marry a second time. Let us say that a man gets married a second time. For that man the second marriage is illegal, the courts will not recognise it; thus he is not married *de jure*. However, from the courts' perspective he is married *de facto*; which allows for the bigamy case to proceed.

A further example gets us closer to a consideration of the essence of the definition of slavery. Consider the dispute between two drug dealers over a kilogram of heroin. While neither has a *de jure* right of ownership of the drugs, the courts will recognise the exercise of a power attaching to such a right of ownership in a *de facto* sense so as to hold one or the other in violation of the laws related to possessing controlled substances. This example is instructive as it functions within a property law paradigm that is also applicable in cases of contemporary slavery. While the judge could make a determination of *de facto* ownership if a drug dealer was caught selling heroin, typically such cases are resolved on the simple issue of possession: did the individual have control over the heroin, did she possess it.

In the case of slavery the element of possession is fundamental and allows us to drain the swamp and walk out of the definitional quagmire which has marginalised the legal definition of slavery. The definition has been often bogged down, since at least the 1930s, by individuals and organisations trying to expand the notion of slavery to fit their agenda and thus benefit from the visceral power of a claim that what they were railing against is 'slavery'. Consider, for instance, attempts within the United Nations during the 1960s to equate colonialism and apartheid to slavery; or in the 1990s with UN studies considering incest and juvenile detention under the heading of contemporary forms of slavery.[7]

With the legal definition of slavery marginalised, peopled looked elsewhere to define slavery. A survey of the academic literature on contemporary slavery – including much of the legal literature on the subject – would show that, in the main, it has turned to the work of Kevin Bales and his sociological reading of what constitutes slavery. For more than fifteen years, Bales has attempted to build discussions on contemporary slavery and propose an agenda for both research and effective intervention.[8] Reduced to its essence, Bales' definition turns on the following elements: the use of violence, the ability to control, for economic exploitation.[9] The primary indicator of slavery is that of control;

---

7 See United Nations, Economic and Social Council, Resolution 1126 (XLI), 26 July 1966; and United Nations, Economic and Social Council, Commission on Human Rights, Sub-Commission on Prevention of Discrimination and Protection of Minorities, Contemporary Forms of Slavery: Report of the Working Group on Slavery on its Eighteenth Session, UN Doc. E/CN.4/Sub.2/1993/30, 23 June 1993, pp. 67–68 and 76–79.

With regard to the 1930s, see the International Commission of Inquiry into the Existence of Slavery and Forced Labour in the Republic of Liberia. 8 September 1930.

8 See Kevin Bales, *Disposable People: New Slavery in the Global Economy*, 1999; Kevin Bales, *Understanding Global Slavery*, 2005; Kevin Bales, *Ending Slavery: How We Free Today's Slaves* 2007; Kevin Bales, Zoe Trodd and Alex Williamson; *To Plead Our Own Cause: Personal Stories by Today's* Slaves, 2008; and Kevin Bales and Ron Soodalter, *The Slave Next Door: Human Trafficking and Slavery in America Today*, 2009.

9 See for instance: "the use of violence to control the slave, the resulting loss of free will, and the economic exploitation that normally precludes the slave receiving any recompense for their work." Kevin Bales, *Understanding Global Slavery: A Reader*, 2005, p. 91.

By Bales' own admission, his definition has evolved as this thinking on the subject has evolved. His most recent understanding of slavery, not yet in print reads:

Slavery is the control of one person (the slave) by another (the slaveholder or slaveholders). This control transfers agency, freedom of movement, access to the body, and labor and its product and benefits to the slaveholder. The control is supported and exercised control that diminishes the agency of the slave, normally demonstrated by the physical control of the slave that prevents their escape from enslavement and forces them to work. The primacy of control is often additionally demonstrated by the sexual use of the body of the slave by the slaveholder in addition to other forms of exploitation.

Bales also argues that slavery as a status or condition is not defined by the customs, practices, methods, or mechanisms of enslavement. A person might be taken into slavery by many paths, but the means of enslavement, the vehicle by which a person arrives in the state or condition of slavery, while important for understanding the particular nature of a case of slavery, does not determine that state, it is simply the means by which a person arrives under the control of another.

A number of examples help to shed light on this last distinction and clear up the confusion arising from disparate definitions based on pathways to enslavement as opposed to the condition of slavery itself. Imagine there are four women all of whom are experiencing the following conditions. All four women are held under the physical control of another person against their will, this control prevents them from exercising agency or leaving the place where they are held. The person in control manages the activities of each woman, and they are required to undertake activities that benefit the person who controls them. The control is such that any of the women can be transferred to another individual against her will, or destroyed by the person who controls them. All of the women experience intermittent rape at the hands of the person controlling them as well as by other men as allowed by the person who controls them.

What is telling is that while few would disagree that these four women are enslaved based on this description, some commentators would argue that some of these women are not in slavery when the means by which they were enslaved are introduced. Now let us assume that the first woman arrived at this condition after being falsely arrested, 'fined', and then handed over to the person who controls her to 'work off her fine' in an open pit mine in Eastern Congo. The second woman, seeking a better life, paid a smuggler to help her enter another country and upon arrival was handed over to, and then sexually assaulted by, the person who would control her, who also told her that she owed a sum of money in addition to what she paid to be smuggled, and was

---

through violence and its threat. The aim of this control is primarily economic exploitation, but may include sexual use or psychological benefit.

See Kevin Bales, "Professor Kevin Bales Response to Professor Orlando Patterson," in the *forthcoming* Jean Allain (ed.) *The Legal Understanding of Slavery: The Historical to the Contemporary*, 2012.

then placed in a brothel in the United States owned by the person controlling her where she was sold for sex. The third woman arrived in the condition of control when her husband took a loan and placed himself and his family as collateral against that loan, the family continued in the agricultural work in India they had done previously but which now profited the person who controlled them. The fourth woman entered this situation as a child when her parents were offered the opportunity of a 'placement', a sort of apprenticeship, for their child in the family of the person who would come to control her in Haiti.

There are proponents of specific definitions of slavery that rely on reference to mechanisms of acquisition or cultural context that would deny that these women are enslaved. And yet, there are three important points to make about these four women: (1) These are not hypothetical examples; all of these are real women, living today.[10] (2) Most would recognize the situations of each of these women as constituting slavery. (3) The path or mechanism by which they arrived at this condition is important in understanding their situation but is not relevant in the determination of whether they are slaves.

This last point is especially important. For example, in the case of the first woman some academic commentators, as well as members of local power elites, and specifically the leaders of the rebel groups illegally operating the mines of Eastern Congo and exercising control over each of the first women as slaveholders, would argue that the she is not enslaved but simply in a situation of *peonage*, a legitimate exercise of legal control over miscreants. In the case of the second woman, some commentators, and typically criminals who engage in human trafficking for commercial sexual exploitation, would argue the second woman was not in slavery because she was in a situation of debt obligation, while other commentators would argue that she was not a slave but a *sex*

10 These cases are drawn from the files of the Program Team of Free the Slaves, and from their partner organizations in Congo, India, Haiti, and the United States. The identities of these survivors are concealed in order to protect them. However, with regard to open-pit mining in the Democratic Republic of the Congo, see Free the Slaves, *The Congo Report: Slavery in Conflict Minerals,* 2011; for considerations of a case of being smuggled then forced into prostitution see *United States v. Francisco Cortes-Meza and Juan Cortes-Meza,* United States Court of Appeals (Eleventh Circuit), D.C. Docket No. 1:08-cr-00055-RWS-GGB-3. 1 February 2011; with reference to agricultural workers and collateral debt, see Krishna Prasad Upadhyaya, *Poverty, Discrimination and Slavery: The Reality of Bonded Labour in India, Nepal and Pakistan* (Anti-Slavery International) 2008; finally with regard to the placement of children in more affluent homes, see United Nations, General Assembly, Human Rights Council, *Report of the Special Rapporteur on Contemporary Forms of Slavery, including its Causes and Consequences, Gulnara Shahinian,* Addendum: Mission to Haiti, UN Doc. A/HRC/12/21/Add.1, 4 September 2009.

trafficking victim. In the case of the third woman some commentators, and typically the slave masters of India, would argue that she was not in slavery because this form of hereditary *debt bondage* is not slavery but a traditional contracting of obligated labor. And some commentators, and typically the adults in the households exploiting her labour and using her sexually, would argue that the fourth woman was not in slavery because she was in fact benefit ing from a traditional practice of *placement* that allows the poor access to alternative ladders of opportunity.

Put simply, it is illogical to name the mechanism of acquisition of a person as an essential component in defining whether a person is in slavery. Slavery is a status or condition, not the means by which a person is removed into that state or condition of control.

However, for most academics and practitioners turning to Bales' sociological definition of slavery leaves us with a dilemma: on the one hand it provides us with the nearest approximation to the lived experience of a slave today, and it serves well as a methodological tool supporting predictive validity in the social scientific study of slavery, but it is not legally binding; on the other hand, the failure, more generally to engage with the legal definition has made it redundant as an anti-slavery tool within the rule of law.

We believe that there is a way out of the dilemma; and it is here that our earlier discussion of possession comes into play. It was not realised until recently, when property lawyers sat down with slavery experts – both historians and contemporary scholars – that, not only could the 1926 definition be read in a such a manner as to be consistent with what would be considered in social scientific terms as slavery, but that such a reading was, in fact and in law, internally consistent with a reading of the legal definition.[11]

That reading turns on the understanding that possession is about control, which is very much the orthodoxy in property law. In his seminal piece, now more than fifty years old, Antony Honoré wrote that possession is "the foundation on which the whole superstructure of ownership rests."[12] Thus, when considering the legal definition and seeking to apply it to a case of contemporary slavery, one should look for the exercise of control over a person

11 The property lawyers and slavery experts were brought together as a Research Network, as a result of funding provided by the British Arts & Humanities Research Council. Research Network consists of Jean Allain, Kevin Bales, Annie Bunting, John Cairns, William M. Carter Jr, Holly Cullen, Seymour Drescher, Stanley Engerman, Paul Finkelman, Bernard Freamon, Allison Gorsuch, Richard Helmholz, Robin Hickey, Tony Honoré, Aidan McQuade, Orlando Patterson, James Penner, Joel Quirk, Jody Sarich, and Rebecca Scott.

12 A.M. Honoré, "Ownership," A.G. Guest (ed.) *Oxford Essays in Jurisprudence*, 1961, p. 113.

tantamount to possession. Possession is the *sine qua non* of slavery – it is, as in the case of illegal drugs, what judges and prosecutors should focus upon. Why? Because possession is the most important of the – in the language of definition – powers attaching to the right of ownership. This is so as the other powers do not catch the essence of slavery unless control tantamount to possession is present.

In the language of property lawyers, ownership entails a number of rights, thus there "is the right to walk about the field, to till it, to allow others to till it…, to sell it…, to give it away, …and so forth."[13] Yet, as Honoré makes plain, what underlies these rights is possession. You cannot sell a thing or profit from it to the exclusion of others unless you possess it. And possession in law ultimately turns on demonstrating control.

The same can be said about contemporary slavery. There would be no case to answer over a charge of slavery, in a case where a manager determines – within the limits of the law – what, where, and how her employees are deployed. This is so as the essential ingredient of possession is lacking. Consider the opposite now: the only manner to buy or sell a person is through effecting control tantamount to possession as a precondition. That is a banal way of saying that, in a typical case of the selling of a slave, the enslaved has been beaten, often raped, until they can no longer resist being the object of such a transaction. Slavery, after all, is not pretty; it is nasty business where control tantamount to possession is achieved through violence. In such instances, personal liberty is lost; the free will of the person has been taken away, transferred from the slave to the owner – the slaveholder. Once this is achieved, the slave can then be exploited, their labour used, their sexual autonomy disregarded, all at the whim of the person who now possess the enslaved.

We have already mentioned that in a case of slavery, once a person has established control tantamount to possession, they can manage them or sell them. These, along with possession, are three prime examples of the exercise of "the powers attaching to the right of ownership," which are central to the legal definition of slavery. Further examples of such powers are the use, profit, transfer of a person, as well as the treating of a person as though they were disposable. This reading is an important breakthrough which gives fundamental traction to the law as an anti-slavery tool. Property lawyers recognise that a proper reading of the exercise of the powers attaching to the right of ownership speaks to the contemporary understanding of what constitutes slavery in fact. Those leading property scholars and the slavery experts who first sat down

13 William Markby, *Elements of Law*, 1905, para. 307.

together in Italy and later in the United States give pay to their reading of the legal definition of slavery by developing the *Bellagio-Harvard Guidelines on the Legal Parameters of Slavery*.[14] While these Guidelines unpack the various powers attaching to the right of ownership just mentioned, they recognise fundamentally that:

> In cases of slavery, the exercise of 'the powers attaching to the right of ownership' should be understood as constituting control over a person in such a way as to significantly deprive that person of his or her individual liberty, with the intent of exploitation through the use, management, profit, transfer or disposal of that person. Usually this exercise will be supported by and obtained through means such as violent force, deception and/or coercion.

From the 1930s until recently, the general outlook towards the legal definition of slavery has been a negative one: why it is *not* applicable to cases of slavery. Spurred on by determination of the High Court of Australia, that the legal definition was applicable to contemporary cases of *de facto* slavery; a group of property scholars and experts in slavery set about unpacking those powers attaching to the right of ownership. Much to their surprise, there is no true gap existing between a legal reading of ownership and the factual circumstances of contemporary enslavement. As such, what is left to be done is to harness the latent potential of the accepted definition of slavery and simply hold people responsible for enslaving others.

The neo-abolitionist era holds out this promise, as States are in the midst of moving from having slavery on the books to dealing with slavery in the courtroom. For many countries, this is novel. With no established jurisprudence in the area and having to rely, in the main, on constitutional provisions which simply read: "No one shall be subject to slavery;" judges and prosecutors will need to seek to understand what, in law, slavery means. Inevitably they will look to the definition established in international law. In coming together and developing the *Bellagio-Harvard Guidelines on the Legal Parameters of Slavery*, we have provided an internally consistent reading of that definition within its property paradigm that fundamentally reflects the lived experience of contemporary slaves. As such, we provide the most coherent reading of the legal definition of slavery, one that gets us beyond the

14 *The Bellagio-Harvard Guidelines on the Legal Parameters of Slavery*. [Reproduced in Appendix 6 of this volume.]

dilemma of having to choose between the legal definition and a definition which reflects reality. As a result, the definition provides the type of legal certainty which is fundamental to any prosecution of contemporary slavery: within an ordinary reading of its terms, based as it is on a property paradigm, it captures the factual reality of slavery.

APPENDICES

APPENDIX 1

The Slavery Convention

Whereas the signatories of the General Act of the Brussels Conference of 1889–90 declared that they were equally animated by the firm intention of putting an end to the traffic in African slaves;

Whereas the signatories of the Convention of Saint Germain-en-Laye of 1919, to revise the General Act of Berlin of 1885, and the General Act and Declaration of Brussels of 1890, affirmed their intention of securing the complete suppression of slavery in all its forms and of the slave trade by land and sea;

Taking into consideration the report of the Temporary Slavery Commission appointed by the Council of the League of Nations on June 12th, 1924;

Desiring to complete and extend the work accomplished under the Brussels Act and to find a means of giving practical effect throughout the world to such intentions as were expressed in regard to slave trade and slavery by the signatories of the Convention of Saint Germain-en-Laye, and recognising that it is necessary to conclude to that end more detailed arrangements than are contained in that Convention;

Considering, moreover, that it is necessary to prevent forced labour from developing into conditions analogous to slavery,

Have decided to conclude a Convention and have accordingly appointed as their Plenipotentiaries:

[omitted]

Who, having communicated their full powers, have agreed as follows:

ARTICLE 1

1. Slavery is the status or condition of a person over whom any or all of the powers attaching to the right of ownership are exercised.
2. The slave trade includes all acts involved in the capture, acquisition or disposal of a person with intent to reduce him to slavery; all acts involved in the acquisition of a slave with a view to selling or exchanging him; all acts of disposal by sale

 | DOI 10.1163/9789004279896_025

or exchange of a slave acquired with a view to being sold or exchanged, and, in general, every act of trade or transport in slaves.

ARTICLE 2

The High Contracting Parties undertake, each in respect of the territories placed under its sovereignty, jurisdiction, protection, suzerainty or tutelage, so far as they have not already taken the necessary steps:

(a) To prevent and suppress the slave trade;
(b) To bring about, progressively and as soon as possible, the complete abolition of slavery in all its forms.

ARTICLE 3

The High Contracting Parties undertake to adopt all appropriate measures with a view to preventing and suppressing the embarkation, disembarkation and transport of slaves in their territorial waters and upon all vessels flying their respective flags.

The High Contracting Parties undertake to negotiate as soon as possible a general Convention with regard to the slave trade which will give them rights and impose upon them duties of the same nature as those provided for in the Convention of June 17th, 1925, relative to the International Trade in Arms (Articles 12, 20, 21, 22, 23, 24, and paragraphs 3, 4 and 5 of Section II of Annex II), with the necessary adaptations, it being understood that this general Convention will not place the ships (even of small tonnage) of any High Contracting Parties in a position different from that of the other High Contracting Parties.

It is also understood that, before or after the coming into force of this general Convention the High Contracting Parties are entirely free to conclude between themselves, without, however, derogating from the principles laid down in the preceding paragraph, such special agreements as, by reason of their peculiar situation, might appear to be suitable in order to bring about as soon as possible the complete disappearance of the slave trade.

ARTICLE 4

The High Contracting Parties shall give to one another every assistance with the object of securing the abolition of slavery and the slave trade.

ARTICLE 5

The High Contracting Parties recognise that recourse to compulsory or forced labour may have grave consequences and undertake, each in respect of the territories placed under its sovereignty, jurisdiction, protection, suzerainty or tutelage, to take all necessary measures to prevent compulsory or forced labour from developing into conditions analogous to slavery.

It is agreed that:

(1) Subject to the transitional provisions laid down in paragraph (2) below, compulsory or forced labour may only be exacted for public purposes.
(2) In territories in which compulsory or forced labour for other than public purposes still survives, the High Contracting Parties shall endeavour progressively and as soon as possible to put an end to the practice. So long as such forced or compulsory labour exists, this labour shall invariably be of an exceptional character, shall always receive adequate remuneration, and shall not involve the removal of the labourers from their usual place of residence.
(3) In all cases, the responsibility for any recourse to compulsory or forced labour shall rest with the competent central authorities of the territory concerned.

ARTICLE 6

Those of the High Contracting Parties whose laws do not at present make adequate provision for the punishment of infractions of laws and regulations enacted with a view to giving effect to the purposes of the present Convention undertake to adopt the necessary measures in order that severe penalties may be imposed in respect of such infractions.

ARTICLE 7

The High Contracting Parties undertake to communicate to each other and to the Secretary-General of the League of Nations any laws and regulations which they may enact with a view to the application of the provisions of the present Convention.

ARTICLE 8

The High Contracting Parties agree that disputes arising between them relating to the interpretation or application of this Convention shall, if they cannot be settled by direct negotiation, be referred for decision to the Permanent Court of International

Justice. In case either or both of the States Parties to such a dispute should not be parties to the Protocol of December 16th, 1920 relating to the Permanent Court of International Justice, the dispute shall be referred, at the choice of the Parties and in accordance with the constitutional procedure of each State either to the Permanent Court of International Justice or to a court of arbitration constituted in accordance with the Convention of October 18th, 1907, for the Pacific Settlement of International Disputes, or to some other court of arbitration.

ARTICLE 9

At the time of signature or of ratification or of accession, any High Contracting Party may declare that its acceptance of the present Convention does not bind some or all of the territories placed under its sovereignty, jurisdiction, protection, suzerainty or tutelage in respect of all or any provisions of the Convention; it may subsequently accede separately on behalf of any one of them or in respect of any provision to which any one of them is not a party.

ARTICLE 10

In the event of a High Contracting Party wishing to denounce the present Convention, the denunciation shall be notified in writing to the Secretary-General of the League of Nations, who will at once communicate a certified true copy of the notification to all the other High Contracting Parties, informing them of the date on which it was received.

The denunciation shall only have effect in regard to the notifying State, and one year after the notification has reached the Secretary-General of the League of Nations.

Denunciation may also be made separately in respect of any territory placed under its sovereignty, jurisdiction, protection, suzerainty or tutelage.

ARTICLE 11

The present Convention, which will bear this day's date and of which the French and English texts are both authentic, will remain open for signature by the States Members of the League of Nations until April 1st, 1927.

The Secretary-General of the League of Nations will subsequently bring the present Convention to the notice of States which have not signed it, including States which are not Members of the League of Nations, and invite them to accede thereto.

A State desiring to accede to the Convention shall notify its intention in writing to the Secretary-General of the League of Nations and transmit to him the instrument of accession, which shall be deposited in the archives of the League.

The Secretary-General shall immediately transmit to all the other High Contracting Parties a certified true copy of the notification and of the instrument of accession, informing them of the date on which he received them.

ARTICLE 12

The present Convention will be ratified and the instruments of ratification shall be deposited in the office of the Secretary-General of the League of Nations. The Secretary-General will inform all the High Contracting Parties of such deposit.

The Convention will come into operation for each State on the date of the deposit of its ratification or of its accession.

In faith whereof the Plenipotentiaries have signed the present Convention.

DONE at Geneva the twenty-fifth day of September, one thousand nine hundred and twenty-six, in one copy, which will be deposited in the archives of the League of Nations. A certified copy shall be forwarded to each signatory State.

APPENDIX 2

The Forced Labour Convention

The General Conference of the International Labour Organisation,

Having been convened at Geneva by the Governing Body of the International Labour Office, and having met in its fourteenth session on 10 June 1930, and

Having decided upon the adoption of certain proposals with regard to forced or compulsory labour, which is included in the first item on the agenda of the session, and

Having determined that these proposals shall take the form of an international Convention,

Adopts this twenty-eighth day of June of the year one thousand nine hundred and thirty the following Convention, which may be cited as the Forced Labour Convention, 1930, for ratification by the Members of the International Labour Organisation in accordance with the provisions of the Constitution of the International Labour Organisation:

ARTICLE 1

1. Each Member of the International Labour Organisation which ratifies this Convention undertakes to suppress the use of forced or compulsory labour in all its forms within the shortest possible period.
2. With a view to this complete suppression, recourse to forced or compulsory labour may be had, during the transitional period, for public purposes only and as an exceptional measure, subject to the conditions and guarantees hereinafter provided.
3. At the expiration of a period of five years after the coming into force of this Convention, and when the Governing Body of the International Labour Office prepares the report provided for in article 31 below, the said Governing Body shall consider the possibility of the suppression of forced or compulsory labour in all its forms without a further transitional period and the desirability of placing this question on the agenda of the Conference.

ARTICLE 2

1. For the purposes of this Convention the term "forced or compulsory labour" shall mean all work or service which is exacted from any person under the menace of any penalty and for which the said person has not offered himself voluntarily.

 | DOI 10.1163/9789004279896_026

2. Nevertheless, for the purposes of this Convention the term "forced or compulsory labour" shall not include:

   (a) Any work or service exacted in virtue of compulsory military service laws for work of a purely military character;
   (b) Any work or service which forms part of the normal civic obligations of the citizens of a fully self-governing country;
   (c) Any work or service exacted from any person as a consequence of a conviction in a court of law, provided that the said work or service is carried out under the supervision and control of a public authority and that the said person is not hired to or placed at the disposal of private individuals, companies or associations;
   (d) Any work or service exacted in cases of emergency, that is to say, in the event of war or of a calamity or threatened calamity, such as fire, flood, famine, earthquake, violent epidemic or epizootic diseases, invasion by animal, insect or vegetable pests, and in general any circumstance that would endanger the existence or the well-being of the whole or part of the population;
   (e) Minor communal services of a kind which, being performed by the members of the community in the direct interest of the said community, can therefore be considered as normal civic obligations incumbent upon the members of the community, provided that the members of the community or their direct representatives shall have the right to be consulted in regard to the need for such services.

ARTICLE 3

For the purposes of this Convention the term "competent authority" shall mean either an authority of the metropolitan country or the highest central authority in the territory concerned.

ARTICLE 4

1. The competent authority shall not impose or permit the imposition of forced or compulsory labour for the benefit of private individuals, companies or associations.
2. Where such forced or compulsory labour for the benefit of private individuals, companies or associations exists at the date on which a Member's ratification of this Convention is registered by the Director-General of the International Labour Office, the Member shall completely suppress such forced or compulsory labour from the date on which this Convention comes into force for that Member.

ARTICLE 5

1. No concession granted to private individuals, companies or associations shall involve any form of forced or compulsory labour for the production or the collection of products which such private individuals, companies or associations utilise or in which they trade.
2. Where concessions exist containing provisions involving such forced or compulsory labour, such provisions shall be rescinded as soon as possible, in order to comply with article 1 of this Convention.

ARTICLE 6

Officials of the administration, even when they have the duty of encouraging the populations under their charge to engage in some form of labour, shall not put constraint upon the said populations or upon any individual members thereof to work for private individuals, companies or associations.

ARTICLE 7

1. Chiefs who do not exercise administrative functions shall not have recourse to forced or compulsory labour.
2. Chiefs who exercise administrative functions may, with the express permission of the competent authority, have recourse to forced or compulsory labour, subject to the provisions of article 10 of this Convention.
3. Chiefs who are duly recognised and who do not receive adequate remuneration in other forms may have the enjoyment of personal services, subject to due regulation and provided that all necessary measures are taken to prevent abuses.

ARTICLE 8

1. The responsibility for every decision to have recourse to forced or compulsory labour shall rest with the highest civil authority in the territory concerned.
2. Nevertheless, that authority may delegate powers to the highest local authorities to exact forced or compulsory labour which does not involve the removal of the workers from their place of habitual residence. That authority may also delegate, for such periods and subject to such conditions as may be laid down in the regulations provided for in article 23 of this Convention, powers to the highest local authorities to exact forced or compulsory labour which involves the removal of the workers from their place of habitual residence for the purpose of facilitating

the movement of officials of the administration, when on duty, and for the transport of Government stores.

ARTICLE 9

Except as otherwise provided for in article 10 of this Convention, any authority competent to exact forced or compulsory labour shall, before deciding to have recourse to such labour, satisfy itself:

(a) That the work to be done or the service to be rendered is of important direct interest for the community called upon to do the work or render the service;
(b) That the work or service is of present or imminent necessity;
(c) That it has been impossible to obtain voluntary labour for carrying out the work or rendering the service by the offer of rates of wages and conditions of labour not less favourable than those prevailing in the area concerned for similar work or service; and
(d) That the work or service will not lay too heavy a burden upon the present population, having regard to the labour available and its capacity to undertake the work.

ARTICLE 10

1. Forced or compulsory labour exacted as a tax and forced or compulsory labour to which recourse is had for the execution of public works by chiefs who exercise administrative functions shall be progressively abolished.
2. Meanwhile, where forced or compulsory labour is exacted as a tax, and where recourse is had to forced or compulsory labour for the execution of public works by chiefs who exercise administrative functions, the authority concerned shall first satisfy itself:

    (a) That the work to be done or the service to be rendered is of important direct interest for the community called upon to do the work or render the service;
    (b) That the work or the service is of present or imminent necessity;
    (c) That the work or service will not lay too heavy a burden upon the present population, having regard to the labour available and its capacity to undertake the work;
    (d) That the work or service will not entail the removal of the workers from their place of habitual residence;
    (e) That the execution of the work or the rendering of the service will be directed in accordance with the exigencies of religion, social life and agriculture.

ARTICLE 11

1. Only adult able-bodied males who are of an apparent age of not less than 18 and not more than 45 years may be called upon for forced or compulsory labour. Except in respect of the kinds of labour provided for in article 10 of this Convention, the following limitations and conditions shall apply:

   (a) Whenever possible prior determination by a medical officer appointed by the administration that the persons concerned are not suffering from any infectious or contagious disease and that they are physically fit for the work required and for the conditions under which it is to be carried out;
   (b) Exemption of school teachers and pupils and of officials of the administration in general;
   (c) The maintenance in each community of the number of adult able-bodied men indispensable for family and social life;
   (d) Respect for conjugal and family ties.

2. For the purposes of subparagraph (c) of the preceding paragraph, the regulations provided for in article 23 of this Convention shall fix the proportion of the resident adult able-bodied males who may be taken at any one time for forced or compulsory labour, provided always that this proportion shall in no case exceed 25 per cent. In fixing this proportion the competent authority shall take account of the density of the population, of its social and physical development, of the seasons, and of the work which must be done by the persons concerned on their own behalf in their locality, and, generally, shall have regard to the economic and social necessities of the normal life of the community concerned.

ARTICLE 12

1. The maximum period for which any person may be taken for forced or compulsory labour of all kinds in any one period of twelve months shall not exceed sixty days, including the time spent in going to and from the place of work.
2. Every person from whom forced or compulsory labour is exacted shall be furnished with a certificate indicating the periods of such labour which he has completed.

ARTICLE 13

1. The normal working hours of any person from whom forced or compulsory labour is exacted shall be the same as those prevailing in the case of voluntary

labour, and the hours worked in excess of the normal working hours shall be remunerated at the rates prevailing in the case of overtime for voluntary labour.

2. A weekly day of rest shall be granted to all persons from whom forced or compulsory labour of any kind is exacted and this day shall coincide as far as possible with the day fixed by tradition or custom in the territories or regions concerned.

ARTICLE 14

1. With the exception of the forced or compulsory labour provided for in article 10 of this Convention, forced or compulsory labour of all kinds shall be remunerated in cash at rates not less than those prevailing for similar kinds of work either in the district in which the labour is employed or in the district from which the labour is recruited, whichever may be the higher.
2. In the case of labour to which recourse is had by chiefs in the exercise of their administrative functions, payment of wages in accordance with the provisions of the preceding paragraph shall be introduced as soon as possible.
3. The wages shall be paid to each worker individually and not to his tribal chief or to any other authority.
4. For the purpose of payment of wages the days spent in travelling to and from the place of work shall be counted as working days.
5. Nothing in this article shall prevent ordinary rations being given as a part of wages, such rations to be at least equivalent in value to the money payment they are taken to represent, but deductions from wages shall not be made either for the payment of taxes or for special food, clothing or accommodation supplied to a worker for the purpose of maintaining him in a fit condition to carry on his work under the special conditions of any employment, or for the supply of tools.

ARTICLE 15

1. Any laws or regulations relating to workmen's compensation for accidents or sickness arising out of the employment of the worker and any laws or regulations providing compensation for the dependants of deceased or incapacitated workers which are or shall be in force in the territory concerned shall be equally applicable to persons from whom forced or compulsory labour is exacted and to voluntary workers.
2. In any case it shall be an obligation on any authority employing any worker on forced or compulsory labour to ensure the subsistence of any such worker who, by accident or sickness arising out of his employment, is rendered wholly or partially incapable of providing for himself, and to take measures to ensure the

maintenance of any persons actually dependent upon such a worker in the event of his incapacity or decease arising out of his employment.

ARTICLE 16

1. Except in cases of special necessity, persons from whom forced or compulsory labour is exacted shall not be transferred to districts where the food and climate differ so considerably from those to which they have been accustomed as to endanger their health.
2. In no case shall the transfer of such workers be permitted unless all measures relating to hygiene and accommodation which are necessary to adapt such workers to the conditions and to safeguard their health can be strictly applied.
3. When such transfer cannot be avoided, measures of gradual habituation to the new conditions of diet and of climate shall be adopted on competent medical advice.
4. In cases where such workers are required to perform regular work to which they are not accustomed, measures shall be taken to ensure their habituation to it, especially as regards progressive training, the hours of work and the provision of rest intervals, and any increase or amelioration of diet which may be necessary.

ARTICLE 17

Before permitting recourse to forced or compulsory labour for works of construction or maintenance which entail the workers remaining at the workplaces for considerable periods, the competent authority shall satisfy itself:

1. That all necessary measures are taken to safeguard the health of the workers and to guarantee the necessary medical care, and, in particular,

   (a) that the workers are medically examined before commencing the work and at fixed intervals during the period of service,
   (b) that there is an adequate medical staff, provided with the dispensaries, infirmaries, hospitals and equipment necessary to meet all requirements, and
   (c) that the sanitary conditions of the workplaces, the supply of drinking water, food, fuel, and cooking ustensils, and, where necessary, of housing and clothing are satisfactory;

2. That definite arrangements are made to ensure the subsistence of the families of the workers, in particular by facilitating the remittance, by a safe method, of part of the wages to the family, at the request or with the consent of the workers;

3. That the journey of the workers to and from the workplaces are made at the expense and under the responsibility of the administration, which shall facilitate such journeys by making the fullest use of all available means of transport;
4. That, in case of illness or accident causing incapacity to work of a certain duration, the worker is repatriated at the expense of the administration;
5. That any worker who may wish to remain as a voluntary worker at the end of his period of forced or compulsory labour is permitted to do so without, for a period of two years, losing his right to repatriation free of expense to himself.

ARTICLE 18

1. Forced or compulsory labour for the transport of persons or goods, such as the labour of porters or boatmen, shall be abolished within the shortest possible period. Meanwhile the competent authority shall promulgate regulations determining, inter alia,

   (a) that such labour shall only be employed for the purpose of facilitating the movement of officials of the administration, when on duty, or for the transport of Government stores, or, in cases of very urgent necessity, the transport of persons other than officials,
   (b) that the workers so employed shall be medically certified to be physically fit, where medical examination is possible, and that where such medical examination is not practicable the person employing such workers shall be held responsible for ensuring that they are physically fit and not suffering from any infectious or contagious diseases,
   (c) the maximum load which these workers may carry,
   (d) the maximum distance from their homes to which they may be taken,
   (e) the maximum number of days per month or other period for which they may be taken, including the days spent in returning to their homes, and
   (f) the persons entitled to demand this form of forced or compulsory labour and the extent to which they are entitled to demand it.

2. In fixing the maxima referred to under (c), (d) and (e) in the foregoing paragraph, the competent authority shall have regard to all relevant factors, including the physical development of the population from which the workers are recruited, the nature of the country through which they must travel and the climatic conditions.
3. The competent authority shall further provide that the normal daily journey of such workers shall not exceed a distance corresponding to an average working day of eight hours, it being understood that account shall be taken not only of the weight to be carried and the distance to be covered, but also of the nature of the road, the season and all other relevant factors, and that, where hours of journey

in excess of the normal daily journey are exacted, they shall be remunerated at rates higher than the normal rates.

ARTICLE 19

1. The competent authority shall only authorise recourse to compulsory cultivation as a method of precaution against famine or a deficiency of food supplies and always under the condition that the food or produce shall remain the property of the individuals or the community producing it.
2. Nothing in this article shall be construed as abrogating the obligation on members of a community, where production is organised on a communal basis by virtue of law or custom and where the procedure or any profit accruing from the sale thereof remain the property of the community, to perform the work demanded by the community by virtue of law or custom.

ARTICLE 20

Collective punishment laws under which a community may be punished for crimes committed by any of its members shall not contain provisions for forced or compulsory labour by the community as one of the methods of punishment.

ARTICLE 21

Forced or compulsory labour shall not be used for work underground in mines.

ARTICLE 22

The annual reports that Members which ratify this Convention agree to make to the International Labour Office, pursuant to the provisions of article 22 of the Constitution of the International Labour Organisation, on the measures they have taken to give effect to the provisions of this Convention, shall contain as full information as possible, in respect of each territory concerned, regarding the extent to which recourse has been had to forced or compulsory labour in that territory, the purposes for which it has been employed, the sickness and death rates, hours of work, methods of payment of wages and rates of wages, and any other relevant information.

ARTICLE 23

1. To give effect to the provisions of this Convention the competent authority shall issue complete and precise regulations governing the use of forced or compulsory labour.

2. These regulations shall contain, inter alia, rules permitting any person from whom forced or compulsory labour is exacted to forward all complaints relative to the conditions of labour to the authorities and ensuring that such complaints will be examined and taken into consideration.

ARTICLE 24

Adequate measures shall in all cases be taken to ensure that the regulations governing the employment of forced or compulsory labour are strictly applied, either by extending the duties of any existing labour inspectorate which has been established for the inspection of voluntary labour to cover the inspection of forced or compulsory labour or in some other appropriate manner. Measures shall also be taken to ensure that the regulations are brought to the knowledge of persons from whom such labour is exacted.

ARTICLE 25

The illegal exaction of forced or compulsory labour shall be punishable as a penal offence, and it shall be an obligation on any Member ratifying this Convention to ensure that the penalties imposed by law are really adequate and are strictly enforced.

ARTICLE 26

1. Each Member of the International Labour Organisation which ratifies this Convention undertakes to apply it to the territories placed under its sovereignty, jurisdiction, protection, suzerainty, tutelage or authority, so far as it has the right to accept obligations affecting matters of internal jurisdiction; provided that, if such Member may desire to take advantage of the provisions of article 35 of the Constitution of the International Labour Organisation, it shall append to its ratification a declaration stating:

    (1) The territories to which it intends to apply the provisions of this Convention without modification;
    (2) The territories to which it intends to apply the provisions of this Convention with modifications, together with details of the said modifications;
    (3) The territories in respect of which it reserves its decision.

2. The aforesaid declaration shall be deemed to be an integral part of the ratification and shall have the force of ratification. It shall be open to any Member, by a subsequent declaration, to cancel in whole or in part the reservations made, in

pursuance of the provisions of subparagraphs (2) and (3) of this article, in the original declaration.

ARTICLE 27

The formal ratifications of this Convention under the conditions set forth in the Constitution of the International Labour Organisation shall be communicated to the Director-General of the International Labour Office for registration.

ARTICLE 28

1. This Convention shall be binding only upon those Members whose ratifications have been registered with the International Labour Office.
2. It shall come into force twelve months after the date on which the ratifications of two Members of the International Labour Organisation have been registered with the Director-General.
3. Thereafter, this Convention shall come into force for any Member twelve months after the date on which the ratification has been registered.

ARTICLE 29

As soon as the ratifications of two Members of the International Labour Organisation have been registered with the International Labour Office, the Director-General of the International Labour Office shall so notify all the Members of the International Labour Organisation. He shall likewise notify them of the registration of ratifications which may be communicated subsequently by other Members of the Organisation.

ARTICLE 30

1. A Member which has ratified this Convention may denounce it after the expiration of ten years from the date on which the Convention first comes into force, by an act communicated to the Director-General of the International Labour Office for registration. Such denunciation shall not take effect until one year after the date on which it is registered with the International Labour Office.
2. Each Member which has ratified this Convention and which does not, within the year following the expiration of the period of ten years mentioned in the preceding paragraph, exercise the right of denunciation provided for in this article, will be bound for another period of five years and, thereafter, may denounce this Convention at the expiration of each period of five years under the terms provided for in this article.

ARTICLE 31

At the expiration of each period of five years after the coming into force of this Convention, the Governing Body of the International Labour Office shall present to the General Conference a report on the working of this Convention and shall consider the desirability of placing on the agenda of the Conference the question of its revision in whole or in part.

ARTICLE 32

1. Should the Conference adopt a new Convention revising this Convention in whole or in part, the ratification by a Member of the new revising Convention shall ipso jure involve denunciation of this Convention without any requirement of delay, notwithstanding the provisions of article 30 above, if and when the new revising Convention shall have come into force.
2. As from the date of the coming into force of the new revising Convention, the present Convention shall cease to be open to ratification by the Members.
3. Nevertheless, this Convention shall remain in force in its actual form and content for those Members which have ratified it but have not ratified the revising Convention.

ARTICLE 33

The French and English texts of this Convention shall both be authentic.

APPENDIX 3

The Supplementary Convention on the Abolition of Slavery, the Slave Trade, and Institutions and Practices Similar to Slavery

PREAMBLE

The States Parties to the present Convention,

Considering that freedom is the birthright of every human being;

Mindful that the peoples of the United Nations reaffirmed in the Charter their faith in the dignity and worth of the human person;

Considering that the Universal Declaration of Human Rights, proclaimed by the General Assembly of the United Nations as a common standard of achievement for all peoples and all nations, states that no one shall be held in slavery or servitude and that slavery and the slave trade shall be prohibited in all their forms;

Recognizing that, since the conclusion of the Slavery Convention signed at Geneva on 25 September 1926, which was designed to secure the abolition of slavery and of the slave trade, further progress has been made towards this end;

Having regard to the Forced Labour Convention of 1930 and to subsequent action by the International Labour Organisation in regard to forced or compulsory labour;

Being aware, however, that slavery, the slave trade and institutions and practices similar to slavery have not yet been eliminated in all parts of the world;

Having decided, therefore, that the Convention of 1926, which remains operative, should now be augmented by the conclusion of a supplementary convention designed to intensify national as well as international efforts towards the abolition of slavery, the slave trade and institutions and practices similar to slavery;

 | DOI 10.1163/9789004279896_027

Have agreed as follows:

SECTION I

INSTITUTIONS AND PRACTICES SIMILAR TO SLAVERY

ARTICLE 1

Each of the States Parties to this Convention shall take all practicable and necessary legislative and other measures to bring about progressively and as soon as possible the complete abolition or abandonment of the following institutions and practices, where they still exist and whether or not they are covered by the definition of slavery contained in article 1 of the Slavery Convention signed at Geneva on 25 September 1926:

(a) Debt bondage, that is to say, the status or condition arising from a pledge by a debtor of his personal services or of those of a person under his control as security for a debt, if the value of those services as reasonably assessed is not applied towards the liquidation of the debt or the length and nature of those services are not respectively limited and defined;

(b) Serfdom, that is to say, the condition or status of a tenant who is by law, custom or agreement bound to live and labour on land belonging to another person and to render some determinate service to such other person, whether for reward or not, and is not free to change his status;

(c) Any institution or practice whereby:

  (i) A woman, without the right to refuse, is promised or given in marriage on payment of a consideration in money or in kind to her parents, guardian, family or any other person or group; or

  (ii) The husband of a woman, his family, or his clan, has the right to transfer her to another person for value received or otherwise; or

  (iii) A woman on the death of her husband is liable to be inherited by another person;

(d) Any institution or practice whereby a child or young person under the age of 18 years is delivered by either or both of his natural parents or by his guardian to another person, whether for reward or not, with a view to the exploitation of the child or young person or of his labour.

ARTICLE 2

With a view to bringing to an end the institutions and practices mentioned in article 1 (c) of this Convention, the States Parties undertake to prescribe, where appropriate, suitable minimum ages of marriage, to encourage the use of facilities whereby the consent of both parties to a marriage may be freely expressed in the presence of a competent civil or religious authority, and to encourage the registration of marriages.

SECTION II

THE SLAVE TRADE

ARTICLE 3

1. The act of conveying or attempting to convey slaves from one country to another by whatever means of transport, or of being accessory thereto, shall be a criminal offence under the laws of the States Parties to this Convention and persons convicted thereof shall be liable to very severe penalties.
2. (a) The States Parties shall take all effective measures to prevent ships and aircraft authorized to fly their flags from conveying slaves and to punish persons guilty of such acts or of using national flags for that purpose.
   (b) The States Parties shall take all effective measures to ensure that their ports, airfields and coasts are not used for the conveyance of slaves.
3. The States Parties to this Convention shall exchange information in order to ensure the practical co-ordination of the measures taken by them in combating the slave trade and shall inform each other of every case of the slave trade, and of every attempt to commit this criminal offence, which comes to their notice.

ARTICLE 4

Any slave who takes refuge on board any vessel of a State Party to this Convention shall *ipso facto* be free.

SECTION III

SLAVERY AND INSTITUTIONS AND PRACTICES SIMILAR TO SLAVERY

ARTICLE 5

In a country where the abolition or abandonment of slavery, or of the institutions or practices mentioned in article 1 of this Convention, is not yet complete, the act of mutilating, branding or otherwise marking a slave or a person of servile status in order to indicate his status, or as a punishment, or for any other reason, or of being accessory thereto, shall be a criminal offence under the laws of the States Parties to this Convention and persons convicted thereof shall be liable to punishment.

ARTICLE 6

1. The act of enslaving another person or of inducing another person to give himself or a person dependent upon him into slavery, or of attempting these acts, or being accessory thereto, or being a party to a conspiracy to accomplish any such acts, shall be a criminal offence under the laws of the States Parties to this Convention and persons convicted thereof shall be liable to punishment.
2. Subject to the provisions of the introductory paragraph of article 1 of this Convention, the provisions of paragraph 1 of the present article shall also apply to the act of inducing another person to place himself or a person dependent upon him into the servile status resulting from any of the institutions or practices mentioned in article 1, to any attempt to perform such acts, to bring accessory thereto, and to being a party to a conspiracy to accomplish any such acts.

SECTION IV

DEFINITIONS

ARTICLE 7

For the purposes of the present Convention:

(a) "Slavery" means, as defined in the Slavery Convention of 1926, the status or condition of a person over whom any or all of the powers attaching to the right of ownership are exercised, and "slave" means a person in such condition or status;
(b) "A person of servile status" means a person in the condition or status resulting from any of the institutions or practices mentioned in article 1 of this Convention;
(c) "Slave trade" means and includes all acts involved in the capture, acquisition or disposal of a person with intent to reduce him to slavery; all acts involved in the acquisition of a slave with a view to selling or exchanging him; all acts of disposal by sale of exchange of a person acquired with a view to being sold or exchanged; and, in general, every act of trade or transport in slaves by whatever means of conveyance.

SECTION V

CO-OPERATION BETWEEN STATES PARTIES AND COMMUNICATION OF INFORMATION

ARTICLE 8

1. The States Parties to this Convention undertake to co-operate with each other and with the United Nations to give effect to the foregoing provisions.
2. The Parties undertake to communicate to the Secretary-General of the United Nations copies of any laws, regulations and administrative measures enacted or put into effect to implement the provisions of this Convention.
3. The Secretary-General shall communicate the information received under paragraph 2 of this article to the other Parties and to the Economic and Social Council as part of the documentation for any discussion which the Council might undertake with a view to making further recommendations for the abolition of slavery, the slave trade or the institutions and practices which are the subject of this Convention.

SECTION VI

FINAL CLAUSES

ARTICLE 9

No reservations may be made to this Convention.

ARTICLE 10

Any dispute between States Parties to this Convention relating to its interpretation or application, which is not settled by negotiation, shall be referred to the International Court of Justice at the request of any one of the parties to the dispute, unless the parties concerned agree on another mode of settlement.

ARTICLE 11

1. This Convention shall be open until 1 July 1957 for signature by any State Member of the United Nations or of a specialized agency. It shall be subject to ratification by the signatory States, and the instruments of ratification shall be deposited

with the Secretary-General of the United Nations, who shall inform each signatory and acceding State.

2. After 1 July 1957 this Convention shall be open for accession by any State Member of the United Nations or of a specialized agency, or by any other State to which an invitation to accede has been addressed by the General Assembly of the United Nations. Accession shall be effected by the deposit of a formal instrument with the Secretary-General of the United Nations, who shall inform each signatory and acceding State.

ARTICLE 12

1. This Convention shall apply to all non self-governing, trust, colonial and other non-metropolitan territories for the international relations of which any State Party is responsible; the Party concerned shall, subject to the provisions of paragraph 2 of this article, at the time of signature, ratification or accession declare the non-metropolitan territory or territories to which the Convention shall apply *ipso facto* as a result of such signature, ratification or accession.
2. In any case in which the previous consent of a non-metropolitan territory is required by the constitutional laws or practices of the Party or of the non-metropolitan territory, the Party concerned shall endeavour to secure the needed consent of the non-metropolitan territory within the period of twelve months from the date of signature of the Convention by the metropolitan State, and when such consent has been obtained the Party shall notify the Secretary-General. This Convention shall apply to the territory or territories named in such notification from the date of its receipt by the Secretary-General.
3. After the expiry of the twelve-month period mentioned in the preceding paragraph, the States Parties concerned shall inform the Secretary-General of the results of the consultations with those non-metropolitan territories for whose international relations they are responsible and whose consent to the application of this Convention may have been withheld.

ARTICLE 13

1. This Convention shall enter into force on the date on which two States have become Parties thereto.
2. It shall thereafter enter into force with respect to each State and territory on the date of deposit of the instrument of ratification or accession of that State or notification of application to that territory.

ARTICLE 14

1. The application of this Convention shall be divided into successive periods of three years, of which the first shall begin on the date of entry into force of the Convention in accordance with paragraph I of article 13.
2. Any State Party may denounce this Convention by a notice addressed by that State to the Secretary-General not less than six months before the expiration of the current three-year period. The Secretary-General shall notify all other Parties of each such notice and the date of the receipt thereof.
3. Denunciations shall take effect at the expiration of the current three-year period.
4. In cases where, in accordance with the provisions of article 12, this Convention has become applicable to a non-metropolitan territory of a Party, that Party may at any time thereafter, with the consent of the territory concerned, give notice to the Secretary-General of the United Nations denouncing this Convention separately in respect of that territory. The denunciation shall take effect one year after the date of the receipt of such notice by the Secretary-General, who shall notify all other Parties of such notice and the date of the receipt thereof.

ARTICLE 15

This Convention, of which the Chinese, English, French, Russian and Spanish texts are equally authentic, shall be deposited in the archives of the United Nations Secretariat. The Secretary-General shall prepare a certified copy thereof for communication to States Parties to this Convention, as well as to all other States Members of the United Nations and of the specialized agencies.

IN WITNESS WHEREOF the undersigned, being duly authorized thereto by their respective Governments, have signed this Convention on the date appearing opposite their respective signatures.

DONE at the European Office of the United Nations at Geneva, this seventh day of September one thousand nine hundred and fifty-six.

APPENDIX 4

The Abolition of Forced Labour Convention

The General Conference of the International Labour Organisation,

Having been convened at Geneva by the Governing Body of the International Labour Office, and having met in its fortieth session on 5 June 1957, and

Having considered the question of forced labour, which is the fourth item on the agenda of the session, and

Having noted the provisions of the Forced Labour Convention, 1930, and

Having noted that the Slavery Convention, 1926, provides that all necessary measures shall be taken to prevent compulsory or forced labour from developing into conditions analogous to slavery and that the Supplementary Convention on the Abolition of Slavery, the Slave Trade, and Institutions and Practices Similar to Slavery, 1956, provides for the complete abolition of debt bondage and serfdom, and

Having noted that the Protection of Wages Convention, 1949, provides that wages shall be paid regularly and prohibits methods of payment which deprive the worker of a genuine possibility of terminating his employment, and

Having decided upon the adoption of further proposals with regard to the abolition of certain forms of forced or compulsory labour constituting a violation of the rights of man referred to in the Charter of the United Nations and enunciated by the Universal Declaration of Human Rights, and

Having determined that these proposals shall take the form of an international Convention,

Adopts this twenty-fifth day of June of the year one thousand nine hundred and fifty-seven the following Convention, which may be cited as the Abolition of Forced Labour Convention, 1957:

ARTICLE 1

Each Member of the International Labour Organisation which ratifies this Convention undertakes to suppress and not to make use of any form of forced or compulsory labour:

 | DOI 10.1163/9789004279896_028

(a) As a means of political coercion or education or as a punishment for holding or expressing political views or views ideologically opposed to the established political, social or economic system;
(b) As a method of mobilising and using labour for purposes of economic development;
(c) As a means of labour discipline;
(d) As a punishment for having participated in strikes;
(e) As a means of racial, social, national or religious discrimination.

ARTICLE 2

Each Member of the International Labour Organisation which ratifies this Convention undertakes to take effective measures to secure the immediate and complete abolition of forced or compulsory labour as specified in article 1 of this Convention.

ARTICLE 3

The formal ratifications of this Convention shall be communicated to the Director-General of the International Labour Office for registration.

ARTICLE 4

1. This Convention shall be binding only upon those Members of the International Labour Organisation whose ratifications have been registered with the Director-General.
2. It shall come into force twelve months after the date on which the ratifications of two Members have been registered with the Director-General.
3. Thereafter, this Convention shall come into force for any Member twelve months after the date on which its ratification has been registered.

ARTICLE 5

1. A Member which has ratified this Convention may denounce it after the expiration of ten years from the date on which the Convention first comes into force, by an act communicated to the Director-General of the International Labour Office for registration. Such denunciation shall not take effect until one year after the date on which it is registered.
2. Each Member which has ratified this Convention and which does not, within the year following the expiration of the period of ten years mentioned in the preceding paragraph, exercise the right of denunciation provided for in this

article, will be bound for another period of five years and, thereafter, may denounce this Convention at the expiration of each period of five years under the terms provided for in this article.

ARTICLE 6

1. The Director-General of the International Labour Office shall notify all Members of the International Labour Organisation of the registration of all ratifications and denunciations communicated to him by the Members of the Organisation.
2. When notifying the Members of the Organisation of the registration of the second ratification communicated to him the Director-General shall draw the attention of the Members of the Organisation to the date upon which the Convention will come into force.

ARTICLE 7

The Director-General of the International Labour Office shall communicate to the Secretary-General of the United Nations for registration in accordance with Article 102 of the Charter of the United Nations full particulars of all ratifications and acts of denunciation registered by him in accordance with the provisions of the preceding articles.

ARTICLE 8

At such times as it may consider necessary the Governing Body of the International Labour Office shall present to the General Conference a report on the working of the Convention and shall examine the desirability of placing on the agenda of the Conference the question of its revision in whole or in part.

ARTICLE 9

1. Should the Conference adopt a new Convention revising this Convention in whole or in part, then, unless the new Convention otherwise provides:

    (a) The ratification by a Member of the new revising Convention shall ipso jure involve the immediate denunciation of this Convention, notwithstanding the provisions of article 5 above, if and when the new revising Convention shall have come into force;
    (b) As from the date when the new revising Convention comes into force this Convention shall cease to be open to ratification by the Members.

2. This Convention shall in any case remain in force in its actual form and content for those Members which have ratified it but have not ratified the revising Convention.

ARTICLE 10

The English and French versions of the text of this Convention are equally authoritative.

The foregoing is the authentic text of the Convention duly adopted by the General Conference of the International Labour Organisation during its fortieth session which was held at Geneva and declared closed the twenty-seventh day of June 1957.

In faith whereof we have appended our signatures this fourth day of July 1957.

APPENDIX 5

2000 Protocol to Prevent, Suppress and Punish Trafficking in Persons, Especially Women and Children, Supplementing the United Nations Convention against Transnational Organized Crime

Preamble

The States Parties to this Protocol,

Declaring that effective action to prevent and combat trafficking in persons, especially women and children, requires a comprehensive international approach in the countries of origin, transit and destination that includes measures to prevent such trafficking, to punish the traffickers and to protect the victims of such trafficking, including by protecting their internationally recognized human rights,

Taking into account the fact that, despite the existence of a variety of international instruments containing rules and practical measures to combat the exploitation of persons, especially women and children, there is no universal instrument that addresses all aspects of trafficking in persons,

Concerned that, in the absence of such an instrument, persons who are vulnerable to trafficking will not be sufficiently protected,

Recalling General Assembly resolution 53/111 of 9 December 1998, in which the Assembly decided to establish an open-ended intergovernmental ad hoc committee for the purpose of elaborating a comprehensive international convention against transnational organized crime and of discussing the elaboration of, inter alia, an international instrument addressing trafficking in women and children,

Convinced that supplementing the United Nations Convention against Transnational Organized Crime with an international instrument for the prevention, suppression and punishment of trafficking in persons, especially women and children, will be useful in preventing and combating that crime,

 | DOI 10.1163/9789004279896_029

Have agreed as follows:

I. GENERAL PROVISIONS

ARTICLE 1

Relation with the United Nations Convention against Transnational Organized Crime

1. This Protocol supplements the United Nations Convention against Transnational Organized Crime. It shall be interpreted together with the Convention.
2. The provisions of the Convention shall apply, mutatis mutandis, to this Protocol unless otherwise provided herein.
3. The offences established in accordance with article 5 of this Protocol shall be regarded as offences established in accordance with the Convention.

ARTICLE 2

Statement of purpose

The purposes of this Protocol are:

(a) To prevent and combat trafficking in persons, paying particular attention to women and children;
(b) To protect and assist the victims of such trafficking, with full respect for their human rights; and
(c) To promote cooperation among States Parties in order to meet those objectives.

ARTICLE 3

Use of terms

For the purposes of this Protocol:

(a) "Trafficking in persons" shall mean the recruitment, transportation, transfer, harbouring or receipt of persons, by means of the threat or use of force or other forms of coercion, of abduction, of fraud, of deception, of the abuse of power or of a position of vulnerability or of the giving or receiving of payments or benefits to achieve the consent of a person having control over another person, for the purpose of exploitation. Exploitation shall include, at a minimum, the exploitation of the prostitution of others or other forms of sexual exploitation, forced labour or services, slavery or practices similar to slavery, servitude or the removal of organs;

(b) The consent of a victim of trafficking in persons to the intended exploitation set forth in subparagraph (a) of this article shall be irrelevant where any of the means set forth in subparagraph (a) have been used;

(c) The recruitment, transportation, transfer, harbouring or receipt of a child for the purpose of exploitation shall be considered "trafficking in persons" even if this does not involve any of the means set forth in subparagraph (a) of this article;

(d) "Child" shall mean any person under eighteen years of age.

ARTICLE 4

Scope of application

This Protocol shall apply, except as otherwise stated herein, to the prevention, investigation and prosecution of the offences established in accordance with article 5 of this Protocol, where those offences are transnational in nature and involve an organized criminal group, as well as to the protection of victims of such offences.

ARTICLE 5

Criminalization

1. Each State Party shall adopt such legislative and other measures as may be necessary to establish as criminal offences the conduct set forth in article 3 of this Protocol, when committed intentionally.

2. Each State Party shall also adopt such legislative and other measures as may be necessary to establish as criminal offences:

   (a) Subject to the basic concepts of its legal system, attempting to commit an offence established in accordance with paragraph 1 of this article;

   (b) Participating as an accomplice in an offence established in accordance with paragraph 1 of this article; and

   (c) Organizing or directing other persons to commit an offence established in accordance with paragraph 1 of this article.

II. PROTECTION OF VICTIMS OF TRAFFICKING IN PERSONS

ARTICLE 6

Assistance to and protection of victims of trafficking in persons

1. In appropriate cases and to the extent possible under its domestic law, each State Party shall protect the privacy and identity of victims of trafficking in persons, including, inter alia, by making legal proceedings relating to such trafficking confidential.
2. Each State Party shall ensure that its domestic legal or administrative system contains measures that provide to victims of trafficking in persons, in appropriate cases:

    (a) Information on relevant court and administrative proceedings;
    (b) Assistance to enable their views and concerns to be presented and considered at appropriate stages of criminal proceedings against offenders, in a manner not prejudicial to the rights of the defence.

3. Each State Party shall consider implementing measures to provide for the physical, psychological and social recovery of victims of trafficking in persons, including, in appropriate cases, in cooperation with non-governmental organizations, other relevant organizations and other elements of civil society, and, in particular, the provision of:

    (a) Appropriate housing;
    (b) Counselling and information, in particular as regards their legal rights, in a language that the victims of trafficking in persons can understand;
    (c) Medical, psychological and material assistance; and
    (d) Employment, educational and training opportunities.

4. Each State Party shall take into account, in applying the provisions of this article, the age, gender and special needs of victims of trafficking in persons, in particular the special needs of children, including appropriate housing, education and care.
5. Each State Party shall endeavour to provide for the physical safety of victims of trafficking in persons while they are within its territory.
6. Each State Party shall ensure that its domestic legal system contains measures that offer victims of trafficking in persons the possibility of obtaining compensation for damage suffered.

ARTICLE 7

Status of victims of trafficking in persons in receiving States

1. In addition to taking measures pursuant to article 6 of this Protocol, each State Party shall consider adopting legislative or other appropriate measures that permit victims of trafficking in persons to remain in its territory, temporarily or permanently, in appropriate cases.
2. In implementing the provision contained in paragraph 1 of this article, each State Party shall give appropriate consideration to humanitarian and compassionate factors.

ARTICLE 8

Repatriation of victims of trafficking in persons

1. The State Party of which a victim of trafficking in persons is a national or in which the person had the right of permanent residence at the time of entry into the territory of the receiving State Party shall facilitate and accept, with due regard for the safety of that person, the return of that person without undue or unreasonable delay.
2. When a State Party returns a victim of trafficking in persons to a State Party of which that person is a national or in which he or she had, at the time of entry into the territory of the receiving State Party, the right of permanent residence, such return shall be with due regard for the safety of that person and for the status of any legal proceedings related to the fact that the person is a victim of trafficking and shall preferably be voluntary.
3. At the request of a receiving State Party, a requested State Party shall, without undue or unreasonable delay, verify whether a person who is a victim of trafficking in persons is its national or had the right of permanent residence in its territory at the time of entry into the territory of the receiving State Party.
4. In order to facilitate the return of a victim of trafficking in persons who is without proper documentation, the State Party of which that person is a national or in which he or she had the right of permanent residence at the time of entry into the territory of the receiving State Party shall agree to issue, at the request of the receiving State Party, such travel documents or other authorization as may be necessary to enable the person to travel to and re-enter its territory.
5. This article shall be without prejudice to any right afforded to victims of trafficking in persons by any domestic law of the receiving State Party.

6. This article shall be without prejudice to any applicable bilateral or multilateral agreement or arrangement that governs, in whole or in part, the return of victims of trafficking in persons.

III. PREVENTION, COOPERATION AND OTHER MEASURES

ARTICLE 9

Prevention of trafficking in persons

1. States Parties shall establish comprehensive policies, programmes and other measures:

   (a) To prevent and combat trafficking in persons; and
   (b) To protect victims of trafficking in persons, especially women and children, from revictimization.

2. States Parties shall endeavour to undertake measures such as research, information and mass media campaigns and social and economic initiatives to prevent and combat trafficking in persons.
3. Policies, programmes and other measures established in accordance with this article shall, as appropriate, include cooperation with non-governmental organizations, other relevant organizations and other elements of civil society.
4. States Parties shall take or strengthen measures, including through bilateral or multilateral cooperation, to alleviate the factors that make persons, especially women and children, vulnerable to trafficking, such as poverty, underdevelopment and lack of equal opportunity.
5. States Parties shall adopt or strengthen legislative or other measures, such as educational, social or cultural measures, including through bilateral and multilateral cooperation, to discourage the demand that fosters all forms of exploitation of persons, especially women and children, that leads to trafficking.

ARTICLE 10

Information exchange and training

1. Law enforcement, immigration or other relevant authorities of States Parties shall, as appropriate, cooperate with one another by exchanging information, in accordance with their domestic law, to enable them to determine:

(a) Whether individuals crossing or attempting to cross an international border with travel documents belonging to other persons or without travel documents are perpetrators or victims of trafficking in persons;
(b) The types of travel document that individuals have used or attempted to use to cross an international border for the purpose of trafficking in persons; and
(c) The means and methods used by organized criminal groups for the purpose of trafficking in persons, including the recruitment and transportation of victims, routes and links between and among individuals and groups engaged in such rafficking, and possible measures for detecting them.

2. States Parties shall provide or strengthen training for law enforcement, immigration and other relevant officials in the prevention of trafficking in persons. The training should focus on methods used in preventing such trafficking, prosecuting the traffickers and protecting the rights of the victims, including protecting the victims from the traffickers. The training should also take into account the need to consider human rights and child- and gender-sensitive issues and it should encourage cooperation with non-governmental organizations, other relevant organizations and other elements of civil society.
3. A State Party that receives information shall comply with any request by the State Party that transmitted the information that places restrictions on its use.

ARTICLE 11

Border measures

1. Without prejudice to international commitments in relation to the free movement of people, States Parties shall strengthen, to the extent possible, such border controls as may be necessary to prevent and detect trafficking in persons.
2. Each State Party shall adopt legislative or other appropriate measures to prevent, to the extent possible, means of transport operated by commercial carriers from being used in the commission of offences established in accordance with article 5 of this Protocol.
3. Where appropriate, and without prejudice to applicable international conventions, such measures shall include establishing the obligation of commercial carriers, including any transportation company or the owner or operator of any means of transport, to ascertain that all passengers are in possession of the travel documents required for entry into the receiving State.

4. Each State Party shall take the necessary measures, in accordance with its domestic law, to provide for sanctions in cases of violation of the obligation set forth in paragraph 3 of this article.
5. Each State Party shall consider taking measures that permit, in accordance with its domestic law, the denial of entry or revocation of visas of persons implicated in the commission of offences established in accordance with this Protocol.
6. Without prejudice to article 27 of the Convention, States Parties shall consider strengthening cooperation among border control agencies by, inter alia, establishing and maintaining direct channels of communication.

ARTICLE 12

Security and control of documents

Each State Party shall take such measures as may be necessary, within available means:

(a) To ensure that travel or identity documents issued by it are of such quality that they cannot easily be misused and cannot readily be falsified or unlawfully altered, replicated or issued; and
(b) To ensure the integrity and security of travel or identity documents issued by or on behalf of the State Party and to prevent their unlawful creation, issuance and use.

ARTICLE 13

Legitimacy and validity of documents

At the request of another State Party, a State Party shall, in accordance with its domestic law, verify within a reasonable time the legitimacy and validity of travel or identity documents issued or purported to have been issued in its name and suspected of being used for trafficking in persons.

IV. FINAL PROVISIONS

ARTICLE 14

Saving clause

1. Nothing in this Protocol shall affect the rights, obligations and responsibilities of States and individuals under international law, including international

humanitarian law and international human rights law and, in particular, where applicable, the 1951 Convention and the 1967 Protocol relating to the Status of Refugees and the principle of non-refoulement as contained therein.

2. The measures set forth in this Protocol shall be interpreted and applied in a way that is not discriminatory to persons on the ground that they are victims of trafficking in persons. The interpretation and application of those measures shall be consistent with internationally recognized principles of non-discrimination.

ARTICLE 15

Settlement of disputes

1. States Parties shall endeavour to settle disputes concerning the interpretation or application of this Protocol through negotiation.
2. Any dispute between two or more States Parties concerning the interpretation or application of this Protocol that cannot be settled through negotiation within a reasonable time shall, at the request of one of those States Parties, be submitted to arbitration. If, six months after the date of the request for arbitration, those States Parties are unable to agree on the organization of the arbitration, any one of those States Parties may refer the dispute to the International Court of Justice by request in accordance with the Statute of the Court.
3. Each State Party may, at the time of signature, ratification, acceptance or approval of or accession to this Protocol, declare that it does not consider itself bound by paragraph 2 of this article. The other States Parties shall not be bound by paragraph 2 of this article with respect to any State Party that has made such a reservation.
4. Any State Party that has made a reservation in accordance with paragraph 3 of this article may at any time withdraw that reservation by notification to the Secretary-General of the United Nations.

ARTICLE 16

Signature, ratification, acceptance, approval and accession

1. This Protocol shall be open to all States for signature from 12 to 15 December 2000 in Palermo, Italy, and thereafter at United Nations Headquarters in New York until 12 December 2002.
2. This Protocol shall also be open for signature by regional economic integration organizations provided that at least one member State of such organization has signed this Protocol in accordance with paragraph 1 of this article.

3. This Protocol is subject to ratification, acceptance or approval. Instruments of ratification, acceptance or approval shall be deposited with the Secretary-General of the United Nations. A regional economic integration organization may deposit its instrument of ratification, acceptance or approval if at least one of its member States has done likewise. In that instrument of ratification, acceptance or approval, such organization shall declare the extent of its competence with respect to the matters governed by this Protocol. Such organization shall also inform the depositary of any relevant modification in the extent of its competence.
4. This Protocol is open for accession by any State or any regional economic integration organization of which at least one member State is a Party to this Protocol. Instruments of accession shall be deposited with the Secretary-General of the United Nations. At the time of its accession, a regional economic integration organization shall declare the extent of its competence with respect to matters governed by this Protocol. Such organization shall also inform the depositary of any relevant modification in the extent of its competence.

ARTICLE 17

Entry into force

1. This Protocol shall enter into force on the ninetieth day after the date of deposit of the fortieth instrument of ratification, acceptance, approval or accession, except that it shall not enter into force before the entry into force of the Convention. For the purpose of this paragraph, any instrument deposited by a regional economic integration organization shall not be counted as additional to those deposited by member States of such organization.
2. For each State or regional economic integration organization ratifying, accepting, approving or acceding to this Protocol after the deposit of the fortieth instrument of such action, this Protocol shall enter into force on the thirtieth day after the date of deposit by such State or organization of the relevant instrument or on the date this Protocol enters into force pursuant to paragraph 1 of this article, whichever is the later.

ARTICLE 18

Amendment

1. After the expiry of five years from the entry into force of this Protocol, a State Party to the Protocol may propose an amendment and file it with the Secretary-General of the United Nations, who shall thereupon communicate the proposed

amendment to the States Parties and to the Conference of the Parties to the Convention for the purpose of considering and deciding on the proposal. The States Parties to this Protocol meeting at the Conference of the Parties shall make every effort to achieve consensus on each amendment. If all efforts at consensus have been exhausted and no agreement has been reached, the amendment shall, as a last resort, require for its adoption a two-thirds majority vote of the States Parties to this Protocol present and voting at the meeting of the Conference of the Parties.

2. Regional economic integration organizations, in matters within their competence, shall exercise their right to vote under this article with a number of votes equal to the number of their member States that are Parties to this Protocol. Such organizations shall not exercise their right to vote if their member States exercise theirs and vice versa.
3. An amendment adopted in accordance with paragraph 1 of this article is subject to ratification, acceptance or approval by States Parties.
4. An amendment adopted in accordance with paragraph 1 of this article shall enter into force in respect of a State Party ninety days after the date of the deposit with the Secretary-General of the United Nations of an instrument of ratification, acceptance or approval of such amendment.
5. When an amendment enters into force, it shall be binding on those States Parties which have expressed their consent to be bound by it. Other States Parties shall still be bound by the provisions of this Protocol and any earlier amendments that they have ratified, accepted or approved.

ARTICLE 19

Denunciation

1. A State Party may denounce this Protocol by written notification to the Secretary-General of the United Nations. Such denunciation shall become effective one year after the date of receipt of the notification by the Secretary-General.
2. A regional economic integration organization shall cease to be a Party to this Protocol when all of its member States have denounced it.

ARTICLE 20

Depositary and languages

1. The Secretary-General of the United Nations is designated depositary of this Protocol.

2. The original of this Protocol, of which the Arabic, Chinese, English, French, Russian and Spanish texts are equally authentic, shall be deposited with the Secretary-General of the United Nations.

IN WITNESS WHEREOF, the undersigned plenipotentiaries, being duly authorized thereto by their respective Governments, have signed this Protocol.

APPENDIX 6

Bellagio-Harvard Guidelines on the Legal Parameters of Slavery

We, the Members of the Research Network on the Legal Parameters of Slavery,

Recognizing that there has been a lack of legal clarity with regard to the interpretation of the definition of slavery in international law;

Conscious that the starting point for understanding that definition is Article 1(1) of the 1926 Slavery Convention which reads: '*Slavery is the status or condition of a person over whom any or all of the powers attaching to the right of ownership are exercised*';

Recalling that this definition is reproduced in substance in Article 7(a) of the 1956 Supplementary Convention on the Abolition of Slavery, the Slave Trade, and Institutions and Practices Similar to Slavery;

Also noting that the 1926 definition of slavery is once again reproduced in substance in the definition of enslavement found in Article 7(2)(c) of the 1998 Statute of the International Criminal Court and developed in more detail in the secondary legislation of the Court, in its Elements of Crimes;

Bearing in mind the provisions in international human rights law regarding slavery within the 1948 Universal Declaration and 1966 International Covenant on Civil and Political Rights; as well as the provisions regarding slavery in regional human rights conventions of the African, European, and Inter-American systems;

Considering the inclusion of slavery as an enumerated type of human exploitation in both the 2000 United Nations Palermo Protocol on Trafficking in Persons and the 2005 Council of Europe Convention on Action against Trafficking in Human Beings;

Mindful of the pronouncements and case-law related to slavery of international, regional and domestic courts;

 | DOI 10.1163/9789004279896_030

Having met to consider the issue at the 2010 symposium entitled: 'The Parameters of Slavery' at the Rockefeller Foundation's Bellagio Conference Centre in Bellagio, Italy; having further deliberated in 2011 at a meeting under the auspices of the Harriet Tubman Institute for Research on the Global Migrations of African Peoples, York University, Canada; and came together once more at a 2011 symposium entitled: 'The Legal Parameters of Slavery: Historical to the Contemporary' at Harvard University, under the auspices of the Charles Hamilton Houston Institute for Race and Justice, Harvard Law School; the Harvard Sociology Department; the W.E.B. DuBois Institute;

Recommend the following Guidelines related to the legal parameters of slavery:

Guideline 1 – The Legal Definition

The legal definition of slavery is found at Article 1(1) of the 1926 Slavery Convention, which reads: 'Slavery is the status or condition of a person over whom any or all of the powers attaching to the right of ownership are exercised'.

Guideline 2 – The Exercise of the Powers Attaching to the Right of Ownership

In cases of slavery, the exercise of 'the powers attaching to the right of ownership' should be understood as constituting control over a person in such a way as to significantly deprive that person of his or her individual liberty, with the intent of exploitation through the use, management, profit, transfer or disposal of that person. Usually this exercise will be supported by and obtained through means such as violent force, deception and/or coercion.

Guideline 3 – Possession is Foundational to Slavery

Where there is a right of ownership in respect of a thing, ownership implies a background relation of control. That control is the power attaching to the right of ownership known as possession.

Possession is foundational to an understanding of the legal definition of slavery, even when the State does not support a property right in respect of persons. To determine, in law, a case of slavery, one must look for possession.

While the exact form of possession might vary, in essence it supposes control over a person by another such as a person might control a thing. Such control may be physical, but physical constraints will not always be necessary to the maintenance of effective control over a person. More abstract manifestations of control of a person may be evident in attempts to withhold identity documents; or to otherwise restrict free movement or access to state authorities or legal processes; or equally in attempts to forge a new identity through compelling a new religion, language, place of residence, or forcing marriage.

Fundamentally, where such control operates, it will significantly deprive that person of his or her individual liberty for a period of time which is, for that person, indeterminate.

Cases of slavery are to be distinguished from those where, though there has been control exercised, it does not constitute control tantamount to possession, such as where employers make legitimate decisions about the management of workers.

Possession is foundational in that, not only is it a power attaching to the right of ownership, it also creates the factual conditions for the exercise of any or all of other powers attaching to the right of ownership, such as those set out in *Guideline 4*.

Guideline 4 – Further Examples of Powers Attaching to the Right of Ownership

Where a person controls another such as he or she would control a thing owned, such possession makes possible the exercise of any or all of the powers attaching to the right of ownership.

Correlatively, the exercise of any or all of the powers attaching to the right of ownership may serve to indicate the presence of control of a person tantamount to possession, and so provide evidence of slavery.

The following are further examples of powers attaching to the right of ownership:

(a) Buying, Selling or Transferring a Person

Buying, selling or otherwise transferring a person may provide evidence of slavery. Having established control tantamount to possession; the act of buying, selling or transferring that person will be an act of slavery.

Evidence of slavery may also be found in similar transactions, such as bartering, exchanging, or giving or receiving a person as a gift, where control tantamount to possession has been established.

(b) Using a Person

Using a person may provide evidence of slavery. Having established control tantamount to possession; the act of using that person will be an act of slavery.

Evidence of such use of a person may include the derived benefit from the services or labour of that person. In such cases, a person might be used by working for little or no pay, utilised for sexual gratification, or used by providing a service.

(c) Managing the Use of a Person

Managing the use of a person may provide evidence of slavery. Having established control tantamount to possession; the act of managing that person will be an act of slavery.

Evidence of such management of the use of a person may include direct management such as a brothel owner delegating power to a day manager in a situation of slavery in the context of sex work.

(d) Profiting from the Use of a Person

Profiting from the use of a person may provide evidence of slavery. Having established control tantamount to possession; the act of profiting from the use of that person will be an act of slavery.

Evidence of profiting from the use of a person may include cases where a person is mortgaged, lent for profit, or used as collateral.

Evidence of profiting from the use of a person may also include making money or deriving any other kind of income or benefit from the use of the person. Such as the use of an agricultural worker in a situation of slavery, where the profit from the picking of a crop is taken or received by another whether in the form of wages or of the harvest.

(e) Transferring a Person to an Heir or Successor

Transferring a person to an heir or successor may provide evidence of slavery. Having established control over a person tantamount to possession; the act of willing that person to a child or other heir or successor will be an act of slavery.

Evidence of such transferring of a person may include a case of inheritance where a woman, on the death of her husband, is deemed to be inherited by another person.

Evidence of such a transferring of a person may also include the conveying of a status or condition of a person to that of a successive generation, such as from mother to daughter.

(f) Disposal, Mistreatment or Neglect of a Person

Disposing of a person following his or her exploitation may provide evidence of slavery. Having established control over a person tantamount to possession; the act of disposing of a person will be an act of slavery.

Mistreatment or neglect of a person may provide evidence of slavery. Having established control tantamount to possession, such disregard may lead to the physical or psychological exhaustion of a person, and ultimately to his or her destruction; accordingly the act of bringing about such exhaustion will be an act of slavery.

Evidence of such mistreatment or neglect may include sustained physical and psychological abuse, whether calculated or indiscriminate; or the imposition of physical demands that severely curtail the capacity of the human body to sustain itself or function effectively.

Guideline 5 – Making a Determination as to whether Slavery Exists

The exercise of any or all of the powers attaching to the right of ownership just considered shall provide evidence of slavery, insofar as they demonstrate control over a person tantamount to possession.

Accordingly, in determining whether slavery exists in a given case, it is necessary to examine the particular circumstances, asking whether *'powers attaching to the right of ownership'* are being exercised, so as to demonstrate control of a person tantamount to their possession.

In evaluating the particular circumstances to determine whether slavery exists, reference should be made to the substance and not simply to the form of the relationship in question.

The substance of the relationship should be determined by investigating whether in fact there has been an exercise of one or more of the powers attaching to the right of ownership. This will include a determination as to whether control tantamount to possession is present.

Guideline 6 – Expropriation

Ordinarily exclusion from expropriation or 'security of holding' would be deemed a power attaching to the right of ownership. However, as the State generally does not support a property right in persons, a negative obligation against the State generally no longer exists.

However, the State has *at minimum* the positive obligation to bring about the end of either the status or condition of a person over whom any or all of the powers attaching to the right of ownership are exercised.

The State may have further positive obligations with regard to the prohibition against slavery on the basis of domestic law as well as regional or international instruments.

Guideline 7 – Terminology

The term 'slavery' has often been utilised to describe circumstances that go beyond the legal definition as established by the 1926 Slavery Convention.

In law, only 'slavery' and 'institutions and practices similar to slavery', which is often abbreviated to 'practices similar to slavery' have standing and are defined in international law via the 1926 Slavery Convention and the 1956 Supplementary Convention.

Guideline 8 – Distinction between Slavery and Forced Labour

The 1926 Slavery Convention recognises that forced labour can develop 'into conditions analogous to slavery'.

Although forced or compulsory labour is defined by the 1930 Forced Labour Convention as 'all work or service which is exacted from any person under the menace of any penalty and for which the said person has not offered himself voluntarily'; forced labour will only amount to slavery when, in substance, there is the exercise of the powers attaching to the right of ownership.

Slavery will not be present in cases of forced labour where the control over a person tantamount to possession is not present.

Guideline 9 – Distinction between Slavery and 'Institutions and Practices Similar to Slavery'

Article 1 of the 1956 Supplementary Convention recognises that the 'institutions and practices similar to slavery', that is: debt bondage, serfdom, servile marriages, or child exploitation; may be 'covered by the definition of slavery contained in article 1 of the Slavery Convention of 1926'.

The distinction between these servile statuses as defined by the 1956 Supplementary Convention in the following terms and slavery is that slavery is present where in substance there is the exercise of the powers attaching to the right of ownership.

It should be emphasised that slavery will only be present in cases of such 'institutions and practices similar to slavery' where control over a person tantamount to possession is present.

The following are the conventional servitudes set out in the 1956 Supplementary Convention on the Abolition of Slavery, the Slave Trade, and Institutions and Practices Similar to Slavery:

(a) Debt bondage, that is to say, the status or condition arising from a pledge by a debtor of his personal services or of those of a person under his control as security for a debt, if the value of those services as reasonably assessed is not applied towards the liquidation of the debt or the length and nature of those services are not respectively limited and defined;
(b) Serfdom, that is to say, the condition or status of a tenant who is by law, custom or agreement bound to live and labour on land belonging to another person and to render some determinate service to such other person, whether for reward or not, and is not free to change his status;
(c) Any institution or practice whereby:

    (i) A woman, without the right to refuse, is promised or given in marriage on payment of a consideration in money or in kind to her parents, guardian, family or any other person or group; or
    (ii) The husband of a woman, his family, or his clan, has the right to transfer her to another person for value received or otherwise; or
    (iii) A woman on the death of her husband is liable to be inherited by another person;

(d) Any institution or practice whereby a child or young person under the age of 18 years is delivered by either or both of his natural parents or by his guardian to another person, whether for reward or not, with a view to the exploitation of the child or young person or of his labour.

Guideline 10 – When Slavery and Lesser Servitudes are Present

Accepting that both slavery and lesser servitudes such as forced labour or 'institutions and practices similar to slavery' may be found in substance in a particular circumstance; the manner to proceed is by making reference to that substance and not simply to the form, and first ask whether there has been an exercise of the powers attaching to the right of ownership. If so, then the more serious offence of slavery is present.

If not, reference should be made to the legal definition of the lesser servitude which corresponds in substance to the particular circumstance in question.

Adopted on this day, 3 March 2012, by the Members of the Research Network on the Legal Parameters of Slavery.

Jean Allain, Queen's University, Belfast
Kevin Bales, Free the Slaves
Annie Bunting, York University
John Cairns, University of Edinburgh
William M. Carter Jr., Temple University
Holly Cullen, University of Western Australia
Seymour Drescher, University of Pittsburgh
Stanley Engerman, University of Rochester
Paul Finkelman, Albany Law School
Bernard Freamon, Seton Hall University
Allison Gorsuch, Yale University
Robin Hickey, Durham University
Richard Helmholz, University of Chicago
Antony Honoré, University of Oxford
Aidan McQuade, Anti-Slavery International
Orlando Patterson, Harvard University
James Penner, University College, London
Joel Quirk, University of Witwatersrand
Jody Sarich, Free the Slaves
Rebecca Scott, University of Michigan

APPENDIX 7

The Protocol to the Forced Labour Convention, 1930

The General Conference of the International Labour Organization,

Having been convened at Geneva by the Governing Body of the International Labour Office, and having met in its 103rd Session on 28 May 2014, and

Recognizing that the prohibition of forced or compulsory labour forms part of the body of fundamental rights, and that forced or compulsory labour violates the human rights and dignity of millions of women and men, girls and boys, contributes to the perpetuation of poverty and stands in the way of the achievement of decent work for all, and

Recognizing the vital role played by the Forced Labour Convention, 1930 (No. 29), hereinafter referred to as "the Convention," and the Abolition of Forced Labour Convention, 1957 (No. 105), in combating all forms of forced or compulsory labour, but that gaps in their implementation call for additional measures, and

Recalling that the definition of forced or compulsory labour under Article 2 of the Convention covers forced or compulsory labour in all its forms and manifestations and is applicable to all human beings without distinction, and

Emphasizing the urgency of eliminating forced and compulsory labour in all its forms and manifestations, and

Recalling the obligation of Members that have ratified the Convention to make forced or compulsory labour punishable as a penal offence, and to ensure that the penalties imposed by law are really adequate and are strictly enforced, and

Noting that the transitional period provided for in the Convention has expired, and the provisions of Article 1, paragraphs 2 and 3, and Articles 3 to 24 are no longer applicable, and

Recognizing that the context and forms of forced or compulsory labour have changed and trafficking in persons for the purposes of forced or compulsory labour, which may

 | DOI 10.1163/9789004279896_031

involve sexual exploitation, is the subject of growing international concern and requires urgent action for its effective elimination, and

Noting that there is an increased number of workers who are in forced or compulsory labour in the private economy, that certain sectors of the economy are particularly vulnerable, and that certain groups of workers have a higher risk of becoming victims of forced or compulsory labour, especially migrants, and

Noting that the effective and sustained suppression of forced or compulsory labour contributes to ensuring fair competition among employers as well as protection for workers, and

Recalling the relevant international labour standards, including, in particular, the Freedom of Association and Protection of the Right to Organise Convention, 1948 (No. 87), the Right to Organise and Collective Bargaining Convention, 1949 (No. 98), the Equal Remuneration Convention, 1951 (No. 100), the Discrimination (Employment and Occupation) Convention, 1958 (No. 111), the Minimum Age Convention, 1973 (No. 138), the Worst Forms of Child Labour Convention, 1999 (No. 182), the Migration for Employment Convention (Revised), 1949 (No. 97), the Migrant Workers (Supplementary Provisions) Convention, 1975 (No. 143), the Domestic Workers Convention, 2011 (No. 189), the Private Employment Agencies Convention, 1997 (No. 181), the Labour Inspection Convention, 1947 (No. 81), the Labour Inspection (Agriculture) Convention, 1969 (No. 129), as well as the ILO Declaration on Fundamental Principles and Rights at Work (1998), and the ILO Declaration on Social Justice for a Fair Globalization (2008), and

Noting other relevant international instruments, in particular the Universal Declaration of Human Rights (1948), the International Covenant on Civil and Political Rights (1966), the International Covenant on Economic, Social and Cultural Rights (1966), the Slavery Convention (1926), the Supplementary Convention on the Abolition of Slavery, the Slave Trade, and Institutions and Practices Similar to Slavery (1956), the United Nations Convention against Transnational Organized Crime (2000), the Protocol to Prevent, Suppress and Punish Trafficking in Persons, especially Women and Children (2000), the Protocol against the Smuggling of Migrants by Land, Sea and Air (2000), the International Convention on the Protection of the Rights of All Migrant Workers and Members of Their Families (1990), the Convention against Torture and Other Cruel, Inhuman or Degrading Treatment or Punishment (1984), the Convention on the Elimination of All Forms of Discrimination against Women (1979), and the Convention on the Rights of Persons with Disabilities (2006), and

Having decided upon the adoption of certain proposals to address gaps in implementation of the Convention, and reaffirmed that measures of prevention, protection, and remedies, such as compensation and rehabilitation, are necessary to achieve the effective and sustained suppression of forced or compulsory labour, pursuant to the fourth item on the agenda of the session, and

Having determined that these proposals shall take the form of a Protocol to the Convention;

adopts this eleventh day of June two thousand and fourteen the following Protocol, which may be cited as the Protocol of 2014 to the Forced Labour Convention, 1930.

ARTICLE 1

1. In giving effect to its obligations under the Convention to suppress forced or compulsory labour, each Member shall take effective measures to prevent and eliminate its use, to provide to victims protection and access to appropriate and effective remedies, such as compensation, and to sanction the perpetrators of forced or compulsory labour.
2. Each Member shall develop a national policy and plan of action for the effective and sustained suppression of forced or compulsory labour in consultation with employers' and workers' organizations, which shall involve systematic action by the competent authorities and, as appropriate, in coordination with employers' and workers' organizations, as well as with other groups concerned.
3. The definition of forced or compulsory labour contained in the Convention is reaffirmed, and therefore the measures referred to in this Protocol shall include specific action against trafficking in persons for the purposes of forced or compulsory labour.

ARTICLE 2

The measures to be taken for the prevention of forced or compulsory labour shall include:

(a) educating and informing people, especially those considered to be particularly vulnerable, in order to prevent their becoming victims of forced or compulsory labour;
(b) educating and informing employers, in order to prevent their becoming involved in forced or compulsory labour practices;
(c) undertaking efforts to ensure that:

   (i) the coverage and enforcement of legislation relevant to the prevention of forced or compulsory labour, including labour law as appropriate, apply to all workers and all sectors of the economy; and
   (ii) labour inspection services and other services responsible for the implementation of this legislation are strengthened;

(d) protecting persons, particularly migrant workers, from possible abusive and fraudulent practices during the recruitment and placement process;
(e) supporting due diligence by both the public and private sectors to prevent and respond to risks of forced or compulsory labour; and
(f) addressing the root causes and factors that heighten the risks of forced or compulsory labour.

ARTICLE 3

Each Member shall take effective measures for the identification, release, protection, recovery and rehabilitation of all victims of forced or compulsory labour, as well as the provision of other forms of assistance and support.

ARTICLE 4

1. Each Member shall ensure that all victims of forced or compulsory labour, irrespective of their presence or legal status in the national territory, have access to appropriate and effective remedies, such as compensation.
2. Each Member shall, in accordance with the basic principles of its legal system, take the necessary measures to ensure that competent authorities are entitled not to prosecute or impose penalties on victims of forced or compulsory labour for their involvement in unlawful activities which they have been compelled to commit as a direct consequence of being subjected to forced or compulsory labour.

ARTICLE 5

Members shall cooperate with each other to ensure the prevention and elimination of all forms of forced or compulsory labour.

ARTICLE 6

The measures taken to apply the provisions of this Protocol and of the Convention shall be determined by national laws or regulations or by the competent authority, after consultation with the organizations of employers and workers concerned.

ARTICLE 7

The transitional provisions of Article 1, paragraphs 2 and 3, and Articles 3 to 24 of the Convention shall be deleted.

ARTICLE 8

1. A Member may ratify this Protocol at the same time as or at any time after its ratification of the Convention, by communicating its formal ratification to the Director-General of the International Labour Office for registration.
2. The Protocol shall come into force twelve months after the date on which ratifications of two Members have been registered by the Director-General. Thereafter, this Protocol shall come into force for a Member twelve months after the date on which its ratification is registered and the Convention shall be binding on the Member concerned with the addition of Articles 1 to 7 of this Protocol.

ARTICLE 9

1. A Member which has ratified this Protocol may denounce it whenever the Convention is open to denunciation in accordance with its Article 30, by an act communicated to the Director-General of the International Labour Office for registration.
2. Denunciation of the Convention in accordance with its Articles 30 or 32 shall *ipso jure* involve the denunciation of this Protocol.
3. Any denunciation in accordance with paragraphs 1 or 2 of this Article shall not take effect until one year after the date on which it is registered.

ARTICLE 10

1. The Director-General of the International Labour Office shall notify all Members of the International Labour Organization of the registration of all ratifications, declarations and denunciations communicated by the Members of the Organization.
2. When notifying the Members of the Organization of the registration of the second ratification, the Director-General shall draw the attention of the Members of the Organization to the date upon which the Protocol shall come into force.

ARTICLE 11

The Director-General of the International Labour Office shall communicate to the Secretary-General of the United Nations, for registration in accordance with article 102 of the Charter of the United Nations, full particulars of all ratifications, declarations and denunciations registered by the Director-General.

ARTICLE 12

The English and French versions of the text of this Protocol are equally authoritative.

HIGH COURT OF AUSTRALIA*

GLEESON CJ,
GUMMOW, KIRBY, HAYNE, HEYDON, CRENNAN, KIEFEL JJ

THE QUEEN APPELLANT

AND

WEI TANG RESPONDENT

The Queen v Tang [2008] HCA 39
28 August 2008
M5/2008

ORDER

1. *Appeal allowed.*
2. *Special leave to cross-appeal on the first and second grounds in the proposed notice of cross-appeal granted. Cross-appeal on those grounds treated as instituted, heard instanter, and dismissed.*
3. *Special leave to cross-appeal on the third ground in the proposed notice of cross-appeal refused.*
4. *Set aside orders 3, 4 and 5 of the orders of the Court of Appeal of the Supreme Court of Victoria made on 29 June 2007 and, in their place, order that the appeal to that Court against conviction be dismissed.*
5. *The appellant to pay the respondent's costs of the application for special leave to appeal and of the appeal to this Court.*
6. *Remit the matter to the Court of Appeal of the Supreme Court of Victoria for that Court's consideration of the application for leave to appeal against sentence.*

On appeal from the Supreme Court of Victoria

Representation

W J Abraham QC with R R Davis for the appellant (instructed by Director of Public Prosecutions (Cth))

N J Young QC with M J Croucher and K L Walker for the respondent (instructed by Slades & Parsons Solicitors)

Interveners

D M J Bennett QC, Solicitor-General of the Commonwealth with S P Donaghue intervening on behalf of the Attorney-General of the Commonwealth (instructed by Australian Government Solicitor)

B W Walker SC with R Graycar intervening on behalf of the Human Rights and Equal Opportunity Commission (instructed by Human Rights and Equal Opportunity Commission)

CATCHWORDS

The Queen v Tang

Criminal law – Slavery – Licensed brothel – Foreign sex workers – Whether respondent "intentionally possesses a slave or exercises over a slave any of the other powers attaching to the right of ownership" contrary to *Criminal Code* (Cth) ("the Code"), s 270.3(1)(a) – Elements of offence.

Criminal procedure – Directions to jury – Fault element of offence – Relevance of respondent's state of mind – "Intention" – Whether court required to direct on all aspects of definition of "intention" in Code, s 5.2 or only on aspect of definition attaching to physical element or elements of offence.

Criminal law – Conviction – Whether verdicts unreasonable or not supported by evidence – "Proviso" in *Crimes Act* 1958 (Vic), s 568(1) – Whether verdict of acquittal or re-trial appropriate.

Constitutional law – External affairs power – International Convention to Suppress the Slave Trade and Slavery (1926) – Supplementary Convention on the Abolition of Slavery, the Slave Trade, and Institutions and Practices similar to Slavery (1956) – Implementation of treaty by legislation regulating conduct in Australia – Whether Code, ss 270.1 and 270.3(1)(a) within legislative power – Constitution, s 51(xxix).

Words and phrases – "possess," "powers attaching to the right of ownership," "slave," "slavery."

Criminal Code (Cth), ss 5.1, 5.2, 5.6, 270.1, 270.2, 270.3.

1 GLEESON CJ. Following a trial in the County Court of Victoria, before Judge McInerney and a jury, the respondent was convicted of five offences of intentionally possessing a slave, and five offences of intentionally exercising over a slave a power attaching to the right of ownership, namely the power to use, contrary to s 270.3(1)(a) of the *Criminal Code* (Cth) ("the Code"). She was sentenced to a lengthy term of imprisonment. The Court of Appeal of the Supreme Court of Victoria upheld an appeal against each of the convictions, quashed the convictions, and ordered a new trial on all counts.[1] The prosecution, by special leave, has appealed to this Court. The respondent seeks special leave to cross-appeal against the order for a new trial.

2 The Court of Appeal rejected a number of grounds of appeal which, if upheld, would have resulted in an acquittal on all counts. It upheld one ground of appeal, which complained that the directions given to the jury were inadequate. The proposed cross-appeal raises three grounds. The first two grounds concern the meaning and constitutional validity of s 270.3(1)(a). Both grounds were rejected by the Court of Appeal. Logically, a consideration of those grounds should come before consideration of the Court of Appeal's decision on the directions given to the jury. Special leave to cross-appeal on those two grounds should be granted. It will be convenient to deal with them before turning to the prosecution appeal. It is also convenient to leave to one side for the moment the proposed third ground of cross-appeal, which is that the Court of Appeal erred in failing to hold that the jury verdicts were unreasonable or could not be supported having regard to the evidence.

The Legislation

3 Chapter 8 of the Code deals with "Offences against humanity." It includes Div 270 which deals with "Slavery, sexual servitude and deceptive recruiting." Division 270, which was introduced by the *Criminal Code Amendment (Slavery and Sexual Servitude) Act* 1999 (Cth), was based on recommendations made by the Australian Law Reform Commission in 1990.[2] It includes the following:

"270.1 **Definition of *slavery***

For the purposes of this Division, *slavery* is the condition of a person over whom any or all of the powers attaching to the right of ownership are exercised, including where such a condition results from a debt or contract made by the person.

1 *R v Wei Tang* (2007) 16 VR 454.

2 Australian Law Reform Commission, *Criminal Admiralty Jurisdiction and Prize*, Report No 48, (1990) at 72–92.

270.2 Slavery is unlawful

Slavery remains unlawful and its abolition is maintained, despite the repeal by the *Criminal Code Amendment (Slavery and Sexual Servitude) Act 1999* of Imperial Acts relating to slavery.

270.3 Slavery offences

(1) A person who, whether within or outside Australia, intentionally:
- (a) possesses a slave or exercises over a slave any of the other powers attaching to the right of ownership; or
- (b) engages in slave trading; or
- (c) enters into any commercial transaction involving a slave; or
- (d) exercises control or direction over, or provides finance for:
  - (i) any act of slave trading; or
  - (ii) any commercial transaction involving a slave;

is guilty of an offence.

Penalty: Imprisonment for 25 years.

(2) A person who:
- (a) whether within or outside Australia:
  - (i) enters into any commercial transaction involving a slave; or
  - (ii) exercises control or direction over, or provides finance for, any commercial transaction involving a slave; or
  - (iii) exercises control or direction over, or provides finance for, any act of slave trading; and
- (b) is reckless as to whether the transaction or act involves a slave, slavery or slave trading;

is guilty of an offence.

Penalty: Imprisonment for 17 years.

(3) In this section:

slave trading includes:

- (a) the capture, transport or disposal of a person with the intention of reducing the person to slavery; or
- (b) the purchase or sale of a slave.

(4) A person who engages in any conduct with the intention of securing the release of a person from slavery is not guilty of an offence against this section.
(5) The defendant bears a legal burden of proving the matter mentioned in subsection (4)."

4 Later, at a time after the alleged offences the subject of these proceedings, a further offence described as "debt bondage" was added to Ch 8 (s 271.8). That offence carries a lesser maximum penalty than an offence against s 270.3. It may be that the facts of this case would have fallen within s 271.8 had it been in force. If so, that is immaterial. There are many statutes, Commonwealth and State, which create offences of such a kind that particular conduct may fall within both a more serious and a less serious offence. There is a question, to be considered, whether the facts alleged in this case fall within s 270.3. If they had occurred at a later time, they might also have fallen within s 271.8. The two provisions are not mutually exclusive.

It is necessary also to refer to Ch 2 of the Code. It includes the following:

"Chapter 2 – General principles of criminal responsibility

Part 2.1 – Purpose and application

Division 2

2.1 Purpose

The purpose of this Chapter is to codify the general principles of criminal responsibility under laws of the Commonwealth. It contains all the general principles of criminal responsibility that apply to any offence, irrespective of how the offence is created.

...

Part 2.2 – The elements of an offence

Division 3 – General

3.1 Elements

(1) An offence consists of physical elements and fault elements.
(2) However, the law that creates the offence may provide that there is no fault element for one or more physical elements.

(3) The law that creates the offence may provide different fault elements for different physical elements.

3.2 Establishing Guilt in Respect of Offences

In order for a person to be found guilty of committing an offence the following must be proved:

(a) the existence of such physical elements as are, under the law creating the offence, relevant to establishing guilt;
(b) in respect of each such physical element for which a fault element is required, one of the fault elements for the physical element.

...

Division 4 – Physical elements

4.1 Physical Elements

(1) A physical element of an offence may be:
(a) conduct; or
(b) a result of conduct; or
(c) a circumstance in which conduct, or a result of conduct, occurs.
(2) In this Code:

conduct means an act, an omission to perform an act or a state of affairs.
engage in conduct means:

(a) do an act; or
(b) omit to perform an act.

4.2 Voluntariness

(1) Conduct can only be a physical element if it is voluntary.
(2) Conduct is only voluntary if it is a product of the will of the person whose conduct it is.

...

4.3 Omissions

An omission to perform an act can only be a physical element if:

(a) the law creating the offence makes it so; or
(b) the law creating the offence impliedly provides that the offence is committed by an omission to perform an act that by law there is a duty to perform.

Division 5 – Fault elements

5.1 Fault Elements

(1) A fault element for a particular physical element may be intention, knowledge, recklessness or negligence.
(2) Subsection (1) does not prevent a law that creates a particular offence from specifying other fault elements for a physical element of that offence.

5.2 Intention

(1) A person has intention with respect to conduct if he or she means to engage in that conduct.
(2) A person has intention with respect to a circumstance if he or she believes that it exists or will exist.
(3) A person has intention with respect to a result if he or she means to bring it about or is aware that it will occur in the ordinary course of events.

5.3 Knowledge

A person has knowledge of a circumstance or a result if he or she is aware that it exists or will exist in the ordinary course of events.

5.4 Recklessness

(1) A person is reckless with respect to a circumstance if:
   (a) he or she is aware of a substantial risk that the circumstance exists or will exist; and
   (b) having regard to the circumstances known to him or her, it is unjustifiable to take the risk.
(2) A person is reckless with respect to a result if:
   (a) he or she is aware of a substantial risk that the result will occur; and
   (b) having regard to the circumstances known to him or her, it is unjustifiable to take the risk.

(3) The question whether taking a risk is unjustifiable is one of fact.
(4) If recklessness is a fault element for a physical element of an offence, proof of intention, knowledge or recklessness will satisfy that fault element.

5.5 Negligence

A person is negligent with respect to a physical element of an offence if his or her conduct involves:

(a) such a great falling short of the standard of care that a reasonable person would exercise in the circumstances; and
(b) such a high risk that the physical element exists or will exist;

that the conduct merits criminal punishment for the offence.

5.6 Offences that Do Not Specify Fault Elements

(1) If the law creating the offence does not specify a fault element for a physical element that consists only of conduct, intention is the fault element for that physical element.
(2) If the law creating the offence does not specify a fault element for a physical element that consists of a circumstance or a result, recklessness is the fault element for that physical element."

The Background

5 The respondent was the owner of a licensed brothel at 417 Brunswick Street, Fitzroy known as Club 417. The ten counts in the indictment contained two charges (possessing and using) under s 270.3(1)(a) in relation to each of five women (sometimes described as the complainants). The women were Thai nationals. They all came to Australia to work as prostitutes. They had all previously worked in what was described as the sex industry. They became "contract workers." There was no written contract, but there were agreed conditions. Each complainant came to Australia voluntarily.

6 In an appeal to the Court of Appeal of Victoria by a woman, DS, who originally had been a co-accused of the respondent, Chernov JA described the practice that was followed:[3]

---

3 *R v* DS (2005) 191 FLR 337 at 340 [6].

> The organisers in Australia arranged for an appropriate visa to be issued to a [complainant], no doubt on the basis of false information being provided to the immigration authorities. Sometimes that required funds to be deposited temporarily in a bank account in the name of the [complainant] in order to ensure that her visa could be obtained. The woman was then flown to Sydney from Bangkok, 'escorted' by one or two people, usually an elderly couple (so as not to arouse suspicion as to the [complainant's] real purpose in coming to Australia). Generally, once the [complainant] arrived here she was treated as being 'owned' by those who had procured her passage. The [complainant] would be met at the airport by a representative of the Australian 'owner', who would pay off the 'escorts' and take the [complainant] to an apartment or hotel in Sydney and keep her there until a decision was made as to the brothel at which she was to work.

The "Purchase" of the Complainants and the "Debts" Incurred by Them

DS gave evidence at the trial of the respondent. DS's involvement included negotiating with people in Thailand who recruited the women, and settling the women in brothels in Australia.[4] In her evidence in the trial of the respondent, DS described the process that was followed in relation to one of the complainants, once she had arrived in Australia. She gave a similar account in relation to three of the other complainants. After receiving a telephone call from the woman's "boss," DS collected this particular complainant from a hotel. She then contacted the respondent, who agreed to accept the complainant as a contract worker in her brothel, and who also agreed to take up a 70% interest in a syndicate which would "purchase" the woman, DS and her associates taking up the other 30%. The syndicate agreed to pay the "boss" the sum of $20,000. That sum was described by DS as "the amount for this girl," "the amount of money we purchased this woman" and "the money for purchasing women from Thailand to come here." The $20,000 was sent to Thailand.

7 An amount of $110 was to be charged to customers for the complainant's services. It was agreed that the respondent would retain $43 in her capacity as brothel owner. The remaining $67 was divided between the "owners" of the complainant. In this case, the respondent retained 70% of $67 and DS and her associates took 30%.

8 The complainant acknowledged a "debt" to the syndicate in an amount of $45,000. For each customer serviced, the complainant's "debt" would be reduced by $50. In the

---

4 *R v* DS (2005) 191 FLR 337 at 340 [7].

particular case, the amount of the debt was the subject of subsequent negotiation between DS, the respondent and the complainant. DS said:

> It was agreed in Sydney that the debt would be $45,000, but [the complainant] was not happy to pay that amount. So, I asked [the respondent] if she could review the amount on her. So, it was finally agreed that the amount would be I'm not sure $43,000 or $42,000.

It was also agreed that there would be a "free day" for the complainant. On that day, the complainant retained $50 per customer and $17 was divided between the syndicate members (70% to the respondent and 30% to DS and her associates). The respondent was also paid $43 per customer, in her capacity as owner of the brothel. Prior to coming to Australia the complainants were not always aware of the precise terms of the debt or of the living conditions in Australia.

9 There were five complainants. All of them consented to come to Australia to work, on the understanding that, once they had paid off their "debt," they would have the opportunity to earn money on their own account as prostitutes. Upon their arrival the women had very little, if any, money in their possession, spoke little, if any, English, and knew no-one.

10 Four of the complainants went to work in the respondent's brothel in the circumstances described above. In respect of each of those four complainants, the respondent had a share in a syndicate which, according to DS, "purchased" the complainant for $20,000. The contract "debt" was $45,000, or, in the particular case earlier mentioned, $42,000 or $43,000. In his remarks on sentencing, which were based on the evidence that went to the jury, the trial judge said that this sum took account of the $20,000 paid to the recruiters in Thailand, as well as costs of travel and the complainant's living expenses during the term of the contract. It included a profit margin, but the margin was not the subject of any calculation. The "debt" was a notional liability by reference to which aspects of the complainant's obligations were regulated. It was the amount she had to work off, at the rate of $50 per customer, under her "contract." Two of the complainants ultimately worked off their debts, and were thereafter paid for their prostitution.

11 The respondent herself paid nothing to the recruiters in the case of the fifth complainant. The evidence was that, after the fifth complainant was brought to Australia, she worked for others at a different brothel. Later, DS arranged for her to work at the respondent's brothel. The arrangements in relation to the fifth complainant were

the same as for the other four, save that she had different "owners." DS's evidence was that, in relation to the $110 paid by each of the fifth complainant's customers, the respondent retained $43 as brothel owner and the remaining $67 would be paid to DS, who divided the amount between that complainant's owners. The fifth complainant's "debt" of $45,000 also was being worked off at the rate of $50 per customer.

12 In summary, then, while under contract, each complainant was to work in the respondent's brothel in Melbourne six days per week, serving up to 900 customers over a period of four to six months. The complainants earned nothing in cash while under contract except that, by working on the seventh, "free," day each week, they could keep the $50 per customer that would, during the rest of the week, go to offset their contract debts.

The Conditions of the Complainants

13 The trial judge said in his sentencing remarks that he was satisfied on the evidence that the complainants were financially deprived and vulnerable upon arriving in Australia. He found that the complainants entered Australia on visas that were obtained illegally. Continued receipt of the benefits of the complainants' contracts depended on their not being apprehended by immigration authorities. The benefits were more certain to be obtained when the complainants were kept hidden.

14 While on contract, the complainants' passports and return airfares were retained by the respondent. This was done so that the passports could be produced to immigration authorities if necessary, and also so that the complainants could not run away. The complainants lived in premises arranged by the respondent, where they were lodged and fed, and their medical requirements attended to. The evidence was that the complainants were well-provisioned, fed, and provided for. The complainants were not kept under lock and key. Nevertheless, the trial judge said that, in the totality of the circumstances, the complainants were effectively restricted to the premises. On rare occasions they ventured out with consent or under supervision. The circumstances to which the trial judge referred included the hours of work involved, as well as control by way of fear of detection from immigration authorities, fear of visa offences, advice to be aware of immigration authorities, advice to tell false stories to immigration authorities if apprehended, and instructions not to leave their accommodation without the respondent, DS or the manager of the brothel. In the case of some of the contract workers, the regime became more relaxed as the contract progressed and, towards the end of their contracts, they were at liberty to go out as they wished. At work, the trial judge found that, while they were occasionally permitted to go out to shop, the

complainants were, because of the nature and hours of their work, effectively restricted to the premises.

15 In the case of the two complainants who ultimately paid off their debts, the restrictions that had been placed on them were then lifted, their passports were returned, and they were free to choose their hours of work, and their accommodation.

16 In addition to the restrictions that were placed on the complainants, the prosecution pointed to the demands placed upon them as to the numbers of clients they were required to service, their lack of payment, and the days and hours they were required to work as demonstrating that their situation differed materially from that of other sex workers who, however exploited they may have been, were not slaves. The Court of Appeal accepted that the evidence was capable of supporting the jury verdicts, which were held not to have been unreasonable.

The Meaning and Validity of s 270.3(1)(a)

17 The first two grounds of the respondent's proposed cross-appeal are that:

(1) the Court of Appeal erred in holding that ss 270.1 and 270.3(1)(a) of the Code were within the legislative power of the Commonwealth; and
(2) the Court of Appeal erred in holding that the offences created by s 270.3(1)(a) extended to the behaviour alleged in the present case and that they were not confined to situations akin to "chattel slavery" or in which the complainant is notionally owned by the accused or another at the relevant time.

18 As to ground (1), the Court of Appeal held that the relevant provisions of the Code were enacted pursuant to, and sustained by, the power of the Parliament to make laws with respect to external affairs (Constitution, s 51(xxix)). As to ground (2), the Court of Appeal held that s 270.3(1)(a) was not confined to what is sometimes called "chattel slavery." Presumably, the reference in ground (2) to "situations akin to" chattel slavery, and to notional ownership, was prompted by the consideration that chattel slavery is, in Australia, a legal impossibility. If s 270.3(1)(a), in its application to conduct within Australia, were confined to chattel slavery and legal ownership it would have no practical operation. Section 270.2 would eliminate chattel slavery and ownership and s 270.3(1)(a) would be otiose. The Court of Appeal held that the facts alleged in the present case were capable of being regarded as within the scope of s 270.3(1)(a). For the reasons that follow, the decision of the Court of Appeal on these issues should be upheld.

19 The word "slave" in s 270.3(1)(a) is not defined. It takes its meaning from the definition of "slavery" in s 270.1. That definition, in turn, derives from, although it is not identical to, the definition of "slavery" in Art 1 of the 1926 International Convention to Suppress the Slave Trade and Slavery ("the 1926 Slavery Convention").[5] That definition was taken up in Art 7 of the 1956 Supplementary Convention on the Abolition of Slavery, the Slave Trade, and Institutions and Practices similar to Slavery ("the 1956 Supplementary Convention"),[6] which dealt with institutions and practices similar to slavery "where they still exist and whether or not they are covered by the definition of slavery contained in article 1 of the [1926] Slavery Convention."[7]

20 The 1926 Slavery Convention, in its Preamble, recited the declaration in the General Act of the Brussels Conference of 1889–1890 of an intention to put an end to the traffic in African slaves, the intention, affirmed at the Convention of Saint-Germain-en-Laye of 1919, to secure the complete suppression of slavery in all its forms, and the need to prevent forced labour from developing into conditions analogous to slavery. Article 2 contained an undertaking by the parties to prevent and suppress the slave trade and to bring about the complete abolition of slavery "in all its forms."

21 Article 1 of the 1926 Slavery Convention was in the following terms:

> For the purpose of the present Convention, the following definitions are agreed upon:
>
> (1) Slavery is the status or condition of a person over whom any or all of the powers attaching to the right of ownership are exercised.
> (2) The slave trade includes all acts involved in the capture, acquisition or disposal of a person with intent to reduce him to slavery; all acts involved in the acquisition of a slave with a view to selling or exchanging him; all acts of disposal by sale or exchange of a slave acquired with a view to being sold or exchanged, and, in general, every act of trade or transport in slaves.

22 The definition in Art 1(1) has continued to be used in international instruments. For example, the Rome Statute of the International Criminal Court, which entered into force in 2002, defined "enslavement," a crime against humanity, as "the exercise of any

5 212 UNTS 17.
6 266 UNTS 3.
7 Article 1.

or all of the powers attaching to the right of ownership over a person…includ[ing] the exercise of such power in the course of trafficking in persons."[8]

23 The travaux préparatoires of the 1926 Slavery Convention are not especially illuminating as to the meaning of Art 1.[9] Nevertheless, certain observations may be made as to the text and context, including the purpose, of the Convention. First, in 1926, in the case of many of the parties to the Convention, including Australia, the legal status of slavery did not exist, and legal ownership by one person of another was impossible. (In Australia, the law on slavery was based on four 19th century Imperial Acts,[10] a matter adverted to in s 270.2 of the Code.) Secondly, a principal object of the Convention was to bring about the same situation universally, as soon as possible. Thirdly, the definition of slavery in Art 1 referred to the status *or* condition of a person. Status is a legal concept. Since the legal status of slavery did not exist in many parts of the world, and since it was intended that it would cease to exist everywhere, the evident purpose of the reference to "condition" was to cover slavery de facto as well as de jure. This is hardly surprising. The declared aim of the parties to the Convention was to secure the complete suppression of slavery in all its forms, and to prevent forced labour from developing into conditions analogous to slavery. They undertook to bring about "the complete abolition of slavery in all its forms." It would have been a pitiful effort towards the achievement of those ends to construct a Convention that dealt only with questions of legal status. The slave trade was not, and is not, something that could be suppressed merely by withdrawal of legal recognition of the incidents of slavery. It is one thing to withdraw legal recognition of slavery; it is another thing to suppress it. The Convention aimed to do both. Fourthly, the definition turns upon the exercise of power over a person. The antithesis of slavery is freedom. The kind of exercise of power that deprives a person of freedom to the extent that the person becomes a slave is said to be the exercise of *any or all* of the powers attaching to the right of ownership. As already noted, there was no legal right of ownership in many of the states which were parties to the Convention, and one purpose of the Convention was that there would be no such legal right anywhere.

---

8 2187 UNTS 90, Art 7(2)(c).

9 Allain, "A Legal Consideration of 'Slavery' in Light of the *Travaux Préparatoires* of the 1926 Convention," paper delivered at the conference, *Twenty-First Century Slavery: Issues and Responses*, 23 November 2006; Allain, "The Definition of 'Slavery' in General International Law and the Crime of Enslavement within the Rome Statute," paper delivered at the International Criminal Court, *Guest Lecture Series of the Office of the Prosecutor*, 26 April 2007; Allain, *The Slavery Conventions: The Travaux Préparatoires of the 1926 League of Nations Convention and the 1956 United Nations Convention*, (2008).

10 *Slave Trade Act* 1824 (Imp); *Slavery Abolition Act* 1833 (Imp); *Slave Trade Act* 1843 (Imp); *Slave Trade Act* 1873 (Imp).

24 In its application to the de facto condition, as distinct from the de jure status, of slavery, the definition was addressing the exercise over a person of powers of the kind that attached to the right of ownership when the legal status was possible; not necessarily all of those powers, but any or all of them. In a 1953 Memorandum, the Secretary-General of the United Nations[11] listed such powers as including the capacity to make a person an object of purchase, the capacity to use a person and a person's labour in a substantially unrestricted manner, and an entitlement to the fruits of the person's labour without compensation commensurate to the value of the labour. Each of those powers is of relevance in the present case. On the evidence it was open to the jury to conclude that each of the complainants was made an object of purchase (although in the case of one of them the purchaser was not the respondent); that, for the duration of the contracts, the owners had a capacity to use the complainants and the complainants' labour in a substantially unrestricted manner; and that the owners were entitled to the fruits of the complainants' labour without commensurate compensation.

25 The reference to "chattel slavery" in the second ground of cross-appeal is a reference to the legal capacity of an owner to treat a slave as an article of possession, subject to the qualification that the owner was not allowed to kill the slave; power over "the slave's person, property, and limbs, life only excepted."[12] Without doubt, chattel slavery falls within the definition in Art 1 of the 1926 Slavery Convention, but it would be inconsistent with the considerations of purpose, context and text referred to in the preceding paragraph to read the definition as limited to that form of slavery.

26 In the case of *Prosecutor v Kunarac*, before the International Criminal Tribunal for the Former Yugoslavia, where the charges were of "enslavement," both the Trial Chamber[13] and the Appeals Chamber[14] adopted a view of the offence that was not limited to chattel slavery. The Trial Chamber, after an extensive review of relevant authorities and materials, concluded that enslavement as a crime against humanity in customary international law consisted of the exercise of any or all of the powers attaching to the right of ownership over a person; the actus reus of the violation being the exercise of any or all of such powers and the mens rea consisting in the intentional exercise of such powers.[15] The Trial Chamber identified, as factors to be taken into

---

11 United Nations Economic and Social Council, *Slavery, the Slave Trade, and Other Forms of Servitude*, Report of the Secretary-General, UN Doc E/2357, (1953) at 28.

12 *Somerset v Stewart* (1772) Lofft 1 at 2 [98 ER 499 at 500]. See also *Smith v Gould* (1706) 2 Salk 666 [91 ER 567]; *Forbes v Cochrane* (1824) 2 B & C 448 at 471–472 [107 ER 450 at 459].

13 Case No IT-96-23-T & IT-96-23/1-T, 22 February 2001.

14 Case No IT-96-23 & IT-96-23/1-A, 12 June 2002.

15 Case No IT-96-23-T & IT-96-23/1-T, 22 February 2001 at 192 [539]-[540].

account, control of movement, control of physical environment, psychological control, measures taken to prevent or deter escape, force, threat of force or coercion, duration, assertion of exclusivity, subjection to cruel treatment and abuse, control of sexuality and forced labour.[16] The Appeals Chamber agreed with those factors.[17] However, it preferred to leave open, as a matter that was unnecessary for decision in that case, the Trial Chamber's added factor of an ability to buy and sell a person, and it disagreed with the Trial Chamber's view that lack of consent was an element of the offence, although accepting that it may be of evidential significance.[18]

27 It is unnecessary, and unhelpful, for the resolution of the issues in the present case, to seek to draw boundaries between slavery and cognate concepts such as servitude, peonage, forced labour, or debt bondage. The 1956 Supplementary Convention in Art 1 recognised that some of the institutions and practices it covered might also be covered by the definition of slavery in Art 1 of the 1926 Slavery Convention. To repeat what was said earlier, the various concepts are not all mutually exclusive. Those who engage in the traffic in human beings are unlikely to be so obliging as to arrange their practices to conform to some convenient taxonomy.

28 In *Siliadin v France*,[19] the European Court of Human Rights dealt with a complaint by a domestic worker that the French criminal law did not afford her sufficient and effective protection against "servitude" or at least "forced or compulsory" labour. Reference was made to legislative materials which used the term "modern slavery" to apply to some females, working in private households, who started out as migrant domestic workers, au pairs or "mail-order brides."[20] The Court referred briefly and dismissively to the possibility that the applicant was a slave within the meaning of Art 1 of the 1926 Slavery Convention, saying:[21]

> "[The Court] notes that this definition corresponds to the 'classic' meaning of slavery as it was practised for centuries. Although the applicant was, in the instant case, clearly deprived of her personal autonomy, the evidence does not suggest that she was held in slavery in the proper sense, in other words that

16 Case No IT-96-23-T & IT-96-23/1-T, 22 February 2001 at 194 [543].
17 Case No IT-96-23 & IT-96-23/1-A, 12 June 2002 at 35–36 [117]-[119].
18 Case No IT-96-23 & IT-96-23/1-A, 12 June 2002 at 36–37 [119]-[120].
19 (2006) 43 EHRR 16.
20 (2006) 43 EHRR 16 at 301–304 [49].
21 (2006) 43 EHRR 16 at 319 [122] (emphasis added).

> Mr and Mrs B exercised a *genuine right of legal ownership* over her, thus reducing her to the status of an 'object'."[22]

29 It is understandable, in the context of that case, that the definition of "slavery" was dealt with only in passing and briefly. Nevertheless, it is to be noted that the Court did not refer to the definition's reference to condition in the alternative to status, or to powers as well as rights, or to the words "any or all." It may be assumed that there is, in France, no such thing as "a genuine right of legal ownership" of a person. That Mr and Mrs B did not exercise a genuine right of legal ownership over the applicant was self-evident, but it would not have been a complete answer if there had been a serious issue of slavery in the case.

30 It is important not to debase the currency of language, or to banalise crimes against humanity, by giving slavery a meaning that extends beyond the limits set by the text, context, and purpose of the 1926 Slavery Convention. In particular it is important to recognise that harsh and exploitative conditions of labour do not of themselves amount to slavery. The term "slave" is sometimes used in a metaphorical sense to describe victims of such conditions, but that sense is not of present relevance. Some of the factors identified as relevant in *Kunarac*, such as control of movement and control of physical environment, involve questions of degree. An employer normally has some degree of control over the movements, or work environment, of an employee. Furthermore, geographical and other circumstances may limit an employee's freedom of movement. Powers of control, in the context of an issue of slavery, are powers of the kind and degree that would attach to a right of ownership if such a right were legally possible, not powers of a kind that are no more than an incident of harsh employment, either generally or at a particular time or place.

31 Although the definition of "slavery" in s 270.1 of the Code is plainly based on the definition in Art 1 of the 1926 Slavery Convention, the wording is not identical. First, s 270.1 refers to "condition," not "status or condition." The explanation for the difference appears from s 270.2. There is no status of slavery under Australian law. Legal ownership of a person is impossible. Consequently s 270.1, in its application to conduct within Australia, is concerned with de facto slavery. In s 270.1, the reference to powers attaching to the right of ownership, which are exercised over a person in a condition described as slavery, is a reference to powers of such a nature and extent that they are

---

22 In the authoritative French text, "…c'est-à-dire que les époux B aient exercé sur elle, *juridiquement, un véritable droit de propriété*, la réduisant à l'état d'« objet »": *Affaire Siliadin c France*, Requête No 73316/01, 26 July 2005 at 33 [122] (emphasis added).

attributes of effective (although not legal, for that is impossible) ownership.[23] Secondly, the concluding words of the definition in s 270.1 ("including where such a condition results from a debt or contract made by the person") do not alter the meaning of the preceding words because it is only where "such a condition" (that is, the condition earlier described in terms of the 1926 Slavery Convention) results that the words of inclusion apply. The words following "including," therefore, do not extend the operation of the previous words but make it plain that a condition that results from a debt or a contract is not, on that account alone, to be excluded from the definition, provided it would otherwise be covered by it. This is a common drafting technique, and its effect is not to be confused with that of cases where "including" is used as a term of extension.[24]

32 In the result, the definition of "slavery" in s 270.1 falls within the definition in Art 1 of the 1926 Slavery Convention, and the relevant provisions of Div 270 are reasonably capable of being considered appropriate and adapted to give effect to Australia's obligations under that Convention.[25] They are sustained by the external affairs power. They are not limited to chattel slavery.

33 The factors accepted by both the Trial Chamber and the Appeals Chamber in *Kunarac* are relevant to the application of s 270.3(1)(a) of the Code. The Appeals Chamber was right to point out that consent is not inconsistent with slavery. In some societies where slavery was lawful, a person could sell himself into slavery. Peonage could be voluntary as well as involuntary, the difference affecting the origin, but not the character, of the servitude.[26] Consent may be factually relevant in a given case, although it may be necessary to make a closer examination of the circumstances and extent of the consent relied upon, but absence of consent is not a necessary element of the offence. On the point left open by the Appeals Chamber, it should be concluded that, for the purpose of s 270.3(1)(a) of the Code, the commodification of an individual by treating him or her as an object of sale and purchase, if it exists, is a material factor when a tribunal of fact comes to assess the circumstances of a case, and may involve

---

23 Allain, "The Definition of 'Slavery' in General International Law and the Crime of Enslavement within the Rome Statute," paper delivered at the International Criminal Court, *Guest Lecture Series of the Office of the Prosecutor*, 26 April 2007 at 12–13.

24 That this construction conforms to the legislative purpose appears from the Minister's Second Reading Speech: Australia, Senate, *Parliamentary Debates* (Hansard), 24 March 1999 at 3076; and Model Criminal Code Officers Committee of the Standing Committee of Attorneys-General, *Model Criminal Code, Chapter 9, Offences Against Humanity: Slavery*, Report, (1998) at 29.

25 cf *Victoria v The Commonwealth* (*Industrial Relations Act Case*) (1996) 187 CLR 416 at 486–488; [1996] HCA 56.

26 *Clyatt v United States* 197 US 207 at 215 (1905).

the exercise of a power attaching to a right of ownership. Having regard to all those matters, there was in the present case evidence to go to a jury that was capable of sustaining verdicts of guilty.

The Appeal

34 The Court of Appeal quashed the respondent's convictions, and ordered a new trial, substantially upon a single ground of criticism of the primary judge's directions to the jury. The point on which the Court of Appeal differed from the primary judge comes down to a question of the application of the provisions of Ch 2 of the Code to charges of breaches of s 270.3(1)(a). Before turning to those provisions, it is convenient to set out what was said in the Court of Appeal by Eames JA, with whom Maxwell P and Buchanan JA agreed.

35 Eames JA described as "the critical issue" one that "concerns the character of the exercise of power by the accused over the victim." He said that the prosecutor's argument and the trial judge's directions "did not, in terms, [invite or] direct the jury to consider the subjective intention of the [respondent] – her state of mind – when dealing with the complainants." This, he said, "was a critical element of the offence that had to be established if the [respondent] was to be convicted." The jurors, Eames JA held, "were not alerted as to the relevance, when considering the question of intention, of the belief which the [respondent] may have held as to the basis on which she was dealing with each of the complainants." What his Honour understood to be the relevance of that belief was made clear in his reasons. The primary judge had told the jury that, in order to convict, they had to find that the complainants were slaves in accordance with the statutory definition as he explained it to them, that the respondent knew the facts that brought the complainants within that definition (although not that she was aware of the legislation, or the legal definition of slavery) and that she intended to possess or use persons in the condition disclosed by those facts. (It may be noted that the elements of the offence as explained by the primary judge in his directions were somewhat similar to what the Trial Chamber in *Kunarac* identified as the actus reus and the mens rea for the crime of enslavement.)

36 Eames JA said that the critical element of the offence of possessing a slave, missing from the primary judge's directions, was "[the respondent's] *appreciation* of the character of her own actions" (emphasis added). He described the element as follows (references omitted):

> "Fourthly, the accused must have possessed the worker in the intentional exercise of what constitutes a power attaching to a right of ownership, namely, the

power of possession. For that to be the case the accused must be shown to have regarded the worker as though she was mere property, a thing, thereby intending to deal with her not as a human being who had free will and a right to liberty, but as though she was mere property. However harsh or oppressive her conduct was towards the worker it would not be sufficient for a conviction if, rather than having possessed the worker with the knowledge, intention, or in the belief that she was dealing with her as though she was mere property, the accused possessed her in the knowledge or belief that she was exercising some different right or entitlement to do so, falling short of what would amount to ownership, such as that of an employer, contractor, or manager."

37 In a footnote to his reasons on this point, Eames JA said that it was not necessary to prove that an offender knew that the power to possess or use property was an incident of the right of ownership. That is correct, but it is not easy to relate that to the concluding words of the paragraph just quoted, which seem to postulate, as exculpatory, a knowledge or belief that the offender was exercising some other right or entitlement. If it were not necessary to prove that the respondent knew what rights of ownership were, it would be curious if it were relevant to consider what she knew or believed about other rights or entitlements. One would have expected that a person could be convicted of the offence of possessing a slave without knowing, or caring, anything about possible alternative sources of rights or entitlements.

38 In a further footnote, Eames JA supported the above paragraph by references to ss 5.2(2) and 5.2(3) of the Code, which, he said, were both relevant. This is a matter to which it will be necessary to return.

39 Later, Eames JA said (in a passage that also is difficult to reconcile with the first of the footnotes mentioned above):

> "What the judge omitted to state was that the Crown had to prove intention to exercise power over the slave in the knowledge or belief that the power that was being exercised was one attaching to ownership. That is, the power must have been intentionally exercised as an owner of property would exercise power over that property, acting in the knowledge or belief that the victim could be dealt with as no more than a chattel. It would not suffice for the power to have been exercised by the accused in the belief that she was dealing with the victim as her employee, albeit one in a subservient position and being grossly exploited."

40 These passages, notwithstanding the footnote, indicate that Eames JA had in mind that it was necessary for the prosecution to establish a certain state of knowledge or

belief on the part of the respondent as to the source of the powers she was exercising, in addition to an intention to exercise those powers. They appear to require advertence by the respondent to the different capacities (owner or employer) by virtue of which she might have been able to exercise powers. This was made even clearer by the form of an answer which his Honour said should have been given to a question asked by the jury:

> "You must be satisfied that the accused was intentionally exercising a power that an owner would have over property *and was doing so with the knowledge or in the belief that the complainant was no more than mere property.*

If it is reasonably possible that the accused acted to possess or to use the complainant with the knowledge or in the belief that she was exercising her rights and entitlements as her employer or contractor and not in the belief that the complainant had no rights or free will, but was property, a thing, over whom she could exercise power as though she owned her then, however exploitative and unfair you may think her treatment of the complainant was, it would not constitute the offences of intentionally possessing or using a slave." (emphasis added)

This cannot be accepted. What the respondent knew or believed about her rights and entitlements as an employer or contractor, as distinct from rights of property, in the perhaps unlikely event that she knew or believed anything on that subject, was not something that the prosecutor had to establish or that the jury had to consider.

It seems likely that the Court of Appeal was, with good reason, concerned about a problem presented by s 270.3(1)(a), at least in a borderline case: how is a jury to distinguish between slavery, on the one hand, and harsh and exploitative conditions of labour, on the other? The answer to that, in a given case, may be found in the nature and extent of the powers exercised over a complainant. In particular, a capacity to deal with a complainant as a commodity, an object of sale and purchase, may be a powerful indication that a case falls on one side of the line. So also may the exercise of powers of control over movement which extend well beyond powers exercised even in the most exploitative of employment circumstances, and absence or extreme inadequacy of payment for services. The answer, however, is not to be found in the need for reflection by an accused person upon the source of the powers that are being exercised. Indeed, it is probably only in a rare case that there would be any evidence of such consideration.

It should also be noted that the concluding words of the definition of slavery in s 270.1 of the Code show that the existence of a contract between an alleged offender and a complainant is not inconsistent with the commission of an offence. The legislation, in terms, accepts that a condition of slavery may result from a contract. The above reasoning appears to construct a false dichotomy between employment and effective ownership, in addition to importing a requirement of rights analysis by the offender which is unnecessary.

Chapter 2 of the Code does not provide support for the Court of Appeal's reasoning. In the case of both of the offences alleged in relation to each complainant, the physical element of the offence was conduct, which is defined to include both an act and a state of affairs. It was not suggested by the Court of Appeal that recklessness, as the default element in relation to circumstances, had a role to play.[27] As Brennan J pointed out in *He Kaw Teh v The Queen*,[28] having something in possession is more easily seen as a state of affairs that exists because of what the person who has possession does in relation to the thing possessed. Both possessing a slave and using a slave are conduct, and the prosecution had to establish the existence of the conduct and *one* of the fault elements specified in s 5.1(1). The prosecution case was conducted on the basis that the relevant fault element was intention. In a footnote earlier mentioned, Eames JA said that all of sub-ss (1), (2) and (3) of s 5.2 were relevant. This is not easy to understand: sub-s (1) applies where the physical element is conduct; sub-s (2) applies where the physical element is a circumstance; sub-s (3) applies where the physical element is a result. Section 4.1 says a physical element may be conduct *or* a result of conduct *or* a circumstance in which conduct or a result of conduct occurs.

41 The physical element was conduct (which includes a state of affairs); the fault element was intention. It was, therefore, s 5.2(1) that was relevant. A person has intention with respect to conduct if he or she means to engage in that conduct. Knowledge or belief is often relevant to intention.[29] If, for example, it is the existence of a state of affairs that gives an act its criminal character, then proof of knowledge of that state of affairs ordinarily will be the best method of proving that an accused meant to engage in the proscribed conduct.

42 The terms of s 270.3(1) reinforce the conclusion that intention is the relevant fault element. The offences in question were of intentionally possessing a slave or intentionally exercising over a slave another power (here, using) attaching to the right of ownership. It is agreed on all sides that it was unnecessary for the prosecution to prove that the respondent knew or believed that the complainant was a slave, or even that she

27 cf *R v Saengsai-Or* (2004) 61 NSWLR 135.

28 (1985) 157 CLR 523 at 564; [1985] HCA 43.

29 *He Kaw Teh v The Queen* (1985) 157 CLR 523 at 570.

knew what a slave was. Thus, Eames JA said that the respondent "does not have to have known the definition of a slave, nor even that there was an offence of slavery." So much is uncontroversial. If a person is known by an accused to possess the qualities that, by virtue of s 270.1, go to make that person a slave, then the state of knowledge relevant to intention, and therefore intention itself, may be established regardless of whether the accused appreciates the legal significance of those qualities. An accused does not have to know anything about the law in order to contravene s 270.3(1)(a).

43 Insofar as a state of knowledge or belief is factually relevant to intention as the fault element of the offence, it is knowledge or belief about the facts relevant to possession or using, and knowledge or belief about the facts which determine the existence of the condition described in s 270.1. This is a condition that results from the exercise of certain powers. Whether the powers that are exercised over a person are "any or all of the powers attaching to the right of ownership" is for a jury to decide in the light of a judge's directions as to the nature and extent of the powers that are capable of satisfying that description. This is not to ignore the word "intentionally" in s 270.3(1). Rather, it involves no more than the common exercise of relating the fault element to the physical elements of the offence.[30]

44 In this case, the critical powers the exercise of which was disclosed (or the exercise of which a jury reasonably might find disclosed) by the evidence were the power to make the complainants an object of purchase, the capacity, for the duration of the contracts, to use the complainants and their labour in a substantially unrestricted manner, the power to control and restrict their movements, and the power to use their services without commensurate compensation. As to the last three powers, their extent, as well as their nature, was relevant. As to the first, it was capable of being regarded by a jury as the key to an understanding of the condition of the complainants. The evidence could be understood as showing that they had been bought and paid for, and that their commodification explained the conditions of control and exploitation under which they were living and working.

45 It was not necessary for the prosecution to establish that the respondent had any knowledge or belief concerning the source of the powers exercised over the complainants, although it is interesting to note that, in deciding to order a new trial, the Court of Appeal evidently took the view that the evidence was capable of satisfying a jury, beyond reasonable doubt, of the existence of the knowledge or belief that the Court of Appeal considered necessary.

---

30 cf *He Kaw Teh v The Queen* (1985) 157 CLR 523 at 568.

46 The ground on which the Court of Appeal regarded the primary judge's directions as inadequate has not been sustained.

The Third Ground of Proposed Cross-appeal

This ground is:

> "The Court of Appeal erred in failing to hold that the verdicts are unreasonable or cannot be supported having regard to the evidence."

47 The argument that the jury's verdict was unreasonable, because of the inadequacy of the evidence, was considered and rejected by the Court of Appeal, applying the principles stated by this Court in *M v The Queen*.[31] Eames JA noted that much of the evidence in the case was uncontested, although there were some disputes of fact, especially in relation to some testimony as to aspects of the restraint applied to the movements of the complainants.

48 A cognate question was the subject of further argument and further reasons for judgment. When the Court of Appeal delivered its reasons for quashing the convictions (on the ground discussed earlier) it left open for further argument and consideration the question whether there should be an order for a new trial. After further argument, Eames JA said that his earlier reasons were intended to embrace a conclusion that the evidence in the case had sufficient cogency to justify a conviction. He said it did not follow automatically that there should be a new trial, but went on to deal with other relevant considerations. Finally, the Court of Appeal ordered a new trial.

49 It is likely that a good deal would have turned on the jury's assessment of DS and the complainants. Subject to that, there was cogent evidence of the intentional exercise of powers of such a nature and extent that they could reasonably be regarded as resulting in the condition of slavery, and the conduct, to which s 270.3(1)(a) was directed. There was no error of principle by the Court of Appeal on this aspect of the case, and it has not been shown that the interests of justice require a grant of special leave to cross-appeal on this ground.

Orders

50 I propose that the following orders be made:

---

31 (1994) 181 CLR 487; [1994] HCA 63.

1. Appeal allowed.
2. Special leave to cross-appeal on the first and second grounds in the proposed notice of cross-appeal granted. Cross-appeal on those grounds treated as instituted, heard instanter, and dismissed.
3. Special leave to cross-appeal on the third ground in the proposed notice of cross-appeal refused.
4. Set aside orders 3, 4 and 5 of the orders of the Court of Appeal of the Supreme Court of Victoria made on 29 June 2007 and, in their place, order that the appeal to that Court against conviction be dismissed.

51 Notwithstanding that these are criminal proceedings, the appellant, on the hearing of the application for special leave to appeal, undertook to pay the costs of the respondent of the application for special leave to appeal and of the appeal to this Court. Consistently with that undertaking, the Court should order that the appellant pay the respondent's costs of the application for special leave to appeal and of the appeal to this Court.

52 There was also an application to the Court of Appeal for leave to appeal against sentence. Because the Court of Appeal allowed the appeal against conviction, it did not deal with the matter of sentence. The matter should be remitted to the Court of Appeal for its consideration of the application for leave to appeal against sentence.

53 GUMMOW J. I agree with the orders proposed by the Chief Justice and with his Honour's reasons. I agree also with the reasons of Hayne J.

54 KIRBY J. These proceedings arise out of convictions entered against Wei Tang ("Ms Tang") following jury verdicts. The convictions are said to be the "first convictions in Australia" of "slavery offences" contrary to s 270.3(1)(a) of the *Criminal Code* (Cth) ("the Code").[32] These offences are found in Ch 8 of the Code dealing with "Offences against humanity."

55 Ms Tang sought, and obtained, leave to appeal against her convictions to the Court of Appeal of the Supreme Court of Victoria.[33] That Court, whilst rejecting her submission that verdicts of acquittal should be entered, set aside the convictions and ordered a retrial of the charges.[34]

---

32 *R v Wei Tang* (2007) 16 VR 454 at 456 [4].

33 (2007) 16 VR 454 at 497 [200].

34 *R v Wei Tang* [2007] VSCA 144 at [13]-[14]. See (2007) 16 VR 454 at 497 [199]-[200].

56 The prosecution, by special leave, has appealed to this Court seeking restoration of Ms Tang's convictions. For her part, Ms Tang has sought special leave to cross-appeal on three grounds. If successful on the cross-appeal, Ms Tang again seeks the substitution of verdicts of acquittal.

57 The other members of this Court[35] have concluded that the prosecution is entitled to succeed; its appeal should be allowed; the convictions of Ms Tang should be restored; and the cross-appeal rejected. I agree with most of their reasons. However, upon what Eames JA, in the Court of Appeal, described as "the critical issue" in the proceedings,[36] I disagree with my colleagues. On that issue, in effect, I concur in the approach and conclusion expressed in the Court of Appeal by Eames JA (with whom Maxwell P and Buchanan JA agreed without additional reasons[37]).

58 The "critical issue" concerns the accuracy and adequacy of the directions given to the jury at the second trial of Ms Tang. (In the first trial, the jury failed to agree on verdicts in relation to Ms Tang.[38]) The controversial point involves the meaning and application of the provisions of the Code that define the offences with which Ms Tang was charged and the content of the "fault elements"[39] (relevantly the "intention" aspect) necessary to constitute those offences. It concerns what the trial judge was obliged to tell the jury in that respect about the law governing these offences.

59 I concede that there is room for differences of opinion on the issue that separates my opinion from that reached by the majority in this Court. Such differences may arise because of the difficulties in interpreting the novel provisions of the Code[40]; the absence of earlier explorations of those provisions by appellate decisions[41]; the necessary interaction of the applicable Australian law with the relevant provisions of international law – in particular, the Convention to Suppress the Slave Trade and Slavery ("the 1926 Slavery Convention")[42] and the Supplementary Convention on the Abolition of Slavery, the Slave Trade, and Institutions and Practices Similar to Slavery ("the 1956

35 Reasons of Gleeson CJ at [57] and reasons of Hayne J at [168]. Gummow, Heydon, Crennan and Kiefel JJ agreeing with both.
36 (2007) 16 VR 454 at 469 [66]; see also reasons of Hayne J at [133].
37 (2007) 16 VR 454 at 456 [1], [2].
38 (2007) 16 VR 454 at 458 [17].
39 The Code, Ch 2, Div 5, s 5.1. The relevant provisions are set out in the reasons of Gleeson CJ at [5].
40 See (2007) 16 VR 454 at 468 [60], 487 [143].
41 (2007) 16 VR 454 at 475 [93].
42 Opened for signature in 1926 and entered into force in 1927. See [1927] ATS 11; 212 UNTS 17.

Supplementary Convention");[43] and the mass of evidentiary material from the lengthy trial of Ms Tang. Such evidence was relevant for two purposes: first, as to the quality of the relationship between Ms Tang and the five women ("the complainants") whom she was charged with possessing as "a slave" or using as "a slave" contrary to s 270.3(1)(a) of the Code; and secondly, as to the suggested "fault element" ("intention") that the prosecution was required to prove in order to secure convictions.[44]

60 Whilst I agree that the other challenges mounted for Ms Tang fail, in my opinion the approach of the Court of Appeal to the "critical issue" was correct. That approach is more consonant with:

The proper analysis of the Code;

- The basic doctrine of criminal law in Australia, against the background of which the Code is written, on the operation of "intention" in respect of serious criminal offences;
- The principles of interpretation applicable to the legislation in question;
- A proper view of the relationship between the Code provisions and the international law that they seek to apply in Australia; and
- The various other considerations of legal principle and policy to which regard may properly be had.

61 We do not advance the correct application in Australia of a contemporary statutory provision to tackle modern issues of "slavery" and trafficking in "sexual slaves" by distorting the essential ingredients of serious criminal offences as provided by the Parliament. Nor do we do so by diminishing the elements that the prosecution must prove and that the trial judge must accurately explain to the jury. In this case, that element is the "intention" necessary to constitute such a serious offence, with the exposure that it brings, upon conviction, to special calumny and to extremely severe punitive consequences.

62 In a case such as the present, there is an inescapable dilemma in the operation of fundamental principles of human rights, reflected in the Code and in Australian law more generally. Protection of persons alleged to have been trafficked as "sexual slaves" is achieved in this country in a trial system that also provides fundamental legal protections for those who are accused of having been involved in such offences. As is often

43 Opened for signature in 1956 and entered into force in 1957. See [1958] ATS 3; 266 UNTS 3.

44 cf (2007) 16 VR 454 at 489 [157].

observed, the protection of the law becomes specially important when it is claimed by the unpopular and the despised accused of grave wrong-doing.[45]

63 In my opinion, the appeal fails and so does Ms Tang's attempt, by cross-appeal, to secure the substitution of verdicts of acquittal. As the Court of Appeal proposed, an order for a retrial, freed from the legal errors of the second trial, is the correct outcome.

The Facts

The general background: The general factual background is explained in the reasons of Gleeson CJ.[46] There were various points of difference in the extensive evidence called at the trial. For example, in respect of one of the complainants, there were differences as to the arrangements whereby she had travelled to Australia from Thailand and as to the persons involved in making those arrangements. However, much of the evidence tendered against Ms Tang was not in dispute.[47] The battleground, instead, lay in the interpretation of that evidence and its legal effect. The relevant question was whether the evidence fell within the particular provisions of the Code governing, first, the "physical elements" of the offences provided in s 270.3(1) with which Ms Tang was charged, and secondly, the "fault elements" that also had to be proved in order to satisfy those charges.[48]

64 In this appeal, the novelty of the meaning of the "slavery offences" provided by s 270.3 of the Code gives rise to the first problem of interpretation. This country has never lawfully had "slavery" in the conventional meaning of that term and still does not. The novelty of the "general principles of criminal responsibility"[49] and the specification of the essential elements of an offence under the Code give rise to the second problem of interpretation. Those problems of interpretation must be made concrete by reference to the evidence at the trial. Such evidence will help to test whether the trial judge properly understood, and explained, the provisions of the Code so as to render the verdicts of the second jury (and the convictions that followed) both lawful and reasonable. The evidence will also help to answer the legal propositions advanced by the contesting parties.

---

45 cf *Adelaide Company of Jehovah's Witnesses Inc v The Commonwealth* (1943) 67 CLR 116 at 124 per Latham CJ; [1943] HCA 12.

46 Reasons of Gleeson CJ at [6]-[18].

47 (2007) 16 VR 454 at 495 [191].

48 See the Code, ss 2.1, 3.1, 3.2, 5.1. These provisions are set out in the reasons of Gleeson CJ at [5].

49 The chapter heading to Ch 2 of the Code. See reasons of Gleeson CJ at [5].

65 At the outset, it is important to acknowledge that the evidence was by no means incontestable or clear-cut. There are two particular indications of this:

- First, upon basically the same evidence, the first jury summoned to try Ms Tang and a co-accused (Mr Paul Pick, who was the manager of the licensed brothel "Club 417") acquitted Mr Pick on eight counts. The jury were unable to agree on two further counts against him or upon any of the counts presented against Ms Tang. Mr Pick subsequently applied successfully for a *nolle prosequi*;[50] and
- Secondly, following very extensive directions given by the trial judge to the jury in the second trial, the jury returned twice to seek judicial clarification about the requirements of intention. This became the "critical issue" in the Court of Appeal as it is likewise in this Court. What took place and the terms of the questions asked by the jury and directions given by the trial judge are explained in detail by Eames JA.[51]

66 The first question was asked on the first day of the jury's deliberations (after a charge that had proceeded over three days). The question was presented after the jury had already been deliberating for five hours. The second question was asked the following afternoon, after the jury had been deliberating for over a day. It will be necessary to return to these developments.[52]

67 For a complete understanding of my reasons, it is essential to appreciate how the questions emerged; the preceding complex and confusing instructions given to the jury on the subject; and the further instruction that followed which, with respect, was partly non-responsive and partly added to the uncertainty and confusion. This is all set out with admirable clarity by Eames JA. If nothing else, it indicates the confusion of the instructions given to the jury on the subject of the intention necessary to justify guilty verdicts; the correct focus that the jury themselves were giving to the "critical issue"; and thus the great importance of that issue to their deliberations in the forensic circumstances of the second trial.

68 The successive questions from the jury indicate the significance that they were assigning to the quality and content of the "intention" of Ms Tang which the prosecution had to prove to secure guilty verdicts. The length of the jury's deliberations and their repeated questions on this issue also indicate (correctly in my view) that this jury,

50 (2007) 16 VR 454 at 458 [17].

51 (2007) 16 VR 454 at 481–483 [122]-[129].

52 See these reasons below at [123]-[125].

like the earlier jury in the first trial, did not find reaching their verdicts in these proceedings an easy task, considering the way in which the evidence emerged in the second trial.

69 In these reasons, I incorporate by reference the chronicle set out by Eames JA in the Court of Appeal. This includes the lengthy directions given to the jury about the meaning of the words "possession" and "use" of a "slave," contrary to the Code; the jury's successive questions; the supplementary directions then given by the trial judge; and the further supplementary directions given after trial counsel for Ms Tang took exception to aspects of the judge's first attempt.[53]

70 Although additional reference will be made below to these questions and the resulting redirections, because mine is a minority opinion in this Court, I will not set the passages out *seriatim*. They are not set out in other reasons. Nevertheless, to understand the conclusion that Eames JA and the other members of the Court of Appeal reached, it is essential to appreciate the deficiencies in the directions given to the jury on the critical subject of "intention." No other course would do justice to Ms Tang's case or to the Court of Appeal's analysis.

71 *Evidence against statutory slavery*: Allowing, for the moment, that the Code expands somewhat the traditional definition of "slavery" in international law (and in more recent times under the 1926 Slavery Convention and the 1956 Supplementary Convention), and that it may do this in Australia in conformity with the Constitution, there was certainly evidence before the jury in the second trial that, in combination, could have supported the acquittal of Ms Tang:

> (1) The trial was conducted on the footing that each of the complainants, in their country of nationality (Thailand), had earlier worked in the sex industry.[54] In this sense, they were not tricked into employment in Australia on a false premise or led to believe that they would be working in tourism, entertainment or other non-sexual activities.[55] Whilst trafficking in persons for sexual or like purposes is an undeniable feature of modern population movements, equally, some such movements are undoubtedly economically motivated.[56] As such,

53 This is set out, with extracts from the trial, at (2007) 16 VR 454 at 475–487 [93]-[141].

54 (2007) 16 VR 454 at 456–457 [5].

55 cf Dorevitch and Foster, "Obstacles on the Road to Protection: Assessing the Treatment of Sex-Trafficking Victims under Australia's Migration and Refugee Law," (2008) 9 *Melbourne Journal of International Law* 1 at 8, 38 ("Dorevitch and Foster").

56 See Dorevitch and Foster, (2008) 9 *Melbourne Journal of International Law* 1 at 38–39.

they would not constitute "slavery" offences under s 270.3(1)(a) of the Code if undertaken with appropriate knowledge and consent by an adult person who was able to give such consent;

(2) Each complainant was above the legal age of consent. It was not suggested (and it did not appear from the evidence) that they were in any way legally incompetent or that they had been subjected to coercion to persuade them to come to Australia to work in the sex industry. It was accepted that they came to this country voluntarily, knowing at least the general nature and incidents of the work they were agreeing to perform;[57]

(3) Whilst the evidence revealed several offences against the *Migration Act* 1958 (Cth) and Regulations and perhaps State offences, the brothel in Melbourne in which the complainants worked as commercial sex workers and their work were not illegal under Victorian law. The brothel held a licence pursuant to the *Prostitution Control Act* 1994 (Vic).[58] Although activities of prostitution were previously illegal under Australian law (as they still are in many countries) they were not, without more, illegal in the subject brothel. Necessarily, Ms Tang's trial was unconcerned with any migration or other offences that she, the complainants or others might have committed. No such offences were before the jury;

(4) The evidence indicated that the complainants were not imprisoned in the brothel or in their place of residence. The largest evidentiary dispute at trial concerned the extent to which the complainants were able to move freely and whether their accommodation was subject to a deadlock controlling access and egress.[59] It is appropriate to accept the trial judge's finding on sentencing that the complainants were *not* kept under lock and key[60] although initially they were "effectively restricted." In part, such restrictions were adopted because of the common objective of the complainants and Ms Tang to avoid detection by migration authorities and deportation from Australia as unlawful aliens present in the country without relevant visas;[61]

57 Reasons of Gleeson CJ at [6]; reasons of Hayne J at [166].

58 (2007) 16 VR 454 at 457 [8].

59 (2007) 16 VR 454 at 495 [191].

60 (2007) 16 VR 454 at 495 [192]. See also at 496 [196].

61 (2007) 16 VR 454 at 457 [8].

(5) The "fee" paid to the "recruiters" in Thailand who arranged for the complainants to travel to Australia (and eventually to Melbourne)[62] was never fully explained, still less justified, to the complainants. However, there was no doubt that some costs were incurred by the "recruiters." These included, by inference, procuring visas; arranging land and air transport;[63] providing return airfares for the complainants; arranging and paying for accompanying persons (usually an elderly couple so as to avoid detection at the border); providing initial and later accommodation; and a "profit margin."[64] The "fee" extracted would arguably fall to be considered (at least in part) in the context of the law, culture and economy of Thailand where it was orally agreed. It would also arguably need to be judged in the context that the complainants voluntarily entered Australia aware of the type of work they were to perform, inferentially so as to make their lives better as a consequence and appreciating that it would result in a debt to those who had made the necessary arrangements to facilitate their travel and relocation;[65]

(6) As was essential to their successful initiation into the sex industry in Australia, the complainants themselves participated in the subterfuge of pretending to visit Australia on a tourist visa;[66]

(7) After the complainants commenced work in the brothel, their passports and return air tickets were taken and retained in a secure place. It was stated that this was done to permit the nationality and identity of the complainants to be established, in the event of investigations by migration authorities. Also, it was done to avoid loss or theft of the documents. This is in addition to any motive to prevent the non-consensual departure of the complainants;

(8) It was agreed that the complainants enjoyed a "free day" each week; that each was credited with a notional sum of $50 per customer in the reduction of their outstanding debt; and that, on the free day, each complainant could either rest or continue to work and receive $50 per customer for themselves.[67] The evidence also showed that the complainants were well fed and provided for.[68] Two had

62 The "fee" varied but was about $20,000. See reasons of Gleeson CJ at [12].
63 Reasons of Gleeson CJ at [8].
64 Reasons of Gleeson CJ at [8], [12].
65 (2007) 16 VR 454 at 488 [149].
66 (2007) 16 VR 454 at 457 [6].
67 Reasons of Gleeson CJ at [14].
68 Reasons of Gleeson CJ at [16].

actually paid off their debts[69] within six months of arrival. Assuming that they worked every day of the week (as most did), this would mean attending to an average of five clients a day. The two who had paid off their debts stayed and continued to work in the brothel. This was strongly relied on as contradicting a relationship that could be characterised as "slavery" in any meaningful sense of that word. It was common ground that once the debt was paid, each complainant was completely free to choose for herself the hours of work and place of accommodation.[70] There was conflicting and unclear evidence about the freedom of movement permitted before the debt was paid, other than transfer between the brothel and the residence. Some evidence suggested that at least one complainant had formed a personal relationship which she pursued during that interval;

(9) Once the complainants and their migration status were discovered, they were, by law, subject to immediate detention and deportation from Australia. The availability of legal relief against that course was limited. One such form of relief, introduced soon after these events took place, was the provision of both temporary and longer-term visas to stay in Australia.[71] The latter were available only to permit a person, such as one or more of the complainants, to stay if they made a "significant contribution" to a prosecution of an accused offender for criminal offences; and

(10) There was no evidence that the complainants were subjected to rape, violence or other such offences.[72] This sometimes marks the predicament of those (generally women and children) who are trafficked for the purpose of sexual slavery and sexual debt bondage.[73]

72 *Evidence favouring statutory slavery*: The foregoing evidence was available to Ms Tang to contest the charge that she had "within… Australia, intentionally…possesse[d]

69 The debt varied but was about $45,000, inclusive of the "fee" paid or payable to the Thai "recruiters."

70 Reasons of Gleeson CJ at [12], [17].

71 Dorevitch and Foster, (2008) 9 *Melbourne Journal of International Law* 1 at 10: "Effective since 1 January 2004, the…framework consists of four types of visa: a new Bridging Visa F (Subclass 060) ('BVF'); the existing Criminal Justice Stay Visa ('CJSV'); a Temporary Witness Protection (Trafficking) Visa ('TWPTV'); and a Permanent Witness Protection (Trafficking) Visa ('PWPTV')" (footnotes omitted).

72 cf Halley, "Rape in Berlin: Reconsidering the Criminalisation of Rape in the International Law of Armed Conflict," (2008) 9 *Melbourne Journal of International Law* 78 at 113.

73 Dorevitch and Foster, (2008) 9 *Melbourne Journal of International Law* 1 at 19–20.

a slave or exercise[d] over a slave any of the other powers attaching to the right of ownership."[74] However, as noted by the Court of Appeal, there was also evidence capable of supporting the conclusions that Ms Tang was guilty of the offences charged and that such verdicts were not unreasonable.[75]

73 The relevant evidence included:

> (1) The meaning to be given to the language of Div 270 of the Code is not controlled by considerations prevailing in the law, culture or economy of Thailand. The applicable Code provisions draw upon international law, specifically the 1926 Slavery Convention and the 1956 Supplementary Convention. They thus purport to express universal offences against humanity. However, ultimately it is the duty of an Australian court to give effect to the language stated in the Code, an Australian statute. It is to measure the evidence accepted against the standards expressed in the Code, as that law is understood in Australia.
>
> In determining what constitutes employment conditions that are extremely harsh, unconscionable and oppressive but which do not answer to the defined description of "slavery," it is proper that the criteria expressed in the Code[76] should be given a meaning that reflects Australian understandings. The definition of "slavery" in the Code is not intended to attract merely harsh, unconscionable and oppressive employment conditions. As such, the *discrimen* for "slavery offences" will properly take into account the normal features of working conditions in Australia and not working conditions that may exist in Thailand or elsewhere.
>
> Such conditions in Australia are closely regulated by federal and State laws. They have been so regulated since colonial times. Commonly, the applicable laws are designed to ensure a "fair go all round."[77] (Some would argue the purpose of s 51(xxxv) of the Constitution was to protect and entrench in law that basic feature of Australian society.) Measured against that feature, as this Court

74 The Code, s 270.3(1)(a).

75 cf reasons of Gleeson CJ at [18].

76 The Code, s 270.1 (definition of slavery): "the condition of a person over whom any or all of the powers attaching to the right of ownership are exercised, including where such a condition results from a debt or contract made by the person."

77 *Blackadder v Ramsey Butchering Services Pty Ltd* (2005) 221 CLR 539 at 548–549 [30]; [2005] HCA 22 citing *In re Loty and Holloway and Australian Workers' Union* [1971] AR (NSW) 95 at 99 per Sheldon J; cf *New South Wales v The Commonwealth* (*Work Choices Case*) (2006) 229 CLR 1 at 244 [609]; [2006] HCA 52.

may take judicial notice and as a jury would have been aware, the working conditions of the complainants were substantially different. The differences were most evident in the hours, conditions and circumstances of the work; the closely restricted accommodation; and the onerous requirements for the reduction of the "employment" debts.

At trial, counsel for Ms Tang suggested analogies between the situation of the complainants and those of an oil rig employee or of students obliged to repay HECS debts. These comparisons are unconvincing when contrasted with the seriously exploitative conditions of the complainants that were revealed by the evidence. At the very least, in an Australian setting, it was open to the jury to conclude that such circumstances bore no comparison or analogy to (even harsh) employment conditions as understood in Australia;[78]

(2) If it be accepted that the complainants came voluntarily to Australia to work in the sex industry, the counts charging Ms Tang with offences against s 270.3(1)(a) of the Code still raised a critical question. That question was what happened to the complainants after they arrived at their place of employment and what was the quality and content of Ms Tang's intention in that regard. Allowing for the existence of some kind of agreement with the complainants before they left Thailand, the fact is that the agreement was not in writing; its terms were in some respects unclear and disputed; and the "fees" payable to the Thai "recruiters" and to Ms Tang were never fully explained or justified to the complainants. At the very least, the complainants were economically vulnerable in Thailand. They were particularly vulnerable once they arrived in Australia. In this country, they found themselves in an alien culture; were exposed to the possibility of sudden immigration expulsion; had severe practical restrictions affecting their movements, work and accommodation; had little skill in the English language; and had few, if any, local friends or acquaintances outside the brothel, its personnel and customers;

(3) The taking of the passports and return air tickets from the complainants can, it is true, be explained in other ways; likewise the confiscation of the funds lent to them to afford evidence upon arrival of an apparent capacity of self-support. However, the consequence of these steps was to remove from the complainants the wherewithal to enquire about or pursue their legal rights or to escape from the conditions in which they found themselves, if that was their desire.[79]

78 See (2007) 16 VR 454 at 457 [8], 458 [12].

79 (2007) 16 VR 454 at 495 [192]-[193]. See also at 489 [155].

Particular employment arrangements, including in Australia, can sometimes seem oppressive to those engaged in conventional employment. Relevant here, however, was the work that the complainants had agreed to perform; the regime of effective discipline governing the complainants' place of employment and accommodation; their sleeping arrangements; the long hours of service; and the effective contemplation of a seven day week. These factors combine to portray a level of oppression having few analogies in contemporary consensual Australian employment conditions. The Court of Appeal did not err in reaching the opinion that it was open to the jury to so conclude;[80]

(4) There was a lively dispute at the trial as to whether the arrangements with the Thai "recruiters" or the "syndicate" amounted to a "purchase [of] the women."[81] This is distinct from "purchasing the contracts" under which they allegedly agreed to travel to Australia to work in their own interests. However, at least one witness used the term "we purchased this woman." To that extent, evidence was available that the jury could accept about the attitude of human purchase towards procuring the complainants' services for Ms Tang;[82]

(5) Not every exploitative employment arrangement will warrant the description of "slavery," including in its extended Australian statutory form under the Code. Making the distinction between harsh, unconscionable and oppressive employment and "slavery" may sometimes be difficult. The notion of "slavery" should not be debased by metaphorical applications to non-"slave" conditions. Nevertheless, it was open to the Court of Appeal to reach its conclusion that the burdens imposed on the complainants were different in kind from even the harshest conditions of "employment," as such, in contemporary Australia.[83] Upon this basis, it was competent for a properly instructed jury to conclude that the "employment" conditions of the complainants involved the exercise over them of at least some of the "powers attaching to the right of ownership." That expression is to be understood in the Australian context where full ownership (in the sense of "chattel slavery") was unlawful under Imperial legislation dating back to colonial times and remains unlawful under the Code;[84]

---

80 (2007) 16 VR 454 at 468 [59], 489 [155], 495 [193].

81 (2007) 16 VR 454 at 465 [46].

82 (2007) 16 VR 454 at 465 [46].

83 (2007) 16 VR 454 at 468 [59].

84 The Code, s 270.2.

(6) "Full ownership" of another human being (and thus "chattel slavery") is, and has always been, expressly excluded as a possibility under Australian law. This makes it clear that, in creating "slavery offences" as it does, s 270.3 of the Code provides such offences in another, different and extended (statutory) sense. Subject to any constitutional problems in so providing, it is therefore in this extended sense that the charges of "slavery offences" preferred against Ms Tang under the Code needed to be understood. This involved some awareness on the part of the court of important changes in international law since earlier times. It also involved responding to the evidence of new forms of people trafficking and exploitation. Subject to the Constitution, there are good reasons why the "slavery offences" in s 270.3 of the Code should be given an operation that accords with the language in which the offences are expressed. The language of s 270.3 should not be artificially narrowed nor its application circumscribed when invoked for suggested application to new and emerging fact situations; and

(7) It is possible that the complainants, especially when faced with the prospect of deportation as illegal immigrants, may have been motivated to cooperate with the prosecution of Ms Tang in order to obtain visas to remain in Australia.[85] However, such visas themselves present serious deficiencies. They are readily cancelled. Their provision does not found an inference that the complainants falsely elaborated the circumstances of their living and working arrangements with Ms Tang simply to stay in Australia and to further the economic opportunities that allegedly motivated their journey to Australia in the first place.

74 *Conclusion: verdicts arguably available*: Subject therefore to what follows, to respond to the issues raised by the appeal and by Ms Tang's application for special leave to cross-appeal (including on constitutional grounds), no error has been demonstrated in the conclusion of the Court of Appeal that there was evidence available at the trial to support the second jury's guilty verdicts and the subsequent convictions of Ms Tang. As long as that trial was not flawed by inaccurate or imperfect directions on the applicable law, the resulting convictions must therefore stand.

The Legislation

75 The reasons of Gleeson CJ set out the relevant provisions of the legislation,[86] which I incorporate by reference. That legislation consists of the specific provisions of the Code in respect of the "slavery offences," introduced by the *Criminal Code Amendment*

---

85 Dorevitch and Foster, (2008) 9 *Melbourne Journal of International Law* 1 at 44–45.

86 Reasons of Gleeson CJ at [5].

(*Slavery and Sexual Servitude*) *Act* 1999 (Cth), and the general provisions, under Ch 2 of the Code, that govern the required approach to the "general principles of criminal responsibility" under the laws of the Commonwealth (including the Code). It is unnecessary for me to repeat those provisions.

The Issues

76 The following issues are raised by these proceedings:

(1) *The meaning of "slavery" issue*: Upon consideration of Div 270 of the Code and relevant provisions of international law, did the Court of Appeal err in the "slavery" definition that it adopted (and, by extension, the definition of "slave" in s 270.3(1)(a) of the Code)? Should Ms Tang be granted special leave to cross-appeal to challenge the approach adopted by the Court of Appeal with respect to the stated ambit of the offence?

Before tackling propounded issues of constitutional *validity*, it is the conventional methodology of this Court to identify first the *meaning* to be attributed to the impugned legislation.[87] Subject to what I have said in these reasons, I am in general agreement on this issue with Gleeson CJ[88] and Hayne J[89] about the meaning of "slavery" and "slave" in the Code. Accordingly, the order proposed by Gleeson CJ in respect of the first ground of Ms Tang's notice of cross-appeal should be made;

(2) *The constitutional validity issue*: The Court of Appeal rejected Ms Tang's challenge to the constitutional validity of the offences expressed in s 270.3(1)(a) under which Ms Tang had been charged. It affirmed the validity of the offences on the footing that the provisions give effect to Australia's obligations under the 1926 Slavery Convention.[90] Did the Court of Appeal err in making such findings? Alternatively, was s 270.3(1)(a) constitutionally valid as within the powers of the Federal Parliament on any of the alternative bases propounded by the

87 *Bank of* NSW *v The Commonwealth* (1948) 76 CLR 1 at 186 per Latham CJ; [1948] HCA 7; *Residual Assco Group Ltd v Spalvins* (2000) 202 CLR 629 at 662 [81]; [2000] HCA 33; *Northern Territory of Australia v Arnhem Land Aboriginal Land Trust* [2008] HCA 29 at [65].

88 Reasons of Gleeson CJ at [21]-[35].

89 Reasons of Hayne J at [135]-[159].

90 (2007) 16 VR 454 at 460 [24].

prosecution,[91] as supported by the Attorney-General of the Commonwealth intervening in this Court?

The Court of Appeal did not err in concluding this issue as it did. The definition of "slavery" in s 270.1 of the Code, and the consequential offences expressed in s 270.3(1)(a) of the Code, are reasonably proportionate to a law giving effect to Australia's obligations under the 1926 Slavery Convention.[92] In any case, besides the constitutional support afforded by that treaty, other well-established foundations for constitutional validity exist in the present case. Following the decision of this Court in *XYZ v The Commonwealth*,[93] I regard the challenge to the constitutional validity of the contested provisions of the Code as barely arguable. Even on the narrowest view expressed in that case, and assuming that the external affairs power in s 51(xxix) of the Constitution does not support laws that are solely concerned with matters geographically external to Australia,[94] there is no such disqualifying defect in the present case. The provisions of the Code are valid. Accordingly the order proposed by Gleeson CJ, in relation to this ground, should also be made;

(3) *The accuracy of the judicial directions issue*: This is the "critical issue" presented by the appeal. It constitutes the ground upon which the Court of Appeal concluded that the second trial of Ms Tang had miscarried.[95] For reasons that I will explain, the Court of Appeal was right in its conclusion. Accordingly, subject to what follows, Ms Tang was entitled to have her convictions set aside. That order, and the consequential orders that followed, should be confirmed by this Court;

(4) *The unreasonable verdicts issue*: Did the Court of Appeal err in concluding that the verdicts of the jury were not unreasonable or unsupported by the evidence so

---

91 (2007) 16 VR 454 at 460 [23].

92 The "reasonable proportionality" test is to be preferred to the opaque and partly circular "reasonably capable of being considered appropriate and adapted" test expressed in *Victoria v The Commonwealth* (*Industrial Relations Act Case*) (1996) 187 CLR 416 at 486–489; [1996] HCA 56. However, there is no basic difference in these two propounded tests of constitutional connection: *Lange v Australian Broadcasting Corporation* (1997) 189 CLR 520 at 562, 567 (fn 272); [1997] HCA 25; *Mulholland v Australian Electoral Commission* (2004) 220 CLR 181 at 252 [205]-[206]; [2004] HCA 41.

93 (2006) 227 CLR 532; [2006] HCA 25.

94 (2006) 227 CLR 532 at 612 [226] per Callinan and Heydon JJ.

95 (2007) 16 VR 454 at 488 [146].

that (besides the allegedly inaccurate and inadequate directions on the applicable law) they should otherwise stand?[96]

For the reasons explained by the Court of Appeal,[97] by Gleeson CJ[98] and by myself,[99] the evidence before the jury was otherwise capable of sustaining the verdicts of guilty that the second jury returned against Ms Tang. This ground of Ms Tang's application for special leave to cross-appeal therefore fails. The order proposed by Gleeson CJ in that respect should be made. It follows that the attempt by Ms Tang to persuade this Court to substitute orders of acquittal, so as to spare her a further (third) trial, fails; and

(5) *The miscarriage/proviso issue*: The Court of Appeal declined to apply the "proviso" stated in s 568(1) of the *Crimes Act* 1958 (Vic) with respect to the inaccurate and inadequate directions that it found the trial judge had given to the jury on the ingredients of the slavery offences.[100] Did the Court of Appeal err in so deciding? In this Court, the prosecution ultimately contested an order for a retrial on the basis of the conclusion reached by the Court of Appeal on the "essential issue" as it defined it. There was no error in the reasoning of that Court.[101] If the conclusion of the Court of Appeal on the errors and inadequacies of the impugned directions is otherwise sustained by this Court, the dispositive orders made below will likewise be upheld. This would result in a retrial of Ms Tang even though a third trial would be most unfortunate.[102] Any relief against a third trial would have to rest in the discretion of the prosecution.

77 From the foregoing it follows that all but one of the issues that have been propounded in these proceedings (including some that were not continued in this Court[103]) fall away. That leaves only the accuracy of the judicial directions issue

96 (2007) 16 VR 454 at 496 [194].
97 (2007) 16 VR 454 at 495 [190]-[193].
98 Reasons of Gleeson CJ at [35].
99 These reasons above at [80]-[82].
100 (2007) 16 VR 454 at 496–497 [195]-[197].
101 cf *Weiss v The Queen* (2005) 224 CLR 300 at 317–318 [45]-[46]; [2005] HCA 81. See also AK *v Western Australia* (2008) 82 ALJR 534 at 546 [59] per Gummow and Hayne JJ, 553 [87] per Heydon J; 243 ALR 409 at 423, 433–434; [2008] HCA 8 and CTM *v The Queen* (2008) 82 ALJR 978 at 1001 [132]; [2008] HCA 25.
102 See *R v Wei Tang* [2007] VSCA 144 at [10].
103 For example, the ground complaining of lack of balance in the trial judge's charge to the jury and the ground complaining of excessive judicial intervention during cross-examination. See (2007) 16 VR 454 at 489–495 [159]-[189].

relating to the intention of Ms Tang necessary for her to be found guilty of the "slavery offences" charged. I turn to that issue to explain why I come to a conclusion different from my colleagues.

Remaining Issue: Judicial Directions on Intention

78 *The issue defined*: The issue that divides this Court is whether, in the second trial, the trial judge gave sufficiently accurate and clear directions to the jury on the ingredients of the offences with which Ms Tang was charged.

79 Juries cannot be expected to know the law. They must rely on the judge, presiding in the trial, to explain to them, accurately and clearly, the legal ingredients of the offences with which the accused stands charged and of any defences that arise for consideration. It is not the duty of the judge to give the jury a general disquisition on the law or to burden them with immaterial or unnecessary directions.[104] However, unless the charges are explained to the jury accurately and clearly, with assistance on the application of the law to the facts as appropriate, a fundamental assumption of trial by jury is undermined.

80 As the Court of Appeal pointed out, the "trial judge had the misfortune to be the first judge in Australia called on to devise directions for these novel offences."[105] This is a reason to avoid overly pernickety approaches to Ms Tang's challenge to those directions. But it cannot be a reason for denying Ms Tang an accurate trial that conforms to the law as stated by the Parliament.

81 The matter that concerned the Court of Appeal was the explanation given by the trial judge "as to the elements of the offences created by s 270.3(1)(a)." Relevantly, that issue concerns the character and quality of the exercise of power by the accused over the victim who is alleged to be a "slave."[106] In the Court of Appeal, Eames JA, a judge with much experience in criminal trials and law, concluded that the approach urged by the prosecution, and adopted by the judge at the trial, "did not correctly identify the elements of the offences which the [prosecution] had to establish." Specifically, by reference to s 5.2 of the Code (which contains the explanation of the general principles of criminal responsibility in respect of "intention"), Eames JA concluded that, to make

104 *Alford v Magee* (1952) 85 CLR 437 at 466; [1952] HCA 3. See *Melbourne v The Queen* (1999) 198 CLR 1 at 52–53 [143] per Hayne J; [1999] HCA 32.

105 (2007) 16 VR 454 at 475 [93].

106 (2007) 16 VR 454 at 469 [66].

good the offences in s 270.3(1)(a), the prosecution had to prove the following against Ms Tang:[107]

> First, the worker must have been reduced to the condition that would constitute her a slave, as defined in the [Code]. The jury must be satisfied that she had had powers exercised over her as though she was mere property, with the result that she had been reduced to the status of mere property, a thing, over whom powers attaching to the right of ownership could be exercised.
>
> Secondly, the accused must have known that the worker had been reduced to a condition where she was no more than property, a thing, over whom persons could exercise powers as though they owned her.
>
> Thirdly, the accused must have intentionally possessed the worker, that is, must have intentionally held her in her custody or under her physical control.
>
> Fourthly, the accused must have possessed the worker in the intentional exercise of what constitutes a power attaching to a right of ownership, namely, the power of possession. For that to be the case the accused must be shown to have regarded the worker as though she was mere property, a thing, thereby intending to deal with her not as a human being who had free will and a right to liberty, but as though she was mere property. However harsh or oppressive her conduct was towards the worker it would not be sufficient for a conviction if, rather than having possessed the worker with the knowledge, intention, or in the belief that she was dealing with her as though she was mere property, the accused possessed her in the knowledge or belief that she was exercising some different right or entitlement to do so, falling short of what would amount to ownership, such as that of an employer, contractor, or manager.

82 I do not take there to be a present dispute concerning the first three "elements of the offences" identified in the foregoing passage. There was also no disagreement over the trial judge's direction to the jury that it was not essential that Ms Tang should know that the "worker" was, in law, a "slave." Although ignorance of the law is no excuse, the provisions of s 270.3(1)(a) of the Code do not postulate that a person, such as Ms Tang, will necessarily be aware of the categories and classifications of Australian law. Still less would such a person be expected to know the provisions of an

107 (2007) 16 VR 454 at 471–472 [77] (citations omitted). Eames JA explained that he would use the "neutral descriptor of 'worker'," inferentially instead of using the conclusory word "victim."

international treaty dating back to 1926. The Code, however, is intended to bring proved "physical" and "fault" elements together in particular evidentiary circumstances to render a person answerable for "criminal responsibility under laws of the Commonwealth."[108] This befits a contemporary federal statute that imposes criminal liability on people for their acts and omissions within Australia.

83 The basic reason for adopting this view arises from the language and structure of the Code itself. That is the starting point for an analysis of the offences with which Ms Tang was charged. However, there are several other reasons that support the approach to the construction of the Code adopted by the Court of Appeal. In the balance of these reasons, I will explain what I consider to be the most important arguments favouring the approach that the Court of Appeal adopted.

84 *Analysis of the statute*: Relevant here are not only the "slavery offences" with which Ms Tang was charged under s 270.3(1)(a) of the Code but also the more general "physical" and "fault" element provisions under Ch 2 of the Code. These latter elements are declared by the Parliament to be necessary in Australia for criminal responsibility under federal law.[109]

85 The starting point is the structure of s 270.3(1). In expressing the relevant "slavery offence," the word "intentionally" is placed in the chapeau, above the particular offences that follow. These include the provisions of par (a) under which Ms Tang was charged. By the ordinary application of the principles of statutory construction, it must therefore be accepted that the adverb "intentionally" was designed to modify the entirety of the subsequent paragraphs. Thus, it is not enough for the accused to "possess" a slave or to "exercise" over a slave "any of the other powers attaching to the right of ownership." To be guilty of the offence provided by the Code, the accused must do these things, and all of them, "intentionally."

86 That paragraph contains descriptors of "physical elements," such as "possessing" a slave or "exercising" powers "attaching to the right of ownership" over a slave. However, the general principles of criminal responsibility contained in Ch 2 of the Code also make it clear that such "physical elements" alone are not sufficient to secure a conviction. There must be a relevant combination of both "physical" and "fault" elements. In the present appeal (as was properly acknowledged by the prosecution in its conduct of Ms Tang's trial) it was common ground that the applicable "fault element" was the

108 The Code, s 2.1. See also s 3.1(1).

109 Pursuant to ss 3.1(1) and 5.2(1) of the Code.

"intention" of the accused. This is clear enough because of the inclusion of the adverb "intentionally" in the chapeau to s 270.3(1).

87 Where "intention" is the applicable "fault element," as here, s 5.2(1) of the Code provides that "[a] person has intention with respect to conduct if he or she means to engage in that conduct." Quite apart from the introductory adverb in the language of s 270.3(1) of the Code, it is clear that the prosecution must prove beyond reasonable doubt that the accused had the "intention" to engage in the relevant conduct. Thus, in a case brought under s 270.3(1) of the Code, the "intention" is not simply an "intention" addressed to the "physical elements" concerned with "possession" or the exercise of powers attaching to the "right of ownership." It is also an intention directed to the underlying entitlement that gives rise to those elements. Without that ingredient of the offence, the word "intentionally" might just as well not have been present in s 270.3(1).

88 In effect, the construction urged by the prosecution (and now adopted by this Court) either ignores the word "intentionally" at the head of the sub-section or treats it as relevant only to the physical elements involved in the treatment of a person. It does not, as s 270.3(1)(a) indicates by its language and structure, also govern the *quality* and *character* of those physical elements so that they amount, in law, to "possession" or to "exercis[ing] over a slave any of the other powers attaching to the right of ownership."

89 Paragraph (a) of s 270.3(1) of the Code uses legal notions such as "possession" and "rights of ownership" preceded by the statutory requirement that such "physical elements" should be exercised "intentionally." This imports into the constituent elements of the offences charged an appreciation, belief or realisation by the accused ("intentionally") of the entitlement to assert the "physical elements" that go to make up the offences.

90 *Relevant canons of construction*: A fundamental canon of construction that supports the Court of Appeal's approach is reflected in the acknowledgment, in extrinsic statutory material, that:[110]

> slavery is more than merely the exploitation of another. It is where the power a person exercises over another effectively amounts to the power a person would exercise over property he or she owns.

110 The revised Explanatory Memorandum to the Criminal Code Amendment (Slavery and Sexual Servitude) Bill 1999 (Cth) at 4 cited by the Court of Appeal: (2007) 16 VR 454 at 461 [27].

91 To exercise such a power, as if over property that the person owns or possesses, it is inherent that the person deploying that power does so based upon a notion of that person's entitlement to act as he or she does. What is done is not done mindlessly, thoughtlessly or carelessly. It is done out of a sense of power, founded on a sense of entitlement. Thus the language and structure of the legislation, and the terms of the Explanatory Memorandum, support the approach of the Court of Appeal. And basically that is enough.

92 Two additional considerations further reinforce the conclusion adopted by the Court of Appeal. The first, which Eames JA noted,[111] is that the Code comprises penal legislation which is conventionally construed strictly because of the consequences of serious punishment that may follow from a conviction.[112] To the extent that there is any residual doubt about the meaning and requirement of the provisions of the Code to Ms Tang's case, the Court of Appeal adopted such an approach and that approach is to be preferred.

93 Secondly, the introduction of "slavery offences" into the Code enacted novel crimes that have to be read together with general principles of the Code governing criminal responsibility. Those principles are, in turn, in some ways new. They must be given meaning according to their terms and in consideration of the context and purpose of the reforms they introduce. Nevertheless, these provisions are themselves written against the background of the basic doctrines of criminal law as they operate throughout Australia. It will generally be presumed that the language of a code that is designed to state criminal offences applicable in Australia is intended generally to reflect, and not to depart from, long-observed basic principles of criminal liability.[113]

94 With respect, it is not persuasive to suggest[114] that the approach favoured by the majority is supported by the "common exercise of relating the fault element to the physical elements of the offence."[115] The ultimate duty of this Court is to construe the language of the Code.[116] This must be done by reference to the text of the Code and

111 (2007) 16 VR 454 at 473 [85].

112 cf *He Kaw Teh v The Queen* (1985) 157 CLR 523 at 583 per Brennan J; [1985] HCA 43; *Murphy v Farmer* (1988) 165 CLR 19 at 28–29; [1988] HCA 31.

113 *R v Barlow* (1997) 188 CLR 1 at 32; [1997] HCA 19. The passage cites *Vallance v The Queen* (1961) 108 CLR 56 at 75–76; [1961] HCA 42 and *Parker v The Queen* (1997) 186 CLR 494 at 517–519; [1997] HCA 15.

114 Reasons of Gleeson CJ at [49].

115 Referring to *He Kaw Teh* (1985) 157 CLR 523 at 568.

116 This is a special example of the general rule mandating the primacy of statutory language as the source of, and starting point for deriving, legislative obligations. Recent cases are

a consideration of the context of the relevant provisions and their purpose of expressing a new approach to the application of the "fault elements" of federal offences. When this approach is adopted, the language of the Code, and especially the structure of the provisions in which that language appears (the chapeau of s 270.3(1)), argue powerfully against the conclusion reached by the majority. This approach instead supports the analysis adopted by the Court of Appeal.

95 In any case, when considering basic principles of criminal law, one such principle is the common law presumption that no person will be punished criminally "for doing an act which he honestly and reasonably believes to be lawful and right."[117] To the extent that they are consistent with the Code, fundamental principles of criminal responsibility inform the construction of such statutory provisions.[118] It would require very clear statutory language to render the mere performance of an act criminally blameworthy, without regard being had to the "golden thread"[119] which has been present in Australian (and earlier English) criminal law for at least seventy years. In the present case, this is not to oblige (in effect) that the accused should know the precise terms of the statute or of antecedent treaties. It is simply to apply the statutory postulate of "intention" not only to the physical elements but also to their quality and the "circumstances [that] make [them] criminal."[120]

96 General considerations such as these[121] confirm the conclusion of the Court of Appeal in this case. The mere existence of what the Code now describes as "physical elements" (relevantly "possession" and "the right of ownership") does not, on conventional theory, ordinarily attract criminal liability to a person accused in Australia of a serious criminal offence. Something more is required. That something is the "mental element" (*mens rea* as formerly described) on the part of the accused, or as is now described in the Code, the "fault element." This element is essential to constitute, with a "particular physical element," responsibility in law for an offence against federal criminal provisions.

---

set out in *Central Bayside General Practice Association Ltd v Commissioner of State Revenue (Vic)* (2006) 228 CLR 168 at 198 [84], fn 86; [2006] HCA 43. See also *Barlow* (1997) 188 CLR 1 at 31–33.

117 *R v Tolson* (1889) 23 QBD 168 at 182. See CTM (2008) 82 ALJR 978 at 981 [4] per Gleeson CJ, Gummow, Crennan and Kiefel JJ, 991–992 [61] of my own reasons.

118 CTM (2008) 82 ALJR 978 at 981 [5] per Gleeson CJ, Gummow, Crennan and Kiefel JJ, 991–992 [61] of my own reasons, 1004 [146] per Hayne J.

119 *Woolmington v Director of Public Prosecutions* [1935] AC 462 at 481.

120 *He Kaw Teh* (1985) 157 CLR 523 at 572 per Brennan J.

121 cf CTM (2008) 82 ALJR 978 at 982 [6] per Gleeson CJ, Gummow, Crennan and Kiefel JJ, 998 [108] of my own reasons.

97 The Court of Appeal's approach gives full force and effect to these basic notions of our criminal law. So much is required by the language and structure of the Code. However, if there were any ambiguity, this is the approach that this Court should take. It conforms more closely to the "general principles of criminal responsibility" expressed in Ch 2 of the Code and also in the basic doctrines of contemporary Australian criminal law. It is against this background that the Code provisions were formulated and enacted.

98 *Further considerations in support*: A number of additional considerations lend still further support to the approach adopted by the Court of Appeal.

99 *Traditional approach to "intention"*: Having something in "possession" (or asserting over something "powers attaching to the right of ownership") will not ordinarily render a person liable for a criminal act unless the mind ("intention") of the person combines with the physical elements. Take, for example, someone who carries a suitcase containing a prohibited drug over a border. The physical elements involved in such "possession" of that drug (or the assertion of powers attaching to the "right of ownership" over the suitcase) would not, on conventional theory, alone be sufficient to render the carrier criminally liable. The prosecution would have to identify and prove that the accused was aware of the nature and quality of the control asserted over the import in question. It is not enough that the suitcase should, in physical fact, contain a prohibited drug. The prosecution must establish, to the requisite standard, that the accused knew that the drug was present and intended to perform the physical acts amounting to a criminal importation.[122]

100 Innocent parties fall outside the ambit of the offences provided by s 270.3(1) of the Code. This is precisely because the requirement of "intentionally," as expressed in the chapeau to the sub-section, imports a necessity of consciousness of the quality, source and purported basis or justification of the "possession" and "right of ownership" being asserted. All of this is simply to insist that, under the Code, as conventionally at common law, the mere *acts* of "possession" or "ownership" alone are not enough to constitute the criminal offence. The necessary added ingredient is the presence of the *intention* to which s 270.3(1) refers, addressed to the quality and character of the acts charged.

101 The Court of Appeal correctly insisted upon the necessity of this ingredient. Correctly, it concluded that its absence from the directions of the trial judge to the jury

---

122 *He Kaw Teh* (1985) 157 CLR 523 at 585–586 per Brennan J.

constituted a serious omission in explaining to the jury the legal components of the offences charged.

Conformability with international law: The present task is to construe and apply the Code, an Australian statute. However, the ostensible purpose of the relevant provisions was to introduce into Australian municipal law offences derived substantially from the 1926 Slavery Convention.

The interpretation of s 270.3(1) favoured by the Court of Appeal is more consonant with that Convention and the extremely grave international crime that "slavery," so expressed, involves. As stated in the Code,[123] slavery, like piracy,[124] is a crime against humanity.[125] Thus those who engage in "slavery," piracy and other special crimes are enemies of mankind.[126] Such offences arguably attract obligations that attach to crimes of universal jurisdiction.[127] As a rule *jus cogens*,[128] slavery is prohibited as a peremptory norm from which no derogation is permitted.[129] This further reinforces the seriousness of slavery and hence the need to define it very carefully and precisely.

123 The Code, s 268.10.

124 Simpson, *Law, War and Crime: War Crimes Trials and the Reinvention of International Law*, (2007) at 159.

125 *Prosecutor v Kunarac, Kovac and Vukovic*, International Criminal Tribunal for the Former Yugoslavia, Case No IT-96-23-T & IT-96-23/1-T, 22 February 2001 at 179 [522], 183 [526], 191 [537], 192 [539] ("*Kunarac* (*Trial*)") and Case No IT-96-23 & IT-96-23/1-A, 12 June 2002 at 4 [13] ("*Kunarac* (*Appeal*)"); Jennings and Watts (eds), *Oppenheim's International Law*, 9th ed (1992), vol 1, Pts 2 to 4, §429; Bassiouni, "Enslavement as an International Crime," (1991) 23 *New York University Journal of International Law and Politics* 445 at 448. Some of the above references refer to the term "enslavement," which is nonetheless applicable in the present circumstances. As noted in *Kunarac* (*Trial*) at 192 [539], "enslavement" consists of the "exercise of any or all of the powers attaching to the right of ownership over a person." Further, *Kunarac* (*Appeal*) at 38 [123] equates the terms "slavery" and "enslavement."

126 See Simpson, *Law, War and Crime: War Crimes Trials and the Reinvention of International Law*, (2007) at 159.

127 cf *R v Bow Street Metropolitan Stipendiary Magistrate; Ex parte Pinochet Ugarte* (*No 3*) [2000] 1AC 147 at 189, 200–204, 278–279.

128 Hannikainen, *Peremptory Norms (Jus Cogens) in International Law*, (1988) at 446–447; Meron, *Human Rights and Humanitarian Norms as Customary Law*, (1989) at 20–21; Henkin, *International Law: Politics and Values*, (1995) at 39; Schachter, *International Law in Theory and Practice*, (1991) at 343; Drew, "Human Trafficking: A modern form of slavery?" (2002) 7 *European Human Rights Law Review* 481 at 481.

129 Vienna Convention on the Law of Treaties 1969, Art 53.

102 I therefore agree with Gleeson CJ that, without the clearest statutory authority, it is undesirable to banalise slavery crimes by applying them to circumstances that would amount to no more than a seriously exploitative employment relationship.[130] The approach of the Court of Appeal requires consideration by the decision-maker of the quality and extent of the accused's "intention." To that extent, in asserting "possession" and "rights of ownership" over another person as a "slave," the crimes provided by s 270.3(1) are reserved to indisputably serious offences containing a substantial, not trivial, intention element.

103 To the extent that the intention element is restricted to conduct in relation to a person, with no attention being given to the perpetrator's intention, there is a serious risk of over-expansion of the notion of "slavery." The approach of the Court of Appeal is more rigorous. Such rigour is more appropriate to a crime defined by reference to the universal international offence of "slavery."

104 *Consistency with severe punishment*: All of the foregoing is yet further reinforced by a reflection upon the maximum penalty that the Code provides upon conviction of the s 270.3(1) slavery offences.

105 The maximum penalty of imprisonment for twenty-five years[131] is one of the highest now provided under Australian legislation. This feature helped to reinforce the conclusion of the Court of Appeal that the applicable "fault element" of "intention" should apply in the manner adopted by Eames JA.[132] His Honour remarked:[133]

> Lack of control of the 'slave' over her life, and her lack of personal liberty, may well suggest that she is being treated as though she were mere property – as a thing – but more is required to be proved for an offence under s 270.3(1)(a). And much more is required than that the person be shown to have been exploited, abused or humiliated, whether physically, emotionally or financially. To be a slave, the person must be in a state where he or she is dealt with by others as though he or she was mere property – a thing. For the exercise of the power to contravene s 270.3(1)(a) the accused must have knowingly treated the person as though he or she was the accused's property. Only when that state of mind exists is the exercise of power referable to a right of ownership, as the section requires.

---

130 Reasons of Gleeson CJ at [32].

131 (2007) 16 VR 454 at 466 [53].

132 cf *He Kaw Teh* (1985) 157 CLR 523 at 583 per Brennan J.

133 (2007) 16 VR 454 at 473 [84].

106 *Comparison with human trafficking*: In a case such as the present it is important for the judicial decision-maker to be familiar with contemporary instances of human trafficking. Human trafficking involves the movement, recruitment or receipt of persons, often by means of the threat or use of force, for the purpose of exploitation.[134] As such, it commonly operates in conjunction with, or as part of, slavery.[135] Women and children are particularly vulnerable to human trafficking and they are often subjected to sexual and other physical and emotional exploitation. This abhorrent activity commonly involves conditions of infancy, serious vulnerability, shocking living and working conditions and repeated violence, oppression and humiliation.

107 The close connection between human trafficking, as described, and "slavery" serves to reinforce the extremely serious nature of such "slavery offences." Given the nature of "slavery," as understood in international law, there is a great need to not over-extend "slavery offences" to apply to activities such as seriously oppressive employment relationships. The approach adopted by the Court of Appeal is more consistent with such an aim. The approach of the majority in this Court is not.

108 *Distinguishing "slavery" from debt bondage*: Since the actions occurred for which Ms Tang was charged, the Parliament has amended the Code to introduce into Australian law[136] a new and discrete offence of "debt bondage."[137] As Eames JA remarked:[138]

---

134 See Protocol to Prevent, Suppress and Punish Trafficking in Persons, Especially Women and Children, Supplementing the United Nations Convention Against Transnational Organized Crime 2000, Art 3; International Labour Office, *Trafficking in Human Beings: New Approaches to Combating the Problem*, (2003) at 6; International Labour Office (Belser, de Cock and Mehran), ILO *Minimum Estimate of Forced Labour in the World*, (2005) at 4–6.

135 See Rome Statute of the International Criminal Court 1998, Art 7(2)(c); United Nations Economic and Social Council, *Contemporary Forms of Slavery*, UN Doc E/CN.4/Sub.2/2000/3 (2000) at 13 [48]; Tessier, "The New Slave Trade: The International Crisis of Immigrant Smuggling," (1995) 3 *Indiana Journal of Global Legal Studies* 261 at 261–262; Bassiouni, *Crimes Against Humanity in International Criminal Law*, 2nd rev ed (1999) at 212; Levchenko, *Combat of Trafficking in Women for the Purpose of Forced Prostitution – Ukraine* (*Country Report*), (1999) at 23. For a comprehensive analysis of the relationship between slavery and trafficking, see Hathaway, "The Human Rights Quagmire of 'Human Trafficking'," (2008) 49 *Virginia Journal of International Law* (forthcoming).

136 (2007) 16 VR 454 at 473–474 [86].

137 The Code, s 271.8. "Slavery" and "debt bondage" are often treated separately in international instruments. See, for example, the 1956 Supplementary Convention, Arts 1(a), 7(b) ("debt bondage" as a "person of servile status") and Art 7(a) ("slavery").

138 (2007) 16 VR 454 at 474 [87] (footnote omitted).

> 'Debt bondage' is defined in the Dictionary of the Code as arising when a person pledges personal services as security for a debt and the debt is manifestly excessive, or the reasonable value of the services provided is not applied in reduction of the debt, or the length and nature of the services are not limited and defined. Arguably, that offence would have been proved on the evidence in this case and, if so, it would have carried a maximum sentence of 12 months' imprisonment. There being no such provision, [Ms Tang] was charged with slavery offences, which carried a maximum sentence of 25 years. ... [S]he received a total effective sentence of 10 years' imprisonment with a non-parole period of six years, although she had no prior convictions.

109 Responding to a question asked during the hearing, the Attorney-General of the Commonwealth acknowledged that:

> After examining the legislation of the United States, Canada, South Africa, New Zealand and the United Kingdom, we have not identified any provisions that implement the Convention in terms similar to those found in Australia's *Criminal Code*.

The closest analogy to the Australian provisions was said to be s 98(1) of the *Crimes Act* 1961 (NZ).[139]

110 None of the states mentioned above have implemented the Convention in a similar way to that of the Code here. This affords a further reason why, in respect of the "slavery offences" in s 270.3(1)(a) of the Code, this Court should adopt the more stringent requirement of proof of intention favoured by the Court of Appeal. Doing so would ensure that Australian law remained in broad harmony with the law of similar countries. Especially in relation to crimes having a universal or transnational character, that is a proper interpretive consideration.

111 *Shift in law on sex work*: As to the extension of "slavery" to adult consensual participation in the commercial sex industry, it is also important for courts such as this to give due weight to recent changes in Australian law (including in Victoria). Those changes reflect a recognition by Parliament that adults (as the prosecution conceded before this Court) are entitled to participate in the sex industry lawfully. This includes participation as sex workers, consensually, for economic reasons. Attempts to use

139 This section creates an offence of dealing with, using or detaining a person as a slave and defines "debt bondage" in terms similar to the 1956 Supplementary Convention (Art 1). See also *R v Decha-Iamsakun* [1993] 1 NZLR 141.

"slavery offences" to suppress commercial sex work, based upon individual repugnance towards adult sexual behaviour, potentially contradict the law enacted by the Victorian Parliament. The simple fact is that some commercial sex workers have no desire to exit the industry. Some people may find that shocking; but it matters not. In Victoria, so long as the sex worker is a consenting adult with no relevant disability, that is a choice open to her or him. The contrary approach risks returning elements of the sex industry to operate, as was previously the case, covertly, corruptly and underground. This would undermine the fundamental objectives of the recent Australian legislation in this area, such as that of Victoria under which the brothel where the complainants worked was licensed.[140]

112 Such developments could also prove counterproductive to important purposes of the recent legislation. Specifically, such purposes include empowering sex workers to safeguard their own lives and wellbeing and thereby assisting in the reduction of the spread of sexually transmitted diseases, including the human immunodeficiency virus.[141] These policy considerations (although not mentioned by the Court of Appeal) offer additional reasons of legal principle and policy to confine "sexual slavery" offences in Australia to cases where the specific element of "intention" includes exerting powers of possession or ownership over a person because of an established belief, on the part of the accused, that it is his or her right and entitlement to do so.

113 *The jury's repeated questions*: The Court of Appeal's approach on this issue was by no means an esoteric one. This is made clear by the questions which the jury in the second trial returned twice to ask. The first question was:[142]

> Does the defendant have to have known what the definition of a slave is 'to intentionally possess a slave' as stated in the indictment.

114 The second question, presented the following afternoon, was:[143]

140 *Prostitution Control Act* 1994 (Vic).

141 See United Kingdom, Committee on Homosexual Offences and Prostitution, *Report of the Committee on Homosexual Offences and Prostitution*, (1957) Cmnd 247 at 95–96 [286] (Wolfenden Report); Lacey, Wells and Meure, *Reconstructing Criminal Law*, (1990) at 357–368; cf *Bodyline Spa and Sauna (Sydney) Pty Ltd v South Sydney City Council* (1992) 77 LGRA 432 at 433–438; Gostin and Lazzarini, *Human Rights and Public Health in the AIDS Pandemic*, (1997) at 50–51, 124–125.

142 (2007) 16 VR 454 at 481 [122].

143 (2007) 16 VR 454 at 483 [129].

> To intentionally possess a slave is it necessary for the accused to have knowledge that her actions amount to slavery?
>
> or
>
> Is it sufficient that the accused only have knowledge of the conditions she has imposed (ie slavery has not entered her mind) and the law has decided those conditions amount to slavery.

The members of the jury in the second trial were obviously puzzled over these questions and the members of the jury in the first trial were unable to reach verdicts. It is thus reasonable to infer that considerations as to the requisite *intention* of Ms Tang may be foremost in the minds of Australian jurors as they seek to differentiate activities that amount to seriously oppressive employment from those that justify conviction of "slavery offences" against s 270.3(1)(a) of the Code.

Court of Appeal's answers: Instead of the partly unresponsive, generally unclear and confusing answers given by the trial judge to the foregoing questions, the Court of Appeal (consistent with its approach) favoured the following answers. In my opinion, they are correct. They are not confusing. They respond precisely to the concern expressed by the jury about the "fault element" of "intention" that the Code requires to be proved to establish the "slavery offences." Eames JA said:[144]

> With the benefit of hindsight, and the luxuries of time and the provision of comprehensive submissions of counsel on the appeal, I would respectfully suggest that the answers to the jury questions might have been along the following lines:
>
> [As to the first question]
>
> A – No, she does not have to have known the definition of a slave, nor even that there was an offence of slavery in the laws of Australia. Ignorance of the law is no defence.[145]
>
> The Crown has to prove that she did know that in each case the worker had been reduced to a condition in which she was treated as though she was mere property, just a thing, who had no say in how she was treated.

144 (2007) 16 VR 454 at 487–488 [145].

145 See s 9.3 of the Code.

[As to the second question]

A – It is not necessary for the accused to have knowledge that her actions amount, in law, to slavery.

For the offence of intentionally possessing a slave, the accused must have known that the complainant had been reduced to a condition where she was no more than property, merely a thing, over which the accused could exercise powers as though she owned the complainant.

Furthermore, the Crown must prove that in exercising the relevant power over a particular complainant (that is, possessing or using the complainant) the accused was treating that complainant as though she was property, as if she owned her, as if she could do with her whatever she chose to do. You must be satisfied that the accused was intentionally exercising a power that an owner would have over property and was doing so with the knowledge or in the belief that the complainant was no more than mere property.

If it is reasonably possible that the accused acted to possess or to use the complainant with the knowledge or in the belief that she was exercising her rights and entitlements as her employer or contractor and not in the belief that the complainant had no rights or free will, but was property, a thing, over whom she could exercise power as though she owned her then, however exploitative and unfair you may think her treatment of the complainant was, it would not constitute the offences of intentionally possessing or using a slave.

115 Such answers would have provided accurate and adequate instructions to the jury and clear responses to their questions. These suggested answers may be contrasted with the very confusing directions actually presented to the jury by the trial judge.[146]

116 *Conclusion: miscarriage of the trial*: I leave aside the justifiable criticisms by the Court of Appeal of the unresponsiveness, ambiguity and uncertainty of the directions given to the jury. These criticisms alone raise serious questions about the compliance of Ms Tang's trial with the standards established by this Court for the comprehensibility and accuracy of jury directions.[147] The Court of Appeal considered authorities of

146 Set out at length by the Court of Appeal: (2007) 16 VR 454 at 481–486 [122]-[139].

147 *Ahern v The Queen* (1988) 165 CLR 87 at 103; [1988] HCA 39; *Zoneff v The Queen* (2000) 200 CLR 234 at 260–261 [65]-[67]; [2000] HCA 28; *Doggett v The Queen* (2001) 208 CLR 343 at 346 [2] per Gleeson CJ; [2001] HCA 46.

this Court and came to the correct conclusion on this "critical issue." It is the conclusion that I also reach. It leaves a continuing substantive operation for "slavery offences" under Australian law, as the valid provisions of s 270.3(1)(a) of the Code require. It allows such offences to apply in contemporary circumstances warranting the appellation of "slavery." It properly confines such offences to the grave affront to humanity that is "slavery" *eo nomine*, as expanded by statute in Australia to include modern instances, and not to employment deemed harsh, oppressive or repulsive.

117 As the Court of Appeal concluded, there was evidence upon which a reasonable jury, properly instructed, might have arrived at the decision that "slavery offences" of the kind provided for in the Code had been proved against Ms Tang. However, it was essential for the "fault element" of "intention" to be applied to *all*, and not just *some*, of the ingredients of the offences and to be accurately and clearly explained to the jury. Despite the jury's repeated questions, this was not done. The result is that Ms Tang's second trial miscarried. The outcome favoured by the Court of Appeal was then inevitable. There should be a new trial.

Orders

118 It follows that I agree with Gleeson CJ that special leave to cross-appeal on the first and second grounds in the proposed notice of cross-appeal should be granted. That cross-appeal should be treated as instituted and heard instanter and dismissed. I also agree with Gleeson CJ that special leave to cross-appeal on the third ground in the proposed notice of cross-appeal should be refused.

119 However, the appeal from the orders of the Court of Appeal of the Supreme Court of Victoria should be dismissed.

120 HAYNE J. I agree with Gleeson CJ that, for the reasons he gives, the appeal to this Court should be allowed. I also agree with Gleeson CJ that, for the reasons he gives, orders should be made granting the respondent special leave to cross-appeal, limited to the first two proposed grounds of cross-appeal, but dismissing the cross-appeal. I agree that consequential orders should be made in the form proposed by Gleeson CJ.

121 Section 270.3(1)(a) of the *Criminal Code* (Cth) ("the Code") makes it an offence intentionally to possess a slave or to exercise over a slave "any of the other powers attaching to the right of ownership." The central issue in the appeal concerns what directions should have been given to the jury at the respondent's trial about the mental element of the offences of possessing or using a slave. I agree with Gleeson CJ that,

contrary to the holding of the Court of Appeal,[148] the prosecution did not have to prove that the respondent had any knowledge or belief about the source of the powers she exercised over the complainants. What was to be proved was the intentional possession and use of each complainant as a slave, which is to say as a person over whom any or all of the powers attaching to the right of ownership were exercised.

122 I agree with what Gleeson CJ has said about the application of Ch 2 of the Code to s 270.3(1). The relevant fault element of each of the offences with which the respondent was charged was intention.[149] The conduct, which is to say the act or state of affairs,[150] in question in this matter was possessing a slave or using a slave. To establish the relevant fault element in this case it was necessary to show that the respondent meant to engage in the conduct, in respect of each complainant, of exercising powers attaching to the right of ownership.

123 The remaining part of these reasons is directed to the meaning, and application in this case, of the terms "slavery" and "slave" when used in the relevant provisions of the Code. "Slavery" is defined[151] as follows:

> For the purposes of this Division, *slavery* is the condition of a person over whom any or all of the powers attaching to the right of ownership are exercised, including where such a condition results from a debt or contract made by the person.

"Slave" is not separately defined but must take its meaning from the definition of "slavery."

124 As Gleeson CJ has pointed out, the definition of "slavery" in the Code derives from, but is not identical with, the definition of "slavery" in Art 1(1) of the 1926 International Convention to Suppress the Slave Trade and Slavery.[152] Because the purpose of the Convention was to suppress the slave trade and slavery it was directed to both the status of slavery and the condition of slavery. The status of slavery, in the context of the Convention, is to be understood as referring to a legal status created by or recognised under relevant municipal law. By contrast, the condition of slavery is to be understood as referring to a factual state of affairs which need not, but may, depend upon recognition by the relevant municipal legal system. Yet both that status and that

148 *R v Wei Tang* (2007) 16 VR 454 at 471-472 [77], 482 [124], 487-488 [145].
149 *Criminal Code* (Cth), ss 5.1, 5.2.
150 s 4.1(2).
151 s 270.1.
152 [1927] Australian Treaty Series 11.

condition were defined in the Convention in identical terms: as a status or condition of a person over whom any or all of the powers attaching to the right of ownership are exercised.

125 The language of the Convention, whether in its definition of slavery or otherwise, cannot be read as if it gave effect to or reflected particular legal doctrines of ownership or possession developed in one or more systems of municipal law. Nothing in the preparatory materials relating to the Convention suggests that it was intended to embrace any particular legal doctrine of that kind and the text of the Convention itself does not evidence any such intention. Rather, slavery (both as a legal status and as a factual condition) was defined only by a description that assumed an understanding, but did not identify the content, of "the powers attaching to the right of ownership." Yet for the purposes of creating particular norms of individual behaviour enforceable by application of the criminal law, the definition of "slavery" that is adopted in s 270.1 of the Code takes as its origin the definition of slavery, as a condition, that was given in the Convention.

126 What are the "powers attaching to the right of ownership?" How are they to be identified when the Code is applied, given that the Convention did not use the term "ownership," or the expression "powers attaching to the right of ownership," with a legal meaning that was anchored in any particular legal system? Both "ownership" and the "powers attaching to the right of ownership" must be understood as ordinary English expressions and applied having regard to the context in which they are to be applied. The chief feature of that context is that the subject of "ownership," the subject of the exercise of "powers attaching to the right of ownership," is a human being.

127 Because "ownership" cannot be read in s 270.1 of the Code as a technical legal term whose content is spelled out by a particular legal system, it is a word that must be read as conveying the ordinary English meaning that is captured by the expression "dominion over" the subject matter. That is, it must be read as identifying a form of relationship between a person (the owner) and the subject matter (another person) that is to be both described and identified by the powers that the owner has over that other.

128 "Ownership" ordinarily is to be understood as referring to a *legal* relationship between owner and subject matter. An "owner" has an aggregation of powers that are recognised in law as the powers permissibly exercised over the subject matter.[153] It is a term that connotes at least an extensive aggregation of powers, perhaps the fullest and

153 cf *Yanner v Eaton* (1999) 201 CLR 351 at 365-366 [17], 388-389 [85]-[86]; [1999] HCA 53.

most complete aggregation that is possible. But s 270.1 cannot be read as requiring the identification of an aggregation of powers that the law permits to be exercised over a person because Australian law does not recognise, and never has recognised, the possibility that one person may own another. There is not, and never has been, legal endorsement in Australia for the creation or maintenance of such a concentration of legally recognised powers in one person over another as would amount to "ownership" of that person. In particular, Australian law does not recognise, and never has recognised, any right to "possess" a person.

It follows that neither the definition of slavery in s 270.1, nor the references to "a slave" in s 270.3, invite attention to what legal rights the "owner" has over the person who it is alleged is "a slave." Rather, the references in s 270.3(1)(a) of the Code to possessing a slave, and exercising over a slave "any of the other powers attaching to the right of ownership," invite attention to what the alleged offender has done. In particular, what powers has the alleged offender exercised over the person who is alleged to be a slave? And what the alleged offender has done must then be measured against a factual construct: the powers that an owner would have over a person if, contrary to the fact, the law recognised the right to own another person.

129 As explained earlier, to constitute "ownership," one person would have dominion over that other person. That is, the powers that an owner of another person would have would be the powers which, taken together, would constitute the complete subjection of that other person to the will of the first. Or to put the same point another way, the powers that an owner would have over another person, if the law recognised the right to own that other, would be powers whose exercise would not depend upon the assent of the person over whom the powers are exercised.

130 How are those abstract ideas to be given practical application? It is convenient to approach that question by reference to the particular allegations in this matter, where it was alleged that the respondent had "possessed" each complainant as a slave and that she had "used" each complainant as a slave.

131 The first step to take is to recognise that both the offence of possessing a slave, and the offence of exercising over a slave any of the powers attaching to the right of ownership, are cast in terms that appear to present two questions: first, did the accused possess, or exercise some other power attaching to the right of ownership over, the complainant and second, was the complainant a slave? But the two questions merge.

132 The condition that must be proved is that the person meets the description "a slave." The offence is intentionally to possess a slave or intentionally to exercise over a

slave any of certain powers. The condition of slavery (which is what provides the content of the term "a slave") is defined as the condition of a person over whom any or all of the powers attaching to the right of ownership are exercised. It thus follows that proof of the intentional exercise of *any* of the relevant powers over a person suffices to establish both that the victim is a slave and that the accused has done what the legislation prohibits.

133 The next step to take is to observe that the Code's definition of "slavery" in s 270.1 speaks of "the *powers* attaching to the *right* of ownership" (emphasis added). Section 270.3 of the Code shows that possessing a slave is one particular power attaching to the right of ownership. And it is also clear that possessing a slave is not the only power attaching to the right of ownership. So much is made clear by the use of the word "other" in the phrase "*other* powers attaching to the right of ownership." But s 270.1 does not further identify what those powers are.

134 As Brennan J said in *He Kaw Teh v The Queen*,[154] "'possession' is a term which implies a state of mind with respect to the thing possessed." In that case, Brennan J identified[155] the actus reus of possession of a prohibited import as being that the object of possession was physically in the custody or under the control of the accused. And as Dawson J pointed out in the same case,[156] "[p]ossession may be an intricate concept for some purposes, but the intricacies belong to the civil rather than the criminal law." That is why, in the criminal law, "possession" is best understood as a reference to a state of affairs in which there is[157] "the intentional exercise of physical custody or control over something." In considering s 270.3(1)(a) of the Code, however, it will also be important to recognise that the right to possess a subject matter, coupled with a power to carve out and dispose of subsidiary possessory rights, is an important element in that aggregation of powers over a subject matter that is commonly spoken of as "ownership."

135 Just as the word "ownership" evokes notions of the dominion of one person over another, to speak of one person possessing another (in the sense of having physical custody of or control over that other) connotes one person having dominion over the other. Or to put the same point in different words, possession, like ownership, refers to a state of affairs in which there is the complete subjection of that other by the first person.

154 (1985) 157 CLR 523 at 585; [1985] HCA 43.
155 (1985) 157 CLR 523 at 585-586.
156 (1985) 157 CLR 523 at 599.
157 *He Kaw Teh v The Queen* (1985) 157 CLR 523 at 599 per Dawson J.

136 One, and perhaps the most obvious, way in which to attempt to give practical content to the otherwise abstract ideas of ownership or possession (whether expressed by reference to subjection, dominion or otherwise) is to explore the antithesis of slavery. That is, because both the notion of ownership and of possession, when applied to a person, can be understood as an exercise of power over that person that does not depend upon the assent of the person concerned, it will be relevant to ask *why* that person's assent was irrelevant. Or, restating the proposition in other words, in asking whether there was the requisite dominion over a person, the subjection of that person, it will be relevant to ask whether the person concerned was deprived of freedom of choice in some relevant respect and, if so, what it was that deprived the person of choice. In that inquiry some assistance is to be had from United States decisions about legislation giving effect to the Thirteenth Amendment to the United States Constitution.

137 Those cases explore what is meant when it is said that a person had no choice but to continue to serve a person accused of holding the first in "involuntary servitude." And they show that a person may be deprived of choice to the requisite extent, not just by force or the threat of force, but also by threats to invoke the proper application of the law to the detriment of the person threatened. But examination of the cases will also show why analysis of who is "a slave" by reference only to freedom or absence of choice of the alleged victim, or by reference only to the nature of the coercion applied by an accused, is not determinative of that question.

138 The Thirteenth Amendment provides, in s 1, that:

> Neither slavery nor involuntary servitude, except as a punishment for crime whereof the party shall have been duly convicted, shall exist within the United States, or any place subject to their jurisdiction.

Part 2 of the Amendment gives the Congress power to make appropriate laws to enforce the Amendment.

139 The prime purpose of outlawing "involuntary servitude" in the Thirteenth Amendment, and in statutes enacted to enforce it, was described by Judge Friendly, speaking for the plurality of the United States Court of Appeals for the Second Circuit in *United States v Shackney*,[158] as being:

> to abolish all practices whereby subjection having some of the incidents of slavery was legally enforced, either directly, by a state's using its power to return the

158 333 F 2d 475 at 485-486 (1964).

> servant to the master...or indirectly, by subjecting persons who left the employer's service to criminal penalties.

But as Judge Friendly went on to point out, the Thirteenth Amendment is not addressed solely to State action. In the United States it has been held to apply in cases of physical restraint,[159] threats of imprisonment, or physical violence.[160] In *Shackney*, the plurality held[161] that:

> a holding in involuntary servitude means to us *action by the master causing the servant to have, or to believe he has, no way to avoid continued service or confinement*...not a situation where the servant knows he has a choice between continued service and freedom, even if the master has led him to believe that the choice may entail consequences that are exceedingly bad. (emphasis added)

The third member of that Court, Judge Dimock, held[162] that servitude is involuntary only "[w]here the subjugation of the will of the servant is so complete as to render him incapable of making a rational choice."

140 Twenty years later, in 1984, the United States Court of Appeals for the Ninth Circuit expressed the test differently. In *United States v Mussry*,[163] a case about Indonesian domestic workers, the Court of Appeals held that:

> A holding in involuntary servitude occurs when an individual *coerces another into his service by improper or wrongful conduct* that is intended to cause, and does cause, the other person to believe that he or she has no alternative but to perform the labor. (emphasis added)

In that case the prosecution alleged that:[164]

> [the defendants] knowingly placed [the Indonesian servants] in a strange country where [they] had no friends, had nowhere to go, did not speak English, had no work permit, social security card, or identification, no passport or return

159 *Davis v United States* 12 F 2d 253 (1926).

160 *Bernal v United States* 241 F 339 (1917); *Pierce v United States* 146 F 2d 84 (1944); *United States v Ingalls* 73 F Supp 76 (1947).

161 333 F 2d 475 at 486 (1964).

162 333 F 2d 475 at 488 (1964).

163 726 F 2d 1448 at 1453 (1984).

164 726 F 2d 1448 at 1453 (1984).

> airline ticket to return to Indonesia, [were] here as...illegal alien[s], with no means by which to seek other employment, and with insufficient funds to break [their] contract[s] by paying back to defendant[s] the alleged expenses incurred in getting...here.

The Court held that the conduct alleged by the prosecution, if proved, was sufficient to demonstrate improper or wrongful acts by the defendants intended to coerce the Indonesian servants into performing service for the defendants. The Court further held[165] that "the use, or threatened use, of law or physical force is not an essential element of a charge of 'holding' in involuntary servitude." Other forms of coercion may also result in a violation of the involuntary servitude statutes.

141 Subsequently, the Supreme Court of the United States held in *United States v Kozminski*[166] that the use, or threatened use, of physical or legal coercion was essential to proof of involuntary servitude.[167] The Court rejected the view that the statute then in question extended to cases the Court identified[168] as the compulsion of services "through psychological coercion." Such a test was rejected[169] as depending "entirely upon the victim's state of mind." Accordingly, while deprivation of the victim's will was essential, the Court held that the deprivation must be enforced by the use or threatened use of the means identified. But as the reference to "legal coercion" reveals, the Court held that involuntary servitude could be established in cases where the coercion applied was not in itself illegal. Thus, threatening an immigrant with deportation was identified[170] as one possible form of threatened legal coercion.

142 The discussion in the United States cases reveals three points of immediate relevance to the application of the provisions of the Code in issue in this case. First, they show that some assistance can be obtained in the practical application of the abstract concepts of ownership and possession by considering the antithesis of slavery and asking whether, and in what respects, the person alleged to be a slave was free. But the second point revealed by the United States cases is that to ask whether a person was "free," or to ask the more particular questions of when and how a person was deprived of will or freedom of choice, is in each case a question of fact and degree. And because that is the nature of the question, the answer may often be expressed using some word

165 726 F 2d 1448 at 1455 (1984).
166 487 US 931 (1988).
167 487 US 931 at 944, 952 (1988).
168 487 US 931 at 949 (1988).
169 487 US 931 at 949 (1988).
170 487 US 931 at 948 (1988).

like "real" or "substantial" to describe the quality of the freedom or the denial of freedom that is identified. The third point that emerges from the United States cases is that to ask whether a person has been deprived of free choice presents two further questions. First there is the question: choice about what? Then there is the question: how is the deprivation effected? The United States cases that have been discussed explore choice about provision of labour, and deprivation by means other than close physical confinement. The detail of that discussion may or may not be immediately relevant to the facts of a case brought under the provisions of the Code that are in issue in this case.

143 Asking what freedom a person had may shed light on whether that person was a slave. In particular, to ask whether a complainant was deprived of choice may assist in revealing whether what the accused did was exercise over that person a power attaching to the right of ownership. To ask how the complainant was deprived of choice may help to reveal whether the complainant retained freedom of choice in some relevant respect. And if the complainant retained freedom to choose whether the accused used the complainant, that freedom will show that the use made by the accused of the complainant was not as a slave. But it is essential to bear three points at the forefront of consideration.

144 First, asking what freedom a person had is to ask a question whose focus is the reflex of the inquiries required by ss 270.1 and 270.3 of the Code. It is a question that looks at the person who it is alleged was a slave whereas the definition of slavery in s 270.1 looks to the exercise of power over that person. The question looks at freedom, but the Code requires a decision about ownership.

145 Secondly, what is proscribed by the Code is conduct of the accused. An absence of choice on the part of the complainant may be seen to result from the combined effect of multiple factors. Some of these, such as the complainant's immigration status or the conduct of third parties, may be present independently of the conduct of the accused. Such factors are part of the context in which the conduct of the accused falls to be assessed. However, it is that conduct which must amount to the exercise by the accused of a power attaching to the right of ownership for the offence to be made out.

145 Thirdly, because the Code requires consideration of whether the accused exercised *any* of the powers attaching to the right of ownership, it will be important to consider the particular power that it is alleged was exercised and the circumstances that bear upon whether the exercise of that power was the exercise of a power attaching to the right of ownership. To ask only the general question – was a complainant "free" – would not address the relevant statutory questions.

147 There were two aspects in the present case that were of critical importance in deciding whether the respondent possessed each complainant as a slave and used each as a slave. There was the evidence that each complainant came to Australia following a transaction described as purchase and sale. There was the evidence of how each complainant was treated in Australia, in particular evidence about the living and the working conditions of each. And a critical feature of that evidence was that each woman was treated as having incurred a debt that had to be repaid by working in the brothel. Although there was evidence that one of the complainants was able to secure a reduction in the amount of her initial debt, there was no satisfactory explanation in the evidence of how the so-called debt of any of the complainants was calculated, or of what had been or was to be provided in return for the incurring of the obligation. To be put against this evidence about the purchase and sale of the women and their living and working conditions was the concession made by the prosecution at the outset of these proceedings that each complainant came to Australia voluntarily.

148 The evidence at trial showed that the respondent had bought a "share" in four of the five women. The fifth woman had also been bought by a syndicate but the respondent was not a member of that syndicate.

149 In argument at trial, and on appeal to the Court of Appeal, there was much attention given to what was meant by "buying" the women or a share in some of them. A deal of that debate appears to have proceeded by reference to a supposed distinction between the respondent buying a contract under which a person agreed to provide services, and buying the person.[171] The distinction asserted depends upon directing attention to the legal rights and duties of the parties affected by the transaction. But it is a distinction that is necessarily flawed. One of the asserted alternatives (buying a person) is legally impossible. It is a transaction that could not give rise to legal rights and duties. To the extent, therefore, that the comparison seeks to direct attention to legal rights and duties, it is of no assistance.

150 Yet because reference to buying or selling the complainants is to speak of what, in Australian law, is a legal impossibility, the significance that is to be attached to the transaction depends upon what the respondent did. And in that respect, each of the transactions identified as a syndicate "buying" one of the women had to take its significance in a context provided by all of the evidence. The way in which all five women were treated in Australia by setting them to work as they did, on the terms that they did, coupled with the restraints on their movement and freedom of other action,

171 See, for example, (2007) 16 VR 454 at 488-489 [149]-[158].

permitted a jury to conclude that what the respondent did, when she took up a "share" in four of the women, was to buy them as if they were articles of trade or commerce and thereafter possess and use them.

151 In the case of the fifth woman, where the respondent was not a member of the syndicate, the respondent's acceptance of that woman as a worker in her brothel on terms that payments were made to the syndicate members for her services was evidence which, when coupled with the evidence of her working conditions and restraints on movement and freedom, was again capable of demonstrating to a jury's satisfaction that the respondent possessed her as if she were an article of trade or commerce that others had bought and sold, and that the respondent thereafter possessed and used her. That is, what was done with respect to the fifth of the complainants could be understood as her "owners" giving the respondent the right to possess her and use her. Those who exercised over the fifth complainant the powers attaching to the right of ownership carved out of that "ownership," and disposed of to the respondent, subsidiary possessory "rights" over the woman.

152 What permitted the conclusion, in respect of each complainant, that she had been bought and sold as if an article of trade or commerce and thereafter possessed and used by the respondent, was the combination of the evidence about the treatment of each in Australia with the evidence of sale and purchase in Thailand. The respondent's use of each woman in the respondent's business, coupled with the restraints on the freedom of action of the complainants, permitted the conclusion that the reference to their sale and purchase was an accurate reflection of the relationship that the respondent was to have with each complainant. That relationship was to be one in which the respondent was to have the possession and use of each as if the respondent owned her.

153 Accepting, as the prosecution did at the outset of the trial, that each of the women came to Australia voluntarily did not preclude the conclusion that each was possessed and used by the respondent as if owned by her. Taking the concession at its highest (that each woman had consciously, freely and deliberately submitted herself to the conditions that she encountered in Australia), the evidence permitted the jury to conclude that none of the women thereafter retained *any* freedom to choose what was done with them in Australia. The practical impediments and economic consequences for each woman, if she refused to complete her performance of the arrangement, were such as permitted the jury to conclude that, if there were choices to be made about those matters, they were to be made by others. In this case the evidence permitted the conclusion that the respondent used and possessed each complainant as a slave because it permitted the conclusion, in each case, that the respondent used and

possessed the complainant as an item of property at the disposal of those who had bought the complainant regardless of *any* wish she might have.

154 There is one further point to make about the evidence of purchase and sale. There was no evidence at trial about the circumstances in which the transactions were made. In particular, there was no evidence of how it came about that the "vendor" asserted the right to make the sales that were made. Exploration of those matters would very likely have cut down, even eliminated altogether, the notion that the women came to Australia voluntarily. Not least is that so because it is possible, even probable, that examination of those matters would reveal not just great disparities of knowledge and power as between the "vendor" and each of the women concerned, but other circumstances touching the reality of the assent which it was accepted each had expressed. But assuming that each of the women was to be taken to have voluntarily agreed to be the subject of sale and purchase, her assent does not deny that the result of the transaction to which each agreed was her subjection to the dominion of her purchasers.

155 It was open to the jury at the respondent's trial to find that each complainant was a person over whom was exercised, by the respondent, one or more powers attaching to the right of ownership. The respondent's appeal to the Court of Appeal of Victoria against her convictions should have been dismissed.

156 HEYDON J. I agree with both Gleeson CJ and Hayne J.

157 CRENNAN J. I agree with the orders proposed by the Chief Justice, for the reasons given by his Honour. I agree also with the reasons given by Hayne J for concurring in those orders.

158 KIEFEL J. I agree with Gleeson CJ and with Hayne J.

Index